THE ROUGH GUIDE TO
GAME PARKS
OF SOUTH AFRICA

Written by
Philip Briggs

ROUGH
GUIDES

Contents

NILE CROCODILE, KRUGER NATIONAL PARK

Introduction to
Game parks of
South Africa

South Africa is a large, diverse and incredibly beautiful country. It is home to a stunning collection of wildlife, much of which lives protected within the borders of the country's bountiful game parks. The size of France and Spain combined, and roughly twice the size of Texas, South Africa varies from picturesque Cape Town and the Garden Route towns of the Western Cape to the raw subtropical coast of northern KwaZulu-Natal, with the vast semi-desert Karoo and Kalahari extending across its central plains, and the hulking sandstone cliffs of the uKhahlamba-Drakensberg at its elevated heart.

For many, South Africa's most outstanding feature is its wildlife. Foremost among its quite wonderful game parks is the immense **Kruger National Park**, which ranks as one of Africa's premier **Big Five** destinations. Elsewhere, **Hluhluwe-iMfolozi** harbours the world's densest population of rhinos, the remote **Kgalagadi Transfrontier Park** protects a starkly beautiful dunescape inhabited by lions, leopards, cheetahs and a host of smaller carnivores, while the lakes and waterways of **iSimangaliso Wetland Park** are alive with hippos, crocs and aquatic birds.

For budget- and independent-minded travellers, a joy of South Africa's many national parks and other public reserves is that most are well suited to **self-drive safaris**. The Kruger, for instance, must rank as the top DIY safari destination anywhere in Africa. Like most of the country's other state- and provincially run reserves, it boasts a good network of surfaced or all-weather dirt roads along with affordable restcamps and campsites offering amenities suited both to first-time safarigoers and to more experienced hands.

South Africa is also a continental leader when it comes to **private reserves**. The many privately owned conservancies that share open borders with Kruger lead the pack when

VIEWING AN ELEPHANT ON SAFARI

it comes to superlative guided Big Five viewing in open vehicles based out of luxurious **lodges** steeped in bush chic. And there are dozens of other such reserves dotted around the rest of country, from Tswalu in the deep Kalahari and Phinda in subtropical KwaZulu-Natal to Shamwari near Port Elizabeth and Gondwana on the Garden Route east of Cape Town.

Many visitors are pleasantly surprised by South Africa's excellent **infrastructure**. Good air links and bus routes, excellent roads, and plenty of accommodation suited to all budgets make the country perfect for touring. Despite this, after 25 years of democracy, the "**rainbow nation**" is still struggling to find a new identity. Apartheid is dead, but its heritage still shapes South Africa in many ways and has left it as one of the world's most unequal societies.

Culturally, South Africa doesn't reduce simply to black and white. More than eighty percent of the population comprises black **Africans** whose diverse cultural heritages are reflected in the existence of eleven official languages (and several more unofficial ones). **White people** of European descent make up just under nine percent of the population, split roughly evenly between those who speak English as a first language, and those who speak Afrikaans (a derivative of Dutch). There are a similar number of (mostly Afrikaans-speaking) **Coloureds**, the mixed-race descendants of white settlers, Africans and slaves from Southeast Asia, while 2.5 percent of the population is descended from indentured **Indian** labourers who came to KwaZulu-Natal in the late nineteenth century. Unsurprisingly,

FACT FILE

- With a **population** estimated at almost 58 million people, South Africa has eleven official **languages**: isiZulu, isiXhosa, Afrikaans, English, Sepedi, Setswana, Sesotho, Xitsonga, siSwati, Tshivenda and isiNdebele.

- The country is a **multiparty democracy**, the head of state being President Cyril Ramaphosa of the African National Congress (ANC). Parliament sits in Cape Town, the **legislative capital**, while Pretoria is the **executive capital**, from where the president and his cabinet run the country, and Bloemfontein is the judicial capital. Each of the nine provinces has its own government.

- South Africa has a **2850km coastline** split between the Atlantic Ocean to the west and the Indian Ocean to the east. The two oceans meet at Cape Agulhas, the most southerly point in Africa. The interior rises to the **uKhahlamba-Drakensberg**, which is both the most extensive and the highest range in southern Africa, with several peaks topping 3400m.

- South Africa is listed as one of the world's seventeen **megadiverse** countries thanks mainly to its **flora**, which includes 22,000 described species of vascular plant, sixty percent of then unique to this one country. It also boasts an impressive **fauna** including roughly 300 mammal, 850 bird and 350 reptile species.

- Despite a dramatic increase in **rhino** poaching since 2010, South Africa is far and away the world's most important stronghold for these vulnerable giants. Indeed, the largest surviving populations of both black and white rhino live within its borders, representing around **eighty percent** of the world's individual rhinos, of *all* five species!

then, each of South Africa's nine provinces has its own style of architecture, craftwork, food and sometimes dress.

Crime isn't the indiscriminate phenomenon that press reports suggest, but it is an issue. Really, it's a question of perspective – taking care, but not becoming paranoid. The odds of becoming a victim are highest in downtown Johannesburg, where violent crime is a daily reality; there is less risk in other cities, and less still in the most rural areas surrounding game reserves.

Where to go

While you could circuit South Africa and visit several scattered game parks in a matter of weeks, it's more satisfying to focus on one or two specific regions, depending on the time of year and your interests. Broadly speaking, the county's game parks can be divided into **five safari regions**, all of which have much in common in terms of wildlife, but each with its own distinct character and pros and cons.

South Africa's most established and popular safari destination is the **Greater Kruger**, which lies in the eastern lowveld of Mpumalanga and Limpopo provinces, half a day by car, or an hour's hop by air, from the cities of Johannesburg and Pretoria. The regional focal point is the mighty **Kruger National Park**, which extends across an incredible 19,500 square kilometres of bushveld inhabited by scores of large mammals including the country's largest single populations of all the Big Five (lion, leopard, buffalo, elephant and rhino). Kruger itself is relatively budget friendly, ideal for self-drive exploration, and so extensive that you could easily dedicate a fortnight to meandering from the bustling south to the remote and little-visited north. The national park also shares open boundaries with a number of concession lodges and private reserves that offer superlative all-inclusive upmarket guided safari packages within their own small corner of the vast Greater Kruger ecosystem.

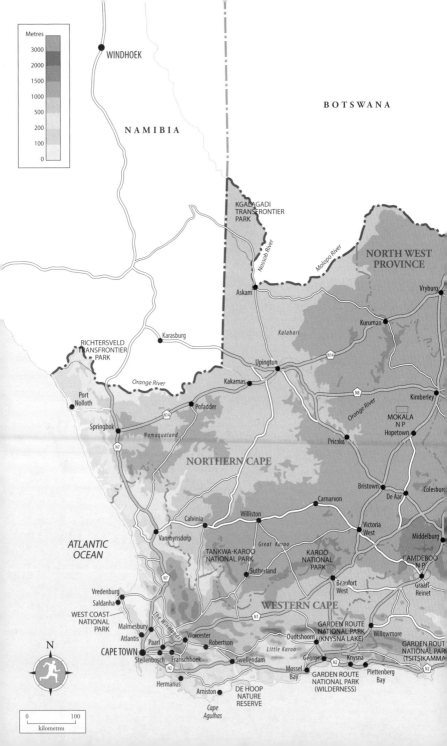

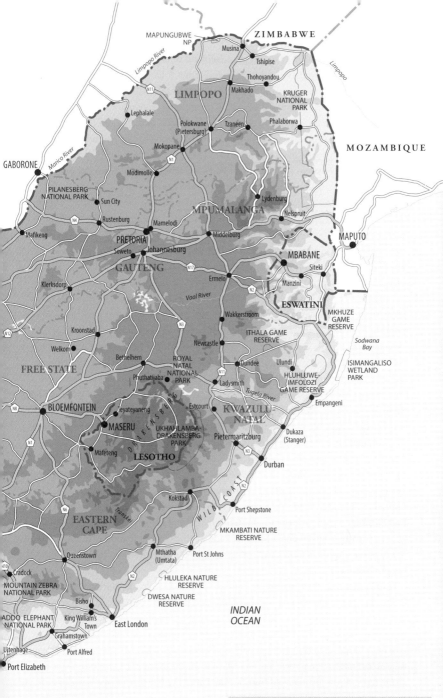

SOUTH AFRICA, LESOTHO AND ESWATINI

Second only to Kruger in stature, the **Zululand safari circuit** is centred on the **isimangaliso Wetland Park**, a 3320-square-kilometre UNESCO World Heritage Site set along the subtropical north coast of **KwaZulu-Natal**. Zululand isn't a single, vast, unfenced conservation area like Greater Kruger, but compensates with its incredible diversity of terrestrial, freshwater and marine habitats. iSimangaliso itself comes across less like a unified conservation area than a patchwork of perhaps a dozen small reserves – of which the most important are **Lake St Lucia** (hippos and waterbirds), **uMkhuze Game Reserve** (Big Five) and **Sodwana Bay** (snorkelling and diving). Outside of iSimangaliso, **Hluhluwe-iMfolozi Park** is a superb self-drive Big Five destination that hosts the world's highest densities of both white and black rhino, while **Phinda** and **Zimanga** are the pick of a pack of top-notch private reserves. As with Kruger, it would be easy to dedicate a couple of weeks to exploring Zululand, the difference being that this subtropical coastal circuit, with its gorgeous beaches and liberal scattering of forests and lakes, offers a far greater scenic, biological and experiential variety.

A negative of the Greater Kruger, and to a lesser extent Zululand, is that they carry a low risk of **malaria**, at least during the wet summer months, when they can also be stiflingly hot. For this reason, an increasing number of visitors to South Africa, especially those with young children, gravitate towards the **North West Circuit**, which is entirely free of malaria, and closer to Johannesburg and Pretoria. The main self-drive Big Five destination in North West Province is **Pilanesberg National Park**, while its counterpart for those seeking the luxurious private reserve treatment is **Madikwe Game Reserve**. Also worth considering, though it actually lies just within Limpopo Province, is the little-known **Marakele National Park** and associated mosaic of private properties that comprise the **Waterberg Biosphere Reserve**.

South Africa boasts two other malaria-free safari circuits. The **Eastern Cape** is perhaps the most ecologically compromised of these, since many of its reserves were recently salvaged from degraded farmland. That said, it has the advantage of being conveniently located at the eastern end of the popular overland tourist route from **Cape Town** to **Port Elizabeth** via the **Winelands** and **Garden Route**. Pride of place in the Eastern Cape goes to **Greater Addo Elephant National Park**, a self-drive destination that now hosts all the Big Five, but the region also hosts several good private reserves, including world-famous **Shamwari**.

At the other end of the remoteness and development scale, the **Northern Cape circuit** is set on a sparse but exhilarating region of open horizons, switchback mountain passes, rocks, scrubby vegetation and isolated *dorps* (small towns) that covers nearly a third of the country. Highlights include the peachy dunescapes and excellent big cat viewing of **Kgalagadi Transfrontier Park**, the spectacular waterfall that lends its name to **Augrabies Falls National Park**, and the Martian landscapes and bizarre succulents that characterize **Ai-Ais Richtersveld Transfrontier Park**. The Northern Cape is the one circuit that genuinely requires time – anything less than two weeks would feel rushed – and it is probably best saved for a second or third visit to South Africa, ideally in August or September, to coincide with the legendary wildflower displays that blanket the **Namaqualand region** in spring.

Five of this book's six regional chapters are dedicated primarily to one of the above safari circuits. The odd-man-out is the chapter that covers the **Western Cape**, which is a bit of a paradox insofar as it is unquestionably the most heavily touristed of South Africa's provinces, thanks to the presence of Cape Town, the Winelands and the Garden Route, but isn't much cop when it comes to safari-type reserves. Despite this, the Western Cape has much to offer wildlife enthusiasts. The world's best land-based **whale-watching** and the only penguin colonies on the African mainland are highlights of the province's exceptional marine fauna, while its fynbos-strewn slopes and evergreen forests are rich in endemic mammals and birds, ranging from the endangered Cape mountain zebra to the spectacular Knysna turaco.

When to go

South Africa is predominantly sunny, but when it does get cold you feel it, since everything is geared to fine weather. **Midwinter** in the southern hemisphere is in June and July, while **midsummer** is during December and January, when the country shuts down for its annual holiday.

South Africa has distinct climatic zones. **Cape Town** and nearby parts of the **Western Cape** have a Mediterranean climate characterized by dry summers and damp winters. Many Capetonians regard March to May, when the summer winds drop, as the perfect season: weather tends to be mild and autumnal, and the tourists have gone along with the stifling February heat. The rest of the country is a summer rainfall area, though the coastal strip running west from the **Garden Route** to Port Elizabeth is a transition zone where rain might fall at any time of year.

Temperatures are strongly influenced by proximity to the equator and altitude. The subtropical **KwaZulu-Natal** coastal belt is very hot and humid in summer, but pleasantly warm and sunny in winter. The **uKhahlamba-Drakensberg** range in western KwaZulu-Natal has warm misty days in summer and mountain snow in winter. **Johannesburg** and **Pretoria** lie on the highveld plateau and have a near-perfect climate; summer days are hot and frequently broken by dramatic thunder showers; winters are warm and dry by day, with chilly nights that frequently drop below freezing. East of Johannesburg, the **lowveld**, the low-lying wedge along the Mozambique border that includes the **Kruger National Park** and much of **Eswatini** (formerly Swaziland) is subject to similar summer and winter rainfall patterns to the highveld, but experiences far greater extremes of temperature because of its considerably lower altitude. The semi-arid **Kalahari** and **Karoo**, which comprise most of the **Northern Cape**, **Western Cape** and **Eastern Cape interior**, are much drier and tend to have a high daily temperature fluctuation, becoming very hot on summer days and seriously chilly on winter nights.

From a game-viewing perspective, winter is the best time to visit most South African game parks, not only because temperatures tend to be more comfortable, but also because the vegetation is lower and animals tends to congregate around limited water sources, making it easier to locate and spot wildlife. This is especially true of **Greater Kruger**, where an added advantage of travelling in the dry season is the greatly reduced risk of malaria infection. A major exception to the above is the reserves of the **Eastern Cape**, a year-round destination that gets prohibitively cold on winter nights, and so tends to be more enjoyable in summer. Another exception is the **Northern Cape**, which is most pleasant climatically in the cusp seasons of March to May and August to September, the latter two months also being spring wildflower season in nearby **Namaqualand**. Finally, while winter is generally the most productive season for viewing large mammals, **birders** will more likely want to visit in summer, when avian variety is boosted by the arrival of various Palaearctic migrants, and many resident species shed their dull eclipse plumage in favour of brighter breeding colours. For serious wildlife photographers, summer might offer slightly less game viewing, but the greener scenery and less hazy skies compensate.

Another not-so-obvious factor in choosing when to visit South Africa is domestic school holidays, which are best avoided especially if you will be focusing on public reserves such as **Kruger**, **Pilanesberg** and **Addo**. The main school break is in midsummer (early December to mid-January), but there are also usually holidays over Easter, late June into July, and late September. Exact dates vary from one year to the next, so check ⓦschoolterms.co.za for up-to-date details.

Author picks

Our author has visited every corner of South Africa to isolate its most rewarding game parks and wildlife-viewing experiences. These are some of the author's favourite spots.

Self-drive safaris Served by a vast network of all-weather roads, a dozen well-equipped restcamps and an excellent choice of interpretive material, the 350km-long Kruger National Park is Africa's ultimate DIY safari destination (see page 105).

That elusive leopard Sabi Sands, MalaMala and the other private reserves that share an open border with Kruger (see page 123) are justifiably renowned for their Big Five viewing, but they stand out above all as the best place anywhere for close-up sightings of the iconic quintet's most secretive member.

Rhino viewing Hluhluwe-iMfolozi, another fine Big Five reserve suited to self-drivers, played a crucial role in saving the white rhino from a near-extinction in the early twentieth century. Today it reputedly hosts the densest remaining population of both African rhino species (see page 147).

Desert delights The compelling red dunescapes of Kgalagadi Transfrontier Park host a varied collection of large mammal fauna, including several prides of black-maned Kalahari lion (see page 285).

Marine wildlife South Africa's busiest tourist hub thanks to its gorgeous seaside setting below Table Mountain, Cape Town is somewhat lacking when it comes to conventional safari opportunities, but the marine fauna – lobtailing whales, cavorting seals, graceful dolphins, comical penguins and a host of pelagic wanderers – is sensational (see page 196).

A bounty of birds A tally of 850 species make South Africa an alluring destination for birders. There's plenty of avian action throughout the country, but when it comes to subtropical variety, the biodiverse iSimangaliso Wetland Park would be tough to beat (see page 350).

Spectacular scenery The Amphitheatre, a sheer 5km-long sandstone crescent bookended by a pair of massive rock buttresses, is the most striking geographic feature in the uKhahlamba-Drakensberg Park, which protects southern Africa's tallest mountain range (see page 190).

Our author recommendations don't end here. We've flagged up our favourite places – a perfectly sited hotel, an atmospheric café, a special restaurant – throughout the Guide, highlighted with the ★ symbol.

WHITE RHINOCEROS CALF, HLUHLUWE–IMFOLOZI PARK

AFRICAN PENGUIN, BOULDERS BEACH

20

things not to miss

It's not possible to see everything that South Africa's game parks have to offer in one trip – and we don't suggest you try. What follows is a selective taste of the country's wildlife highlights, including staggeringly beautiful mammals, unforgettable reserves, and lodges that will cosset you in the lap of luxury. All entries have a page reference to take you straight into the Guide, where you can find out more. Coloured numbers refer to chapters in the Guide section.

1 HLUHLUWE-IMFOLOZI PARK
See page 147

KwaZulu-Natal's finest game reserve provides an unsurpassed variety of wildlife-spotting activities, from night drives to guided wilderness walks.

2 ADDO ELEPHANT NATIONAL PARK
See page 235

Encounter elephants and the rest of the Big Five at the eastern end of the Garden Route.

3 WILDERNESS TRAILS
See pages 108 and 150

Spot wildlife on a guided overnight hike through Kruger or Hluhluwe-iMfolozi.

4 CAPE OF GOOD HOPE
See page 202

A wide variety of endemic wildlife and marine birds inhabit the most southerly sector of Table Mountain National Park, terminating in the rocky promontory of Cape Point, one of the most dramatic coastal locations on the continent.

5 KGALAGADI TRANSFRONTIER PARK
See page 285

View cheetah, gemsbok, meerkat and other desert dwellers amid the harsh beauty of the Kalahari's red dunes.

6 NAMAQUALAND WILD FLOWERS

See page 277

Over August and September, spring rains transform Namaqualand's normally bleak landscape into an explosion of floral colour.

7 KRUGER NATIONAL PARK

See page 104

South Africa's largest national park and ultimate wildlife destination Is home to 147 mammal species, including substantial populations of all the Big Five.

8 MADIKWE GAME RESERVE

See page 72

This underrated malaria-free game park boasts some excellent lodges and superlative wildlife-spotting opportunities, from wild dogs to lions and elephants.

9 DE HOOP NATURE RESERVE

See page 217

Endemic mountain zebras and bontebok, plentiful birds and a varied marine fauna make this one of the Western Cape's most compelling wildlife-viewing destinations. See it all on the five-day Whale Trail.

10 WHALE-WATCHING

See page 216

Southern right whales often approach close below the cliffs around Hermanus during the calving season of July to November.

11 CRUISE LAKE ST LUCIA

See page 153

Hippo and crocodiles are the star attraction of boat trips on the estuarine lake at the heart of the iSimangaliso Wetland Park.

12 AUGRABIES FALLS

See page 282

South Africa's most spectacular waterfall is the focal point of a walker-friendly national park whose dry-country wildlife ranges from colourful lizards and birds to giraffe and zebra.

13 GREATER KRUGER PRIVATE RESERVES

See page 123

Though they're not aimed at tight budgets, the luxurious likes of Sabi Sand, MalaMala and Timbavati offer the world's best leopard viewing on guided drives that also reliably throw up the rest of the Big Five.

14 PHOTOGRAPH FROM A HIDE

See pages 163 and 178

Zululand's uMkhuze Game Reserve is a great place to snap rhino, antelope and colourful birds from a hide, while nearby Zimanga Private Reserve takes it a step further with nine strategically designed hides for the exclusive use of overnight guests.

15 TRACK WHITE RHINO

See page 174

Pongola Game Reserve is perhaps the best place in South Africa to track Africa's second-largest land mammal on foot.

16 GO BIRDING
See page 350
Most visitors are wowed by
South Africa's spectacular
birdlife, which encompasses
850 bird species ranging
from the outsized ostrich
and various mighty eagles
and vultures to brightly
coloured rollers, bee-eaters
and twinspots.

17 SNORKEL AT
SODWANA BAY
See page 167
The world's southernmost
coral reefs harbour giddying
swirls of colourful fish along
with large marine creatures
such as ragged-tooth sharks
and green turtles.

18 TRACK CHEETAHS
ON FOOT
See page 258
Guided cheetah tracking
is a highlight of Mountain
Zebra National Park, a hilly
reserve that also forms the
main stronghold of the
endangered Cape mountain
zebra.

19 SELF-DRIVE
PILANESBERG
See page 66
The closest major self-drive
reserve to Gauteng, set in a
scenic extinct volcano, offers
a good chance of spotting all
the Big Five over the course
of a few days.

20 LOOK FOR
NOCTURNAL SPECIALS
See pages 124, 158 and 267
Night drives in most private
and some public reserves
offer potential encounters
with a host of nocturnal
creatures, from the bizarre
aardvark and pangolin to
the lovely cat-like genet and
impressive giant eagle-owl.

Tailor-made trips

The following four itineraries all focus on game parks and other wildlife-viewing opportunities, from birding to whale-watching. Each is worth at least two weeks, and stitched together they could constitute a grand tour of two months or longer. They give a flavour of what South Africa has to offer and what we can plan and book for you at www.roughguides.com/trips.

KRUGER EXPLORER

South Africa's largest national park extends over an area comparable to many European countries and is ideal for a self-drive safari. Most visitors stick to a two- or three-night visit to southern Kruger, which has the best facilities and is the closest part of the park to Johannesburg, the usual starting point for self-drivers. For those with sufficient time and interest, however, you could easily dedicate two weeks or longer to exploring this vast park from south to north.

❶ **Lower Sabie or Skukuza** The pick of the southern restcamps, low-key Lower Sabie and the much larger and better-equipped Skukuza, both have great locations on the Sabie River and stand at the junction of several fine game-viewing roads. Either camp would make an ideal base for a two- to three-night standalone safari. See page 114.

❷ **Satara** Set in the heart of the park's south-central plains, Satara is not the most characterful or scenic restcamp, but the surrounding grassland supports high densities of lion, cheetah and other carnivores. See page 118.

❸ **Olifants or Balule** Perched on a cliff above the eponymous river, Olifants is Kruger's most scenic camp, and it also offers great in-house game viewing. Nearby Balule is a tiny and super-affordable off-the-grid satellite camp that offers a real taste of old-style safari living. See page 118.

❹ **Letaba** A favourite with repeat Kruger visitors and dedicated birders, this small restcamp has a lovely setting on the Letaba River. Here, you really start to feel the transition from the relatively crowded south of Kruger to the quieter north. See page 118.

❺ **Shingwedzi** Possibly the most underrated restcamp in Kruger, Shingwedzi has a gorgeous riverine setting and is also something of a wildlife-viewing oasis. See page 122.

❻ **Punda Maria** Kruger's most northerly restcamp is a great base for exploring the rewarding Pafuri wildlife viewing circuit as it runs along the south bank of the perennial Luvuvhu River. See page 122.

❼ **Western Limpopo** With an additional five days or so, it is well worth returning

You can book these trips with Rough Guides, or we can help you create your own. Whether you're after adventure or a family-friendly holiday, we have a trip for you, with all the activities you enjoy doing and the sights you want to see. All our trips are devised by local experts who get the most out of the destination. Visit **www.roughguides.com/trips** to chat with one of our travel agents.

to Johannesburg via the west of Limpopo Province, highlights of which include the excellent but unsung Mapungubwe and Marakele National Parks and (summer only) bird-rich Nylsvley Nature Reserve. See page 78.

KWAZULU-NATAL COASTAL SAFARI

Dominated by the iSimangaliso Wetland Park, a UNESCO World Heritage Site known for its rich aquatic and marine fauna, the northern reaches of the subtropical coastal province of KwaZulu-Natal rival Kruger as South Africa's best self-drive safari destination. The difference is that while Kruger is a vast contiguous wilderness where activities are more-or-less limited to game drives, northern KwaZulu-Natal protects a mosaic of smaller reserves that offer a varied palette of drives, boat trips, day walks and beach excursions. It can be explored as a round trip from the port of Durban or as a southern extension of a Kruger safari.

❶ St Lucia Village The urban gateway to iSimangaliso, jungle-bound St Lucia is South Africa's wildest village, home to the likes of porcupine, bushbuck, vervet monkey, warthog and a wealth of forest birds. Boat trips onto

hippo-inundated Lake St Lucia are a highlight, as are drives into the scenic reserves known as Eastern and Western Shores. The beach is lovely too. See page 155.

❷ Hluhluwe-iMfolozi Park This green and hilly self-drive reserve supports all the Big Five and is renowned for its dense population of black and white rhino. Elephant and lion are also common. See page 147.

❸ Mkhuze Game Reserve Part of the iSimangaliso Wetland Park, Mkhuze is a good Big Five reserve famed among photographers and birders for its excellent network of photographic hides. See page 163.

❹ Phinda or Zimanga If your budget stretches to a stay in a private reserve, these two are the pick of Zululand's excellent crop. Bordering iSimangaliso, Phinda offers superb general Big Five viewing and birding, while Zimanga is aimed mainly at dedicated photographers with its network of strategically located hides. See page 176.

❺ Northern iSimangaliso The northern part of iSimangaliso protects a long sliver of pristine Indian Ocean coastline where marine turtles come ashore to nest below tall forested dunes. Highlights include Sodwana Bay (a top diving

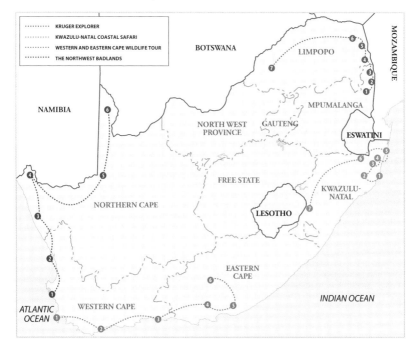

and snorkelling destination, but busy in season) and the more remote Lake Sibaya and Kosi Bay. See page 166.

❻ Pongola Game Reserve This underrated private reserve has two scenic and budget-friendly lodges from where you can track rhino on foot or take a boat onto the wildlife-rich Pongolapoort Dam. See page 174.

❼ uKhahlamba-Drakensberg Head inland to this dramatically mountainous UNESCO World Heritage Site, with its breathtaking hikes, wealth of prehistoric rock-art sites, and varied (and safe) wildlife. See page 186.

WESTERN AND EASTERN CAPE WILDLIFE TOUR

South Africa's most southerly provinces are best known for their sensational coastlines and characterful old cities, but they also offer some superb wildlife viewing. In addition to a dozen or so Big Five reserves offering a condensed version of the safari experience associated with Greater Kruger, there are marine creatures such as whales and penguins, and terrestrial endemics ranging from Cape mountain zebra and bontebok to Cape sugarbird and orange-bellied sunbird.

❶ Table Mountain National Park The scenic backdrop to Cape Town, Southern Africa's oldest and most beautiful city, this piecemeal national park also offers some great marine and terrestrial wildlife viewing. See page 196.

❷ De Hoop Nature Reserve Monumental dunes, wild surf and a few endemic large mammals are reason enough to visit this lovely coastal reserve, but it's also one of the world's top spots for land-based whale-watching. See page 217.

❸ Garden Route Wildlife highlights of South Africa's quintessential coastal route include Gondwana Game Reserve, the only place where you can see the Big Five in a fynbos habitat, and Robberg Nature Reserve, a dramatic peninsula inhabited by large numbers of seals. See page 221.

❹ Greater Addo National Park The Eastern Cape's top self-drive safari destination is renowned for its high density of elephants, but is also home to lion, leopard, black rhino and buffalo. See page 235.

❺ Eastern Cape Private Reserves A cluster of private Big Five reserves to the east of Addo includes prestigious Shamwari, untrammelled Kwandwe, scenic Sibuya and relatively budget-friendly Amakhala. See page 246.

❻ Eastern Karoo Head inland to the semi-arid Eastern Cape interior, where Mountain Zebra National Park is a great self-drive gem offering cheetah-tracking on foot and Samara ranks among South Africa's most exclusive private reserves. See page 257.

THE NORTHWEST BADLANDS

This rewarding alternative route to the N1 between Cape Town and Johannesburg is at its best during the spring wildflower season in August and September. Allow two weeks – or longer – to make the most of it.

❶ West Coast National Park This stunning coastal park, centred on the Langebaan Lagoon, is worth visiting for marine and terrestrial wildlife throughout the year, but is best dressed in wildflower season, when the Postberg sector is not to be missed. See page 207.

❷ Bird Island A breeding colony of handsomely marked Cape gannets is the star attraction at this small island off Lambert's Bay, but penguins, cormorants and seals play a key supporting role. See page 209.

❸ Namaqua National Park As is the case with much of Namaqualand, this dry-country national park supports an intriguing succulent flora that bursts into prodigious multi-hued blossom in spring. See page 276.

❹ Ai-Ais Richtersveld Transfrontier Park A great diversion for those with a sturdy 4WD and plenty of time, this desert park is notable for the bizarre succulents on its mountainous slopes and the presence of a raftable stretch of the Orange River along the border with Namibia. See page 279.

❺ Augrabies Falls National Park South Africa's mightiest waterfall is formed by the Orange River as it crashes into a steep cliff-lined gorge. Walking trails offer an opportunity to a variety of dry country. See page 282.

❻ Kgalagadi Transfrontier Park The most remote of South Africa's major self-drive game parks is a favourite with the cognoscenti for its wild character, scenic red dunes and a varied fauna that includes lion, leopard, bat-eared fox, gemsbok and meerkat. See page 285.

OSTRICH, KRUGER NATIONAL PARK

Basics

Getting there

As sub-Saharan Africa's economic and tourism hub, South Africa is well served with flights from London and the rest of Europe. The majority of these touch down at Johannesburg's OR Tambo International, but there are also frequent flights into Cape Town. From North America there are a relatively small number of nonstop flights into Johannesburg.

Airfares depend on the **season**, with the highest prices and greatest demand in July, August, September, December and the first week of January. Prices drop during April (except for around Easter), May and November, while the rest of the year is "shoulder season".

Flights from the UK and Ireland

From London there are nonstop flights with British Airways (🌐 ba.com), South African Airways (SAA, 🌐 flysaa.com) and Virgin Atlantic (🌐 virgin-atlantic. com) to Johannesburg and Cape Town. Flying time from the UK is around eleven hours to Joburg, about an hour longer to Cape Town; to the latter, average high-season scheduled direct fares from London start around £1000. It's generally cheaper to fly to Cape Town via Joburg; you can make major savings by flying via mainland Europe, the Middle East or Asia, and enduring at least one change of plane.

There are no direct flights from the **Republic of Ireland**, but a number of European and Middle Eastern carriers fly to South Africa via their hub airports.

Flights from the US and Canada

From the US there are regular direct **flights** from New York (JFK) and Washington (IAD) operated by South African Airways in partnership with United Airlines (🌐 united.com). Stopping in West Africa to refuel, these take between fifteen and seventeen hours. Most other flights stop off in Europe, the Middle East or Asia and involve a change of plane. There are no direct flights **from Canada**; you'll have to change planes in the US, Europe or Asia, with journey times that can last over thirty hours.

For flights from New York to Cape Town via Joburg, expect high-season return fares to start around $1200; you will make major savings if you fly via Europe, the Middle East or Asia. High-season return fares from Toronto to Cape Town are similarly priced to those from the US east coast.

Flights from Australia and New Zealand

There are nonstop flights **from Sydney** (which take 14hr) and **Perth** (11hr) to Johannesburg, with onward connections to Cape Town. Flights **from New Zealand** tend to be via Sydney too. South African Airways and Qantas (🌐 qantas.com) fly nonstop to Joburg from Perth and Sydney respectively; several Asian, Middle Eastern and European airlines fly to South Africa via their hub cities, and tend to be less expensive, but their routings often entail long stopovers.

Cape Town is not a cheap destination for travellers from Australia and New Zealand; high-/low-season fares start around Aus$2000/1600 for an indirect return flight **from Sydney** to Cape Town with one change. A flight to Europe with a stopover in South Africa, or even a RTW ticket, may represent better value than a straightforward return. The most affordable return flights tend to travel via Dubai, Doha, Singapore and Kuala Lumpur, with the likes of Qatar Airways and Emirates.

Entry requirements

Nationals of the UK, US, Canada, Australia, New Zealand, Japan, Argentina and Brazil don't require a **visa** to enter South Africa. Most EU nationals don't need a visa, the exceptions being citizens from Bulgaria, Croatia, Estonia, Latvia, Lithuania, Romania, Slovakia and Slovenia, who need to obtain one at a South African diplomatic mission in their home country. Requirements are prone to change, however, so check the official government website

---

A BETTER KIND OF TRAVEL

At Rough Guides we are passionately committed to travel. We believe it helps us understand the world we live in and the people we share it with – and of course tourism is vital to many developing economies. But the scale of modern tourism has also damaged some places irreparably, and climate change is accelerated by most forms of transport, especially flying. We encourage our authors to consider the carbon footprint of the journeys they make in the course of researching the guides.

(W dha.gov.za/index.php/immigration-services/ exempt-countries) for a full and up-to-date list of visa-exempt countries.

As long as you carry a passport that is valid for at least thirty days from the date of exit from South Africa, with at least two empty pages, you will be granted a **temporary visitor's permit**, which allows you to stay in South Africa for up to ninety days for most nationals, and thirty days for EU passport holders from Cyprus, Hungary and Poland. All visitors should have proof of a valid return ticket or another form of onward travel; immigration officers rarely ask to see it, but airlines will often check. Likewise, visitors should have a bank statement showing that they have sufficient funds to cover their stay, but, again, officials seldom ask to see it.

Cross-border "visa runs" are not possible, but you can **extend your visitor's visa** for up to ninety days, or apply to stay for longer periods for purposes such as study. Applications should be made through VFS Global (☎ 012 425 3000, W vfsglobal.com/southafrica), which will ask to see paperwork including proof of sufficient funds to cover your stay.

The easiest option is to use a **consultant** such as the immigration division of the International English School (☎ 021 852 8859, W english.za.net/immigration-services) in Somerset West, just outside Cape Town. Their services are recommended, and paying such a consultant's fees is preferable to bureaucratic headaches.

AGENTS AND OPERATORS

Absolute Africa UK ☎ 020 8742 0226, W absoluteafrica.com. Safaris and adventure camping overland trips.

Acacia Africa Australia ☎ 02 8011 3686; UK ☎ 020 7706 4700; South Africa ☎ 021 556 1157, W acacia-africa.com. Camping and accommodated trips along classic Southern African routes.

Africa Travel UK ☎ 020 7843 3500, W africatravel.com. Experienced Africa specialists, offering flights and packages including a thirteen-day Cape Town, Garden Route and Victoria Falls itinerary.

Classic Safari Company Australia ☎ 1300 130 218, W classicsafaricompany.com.au. Luxury tailor-made safaris to Southern Africa.

Exodus Travels UK ☎ 020 3733 0570, W exodus.co.uk; US ☎ 1 844 227 9087, W exodustravels.com. Small-group adventure tour operator with itineraries in and around Cape Town, overland trips taking in Kruger National Park and themed packages including activities such as cycling. Offices worldwide.

Expert Africa Australia ☎ 1-800-995-397; New Zealand ☎ 04 976 7585; UK ☎ 020 3405 6666; US ☎ 1 800 242 2434, W expertafrica. com. Mostly self-drive safari packages, including Addo Elephant National Park, and with the option of incorporating flights from the UK.

Explore Worldwide UK ☎ 01252 882 946, W explore.co.uk; US ☎ 1 800 715 1746, W exploreworldwide.com. Good range of small-group tours, expeditions and safaris, staying mostly in small hotels and taking in Cape Town and beyond.

Journeys International US ☎ 1 800 255 8735, W journeys.travel. Small-group trips with a range of safaris.

Okavango Tours and Safaris UK ☎ 07721 387 738, W okavango. com. Top-notch outfit with on-the-ground knowledge of sub-Saharan Africa, offering fully flexible and individual tours across the country, including the Western Cape and family-focused packages.

Rainbow Tours UK ☎ 020 8131 7572, W rainbowtours.co.uk. Knowledgeable Africa specialists whose trips include a sixteen-day Cape Town, Garden Route and Kruger holiday.

Rough Guides UK W roughguides.com/trips. Tailor-made trips created by local experts to bring you off the beaten path, effortlessly. Trips can be personalized to take in the best game parks and wildlife-viewing opportunities.

Tribes UK ☎ 01473 890 499, W tribes.co.uk; US ☎ 1 800 608 4651. Unusual and off-the-beaten-track sustainable safaris and cultural tours, including Cape Town itineraries.

Wildlife Worldwide UK ☎ 01962 302 086, W wildlifeworldwide. com; US ☎ 1 800 972 3982. Tailor-made trips for wildlife and wilderness enthusiasts, covering the Cape and the great reserves.

Getting around

Despite the large distances, travelling around most of South Africa is fairly straightforward, with a reasonably well-organized network of public transport, a good range of car rental companies, the best road system in Africa, and the continent's most comprehensive network of internal flights. The only weak point is public transport in urban areas, which is mostly poor and dangerous with the exceptions of Johannesburg's Gautrain and Cape Town's MyCiTi bus and Metrorail Southern Line. Urban South Africans who can afford to do so tend to use private transport, and renting a vehicle is the easiest and safest option (notwithstanding South African drivers). It's virtually impossible to get to the national parks and places off the beaten track by public transport; even if you do manage, you're likely to need a car once you're there.

Buses

South Africa's three established **intercity bus** companies are Greyhound (☎ 087 352 0352, W greyhound.co.za), Intercape (☎ 021 380 4400, W intercape).

CHILDREN TRAVELLING TO SOUTH AFRICA

Rigorous **immigration requirements** for children under eighteen were introduced by the South African government in 2015, and although they were relaxed slightly in December 2018, it is important to be aware of current requirements before you travel; failure to provide all the necessary documents has caused many families to miss flights.

Under the rules introduced in 2015, all children under eighteen travelling into or out of South Africa were required to show an **unabridged (full) birth certificate** (not to be confused with the shorter and equally common abridged birth certificate) showing both parents' details, in addition to their passport. As of 2018, children from visa-exempt countries travelling with *both* parents are not automatically required to produce the birth certificate, but they may still be asked to (especially if the parents have different surnames), so is advisable to have it to hand. Children of South African origin or from a non-visa-exempt country are legally required to show a copy of the unabridged birth certificate, even when accompanied by both parents.

Where only one parent is accompanying a child of any nationality, the following may be required: copy of the unabridged passport and parental or legal consent for the child to travel (such as an affidavit from the other parent or a court order), along with a copy of the absent parent's passport, their contact details, and the reason for their absence (or, if deceased, their death certificate). Requirements for children travelling unaccompanied or with adults who are not their parents are even more exacting. The Department of Home Affairs has more details at ⓦ dha.gov.za, while the British Foreign and Commonwealth Office (ⓦ gov.uk/foreign-travel-advice/south-africa/entry-requirements) offers clear guidance and helpful links.

---

co.za) and Translux (ⓦ translux.co.za); between them, they reach most towns in the country. Travel on these buses is safe, comfortable and inexpensive, and the vehicles are invariably equipped with air conditioning and toilets. Keep your valuables close on overnight journeys, when lone women should find a seat at the front near the driver.

Fares vary according to the time of year, with peak fares corresponding approximately to school holidays. As a rough indication, expect to pay the following Greyhound fares for single journeys from Cape Town: Mossel Bay (7hr) from R560, Johannesburg (19hr) from R650, or Durban (26hr) from R795.

Translux and Greyhound also operate the no-frills budget bus lines City to City (ⓦ www.citytocity.co.za) and Citiliner (ⓦ citiliner.co.za) respectively, which run along a range of routes around the country: check their websites for schedules and prices. You'll also find a host of small private companies running certain routes – your best bet is to enquire at the bus station the day before you travel.

Baz Bus (ⓣ 021 422 5202, ⓦ bazbus.com) operates an extremely useful hop-on/hop-off bus network aimed at backpackers and budget travellers, with minibuses stopping off at backpacker accommodation en route. Its services run up and down the coast in both directions between Cape Town and Port Elizabeth via the Garden Route (five days weekly), and between Port Elizabeth and Durban via the Wild Coast (four days weekly). Inland, it runs buses between Durban and Johannesburg via the Northern Drakensberg (three days weekly). A number of independently run **shuttle services** connect with the Baz Bus and go to Stellenbosch, Hermanus and Oudtshoorn in the Western Cape; to Hogsback and several Wild Coast backpackers in the Eastern Cape; to the Southern Drakensberg in KwaZulu-Natal; and to Pretoria in Gauteng.

The Cape Town–Port Elizabeth fare is R2990 one-way with no time limits, though there are also better-value seven-, fourteen- and 21-day passes costing R3300, R5300 and R6600. Bookings can be made through the website or by telephone.

Minibus taxis

Minibus taxis provide transport to the majority of South Africans, travelling everywhere in the country, covering relatively short hops from town to town, commuter trips from township to town and back, and routes within larger towns and cities. However, their associated problems – dangerous drivers and violent feuds between the different taxi associations competing for custom – mean that you should take local advice before using them. This is particularly true in cities, where minibus taxi ranks tend to be a magnet for petty criminals. The other problem with minibus taxis is that there is rarely much room to place **luggage**. Despite the drawbacks, minibus taxis are often the only option for getting around **remote areas**, where you're unlikely to encounter trouble, although it would be inadvisable for lone women. You should be prepared for some long waits in the countryside, due to the taxis'infrequency.

Fares are low and comparable to what you might pay on the inexpensive intercity buses. Try to have the exact change (on shorter journeys particularly), and pass your fare to the row of passengers in front of you; eventually all the fares end up with the conductor, who dishes out any change. It's a good idea to check with locals which taxi routes are safe to use.

Trains

Travelling by **train** is just about the slowest way of getting around South Africa: the trans-Karoo journey from Johannesburg to Cape Town, for example, takes 27 hours – compared with 19 hours by bus. **Overnighting** on the train, though, is more comfortable than the bus and saves you the cost of a night's accommodation. Families with children get a private compartment on the train, and under-3s travel free, while under-9s receive a twenty percent discount.

Shosholoza Meyl (☎ 086 000 8888 or ☎ 011 774 4555, ⓦ shosholozameyl.co.za) runs most of the intercity rail services, offering comfortable and good-value **Tourist Class** travel in lockable two-person coupés and four-person compartments equipped with washbasins. There are showers and a dining car serving passable food and alcoholic drinks. Seats are comfortable and convert into **bunks**; you can rent sheets and blankets for the night (R40 per person), which are brought around by a bedding attendant who'll make up your bed. It's best to buy your bedding voucher when you book your train ticket. Services run between Johannesburg and Cape Town, Port Elizabeth, East London and Durban; and between Cape Town and Queenstown and East London. Tourist class **fares** from Johannesburg range from R360 per person to Durban (the shortest route) to R690 to Cape Town (the longest route) but vary slightly depending on the time of year. Tickets must be booked in advance at train stations, over the phone or online.

If you are travelling alone, consider buying two tickets to ensure you get a private two-person coupé; otherwise you may end up sharing in a four-person compartment.

Shosholoza Meyl's upmarket, air-conditioned weekly **Premier Classe** (☎ 086 000 8888 or ☎ 011 774 4555, ⓦ premierclasse.co.za) service connects Johannesburg and Cape Town. It offers a choice of single, double, triple and four-person compartments, with gowns, slippers and towels provided, plus high teas and five-course dinners served in a luxury dining car – all included in the fare. The **fare** is R3120 one way.

South Africa also offers a handful of **luxury trains**, with plush carriages and pricey fares. The celebrated **Blue Train** (☎ 012 334 8459, ⓦ bluetrain.co.za) runs between Cape Town and Pretoria weekly, with fares starting at R23,050 per person sharing a double berth for the 27-hour journey. Bookings can be made online or by phone.

Rovos Rail (Cape Town ☎ 021 421 4020; Pretoria ☎ 012 315 8242; ⓦ rovos.com) also runs luxury rail trips between Pretoria and Cape Town (from R22,350 per person sharing), Durban (R22,350) and Victoria Falls in Zimbabwe (R29,950), at three levels of luxury, with prices to match.

A word of warning about **security** on trains: never leave valuables unattended in your compartment unless it is locked, and always close the window if leaving your carriage.

Visit **The Man in Seat 61** (ⓦ seat61.com/South Africa) for more ideas.

Domestic flights

Flying between destinations in South Africa compares favourably with the cost of covering long distances in a rental car and overnighting en route. With several competing **budget airlines**, you can also pick up good deals.

The biggest airline offering **domestic flights** is **South African Airways** (SAA), with its subsidiaries **SA Airlink** and **SA Express** (reservations for all three go through SAA). SAA's main competitors are the budget airlines Kulula, Mango and FlySafair, which have more limited networks, but generally offer better deals on the major routes. There's also British Airways **Comair** for the major routes, while for the coastal towns of Margate and Plettenberg Bay, Cemair runs a limited service from Johannesburg.

On SAA and its associates, one-way economy-class **fares** from Cape Town to Johannesburg cost from around R1000, while the budget airlines might start at around R500 for the same route, provided you're flexible about timing and book well ahead.

Computicket Travel (☎ 0861 915 4000, ⓦ computickettravel.com) is a useful booking engine for flights, buses and car rental.

SOUTH AFRICAN DOMESTIC AIRLINES

British Airways Comair ☎ 011 441 8600, ⓦ britishairways.com. Domestic flights serving Johannesburg, Cape Town, Durban, Port Elizabeth and Nelspruit with links to the rest of Africa, including Harare, Livingstone and Windhoek.

Cemair ☎ 011 395 4473, ⓦ flycemair.co.za. Links Johannesburg to Hoedspruit (for the Kruger Park) and the coastal resorts of Plettenberg Bay in the Western Cape, and Richards Bay and

Margate in KwaZulu-Natal, with additional routes including Bloemfontein–Port Elizabeth.

FlySafair ☎ 087 135 1351, ⓦ flysafair.co.za. Budget airline with a useful network including Johannesburg and all the major coastal cities.

Kulula ☎ 086 158 5852, ⓦ kulula.com. Budget network covering Cape Town, Durban, George, East London, Johannesburg, Nairobi, Victoria Falls, Mauritius and beyond.

Mango ☎ 086 100 1234, ⓦ flymango.com. SAA's budget airline provides cheap flights including Johannesburg to Cape Town, Durban, George, Port Elizabeth and Zanzibar; and Cape Town to Bloemfontein, Durban and Joburg.

South African Airways ☎ 0861 606606, ⓦ flysaa.com. Together with SA Airlink and SA Express, SAA serves the major hubs of Johannesburg, Cape Town and Durban. Other destinations include Bloemfontein, East London, George, Kimberley, Mbombela (for southern Kruger National Park and associated private reserves), Mthatha, Phalaborwa (for northern Kruger National Park), Polokwane, Port Elizabeth, Pretoria, Richards Bay and Upington.

Driving

Short of joining a tour, the only way to get to national parks and the more remote coastal areas is by **car**. Likewise, some of the most interesting places off the beaten track are only accessible in your own vehicle, as buses tend to ply just the major routes.

South Africa is ideal for driving, with a generally **well-maintained** network of highways and a high proportion of secondary and tertiary roads that are tarred and can be driven at a reasonable speed. **Renting a vehicle** is not prohibitively expensive, and for a couple or small group it can work out to be a cheap option.

Filling stations are frequent on the major routes of the country, and usually open 24 hours. Off the beaten track, though, stations are less frequent, so fill up whenever you get the chance. Stations are not self-service; instead, poorly paid attendants fill up your car, check oil, water and tyre pressure if you ask them to, and often clean your windscreen even if you don't. A **tip** of R5–10 is appropriate.

Parking is pretty straightforward, but due to the high levels of car break-ins, attendants, known as "**car guards**", are present virtually anywhere you'll find parking, for example at shopping malls. A tip of R2–5 during the day and around R10 at night is generally appreciated.

Rules of the road and driving tips

Foreign driving licences are valid in South Africa provided they are printed in English. If you don't have such a licence, you'll need to get an **International Driving Permit** (available from national motoring organizations) before arriving in South Africa. When driving, you are obliged by law to carry your driving **licence** and (unless you're a South African resident) your passport (or certified copies) at all times; in reality, in the rare event of your being stopped, showing one of these documents or uncertified photocopies should satisfy most police officers. Leaving these documents lying in your glove box or elsewhere is not recommended.

South Africans drive on the **left-hand side** of the road; speed limits range from 30–40km/h in wildlife parks and reserves and 60km/h in built-up areas to 100km/h on open roads and 120km/h on highways and major arteries. In addition to roundabouts, which follow the British rule of giving way to the right, there are four-way stops, where the rule is that the person who got there first leaves first. Traffic lights are often called **robots** in South Africa.

The main danger you'll face on the roads is other drivers. South Africa has among the world's worst road **accident** statistics – the result of recklessness, drunken drivers (see page 44) and unroadworthy, overloaded vehicles. Keep your distance from cars in front, as cars behind you often won't and domino-style pile-ups are common. Watch out also for overtaking traffic coming towards you: overtakers often assume that you will head for the **hard shoulder** to avoid an accident (it is customary to drive on the hard shoulder, but be careful as pedestrians frequently use it). If you pull into the hard shoulder to let a car behind overtake, the other driver will probably thank you by flashing their hazard lights. It's wise to do so when it's safe, as aggressive and impatient South African drivers will soon start driving dangerously close to your back bumper to encourage you to give way. If oncoming cars flash their headlights at you, it probably means there is a speed trap or hazard ahead.

Another potential **hazard** is animals on the roads in rural areas – from livestock to baboons – so drive slowly even on quiet routes. Also, the large distances between major towns mean that falling asleep at the wheel, especially when travelling through long stretches of flat landscape in the Karoo or the Free State, is a real danger. Plan your car journeys to include breaks and stopovers. Finally, in urban areas, there's a small risk of being car-jacked; you should follow safety advice (see page 45).

South Africa's motoring organization, the **Automobile Association** (AA; ☎ 0861 000234, ⓦ aa.co.za), provides information about road conditions as well as free maps.

Car rental

Prebooking your **rental car** is the cheapest option, and will provide more favourable terms and conditions (such as unlimited mileage and lower insurance

ENGLISH/AFRIKAANS STREET NAMES

Many towns have **bilingual street names** with English and Afrikaans alternatives sometimes appearing along the same road. This applies particularly in Afrikaans areas away from the large cities, and often the Afrikaans name bears little resemblance to the English one – something to be aware of when trying to map read. Some terms you may encounter on Afrikaans signage are listed in Language (see page 393).

excesses). Don't rely on being able to just arrive at the airport and pick up a vehicle without reserving.

As a rough guideline, for a **one-week rental** expect to pay from R255 a day with a R7500 insurance excess and unlimited mileage. Many companies stipulate that drivers must be 23 or over and have been driving for at least two years. Note that to collect your vehicle, you will need to produce a credit (not debit) card.

Major rental companies usually allow you to return the car to a different city from where you rented it, though they will usually levy a charge for this. If you're planning to cross a border, for example to **Lesotho** or **Eswatini**, check that the company allows it and will provide a letter of permission. **Insurance** often doesn't cover you if you drive on unsealed roads, so check for this too. Local firms such as Around About Cars (**W** aroundaboutcars.com) are almost always cheaper than chains, but may include limited mileage of around 200km per day and restrictions on how far you can take the vehicle.

Camper vans and **4WD vehicles** equipped with rooftop tents are a good idea for camping trips and self-drive safaris. For a 4WD, expect to pay from R1200 a day for a week's rental. Some companies knock fifteen to twenty percent off the price if you book at short notice. Vans generally come fully equipped with crockery, cutlery and linen, and usually a toilet and shower. The downside of camper vans and 4WDs is that they struggle up hills and guzzle a lot of fuel (15 litres per 100km in the smaller vans), which could partly offset any savings on accommodation.

CAMPER VAN AND 4WD RENTAL AGENCIES

Britz **W** britz.co.za. Bakkies, 4WDs and SUVs, geared towards safari holidays.

Cheap Motorhome Rental **W** cheapmotorhomes.co.za. Booking agency that sources competitive motorhome rentals.

Drive Africa Cape Town **T** 021 447 1144, **W** driveafrica.co.za. Camper van, 4WD and car rental. They offer long-term deals and rent vehicles to drivers under 21.

Kea Travel **W** kea.co.za. Motorhome and 4WD rental.

Maui **T** 011 230 5200, **W** maui.co.za. One of the biggest rental outlets for camper vans and 4WDs.

Cycling

It's easy to see why **cycling** is popular in South Africa: you can get to stunning destinations on good roads unclogged by traffic, many towns have decent cycle shops for spares and equipment, and many backpacker hostels rent out mountain bikes for reasonable rates, so you don't have to transport your bike into the country. You'll need to be fit though, as South Africa is a hilly place, and many roads have punishing gradients. The **weather** can make life difficult, too: if it isn't raining, there is a good chance of it being very hot, so carry plenty of liquids. Cycling in built-up areas and on the main intercity roads is not recommended due to dangerous drivers.

Hitching

Hitching is risky and not recommended, particularly in large towns and cities, and you should never pick up hitchhikers. If you must hitchhike, avoid hitching alone and being dropped off in isolated areas between settlements. Ask drivers where they are going before you say where you want to go, and keep your **bags** with you: having them locked in the boot makes a hasty escape more difficult. Making a contribution towards petrol is often expected. Check the **notice boards** in backpacker lodges for people offering or looking to share lifts – that way, you can meet the driver in advance.

Accommodation

Accommodation in South Africa can be expensive compared with other African countries, but standards are generally high and you get exceptional value for money. Even modest backpacker lodges provide a minimum of fresh sheets and clean rooms. Other than in the very cheapest rooms, a private bath or shower is practically a given, and you'll often have the use of a garden or swimming pool. South Africa also has some outstanding boutique hotels, luxury guesthouses, lodges and country retreats – invariably in beautiful settings – at fairly reasonable prices. The country's national parks and reserves feature a range of accommo-

dation, from fairly basic restcamps to incredibly slick game lodges (see page 39), while you'll also find a backpacker hostel in most areas, plus no shortage of camping and self-catering options.

Advance booking is vital if you're travelling in high season or if you plan to stay in a national park or in popular areas such as Cape Town and the Garden Route. South Africa's **peak season** is during the midsummer Christmas school holiday period, when South African families migrate to the coast and inland resorts. The Easter school holiday is also busy. At Christmas and Easter, **prices** rise sharply across the spectrum, particularly in the mid-range and top-end categories, and most places get booked up months ahead.

> ## ACCOMMODATION PRICES
>
> Accommodation price codes usually reflect the rate of a standard double/twin unit in high season. As a rule, rates charged by restcamps in parks and reserves are bed only, while those for urban hotels and B&Bs include breakfast, and those in luxury safari lodges and camps include all meals and two safari activities, and in some cases drinks too.
>
> **Price codes:**
> $ - under R1200
> $$ - R1200–2500
> $$$ - R2500–5000
> $$$$ - R5,000–10,000
> $$$$$ - R10,000-plus

Hotels

Most of South Africa's **budget hotels** are throwbacks to the 1950s and 1960s, and little more than watering holes that earn their keep from the bar.

Mid-range hotels usually charge from R1200 a room. Along the coastal holiday strips such as the Garden Route, southern KwaZulu-Natal and the major seaside towns in between, these hotels are ubiquitous and frequently offer rooms on the **beachfront**. Many of the mid-priced hotels – especially those on main routes in the interior – are fully booked during the week by travelling salesmen, but over the weekend, when they're often empty, you can often negotiate **discounts**.

A large number of mid-range and **upmarket establishments** belong to hotel **chains**, which offer reliable but sometimes soulless accommodation. Big players include the Marriott-owned Protea Hotels (W protea.marriott.com), Tsogo Sun (W tsogosunhotels.com), Holiday Inn (W ihg.com) and Aha (W aha.co.za).

Country lodges and boutique hotels

You will find incredible value and a memorable stay at South Africa's many small, characterful establishments – something the country excels at. You'll find hip **boutique hotels** in the cities; cosy guesthouses in the *dorps* (small towns); and luxurious **country lodges** in exceptional natural surroundings, including eco-lodges in the middle of forests, properties perched on the edges of cliffs, and magical hideaways in the middle of nowhere. At these places you can expect to be pampered and there will often be a spa on-site. There are also numerous first-rate **safari camps** and **game lodges**, which fulfil your most romantic African

fantasies (see page 39). You might pay anything from R5000 to R20,000 for a double, though this may include meals and guided wildlife-watching activities.

B&Bs and guesthouses

The most ubiquitous form of accommodation in South Africa is **B&Bs** and **guesthouses**. The official difference between the two is that the owner lives on-site at a B&B. The most basic B&Bs are just one or two rooms in a private home, perhaps with washing facilities shared with the owners in township accommodation. In reality, the distinction is a little hazy once you move up a notch to B&Bs and guesthouses that provide en-suite rooms (as is usually the case). **Rates** for en-suite rooms in both start at around R600, for which you can expect somewhere clean, comfortable and relaxed, but usually away from the beach or other action. Moving up another notch, you'll pay from R800 for a room with extra facilities, space or style, and tariffs from R1200 upwards should offer the works: a great location, comfort and good service. Prices are steeper in Cape Town, Johannesburg and the Garden Route.

Since the late 1990s, **township tours** have become popular, with township dwellers offering **B&B** accommodation to tourists in their homes; expect to pay from R500 per room per night for an authentic South African experience.

Along many roads in the countryside you will see signs for "**Bed en Ontbyt**" (Afrikaans for "bed and breakfast"), signalling **farmstay** accommodation, with rooms in the main homestead, in a cottage in its garden or out on the farm. Some also offer hiking trails, horseriding and other **activities**. Tourist offices have lists of farms in their area that rent out rooms or cottages.

Caravan parks, resorts and camping

Virtually all **national parks** – and many provincial reserves – have well-maintained **campsites**, and in some of the really remote places, such as parts of KwaZulu-Natal, camping may be your only option. Use of a campsite generally **costs** from R250 per site depending on the popularity of the park and the **facilities**. At national parks you can expect sinks and draining boards for washing dishes; often communal kitchen areas or, at the very least, a braai stand and running water; and a decent toilet and shower block (known locally as "ablutions")

Caravanning was once the favourite way to have a cheap family holiday in South Africa, and this accounts for the large number of caravan parks dotted across the length and breadth of the country. However, their popularity has declined and with it the standard of many of the country's **municipal caravan parks and campsites**. Today, municipal campsites are generally pretty scruffy, unsafe and not recommended. You may find the odd pleasant one in rural areas, or near small *dorps*. All in all, you're best off heading for the privately owned resorts, where for roughly the same price you get greater comfort, facilities and safety. Although private resorts sometimes give off a holiday-camp vibe, they usually provide good washing and cooking facilities, self-catering chalets, shops selling basic goods, braai stands and swimming pools.

Camping rough is not recommended anywhere in the country.

Backpacker lodges

The cheapest beds in South Africa are in **dormitories** at **backpacker lodges (or hostels)**, which cost from R150 per person. These are generally well-run operations with clean linen and helpful staff, although standards may slip during busy periods. In the cities and tourist resorts you'll have a number of places to choose from and almost all towns of any significance have at least one.

Apart from dorm beds, most also have **private rooms** (double R450–700) – sometimes even with private bathrooms – and an increasing number have **family rooms** that work out at around R180 per person. They usually have communal kitchens, an on-site café, TV, internet access and other facilities such as bike rental. When choosing a hostel, it's worth checking out the **ambience**, as some are party joints, while others have a quieter atmosphere.

The lodges are invariably good meeting points, with a constant stream of travellers passing through, and **notice boards** filled with advertisements for lifts, hostels and backpacker facilities throughout the country. Many lodges operate reasonably priced **excursions** into the surrounding areas, and will pick you up from train stations or bus stops (especially Baz Bus stops) if you phone in advance.

Self-catering cottages and apartments

Self-catering accommodation in cottages, apartments, cabins and small complexes can provide cheap accommodation in a variety of locations – on farms, near beaches, in forests and wilderness areas, as well as in practically every town and city.

There's a wide range of this type of accommodation, with prices depending on facilities, location and level of luxury: expect to pay from R350 a night for something basic to R1000 or over for a luxurious beach stay. **Apartments** often sleep up to six, so this can be very economical if you're travelling as a family or in a small group. You can save a lot of money by cooking for yourself, and you'll get a sense of **freedom** and **privacy** which is missing from even the nicest guesthouse or B&B. Standards are high: cottages and apartments generally come fully equipped with crockery and cutlery, and even microwaves and TVs in the more modern places. Linen and towels are often provided; check before you book in.

Food and drink

With its myriad culinary influences, South Africa doesn't really have a coherent indigenous cuisine, although Cape Malay dishes come close to this status in the Western Cape. Meat is a big feature of meals nationwide, as is the vast array of available seafood, which includes a wide variety of fish, lobster (crayfish), oysters and mussels. Locally grown fruit and vegetables are generally of a high standard.

Apart from Cape Malay street food such as *salomes* (savoury wraps) and samosas, people on the move tend to pick up a pie, burger or chicken and chips. The fast-food chains still have novelty status here, having steadily appeared since the end of apartheid. Drinking is dominated by the Western Cape's often superb wines and by a handful of unmemorable lagers; order a crisp Namibian Windhoek lager or a craft beer, as the recent upsurge of local microbreweries has dramatically improved the quality of beers on offer. In the cities, and to a lesser extent beyond them, there are numerous excellent restaurants serving local and international dishes.

ONLINE ACCOMMODATION RESOURCES

NATIONAL PARKS AND RESERVES

ⓦ **booking.capenature.co.za** Booking portal for all provincially managed reserves in the Western Cape.

ⓦ **kznwildlife.com/accomodation.html** Online bookings for all accommodation run by Ezemvelo KZN Wildlife, the authority in charge of all non-private reserves in KwaZulu-Natal.

ⓦ **sanparks.org/bookings** User-friendly booking portal for all campsites, restcamps and other SANParks-managed accommodation in the country's nineteen national parks, including Kruger.

B&BS, GUESTHOUSES AND SELF-CATERING

ⓦ **airbnb.com** This ubiquitous B&B booking site usually offers a few affordable options for even the most out-of-the-way places.

ⓦ **booking.com** Offers a pretty across-the-board selection of private accommodation, ranging from B&Bs to upmarket safari lodges, often at better rates that you'll get booking directly.

ⓦ **budget-getaways.co.za** A great resource for affordable self-catering accommodation in the Western Cape.

ⓦ **greenwoodguides.com/south-africa** Although properties pay to be listed, this site's hand-picked selection is interesting and quirky.

ⓦ **lekkeslaap.co.za** Popular homegrown counterpart to airbnb.

ⓦ **portfoliocollection.com** Again, properties pay to be listed, but they also have to meet fairly rigorous standards.

ⓦ **safarinow.com** One of the oldest and best South African online booking sites covers all types of accommodation, with user reviews and rankings.

BACKPACKERS

ⓦ **bazbus.com** Website of South Africa's biggest backpacker bus service also provides links to lodges with an online booking facility.

ⓦ **coasttocoast.co.za** Comprehensive coverage of backpackers all over South Africa; no booking facility but you can email a direct enquiry to the lodge of your choice.

ⓦ **hihostels.com** Hostelling International acts as a booking agent for more than a dozen of South Africa's backpacker lodges.

ⓦ **hostelbookers.com** International website with clear navigation and good coverage of South African hostels, including detailed reviews and ratings.

ⓦ **travelnownow.com** Website of SAYTC (South African Youth Travel Confederation) has links to hostel members.

CAMPING AND CARAVAN PARKS

ⓦ **campsa.co.za** Comprehensive online directory of Southern African campsites and caravan parks.

Breakfast, lunch and dinner

B&Bs, hotels, guesthouses and some backpacker lodges serve a **breakfast** of eggs with bacon and usually some kind of sausage. Muesli, fruit, yoghurt, croissants and pastries are increasingly popular. **Lunch** is eaten around 1pm and **dinner** in the evening around 7pm or 8pm; the two are pretty much interchangeable on more limited menus, usually along the lines of meat, chicken or fish and veg.

Styles of cooking

Traditional African food tends to focus around stiff grain **porridge** called *mielie pap* or *pap* (pronounced: "pup"), made of maize meal and accompanied by meat or vegetable-based sauces. Among white South Africans, Afrikaners have evolved a style of cooking known as **boerekos** (see below), which can be heavy-going if you're not used to it.

Some of the best-known South African **foods** are mentioned below, while there's a list of South African culinary terms, including other local foods, in the Language section (see page 393).

Braais

Braai (which rhymes with "dry") is an abbreviation of *braaivleis*, an Afrikaans word translated as "meat grill". More than simply the process of cooking over an outdoor fire, however, a braai is a cultural event that is central to the South African identity. A braai is an intensely social event, usually among family and friends and accompanied by plenty of **beer**. It's also probably the only occasion you'll catch an unreconstructed South African man cooking.

You can braai anything, but a traditional barbecue meal consists of huge slabs of **steak**, **lamb cutlets** and **boerewors** ("farmer's sausage"), with ostrich and venison becoming increasingly popular. Potatoes, onions and butternut squash wrapped in aluminium foil and placed in the embers are the usual accompaniment.

Potjiekos and boerekos

A variant on the braai is **potjiekos**, pronounced "poy-key-kos": pot food, in which meat and vegetables are cooked in a three-legged cast-iron cauldron (the *potjie*), preferably outdoors over an open fire. In a similar vein, but cooked indoors, **boerekos** (literally

VEGETARIAN FOOD

While not quite a **vegetarian** paradise, South Africa is nevertheless vegetarian-savvy and you'll find at least one vegetarian dish in most restaurants. Even steakhouses will have something palatable on the menu and generally offer good salad bars. If you're self-catering in the larger cities, delicious dips and breads can be found at delis and Woolworths and Pick 'n' Pay supermarkets, as can the range of frozen vegetarian sausages and burgers made by Fry's (wfrysvegetarian.co.za).

"farmer's food") is a style of cooking enjoyed mainly by Afrikaners. Much of it is similar to English food, but taken to cholesterol-rich extremes, with even the vegetables prepared with butter and sugar. *Boerekos* comes into its own in its variety of over-the-top **desserts**, including *koeksisters* (plaited doughnuts saturated with syrup) and *melktert* ("milk tart"), a solid, rich custard in a flan case.

Cape Malay

Styles of cooking brought to South Africa by **Asian** and **Madagascan** slaves have evolved into **Cape Malay** cuisine. Characterized by mild, semi-sweet **curries** with strong Indonesian influences, Cape Malay food is worth sampling, especially in Cape Town, where it developed and is associated with the Muslim community. Dishes include *bredie* (stew), of which *waterblommetjiebredie*, made using water hyacinths, is a speciality; **bobotie**, a spicy minced dish served under a savoury custard; and *sosaties*, a local version of kebabs. For **dessert**, dates stuffed with almonds make a light and delicious end to a meal, while *malva* pudding is a rich combination of milk, sugar, cream and apricot jam.

Although Cape Malay cuisine can be delicious, few restaurants specialize in it. Despite this, most of the dishes considered as Cape Malay have crept into the South African diet, many becoming part of the Afrikaner culinary vocabulary.

Other ethnic and regional influences

Although South Africa doesn't really have distinct **regional** cuisines, you will find local specialities in different parts of the country. KwaZulu-Natal, for instance, is especially good for **Indian** food. South Africa's contribution to this multifaceted tradition is the humble **bunny chow**, a cheap takeaway consisting of a hollowed-out half-loaf of white bread

originally filled with curried beans, but nowadays with anything from curried chicken to sardines.

Portuguese food made early inroads into the country because of South Africa's proximity to Mozambique. The Portuguese influence is predominantly seen in the use of hot and spicy peri-peri seasoning, which goes extremely well with braais. The best-known example of this is peri-peri chicken, which you will find all over the country.

Eating out

Restaurants in South Africa offer good value compared with Britain or North America. In every city you'll find places where you can eat a decent main course for under R150, while for R250 you can splurge on the best. All the cities and larger towns boast some restaurants with imaginative menus. As a rule, restaurants are **licensed**, though Muslim establishments don't allow alcohol.

An attractive phenomenon in the big cities, especially Cape Town, has been the rise of continental-style **cafés** – easy-going places where you can eat as well as in a regular restaurant, or just drink **coffee** all night without feeling obliged to order food. A reasonable meal in one of these cafés is unlikely to set you back more than R100.

Don't confuse these with traditional South African cafés, found in even the tiniest country town. The equivalent of **corner stores** elsewhere, they commonly sell a few Afrikaans magazines, soft drinks, sweets and assorted tins and dry goods.

If popularity is the yardstick, then South Africa's real national cuisine is to be found in its **franchise restaurants**, which you'll find in every town of any size. The usual international names like **KFC**, **McDonald's** and **Wimpy** are omnipresent, as are South Africa's own home-grown offerings, such as the American-style steakhouse chain, **Spur**, and the much-exported **Nando's** chain, which serves Portuguese-style grilled chicken under a variety of spicy sauces. Expect to pay from around R60 for a burger and chips or chicken meal at any of these places, and twice that for a good-sized steak.

Drinking

White South Africans do a lot of their drinking **at home**, so pubs and bars are not quite the centres of social activity they are in the US or the UK, though in the African townships **shebeens** (unlicensed bars) do occupy this role. Sports bars with huge screens draw in crowds when there's a big match on, while many drinking spots in city centres and suburbs conform more to European-style café-bars than British pubs, serving coffee and light meals as well as alcohol. The closest things to British-style pubs are the themed bar-restaurant chains, such as Cape Town's *Slug & Lettuce*, while the city has a few longstanding watering holes with an old-world ambience. Johannesburg and Cape Town in particular have a growing range of hipster bars with eclectic decor and craft beers.

Beer, wines and spirits can by law be sold from Monday to Saturday between 9am and 6pm at **liquor stores** (the equivalent of the British off-licence) and at most supermarkets, although you'll still be able to drink at restaurants and pubs outside these hours.

There are no surprises when it comes to **soft drinks**, with all the usual names available. One proudly South African drink you will encounter is locally produced rooibos (or redbush) tea, made from the leaves of an indigenous plant.

Beer

Although South Africa is a major wine-producing country, **beer** is indisputably the national drink. As much an emblem of South African manhood as the braai, it cuts across all racial and class divisions. As in most countries, South Africans tend to be fiercely loyal to their brand of beer, though they are somewhat interchangeable given that the enormous **South African Breweries** (SAB) produces most of the country's mainstream beers. A number of international labels supplement the local offerings dominated by Castle, Lion, Hansa and Carling Black Label lagers, which taste a bit thin and bland to a British palate, but are certainly refreshing when drunk ice-cold on a sweltering day. The SAB offerings are given a good run for their beer money by Windhoek Lager, produced by Namibian Breweries. Widely available international brands include Peroni, Miller Genuine Draft, Grolsch and Heineken.

In recent years, there has been a rapid growth in the number of **microbreweries** across the country, which produce **craft beers and ciders**. Brew Masters (Ⓦ brewmasters.co.za) lists breweries large and small throughout South Africa with a useful map, while the Brew Mistress (Ⓦ brewmistress.co.za) is a good blog.

Wine and spirits

South Africa is one of the world's top ten **winemaking** countries by volume. Despite having the longest-established New World wine-making tradition (going back over 350 years), this rapid rise has taken place in the post-apartheid decades. Before that, South Africa's stagnant wine industry produced heavy Bordeaux-style wines. After the arrival of democracy in 1994, wine-makers began producing fresher, fruitier New World wines, and now develop highly quaffable vintages that combine the best of the Old and New Worlds.

South Africa produces wines from a whole gamut of major cultivars. Of the **whites**, the top South African Chenin and Sauvignon Blancs can stand up to the best the New World has to offer, and among the **reds** it's the blends that really shine. Also look out for robust reds made from Pinotage grapes, a cross between Pinot Noir and Cinsaut unique to South Africa. **Port** is also made, with the best vintages from the Little Karoo town of Calitzdorp along the R62. There are also numerous excellent **sparkling wines**, including Champagne-style, fermented-in-the-bottle bubbly, known as **Méthode Cap Classique** (MCC).

Wine is available throughout the country, although the cost rises as you move out of the Western Cape. **Prices** in shops and vineyards start at under R30 a bottle, and you can get an easy-drinking, entry-level wine by the likes of Worcester's Alvi's Drift for around R50. Just another R20 or so will buy you something pretty decent – the vast bulk of wines cost less than R100 – but you can spend hundreds of rand for a truly great vintage. All this means that anyone with an adventurous streak can indulge in a bacchanalia of sampling without breaking the bank. Restaurant prices are two to three times those in shops.

South Africa produces the world's largest volume of **brandy** – Klipdrift ("Klippie") is a popular local brand – and the Western Cape turns out spirits including **Bain's Whisky** and Inverroche fynbos-infused **gin**.

WINING AND FINE DINING

Focused around the towns of Stellenbosch, Franschhoek, Paarl and Somerset West, the Western Cape **Winelands** has established itself as one of South Africa's culinary centres, with numerous fine-dining restaurants in a small area. Many restaurants are on wine estates, and offer multi-course menus with wine pairings for each course – and superb views too. Restaurants in the Winelands regularly win the majority of South Africa's annual **Eat Out Restaurant Awards** (eight out of the top twenty in 2019). *Eat Out* magazine provides restaurant reviews of establishments across South Africa (available from bookshops or online at Ⓦ eatout.co.za).

Game parks, reserves and wilderness areas

No other African country has as rich a variety of national parks, reserves and wilderness areas as South Africa. Hundreds of national parks, provincial and municipal reserves and state forests pepper the terrain, creating an enticing breadth of choice, from the iconic Kruger National Park and other reserves protecting the so-called Big Five (lion, leopard, buffalo, elephant and rhino) to dozens upon dozens of more unsung wilderness areas that take in great landscapes and less publicized animal life. There are parks protecting coastal areas, wetlands, endangered species, forests, deserts and mountains, usually with the added attraction of assorted mammals, birds, insects and reptiles – in addition to which, South Africa is one of the top destinations for marine wildlife in general and land-based whale-watching in particular.

It can be difficult to get your head around the multi-tiered layers of **protection** accorded to South Africa's reserves, and the multifarious authorities that control them. The highest level of protection accorded to a conservation area is **national park**. There are roughly twenty of these in South Africa, almost all under the control of the national authority South African National Parks (SANParks, ☎012 428 9111, ⓦsanparks.org). These include premier Big Five destinations such as the **Kruger** and **Addo Elephant National Park**, but also a few more specialized wildlife destinations such as Bontebok, Mountain Zebra and Kgalagadi National Parks, as well as a few areas – for instance Agulhas, Table Mountain or Camdeboo – that score highly when comes to ecological significance or scenery, but that are not primarily "game parks".

National parks aside, South Africa hosts several hundred **provincially or municipally owned reserves**. Most significant, especially in terms of game viewing, are the fifty-odd public reserves in the province of KwaZulu-Natal owned or managed by Ezemvelo KwaZulu-Natal Wildlife (EKZNW; ☎033 845 1000, ⓦwww.kznwildlife.com). These include all the myriad individual reserves that fall within the **iSimangaliso Wetland Park** and **uKhahlamba-Drakensberg Park** (both inscribed as UNESCO World Heritage Sites), along with prominent Big Five destinations such as **Hluhluwe-iMfolozi Park** and **Tembe Elephant Park**. Other prominent provincial reserves in terms of game viewing are the malaria-free Madikwe Game Reserve and Pilanes-

AT A GLANCE BOXES

Most reserves covered in this book are accompanied by an "At a Glance" box designed to help readers isolate which places are best suited to their interests and other requirements. These contain a brief summary of the individual reserve's main attraction (and in some cases drawbacks) followed by the following one- to five-star rankings:

Big Five - Indicates how many of the Big Five you are likely to see over a standard 2–3-night stay. A rating of "none" is given to a few reserves where one or more of the Big Five is present, but sightings are infrequent. N/A means none of the Big Five is present.

General wildlife - This rating typically reflects the overall general density and variety of large terrestrial mammals, though some flexibility is given for places that host a rich marine wildlife.

Birding - How suited the reserve is to birdwatching, taking into account factors such as the number of species recorded, overall visibility of birds, the presence of rare, endemic or iconic species, and the extent to which amenities are geared towards dedicated birders.

Scenery - How much of a scenic impact the reserve has.

Wilderness factor - This can be difficult to pin down, but it reflects the extent to which the reserve forms part of a viable ecosystem as well as the general feeling of how wild or tame it is.

Uncrowded - For public reserves, the extent to which other tourists are likely to impact on your experience; for private reserves it is more about the ratio of guests to land area, and whether there are few enough vehicles that sightings don't get managed like a treadmill.

Affordability - How easy it is to visit the reserve on a tight budget, whether on a day- or overnight trip.

Self-drive - A "yes or no" answer, Y where the reserve is open to self-drives or can easy be accessed by them to explore on foot; N where it is only explorable on guided drives.

berg National Park (both operated by North West Parks; northwestparks.org.za) and various coastal and fynbos-dominated reserves that fall under the jurisdiction of Cape Nature (☎087 087 8250, ⓦcape nature.co.za).

If you had to choose just one of the country's top national parks, **Kruger**, stretching up the eastern flanks of Mpumalanga and Limpopo provinces, would lead the pack for its sheer size (almost as big as Wales), its range of animals, its varied lowveld habitats and its game-viewing opportunities. The unchallenged status of Kruger for sighting the **Big Five** and a cast of thousands of other animals tends to put the KwaZulu-Natal parks in the shade, quite undeservedly. As well as offering some of the world's best rhino viewing, these parks feel less developed than Kruger, and often provide superior accommodation at comparable prices. Both Kruger and the KwaZulu-Natal parks offer walking safaris, accompanied by a gun-toting guide, and night drives, a popular way to catch sight of the elusive denizens that creep around after dark.

Addo Elephant National Park in the Eastern Cape, a long day's drive east of Cape Town, is the third-largest national park in South Africa, and still being expanded. The only non-private Big Five reserve in the southern half of the country, Addo has one of the most diverse landscapes, encompassing five biomes and protecting over six hundred elephants. Other important Big Five destinations, all within half a day's drive of Johannesburg, are Pilanesberg, Madikwe and the Waterberg, all of which – like Addo – are completely malaria-free.

In addition to these state-, provincially and municipally run parks, South Africa is home to a burgeoning number of **private reserves**, most of which offer an upscale safari experience centred upon small four- to five-star lodges and tented camps whose rates include guided game drives and other activities, all meals, and in some cases drinks. The best of these private reserves, the cluster that borders and shares open fences with Kruger, essentially offers an upmarket variation on the Kruger experience, set in the same vast ecosystem, but with a far better chance of ticking all the Big Five in a condensed time frame.

Most other private reserves are fenced-off entities whose ecological significance is a function partly of their size (some cover significantly less than 50 square kilometres, others more than 250 square kilometres) and partly of the extent to which they are clustered with other similar bordering private or public reserves. Smaller isolated private reserves can often feel quite contrived; indeed, some even have separate drive-through enclosures for lion and/or elephant, but the best of the larger ones – for instance Phinda, Samara and Kwandwe – rank among the country's most thrilling wildlife destinations.

Park accommodation

Accommodation at national parks includes campsites (expect to pay R200–350 per site); **safari tents** at some of the Kruger and KwaZulu-Natal restcamps (clusters of accommodation in game reserves, including chalets, safari tents, cottages and campsites; from R580 per tent); one-room **huts** with shared washing and cooking facilities (from R500); one-room en-suite **bungalows** with shared cooking facilities (from R800); and self-contained family **cottages** with private bath or shower and cooking facilities (from R1500). In national park accommodation (excluding campsites) you're supplied with bedding, towels, a fridge and basic cooking utensils. Some restcamps have a **shop** selling supplies for picnics or braais, as well as a **restaurant**.

The ultimate wilderness accommodation is in the **private game reserves**, with high concentrations of these around Kruger and Addo and in northern KwaZulu-Natal. Here you pay big bucks for accommodation, which is almost always luxurious, in large en-suite walk-in tents, small thatched **rondavels** or – in the larger and most expensive lodges – plush rooms with air conditioning. A few places have "bush showers" (a hoisted bucket of hot water with a shower nozzle attached) behind reed screens but open to the sky – one of the great treats of the bush. Some chalets and tents have gaslights or lanterns in the absence of **electricity**. Food is usually good and plentiful, and vegetarians can be catered for. Expect to pay upwards of R5000 per person per night, rising to well over R10,000 at the most fashionable spots. High as these **prices** are, all meals and game drives are included, and as numbers are strictly limited, you get an exclusive experience of the bush.

Game viewing

Spotting wild animals takes skill and **experience**. It's easier than you'd think to mistake a rhino for a large boulder, or to miss the king of the beasts in the tall grass – African wildlife has, after all, evolved with **camouflage** in mind. Don't expect the volume of animals you get in wildlife documentaries: what you see is always a matter of **luck**, patience and skill. If you're new to the African bush and its wildlife, consider shelling out for at least two nights at one of the luxurious lodges on a private reserve (for example, those abutting Kruger); they're staffed by well-informed **rangers** who lead game-viewing outings in open-topped 4WDs.

The section on Kruger National Park (see page 104) gives more advice on spotting game and enjoying and understanding what you see – whether it's a brightly coloured lizard in a restcamp, head-butting giraffes at a waterhole or dust-kicking rhinos. Numerous **books** are available that can enhance your visit to a game reserve – especially if you plan a self-drive safari (see below).

Self-drive safaris

The least expensive way of experiencing a game reserve is by **renting a car** and driving around a national park, taking advantage of the self-catering and camping facilities. Most parks have easily navigable tarred and gravel roads. You'll have the thrill of spotting game at your own pace rather than relying on a ranger, and for people with **children**, a self-drive safari is the usual option, as many upmarket lodges don't admit under-12s. The disadvantage of self-driving is that you can end up jostling with other cars to get a view, especially when it comes to lion watching. Also, you may not know what spoor (animal signs) to look for, and unless you travel in a minibus or 4WD vehicle you're unlikely to be high enough off the ground to see across the veld.

Kruger is arguably the best self-drive safari destination anywhere in Africa. The KwaZulu-Natal game reserves, including Hluhluwe-iMfolozi, Mkhuze and Ithala, offer rewarding opportunities for **self-drive touring**, as does Pilanesberg in North West Province, while the remote Kgalagadi Transfrontier Park that stretches into Botswana promises truly exciting wilderness driving. You might choose to cover a route that combines the substantial Kruger National Park with the more intimate reserves of KwaZulu-Natal.

If you plan to self-drive, consider investing in good animal and bird **field guides**, and a decent pair of **binoculars** – one pair per person is recommended. Whether you're self-catering or not, it's worth taking a flask for tea and a cool bag to keep drinks cold. Finally, remember that the best times to spot animals are **dawn and dusk**, when they are most active.

Escorted safaris

It's possible to book places on a **safari excursion** – such packages are often organized by backpacker lodges located near reserves, and occasionally by hotels and B&Bs. On the downside, these don't give you the experience of waking up in the wild, and entail spending more time on the road than if you

were based inside a reserve. But during South African school holidays, when Kruger, for example, is booked to capacity, you may have no other option. You can also organize guided wildlife drives through national park offices.

Mostly, you get what you pay for as regards game-viewing packages. Be wary of cheap deals on "**safari farms**" in the vicinity of Kruger. Essentially huge zoos, these offer an overnight stop en route to Kruger, but are no substitute for a real wilderness experience – sooner or later you hit fences and gates on your game drive. Some of the better places in this category are listed in the relevant chapters.

Safaris on private reserves

If you choose well, the ultimate South African game experience has to be a **private reserve**. You can relax in comfort while your game-viewing activities are organized, and because you spend time in a small group, you get a stronger sense of the wild than at one of the big Kruger restcamps. Best of all, you have the benefit of knowledgeable **rangers**, who can explain the terrain and small-scale wildlife as they drive you around looking for game.

Privately run safari lodges in concessions inside Kruger and some other national parks, such as Addo, operate along similar lines. The smaller private reserves accommodate between ten and sixteen guests; larger **camps** often cater for two or three times as many people, and resemble hotels in the bush. Many safari lodges have their own **waterholes**, overlooked by the bar or restaurant, from which you can watch animals drinking. Nowhere are the private reserves more developed than along the west flank of the Kruger, where you'll find the top-dollar prestigious lodges as well as some more affordable places.

A typical day at a private camp or lodge starts at **dawn** for tea or coffee, followed by guided **game viewing** on foot, or driving. After a mid-morning brunch/breakfast, there's the chance to spend time on a **viewing platform** or in a **hide**, quietly watching the passing scene. Late-afternoon game viewing is a repeat of early morning but culminates with **sundowners** as the light fades, and often turns into a **night drive** with spotlights looking for nocturnal creatures.

Prices, which include accommodation, meals and game-spotting activities, vary widely. The ultra-expensive camps offer more luxury and social cachet, but not necessarily better game viewing. You might find the cheaper camps in the same areas more to your taste, their plainer and wilder atmosphere more in keeping with the bush.

PARK FEES, RESERVATIONS AND ENQUIRIES

Fees given in our park accounts are generally daily conservation fees, which are essentially the entrance fees. Most expensive is Kruger National Park, for which foreign visitors pay a conservation fee of R372 per adult (R186 per child), followed by Kgalagadi Transfrontier Park, where the adult fee is R356. The majority of the rest charge under R300, and small parks such as Bontebok charge as little as R122. As a rule of thumb, visitors aged under 12 pay half the adult rate.

Accommodation at most national parks can be booked in advance through South African National Parks (SANParks, ☏012 428 9111, ⓦsanparks.org). Booking by phone usually involves a long wait; reserving online is far easier and the better option (see page 35). The KwaZulu-Natal reserves are booked through Ezemvelo KZN Wildlife National (EKZNW; ☏033 845 1000, ⓦwww.kznwildlife.com) and again you are best doing it online. Booking details for other parks and reserves are included under the relevant listings. In high season, try to book accommodation in the reserves several months in advance.

A worthwhile acquisition for anyone who intends spending a lot of time in South Africa's national parks and other reserves is a **Wild Card**, which can be bought online at ⓦwildcard.co.za and allows the holder unlimited entry to around eighty protected areas for up to 365 days. This includes all South African national parks, all other public reserves in the Western Cape, most public reserves in KwaZulu-Natal, and all reserves in the Kingdom of Eswatini, but it excludes all private reserves, all provincial reserves outside the Western Cape and KwaZulu-Natal, and all reserves that fall within the iSimangaliso Wetland Park, as well as Tembe Elephant Park. South African and SADC nationals, or foreigners in possession of a South African residence or work permit, have the choice of a Wild Card that covers all affiliated parks and reserves, or any of five different sub-clusters, with annual fees ranging from R460–640 for individuals, R750–1055 for couples, and R920–1290 for families. International visitors may only buy an All Parks Cluster and this costs R2900/4530/5420 for individuals/couples/families. Depending on which parks and reserves you intend to visit, a Wild Card will probably only make sense for foreign visitors who intend on spending ten days or longer in affiliated parks. With Kruger, for instance, an individual would pass the threshold after eight days, a couple after seven days, and a family with two children after six days, but many parks are significantly cheaper than Kruger.

Hiking trails

South Africa has a comprehensive system of **footpaths**, of various distances and catering to all levels of fitness. Wherever you are – even in the middle of Johannesburg – you won't be far from some sort of trail. The best ones are in wilderness areas, where you'll find waymarked paths, from half-hour strolls to major hiking expeditions of several days, that take you right into the heart of some of the most beautiful parts of the country.

Overnight trails are normally well laid out, with painted route markers, and campsites or huts along the way. Numbers are limited on most, and some trails are so popular that you need to book several months in advance to use them.

There are also guided **wilderness trails**, where you walk in game country accompanied by an armed ranger. These walking safaris are an excellent way to get a feel for the wild, although you are likely to see fewer animals on foot than from a vehicle. Specialist trails cover mountain biking, canoeing and horseriding, while a handful of routes have been set up specifically for people with disabilities, mostly for the visually impaired or those in wheelchairs.

Diving and snorkelling

Scuba diving is popular, and South Africa is an affordable country to get an internationally recognized open-water certificate. Courses start around R3500 (including gear) and are available in most coastal cities as well as a number of resorts. Some of the most rewarding diving is in the iSimangaliso Wetland Park area on the northern KwaZulu-Natal coast, which hosts 100,000 dives every year for its coral reefs and fluorescent fish.

You won't find corals and bright colours along the Cape coast, but the huge number of sunken vessels makes **wreck diving** popular, and you can encounter the swaying rhythms of giant kelp forests. Gansbaai (near Hermanus) is the most popular place to go **shark-cage diving** and come face to face with deadly great whites, with more options on the Garden Route.

KwaZulu-Natal is also good for **snorkelling**, and there are some underwater trails elsewhere in the country, most notably in the Garden Route's Tsitsikamma National Park.

Health

You can put aside most of the health concerns that may be justified in some parts of Africa; run-down hospitals and bizarre tropical diseases aren't typical of South Africa. All tourist areas boast generally high standards of hygiene and safe drinking water. The main hazard you're likely to encounter, and the one the majority of visitors are most blasé about, is the sun. In some parts of the country there is a risk of malaria, and you will need to take precautions.

Public **hospitals** are often well equipped and staffed, but the huge pressure they are under undermines their attempts to maintain standards. Expect long waits and frequently indifferent treatment. **Private hospitals** or clinics are a much better option for travellers and are well up to British and North American standards. You'll get to see a doctor quickly and costs are not excessive, unless you require an operation, in which case health insurance is a must.

Dental care in South Africa is also well up to British and North American standards, and is generally less expensive. You'll find dentists in most towns.

Inoculations

No specific inoculations are compulsory if you arrive in South Africa from the West, although the USA's *CDC* suggests several immunizations as routine for adults. In addition, it recommends inoculations against **typhoid** and **hepatitis A**, both of which can be caught from contaminated food or water. This is a worst-case scenario, however, as typhoid is eminently curable and few visitors to South Africa ever catch it. Vaccination against **hepatitis B** is essential only for people involved in health work; the disease is spread by the transfer of blood products – usually dirty needles.

A **yellow fever** vaccination certificate is necessary if you've come from a country where the disease is endemic, such as Kenya, Tanzania or tropical South America.

It's best to start organizing to have jabs **six weeks** before departure, and some clinics will not administer inoculations less than a fortnight before departure. If you're going to another African country first and need the yellow fever jab, note that a yellow fever certificate only becomes valid ten days after you've had the shot.

MEDICAL RESOURCES FOR TRAVELLERS

Canadian Society for International Health ☎ 613 241 5785, Ⓦ csih.org. Extensive list of travel health centres.
CDC (Centers for Disease Control and Prevention) ☎ 800 232 4636, Ⓦ cdc.gov/travel. Official US government travel health site.
Hospital for Tropical Diseases Travel Clinic Ⓦ www.the htd.org. Health advice for travellers, with a link to the British government's online travel health advice, and a shop selling goods such as first-aid kits, mosquito nets and suncream.
International Society for Travel Medicine ☎ 1 404 373 8282, Ⓦ istm.org. Has a global directory of travel health clinics.
MASTA (Medical Advisory Service for Travellers Abroad) Ⓦ masta-travel-health.com. The UK's largest network of private travel clinics.
The Travel Doctor Ⓦ traveldoctor.co.nz. Travel clinics in New Zealand and an online shop.
Travel Doctor ☎ 0861 300 911, Ⓦ traveldoctor.co.za. Travel clinics in Cape Town, Stellenbosch, George and beyond.
Travel Doctor Ⓦ traveldoctor.com.au. Travel clinics in Australia.
Tropical Medical Bureau ☎ 00353 1 271 5200, Ⓦ tmb.ie. Offers extensive advice for travellers, with a number of clinics in Ireland.

Stomach upsets

Stomach upsets from food are rare. Salad and ice – risky items in some developing countries – are both perfectly safe. As with anywhere, don't keep food for too long, and be sure to wash fruit and vegetables as thoroughly as possible. Tap water is generally fine to drink, but bacteria levels rise as dam levels drop during the increasingly common droughts, when you may prefer to stick to bottled water.

If you do get a **stomach bug**, the best cure is lots of water and rest. Most chemists should have non-prescription anti-diarrhoea remedies and rehydration salts.

Avoid jumping for **antibiotics** at the first sign of illness. Instead keep them as a last resort – they don't work on viruses and they annihilate your gut flora (most of which you want to keep), making you more susceptible next time round. Taking probiotics helps to alleviate the latter side effect. Most tummy upsets will resolve themselves if you adopt a sensible **fat-free diet** for a couple of days, but if they do persist without improvement (or are accompanied by other unusual symptoms), see a doctor as soon as possible.

The sun

The sun is likely to be the worst hazard you'll encounter in Southern Africa, particularly if you're fair-skinned. Short-term effects of **overexposure** to the sun include burning, nausea and headaches. Make sure you wear **high-protection sunscreen**, a broad-brimmed hat and sunglasses, and don't stay too long in the sun – especially when you first arrive.

Extreme cases of overexposure to the sun, accompanied by dehydration, overexertion and intoxication, can lead to **heat exhaustion** or heatstroke.

Take particular care with **children**, who should be kept well covered at the seaside, preferably with UV-protective sun suits. Don't be lulled into complacency on **cloudy days**, when UV levels can still be high.

Bilharzia

One ailment that you need to take seriously throughout sub-Saharan Africa is **bilharzia** (schistosomiasis), carried in many freshwater lakes and rivers in northern and eastern South Africa except in the mountains. Bilharzia is spread by tiny, parasitic worm-like flukes which leave their water-snail hosts and burrow into human skin to multiply in the bloodstream; they then work their way to the walls of the intestine or bladder, where they lay **eggs**.

The chances are you'll avoid bilharzia even if you swim in a suspect river, but it's best to avoid **swimming** in dams, rivers and slow-moving water where possible. If you go **canoeing** or can't avoid the water, have a test for bilharzia when you return home.

Symptoms may be no more than a feeling of lassitude and ill health. Once the infection is established, abdominal pain and blood in the urine and stools are common, occasionally leading to kidney failure and bowel damage. Fortunately, bilharzia is easily and effectively treatable.

Malaria

Most of South Africa is free of **malaria**, a potentially lethal disease that is widespread in tropical and subtropical Africa, where it's a major killer. However, **protection** against malaria is essential if you're planning to travel to any of these areas: northern and northeastern Mpumalanga, notably the Kruger National Park; northern KwaZulu-Natal; or the border regions of Limpopo and, to a lesser degree, North West Province and the Northern Cape. The highest **risk** is during the hot, rainy months between October and May. The risk is reduced during the cooler, dry months from June to September, when some people decide not to take prophylactic medication.

Malaria is caused by a parasite carried in the saliva of the female anopheles mosquito. It has a variable incubation period of a few days to several weeks, so you can become ill long after being bitten. The first symptoms of malaria can be mistaken for **flu**, starting off relatively mildly with a variable combination that includes fever, aching limbs and shivering, which come in waves, usually beginning in the early evening. Deterioration can be rapid as the parasites in the bloodstream proliferate. Malaria is not **infectious**, but can be fatal if not treated quickly: get medical help without delay if you go down with flu-like symptoms a week after entering, or within three months of leaving, a malarial area.

Doctors can advise on which kind of **antimalarial tablets** to take. It's important to keep to the prescribed dose, which covers the period before and after your trip. Consult your **doctor** or **clinic** several weeks before you travel, as you should start taking medication a week or two before entering the affected region – depending on the particular drug you're using.

Whatever you decide to take, be aware that no antimalarial drug is totally effective – the most sure-fire protection is to **avoid getting bitten**. Malaria-carrying mosquitoes are active between **dusk** and **dawn**, so try to avoid being out at this time, or at least cover yourself well. Sleep under a **mosquito net** when possible, making sure to tuck it under the mattress, and burn **mosquito coils** (which you can buy everywhere) for a peaceful, if noxious, night. If you have access to a power supply, electric mosquito destroyers, which you fit with a pad, are less pungent than coils. Mosquito "buzzers" are useless. Whenever the mosquitoes are particularly bad, cover your exposed parts with **insect repellent**; those containing diethyltoluamide (DEET) work best. Other locally produced repellents such as Peaceful Sleep are widely available.

Bites and stings

Bites, **stings** and **rashes** in South Africa are comparatively rare. **Snakes** are present, but rarely seen as they move out of the way quickly. The aggressive puff and berg adders are the most dangerous, because they often lie on paths and don't move when humans approach. The best **advice** if you get bitten is to note what the snake looked like and get yourself to a clinic or hospital. Most bites are not fatal and the worst thing is to panic: desperate measures with razor blades and tourniquets can do more harm than good. It's more helpful to immobilise the bitten limb with a splint and apply a bandage over the bite.

Tick-bite fever is occasionally contracted from walking in the bush, particularly in long wet grass. The offending ticks can be minute and you may not spot them. **Symptoms** appear a week later – swollen glands and severe aching of the joints, backache and fever – and the disease should run its course in three or four days, but it is worth visiting the doctor for antibiotics. Ticks you may find on yourself are not dangerous – just make sure you pull out the head as well as the body (it's not painful). A good way of removing small ones is to press down with tweezers, grab the head and gently pull upwards.

Scorpion stings and **spider bites** are painful but almost never fatal, contrary to popular myth. Scorpions and spiders abound, but they're hardly ever seen unless you turn over logs and stones. If you're collecting wood for a campfire, knock or shake it before picking it up. Another simple **precaution** when camping is to shake out your shoes and clothes in the morning before you get dressed. Seek medical attention for scorpion stings if your condition deteriorates.

Rabies is present throughout Southern Africa, with **dogs** posing the greatest risk, although the disease can be carried by other animals. If you are bitten you should go immediately to a clinic or hospital. Rabies can be treated effectively with a course of **injections**. If you plan to spend time in remote areas without medical facilities close at hand, you can get pre-trip jabs, which will buy you more time to reach a clinic or hospital in the event of being bitten.

Sexually transmitted diseases

HIV/AIDS and venereal diseases are widespread in Southern Africa among both men and women, and the danger of catching the virus through sexual contact is very real. Avoid one-night stands with locals and follow the usual precautions regarding **safe sex**. There's very little risk from treatment in private medical facilities, but unsterilized equipment could be an issue in remote public hospitals. If you're travelling overland and want to play it safe, take your own well-stocked first-aid kit, including equipment such as needles.

Tuberculosis

TB is a serious problem in South Africa, but most travellers are at low risk. At higher risk are healthcare workers, long-term travellers and anyone with an impaired immune system, such as people infected with HIV. A **BCG vaccination** is routinely given to babies in South Africa, but its use elsewhere varies. Take medical advice on the question of **immunization** if you feel there may be a risk.

Crime and personal safety

Despite horror stories of sky-high crime rates, most people visit South Africa without incident; be careful, but not paranoid. This is not to underestimate the issue – crime is probably the most serious problem facing the country. But some perspective is in order: crime is disproportionately concentrated in the poor African and coloured townships. Violent crime is a problem throughout Johannesburg, from the city centre to the townships, and travellers are most at risk here. However, the greatest peril facing most visitors is navigating South Africa's roads, which claim well over ten thousand lives a year.

Drugs and drink-driving

Alcohol and **cannabis** in dried leaf form are South Africa's most widely used and abused drugs. The latter, known as *dagga* (pronounced like "dugger" with the "gg" guttural, as in the Scottish pronunciation of "loch"), is grown in hot regions like KwaZulu-Natal (the source of Durban Poison), Eswatini (Swazi Gold) and the Wild Coast. It is fairly easily available and the quality is generally good – but this doesn't alter the fact that it is **illegal**. If you do decide to partake, take particular care when scoring, as visitors have run into trouble dealing with unfamiliar local conditions.

Strangely, for a country that sometimes seems to be on one massive binge, South Africa has laws that prohibit **drinking** in public – not that anyone pays any attention. The drink-drive laws are routinely and brazenly flouted, making the country's **roads** the one real danger you should be concerned about. People routinely stock up their cars with booze for long journeys and levels of alcohol consumption go some way to explaining why, during the Christmas holidays, over a thousand people die in an annual period of road carnage. Don't risk drinking and

SAFETY TIPS

IN GENERAL:
- Dress down and try not to look too like a tourist.
- Avoid wearing expensive jewellery, eye gear and timepieces, carrying a camera or waving your phone around in cities.
- Use hotel safes.
- If you are accosted, remain calm and cooperative.

WHEN ON FOOT:
- Grasp bags firmly under your arm.
- Don't carry excessive sums of money on you.
- Don't put your wallet in your back trouser pocket.
- Always know where your valuables are.
- Don't leave valuables exposed (on a seat or the ground) while having a meal or drink.
- Don't let strangers get too close to you – especially people in groups.
- Travel around in pairs or groups and avoid isolated areas.
- Don't walk alone at night.

ON THE ROAD:
- Lock all your car doors, especially in cities.
- Keep rear windows sufficiently rolled up to keep out opportunistic hands.
- Never leave anything worth stealing in view when your car is unattended.
- If you've concealed valuables in the boot, don't open it after parking.

AT ATMS:
Cash machines are favourite hunting grounds for con men. Never underestimate their ability and don't get drawn into any interaction at an ATM, no matter how well spoken, friendly or distressed the other person appears. If they claim to have a problem with the machine, tell them to contact the bank. Don't let people crowd you or see your personal identification number (PIN) when you withdraw money; if in doubt, go to another machine. Finally, if your card gets swallowed, report it without delay.

WHEN PAYING WITH A CARD:
- Never let your plastic out of your sight.
- At a restaurant, ask for a portable card reader to be brought to your table.
- At the till, keep an eye on your card.
- If the transaction fails, don't try a second time; pay with cash or another card.

Protecting property and "security" are major national obsessions, and often a topic of conversation at dinner parties. A substantial percentage of middle-class homes subscribe to the services of armed private security firms. The other obvious manifestation of this obsession is the huge number of alarms, high walls and electronically controlled gates you'll see, not just in the suburbs, but even in less deprived areas of some townships. Guns are openly carried by police.

driving yourself, as nocturnal roadblocks are common in urban areas.

Sexual harassment

South Africa's extremely high incidence of **rape** doesn't as a rule affect tourists. However, sexism is more common and attitudes are not as progressive as in Western countries, especially in black communities. Sometimes your eagerness to be friendly may be taken as a sexual overture – always be sensitive to potential crossed wires and unintended signals.

Women should take care while travelling on their own, and never hitchhike or walk alone in deserted areas. This applies equally to cities, the countryside or anywhere after dark. Minibus taxis should be ruled out as a means of transport after dark, especially if you're not sure of the local geography.

The police

Poorly paid, shot at (and frequently hit), underfunded, badly equipped, barely respected and demoralized, the **South African Police Service** (SAPS) keeps a low profile.

If you ever get stopped, at a **roadblock** for example (one of the likeliest encounters), always be courteous. And if you're driving, note that under South African law you are required to carry your **driver's licence** at all times. If you are fined and you suspect corruption, asking to be issued with a receipt will discourage foul play or at least give you a record of the incident.

If **robbed**, you need to report the incident to the police, who should give you a case reference. Keep all paperwork for insurance purposes.

Travel essentials

Climate

Although South Africa is predominantly a dry, sunny country, bear in mind that the chart below shows average maximums. **June and July** temperatures can drop below zero in some places; be prepared for average minimums of 4°C in Johannesburg, 7°C in Cape Town and 11°C in Durban.

Costs

For budget and mid-range travellers, the most expensive thing about visiting South Africa is getting there. Once you've arrived, you're likely to find it a relatively **inexpensive** and good-value destination. This will depend partly on exchange rates at the time of your visit – since becoming fully convertible (after the advent of democracy in South Africa), the rand has seen some massive fluctuations against sterling, the dollar and the euro.

When it comes to daily budgets, your biggest expense is likely to be **accommodation**. If you limit yourself to backpacker dorms or camping and self-catering, you should be able to sleep and eat for under R500 per person per day. If you stay in restcamps, B&Bs and guesthouses, eat out once a day, and have a snack or two, budget for R1500 per day for a single traveller and R2000 for a couple. In top-end hotels expect to pay upwards of R3000 for a double. In both cases you should probably add around R1000 per day to cover car rental, fuel and park **entrance fees** for any day spent in a national park or provincially managed game reserve. Luxury safari lodges in major game reserves typically charge more than R6000 per double, and in many cases as much as R20,000, for packages inclusive of meals, activities and in some cases drinks.

Electricity

South Africa's electricity supply runs at 220/230V, 50Hz AC. Most **sockets** take unique plugs with three fat, round pins, although sockets taking European-style two-pin plugs are common. Most hotel rooms have sockets that will take 110V electric shavers, but for other appliances US visitors will need an **adaptor**. Power cuts associated with load shedding are sporadic, but most hotels and lodges that are on the grid will have generators. Some more remote lodges and tented camps operate on **solar power** only.

Insurance

It's wise to take out an **insurance** policy to cover against theft, loss and illness or injury. A typical travel insurance policy usually provides cover for the loss of

AVERAGE DAILY MAXIMUM TEMPERATURES

	Jan	Feb	Mar	Apr	May	Jun	Jul	Aug	Sep	Oct	Nov	Dec
CAPE TOWN												
Max (°C)	27	27	26	23	20	19	17	18	19	22	24	26
Max (°F)	81	81	79	73	68	66	63	64	66	72	75	79
DURBAN												
Max (°C)	27	28	27	26	24	23	22	22	23	24	25	26
Max (°F)	81	82	81	79	75	73	72	72	73	75	77	79
JOHANNESBURG												
Max (°C)	26	26	24	22	19	16	16	20	23	25	25	26
Max (°F)	79	79	75	72	66	61	61	68	73	77	77	79
SKUKUZA (KRUGER NATIONAL PARK)												
Max (°C)	31	31	30	29	27	25	25	26	29	29	30	30
Max (°F)	88	88	86	84	81	77	77	79	84	84	86	86

baggage, valuables and – up to a certain limit – cash and bank cards, as well as cancellation or curtailment of your journey. Most of them exclude so-called dangerous sports unless an extra **premium** is paid: in South Africa this can mean scuba diving, whitewater rafting, windsurfing, horseriding, bungee jumping and paragliding. In addition to these, check whether you are covered by your policy if you're hiking, kayaking, pony trekking or game viewing on safari, all activities people commonly take part in when visiting South Africa. Many policies can be chopped and changed to exclude **coverage** you don't need – for example, sickness and accident benefits can often be excluded or included at will.

If you do take **medical coverage**, ascertain whether benefits will be paid as treatment proceeds or only after you return home, if there's a 24-hour medical emergency number and if medical evacuation will be covered. When buying **baggage cover**, make sure that the per-article limit will cover your most valuable possession. If you need to make a **claim**, you should keep receipts for medicines and medical treatment, and in the event of having anything stolen, you must obtain an official statement from the police.

Internet

Finding somewhere to access the **internet** will seldom be a problem in all but the most rural areas. Assuming you bring your own **smartphone**, tablet or other such device, you'll find that practically all lodges, restcamps, hotels and backpacker hostels offer **free WiFi** to their clients, as do an ever increasing number of restaurants, cafés and even airports and malls, though speed might not always be what you're used to at home. Better still, if you don't have international roaming, or your provider charges heavily for it, you may wish to buy a local SIM card and data bundle. South Africa is similar to the West in its increasing reliance on apps for ordering everything from taxis to takeaway food, and it's also wise and reassuring from a security point of view to have access to the likes of Google Maps.

LGBTQ travellers

South Africa has the world's first gay- and lesbi-an-friendly constitution, and Africa's most developed and diverse LGBTQ scene. Not only is homosexuality **legal** for consenting adults of 16 or over, but the constitution outlaws any **discrimination** on the grounds of sexual orientation. Outside the big cities, however, South Africa remains a conservative place, where open displays of public affection by gays and lesbians are unlikely to go down well. It's still

especially hard for African and coloured men and women to come out, and homophobic attacks are a threat whatever your ethnicity, so be discreet and take care outside the city centres.

The tourist industry, on the other hand, is well aware of the potential of pink spending power and actively woos **gay travellers** – an effort that is evidently paying off, with Cape Town ranking among the world's top gay destinations. The gay scene is typically multi-racial in Johannesburg, especially the clubs, while Pretoria has a few gay and lesbian nightspots. There are also small gay scenes in Port Elizabeth and Durban, and you'll find gay-run or gay-friendly establishments in small towns. There are **gay pride** festivals in Cape Town in February and December, Knysna in April and Joburg in October (Ⓦ johannesburgpride.co.za).

The **gay lifestyle magazine** Mamba (Ⓦ mamba online.com) is one of the useful online resources, and you can download the app or listen online to **GaySA Radio** (Ⓦ gaysaradio.co.za).

Mail

The familiar feel of South African post offices can lull you into expecting an efficient British- or US-style service. In fact, mail within the country is very slow, often unreliable, and certainly not safe for sending money or valuables. Expect domestic delivery times from one city to another of about a week – longer if a rural town is involved at either end. Postage is inexpensive, and **stamps** are available at post offices and from newsagents such as the CNA chain.

International airmail deliveries are often quicker, thanks to direct flights to London. A letter or package sent by surface mail can take up to six weeks to get to London. Delivery is even less reliable and trustworthy coming into the country, when items frequently disappear or take weeks to arrive.

Most towns of any size have a **post office**, generally open Monday to Friday 8.30am to 4.30pm and Saturday till noon (closing earlier in some places). The ubiquitous private **PostNet** outlets (Ⓦ postnet. co.za) are a better option, offering many of the same postal services as the post office and more, including **courier services**. Courier companies like FedEx (☎ 0800 033 339, Ⓦ fedex.com/za) and DHL (☎ 086 034 5000, Ⓦ dhl.co.za) – operating only in the larger towns – are far more reliable than the mail.

Maps

Online resources such as **Google Maps** (Ⓦ google. co.za/maps) and **Open Street Maps** (Ⓦ openstreet map.org) tend to be very reliable for towns but rather less so for more remote areas and game reserves. Many **place and street names** in South Africa have been changed since the 1994 elections, so look out for contradictions between online and printed maps and names on the ground, and if you buy a map, make sure it's reasonably up to date. Bartholomew produces an excellent map of South Africa, including Lesotho and Eswatini, as part of its World Travel Map series. **MapStudio** (Ⓦ mapstudio.co.za) produces and sells a range of excellent maps, while Cape Town's **Slingsby Maps** (Ⓦ slingsbymaps.com) publishes the best hiking and touring maps of the Western Cape and beyond. Slingsby's maps, which include the Cape Peninsula, Winelands and Garden Route, are available at bookshops.

The **national park and game reserve maps** in this book will be useful to self-drivers for general orientation but they are no substitute for the larger and more detailed colour road maps offered free at most national park entrance gates. For most major self-drive reserves and national parks (for instance Kruger, Pilanesberg, Addo, Hluhluwe-iMfolozi or Kgalagadi), excellent interpretative booklets with detailed maps can be bought on site, typically for around R40–60.

South Africa's motoring organization, the **Automobile Association** (Ⓦ aa.co.za), has free maps available to download from its website.

Money

South Africa's currency is the **rand** (R), often called the "buck", divided into 100 **cents**. Notes come in R10, R20, R50, R100 and R200 denominations and there are coins of 5, 10, 20 and 50 cents, as well as R1, R2 and R5. The **exchange rate** fluctuates frequently; at the time of writing, it averaged around R18–19 to the pound sterling, R14–15 to the US dollar, R16–17 to the euro and R9–10 to the Australian dollar.

All but the tiniest settlement will have a **bank**, where you can withdraw and change money, or an ATM. **Banking hours** vary, but are at least from Monday to Friday 9am to 3.30pm, and Saturday 8.30am to 11am; banks in smaller towns usually close for lunch. In major cities, large hotels and banks operate **bureaux de change**. Outside banking hours, some hotel receptions will change money, although this entails a fairly hefty **commission**.

You can also change money at branches of American Express (Ⓦ americanexpressforex.co.za). **Keep exchange receipts**, which you'll need to show to convert any leftover rand at the end of your trip.

Cards

Credit and **debit cards** are the most convenient way to access your funds in South Africa. Most international cards can be used to withdraw money at **ATMs**. Plastic comes in very handy for paying for more mainstream and upmarket tourist facilities, and is essential for car rental. **Visa** and **Mastercard** are most widely accepted, American Express rather less so. In remoter areas, you'll need to carry cash to tide you between ATMs, which are unreliable in rural regions. Stash it in a safe place, or even better in a few places on your person and baggage.

Opening hours and holidays

The **working day** starts and finishes early in South Africa: shops and businesses generally open on **weekdays** around 8.30am and close at 4.30pm. In small towns, many places close for an hour over **lunch**. Many shops and businesses close around noon on Saturdays, and most shops are closed on Sundays. However, in urban neighbourhoods, you'll find small shops and supermarkets where you can buy groceries and essentials after hours. Some establishments have different opening times in summer (September to March) and winter (April to August).

School holidays can disrupt your plans, especially if you want to camp, or stay in the national parks and the budget end of accommodation (self-catering, cheaper B&Bs, etc). All are likely to be booked solid during holiday periods, especially along the coast. If you travel to South Africa over a school holiday, book accommodation well in advance, particularly for the national parks.

SOUTH AFRICAN PUBLIC HOLIDAYS

Many tourist-related businesses and some shops remain open over public holidays, although often with shorter opening hours. Most of the country shuts down on Christmas Day and Good Friday. The main holidays are:

New Year's Day (Jan 1)
Human Rights Day (March 21)
Good Friday, Easter Monday (variable)
Freedom Day (April 27)
Workers' Day (May 1)
Youth Day (June 16)
National Women's Day (Aug 9)
Heritage Day (Sept 24)
Day of Reconciliation (Dec 16)
Christmas Day (Dec 25)
Day of Goodwill (Dec 26)

The longest and busiest holiday period is **Christmas** (summer), which for schools stretches from early December to mid-January. Flights and train berths can be hard to get from mid-December to early January, when many businesses and offices close for their annual break. You should book your **flights** – long-haul and domestic – six months in advance for the Christmas period.

The remaining school holidays roughly cover the following periods: **Easter**, late March to mid-April; **winter**, late June to mid-July; and **spring**, late September to early October. Exact **dates** for each year are listed at ⓦschoolterms.co.za.

Phones

South Africa's landline **telephone** system, dominated by Telkom, generally works well, but **mobile phones** (referred to locally as cell phones) are in far greater use. The competing networks – Vodacom, MTN, Cell C, Virgin Mobile and Telkom itself – cover all main areas and the national roads connecting them. You can use phones from outside South Africa, provided you have **roaming** agreement with your provider at home. A far cheaper alternative is to buy an inexpensive prepaid **local SIM card**. These can be bought for about R20 from the ubiquitous mobile phone shops and various other outlets, including supermarkets. You will need your ID and a proof of address, which can be a hotel receipt or a signed letter from your accommodation or host. You can subsequently purchase data bundles as well as call credit.

International codes

South Africa's international country code is ☎27. To dial out of South Africa, the **access code** is ☎00. In both cases, remember to omit the initial zero in the number of the place you're phoning.

Taxes

Value-added tax (**VAT**) of fifteen percent is levied on most goods and services, though it's usually already included in any quoted price. Foreign visitors can claim back VAT on goods over R250 total. To do this, present an official tax receipt, which should carry your name and address in the case of purchases over R5000, along with a proof of payment for purchases over R10,000, a non-South African passport and the purchased goods themselves, at the **airport** just before you fly out. You will also need to fill in a form, which can be obtained at the airport. For more information, call ☎011 979 0055 or visit ⓦtaxrefunds.co.za.

EMERGENCY NUMBERS

Police ☎10111; fire and state ambulance ☎10177; cellphone emergency operator ☎112; ER24 private ambulance and paramedic assistance ☎084 124; Netcare911 ☎082 911.

Time

There is only one **time zone** in South Africa, two hours ahead of GMT/UTC year-round. If you're flying from Europe, you shouldn't experience any jet lag.

Tipping

Ten to fifteen percent of the tab is the normal **tip** at restaurants, while taxi fares are generally rounded up. Don't feel obliged to tip if service has been shoddy, but bear in mind that many of the people who'll be serving you rely on tips to supplement a meagre wage on which they support huge extended families. Hotel **porters** normally get about R10 per bag. At petrol stations, someone will always be on hand to fill your vehicle, clean your windscreen and check your oil, water and tyre pressure, for which you should tip R5–10. Car guards meanwhile expect around R2–5. It is also usual at **hotels** to leave some money for the person who services your room. Tipping standards at upmarket **game lodges** tend to be more substantial; most will include indicative suggestions in their literature, or you could ask management. Typically, however, you would be looking at a minimum of R100 per client per day for the guide, a similar amount for the tracker (assuming you're allocated one), and again for the general staff (this will shared out evenly to ensuring that lower-profile behind-the-scenes workers are included).

Tourist information

Given South Africa's booming tourism industry, it's not surprising that you'll have no difficulty finding **maps**, **books** and **brochures** before you leave. South African Tourism, the official organization promoting the country, is reasonably efficient: if there's an office near you, it's worth visiting for free maps, **information** and inspiration. Alternatively, check its **website** ⓦsouthafrica.net.

In South Africa itself, nearly every town, right down to the sleepiest *dorp*, has some sort of **tourist office** – sometimes connected to the museum, municipal offices or library – where you can pick up local maps, lists of B&Bs and local advice. In larger cities such as

Cape Town, you'll find several branches offering everything from accommodation reservations to **game park bookings**. We've listed the business hours of tourist offices in the Guide, though they generally open at least Monday to Friday 8.30am to 4.30pm, with some also open shorter hours over weekends.

In this fast-changing country the best way of finding out what's happening is often by word of mouth, and for this, backpacker **hostels** are invaluable. If you're seeing South Africa on a budget, their useful notice boards, constant traveller traffic and largely helpful and friendly staff will smooth your travels.

To find out what's on, check out the entertainment pages of the daily **newspapers** or better still buy the *Mail & Guardian* (W mg.co.za), which comes out every Friday and lists the coming week's offerings in a comprehensive pullout supplement.

TRAVEL ADVISORIES

Australian Department of Foreign Affairs W dfat.gov.au.
British Foreign & Commonwealth Office W fco.gov.uk.
Canadian Global Affairs W international.gc.ca.
Irish Department of Foreign Affairs W foreignaffairs.gov.ie.
New Zealand Ministry of Foreign Affairs W mfat.govt.nz.
US State Department W state.gov.

Travellers with disabilities

Facilities for **travellers with disabilities** are not as sophisticated as those you might find in Western European and North American countries, but they're sufficient to ensure you have a satisfactory visit. You will find good **accessibility** to many buildings, as South Africans tend to build low (single-storey bungalows are the norm). As the car is king, you'll frequently find that you can drive to, and park right outside, your destination. There are organized **tours** and **holidays** for people with disabilities, and activity-based packages are available. These offer the possibility for wheelchair-bound visitors to take part in safaris and a range of adventure **activities**. Tours can either be taken as self-drive trips or as packages for groups.

USEFUL CONTACTS

W **brandsouthafrica.com/tourism-south-africa/travel/advice/disabled** Useful overview and links.
W **capetown.travel/wheelchair-friendly-activities-in-cape-town** Cape Town Tourism has a page on wheelchair-friendly activities.
W **disabledtravel.co.za** Website of occupational therapist Karin Coetzee aimed at disabled travellers, with listings of accommodation, restaurants and attractions personally evaluated for accessibility, as well as links to car rental, tours and orthopaedic equipment.

W **epic-enabled.com** Accommodation, tours and safaris.
W **flamingotours.co.za** Flamingo Tours and Disabled Ventures specialize in tours for visitors with special needs.
W **rollingsa.co.za** Accommodation, tours and safaris.
W **sanparks.org/groups/disabilities/general.php** Lists what wheelchair and mobility-impaired access and facilities are available at South African National Parks.

Travelling with children

Many aspects of travel with **children** are straightforward in South Africa (indeed, the major complication for most visitors is the **paperwork requirements** for children entering the country; see page 27). Whether you want to explore a city, relax on the beach or head for the tranquillity of the mountains, you'll find local people friendly, attentive and accepting of babies and young children.

Visiting **game parks** with children is less straightforward. Most enjoy seeing wildlife in concentrated bursts, but visiting game parks involves a lot of driving (and possible disappointment, should the promised beasts fail to appear), which can stretch the attention span of a restless under-12 to the limit, or induce symptoms of gadget withdrawal in easily bored teenagers. A lot depends on the individual child. Assuming, however, that they are old enough and temperamentally suited to enjoy the experience, few kids enjoy watching animals from afar and through a window, so make sure they have their own **binoculars**. Many private reserves refuse to take under-12s, or allocate them to one specify family-friendly lodge, or insist they take private game drives, so as not to disturb other guests. To get in closer, some animal parks, such as Tshukudu Bush Camp (W tshukudu-bushcamp.co.za) near Kruger, have semi-tame animals, while snake and reptile parks are an old South African favourite.

The following information is aimed mainly at families with under-5s. Although children up to 24 months only pay ten percent of the adult **airfare**, they get no seat allowance. Given this, you'd be well advised to secure bulkhead seats and reserve a bassinet or sky cot, which can be attached to the bulkhead. **Bassinets** are often allocated to babies under about nine months, though many airlines use weight (under 10kg) as the criterion.

Given the size of the country, you're likely to **drive** long distances. Go slowly and plan a route that allows frequent stops – or take flights or trains between centres. The Garden Route, for example, is an ideal drive, with easy stops for picnics between Mossel Bay and Storms River. The route between Johannesburg and Cape Town, conversely, is long, dangerous and tedious.

Family accommodation is plentiful, and hotels, guesthouses, B&Bs and a growing number of backpacker lodges have rooms with extra beds or interconnecting rooms. Kids usually stay for half-price. Self-catering options, such as farmstays, generally have a good deal of space to play in, and there'll often be a **pool**.

Eating out with a baby or toddler is easy, with many outdoor venues where they can get on unhindered with their exploration of the world. Some restaurants have highchairs and offer small portions. If in doubt, try the ubiquitous family-oriented **chains** such as Spur, Nando's or Wimpy.

Breast-feeding is practised by the majority of African mothers wherever they are, though you won't see many white women doing it in public. Be discreet, especially in more conservative areas – which is most of the country outside middle-class Cape Town, Johannesburg and Durban. There are relatively few **baby rooms** in public places for changing or feeding, although the situation is improving and you shouldn't have a problem at shopping malls in the cities. You can buy disposable **nappies** wherever you go, as well as wipes, bottles, formula and dummies. High-street chemists and the Clicks chain are the best places to buy baby goods. If you run out of **clothes**, the Woolworths chain has good-quality stuff, while the ubiquitous Pep stores, present in even the smallest towns, are an excellent source of cheap, functional clothes.

Malaria (see page 43) affects only a small part of the country, but think carefully about visiting these areas as some preventatives aren't recommended for babies or pregnant or breastfeeding women. Avoid many of the northeastern **game reserves**, particularly Kruger National Park and those in KwaZulu-Natal or Limpopo; opt instead for malaria-free reserves, such as Addo Elephant National Park, Pilanesberg and Madikwe. Malarial zones have a reduced risk in winter.

USEFUL CONTACTS

Ⓦ **capetownkids.co.za** Resources for parents and children in Cape Town.

Ⓦ **childmag.co.za** South African parenting guide.

Ⓦ **jozikids.co.za** Resources for parents and children in Johannesburg.

Ⓦ **sitters4u.co.za** Babysitters in Cape Town and Gauteng.

Ⓦ **supersitters.net** Babysitters in Cape Town.

Gauteng, North West Province and Western Limpopo

ZEBRA MARE AND FOAL, PILANESBERG
NATIONAL PARK

1

Gauteng, North West Province and Western Limpopo

The smallest and most urban of South Africa's nine provinces, Gauteng – a SeSotho name meaning "Place Of Gold" – stands at an average altitude of 1500m on the sunny grass-swathed uplands of the highveld. Gauteng accounts for less than two percent of South Africa's surface area, extending over 18,176 square kilometres (making it smaller than the Kruger Park), yet its population, estimated at 15 million in 2019, amounts to around 25 percent of the national total. As might be expected of such a tightly packed and industrialized province, wildlife-viewing opportunities are rather scarce. But they do exist. More importantly, the presence of OR Tambo International Airport, the busiest flight hub in subequatorial Southern Africa, ensures that Gauteng is the main springboard for several top-notch malaria-free reserves in neighbouring North West and Limpopo Provinces.

Gauteng's rapid ascent to become Southern Africa's most important centre of commerce was initiated by the discovery of the world's richest gold seams below what is now **Johannesburg** in 1886. Today, this landlocked and densely populated province contains four of South Africa's seven largest municipalities, generates around forty percent of the national **GDP**, and has an unenviable reputation for high rates of crime, pollution, traffic congestion and other urban malaise. Game parks, unsurprisingly, don't feature prominently on the landscape. Yet despite this, a few (relatively contrived) wildlife-viewing opportunities are squeezed in between the skyscrapers, suburbia and slums of Gauteng. These range from the family-friendly **Rhino and Lion Nature Reserve** and conservation-minded **Ann van Dyk Cheetah Centre** to the underpublicized Dinokeng Game Reserve, whose 230 square kilometres are home to introduced but free-ranging populations of the Big Five.

Looking slightly further afield, Gauteng lies within easy driving distance of a trio of superb Big Five safari destinations, any of which could be visited as a worthwhile malaria-free alternative to the Kruger. Closest to Johannesburg, and best suited to self-drivers, is the **Pilanesberg Game Reserve**, which stands in surreal juxtaposition to the neighbouring Sun City gambling and entertainment complex. Better still, **Madikwe Game Reserve** operates rather like a larger and less busy variation on the famous private reserves bordering Kruger, studded with a dozen or more small exclusive lodges offering all-inclusive safari packages. Finally, the more remote **Waterberg Biosphere Reserve** has something for everybody: self-drive Big Five viewing in Marakele National Park, upmarket guided safaris in the Welgevonden Game Reserve, and more active ventures such as horseback and hiking safaris in various neighbouring properties.

Gauteng

Dominated by a sprawling conurbation that incorporates the cities of Johannesburg, Pretoria and Soweto, **GAUTENG** lacks the spectacular natural assets of the Western Cape or Mpumalanga, and its attractions, such as they are, tend towards the urban. Nonetheless, the province possesses a subtle physical power. Startling outcrops of rock known as koppies, with intriguing and often lucrative geology, are found in the sprawling suburbs and grassy plains of deep-red earth that fringe the cities. Northern Gauteng encompasses

EVOCATIVE MAPUNGUBWE ROCK ART

Highlights

❶ Pilanesberg National Park The most accessible Big Five park from Johannesburg and Pretoria, with beautiful landscapes in a former volcano crater and terrific game viewing. See page 66

❷ Madikwe Game Reserve An often-overlooked Big Five reserve in the corner of the province; prepare to be pampered in some of South Africa's classiest wildlife lodges. See page 72

❸ Nylsvley Nature Reserve Best visited in summer, the seasonal floodplain protected in this pedestrian-friendly small reserve is arguably the country's most rewarding site for freshwater birds. See page 79

❹ Horseriding in the Waterberg This biosphere reserve offers some of South Africa's finest wilderness riding and horseback safaris, with outrides among zebra and giraffe, and the occasional rhino tagging along. See page 80

❺ Marakele National Park This little-known self-drive gem in the heart of the Waterberg is mainly of interest for the fantastic scenery, but it also hosts all the Big Five and a varied birdlife and flora. See page 84

❻ Mapungubwe archeology Climb the Hill of Jackals and see the remains of Africa's earliest kingdom, then continue to the fantastic nearby San cave paintings. See page 89

HIGHLIGHTS ARE MARKED ON THE MAP ON PAGE 56

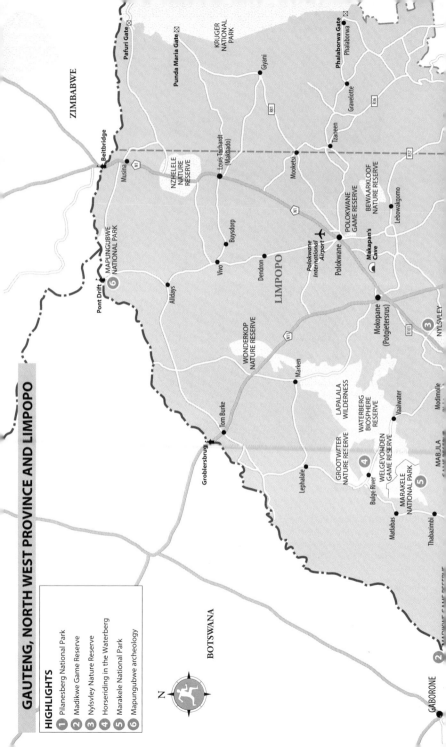

GAUTENG, NORTH WEST PROVINCE AND LIMPOPO

HIGHLIGHTS

1. Pilanesberg National Park
2. Madikwe Game Reserve
3. Nylsvley Nature Reserve
4. Horseriding in the Waterberg
5. Marakele National Park
6. Mapungubwe archeology

ZIMBABWE

BOTSWANA

GABORONE

KRUGER NATIONAL PARK

Pafuri Gate

Punda Maria Gate

Phalaborwa Gate

Phalaborwa

Giyani

Gravelotte

Beitbridge

Musina

Louis Trichardt (Makhado)

Tzaneen

Mooketsi

NZHELELE NATURE RESERVE

BEWAARKLOOF NATURE RESERVE

Lebowakgomo

MAPUNGUBWE NATIONAL PARK

Pont Drift

Buysdorp

POLOKWANE GAME RESERVE

Makapan's Cave

Vivo

Dendron

Polokwane International Airport

Polokwane

LIMPOPO

Alldays

WONDERKOP NATURE RESERVE

Mokopane (Potgietersrus)

NYLSVLEY

Tom Burke

Marken

LAPALALA WILDERNESS

Vaalwater

Groblersbrug

WATERBERG BIOSPHERE RESERVE

Modimolle

GROOTWATER NATURE RESERVE

WELGEVONDEN GAME RESERVE

Bulge River

MARAKELE NATIONAL PARK

MABULA GAME RESERVE

Lephalale

Matlabas

Thabazimbi

1

THE CRADLE OF HUMANKIND

On the R400 50km northwest of central Johannesburg • Daily 9am–5pm • R120-190 • ☏ 014 577 9000, ⓦ maropeng.co.za

Inscribed as a UNESCO World Heritage Site in 1999, the 470-square-kilometre **Cradle of Humankind** comprises a labyrinthine collection of dolomitic caves and subterranean chambers that has yielded roughly one-third of the world's known hominid fossils. It is arguably the world's most important paleoanthropological site, and also perhaps the most accessible, situated a short drive northwest of Johannesburg, and very well developed for tourism. The hominid remains at the Cradle of Humankind date back 3.5 million years, when fossilized pollen, plant material and animal bones also found in the caves indicate that the area supported a cover of tropical rainforest inhabited by giant monkeys, long-legged hunting hyenas and sabre-toothed cats.

The Cradle's most famous fossil is a nearly complete skull unearthed by the palaeontologist Dr Robert Broom in 1947. Originally named *Plesianthropus transvaalensis* ("near-man of the Transvaal") and nicknamed "**Mrs Ples**", the skull was later identified as a 2.6-million-year-old female specimen of *Australopithecus africanus* ("Southern ape of Africa"). For many years after it was discovered, Mrs Ples was the closest thing the world had to "the missing link". More recently, a number of older fossils have been discovered, representing several genera and species. A prominent recent discovery is a cache of 1550 bones identified as a new species *Homo naledi*, and thought to be around 300,000 years old – thus placing it in the same era as *Homo sapiens*. The discovery was made in 2013 inside two almost inaccessible chambers within the Rising Star (*naledi* in the Sesotho language) cave system. Some scientists believe that the unusual location of the bones is suggestive of ritualized behaviour, with a popular current theory being that *Homo naledi* deliberately disposed of their dead.

The best starting point for a tour, **Maropeng Visitors Centre** is an impressive modern installation housed in the Tumulus, a striking building half clad in grassy earth to simulate a burial mound. Maropeng means "return to the place of our ancestors" in SeTswana, and it houses a variety of child-friendly interactive displays dedicated to human origins and evolution. Visitors can take a short underground boat ride into the mists of time, and then browse through other exhibits explaining the history of human development. A fitting finale is provided by a room full of original hominid, plant and animal fossils loaned from various institutions across South Africa, and a display on the recent *Homo naledi* discoveries.

Situated on the R563, 10km southeast of Maropeng, the best known of the Cradle of Humankind sites is the **Sterkfontein Caves** (tours every half-hour from 9am until 4pm), which first came to European attention in 1896, when an Italian lime prospector, Guglielmo Martinaglia, stumbled upon them. It was here in 1947 that Broom discovered Mrs Ples. In 1995 another archeologist, Ronald Clarke, found "Little Foot", the bones of a 3-million-year-old walking hominid, with big toes that functioned like our thumbs do today. In 1998 an Australopithecus skeleton discovered here was the oldest complete specimen known, reckoned to be 3.3 million years old. There's a small museum that you can browse before being taken on a tour through the cave.

---

the **Dinokeng Game Reserve** as well as a section of the **Magaliesberg Mountains**, while the province's eastern flank incorporates the **Cradle of Humankind**, an open-air UNESCO Word Heritage Site whose hominin fossil timeline stretches back 3.5 million years.

More unexpectedly, perhaps, **Johannesburg** and **Pretoria** rank among the most tree-rich cities on Earth. Pretoria is renowned for the jacaranda trees that blossom in October, transforming the city centre and older suburbs in a spectacle of rich purple. Johannesburg, nursery to between six and ten million trees, depending on which thumbsuck you choose to believe, is proudly but contentiously described by locals as the world's largest man-made forest. True, few large mammals survive in Gauteng outside a handful of small fenced reserves, but the province's mosaic of natural and artificial habitats – indigenous highveld grassland, ancient wetlands, leafy suburban gardens and manmade lakes – has attracted more than 450 bird species, including eighty southern African endemics or near-endemics. That said, for most wildlife enthusiasts, Gauteng is not so much a destination in itself as an air gateway for a road safari further afield, be it northwest to Pilanesberg or Madikwe Game Reserves, north to the Waterberg Biosphere Reserve, or east to the Greater Kruger.

Klipriviersberg Nature Reserve

15km south of central Johannesburg on Ormonde Drive, Mondeor • Dawn–dusk • Free • ☎ 011 943 3578, ⓦ klipriviersberg.org.za

Few locals know about this undeveloped, unspoiled six-square-kilometre parkland, which lies just beyond the N12 in the suburb of Mondeor. **Klipriviersberg Nature Reserve** is managed by the Johannesburg City Council on a former farm purchased by it in 1947. It supports a variety of reintroduced wildlife, including Burchell's zebra, springbok, red hartebeest and the endemic black wildebeest and blesbok, along with naturally occurring species such as common duiker, rock hyrax, slender mongoose, Cape clawless otter and small-spotted genet. A picnic spot overlooks the perennial Bloubosspruit (Blue Bush Stream) as it flows through the reserve, and also forms the starting point for an extensive network of easy walking trails through the valley, which is the best place to spot wildlife, as well as the more strenuous hike up well-wooded slopes to a 1785-metre peak that offers wonderful views of the city to the north. Highlights of an impressive bird checklist of 230 species include the African black duck resident in the river, the Verreaux's eagles that frequently soar overhead, and striking bushveld birds that include Acacia pied barbet, chestnut-vented tit-babbler, chin-spot batis, brown-headed tchagra, ashy tit, paradise flycatcher (summer only) and fair flycatcher (winter only).

KLIPRIVIERSBERG AT A GLANCE

A low-key urban park that offers great views over the city and good birding.
Big Five: N/A
General wildlife: **
Birding: ***
Scenery: ***
Wilderness factor: **
Uncrowded: **
Affordability: *****
Self-drive: Y

1

Suikerbosrand Nature Reserve

About 30km southeast of Johannesburg • daily 7am-6pm • R20 • ☎ 011 439 6300, ⓦ gauteng.net

The pedestrian-friendly **Suikerbosrand Nature Reserve** is an underrated gem whose 130 square kilometres of undulating sandstone hills rise to an elevation of 1917m in Southern Gauteng. The largely unspoilt flora includes montane grassland, acacia savannah, riparian woodland and slopes swathed in the eponymous "sugar bush" *Protea caffra* and its unmistakable pink flowers. A wide variety of non-dangerous large mammals have been introduced or occur naturally, notably Burchell's zebra, greater kudu, eland, black wildebeest, red hartebeest, blesbok, springbok, mountain reedbuck, common duiker, steenbok, grey rhebok, oribi, baboon and shy carnivores such as brown hyena, aardwolf and genet. The varied vegetation attracts an equally varied selection of birds, with almost 300 recorded to date. The reserve is serviced by a 60km network of all-weather game-viewing roads, and you can stretch your legs on the 4km interpretive Cheetah Trail or give them a more thorough workout on a 17km day hike. It can get moderately crowded on weekends and public holidays but you'll as likely as not have the trails to yourself on weekdays.

The drive from Johannesburg should take 30–60 minutes, though this depends greatly on traffic, and from where exactly you leave. Follow the N3 highway southeast towards Durban for 25km, then take the R550/Alberton Road off-ramp and turn right, across the highway, from where it is about 6km to the entrance gate.

SUIKERBOSRAND AT A GLANCE

The protea-swathed slopes of these pretty mountains are great for self-drivers and keen walkers.
Big Five: N/A
General wildlife: **
Birding: ****
Scenery: ***
Wilderness factor: ***
Uncrowded: ****
Affordability: *****
Self-drive: Y

1

Marievale Bird Sanctuary

Near Nigel, 67km southeast of Johannesburg • Apr–Sept 5.30am–7pm, Oct–Mar 6am–6pm • Free • ☎ 082 830 5467

Arguably the most important birdwatching hotspot in Gauteng, the 10-square-kilometre **Marievale Bird Sanctuary** forms part of the **Blesbokspruit Ramsar Wetland** and comprises a mosaic of perennial pans, seasonal marshes and open grassland that is frequently inundated during the rainy season. It is serviced by a good network of roads (though walking is permitted throughout) and four hides that are well positioned for spotting and photographing birds on the pans. Of more than 280 species recorded, water-associated birds are particularly well-represented, and a full day here might easily yield upwards of eighty species, especially in summer. Among the more interesting and conspicuous year-round residents are African marsh harrier, great crested grebe, goliath heron, glossy ibis and African purple swamphen. Spur-winged geese often aggregate in large numbers over winter, while Palaearctic migrants present between November and March might include black-tailed godwit and yellow wagtail, along with a wide variety of waders and waterfowl. Mammals likely to be encountered by visitors include Cape clawless otter, three species of mongoose, southern reedbuck and the endemic blesbok.

Marievale can be reached in 45–90 minutes from Johannesburg, depending on exactly where you are coming from and traffic conditions. The best route is to follow the N3 highway southeast towards Durban for 45km to the Heidelberg off-ramp, then to continue northeast along the R42 for 12km to Nigel, from where it is another 10km on the R42 to the sanctuary entrance.

Rhino and Lion Nature Reserve

On the R549 about 50km northwest of Johannesburg • Mon–Fri 8am–5pm, Sat & Sun 8am–6pm • R200 (or R250 including the Wonder Cave, which is visited on conducted tours every hour on the hour) • ☎ 011 957 0349, ⊕ rhinolion.co.za

Situated within the Cradle of Humankind UNESCO World Heritage Site, the 14-square-kilometre **Rhino and Lion Nature Reserve** is more similar to a European-style safari park (albeit with a distinctly African climate and vegetation) than to the game reserves found in other parts of South Africa. Nevertheless, it is the most reliable site in Gauteng for guaranteed large mammal sightings. The main section of the reserve has white rhino, buffalo, wildebeest, hartebeest and zebra roaming free, while the Lion and Predator Camp comprises several large enclosures containing large carnivores such as lion, cheetah and African wild dog. Elsewhere, there's a vulture hide, a series of hippo pools (located opposite the main gate) and a breeding centre. Also situated within the reserve is the so-called **Wonder Cave**, a huge underground chamber which (unlike several others in the Cradle of Humankind) hasn't revealed any paleontological finds, but does contain some extraordinary stalactites, stalagmites and rimstone pools. Once you've descended into the cave by a lift, carefully placed lighting and marked trails make the experience theatrical and unashamedly commercial.

Rietvlei Nature Reserve

14 Game Reserve Avenue, Irene • Sept–Mar 5.30am–7pm, May–Aug 6am–6pm, last entry 1hr before closing • R59 • ☎ 012 358 1811, 🌐 friendsofrietvlei.org

Accessed from the M57 roughly 20km south of central Pretoria, this 40-square-kilometre municipal reserve was established in 1929 at the same time as the bordering **Rietvlei Dam**. It opened to the public as a recreational reserve in 1948, and more than seventy mammal species are present today. The likes of leopard, cheetah, white rhino, Burchell's zebra, hippo, buffalo, black wildebeest, red hartebeest, blesbok, eland, springbok and waterbuck have been introduced to supplement naturally occurring populations of various smaller antelope, primates and carnivores, while a small lion pride is kept in a special camp. A good network of roads can be explored by self-drivers, but the reserve also offers guided group activities such as horseback safaris, day and overnight hikes, lion camp tours (the latter suspended after two of the six lions were found dead of suspected poisoning in October 2019), and day and night drives in an open vehicle. It is a fabulous birding location with around four hundred species recorded, and five hides set at various vantage points alongside Rietvlei Dam and the smaller Marais Dam, where hippos are often seen.

> **RIETVLEI AT A GLANCE**
>
> Decent big game viewing between Joburg and Pretoria.
>
> **Big Five:** ***
> **General wildlife:** ***
> **Birding:** ****
> **Scenery:** **
> **Wilderness factor:** *
> **Uncrowded:** **
> **Affordability:** ****
> **Self-drive:** Y

Dinokeng Game Reserve

Hammanskraal, 40km north of Pretoria; the main Ndlovu Gate is on the R734 1km east of the N1 • Gates open 6am–6pm • R80 per person plus R150 per vehicle • ☎ 012 711 4391, 🌐 dinokengreserve.co.za

The closest Big Five reserve to Johannesburg, **Dinokeng** lies within the crowded confines of Gauteng, only an hour's drive north of OR Tambo Airport and thirty minutes from downtown Pretoria (assuming the traffic cooperates). Divided into a self-drive section and a handful of semi-private concessions, the reserve extends across a total of 230 square kilometres, and possesses a far more remote and wild feel than might reasonably be expected given its location. The creation of Dinokeng – a seTswana name meaning "Place of Rivers" – dates back to a 1996 initiative by the provincial government to develop a game reserve as a source of tourist revenue and social upliftment in a part of northeast Gauteng unsuited to agricultural pursuits. Dinokeng formally opened in 2011 as a partnership between the public sector and more than 170 private landowners, and it is hoped that further negotiations with bordering properties will eventually result in a reserve comparable in extent to the Pilanesberg.

The ancient granitic rocks and sandy Karoo shales of Dinokeng support an archetypically African landscape of open savannah and dense acacia thornbush, coursed through by the north-flowing **Boekenhout** and **Pienaar's** rivers. Alongside naturally occurring species such as black-backed jackal and brown hyena, a wide variety of other wildlife has been reintroduced, notably lion, leopard, cheetah, spotted hyena, elephant, buffalo, giraffe, Burchell's zebra, white rhino, black rhino, hippo and various antelope, of which the most visible are blue wildebeest, greater kudu and impala. More than three hundred bird species have been recorded, a list that include several "bush" species more

> **DINOKENG AT A GLANCE**
>
> The only genuine Big Five reserve in densely populated Gauteng.
>
> **Big Five:** ***
> **General wildlife:** ***
> **Birding:** ****
> **Scenery:** **
> **Wilderness factor:** ***
> **Uncrowded:** ***
> **Affordability:** ****
> **Self-drive:** Y

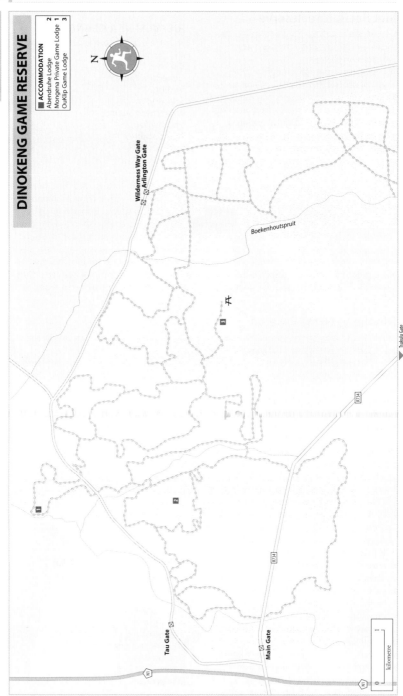

DINOKENG GAME RESERVE

ACCOMMODATION
Abendruhe Lodge 2
Mongena Private Game Lodge 1
Ouklip Game Lodge 3

N

Wilderness Way Gate
Arlington Gate

Boekenhoutspruit

Tsukulu Gate

R734

R734

Tau Gate

Main Gate

N1

N1

0   1

kilometre

1

normally associated with the Kruger than Gauteng, for instance yellow-billed hornbill, magpie shrike, Burchell's starling and various large raptors.

Unlike many private reserves, Dinokeng is well suited to self-drivers, which makes it a realistic option for an affordable day safari out of Johannesburg or Pretoria. The southern part of the reserve is criss-crossed by 140km of well-signposted game-viewing roads, most of which are unsurfaced but suitable to any saloon car, and a good map is supplied free to all self-drive visitors. Wildlife densities are highest in the vicinity of dams and rivers, particularly during the dry winter months, but even then animal numbers tend to be low by comparison to the likes of the Kruger or Pilanesberg. To improve your chances of seeing some of the Big Five, consider booking onto one of the guided game drives offered by *Mongena Lodge*, which has more-or-less exclusive traversing rights to the northern part of the reserve (R350pp, departing 6am, 9am, 2pm, 4.30pm and 8.30pm summer and 6.30am, 9am, 2pm and 4pm winter; see page 66).

Tswaing Meteorite Crater

Onderstepoort Rd, Soshanguve, off the M35 some 40km north of Pretoria • Daily 7.30am–4pm • R30 • ☎ 073 661 5014, ⓦ ditsong.org.za

Centrepiece of a 19.5-square-kilometre nature reserve managed by Ditsong Museums of South Africa, **Tswaing** is one of the world's youngest and best-preserved impact craters, created around 220,000 years ago when a 40m-wide meteorite slammed into the earth, vaporizing itself and everything else within a 3km radius. The resultant crater is 1.4km wide and 200m deep, enclosing a shallow hyper-saline lake alluded to in its seTswana name, which means "Place of Salt". These rich deposits of salt and soda have attracted people for millennia, as evidenced by a wealth of Stone Age tools and artefacts dating back 150,000 years, and they were commercially exploited between 1912 and 1950. The dense thornbush around the crater supports plenty of wildlife, including Burchell's zebra, greater kudu, impala, steenbok, warthog, monitor lizards and around 250 bird species. The reserve also incorporates an extensive wetland fed by the **Soutpansspruit** (Salt Pan Stream). Register at the visitors' centre on the main road before driving to the car park, from where a pleasant 7km circular trail crosses the veld to the crater, down to the lake and back; alternatively, park closer to the rim from where it's a short stroll to the crater.

Ann Van Dyk Cheetah Centre

35km west of Pretoria, just off the R513 towards Brits • Cheetah run and tour Tues, Thurs, Sat & Sun 8am • R400 • Tours daily 1.30pm and Mon, Wed & Fri 8.30am • R380–450 • Book in advance • ☎ 012 504 9906, ⓦ dewildt.co.za

Established in 1971 and originally known as De Wildt, the **Ann Van Dyk Cheetah Centre** is a world-renowned conservation project that is actually situated in North West Province – albeit only 3km from the border with Gauteng. Its mission is to protect the vulnerable cheetah by developing predator-management policies with farmers, and by breeding cubs in captivity (more than 750 have been raised to date) then relocating them into game reserves. Other endangered animals bred and/or cared for at the centre include African wild dogs, vultures and brown hyenas. Visits include an educational tour of the centre and animal enclosures. Photographing cheetahs on the run is a big draw, and the early morning cheetah runs are a unique opportunity to experience the animals in close proximity. Conservation activities are partly funded by a cheetah adoption programme.

> ## TSWAING AT A GLANCE
> Spectacular impact crater hosting some wildlife and plentiful birds.
> **Big Five:** N/A
> **General wildlife:** **
> **Birding:** ****
> **Scenery:** *****
> **Wilderness factor:** ****
> **Uncrowded:** ****
> **Affordability:** *****
> **Self-drive:** Y

ARRIVAL AND DEPARTURE

BY PLANE

OR Tambo International Airport (☎ 011 921 6262 or ☎ 086 727 7888, ⓦ airports.co.za), named after the ANC's greatest leader in exile, lies in Kempton Park some 20km east of central Johannesburg and 50km south of Pretoria. It is the busiest flight hub in Africa, serving more than twenty million domestic and international passengers annually, and offers daily connections to practically every major world city as well as all commercial airports in South Africa. On the ground floor of the international arrivals hall there's a tourist information desk (daily 5.30am–10pm; ☎ 011 390 3614) and 24-hour facilities for changing money; ATMs, a post office and an internet café can be found on the first floor.

ONWARD TRANSPORT

Gautrain The fastest and easiest way to get to the city – especially during the dreaded morning and afternoon rush hours – is on the Gautrain rail link (daily 5.30am–8.30pm; ⓦ gautrain.co.za), which takes 15min to reach Sandton station (R165, plus R15 card), where you can change for trains south to Rosebank and Park stations and north to Pretoria, or use the Gautrain feeder buses to Sandton's hotels.

Shuttle buses EZ Shuttle (☎ 086 139 7488, ⓦ ezshuttle. co.za) and Rhino Shuttles (☎ 010 010 6506, ⓦ rhinoshuttles. co.za) offer a round-the-clock pick-up and drop-off service from the airport; fares are in the ballpark of R500, depending on your drop-off or pick-up point, and it is best to book a day in advance.

Courtesy buses The more expensive hotels often provide courtesy buses, while most backpacker hostels and some smaller guesthouses or B&Bs offer free pick-ups (best booked when making your reservation) and sometimes free drop-offs back to the airport.

Taxis There are plenty of taxi touts floating around the arrival hall proffering price lists with exaggerated (but usually negotiable) fares; however, you are better off using the taxi booking stand next to the tourist office in the arrival hall. Before you set off, make certain to check that the driver knows where you're going, and to get a quote beforehand. You should pay around R500 to get to central Joburg, Rosebank or Sandton, and no more than R600 to reach a far northern or western suburb. Uber also pick up from the airport, though it's best to arrange a pick-up point away from their meter taxi rivals who have been known to harass Uber drivers.

Car rental Standard car rental deals are available from the main companies such as Avis (☎ 011 923 3730), EuropCar (☎ 011 574 1000) and Tempest (☎ 011 394 8626), which all have offices at the airport and in several city locations. It's often much cheaper to rent one of these companies' cars using a broker website like ⓦ carhire.co.za. Alternatively, try Rent-a-Wreck, 343 Louis Botha Ave, Orange Grove (☎ 011 640 2666, ⓦ rentawreck.co.za). Beware of police

checkpoints at the airport; heed all stop signs and speed limits, or you risk getting fined.

Airline information Many major airlines have ticket offices at OR Tambo International Airport, among them Air France/KLM (☎ 011 961 6700); British Airways (☎ 011 441 8400); Lufthansa (☎ 086 184 2538); South African Airways (☎ 011 978 1000); SA Airlink (☎ 011 451 7300); Qantas (☎ 011 978 6414), and Virgin Atlantic (☎ 011 340 3400).

Destinations: Bloemfontein (5–12 daily; 1hr); Cape Town (70 daily; 2hr); Durban (50 daily; 1hr); East London (9 daily; 1hr 25min); Hoedspruit (2 daily; 1hr); Kimberley (3–7 daily; 1hr 30min); Nelspruit (5–6 daily; 1hr 50min); Port Elizabeth (15 daily; 1hr 40min).

LANSERIA AIRPORT

Joburg's secondary Lanseria Airport (☎ 011 367 0300, ⓦ lanseria.co.za) is 30km northwest of the city centre and used by an increasing number of budget airlines. Taxis don't tend to wait at this airport and there's no public transport, so either organize a transfer with your accommodation or call a taxi.

Destinations: Cape Town (12–13 daily; 2hr); Durban (6–7 daily; 1hr); Port Elizabeth (2 daily; 2hr).

BY CAR

Toll roads The much-hated electronic road toll system on the N1, N3, N12 and R21 highways around Joburg and up to Pretoria charges all vehicles about R0.50 per kilometre. Rental cars are fitted with devices to register the toll payments; others must register beforehand at ⓦ www.nra.co.za.

Rush hour When driving to Pretoria, avoid the afternoon rush hour northwards (3.30–5pm), when travel time can double to 2hr; this is also when a quick 45min drive to OR Tambo Airport can turn into a two-hour ordeal.

BY BUS AND MINIBUS

Baz Bus (☎ 086 122 9287, ⓦ bazbus.com) operates 22-seater bus services from Johannesburg to Cape Town via the Drakensberg, Durban, the Eastern Cape coast and the Garden Route (4–5 weekly), stopping at hostels en route. The service is designed to be "hop-on hop-off", with overnight stops in Durban and Port Elizabeth.

Greyhound, Intercape and Translux These intercity buses arrive at Park Station in the centre of town. Once notoriously unsafe, Park Station has been significantly improved and the main concourse is big, open and secure, with information desks for all the bus companies. That said, it's not a good idea to walk around the surrounding area with a lot of luggage, so you're best off taking the Gautrain or a taxi to your final destination or arranging a pick-up with your accommodation. Park Station has a number of car rental offices conveniently located on the upper concourse, usually listed under "Braamfontein" on their websites.

Destinations: Beitbridge (3 daily; 7hr); Bloemfontein (16 daily; 5hr); Cape Town (6 daily; 19hr 30min); Durban (16 daily; 8–11hr); East London (12 daily; 12hr 45min); Kimberley (5 daily; 6hr 30min); King William's Town (3 daily; 12hr 15min); Knysna (daily; 17hr); Kuruman (daily; 7hr); Ladysmith (2 daily; 5hr 45min); Mossel Bay (2 daily; 17hr); Mthatha (daily; 11hr 30min); Nelspruit (6 daily; 5hr); Newcastle (daily; 5hr); Oudtshoorn (2 daily; 14hr 30min); Pietermaritzburg (16 daily; 7hr); Plettenberg Bay (daily; 17hr 30min); Port Elizabeth (4 daily; 13hr 15min); Pretoria (over 30 daily; 1hr).

BY TRAIN

Intercity and Gautrain Long distance Shosholoza Meyl (w shosholozameyl.co.za, ☎ 086 000 8888 or ☎ 011 774 4555) trains pull in at Park Station in the centre of town (see above) and tickets can be booked at the Shosholoza Meyl ticket office in Park Station. The Gautrain service is the fastest and most comfortable rail link to Pretoria. Buy tickets and catch the Gautrain from the Gautrain Park Station at the corner of Wolmarans and Rissik stations (opposite the station's northern concourse entrance). Destinations: Cape Town, via Kimberley (Wed, Fri & Sun; 26hr); Durban (Wed, Fri & Sun; 14hr); East London via Bloemfontein (Wed, Fri & Sun; 20hr); Komatipoort via Nelspruit (Fri; 13hr); Port Elizabeth, via Bloemfontein (Wed, Fri & Sun; 20hr).

ACCOMMODATION AND EATING

There's plenty of accommodation in and around Gauteng, but with the exception of the lodges at Dinokeng Game Reserve, nothing that specifically caters for wildlife enthusiasts. If you are literally just passing through Gauteng in transit to the Kruger or elsewhere, there's no shortage of accommodation close to OR Tambo Airport. For longer stays, the northern suburbs of Johannesburg offer several good options if you are relying on public transport. Melville is relatively close to the CBD and hosts a characterful community with cafés, restaurants and bars within safe walking distance of a great number of guesthouses. Rosebank is well located at the heart of the northern suburbs, and it has a decent selection of places to eat out and shop, plus a Gautrain station. Sandton has a wealth of pricey chain hotels aimed at business executives. The website w johannesburg-guesthouses.co.za is a handy portal for browsing and booking guesthouses based in and around Rosebank and Melville. Pretoria's Bed & Breakfast Association has a central booking site at w bbapt.co.za. Gauteng has a huge range of places to eat out, with authentic French, Italian, Chinese, Greek and Portuguese restaurants, plus increasing numbers of African restaurants – not just South African but also Congolese, Moroccan, Ethiopian and Cape Malay. Prices are higher than most other parts of the country, but an average meal out is still good value. The lodges listed below all serve food, otherwise head out to Parkhurst's Fourth Avenue, Melville's Seventh Street or the Melrose Arch Mall, all of which host a varied cluster of good places to eat.

OR TAMBO AIRPORT

Airport en Route 97 Boden Rd, Benoni Small Farms, Benoni ☎ 011 963 3389, w sa-venues.com/visit/airport enroutebenoni. A tidy, congenial budget lodge located 15min from the airport (pickups can be arranged) in the famously sleepy town where film star Charlize Theron grew up. Accommodation is cosy, three-bed log cabins, some of which are en suite, and two rooms sleeping up to four people; camping is also available. $

City Lodge OR Tambo Airport ☎ 011 552 7600, w clhg. com. Conveniently plonked right on top of the airport parking garage, this is the best value hotel within walking distance of the gates. Rooms are well sized, very quiet and overlook the Gautrain station. $$

JOHANNESBURG NORTHERN SUBURBS

★ **Agterplaas B&B** 66 Sixth Ave, Melville ☎ 011 726 8452 or ☎ 082 902 5799, w agterplaas.co.za. Just a minute's walk from Melville's restaurants and cafés, this neat, tasteful guesthouse has balconied rooms with views over the Melville koppies, and more accommodation in a house across the road. There's a wonderful lounge, where the famed breakfasts are served (until 10am; 11am at weekends); non-guests are welcome as well. $$

★ **Liz at Lancaster** 79 Lancaster Ave, Craighall Park ☎ 011 442 8083, w lizatlancaster.co.za. A classy and very highly regarded guesthouse halfway between the restaurants and boutiques of Parkhurst's 4th Avenue and the upmarket Hyde Park Corner mall. Decorated with local art, the large rooms overlook a garden with a pool. $$

★ **Satyagraha House** 15 Pine Rd, Orchards ☎ 011 485 5928, w satyagrahahouse.com. Peaceful guesthouse named after Gandhi's philosophy of *satyagraha* (non-violent civil disobedience). Gandhi lived here from 1908–09, and there's a small museum dedicated to his life. Vegetarian evening meals can be arranged. $$$

PRETORIA

1322 Backpackers 1322 Arcadia St, Hatfield ☎ 012 362 3905, w 1322backpackers.com. A popular hostel near the embassies and Hatfield's nightlife, with dorms, private rooms, kitchen, pool and travel desk. Just a short walk east of the Gautrain station. $

★ **Moroccan House** 435 Atterbury Rd, Menlo Park, ☎ 012 346 5713, w moroccanhouse.co.za. Modelled on a Moroccan *riad*, the guest suites, each with a private terrace, are a riot of colour, decorated with fabrics, tiles and furniture imported from Morocco. The traditional breakfast served upstairs at the La Terrasse Rooftop Café is excellent. $$

1

CRADLE OF HUMANKIND

Forum Homini Kromdraai Rd ☎ 011 668 7000, ⓦ forum homini.com. Set in a private game farm that's home to antelopes and hippos, this award-winning five-star hotel has beautiful "cave chic" rooms overlooking a lake. The fantastic gourmet restaurant *Roots*, which serves set lunches and dinners, is worth the trip alone; plan to spend several hours eating here. Rates include meals. $$$

Maropeng Hotel Off the R400 ☎ 014 577 9100, ⓦ maropeng.co.za. The chic hotel next to the Maropeng Museum offers good value, with full-board packages available that include museum entrance. Each of its classy earth-toned rooms has a patio commanding a dramatic Magaliesberg view. $$

DINOKENG GAME RESERVE   SEE MAP P.62

Abendruhe Lodge ☎ 078 738 2194, ⓦ abendruhe. co.za. This low-key owner-managed facility comprises four attractive open-plan log cabins, each with a private viewing deck facing a waterhole where wildlife regularly comes to drink. Great value for self-catering self-drivers, especially on weekday nights. Sun–Thurs $, Fri & Sat $$

★ **Mongena Private Game Lodge** ☎ 012 711 8920, ⓦ mongena.co.za. Four-star *Mongena* comprises 24 well-equipped air-conditioned thatched cottages set in an indigenous garden populated by zebra, antelope and a wide variety of birds. It has a genuine bush feel, and rates are inclusive of meals and guided game drives, making for the closest upmarket private safari experience to Johannesburg. $$$$

OuKlip Game Lodge ☎ 071 313 5380 or ☎ 082 476 6214, ⓦ ouklip.co.za. This unpretentious and well-priced tented camp comprises fourteen en-suite standing tents, all with shaded terrace seating, as well as a common self-catering kitchen and boma. Antelope and plentiful birds can be seen in the garden. If you don't fancy self-catering, the helpful owners can point you to a nearby restaurant. $$

North West Province

Running west from Gauteng to the border with Botswana, **NORTH WEST PROVINCE** is a relatively dry and thinly inhabited region dominated by the **Tswana**, who comprise about two-thirds of its population. It was created in April 1994 when the nominally independent homeland of Bophuthatswana was reintegrated into South Africa, and it comprises most of this former "Bantustan" as well as parts of the defunct Cape and Transvaal provinces. Tourism is focused on a pair of fine malaria-free wildlife reserves, both administered by the North West Parks Board (NWPB) and relatively easily visited as a self-contained round-trip from Johannesburg or Pretoria. These are the **Pilanesberg National Park**, an excellent self-drive Big Five destination abutting the equally well-known Sun City entertainment complex, and the larger **Madikwe Game Reserve**, which cannot be explored by self-drivers but is serviced by more than a dozen upmarket lodges that offer all-inclusive guided safari packages similar to those in private reserves such as Sabi Sands or Phinda. Although Pilanesberg and Madikwe are separated by 60km of farmland, NWPB has ambitious long-term expansion plans to create a corridor between them, forming a mega-reserve where animals could migrate between the two protected nodes. Madikwe and Pilanesberg can be visited at any time of year, but as with most reserves in South Africa, game-viewing tends to be best in the dry winter months of April to October, when foliage is lower and animals tend to congregate close to limited water sources. Scenically the reserves are at their best in the wetter summer months, and this is also the best time for birding.

Pilanesberg National Park

Daily: Mar, Apr, Sept & Oct 6am–6.30pm; May–Aug 6.30am–6pm; Nov–Feb 5.30am–7pm • R80, plus R30 per person non-South African visitors' levy and R40 per car • ☎ 014 555 1600, ⓦ pilanesbergnationalpark.org

The 572-square-kilometre **Pilanesberg** is North West Province's biggest tourist draw and the closest self-drive Big Five safari destination of comparable quality to Gauteng. Set within an ancient collapsed volcano, this oasis of conservation, with its huge variety of animals, offers welcome respite from the proliferation of mines that otherwise form the backbone of the region's economy. Pilanesberg's proximity to Gauteng does means it can get busy, especially during long weekends and school holidays, but don't let the crowds put you off. The park offers game-viewing thrills aplenty, with a good chance of seeing all the Big Five, as well as cheetah, brown hyena, hippo, giraffe and zebra. A wide variety of antelope species are here, too, and there's a vast array of birdlife, with more than 365 species recorded so far, including a wealth of eagles and other raptors, along with Kalahari specials such as the gorgeous crimson-breasted shrike, pied babbler and black-faced waxbill at the eastern limit of their range.

> **PILANESBERG AT A GLANCE**
> The closest self-drive Big Five destination reserve to Johannesburg.
> **Big Five:** ★★★★
> **General wildlife:** ★★★★
> **Birding:** ★★★★
> **Scenery:** ★★★
> **Wilderness factor:** ★★★
> **Uncrowded:** ★★
> **Affordability:** ★★★★
> **Self-drive:** Y

As Pilanesberg is the game-viewing location of choice for people based in Gauteng with limited time availability, it does mean that during the day it can become congested around major sightings and in areas known for popular animals. In order to get into the park at dawn, which is prime game-viewing time, it is advisable to stay within the reserve or close to the gate, which allows for some unhindered sightings before the day-visitors stream in.

Brief history
The **Pilanesberg Alkaline Ring Complex**, as it is known by geologists, is one of only three alkaline volcanoes in the world; its beginnings date back roughly 2000 million years. Over time, subsequent volcanic activity, peaking perhaps 1200 million years back, and eons of erosion formed a concentric "onion ring" formation roughly 20km in diameter, whose near-circular outline, though not all that apparent on the ground, is easily recognizable on satellite images on Google Earth and elsewhere.

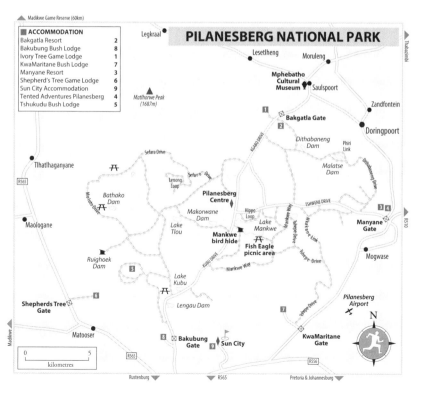

Madikwe Game Reserve (60km)

PILANESBERG NATIONAL PARK

ACCOMMODATION	
Bakgatla Resort	2
Bakubung Bush Lodge	8
Ivory Tree Game Lodge	1
KwaMaritane Bush Lodge	7
Manyane Resort	3
Shepherd's Tree Game Lodge	6
Sun City Accommodation	9
Tented Adventures Pilanesberg	4
Tshukudu Bush Lodge	5

Legkraal
Lesetlheng
Moruleng
Mphebatho Cultural Museum
Saulspoort
Zandfontein
Matlhorwe Peak (1687m)
Bakgatla Gate
Doringpoort
Dithabaneng Dam
Phiri Link
Malatse Dam
Sefara Drive
Tlhatlhaganyane
R565
Lenong Loop
Sefara Drive
Bathako Dam
Pilanesberg Centre
TSHWENE DRIVE
Makorwane Dam
Hippo Loop
Lake Mankwe
Maologane
Lake Tlou
Mankwe bird hide
Fish Eagle picnic area
Manyane Gate
R510
Ruighoek Dam
Mogwase
Lake Kubu
Mankwe Way
Shepherds Tree Gate
Lengau Dam
Pilanesberg Airport
N
Matooser
Bakubung Gate
Sun City
KwaMaritane Gate
R565
R556
0 5 kilometres
Rustenburg
R565
Pretoria & Johannesburg

1

Evidence of **hunter-gatherers** having lived in the area since the Middle Stone Age can still be found in the park. Later the ancestors of the **Batswana** and **Basotho** people began to occupy the area, but it was only in the mid-1700s that major Batswana towns became established. Pilanesberg literally means "Pilane's Mountain" and is named after the chief of the **Bakgatla-ba-Kgafela** clan, who inhabited the northern part of the range prior to the creation of the national park.

In the 1820s, when Mzilikazi (a former lieutenant of Shaka Zulu) invaded the area and his Ndebele followers took control of the region, a few Batswana clans, including the Bakgatla-ba-Kgafela, took refuge in the Pilanesberg mountains. After the removal of Mzilikazi in 1837, Boer farmers began to settle on the land formerly inhabited by Batswana people. As they introduced the concept of registered land ownership, it became difficult for Tswana communities to return to their ancestral land. In the second half of the nineteenth century, **Reverend Henry Godin** established the first missionary church amongst the Bakgatla-ba-Kgafela, and helped them purchase various farms in the Pilanesberg, including Paul Kruger's farm **Saulspoort**.

In the 1960s, white-owned farms in the Pilanesberg were expropriated by the Nationalist government in order to make way for the creation of **Bophuthatswana**, a Tswana "Bantustan" that became a "self-governing homeland" in 1972 and was granted nominal independence as a republic in 1977. A couple of years later, the Bophuthatswana government set aside Pilanesberg as a game reserve to be developed in conjunction with the neighbouring Sun City entertainment complex as the homeland's premier tourist attraction. The remaining Tswana inhabitants were unceremoniously evicted when **Operation Genesis** saw more than 6000 animals relocated here from all over South Africa in the early 1980s. Pilanesberg became Bophuthatswana's first national park in 1984, and confusingly it is still officially referred to as such, despite the subsequent reintegration of the homeland into South Africa, and the fact is the reserve is managed by NWPB as opposed to SANParks.

In 2003 the **Black Rhino Game Reserve** was incorporated into the Pilanesberg. This 18-square-kilometre property, lying in the northwestern section of Pilanesberg, was once a cattle farm before becoming a game farm and later being declared a reserve. This section of the park, with its exclusive lodges, heralded the start of an ambitious plan to incorporate Pilanesberg National Park into a mega reserve that will eventually link it to Madikwe Game Reserve 60km to the northwest.

Game drives

Pilanesberg is traversed by some 200km of tarred and gravel roads, and you will need at least two full days to do them all justice. It is easily explored in a standard sedan vehicle, though extra care might be needed on a few gravel roads, and a high-clearance SUV offers better views over the thatching grass, which can get very long in some areas. A good inexpensive map for self-drivers can be purchased at the entrance gates and camp shops, and intersections are well signposted. The gates also have boards with details of recent wildlife sightings, though they are not always kept up to date. If you're self-driving, don't hesitate to ask the safari jeep drivers for sighting tips; they are all in radio contact with each other and know exactly what's going on.

The sourish mixed bushveld is well stocked with game. Lion, leopard and cheetah are frequently sighted and tend to attract large followings of vehicles. Other big game that is seen regularly includes elephant, white rhino and hippo, the latter being most visible in the cooler winter months when they can be seen grazing out of the water in the middle of the day. Buffalo tend to prefer the Black Rhino concession and the wilderness area in the northwest, but they are starting to make regular forays into the rest of the reserve. Crocodiles inhabit some of the dams.

Main roads and Lake Mankwe

Three main surfaced roads run through Pilanesberg, converging at a central three-way intersection near man-made **Lake Mankwe**. Kubu Drive runs for 12.5km in a broadly northerly direction from the busy Bakubung Gate (the closest point of entry to Sun City), while the 9km Kgabo Drive runs south from Bakgatla Gate, and the 12km Tshwene Drive runs west from Manyane Gate. Another short piece of asphalt, Tau Link, connects Kgabo and Tshwene drives, but numerous potholes and deep speed dips mean it is not much better than most of the unsurfaced roads. The northern part of Tau Link is also hemmed in by very long thatching grass which is not great for game viewing.

The tarred roads are the park's busiest, in part because they converge on Lake Mankwe (seTswana for "Place of the Leopard"), which as the reserve's largest water body forms a natural focus for wildlife and visitors alike. The popular Mankwe bird hide on the southwest shore (recently destroyed by fire but likely to be rebuilt) is a great place to watch hippos, rhinos, crocodiles and other big game on the water's edge. In the evening, the hide's parking area is a regular sundowner stopping point for tour vehicles and can get very crowded.

Hippo loop, running for 2.5km along the lake's northern shore, is known for regular sightings of lion and cheetah, which enjoy hunting animals in the open veld as they come down to drink. The river gulley flowing into the dam at this point is also a good area to view waterbuck, while birders will enjoy the variety of waders usually seen here. A little further east, Thalware and Motlobo drives, although further from the water, can also be rewarding as the grass is fairly short; both roads offer great vistas over the lake as they wind through the rocks.

Located on Kgabo Drive just north of Lake Mankwe is a former district magistrate's court – one of the few buildings that survives from before the reserve was established – that now houses the **Pilanesberg Centre**. Here you will find a small supermarket and gift shop, and an open-air terrace restaurant where you can quaff a cold beer or gorge on a burger whilst the likes of greater kudu, giraffe, wildebeest and zebra come to drink at the waterhole and salt lick below.

Visitors wishing to enjoy their own pre-packed picnic in a quieter setting should consider the elevated Fish Eagle Picnic area on the southeast shore of Lake Mankwe. The site can be reached via a short detour off Mankwe Way, an unsurfaced road that connects Kubu and Tshwene Drive by skirting the southeast side of the lake. The large fenced-in picnic area is a great place to stretch your legs and enjoy some long-distance game viewing and extensive watery vistas. In cooler winter months, be sure to scan the shoreline below for grazing hippos.

Other road loops

At the northern end of Mankwe Way, Tshepe Drive peels off down the valley that drains most of the park, eventually reaching the KwaMaritane Gate near Pilanesberg Airport. While this grassy valley below Lake Mankwe can be rewarding for game viewing, half of Tshepe Drive is near the boundary fence and the views of civilization can be a little distracting. Nkakane Link, a poorly-maintained shortcut between Tshepe and Tshwene Drive, is best avoided by those in a low-slung vehicle, but a small dam on its eastern side about halfway along supports a relatively large bloat of hippos that is even more evident in the dry winter months when the water drops.

Tilodi Loop, close to Manyane Gate, is the access road to an interesting **archeological site** on a rocky outcrop overlooking the valley. While the park is dotted with remnants of Iron Age sites, a walk around this partially restored village offers an interesting introduction to the area's Batswana history.

Heading north from Manyane Gate, Dithabaneng Drive first runs along the park boundary but then turns west towards Kgabo Drive. Climbing steadily, the road passes south of **Malatse Dam** which can be found at the conjunction of two valleys. Access from the short Phiri Link, on the northern side of the dam, takes visitors to a shaded

1

picnic area. A short walk from the car park, a lovely bird hide is situated on a small island on the edge of the dam. The hide is open on three sides, with several dead trees for bird perches placed in front, and it makes a wonderful setting to see elephants coming down to drink, as well as fish eagles and, of course, hippos.

Most of the park's northwestern quarter is a wilderness area that incorporates the Pilanesberg's highest point, 1687m **Matlhorwe Peak**. This mountainous segment is not open to the public, but one can get a sense of the terrain by following the combination of Sefara and Moloto drives (a long loop accessed off Tlou Drive, the main road running from the centre of the park towards the west). Often ignored by visitors, these beautiful hills are in some ways Pilanesberg's finest feature, though wildlife is less conspicuous than elsewhere. Some 2.5km from the eastern side of Sefara Drive, a south turn leads onto Lenong Loop, a surfaced road that zig-zags uphill to the most spectacular viewpoints over the park. Once on top, head straight to the two south-facing viewpoints, as the northern section of the loop is not in good condition. The unrivalled vistas across most of the park make it easy to forget that you are in a Big Five reserve – although it is evident that a wide variety of animals do frequent the area, and due care must be taken.

After descending off the Lenong Loop, head west on Sefara Drive to join with Moloto Drive. These elevated plains, which were once covered in citrus and blue gum plantations, can be wonderful for game viewing as they tend to be less frequented by park visitors. The various picnic spots and hides dotted along the route are ideal for breaking the drive – they make cool and peaceful places to breathe in the natural surroundings. One of these, Moloto picnic spot, is situated among an Iron Age site and has a fantastic view over the remote area to the north. Be sure to stop at **Bathako Dam** on the way down from the high plains, too. It has a lovely hide which is usually good for viewing hippos and crocodiles. Once back on Tlou Drive, there is a short drive to Ruighoek Dam at the end of the road to the west. Another hide, found here, is good for hippo watching, while Makorwana Dam, closer to the Pilanesberg Centre, is better for crocodiles.

Lengau Dam, near Bakubung Gate, can also offer very rewarding game viewing and birdwatching, though being the first dam visitors encounter when approaching from Sun City, it can get congested when there is a special sighting. As so often happens in Pilanesberg, the best sightings come when least expected – and when no one else is about.

Outside the park

Pilanesberg is often explored from **Sun City**, a surreal pocket of high-rise hotels and tinkling gaming machines that stands incongruously on its southern boundary. Comprising four swish hotel resorts and a timeshare complex, the tightly packed resort also incorporates a casino, innumerable restaurants, golf courses, a water park and various other attractions. Sun City was founded in the late 1970s, more or less simultaneously with Pilanesberg, at a time when the government of Bophuthatswana, unlike its Calvinistic South African counterpart, permitted legal **gambling** and partial nudity. Back then, thousands visited every weekend from "across the border" to sample Sun City's racy blend of gaming, topless shows and over-the-top hotels. However, now that gambling is legal in South Africa, Sun City has altered its focus, these days promoting itself as a **family destination**. Indeed, if you have kids to entertain, the Sun City/Pilanesberg combination forms an excellent family-friendly safari destination.

On the opposite side of the reserve, a few kilometres outside the Bakgatla Gate in the sprawling town of Moruleng, lies the **Moruleng Cultural Precinct**. At its heart is the modern Mphebatho Cultural Museum (☏073 097 0504, ⌨tourismnorthwest.co.za/culture/mphebatho-museum.html), dedicated to the Bakgatla-ba-Kgafela. Opened in 2015, it provides fascinating insights into the culture and beliefs of people from the area – stay for at least a couple of hours to do it justice.

ARRIVALS AND DEPARTURE

By car There are four entrance gates to the reserve. The most commonly used are Manyane, on the eastern side of the reserve near Mogwase, and Bakubung in the south, just to the west of Sun City off the R565. Rather peculiarly for a prominent tourist attraction of this size, the park and its gates are not well sign-posted until one is practically upon them. The easiest approach from Pretoria or Johannesburg would be to follow the N4, taking exit 169 after Rustenberg. At the T-junction turn right and continue on the Ottoman Highway for 12km until you reach a roundabout. Take the first exit onto the R565 and continue for just over 23km to Ledig, before turning right onto the R556 towards Sun City. After only 500m turn left again onto the road signposted "Ledig", but don't expect to see a sign for the Pilanesberg National Park. The Bakubung Gate is in the hills 4km further up the road.

PILANESBERG NATIONAL PARK

Opening and closing times vary according to the time of year, and day-visitors should ensure they leave enough time to get to the gate before it closes. Some of the registered lodge vehicles are permitted to stay out well after dark, which is when lucky passengers may see some fantastic nocturnal creatures such as brown hyena, aardwolf, civet, porcupine and caracal. Be sure to pack warm clothes for winter night drives as there can be a temperature change of over twelve degrees Celsius within the park.

By air Until fairly recently, there were scheduled flights to the substantial "international" airport just outside Pilanesberg National Park. Unfortunately, however, administrative bungles have since resulted in the service being suspended. While the situation could change, the best fly-in option would be to charter a plane.

INFORMATION AND TOURS

Information Prices for day-trips from Gauteng average R1500 per person on a scheduled tour; private tours are a bit costlier. Rates for overnight trips vary according to where you stay but expect to pay upwards of R4000. While all activities can be booked on arrival, it's best to reserve them in advance either directly or through your lodge to avoid missing out. The special activities organized by Mankwe Gametrackers (see below) can usually be incorporated into trips run by other operators, particularly if you have the flexibility of a private tour.

Ulysses Tours & Safaris ☎012 653 0018, ⓦulysses. co.za. Well-regarded and professionally run upmarket outfit based in Pretoria, which offers day-trips to Pilanesberg every Saturday or otherwise on demand.

Mankwe Gametrackers ☎014 552 5020, ⓦmankwe gametrackers.co.za. Sun City's activity operator offers spectacular balloon flights over the park (R5000), day and night game drives (from R660) and game walks (R700). Pick-ups from some of the resorts and lodges around the park are possible.

ACCOMMODATION

Pilanesberg's accommodation, mostly situated on the fringes of the park, ranges from upmarket lodges where game drives are included in the price, to large resort-style complexes, and cheaper, more basic camps just outside the park gates. Camping is possible at Golden Leopard's *Bakgatla* and *Manyane* resorts. The more luxurious lodges usually include all meals, game drives and walks in their rates, or can organize them for you; some may insist on two-night stays at weekends. *Bakubung* and *KwaMaritane* have shuttle buses every other hour to and from Sun City. Rates tend to be higher on weekends.

Bakgatla Resort Near Bakgatla Gate at the foot of Garamoga Hills ☎014 555 1045, ⓦgoldenleopard resorts.co.za. A large collection of reasonable chalets, safari tents with attached bathrooms and shady verandas, plus a big campsite. There's a decent restaurant and a large pool, too. Camping $\bar{\underline{S}}$, safari tent $\underline{\underline{SS}}$–$\underline{\underline{SSS}}$, chalet $\underline{\underline{SSS}}$

Bakubung Bush Lodge Entrance next to Bakubung Gate ☎014 552 6000, ⓦlegacyhotels.co.za. The highlight at this lodge is the waterhole, a stone's throw from the restaurant with postcard views over the valley. Rooms are spacious and facilities include a pool, spa and a great restaurant, good for lunch even if you are not staying here. Rates include half-board and a daily game drive. $\underline{\underline{SSSSS}}$

SEE MAP PAGE 67

Ivory Tree Game Lodge Adjacent to Bakgatla Gate ☎014 556 8100 or ☎010 442 5888, ⓦivorytreegamelodge. info. Luxurious lodge with more than sixty stylish rooms which include en-suite bathrooms and outside showers. The extensive facilities, which include a health spa and conference centre, have a rather hotel-like feel. $\underline{\underline{SSSS}}$–$\underline{\underline{SSSSS}}$

KwaMaritane Bush Lodge Near Kwa Maritane Gate ☎014 552 5100, ⓦlegacyhotels.co.za. A beautiful, upmarket resort in the park's southeast corner near Pilanesberg Airport, with decent rooms, a good restaurant and pool with views over the reserve. Rates include half-board and a daily game drive. $\underline{\underline{SSSSS}}$

Manyane Resort Just outside Manyane Gate ☎014 555 1000, ⓦgoldenleopardresorts.co.za. Low cost and convenience compensate for the distinctly un-bushlike atmosphere of the park's main camp. Stay in thatched chalets with a/c, safari tents, or bring a tent or caravan; there's also a restaurant, pool, mini-golf and walking trails. Camping $\bar{\underline{S}}$, safari tent $\underline{\underline{SS}}$, chalet $\underline{\underline{SSS}}$

★ **Shepherd's Tree Game Lodge** Off the R565 in southwestern side of the park ☎014 551 3910 or ☎010 442 5888, ⓦshepherdstreegamelodge.info. Large luxurious bedrooms come with substantial contemporary bathrooms and outside showers. Set on the slopes of a small

1

natural amphitheatre within its own concession inside the park's boundary, the linear layout allows for each room to have a commanding vista over the reserve. Dining room serves delicious meals as well as delectable treats at tea time. Facilities include a health spa, pool, conference centre and a lounge which overlooks a waterhole. $$$$$

Tented Adventures Pilanesberg Within perimeter fence of Manyane Resort ☎076 146 1468 ⓦtented adventures.com. *Tented Adventures* makes a great alternative for those who want to go camping but not have the hassle of packing the car full of gear or setting up camp. These basic but well-equipped safari tents come with electric lights and power points for charging phones and cameras – as well as electric blankets in winter and fans in summer. Meals are also provided in the main dining tent, so there's no need for cooking either. Packages available including or excluding game drives. $$$

Tshukudu Bush Lodge 8km from Bakubung Bush Lodge (parking is at the Bakubung Lodge from where you are chauffeured to Tshukudu) ☎014 552 6255, ⓦlegacyhotels.co.za. Watch big game at the waterhole from your verandah at Pilanesberg's most exclusive lodge, located on a hilltop with sweeping views. The six picturesque thatched cottages offer luxury accommodation with sunken baths and roaring log fires; there's also a swimming pool and four luxury suites. The lodge is unfenced – an especially memorable way to experience the reserve. No children under 12. Rates include full board and game drives. $$$$$

SUN CITY

Cabanas ☎011 780 7810, ⓦsuninternational.com. Close to most of the kids' activities and with a relaxed atmosphere, this is the obvious base for families. The rooms are small but have been refurbished, and there's a good indoor pool and some reasonably priced restaurants. $$

Cascades ☎011 780 7810, ⓦsuninternational.com. After the *Palace*, this is the resort's most comfortable place to stay, though the rooms and service are bland. A stylish pyramid-shaped high-rise with tropical decor and a mini rainforest and aviary; the outside lifts provide splendid views. The inviting pool and bar are for residents only. The quiet *Bocado* restaurant (☎014 557 5850), situated beside the pool, is known for its tasty Mediterranean food including Greek *kleftiko*, grilled prawns and meze, served amid lush subtropical palms. $$$

Palace of the Lost City ☎011 780 7810, ⓦsun international.com. Like something out of an Indiana Jones film, the vast *Palace* is a fantastically opulent and imaginative hotel – a soaring African jungle palace with towers, domes, extravagant carvings and sculptures. Rooms are large and beautifully furnished, and although a stay here is exorbitantly expensive, the experience is unforgettable. There are two recommended dining experiences available to non-guests at the hotel's classically furnished *Crystal Court* (☎014 557 4307): a sumptuous afternoon high tea (served 3–5pm) or à la carte dining in the evening (6.30–10pm). $$$$$

Soho ☎011 780 7810, ⓦsuninternational.com. The resort's original hotel houses its more adult attractions such as the main casino and a nightclub, so is a good choice if gambling is your main reason for visiting Sun City. The large, balconied rooms have great views of the golf courses and there are plenty of restaurants and bars. $$$

Madikwe Game Reserve

Entrances from 85km north of Zeerust on R49 • Daily 6am–6pm • One-off entrance fee of R180 (drive-in guests) and R240 (fly-in guests) plus a daily conservation levy of R165 • ☎018 350 9931, ⓦmadikwereserve.org or ⓦnorthwestparks.org.za

Nestled against the south side of the Botswana border in a secluded corner of North West Province, **Madikwe Game Reserve** is one of South Africa's least-known but finest wildlife-viewing destinations. It also ranks among the country's biggest wildlife sanctuaries, comprising more than 760 square kilometres of malaria-free land sandwiched between the R49 (the main road that runs from Zeerust to Gaborone) to the east, the **Marico River** to the west, and the **Dwarsberg Mountains** in the south. Established in 1991 and subjected thereafter to an intensive program of restocking, Madikwe is home to all the Big Five, along with cheetah, brown hyena, spotted hyena, and most of Southern Africa's large antelopes, including greater kudu, springbok, red hartebeest and tsessebe. It is also renowned as one of the best places in the country to see African

MADIKWE AT A GLANCE

World-class Big Five viewing within easy driving distance of Gauteng.

Big Five: ****
General wildlife: *****
Birding: ****
Scenery: ***
Wilderness factor: ****
Uncrowded: ***
Affordability: *
Self-drive: N

wild dogs, fascinating pack carnivores whose complex social structure and scarcity elsewhere makes them a favourite for many visitors.

Madikwe supports a varied mosaic of vegetation. The distinct geology coupled with an average rainfall that varies from over 600mm in the south to under 500mm in the northeast has resulted in four major veld types converging on the area, namely Arid Sweet Bushveld, Kalahari Thornveld, Mixed Bushveld and Other Turf Thornveld. The more established natural vegetation, with large **trees** such as leadwood and murla, is more commonly found on rocky outcrops such as the Dwarsberg, as well as the primarily quartzite **Tweedepoort Ridge**, which dissect the reserve from east to west, and a series of picturesque gabbro norite inselbergs that protrude 200m above the plains in a north-westerly line from the centre of the park towards Botswana.

More than 350 bird species have been recorded amongst these varying habitats, and while the hot summer months bring various migrants to boost the numbers, the main attraction for twitchers is a number of permanent residents associated with the western Kalahari biome. The pied babbler (dubbed the "flying snowball") is significantly more conspicuous in Madikwe than in the Pilanesberg, as are the likes of yellow-throated sandgrouse and barred wren-warbler, and the lucky few might even get to see the rare yellow morph of the crimson-breasted shrike.

History

Madikwe is steeped in cultural history, with artefacts found on the reserve dating back to the Early Stone Age. Large cores and choppers suggest that the area was inhabited by our early ancestors as far back as 250,000 to one million years ago. In more recent times, **San hunter-gatherers** roamed the land before the first homesteads of the

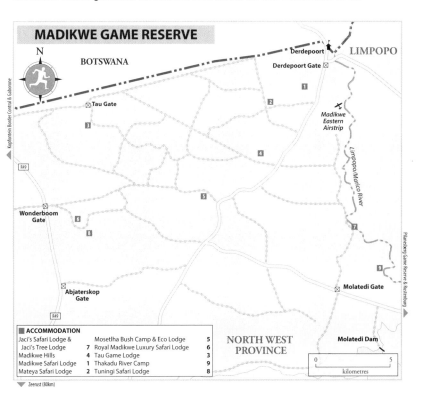

MADIKWE GAME RESERVE

ACCOMMODATION

Jaci's Safari Lodge & Jaci's Tree Lodge	Mosetlha Bush Camp & Eco Lodge	5
	Royal Madikwe Luxury Safari Lodge	6
Madikwe Hills	7	
Madikwe Safari Lodge	1	Tau Game Lodge	4
Mateya Safari Lodge	2	Thakadu River Camp	9
	Tuningi Safari Lodge	8

1

agro-pastoral **Sotho-Tswana** began to appear around 1400 AD. The early part of the nineteenth century heralded upheaval and change in the area largely due to the ripple effect caused by Zulu expansionism under Shaka, as well as the growth of European interest in Southern Africa. The period between 1815 and about 1840, known as the *difaqane* (meaning "the crushing" or "the scattering"), was a period of widespread warfare and forced migration amongst indigenous communities in southern Africa. It was during this time that the renegade Zulu Chief, **Mzilikazi**, settled in the area encompassing Madikwe, resulting in much unrest and bloodshed.

Mzilikazi dominated for several years before a combined force of Voortrekkers, Griquas and Batswana forced him to move north across the Limpopo River, where he eventually founded the Matabele Kingdom centred what is now the city of Bulawayo in western Zimbabwe. After Mzilikazi's departure, Voortrekkers began to farm in the Marico Valley while missionaries, hunters, explorers and fortune seekers made their way north from Mafeking through Zeerust and Madikwe to Bulawayo and beyond. The famous **Mafeking Road**, which ran straight through the centre of the reserve, became the favoured route amongst intrepid travellers as it was malaria-free until well over the Limpopo River.

Dr Andrew Smith, considered by many to be the father of zoology in South Africa, described an abundance of wildlife in the Madikwe area in the mid-nineteenth century, and it was also nearby that William Cornwallis Harris shot the first sable antelope known to science. David Livingstone set up his second mission within a few kilometres of Madikwe and the famous hunter Frederick Courteney Selous passed through Madikwe several times en route to Matabeleland (Zimbabwe). In 1879, the Catholic Church established the Zambesi Mission in Matabeleland, but when the priests struggled with malaria, it decided to establish a more southerly mission station in a malaria-free area to which priests could retreat during bouts of fever.

In the early 1880s, the Church had purchased the **Vleeschfontein** farm for the princely sum of 800 pounds and so begun the first Roman Catholic mission amongst the Batswana. By 1894 the Jesuits had abandoned the Vleeschfontein Mission: travellers no longer used it as a stopping place because of the extension of a railway line from Kimberly via Mafeking to Bulawayo. The railway line later became a prominent venue for skirmishes during the Second Anglo-Boer War. Indeed, the Battle of Derdepoort (25 November 1899) took place a few hundred metres outside what is now the northern boundary of Madikwe. The Oblates of Mary Immaculate purchased Vleeschfontein and went on to run a thriving mission and convent for more than fifty years until events during the early years of apartheid put an end to it.

This period was followed by several decades of **farming**. Then, in the late 1980s, the government of what was then Bophuthatswana earmarked Vleeschfontein and the surrounding ranchland – much of it degraded and rather unproductive – for development as a game reserve. Madikwe was eventually established in 1991 with its primary goal to boost socio-economic growth for the people of the region. The reserve was restocked with more than eight thousand species as part of a massive game translocation programme – at the time, the largest ever undertaken anywhere in the world – called **Operation Phoenix**. The reintroduced wildlife represented 28 large mammal species, among them

---

WHAT'S IN A NAME

Madikwe is another name for the Marico River, which forms most of the eastern boundary of the reserve before combining with the Crocodile River to form the Limpopo. In Setswana, "madi" means "blood" or "genes", while "(di)kwena" means "crocodile". When said together as "madikwena", it means the "blood of the crocodile", a reference to the Madikwe flowing into the Crocodile River. Allusions to blood can also be found in the root of the word "Marico", a corruption of the Setswana word "Malicoe" which means "drenched in blood" – in this case referring to the reddish earth that colours the river.

all the Big Five as well as African wild dog, cheetah, spotted hyena, giraffe, zebra and a wide variety of antelope. An elephant herd from the then drought-affected Gonarezhou National Park in southeast Zimbabwe has thrived in its new habitat and now numbers well over one thousand individuals. Initially a predator-driven ecology, the young reserve took some time to find its feet, but the natural balance has slowly restored itself on the reserve's largely low-lying plains of woodland and grassland. In an unprecedented approach, NWPB, as custodians of the land, joined forces with local communities and partners in the private sector (i.e. lodge owners) to operate Madikwe as a **cooperative venture**. Due to the success of this innovative thinking, Madikwe has become somewhat of a blueprint for other game reserves to follow.

Game drives

Game drives in Madikwe are largely at the discretion of the lodge **guides**, who are in radio contact with one another and usually know where particular sightings are at any given time. Game drives tend to stay relatively close to the lodges from which they are conducted, but the guides are generally very accommodating when it comes to travelling further afield in search of special sightings.

Game is abundant and animals are likely to be seen almost immediately upon entering the reserve. From Abjaterskop Gate it is not uncommon to see impalas and elephants before passing the western airstrip. The proliferation of game seems to increase as one approaches **Vleeschfontein** in the centre of the park – the waterhole which supplied the mission for so many decades is a popular meeting point for a wide variety of game, including all the Big Five. The buildings in the background do take away from the sense of wilderness, however those with a sense for history will be intrigued by the remnants of the Roman Catholic mission station that now houses the reserve's **headquarters**.

The main road heading east from Vleeschfontein towards the Molatedi Gate has a couple of waterholes that draw animals due to their central location. By mid-morning, the first of these, **Vlei Pan**, usually has a host of animals waiting their turn to drink. **Melorane Pan**, a little further down the road, is a circular walled dam that is mostly frequented by elephants. Roughly 1.6km beyond that, spotted hyenas are known to den in a culvert under the road.

North of Vleeschfontein, the Derdepoort Road drops off the Tweedepoort Ridge through "Ambush Alley" – a constriction point on the old Mafeking Road which was allegedly put to use during the **Anglo-Boer War**. The wonderful viewpoints on the cliffs on either side of Ambush Alley are often used for sundowners. It is here too, along a bumpy track, that a deep well – supposedly used by David Livingstone – can be found. When descending Ambush Alley, keep an eye out for baboons as well as a pair of klipspringers that hang around on the slopes that flank the road.

In the past, the flat lands between the Dwarsberg and the Tweedepoort Ridge, as well as the expansive **Madikwe Plains** that make up most of the northern half of the reserve, were extensively farmed. This resulted in degraded soils and some relatively barren areas devoid of large trees. On the eastern side of the reserve, between Ambush Alley and Pipeline Road, impenetrable stands of sicklebush (*Dichrostachys cinerea*) are making significant headway into these previously farmed lands. While the dense foliage can make game-viewing difficult, this type of thicket is a favoured refuge for Cape buffalo.

From the palm tree on the Derdepoort Road, a rather bumpy track runs along the northern edge of Tweedpoort Ridge towards Bat Cave, a distinctive rock formation frequented by little bee-eaters. Continuing on the track will eventually take you into the vicinity of the **Marico River** on the eastern border of the reserve. Here the riverine vegetation provides particularly rewarding birding. Various kingfishers frequent the area, as, on rarer occasions, does the African Finfoot. With a little bit of luck, both hippos and crocodiles can be seen in the Marico River, especially around Tswasa Waterhole, as well as the drift in the northeast. The drift is also a popular point for animals, particularly elephants and wild dogs, to cross the river into an adjacent concession.

1

When denning in the area, the wild dogs like to hunt along the northern and eastern fence lines. Waterbuck are usually found in this corner of the reserve, while in the hot summer months it is a good place to look for the colourful carmine bee-eater.

West of the Derdepoort Road, animals such as springbok, wildebeest, zebra and impala like to congregate around the sparsely vegetated black-cotton soil of the Madikwe Plains, where they can keep a lookout for predators from a distance. Ironically, by congregating in numbers, the grazers actually attract the predators, which means that lion and cheetah are common here too. The extensive plains also offer a good chance of sighting the Kori Bustard (the world's heaviest flying bird), as well as the closely related red-crested korhaan – also known as the "suicide bird" in reference to the male's elaborate courting ritual, which involves flying up thirty metres into the air, then folding away its wings as it plummets straight towards the ground, only to open its wings again just before impact.

While on a game drive, crossing from one side of the reserve to the other is usually done via **Pipeline Road**, which follows the pipeline that pumps water from the Marico River to Gaborone in Botswana; look out for the melanistic form of the gabar goshawk in this area. South of the track, below **Tshwene-Tshwene**, the highest point in the reserve, remnants of a large Tswana community can be found. Nearby, Tlou Dam is ideal for game viewing as its high wall offers a great position overlooking the dam, as well as giving uninterrupted views across the plains towards the inselbergs in the west.

The inselbergs, standing out from the grassy plains, are ideal habitat for leopards. The large trees covering these outcrops are covered with dense foliage which offer some relief from the hot plains, while the heightened vantage points provide some safety as well as a good opportunity to view approaching prey. It is at a choke point between two of these inselbergs that the large **Tau waterhole** can be found. This is almost a compulsory stop for any game moving between the eastern and western side of the reserve and birds also favour the aquatic habitat and adjacent verdant bush. This waterhole, along with the one at Jaci's Lodge, have small permanent crocodile populations.

On the plains west of the inselbergs, the wide-open space makes game viewing relatively easy. Antelope, wildebeest and zebra are all common here, and the area is an ideal hunting ground for cheetahs; once on the move, there is little vegetation to obstruct their trajectory.

Extending along the southern edge of these plains, the **Tweedepoort Ridge** offers a minor obstacle for animals wishing to traverse this rocky area. The dry river valleys provide the paths of least resistance and are therefore best suited for game viewing. Many of the lodges in this area have situated themselves around waterholes in these riverbeds accordingly.

ARRIVAL AND DEPARTURE
MADIKWE GAME RESERVE

By car Madikwe lies 360km from Johannesburg and all lodges can be reached within 4–5 hours of driving from OR Tambo International Airport. For travellers who favour tarred roads, the most straightforward approach is via the R49 that heads north from Zeerust towards Gaborone, as three of the five gates can be reached by this well-maintained provincial road running up the western flank of the reserve.

The first gate, Abjaterskop, is 85km north of Zeerust and leads to the park administration buildings in the centre of the reserve and then on to the lodges in the east. Most of the commercial lodges on the western side of the reserve are accessed via the second gate, Wonderboom, which is a further 7km up the R49. Several hundred metres short of the Kopfontein border post, a road turns off to the right and runs along the northern fenceline to Derdepoort. Tau

Gate can be found 10km down this road, just before the end of the newly tarred section, while Derdepoort Gate is a further 23km of jarringly shaky gravel road beyond that; Derdepoort is accordingly the least used access point for guests approaching Madikwe.

For those who don't mind driving on gravel, the Molatedi Gate offers a short cut from Pilanesberg, which especially benefits guests staying on the eastern side of the reserve. This approach skirts the western side of the Pilanesberg Game Reserve, passing through the village of Tlhatlaganyane with its numerous partially camouflaged speed bumps, before taking a left turn signposted to Kayakulu (15km beyond Tlhatlaganyane). Continue on this road for another 25km before making a right turn at a T-junction. Heading north once again, you will pass a small petrol garage (the

last one before the reserve) about 10km up the road and another 10km beyond that a new junction turns left towards Molatedi Village and Madikwe Game Reserve. From this intersection it is 22km of gravel road to the Molatedi Gate, passing through the Molatedi Village on the way.
Gates open from 6am to 6pm. Should you arrive later, you will need to be escorted from the gate to your lodge. A strict policy dictates that the gates will be impassable after 9pm. Once inside the reserve you will be directed straight to your lodge via one of the main roads, as there are no self-drive options

available. All the roads in the park are gravel – of varying condition – with the three primary roads that converge on Vleeschfontein being in good condition and partially tarred.
By air For those not wanting to be burdened with the long drive, daily scheduled flights are on offer from OR Tambo to the airstrips on either side of Madikwe. The 45min flight can be booked through the lodges or directly with Federal Air (☎ 011 395 9000, ⓦ fedair.com). The lodges take care of transfers to and from the airstrips. Flights cost R4500–5000 per person, one-way, depending on time of year.

ACCOMMODATION

SEE MAP PAGE 73

Madikwe currently has nineteen high-end commercial lodges and no budget accommodation or camping, which makes it one of South Africa's most exclusive reserves. There are no self-drive safari options and there is no access for day-visitors, unless you have booked a package through one of the lodges that includes a game drive and a meal. All this makes for an uncrowded reserve with abundant wildlife sightings. Most of the lodges are situated in nodes on the eastern or western side of the reserve.

EASTERN SECTION

Jaci's Safari Lodge & Jaci's Tree Lodge ☎ 083 700 2071, ⓦ jacislodges.co.za. Two adjacent lodges set amongst the tall trees on the banks of the Marico River, each with their own vibrant and colourful sense of style and laidback luxury. *Jaci's Safari Lodge* is situated on a promontory between the river and a small stream, which allows passing game to be viewed from the balcony of the rooms, while *Jaci's Tree Lodge*'s rooms are built several metres off the ground on stilts around trees. A couple of the suites have the added value of rooftop starbeds which allow for wonderful alfresco sleeping under a ceiling of stars. Spend time in the submerged hide in the middle of the waterhole at *Jaci's Tree Lodge*. $$$$$
Madikwe Safari Lodge ☎ 011 880 9992 (ext. 3), ⓦ madikwesafrilodge.co.za. *Madikwe Safari Lodge*, although one of the biggest lodges in the reserve, has managed to retain a personal touch by running its operation as three smaller lodges, each with its own communal living area. Although all the suites have plunge pools, there is also a large shared swimming pool where guests can enjoy the day while watching animals drink from a waterhole on the other side of a low game fence. Each room has its own wonderful vista across the magnificent plains towards the Tweedepoort Ridge, which is enhanced by the inspired architectural style of natural building material and lack of sharp corners. $$$$$
Mateya Safari Lodge ☎ 014 778 9200, ⓦ mateyasafari. com. Experience the ultimate in bush chic at these five luxurious suites, each with its own swimming pool, as well as indoor and outdoor showers. There's a spa and the lodge's excellent food is best sampled on the terrace overlooking the veld. No children under 16. $$$$$

Thakadu River Camp ☎ 010 442 5888, ⓦ aha.co.za/thakadu-river-camp. This delightful camp, located on a small headland that slightly protrudes into the Marico River, is one of only two community-owned lodges currently in the reserve. *Thakadu*'s peaceful ambiance, enhanced by its position on the riverbank, makes it ideal for a relaxing breakaway. Each of the twelve secluded luxury safari tents is situated under a lush riverine canopy overlooking the water; they come equipped with a large en-suite bathroom, air conditioning and ample lounge space (both indoors and outside on a deck). A small terrace on the water's edge beyond the main boma is a fantastic spot to view elephants bathing in the river. $$$$–$$$$$

WESTERN SECTION

Madikwe Hills ☎ 018 350 9200; reservations ☎ 011 781 5431, ⓦ madikwehills.com. Another gem, this one built around a koppie close to the riverbank. There are pleasant modern rooms, a sundowner terrace and swimming pool with great views, plus a gym, spa and childcare facilities. $$$$$
Royal Madikwe Luxury Safari Lodge ☎ 082 787 1314, ⓦ royalmadikwe.com. As the name suggests, the *Royal Madikwe* exudes luxury and the dedicated staff are committed to service excellence. The large and very comfortable suites are beautifully styled, with the idyllic Honeymoon Suite taking pride of place near the lodge's popular waterhole. Lounge next to the plunge pool, or lie in the soaking bubble bath, while you watch the animals' interactions as they come and go. Boasting a luxurious four-poster bed and cosy wood-burning fireplace, this alluring hideaway offers true romance. A couple of larger suites and a villa, with the same sense of style, are also available for families or small groups of friends. $$$$$
Tau Game Lodge ☎ 011 466 8715 ⓦ taugamelodge. co.za. Each of the 32 rooms at *Tau Game Lodge* overlooks the extensive crescent-shaped waterhole that partially surrounds this green oasis. Situated on the grassy plains between two of the picturesque inselbergs in Madikwe's northwest, *Tau* is by far the biggest lodge in Madikwe – it can comfortably accommodate more than fifty

1

guests. With its three bomas, large conference centre, two swimming pools and relaxing spa, it is ideal for large groups such as conferencing and wedding parties. However, in spite of the size, *Tau* has managed to retain the sense of wilderness and no matter what size the group, the hospitable and attentive staff give each individual their full attention. $$$$–$$$$$

★ **Tuningi Safari Lodge** ☎ 011 781 5384 ⓦ tuningi. com. Intimate and friendly, *Tuningi* is centred around a huge fig tree, *Ficus thonningii*, from which the lodge gets its name. The lodge's luxuriant yet relaxed atmosphere makes for a wonderful bush escape. A well-positioned boma deck under the ficus tree is 25 metres from the waterhole with an option to get within mere metres of the animals at the water's edge via a superb underground hide. Game viewing is also possible while lounging on the deck next to the swimming pool at the reception area, while a smaller, more secluded pool and well-equipped gym are situated a short walk over the low ridge. $$$$$

CENTRAL SECTION

★ **Mosetlha Bush Camp & Eco Lodge** ☎ 011 444 9345, ⓦ thebushcamp.com. *Mosetlha* is a unique eco lodge that has moved away from the sophisticated luxury lodge experience to cater for those who seek adventure by being immersed in the heart of an African Big Five wilderness area. Accommodation is in simple, open-sided log cabins loosely based on an old birdhide design, none of which have en-suite bathroom facilities. As there is no electricity, lighting is provided by means of solar or paraffin lanterns and the hot outdoor showers are delivered by an ingenious boiler and bucket system. What it lacks in luxury it makes up for in atmosphere, with the emphasis placed on game walks as much as drives. $$$–$$$$

Western Limpopo

The most northerly of South Africa's nine provinces, **LIMPOPO** falls entirely within the drainage basin of the "great grey-green, greasy Limpopo River" (to quote Rudyard Kipling) as it arcs sluggishly along the border with Botswana and Zimbabwe before crossing into Mozambique to empty into the Indian Ocean a full 1750km from its most remote source. Limpopo is more culturally diverse than North West Province, and while its population of five million is dominated by the **Pedi** (Northern Sotho), it also includes significant Tsonga, Venda, Tswana, Ndebele and Afrikaner minorities. Hot, dry and rather lacking when it comes to big-name attractions, Limpopo was until recently largely overlooked as a tourist destination, with its best-known attraction being the relatively unknown northern half of the **Kruger Park** that runs along the eastern border with Mozambique (see Chapter 2).

The main tourist focus in western Limpopo today is the **Waterberg**, a vast and sporadically spectacular UNESCO Biosphere Reserve that incorporates the underrated **Marakele National Park**. The Waterberg also hosts a scattering of superb private game reserves, some of which are geared mainly towards Big Five safaris, while others offer horseback and foot excursions amidst a more low-key selection of wildlife. Two other notable conservancies are situated on southeastern fringes of the Waterberg. **Mabula Game Reserve** near Bela Bela is a well-priced private sanctuary that ranks among the closest Big Five destinations to Gauteng, while the **Nylsvley Nature Reserve** near Modimolle protects a Ramsar-recognized seasonal floodplain that offers some of the finest summer birding anywhere in South Africa. More remote than any of the above, **Mapungubwe National Park**, which overlooks the Limpopo as it flows past the tripartite border with Botswana and Zimbabwe, offers the few who venture that far north a memorable combination of wild riverine scenery, fascinating archeological sites and great wildlife viewing and birdwatching.

Mabula Game Reserve

200km northwest of Gauteng's OR Tambo Airport via Bela Bela • Daily • R233 per vehicle • ☎ 014 734 7000 (lodge) or ☎ 011 516 4367 (reservations), ⓦ mabula.com

Set in the southeastern shadow of the Waterberg, the 120-square-kilometre **Mabula Game Reserve** offers a well-priced but slightly compartmentalized Big Five safari experience, a little more than two hours by road from Johannesburg and OR Tambo

Airport. It protects a tract of well-wooded bush denominated by hardy beechwood, silver cluster-leaf and common karee trees, but rather lacking in the acacias and leafy mopanes that respectively form an important part of the diet of giraffe and elephant, both of which struggle in the reserve. As with many other South African private reserves, leopard occur naturally in the area but are seldom seen, while lion, cheetah, elephant, buffalo, white rhino, giraffe, Burchell's zebra, warthog and various large antelope have been reintroduced, alongside a few species that probably never occurred here historically, for instance sable antelope, gemsbok and blesbok.

> **MABULA AT A GLANCE** 1
> Pleasant but packaged Big Five private reserve a shortish drive northwest of Joburg.
> **Big Five:** ****
> **General wildlife:** ****
> **Birding:** ***
> **Scenery:** *
> **Wilderness factor:** **
> **Uncrowded:** ***
> **Affordability:** **
> **Self-drive:** N

Mabula is also home to the **Mabula Ground Hornbill Project**, which was established in 1999 to help the charismatic flagship savannah bird species that has become increasingly rare outside conservation areas in recent decades. In order to protect the reserve's cheetah and more endangered antelope, its lion pride is restricted to the 20-square-kilometre Madjuma ("Place of the Lion's Roar") Enclosure, which is reached via an underpass below the access road to the main gate. The newly annexed Safari Plains, a 120-square-kilometre tract of bush that harbours white rhino, giraffe and various antelope but no dangerous game, is also separated from the main reserve by a public road.

ARRIVAL
MABULA GAME RESERVE

By car Mabula lies about 200km (2.5 hours) northwest of Johannesburg and OR Tambo Airport and 155km (2 hours) northwest of Pretoria. Follow the N1 north from Pretoria for about 100km then turn west onto the R516, which passes through Bela Bela after about 8km and then continues for another 33km before reaching a junction clearly signposted for Mabula to the right. Turn right again after 4km and you will see the reserve entrance to your left after another 7.5km.

ACCOMMODATION

★ **KwaFubesi Tented Camp** ☎ 011 516 4367, ⊛ safari plains.co.za. Named for a pair of spotted eagle-owl ("*fubesi*") that nest close by, this small camp comprises five standing tents spaced sufficiently far apart to offer a private and tranquil bush experience. Set on stilted wooden platforms, the tents feel old school in the best possible way, but come with walk-in nets, en-suite tub and shower, and a balcony overlooking a tract of grassland regularly grazed by white rhinos. The wooded grounds support a varied birdlife and amenities include a plunge pool. Very good value. $$$$ **Mabula Game Lodge** ☎ 014 734 7000 (lodge) or ☎ 011 516 4367 (reservations), ⊛ mabula.com. This well-priced and very agreeable lodge is set in sprawling grounds studded with atmospheric boulder-strewn koppies, inhabited by adorable families of rock hyrax, and shaded by some truly impressive fig trees that attract plenty of frugivorous birds. It is significantly larger than most private reserve camps, and a timeshare complex is attached, but the spacious earthily decorated rooms are very comfortable, the food is good, and the lack of exclusivity is reflected in the relatively down-to-earth rates, which include meals and game drives. Check the website for regular seasonal specials. $$$$ **Safari Plains Tented Camp** ☎ 014 004 0162 (lodge) or ☎ 011 516 4367 (reservations), ⊛ safariplains. co.za. Opened in late 2018, this five-star tented camp is run by the same management as *Mabula Game Lodge*, but stands on a separate property and has an altogether more contemporary and exclusive feel. $$$$$

Nylsvley Nature Reserve

Off the R101 35km east of Modimolle • Daily: Sept–Apr 6am–6pm; May–Aug 6.30am–5.30pm • R30 • ☎ 014 743 6925 or ☎ 071 057 0828, ⊛ nylsvley.co.za

Only 40 square kilometres in extent, but boasting a **bird** checklist of almost four hundred species, provincially managed **Nylsvley** ranks among the country's most

NYLSVLEY AT A GLANCE
Arguably the top wetland birding destination in South Africa, also good for self-guided game walks.
Big Five: N/A
General wildlife: ***
Birding: *****
Scenery: **
Wilderness factor: ***
Uncrowded: ****
Affordability: *****
Self-drive: Y

important ornithological destinations. It is also a very affordable place to see some large wildlife on foot. Its centrepiece is the **Nyl River** – named by an early group of Voortrekkers who mistook a pyramidal hill for a sign they'd made it to the Egyptian Nile – and its marshy seasonal floodplain, which was proclaimed a Ramsar wetland in 1998 and attracts more than one hundred water-associated bird species in wet summers. Nylsvley is famed as one of the best places in South Africa to see several localized species, including European marsh harrier, rufous-bellied heron, Eurasian bittern, dwarf bittern, Allen's gallinule and streaky-breasted flufftail, and it is also an important breeding site for several more widespread herons, rallids and ducks. Even when it isn't flooded, Nylsvley supports a varied selection of woodland birds and more than seventy mammal species, of which the most conspicuous include giraffe, Burchell's zebra, warthog, black-backed jackal, vervet monkey, greater kudu, bushbuck, roan antelope, waterbuck, common reedbuck, tsessebe and impala. The reserve is serviced by a good network of trails and hides, and because there are no dangerous large mammals, visitors can walk or cycle freely throughout.

ARRIVAL   **NYLSVLEY NATURE RESERVE**

By car Nylsvley is about 2.5 hours' drive north of Johannes-burg or OR Tambo Airport. Follow the N2 north from Pretoria for about 130km before turning left onto the R33 for Modimolle. Continue 11km northwest to Modimolle, where you need to turn right onto the R101 to Mookgophong and continue northeast for about 27km before turning right at the sign for Boekenhout railway station. The main entrance gate is about 10km along this gravel road.

ACCOMMODATION

Nylsvley Birding Lodge 500m inside the main entrance gate ☎ 015 293 3612, ⓦ nylsvley.co.za. This unpretentious restcamp offers comfortable and well-priced accommodation in en-suite double chalets with kitchenette, fridge and braai area. It is aimed mainly at self-caterers, but the nearby *Spoonbill Restaurant and Tuck Shop*, set in the original farmhouse, sells a few basic provisions and can also do breakfast, lunch and evening meals by arrangement. A campsite is attached. ⓢ

Waterberg Biosphere Reserve

☎ 078 796 0699, ⓦ waterbergbiospherereserve.org

Rising out of the plains to the west of the Great North Road, the **Waterberg** extends across some 15,000 square kilometres of western Limpopo, where it attains a maximum altitude of 2088m in **Marakele National Park**. As its name suggests, it is an important watershed, feeding four major rivers, but unfortunately rainfall is seasonal and highly erratic, making it prone to severe **droughts** that might endure for several successive years. The Waterberg supports a diverse flora and fauna but is it is thinly populated (around 80,000 people at last count) and poorly suited to agriculture. For much of the twentieth century, it ranked among the least known of South Africa's significant massifs, and its slopes were dominated by low-yield cattle ranches. In the 1990s, however, the Waterberg started to take off as a weekend getaway from Gauteng, just two hours to the southeast. In 2001, the region received international recognition when UNESCO designated a 4000-square-kilometre mosaic of private- and publicly owned land the Waterberg Biosphere Reserve. Since then, as one by one the old ranches have been converted to private reserves, some of which cater to the hunting market, others to photographic or horseback safaris, the Waterberg has also caught on with international visitors seeking a malaria-free alternative game-viewing destination to the lowveld areas around Kruger National Park.

For tourists, the Waterberg remains a rather patchwork region, whose individual components offer a divergence of contrasting experiences. Its centrepiece is Marakele National Park, a rewarding self-drive destination that protects the impressive **Kransberg range** as well as harbouring all the Big Five – though it is arguably of greater interest for its sensational scenery and impressive birdlife than for big game viewing. Nearby, **Welgevonden** is an extensive private reserve where a dozen-or-so individual lodges offer a quality upmarket Big Five safari experience. More exclusive safari options include the stunning **Lapalala Wilderness Area**, which was established in the 1980s but only opened to upmarket tourism in 2019, and **Marataba Game Reserve**, a private concession that shares an open border with Marakele. Elsewhere, a cluster of smaller conservancies exist north of Vaalwater, notably *Ant's Nest* and *Ant's Hill*.

Some background

Like a giant inverted saucer rising between two fault lines running to its north and south, the Waterberg is a geologically stable range of ancient igneous and sedimentary rocks. These rocks were formed between 1.8 and 2.7 billion years ago, supported an inland sea between 400 and 150 million years ago, and have since been exposed by erosion. Today, the mountains are capped by golden sandstone cliffs rich in iron deposits, while the lower strata of the gorges and riverbeds are dominated by quartzite and conglomerate rocks. Up to 500km in width, the Waterberg was named by early Afrikaans settlers impressed by its significance as a watershed, and it is the source of four major tributaries of the Limpopo, namely the **Lephalale** (a sePedi name meaning "Barrier", in reference to the sheer gorge

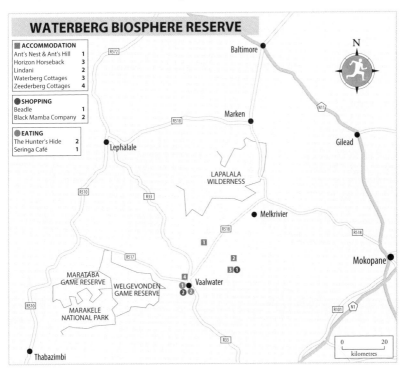

1

it has incised into the Palala Plateau); **Mokolo** ("Surge", due to its propensity for flooding); **Matlabas** ("Sand-bed"); and **Magalakwena** ("Place of Crocodiles"). Despite this, the Voortrekkers who named the Waterberg must have arrived here at the height of a wet summer, because the area receives very little rain between April and September, and it is also prone to extended droughts such as the one that endured for five years prior to the summer of 2019/20. Biodiversity is high and includes more than 2000 plant, 120 mammal, 450 bird, 100 reptile and 25 frog species (for detailed checklists, see ⓦwaterberg-bioquest.co.za).

The Waterberg has a long history of human habitation. **Makapansgat**, a limestone cave formation in the north of the range, has been made a remote annexe of the Cradle of Humankind UNESCO World Heritage Site (see page 58) thanks to its wealth of *Australopithecus* and *Homo* fossils, the oldest of which date back almost three million years. The oldest Stone Age sites in the river valleys are about one million years old, and the range supports a wealth of prehistoric rock art accredited to the San hunter-gatherers who were its sole inhabitants until around 1500 years ago, when the first iron settlements appeared along what was evidently an important trade route running south from Mapungubwe. In the seventeenth century the Waterberg was home to Nguni-speakers ancestral to the modern **Ndebele**, while the **Pedi** used its upper slopes as a place of refuge during the early nineteenth-century Mfecane.

Although the first Europeans arrived in the area in 1808, the mountains were bypassed by most subsequent explorers and Voortrekkers due to the difficulty of traversing its upper slopes. **Bela Bela** is the oldest town in the vicinity of the Waterberg, having been established after President Burger of the Zuid-Afrikaansche Republiek visited the hot springs that gave the place its original name, Warmbad (Hot Bath), in 1873. **Vaalwater**, the only town set within the Waterberg itself, was founded as a mill and transport depot as recently as 1907. It was in the Waterberg that the influential naturalist Eugène Marais (1871–1936) undertook the research into termite behaviour that informed his books *The Soul of the White Ant* (which pioneered the theory that a termite colony ought to be treated as a single organism) and *The Soul of the Ape* (a groundbreaking treatise on baboon behaviour). The endangered cycad *Encephalartos eugene-maraisii*, a striking and prehistoric-looking shrub endemic to the Waterberg, is named in his honour.

Vaalwater and around

Modest **Vaalwater** (Afrikaans for "Pale Water"), the only town set within the Waterberg, forms a useful orientation point on the R33, the trunk road that connects the N1 near Modimolle 70km to the southeast with Lephalale 90km further northwest. The town stands at the junction with the tarred R518 north to Melkrivier ("Milk River") and Marken, a road that provides access to a number of small conservancies that specialize not in Big Five safaris but in more active pursuits (horseriding, hiking, mountain biking and trail running) in areas stocked with non-dangerous game. Vaalwater's oldest and best-known landmark, situated 1.5km northwest of the main crossing along the R33, is the Zeederberg Homestead, which once served as home to the legendary Zeederberg stagecoaches that would crisscross Limpopo and Zimbabwe to service settler outposts. It remains an important service centre today; resuscitated as the **Zeederberg Centre**, it houses the Waterberg tourist office, as well as a filling station, a café, an excellent handicraft shop and good self-catering accommodation. It's positioned alongside a well-stocked Spar supermarket.

ARRIVAL AND INFORMATION
VAALWATER AND AROUND

By car Vaalwater lies about 250km from Johannesburg, a three-hour drive following the N1 north to the Kranskop Toll Plaza then turning left on to the R33 at Modimolle.

Tourist information The Waterberg Tourism information office, set in in the Zeederberg Centre (☎014 161 0930, ⓦwaterbergtourism.co.za, Mon–Fri 9am–5pm, Sat 9am–1pm), has information on accommodation and activities in the region.

ACCOMMODATION

SEE MAP PAGE 81

★ **Ant's Nest & Ant's Hill** North of Vaalwater, turn off the R33 at 19km and 11km respectively ⓣ 087 820 7233 or ⓣ 083 287 2885, ⓦ waterberg.net. Two exclusive and super-luxurious lodges, offering all-inclusive pampering in a private 38-square-kilometre tract of sloping wilderness that supports a wealth of wildlife including giraffe, white rhino, sable and roan antelope, buffalo, greater kudu, eland, blue wildebeest, red hartebeest, Burchell's zebra, warthog, baboon and various small carnivores. The specialist activity here is horseriding, which is aimed at everybody from novices to experienced riders, and offers a fabulous opportunity to get close to wildlife on the saddle. Other activities include mountain biking, game drives, bush walks, trail running and birdwatching, and each day ends with a sundowner at a beautiful viewpoint. The outfit is owned by passionate conservationists who have successfully bred sable antelope on the property and are happy to share their vast knowledge and experience. Both lodges are utterly fabulous, but also very unpretentious and sociable. *Ant's Hill* has the more scenic location, comprising five suites and rooms strung along a ridge offering great views to the plains below, while *Ant's Nest* is an older and more characterful property centred on a converted farmhouse. Rates are inclusive of meals (eaten communally), drinks and activities. $$$$$

Horizon Horseback Triple B Ranch, 24km north on the R518 to Melkrivier, then right onto the gravel road to Sterkstroom and continue for another 4km ⓣ 083 419 1929, ⓦ ridinginafrica.com. A well-established and highly professional outfit with sixty horses and 32,000 acres of beautiful bushland inhabited by hippos, giraffe, zebra and antelope. There's lovely lakeside accommodation in individual chalets, as well as a magical lantern-lit bush camp with a pool and great views. Suitable for riders of all levels, activities include horseback game-viewing, cattle-mustering, polocrosse and a cross-country course. Rates are all-inclusive. $$$$

Lindani Off the R518 around Melkrivier, 36km north of Vaalwater ⓣ 083 631 5579, ⓦ lindani.co.za. On a 31-square-kilometre reserve, *Lindani* comprises eight secluded and attractive thatched self-catering lodges sleeping between four and eighteen people, and a tented camp with twin accommodation and shared ablutions and kitchen. What makes *Lindani* unique is the many hiking and mountain-biking trails crisscrossing the reserve, which guests are free to use unsupervised, making this an ideal spot to explore the bush at your own pace. With tranquil picnic spots along rivers and the potential for encountering giraffe and various antelope, it's not surprising this is one of the most popular game lodges in the Waterberg. Minimum stay two nights. $

Waterberg Cottages Triple B Ranch, for directions see Horizon Horseback (opposite) ⓣ 014 755 4425, ⓦ waterbergcottages.co.za. Pleasant self-catering accommodation in five old farmhouse buildings on a working Bonsmara cattle ranch; some are small thatched cottages sleeping up to four, while the farmhouses can accommodate a couple of large families, and there's a swimming pool, too. The unpolluted wide-open skies above make this an ideal spot for stargazing (two-hour star tours are on offer), and there are walking trails marked out in the bush. $

Zeederberg Cottages Main Rd in Vaalwater, behind the shops and filling station ⓣ 082 332 7088, ⓦ zeederbergs.co.za. The best choice in Vaalwater town, set around a large, relaxing garden with a pool. The cluster of comfortable self-catering cottages includes a Zulu-style rondavel. Guests have access to the kitchen and living room in the main house and all meals are available on request. $

EATING

SEE MAP PAGE 81

The Hunter's Hide Main Rd, 200m south of the main crossing on the R33 ⓣ 072 279 9255. A simple bush-style pub, with TVs for watching the rugby and an outdoor wooden deck where all the lodge employees hang out on their evenings off. The filling menu includes burgers, baked spuds with toppings like creamed spinach, and pizzas, and there's plenty of cold beer. Mon–Sat 7.30am–midnight, Sun 7.30am–9pm.

★ **Seringa Café** Zeederberg Centre ⓣ 014 161 0643. The best place in town for lunch or a coffee, with outside tables under huge shady trees on the grass. It's often very busy and service can be slow, but it's worth it if you are passing through Vaalwater. The menu offers breakfasts, cakes and pastries, and can include light meals like grilled chicken breast with coconut, and hearty soups such as lentil and bacon in winter. Mon–Fri 7.45am–5pm, Sat 8.15am–2.30pm.

SHOPPING

SEE MAP PAGE 81

Beadle Triple B Ranch, for directions see Horizon Horseback ⓣ 014 755 4002. A community project for skills-training and sustainable employment, where you can watch the trainees applying intricate beadwork onto leather items, such as belts, bracelets and sandals, in the workshop. Next door is a tearoom and a shop where you can buy the goods. Mon–Fri 7.30am–5pm, Sat & Sun 7.30am–1pm.

★ **Black Mamba Company** Zeederberg Centre ⓣ 073 701 0543, ⓦ blackmambacompany.webs.com. Next to the Spar supermarket and *Seringa Café*, this excellent gallery sells beautiful crafts from throughout Southern Africa, including basketware, wooden carvings and jewellery, as well as books and nature guides. Mon–Fri 8.30am–5pm, Sat 8.30am–1.30pm, Sun 9.30am–1pm.

MARAKELE AT A GLANCE

Scattered Big Five sightings on the scenic slopes of the Kransberg.

Big Five **/**** public/Marataba
General wildlife: ****
Birding: ****
Scenery: *****
Wilderness factor: ****
Uncrowded: ****
Affordability: *****
Self-drive: Y

Marakele National Park

Main entrance gate 12km from Thabazimbi • Daily: May–Aug 6am–5.30pm; Sept–April 6am–6pm; day-visitors daily 7am–4pm • R218 • Sunrise/sunset game drives and walks R240 • ☎ 014 777 6928, ⓦ sanparks.org/parks/marakele

Set in the mountainous heart of the Waterberg, dramatically scenic **Marakele National Park** was established in 1994. It was originally called Kransberg (literally "Cliff Mountain") after its most impressive prominence, a striking assortment of odd-shaped peaks, boulder-strewn plateaus and sheer sandstone cliffs. Bisected by the **Matlabas River**, Marakele is split almost evenly between two main vegetation types: the relatively well-watered higher slopes support a cover of Waterberg Moist Bushveld, while the lower-lying plains are swathed in dense deciduous woodland dominated by silver cluster leaf, sickle bush and round-leaved bloodwood trees. The public part of Marakele extends over roughly 530 square kilometres and is jointly managed with the more northerly **Marataba Concession**, which effectively functions as a private reserve.

Marakele has been restocked with a wide variety of game, much of it from Kruger Park, and became a Big Five reserve in 2013 following the introduction of a small

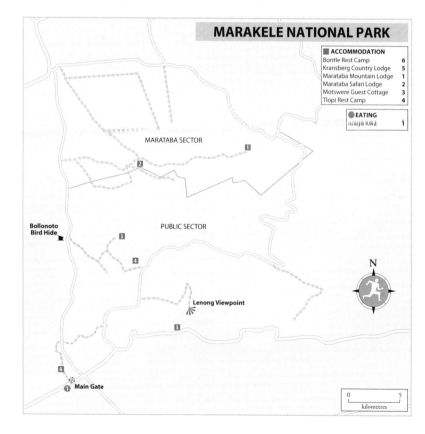

MARAKELE NATIONAL PARK

■ **ACCOMMODATION**
Bontle Rest Camp	6
Kransberg Country Lodge	5
Marataba Mountain Lodge	1
Marataba Safari Lodge	2
Motswere Guest Cottage	3
Tlopi Rest Camp	4

● **EATING**
Kinaya kwa	1

MARATABA SECTOR

Bollonoto Bird Hide

PUBLIC SECTOR

Lenong Viewpoint

Main Gate

0   5
kilometres

buffalo herd. The elephant and lion populations are currently estimated at around 275 and 45 individuals respectively, and it is also home to good numbers of white and black rhino, leopard, cheetah, brown hyena, giraffe, Burchell's zebra, tsessebe, roan antelope, sable antelope, red hartebeest, waterbuck, impala, eland and greater kudu. Marakele also supports more than four hundred bird species, a checklist that includes "dry west" specials such as pied babbler, crimson-breasted shrike, violet-eared waxbill and black-faced waxbill. The world's largest breeding colony of Cape vultures, comprising around eight hundred pairs, resides on the eastern face of the Kransberg. Wildlife can cross freely between Marakele and Marataba, although the border is very mountainous, so the two function as entirely separate tourist destinations with separate entrance gates and wildly divergent price tags.

Self-drive sector

The limited road network through the park's **public sector** doesn't require 4WD, though you might be glad of high clearance on some stretches. The sector can be explored in the space of one long or two short drives – in fact, it is probably better viewed as a scenic drive with a fair chance of wildlife encounters than as a bona fide game drive. Coming from the main entrance gate, the first part of the road network is a series of short loops through a tract of dry deciduous woodland stocked with non-dangerous wildlife such as giraffe, Burchell's zebra and various antelope. A highlight is the **Bollonoto Bird Hide**, which stands next to a small waterhole that attracts plenty of wildlife in the dry season, especially Chacma baboon, greater kudu and impala, though ironically it doesn't seem to be especially rewarding for birds.

East of the hide, Nlopfu Drive crosses through a gated subway below the Rooiberg Road into the main body of the **national park**. From here, the road gradually ascends through dense deciduous woodland into more open grassland overlooked by the stunning cliffs of the **Kransberg** and various other peaks. Elephant, white rhino, buffalo, lion, cheetah and leopard might all be seen along this road, but don't raise your hopes too high, as you're unlikely to see anything more exciting than a few antelope on a slow day. The **scenery** is truly awesome, however, especially as you ascend higher up the Kransberg, past stands of pink-flowering common protea and along a cliffside road so narrow that you'll be praying not to meet a vehicle coming in the opposite direction. Finally, you reach the top of the Kransberg, a gorgeous grassy plateau strewn with clumps of montane heather and mighty boulders where pairs of the localized klipspringer antelope stand sentry. The road terminates at **Lenong View Point**, where the presence of several satellite towers somewhat mars the experience, but the view over the valleys to the north is still fantastic, and bird lovers should be treated to Cape vultures soaring overhead while the likes of Cape rock thrush, mocking cliff-chat and buff-streaked chat hop confidingly around the car-park.

Marataba concession

Altogether different in feel to the public sector of Marakele, the 230-square-kilometre **Marataba Concession** operates as a private reserve serviced by two upmarket lodges with twenty rooms combined. Bisected by the Matlabas River and serviced by three large dams, the concession has far more water than the main body of the park, and this tends to support higher wildlife populations. Visitors spending a couple of days in the concession are likely to see lion, cheetah, elephant, white rhino, buffalo, giraffe and the usual grazers on guided game drives, but black rhino, leopard and brown hyena are scarcer. The lodges also offer boat trips on **Python Dam**, which is home to hippos; it's also a good place to see water-associated birds such as African fish eagle, African darter, greater painted snipe, half-collared kingfisher and swallow-tailed bee-eater. Other guided activities include short nature walks and longer hikes into the mountains.

1

ARRIVAL

MARAKELE NATIONAL PARK

By car The main gate to the public sector of Marakele lies almost 300km from Johannesburg. The most straightforward route follows the N1 north for 100km, past Pretoria then turning onto the R516 at Bela Bela and heading west along it for 95km before turning right on to the R511, which leads to Thabazimbi after 45km. It is 12km along a signposted surfaced road to the park entrance. An alternative route entails following the R511 all the way from the Olifantsfontein Road off-ramp (on the N1 between Johannesburg and Pretoria) to Thabazimbi via Hartebeespoort and Brits. Either way, allow the best part of four hours for the drive.
The gate to the Marataba sector lies 345km from Johannesburg, off the R510 between Thabazimbi and Lephalale. The quickest route entails following the N1 and R33 to Vaalwater, then the R511 to the junction with the R510, where you need to head left towards Thabazimbi.

ACCOMMODATION

SEE MAP PAGE 84

IN THE NATIONAL PARK

All accommodation in the public sector of the national park can be booked through SANParks central reservations (☏ 012 428 9111, ⓦ sanparks.org).

Bontle Rest Camp 2km inside the main gate. This shaded campsite, overlooking Bontle Dam, has a fully kitted kitchen and ablution blocks, obligatory braai area and the option of a power point. There are also pre-erected safari tents on wooden decks with verandas that sleep two with proper beds, en-suite bathrooms and small kitchens. Camping $, safari tents $$

Motswere Guest Cottage 27km from the gate. This secluded old farmhouse has four bedrooms sleeping up to eight, as well as two bathrooms, a lounge with DSTV, a fan, fully equipped kitchen and a veranda and braai area. Great value for groups. $$$

Tlopi Rest Camp 18km from the main gate. A self-catering camp on the banks of the small forest-fringed Tlopi Dam, with ten romantic, luxuriously equipped tents (sleeping two) hovering on stilts over the water's edge. $$

MARATABA CONCESSION

The two small lodges in this private concession – which shares open borders with the public sector of the national park – can be booked through a central reservations office (☏ 011 880 9992, ⓦ marataba.co.za). Rates include all meals and game drives.

Marataba Mountain Lodge Remote off-the-grid eco-lodge powered by solar and gas, with lovely long views across the valley below. Over-16s only. $$$$$

Marataba Safari Lodge This child-friendly, fifteen-room lodge overlooks a busy waterhole set below a tall craggy sandstone escarpment typical of the Waterberg. Public areas are dominated by tall glass walls and have a contemporary African feel, while the imaginatively designed canvas-and-stone rooms resemble a cross between a Mongolian yurt and the curvaceous adobe style typical of Mali. $$$$$

OUTSIDE THE PARK

★ **Kransberg Country Lodge** ☏ 060 452 8061. Situated just outside the national park boundary 15km from the main gate, this friendly family-run lodge stands on a 380-hectare plot with a spectacular setting at the base of the Kransberg, right below the golden cliffs that double as a breeding site for eight hundred pairs of Cape vulture (with binoculars, you can see them nesting). In addition to providing a useful base for day-visits to Marakele, the property supports a diverse birdlife and small game such as warthog and various antelope, and offers plenty of walking, cycling and trail-running opportunities. The six en-suite rooms are unpretentious but comfortable. Amenities include a well-equipped communal kitchen, an honesty bar and a newly built boma for summer evening braais. Bring all your own food. $

EATING

SEE MAP PAGE 84

Aside from *Marataba Safari* and *Mountain* lodges, the accommodation listed above is all self-catering. If you need to stock up locally, there are two very good supermarkets in Thabazimbi, 12km from the park main entrance gate.

Khaya Kwa Opposite the main entrance gate to Marakele National Park, ☏ 083 601 5353. Agreeable pub-like set up, with indoor and terrace seating and an inexpensive menu of burgers, steaks, ribs and such. Tues–Sun 1–10pm.

Welgevonden Game Reserve

The main entrance gate is 25km west of Vaalwater on the tarred R517 towards Lephalale • only accessible to overnight guests, R120 conservation fee per night • ☏ 087 813 0501, ⓦ welgevonden.org

One of South Africa's most exciting Big Five safari destinations outside of Greater Kruger, **Welgevonden** is an ecologically varied 360-square-kilometre private reserve that shares part of its fenced western border with Marakele National Park. Welgevonden was created in 1993 by an association of landowners, but is managed as one large conservation area, which strictly regulates how many lodges can be built and the number of visitors to the park, but there are no internal fences nor any restrictions on individual lodges traversing any part of the 430km internal road network. Its name, which literally translates from Afrikaans as "Well Found", derives from one of the larger farms that has since been co-opted into the reserve. Spanning altitudes of 1080m to 1800m, the ruggedly scenic reserve is cut through by a trio of rivers, the largest of which is the **Matlabas**, and its flat-topped plateaus are incised by a series of steep sandstone

> ### WELGEVONDEN AT A GLANCE
> One of the country's top malaria-free Big Five private reserves.
> **Big Five:** ****
> **General wildlife:** ****
> **Birding:** ****
> **Scenery:** ****
> **Wilderness factor:** ***
> **Uncrowded:** **
> **Affordability:** *
> **Self-drive:** N

gorges whose cliffs are studded with prehistoric-looking euphorbias. It supports a varied cover of grassland, lightly wooded savannah and thick deciduous woodland dominated by the likes of African beechwood, silver cluster-leaf and wild seringa, while drainage lines and watercourses are lined with some impressive marula and fig trees.

Welgevonden supports solid numbers of all the Big Five. The population of 120 elephants is split between eight matriarchal herds, and there are also two lion prides, around fifteen cheetah, sixty-odd buffalo, large numbers of white rhino, and rather fewer black rhino. It is also ideal leopard country and naturally supports a dense population of these secretive nocturnal carnivores, including a number of quite habituated individuals that are most often seen along the main cliff-flanked road to East Gate. A rewarding area for lion and cheetah is the southwesterly tract of open grassland that guides refer to as the Serengeti. Other easily seen wildlife includes giraffe, Burchell's zebra, warthog, greater kudu, eland, waterbuck, blue wildebeest, red hartebeest, impala and black-backed jackal. Klipspringer, Chacma baboon, rock hyrax and Verreaux's eagle are often seen on the boulder-strewn slopes, while hippos are resident in a couple of the larger dams. The bird checklist of almost three hundred species includes such colourful bush dwellers such as crested barbet, brown-hooded kingfisher, lilac-breasted roller and southern yellow-billed hornbill.

ARRIVAL

WELGEVONDEN GAME RESERVE

By car Welgevonden lies about 280km by road from Johannesburg, which generally translates into a three-hour drive. There are four entrance gates. To get to any of them, follow the N1 north from Pretoria for 120km to the Kranskop Toll Plaza, then take the R33 off-ramp and drive northwest through Modimolle to Vaalwater, where you need to continue straight along the R517 towards Lephalale. Main gate is on the left side of the R517 about 25km past Vaalwater. East Gate lies along an 11km dirt road signposted on the left side of the R517 about 13km past Vaalwater. For South Gate, you need to follow the R517 out of Vaalwater for 6km, then turn left on the unsurfaced Bakkerspas road and follow it for 34km. For West Gate, follow the R510 for 47km out of Vaalwater, then turn left onto the Schoongelegen dirt road and continue for 17km. No private vehicles are permitted within the reserve, so all visitors will be collected and transferred to their accommodation from the specific gate used by the lodge where they are staying.

ACCOMMODATION

More than twenty individually managed small lodges are scattered around the reserve. Those listed below are recommended, but a full list with links to the individual lodge websites is available at ⓦ welgevonden.org/accommodation-bookings. There is no central reservations office; bookings must be made with the individual lodges as detailed on the website. **Clifftop Exclusive Safari Hideaway** ☎ 014 755 4920 (lodge) or ☎ 011 516 4367 (reservations), ⓦ clifftop lodge.co.za. Justifiably popular as a romantic weekend getaway from Gauteng, this small (eight-unit) lodge has a stunning location on the side of a cliff, above the scenic gorge carved by the Sterkstroom River in the far east of the reserve. Accommodation is in spacious modern chalets with an outdoor shower, private deck and plunge pool overlooking a stretch of the forest-fringed river where elephants regularly come to drink. Cuisine and service match the superb location. Birdlife around the lodge is excellent and includes very habituated southern masked weavers, Cape robin-chats and mocking cliff-chat. Rates include all activities, meals and drinks. $$$$$

1

Jamila Game Lodge ☎ 010 285 0310, ⓦ jamilalodge. co.za. A good, friendly option in the northern part of the reserve. It has five spacious chalets with wooden decks and outdoor showers and a pool; nearby is a busy watering hole visited by birds, antelope and the occasional elephant. Rates include game drives and all meals. $$$$

Mhondoro Safari Lodge ☎ 087 150 2314, ⓦ mhondoro. com. Centrally located *Mhondoro* is an attractive and modern child-friendly lodge, whose five thatched cottages and six-bed villa all have colourful African decoration, separate sitting rooms, air-conditioning, a well-stocked drinks fridge, state-of-the-art coffeemaker and a large private balcony. Excellent amenities include a gym, a saltwater infinity pool that frequently attracts thirsty elephants at night, and an exceptional underground photographic hide facing a waterhole that attracts a steady trickle of wildlife, from zebra and warthog to white rhino and elephant. The location is ideal for game drives in the productive grassland area known as Serengeti, and the super-keen guides try to encourage their guests to head out earlier than other lodges in the hope of being the first to locate lions or cheetah. Rates are all inclusive. $$$$$

Lapalala Wilderness Reserve

70km north of Vaalwater • ☎ 078 772 7449, ⓦ lapalala.com

The catalyst for the post-millennial transformation of the Waterberg into one of South Africa's most prominent wildlife destinations occurred in 1981, when the renowned conservationists **Dale Parker** and **Clive Walker** bought the first of several former cattle ranches that now comprise **Lapalala Wilderness**. In 1990, Lapalala became the first private reserve in South Africa to acquire a herd of the endangered black rhino, and it subsequently served as a breeding centre for this and other rare large mammal species, notably roan and sable antelope. Since 1985, it has also been home to the highly regarded **Lapalala Wilderness School**, which introduces some three thousand children a year – from all over Africa – to the principles and practices of conservation during week-long courses. Strongly committed both to conservation and community involvement, its founders also spearheaded the campaign to have the Waterberg recognized as a **UNESCO Biosphere Reserve** in 2001. Now extending across an extraordinary 485 square kilometres and likely to be expanded by another fifteen percent by the end of 2020, Lapalala has now remodelled itself as a low-density ecotourist destination, with the first lodge having opened in early 2019 and two more set to follow over the next couple of years.

Lapalala is as much about the thrilling **wilderness** setting as it is to ticking off wildlife, and as such it is better suited to repeat safarigoers seeking a holistic bush experience than to neophytes wanting to tick off the Big Five. The rugged undulating landscape is dominated by the sandstone cliffs of a spectacular gorge incised by the **Lephalale River** as it courses through the reserve for 23km. It only became a Big Five reserve in 2019, following the reintroduction of two lion prides, but it also hosts small numbers of cheetah, elephant and buffalo, as well as one of the country's largest populations of white and black rhino, though the latter is seldom seen. Leopard are prolific but predictably skittish, and the reserve lies within the territory of South Africa's last free-roaming pack of African wild dogs. Other common wildlife includes giraffe, Burchell's zebra, greater kudu and impala, and a few herds of roan and sable antelope will be released from the breeding centre into the main reserve once the current drought ends. Wildlife aside, Lapalala is of great cultural value for its wealth of **prehistoric rock art** (an excellent site lies within 30 minutes' drive of the lodge), and it is also scattered with ancient stone circumcision rings – circles of upright stones erected by young Pedi men at the end of the two-week period of exile in the bush that preceded their initiation ceremony. Also of interest is the shortish guided hike to the plateau

---

LAPALALA AT A GLANCE

Vast and scenically impressive wilderness area that now hosts all the Big Five.

Big Five: ****
General wildlife: ***
Birding: ***
Scenery: *****
Wilderness factor: *****
Uncrowded: *****
Affordability: *
Self-drive: N

of **Palala Hill**, site of a former Nguni settlement that has yielded a host of interesting artefacts, most notably several old burial pots and a clay rhino statue sufficiently similar to its medieval gold-plated counterparts at Mapungubwe to suggest a strong cultural link between the two.

ARRIVAL AND DEPARTURE
LAPALALA WILDERNESS RESERVE

By car Visitors to Tintswalo Lapalala are required to arrive at East Gate, from where they will be transported to the lodge by 4WD. The well signposted gate lies 70km from Vaalwater and can be reached by following the Melkrivier road northeast out of town for 60km then turning left onto the R518 to Marken. Allow four hours coming from Johannesburg.

ACCOMMODATION

Tintswalo Lapalala About one hour's drive from East Gate ☎ 011 300 8888, ⊚ tintswalo.com. This wonderful small lodge comprises seven stand-alone suites spaced out in a semi-circle around a waterhole that attracts plenty of thirsty game. Connected by a stilted wooden walkway, each of the suites is themed around a specific African ethnic group, and individually decorated with related photographs and paraphernalia; all come with air-conditioning, private plunge pool and well-stocked mini-bar. In keeping with the reserve's low-impact ethos, the lodge operates entirely on solar power and gas, and avoids one-use products. Activities are geared to individual client's interests but include game drives in search of specific species, boat trips on the river (rewarding for hippo, crocodiles and water-associated birds), fly-fishing and visits to rock art sites. Rates include all meals, activities and drinks. $$$$$

Mapungubwe National Park

Daily: April–Oct 6.30am–6pm; Sept–March 6am–6.30pm, last entry for day-visitors, two hours before gates close • R219 • Sunset and night drives R318, guided walks R470 • ☎ 015 534 7925, ⊚ sanparks.org/parks/mapungubwe

Set in the far north of Limpopo, **Mapungubwe National Park** is a UNESCO World Heritage Site, primarily due to its famous Iron Age site known as the **Hill of the Jackals**, thought by some experts to be the site of the first kingdom in Africa south of the Zambezi. The park is situated at the confluence of the Limpopo and Shashi rivers, where South Africa, Zimbabwe and Botswana meet. Archeological interest aside, it has a scenic backdrop of unusual sandstone formations, mopane woodland, riverine forest and boulder-strewn slopes scattered with otherworldly baobab trees. It also offers excellent game viewing, with elephant, giraffe and white rhino all common, along with a variety of antelope including eland and gemsbok. If you're lucky, you may spot predators such as lion, leopard and hyena, and there are over four hundred bird species including the African fish eagle, Kori bustard, tropical boubou and magnificent Pel's fishing owl.

The park is divided into an eastern and a western side connected only by the main road, with a large plot of private land in between. The main entrance is on the eastern side nearest Musina, which is also where you'll find the Hill of the Jackals and most of the accommodation. You can explore the park in your own car; 35km of gravel roads are suitable for regular cars, while another 100km can be negotiated in a 4WD. There are also morning and evening three-hour guided game drives and walks for overnight visitors. A restaurant and curio shop are located at the main gate.

Hill of the Jackals
Heritage Tour at 7am, 10am & 3pm from the main gate • R258 plus park fee • Book at the main gate or on ☎ 015 534 7925

The **Hill of the Jackals** is one hour's drive from the main entrance and, to visit, you

> ## MAPUNGUBWE AT A GLANCE
> Stirring riverine scenery, fascinating archeological sites and decent game viewing on the remote Zimbabwe border.
> **Big Five:** **
> **General wildlife:** **
> **Birding:** *****
> **Scenery:** ****
> **Wilderness factor:** *****
> **Uncrowded:** ****
> **Affordability:** ****
> **Self-drive:** N

1

need to join a two-hour Heritage Tour. A knowledgeable guide will talk you through the finds from an archeological dig in front of the hill, before climbing steps up to where the king and his extended family lived. It held a spiritual and mythological importance to local Modimo people long before it was "discovered" in 1932, when a local farmer climbed the dome-shaped granite hill and found various remains, including a tiny one-horned rhinoceros and a bowl, both made out of gold. It is thought that the years 1000–1300 AD were the heyday of a civilization centred at Mapungubwe. Prior to this, the Khoi and San people both left their footprints in the area with numerous sites of important rock art. Most impressive of these is found on land outside the national park (but still within the UNESCO World Heritage Site) at *Kaoxa Bush Camp* (see opposite).

Mapungubwe Museum and Interpretive Centre
Daily 8am–3.30pm • R66 plus park fee

The **Mapungubwe Museum and Interpretive Centre**, near the park's main gate, has won awards for its amazing domed and vaulted architecture, and houses an informative exhibition. However, owing to conservation and security worries only a few of the original gold items found at the site are on display here, but you can see a replica of the golden rhino, and guides bring the Mapungubwe story to life.

ARRIVAL AND DEPARTURE   MAPUNGUBWE NATIONAL PARK

By car There are several routes to the park. The entrance gate lies around 60km west of Musina and the N1 along the R572 road to the Pont Drift border post with Botswana. Another option is to leave the N1 at Polokwane further south and take the R521 via Dendron, Vivo and Alldays and turn right on to the R572 at the park's boundary and follow it to the gate; the distance from Polokwane using this route is about 215km. Note that the nearest fuel stop is in Musina and Alldays, so ensure tanks are filled on the way to the park.

By public transport The only public transport to the park is by a few minibus taxis from Musina. However, in practice this is only really useful if you are visiting the Museum and Interpretive Centre or joining the Heritage Tour, then moving on.

MAPUNGUBWE NATIONAL PARK

ACCOMMODATION

SEE MAP PAGE 90

1

INSIDE THE PARK

All accommodation within the park is operated by SANParks; ☎ 012 428 9111 or ☎ 015 534 7925, ⓦ sanparks.org/parks/mapungubwe.

Leokwe Rest Camp 11km from the main gate. The largest camp in the national park comprises eighteen spacious double and family cottages, in a primally beautiful setting among sandstone boulders close to a viewpoint overlooking the confluence of the Limpopo and Shashi rivers. Amenities include a sundeck, a natural rock pool and a nearby hide. $\overline{\underline{\$\$}}$

Limpopo Forest Tented Camp 40km from the main gate. Set in riverine forest fringing the Limpopo and close to Maloutswa Pan Hide, this small camp consists of eight twin en-suite tents and a shared kitchen. The birding is excellent. $\overline{\underline{\$\$}}$

Mazhou Camping Site 40km from the main gate. Situated close to *Limpopo Forest Tented Camp*, this is a small campsite, with room for only ten tents, but is fully equipped, including power points. $\overline{\underline{\$}}$

Tshugulu Lodge 23km from the main gate. Aimed at groups, this luxury lodge is split between a guest lodge sleeping up to eight and a cottage for four. There is en-suite swimming pool and an exclusive eco-trail. $\overline{\underline{\$\$}}$–$\overline{\underline{\$\$\$}}$

Vhembe Wilderness Camp 13km from the main gate. Four simple cabins and a communal kitchen on a ridge situated within walking distance of the Limpopo River and Mapungubwe Hill. It is unfenced and there's no swimming pool, so it isn't suited to small children. Access by high clearance vehicle (ideally 4WD) only. $\overline{\underline{\$}}$

FURTHER AFIELD

Kaoxa Bush Camp Off the R572 in a private wilderness area between the eastern and western sections of Mapungubwe ☎ 072 536 6297, ⓦ kaoxacamp.com. This rustic self-catering bush camp comprises three stone cottages, whose large terraces offer breathtaking views across the confluence of the Limpopo and Shashi rivers to Zimbabwe and Botswana. There are also three comfortable furnished safari tents with equally wonderful views, and a campsite for those with their own tent. There's electricity but no a/c (and it gets very hot here), and a shared kitchen and dining facilities. The property stretches down to the two rivers and is frequently visited by elephants and other wildlife from Zimbabwe and Botswana. In contrast to the national park, visitors are free to move around independently (after signing lengthy indemnity forms) on foot or by car, though as signs at the camp make clear, elephants have the right of way. Bearing in mind the many hungry animals you may encounter, it's a good idea to seek advice before setting off. The only area that you're not allowed to explore by yourself is the amazing rock-art site with its unique locust images, which one of the camp staff will take you to.

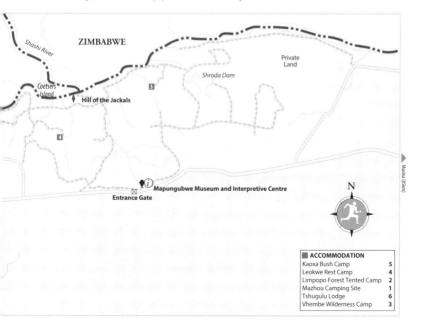

■ ACCOMMODATION	
Kaoxa Bush Camp	5
Leokwe Rest Camp	4
Limpopo Forest Tented Camp	2
Mazhou Camping Site	1
Tshugulu Lodge	6
Vhembe Wilderness Camp	3

Kruger National Park and environs

HIPPOS IN LAKE PANIC

Kruger National Park and environs

Rivalling Cape Town as South Africa's biggest tourist draw, Kruger is indisputably one of Africa's finest "Big Five" parks, thanks both to its vast area – almost 20,000 square kilometres, comparable to Israel or El Salvador – and to a rich biodiversity that includes almost 150 mammal and more than 500 bird species. It stands in the far northeast of the country, where it is split more-or-less equally between two provinces, Mpumalanga in the south and Limpopo in the north, and shares a 300km border with Mozambique.

Unashamedly populist, **Kruger** boasts a great network of surfaced roads and well-equipped **restcamps**, making it the easiest major African game park to explore on a **self-drive** basis, whether you stick to the more densely trafficked south or venture deeper into the remote and untrammelled north. Kruger also incorporates a number of **private concessions** leased to five-star **lodges** where well-informed rangers conduct guided safaris in open vehicles, while the park's western flank shares open borders with a patchwork of similarly exclusive private reserves famed for their close-up encounters with the normally elusive leopard. Also covered in this chapter is the Kingdom of **Eswatini** (formerly Swaziland), which actually lies outside South Africa but is surrounded by it on three sides – consequently, it's often visited by self-drivers crossing between Kruger and northern Kwazulu-Natal.

Approaching Kruger

Most visitors to Kruger fly into Kruger Mpumalanga International Airport (KMIA), which lies a short distance outside the park near the provincial capital **Mbombela**, or drive there from **Johannesburg, Pretoria** or elsewhere in Gauteng. However, Kruger's vast area and elongated shape means that there are a great many possible approach routes – to place this in some perspective, the most southwesterly gates at Malelane and Numbi are less than 400km east of Gauteng's OR Tambo Airport, and under an hour by road from KMIA, whereas the most northerly gate at Pafuri is more than 600km by road from Johannesburg and something like seven hours' drive from KMIA. Bearing this in mind, it is unsurprising that almost all tourist activity in Kruger is focused on the more accessible southern third, which is also the best developed section of the park in terms of **restcamps**, game-drive road and other tourist **amenities**. The ideal way to explore southern Kruger is to book into one or more of its internal restcamps and self-drive, but it is also possible – and, in peak seasons, might sometimes be necessary – to base yourself outside the park and explore it on a series of day trips, either on a self-drive basis or by booking on to a day-safari. The largest urban centre within day-tripping distance of Kruger is Mbombela, which also serves as a useful regional point of entry for those using public transport, but there are more popular and better options for those with wheels, for instance along the N4 running east from Mbombela to **Komatipoort**, or the small towns of Hazyview, Hoedspruit and Phalaborwa further north along the R40.

Mbombela (Nelspruit) and the N4 to Komatipoort

Prosperous **MBOMBELA**, the provincial capital of Mpumalanga ("Place of the Rising Sun" to its siSwati- and isiZulu-speaking residents), stands on the banks of the

SABI SAND LEOPARD

Highlights

❶ Drive the R40 This road, which takes you along Kruger's western flank, is the best way to experience how rural Shangaan and Tsonga people really live. See page 99

❷ African meals at the Shangana Cultural Village Sample crocodile and unusual vegetables, cooked over open fires, and watch stirring traditional dances. See page 101

❸ Self-driving Kruger Whether you spend two days or a fortnight here, there's no more user-friendly self-drive safari destination anywhere in Africa. See page 105

❹ Walking safaris Leave behind your vehicle for the thrill of close encounters with animals on

Kruger's guided wilderness trails. See page 108

❺ Makuleke Contractual Park The most northerly wedge of Kruger is renowned for its tropical feel, high biodiversity and superb birdlife. See page 122

❻ Leopard-spotting in MalaMala or Sabi Sand Guided game drives in these luxury private reserves, which share open borders with the Kruger, offer the world's most reliable leopard viewings. See page 126

❼ Mkhaya Game Reserve Eswatini's best wildlife experience, where you can walk with rhino before sleeping in luxurious open-sided cottages in the bush. See page 141

HIGHLIGHTS ARE MARKED ON THE MAP ON PAGE 96

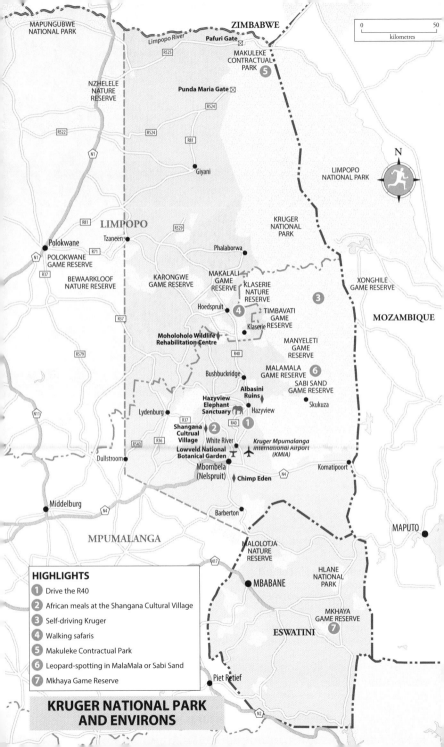

HIGHLIGHTS

1 Drive the R40

2 African meals at the Shangana Cultural Village

3 Self-driving Kruger

4 Walking safaris

5 Makuleke Contractual Park

6 Leopard-spotting in MalaMala or Sabi Sand

7 Mkhaya Game Reserve

KRUGER NATIONAL PARK AND ENVIRONS

Crocodile River some 320km east of central Gauteng along the N4. Originally called **Nelspruit** and still often referred to by that name, it was founded by the Nel brothers in the 1890s as a base for traders, farmers and prospectors, and soon afterwards emerged as an important stop on the Pretoria–Delagoa Bay railway line, which linked the goldfields of **Gauteng** to the Mozambican port now called **Maputo**. Something of a backwater prior to being chosen as **provincial capital** in 1994, Mbombela has since undergone a striking transformation to become a bustling commercial centre serving not only the Mpumalanga lowveld but also shoppers from Eswatini and Mozambique. For all that, the town holds little appeal to travellers, though it remains an important **gateway** to the Kruger, situated at the junction of the two main access roads to the southern part of the park, namely the N4 east to Malelane and Komatipoort and the R40 north to Hazyview, Hoedspruit and Phalaborwa.

East of Mbombela, the N4 roughly follows the course of the Crocodile River for 100km before terminating at the small town of **Komatipoort** on the border with Mozambique. For 58km to the tiny farming settlement of Malelane, the road travels within view of the Crocodile's riverine forest, passing lush subtropical farmlands and the Dalí-esque formations of **granite koppies** that punctuate the southwest Kruger, the only blight on the journey being the smoke stacks from Malelane sugar-cane mill. Here, a 4km side road branches north to Kruger's **Malelane Gate**, the most useful entry point for *Berg-en-Dal* restcamp (see page 114); alternatively, you can continue east along the N4, which runs roughly parallel to the river as it traces the southern boundary of Kruger National Park, into Komatipoort, from where a 12km road curves back northwest to **Crocodile Bridge Gate**, which is a convenient point of entry for *Lower Sabie* restcamp (see page 114).

Lowveld National Botanical Garden

Signposted off the R40 to White River • Daily 8am–5pm • R35 • ☎ 013 752 5531, ⓦ sanbi.org/gardens/lowveld

Mbombela's major attraction is the **Lowveld National Botanical Garden**. Situated at the confluence of the Nels and Crocodile rivers, it is a delightful place to wander about, with a large natural waterfall and an aerial boardwalk through a cultivated patch of **rainforest**, making a pleasant break from the midday heat. The garden specializes in **cycads** from around the world, and there's also a grove of baobabs from South Africa and other African countries, with trees grouped according to habitat and helpfully identified with labels. Wildlife includes hippo, crocodile and African finfoot along the river, as well as vervet monkey, dwarf mongoose, tree squirrel and more than 240 other bird species. A useful brochure sold at the entrance gate has a map showing the highlights of the garden and the paths through it, and you'll find a tea room open for refreshments, as well as a restaurant with good views of the waterfall.

Chimp Eden

15km out of Mbombela off the R40 to Barberton • Daily 8am–4pm • R190 • ☎ 079 777 1514, ⓦ chimpeden.com

Situated within the small but beautiful Umhloti Nature Reserve in the hills south of Mbombela, **Chimp Eden** was established by the Jane Goodall Institute in 2006 as a facility dedicated to the rescue and rehabilitation of **chimpanzees**. There are currently three different chimp groups and enclosures, comprising a total of more than thirty individuals, with viewpoints overlooking the forest. During the 45min tour you get to see the primates – many of them rescued from terrible conditions in places like Angola and Sudan – re-learning how to climb trees, foraging for food in the leaves, carefully grooming each other and establishing troop relationships. Light meals and refreshment are available from the restaurant before or after the tour, and there's also budget accommodation available (see page 98). Book online well in advance to be sure of a place.

ARRIVAL AND DEPARTURE

By plane Kruger Mpumalanga International Airport (KMIA; ☎013 753 7500, ⓦkmiairport.co.za) stands alongside the R368 about 25km northeast of town, and although small, its 7350-square-metre terminal is claimed to be the largest thatched structure in Africa. SA Airlink (ⓦflyairlink.com) operates flights in either direction to/from Johannesburg, Cape Town and Durban. Unfortunately, these are among the most expensive flights in the country, so it may work out cheaper to fly into Johannesburg and continue from there by car. All the major car rental companies, including Avis (☎013 750 1015), have rental desks at the airport. If you're not renting a car, your best option for onward travel is a private shuttle: Summit Tours and Safaris (☎013 516 0067 or ☎078 326 1041, ⓦsummittoursandsafaris.com) meets flights on request and provides reliable transfers into Mbombela (or into Kruger and the private reserves) as well as offering day and overnight guided tours into Kruger. Destinations: Cape Town (daily; 3hr); Durban (daily except

MBOMBELA

Sunday; 1hr); Johannesburg (4–7 daily; 1hr).

By bus From Johannesburg, the City Bug (☎0861 33 44 33, ⓦcitybug.co.za) is the best option, with six departures daily 8am–6pm (4hr), leaving from OR Tambo Airport and arriving in Mbombela at the BP garage in the Sonpark Centre, Piet Retief St, just south of the city centre. You'll need to arrange a taxi beforehand (it's too far to walk into town): Kelly's Taxi (☎082 352 5728) is recommended; alternatively, Uber is available in Mbombela or you could arrange for someone from your accommodation to meet you.

By road Mbombela, the main road gateway to the Kruger Park, lies about 320km east of Pretoria along the N4, a drive of around 3.5 hours once you clear the city. Coming from Johannesburg or OR Tambo Airport, the distance and driving time are similar, but you need to follow the N12 east until it connects with the N4 near Emalahleni (formerly Witbank). Coming from KwaZulu-Natal, it is a 680km/8hr drive from Durban or 360km/5hr from Pongola.

INFORMATION

Tourist information Kruger Lowveld Tourism (Mon–Fri 7am–6pm, Sat 8am–1.30pm; ☎013 755 1988, ⓦkrugerlowveld.com), at the Crossings Centre, corner of the N4 and General Dan Pienaar St, is the town's main

tourist office. It provides maps and basic information, and arranges accommodation, including bookings for Kruger's restcamps, as well as day-trips with various tour operators.

ACCOMMODATION

MBOMBELA

Accommodation close to town is largely geared towards business travellers, and none is close to restaurants. Most places have swimming pools, outdoor eating areas and tropical gardens, and can also arrange Kruger tours at short notice.

Chimp Eden 15km out of town off the R40 to Barberton ☎079 777 1514, ⓦchimpeden.com. This Jane Goodall Institute-affiliated chimpanzee sanctuary offers charming accommodation in a quartet of simple twin cabins that share a communal self-catering kitchen and private garden. One chimpanzee tour per person per night stay is included in the room rate, as is breakfast. $

Funky Monkeys Backpacker Lodge 102 Van Wijk St ☎013 744 1310 or 083 310 4755, ⓦfunkymonkeys. co.za. Popular hostel with a licensed bar, pool table, shady veranda, swimming pool, ATM, broadband and the choice of dorm beds or private doubles. It offers one- to three-day tours into Kruger and can arrange pick-ups from the town centre or airport. $

Lakeview Lodge Take the Kaapsehoop road off the N4; the lodge is on your left after 4km ☎013 741 4312, ⓦlakeviewlodge.co.za. Eleven thatched self-catering chalets in a rural garden setting, with a swimming pool, restaurant, caravan park and campsite. There's also a swimming pool and play area for kids, and a restaurant. $

The Loerie's Call 2 Du Preez St ☎013 744 9507 or ☎086 548 7297, ⓦloeriescall.co.za. This modern guesthouse, with a pool and subtropical gardens, offers upmarket en-suite rooms with private verandas, as well as an appealing lounge and terrace. It's often fully booked, so reserve well ahead. There is also a restaurant on-site and an upmarket spa. $$

Old Vic Travellers Inn 12 Impala St, 3km from town ☎013 744 0993 or ☎082 340 1508, ⓦoldvictravellers inn.com. Clean, comfortable doubles, en suite, luxury & budget options, and a dorm in a quiet backpacker hostel with a pool, garden and walks in the adjoining nature reserve. There are also three self-catering units suitable for families. The owners can arrange transport from the centre of town and from the airport, and their in-house tour company specializes in guided Kruger tours and booking accommodation within the park. Extras include horseriding and a beauty salon. $

★ **Torburnlea Guest House** Mataffin Macadamia Village, 5km east of town ☎013 007 0241 or ☎072 884 8872, ⓦtorburnlea.co.za. Pick of the Mbombela guesthouses, Torburnlea is the beautifully renovated 1920s family home of friendly and informed hosts Andrew and Kim Hall, with a gracious colonial-style veranda looking from a hill onto orchards and sugarcane fields. The rooms are spacious and elegant, with luxurious fittings and linen, and you'll get fresh fruit juice and tropical fruit from the farm for breakfast. $\overline{\$\$}$

TOWARDS KOMATIPOORT

A few midrange lodges are scattered outside the park's southern border, most offering some in-house game viewing as well easy access to Malelane and/or Crocodile Bridge gates.

Buhala Game Lodge 12km east of Malelane Gate ☎ 082 909 5941 or ☎ 083 272 2150, ⓦ buhala.co.za. A fabulous guesthouse on a mango, sugar-cane and papaya farm, set on the banks of the Crocodile River, with views from a wooden deck across the slow water into Kruger, plus a swimming pool, a spa, and ten elegant doubles with a/c. Day drives with a ranger into Kruger can be arranged from here, as well as three-hour walks. It's also popular with golfers, as it's close to the exclusive Leopard Creek course, designed by Gary Player. $\overline{\$\$\$}$

Crocodile Bridge Safari Lodge 200m outside Crocodile Bridge gate ☎ 013 793 7859 or ☎ 072 3888 408, ⓦ crocbridge.co.za. Ideally situated for self-drivers, this riverfront self-catering resort offers the choice of luxury standing tents or cottages, all with air-conditioning, fridge and a view into the park. Evening meals are an optional communal "bring and braai", where guests bring their own choice of meat and drink, while management provides complimentary salads, freshly baked bread, cutlery and crockery. No under-14s permitted for safety reason. $\overline{\$\$}$

Elephant Walk Retreat Immediately outside Crocodile Bridge gate ☎ 013 793 7543 or ☎ 083 4144 683, ⓦ elephantwalk.co.za. This attractive self-catering bush lodge comprises nine stilted and thatched wooden cottages, each sleeping between three and six, set in leafy park-like grounds that run down to Crocodile River and offer views into Kruger. $\overline{\$\$}$

★ **Manyatta Rock Camp** Signposted off the N4, between Malelane and Crocodile Bridge gates, ☎ 082 779 2153 or ☎ 013 790 4214 ⓦ kwamadwala.net. Offering a game-lodge experience at B&B prices, family-friendly Manyatta consists of 27 air-conditioned chalets built around a pair of massive granite outcrops in the Kwa Madwala Game Reserve, a small but beautiful area of bushveld dotted with rocky hills and roamed by elephant, giraffe, warthog, zebra and various antelope. There's a nice pool and good views, though with farmland close by it doesn't have a totally wild feeling. Horse rides are also offered, ranging in duration from one-hour to a half-day including breakfast. Other activities include an elephant interaction experience (provided you have no ethical objections), and full- or half-day drives into Kruger. $\overline{\$\$}$

Ngwenya Lodge Signposted off the N4, between Malelane and Crocodile Bridge gates ☎ 013 793 9300, ⓦ ngwenya.co.za. Boasting 2km of Crocodile River frontage facing the Kruger Park about 10km upstream of Crocodile Bridge, this large family-friendly self-catering resort stands in a patch of indigenous bushveld studded with dams. Ask for one of the riverview chalets, which face a scenic floodplain often frequented by lion and other predators. Amenities include guided game drives into Kruger, three riverfront hides, six swimming pools, an 18-hole mini-golf course, two tennis courts, a children's playground, a beauty salon and a restaurant and pub. $\overline{\$\$}$

EATING

The Food Fundi Coffee Café Pick N Pay Centre, 5–7 Sitrus Crescent ☎ 013 755 1091, ⓦ thefoodfundi.co.za. A local favourite serving really good coffee, home-made bread and craft beer, with a seasonal fresh menu of open sandwiches, wraps, cakes and salads. The rooibos-smoked chicken sandwich with cashew nuts is very tasty, as is the variety of all-day breakfast dishes. Mon–Fri 7.30am–5pm, Sat 8am–4pm, Sun 9am–2pm.

Mediterranean I'langa Mall, cnr Flamboyant and Bitterbessie sts ☎ 013 742 2235; Riverside Mall, White River Rd (R40) ☎ 013 757 0170, ⓦ mediterranean seafood.co.za. A popular seafood and sushi choice, where you can try Greek-style Mozambican prawns, or a whole fish baked, steamed or fried. The menu is extensive – ask to see the display of fresh fish from the kitchen. Mon–Thurs & Sun 11.30am–9pm, Fri & Sat 11.30am–10pm.

Orange Restaurant 4 Du Preez St ☎ 083 628 7759, ⓦ eatatorange.co.za. Sleek wood, glass and steel restaurant, adjacent to *The Loerie's Call* guesthouse with a balcony providing panoramic views of the city and the mountains. The food is pretty good too: fine dining with an eclectic menu, from Norwegian salmon to South African kudu (R150). Daily noon–3pm, Mon–Sat 6–10pm, Sun 6–9pm.

The R40 and Kruger's western flank

The main road skirting the western boundary of the Kruger National Park, the **R40** runs for 230km between Mbombela in the south and **Phalaborwa** in the north via **Hazyview**, **Klaserie** and **Hoedspruit**. The road passes through some prosperous tropical-fruit-growing farmlands around Hazyview, but for the most part it is flanked by a mosaic of densely populated and very poor semi-rural African areas, the biggest conglomeration of which is called **Bushbuckridge**. A fascinating slice of busy, rural

2

DRIVING THE R40

If you're driving the **R40**, take special care as the road has many potholes that can easily damage a wheel, as well as wandering goats and cattle, oblivious pedestrians and a hair-raising combination of minibus taxis tearing along and heavy trucks travelling between Phalaborwa Mine and Mozambique. Given the potential hazards, don't travel along this route in the dark, and allow for a slow journey – it's a very busy road, with only a single lane in each direction.

South African life, in which tiny brick houses and shacks exist alongside much more prosperous dwellings, it makes for a stark contrast to wild, protected Kruger – a reserve that the majority of people in the area have never had the means to enter.

The R40 yields access to five of Kruger's busiest entrance gates, namely **Numbi, Phabeni, Paul Kruger, Orpen** and **Phalaborwa**, as well as to many private game reserves along the park's western boundary, for instance **Sabi Sand, Manyeleti** and **Timbavati**. Its most important settlement in terms of access to Kruger and Sabi Sand is Hazyview, which lies just 50km north of Kruger Mpumalanga International Airport, a mere 13km from Phabeni Gate. Further north, on the border of Mpumalanga and Limpopo Province, Klaserie, though marked prominently on maps, is easily missed, being little more than a petrol station and shop, surrounded by a number of private game farms. Continuing northwards into Limpopo, you reach Hoedspruit, a shopping and service centre that is good for access to several large private game reserves and to Orpen Gate (69km away). Further north is the mining town of Phalaborwa, a convenient 2km from Phalaborwa Gate into central Kruger and the rewarding camps of Letaba and Olifants.

Hazyview

Located a mere 13km from **Phabeni Gate**, 16km from Numbi Gate and 40km from the major Paul Kruger Gate (the closest point of entry to Skukuza, Kruger's "capital"), **HAZYVIEW**, 65km north of Mbombela, is the main service centre for the southern Kruger and Sabi Sand. Far from being the idyllic African backwater this might suggest, the spread-out town centre heaves with traffic and pedestrians, and is dense with shopping malls and busy roadside market stalls; Hazyview isn't just a safari launchpad, but also the main commercial centre serving a large swathe of fruit farms and densely populated rural areas set outside Kruger. Nevertheless, it makes a useful base for visitors who want to stay outside the park and take part in some adventure **activities** and **tours**, as well as viewing game. The town's main tourist hub is **Perry's Bridge Trading Post**, a mock Victorian arcade that houses several luxury shops, craft outlets and restaurants, and stands in green gardens at the junction of the R536 and R40.

Hazyview Elephant Sanctuary

5km from Hazyview on the R536 road to Sabie • ☎ 013 737 6609, ⓦ hazyview.elephantsanctuary.co.za. Book elephant activities ahead on the website

The **Elephant Sanctuary** offers the opportunity to touch and feed orphaned elephants rescued from a culling programme. There's a variety of daily programmes which provide close interaction with the elephants (so long as you have no ethical objections). These are "Early Morning Brush Down", where you groom the animals and feel the texture of their skin and ears (7.30am, R885); an "Elephant Interaction Program", where you walk alongside them lightly holding their trunks (8am, 10am, 1pm, 3pm, R675); an "Elephant Sundowner Experience" (3pm, R1020); and an "immersive Full-Day Bigfoot Experience" (7.30am, R1925).

ARRIVAL AND DEPARTURE   **HAZYVIEW**

By car The shortest and quickest route here from Johannesburg, 421km away, is via the N4 and Mbombela (65km south). | **By minibus taxi** The only form of public transport serving Hazyview is minibus taxis.

INFORMATION

Tourist information Big 5 Country Tourism, Perry's Bridge, R40 (Mon–Sat 8am–7pm, Sat 8am–6pm, Sun 9am–3pm; ☎013 737 8191 or ☎082 574 2345, ⓦtourstickets.co.za), is the best information office in Mpumalanga, and able to book accommodation, safaris into Kruger Park, adventure activities and transfers. It publishes the clearest map of the region and has its own activity booklets. You can purchase tickets online for almost everything worth doing around Kruger and the Escarpment, including ballooning, horseriding and visiting animal rehab centres, as well as game drives and walks in Kruger and Sabi Sand.

ACCOMMODATION

Guesthouses here are set mostly in farmland strung along the roads radiating out to the neighbouring towns of Sabie (the R536), Graskop (the R535) and White River (the R538), as well as to Kruger's Paul Kruger Gate (the R40). Practically all of them can organize day tours into Kruger and elsewhere.

Böhm's Zeederberg Country House 17km from Hazyview, on the R536 ☎013 737 8101 or ☎082 576 5231, ⓦbohms.co.za. Well-run B&B chalets with an old-fashioned feel, set in subtropical gardens around a swimming pool, with magnificent views and walking trails to the river below. Wheelchair-friendly. $\overline{\underline{\$\$}}$

Gecko Lodge 3km from Hazyview on the R536 ☎013 590 1020, ⓦgeckolodge.co.za. Situated on a large farm with Sabie River frontage, this brightly decorated family-run lodge enjoys the nicest setting in Hazyview, with lush riverine vegetation and a stream running through the grounds. Rooms are decent and well priced, and there is an on-site pub as well as a restaurant. $\overline{\underline{\$\$}}$

Hazyview Adventure Backpackers 5km south of Hazyview on the R40 ☎083 859 0212 or ☎082 543 3594, ⓦhazybackpack.weebly.com. Bright ethnic decor and a friendly, fun atmosphere are the hallmarks of this family-run backpackers, which offers a choice of private rooms, dorms and standing tents. The attached *Jungle Café* serves home-cooked, traditional South African fare and hosts occasional live music. It can arrange well-priced day and overnight camping tours into nearby Kruger. $\overline{\underline{\$}}$

Hotel Numbi Main Rd ☎013 737 7301/2, ⓦhotelnumbi.co.za. An old-fashioned, comfortable place, right in the centre, offering garden suites and hotel rooms. The grounds are shady, and the hotel's restaurant serves excellent steaks. $\overline{\underline{\$\$}}$

Idle and Wild 6km from Hazyview, on the R536 ☎013 737 8173 or ☎082 381 7408, ⓦidleandwild.co.za. This mango farm in a lush valley on the banks of the Sabie River offers two thatched rondavels, a cottage (sleeping up to four) and two honeymoon suites (with their own spa bath) in the garden, as well as two en-suite bedrooms in the main house. All have kitchenettes, and there's a jacuzzi, sauna and swimming pool. Quad biking and river rafting on-site. $\overline{\underline{\$\$}}$

Nkambeni Safari Camp Numbi Gate, 25km south of Hazyview ☎013 590 1011 or ☎081 265 1658, ⓦnkambeni.com. A large, popular safari camp just inside the Kruger park boundaries, offering a no-frills game-viewing experience at reasonable prices. Accommodation is in pleasant safari tents with indoor and outdoor showers, though a bit too close together. Massive buffet meals are served in an open-air thatched dining room overlooking the bush and swimming pool. Day and sunset safaris are available, though you can also use it as a base for self-driving in Kruger. Rates include half board. $\overline{\underline{\$\$}}$

Numbi Caravan Park Main Rd ☎013 737 7301/2, ⓦhotelnumbi.co.za. Secure and attractive campsite, conveniently located in the heart of town. It can get busy during local school holidays but tends to be very tranquil at other times. $\overline{\underline{\$}}$

Perry's Bridge Hollow Perry's Bridge, R40 ☎013 737 7752, ⓦperrysbridgehollow.co.za. Convenient, comfortable and stylish boutique hotel set in wooded grounds immediately behind Perry's Bridge Trading Post. The spacious air-conditioned rooms come with indoor and outdoor showers, and there's a swimming pool to boot. $\overline{\underline{\$\$\$}}$

Rissington Inn 2km south of town, just off the R40 ☎013 737 7700 or ☎082 327 6842, ⓦrissington.co.za. Relaxed, well run and informal, this large thatched homestead has fourteen rooms. The best are the garden suites, which have roofless outside showers, so you feel as if you are in a bush-lodge. There's also a swimming pool, a bar and a good restaurant. $\overline{\underline{\$\$}}$

EATING AND DRINKING

Hippo Hollow Restaurant Hippo Hollow Country Estate, Perry's Bridge Centre ☎013 737 7752 or ☎072 752 0952. Enjoy a sundowner, or a meal using local seasonal food, on the expansive deck overlooking the Sabie River, while watching birds, elephants and hippos. Daily 6.30–10pm.

Kuka Cafe Perry's Bridge Centre ☎013 737 6957, ⓦkukasoup.co.za. Smart Afro-chic restaurant and cocktail bar with colourful, modern decor and indoor and outdoor seating. As well as meat and game dishes, such as kudu, there are also decent salads. Daily 7am–10pm.

Shangana Cultural Village 4km out of town on the R535 to Graskop ☎013 737 5804 or ☎086 653 3452, ⓦshangana.co.za. Delicious African dinners cooked in massive pots over an open fire. The menu might include crocodile in spicy peanut sauce and beef and honey-glazed sweet potato, but vegetarians are also well catered for. You

2

2

ACTIVITIES IN AND AROUND HOEDSPRUIT

Hot-air ballooning is a fabulous way to appreciate the surrounding landscape, and recommended flights are offered by Sun Catchers, based near Hoedspruit (☎ 087 806 2079 or 082 572 2223, ✆ suncatchers.co.za; R4050). Conditions have to be perfect, and flights are generally very early in the morning when the weather is at its most stable. They leave from different locations depending on the weather – you'll be advised in good time where to meet your flight, and when to set your alarm clock!

Horseriding is on offer in Hoedspruit itself, at the Hoedspruit Wildlife Estate, where both beginners and experienced riders can view the reserve's game – zebra, giraffe and antelope, among others. Book through African Dream Horse Safaris (☎ 084 582 5442, ✆ africandreamhorsesafari.co.za).

For experienced riders, Wait a Little Safaris (☎ 083 273 9788, ✆ waitalittle.co.za) offers the unforgettable experience of horseriding through big game country. Running from their base in the Karongwe Nature Reserve, 70km north of Hoedspruit, their **Big Five horseriding safaris** range from six to ten days, on highly disciplined horses, with first-class accommodation and food; the trails also venture into Makali Reserve, dependent on date and package. Prices start at R30,000 per person.

eat in huts and are served by women from the household. The meals form the climax of a village tour and an energetic display of dancing, all of which is included in the price; a minimum of fifteen people is required. Booking essential. Daily 5pm.

Summerfields River Café 4.5km out of town on the R536 Sabie Rd ☎ 013 737 6500, ✆ summerfields.co.za.

Beauty, harmony and healthy living are offered at this award-winning spa and restaurant on a rose farm. Breakfast and light lunches are served outdoors on a wooden deck next to the Sabie River, with fresh organic vegetables and salads grown on the property. Daily 8am–11am, noon–3pm & 6.30–9pm.

Orpen Gate

After Hazyview, the R40 passes through Bushbuckridge – although any bushbucks that might once have wandered here have long since been eaten and displaced by cattle and goats. People live crammed in at a density six times greater than the provincial average, a leftover from apartheid land divisions. Forty-five kilometres east from here lies **Orpen Gate**, and the road heading east to Satara into the centre of the Park. Orpen is also the access point for the Manyeleti and Timbavati private game reserves.

ACCOMMODATION   ORPEN GATE

Timbavati Safari Lodge Orpen Gate Rd, 20km from Orpen Gate ☎ 015 793 0415, ✆ timbavatisafarilodge. com. The pick of the places to stay in the vicinity, with space for couples or large groups in thatched Ndebele-styled huts, plus a pool, bar and pleasant outdoor dining with wholesome, hearty dinners under the stars. It has an established feel with well-tended grounds full of trees and tropical vegetation, and a lawn kept cropped by resident warthogs. The lodge has traversing rights into Manyeleti for their own game drives; these are rich in game with very few vehicles around to share the sightings, and thus superior in many ways to going into Kruger itself. The good value for money makes it a popular base for self-drives into Kruger; prices include half-board. The visits into the traditional African village across the road are also worthwhile. 💲💲

Hoedspruit

Lurking in the undulating lowveld, 160km north of Mbombela, with the hazy blue mountains of the Escarpment visible on the distant horizon, is the small but busy service centre of **HOEDSPRUIT** ("hood-sprait"). The town lies at the heart of a concentration of **private game reserves** and lodges, and is a good base for specialist **activities**, such as horseriding, rafting on the Blyde River, visiting animal rehabilitation centres and lazy hot-air ballooning over the bush. Hoedspruit is a significant arrival point for air travellers heading to Kruger and the nearby private reserves, which include Timbavati, Manyeleti and Balule.

Moholoholo Wildlife Rehabilitation Centre

17km from Hoedspruit, on the R531 between the R40 and R527, about 3km from the tarred turn-off to the Blydepoort Dam • **Tours** Mon–Sat 9.30am & 3pm, and during school holidays Sun at 3pm • R170 • Booking essential • ☎ 015 795 5236, ⓦ moholoholo.co.za

At the **Moholoholo Wildlife Rehabilitation Centre**, ex-ranger Brian Jones has embarked on an individual crusade to rescue and rehabilitate injured and abandoned animals, notably raptors, but also lions, leopards and others. Tours are informative and you get to see a lot of endangered animals close up. The centre is part of a wider reserve and both night drives and early-morning walks are offered, and there is also accommodation (see below).

2

ARRIVAL, DEPARTURE AND TOURS   HOEDSPRUIT

By plane Hoedspruit Airport (formerly Eastgate Airport; ☎ 015 793-3681, ⓦ eastgateairport.co.za), 14km south of town, is served by two or three daily flights from Johannesburg and a few flights from Cape Town every week; both routes are run by South African Airlink (☎ 011 451 7300, ⓦ flyairlink.com) and ticket prices are expensive. Car rental is available at the airport through Avis (☎ 015 793 2014, ⓦ avis.co.za). For transfers to game lodges from the airport, contact Eastgate Safaris (☎ 015 793 3678 or 082 774 9544, ⓦ eastgatesafaris.co.za), though most lodges send their own vehicles to meet guests.

By shuttle Ashton's Tours and Safaris (☎ 021 683 0234, ⓦ ashtonstours.com) runs a daily shuttle (R985) from Johannesburg OR Tambo Airport (6.45am daily) to Hoedspruit, and will pick up within a 5km radius of OR Tambo. It drops off in town, at the airport, or at your safari lodge; the journey takes just under six hours.

Tours Eastgate Safaris (☎ 015 793 3678 or 082 774 9544, ⓦ eastgatesafaris.co.za) offers a number of tours in the area, including a full-day game drive in Kruger National Park (from R1805 per person for min 2 people, depending on pick-up point; the more people in the group the less the cost).

ACCOMMODATION

★ **Blue Cottages** 27km from Hoedspruit on the R527 ☎ 084 250 1233, ⓦ bluecottages.co.za. Comfortable suites in a farmhouse filled with African artefacts and fabrics, set in an enticingly cool and colourful tropical garden; more modest, but also lovely, are the garden cottages. You can have dinner served in the garden or on the veranda, if you book in advance, and the adjacent *Mad Dogz Café* is open for light meals from 7.30am–4.30pm daily. ⎎

Marepe Country Lodge Orpen Rd, on the R531 ☎ 072 520 9636, ⓦ marepecountrylodge.co.za. B&B accommodation in chalets and hotel-style rooms in a peaceful garden setting, with swimming pool. Birdwatchers will love it here, as they offer several birding tours. There is also a licensed restaurant and bar. ⎎

Moholoholo Forest Camp 26km from Hoedspruit, on the R531 ☎ 013 795 5236, ⓦ moholoholo.co.za. In the foothills of the Drakensberg Escarpment, this is an unshowy safari camp with plenty of game on the property. The price includes meals, a night drive, morning walk and a tour to the nearby wildlife rehabilitation centre. ⎎⎎⎎

Phalaborwa

PHALABORWA ("pal-a-bore-wa"), 75km north of Hoedspruit, gives access to the central and northern part of Kruger Park. The name Phalaborwa means "better than the south", a cheeky sobriquet coined as the town developed on the back of its extensive mineral wealth. During the 1960s, the borders of the park near Phalaborwa suddenly developed a kink, and large copper deposits were found, miraculously, just outside the protected national park area. Mining actually began at Phalaborwa some time after 200 AD, and the **Masorini Heritage Site**, close to Phalaborwa Gate, is a reconstruction of an iron-smelting village.

ARRIVAL AND DEPARTURE   PHALABORWA

By plane SA Airlink (☎ 015 781 5823, ⓦ flyairlink. com) flights arrive daily from Johannesburg (1hr) at Phalaborwa's Hendrik Van Eck Airport, a 5min drive from Kruger's Phalaborwa Gate, off President Steyn St, and virtually in the town itself. Unfortunately, this is one of the most expensive flights in the country. There are a number of car rental firms represented at the airport, including Avis (☎ 015 781 3169); alternatively, arrange for your accommodation to pick you up.

By bus There are seven bus schedules running daily from Johannesburg to Phalaborwa (ⓦ busticket.co.za); the journey takes about 6hr.

2

ACTIVITIES AROUND PHALABORWA

Keen **golfers** shouldn't miss the chance of a round at the signposted *Hans Merensky Hotel & Spa* (see page 104), where it's not unusual to see giraffes and elephants sauntering across the fairways, built over a vast area of indigenous bush (18 holes; hotel guest R150, day-visitor R400).

You can whet your appetite before heading into Kruger Park with a 3hr **boat trip** with Kambaku Olifants River Safaris (booking essential; ☎082 889 4797 or 082 889 4845, ⓦolifantsriversafaris.co.za), on the Olifants River, frequently encountering game – including elephants – and guaranteeing sightings of crocs and hippos (R350, 8–11am or 3–5.45pm).

INFORMATION

Tourist information Sure Turnkey Travel, 73a Sealene St (Mon–Fri 8am–5pm; ☎015 781 7760, ⓦphalaborwa. co.za), can make bookings for Kruger and help with accommodation and car rental.

ACCOMMODATION

Bushveld Terrace 2 Hendrik Van Eck St ☎015 781 3447, ⓦbushveldterrace.co.za. Enjoy a luxury hotel room with patio and bush or pool view, or one of the elegantly furnished rooms in the guesthouse, some with their own bush view. There is also a swimming pool and a good restaurant. ₅₅
Elephant Walk 30 Anna Scheepers St ☎015 781 5860 or ☎082 495 0575, ⓦelephantwalkguesthouse.co.za. A small and friendly guesthouse and backpackers in a pleasant suburban home with a large garden, 2km from the Kruger Gate, with camping facilities and budget tours into the park, plus a booking service for Phalaborwa/Kruger activities. Besides dorms and twins, they have four en-suite garden rooms, and a swimming pool in the garden. ₅
Hans Merensky Hotel & Spa Copper Road ☎015 781 3931/7, ⓦhansmerensky.com. This is the largest and

most luxurious hotel in Phalaborwa, boasting 166 rooms and suites, with a wonderful location on a golf estate interspersed with indigenous bush – great for birding and also frequently visited by wildlife from the neighbouring Kruger Park. Check the website for low-season bargains. There are three restaurants on site offering a breakfast buffet, light lunches and dinner. ₅₅
Kaia Tani Guest House 29 Boekenhout St ☎015 781 1358, ⓦkaiatani.com. Almost at the gate into Kruger, this upmarket and comfortable B&B guesthouse is run by an energetic Italian couple, Paolo and Barbra, who can meet you at the airport. There is a lounge with library, a bar overlooking a rock swimming pool, a tropical garden, and lunch or dinner from the kitchen can be ordered too – a mixture of Mediterranean and African dishes. ₅₅

EATING AND DRINKING

Buffalo Pub & Grill 1 Raasblaar Ave ☎015 781 0829. Meat lovers will love this place. The house speciality, Eisbein, is especially good – smoked pork shank slow cooked with an apricot and parsley glaze (R120). Mon–Sat 11am–11pm, Sun 11am–8pm.

Bushveld Terrace Restaurant 2 Hendrik Van Eck St ☎015 781 3447, ⓦbushveldterrace.co.za. Excellent, if expensive, food in an atmospheric garden setting; try the tasty chicken and prawn pasta. Mon–Sat 11am–11pm.

Kruger National Park

KRUGER NATIONAL PARK is the emblem of the South African safari industry, and together with the private reserves that open onto its western border, it best delivers what most visitors to Africa come to see – scores of elephants, lions, giraffes, rhinos and other magnificent wild animals roaming the savannah. A narrow leg of land hugging the Mozambique border, the 19,500-square-kilometre park is nowhere more than 85km in width, but from north to south it is an astonishing 414km drive from Pafuri Gate, close to the Zimbabwe border, to Malelane Gate near Mbombela, all of it along tar, with many well-kept gravel roads looping off to provide routes for game drives. Visiting Kruger (see page 105) invariably means choosing between self-driving (staying either in the park itself, or in one of the nearby towns), an organized safari tour, or staying on an exclusive private reserve or concession lodge. How you experience the park will largely depend on your budget – the cost of accommodation

VISITING KRUGER NATIONAL PARK

Kruger National Park, stretching for 350km along the border with Mozambique, remains South Africa's biggest wildlife draw. The park is run by the South African National Parks (SANParks; ⓦsanparks.org), while on its western flank, thousands of square kilometres of land are divided into privately administered farms and reserves, known as Greater Kruger. As far as wildlife is concerned, the private and public areas are joined in an enormous, seamless whole. How you experience the park – or Greater Kruger – depends to a large extent on what you can afford; at the top end, expect exclusivity and a greater sense of the wilderness, while those on a tight budget may want to consider either a self-drive visit or an organized tour. Whatever you choose, don't get too obsessed with seeing the **Big Five** – wildlife-viewing always involves an element of luck, and the very experience of being in Kruger is undeniably exciting in itself.

GETTING TO THE PARK

Johannesburg has the best transport connections to Kruger, with regular flights and buses, as well as organized tours. It is also the best major entry point, if you're planning on driving yourself. If visiting from **Cape Town**, your best option is to fly the two-thousand-odd kilometres to get here – though prices are high as only one airline (SAA; ⓦflysaa.com) offers (daily) flights. A cheaper option is to take a budget flight from Cape Town to Johannesburg, rent a car from OR Tambo Airport and head straight off east to the park. Mbombela, the modern capital of Mpumalanga, boasts the best transport connections in the region, and makes a good jumping-off point for the southern section of the park; flights arrive into Kruger Mpumalanga International (KMI), 20km north of the town.

The other airports serving the park are at Hoedspruit, Phalaborwa and Skukuza, all with expensive daily flights to and from Johannesburg (SA Airlink; ⓦflyairlink.com) and all with car rental facilities. You might choose one of these airports if it is closest to the section of the park you wish to explore.

BUDGET AND MID-RANGE OPTIONS

Kruger is designed for **self-driving** and **self-catering**; if you're travelling with young children, on a budget, or want to manage your own time, this is likely to be the best way of seeing the park's animals. There are restaurants and shops at all the main camps, and the roads are a mix of tar and dirt, making it possible to explore the whole of Kruger in a normal car. The park's popularity does mean that you are likely to share major animal sightings with several other motorists, some of whom may behave badly – hogging the sighting, for instance, or making noises to frighten the animals. A number of game drives are run by the park, operating out of each camp, which offer a greater chance of spotting the more elusive animals. On the plus side, it is very exciting when you are able to find animals yourself and watch them at your leisure. It's also possible to explore Kruger on a walking safari (see page 108).

Accommodation in the park can be over-subscribed, and you may want to consider staying in nearby Hazyview or close to an entry gate, where there are well-priced accommodation options, and then either driving into Kruger each day, or taking one of the organized game-drives. Another option is to stay in a backpackers' lodge in Mbombela, Hazyview or Phalaborwa, all of which offer their own trips into the park; alternatively, you can take a three-to-four-day trip with a tour operator from Johannesburg (see page 109).

LUXURY OPTIONS

With more to spend, the conventional choice is one of the private reserves in Greater Kruger (and it's worth noting that some are more reasonably priced than others). The three major private reserves are **Sabi Sand** to the south (see page 126), and **Timbavati** and **Manyeleti**, both of which adjoin the central section of the national park (see page 130). Another option within Kruger itself is one of several private concessions that are now leased by SANParks to a single concessionaire. With no tarred roads, and no self-driving, the private reserves and concessions offer a much greater sense of the wilderness, and you can be assured that you won't be sharing your sightings with a bunch of other cars. Accommodation is often in very romantic rooms or luxury "tents", overlooking the savannah or a river, and you'll be taken out on guided game drives in comfortable, open-topped 4WDs, with plenty of information and photo opportunities provided. Several luxury camps cater for children, offering special kids' safaris and activities. Others don't, on the basis that they can be intrusive to other guests.

2

is extremely wide-ranging – but regardless of whether you are roughing it on a backpacker tour, or in your own luxury riverside suite, your experience of Kruger, and its animals, is bound to be highly memorable.

Brief history

People have lived in and around the Kruger National Park for hundreds of thousands of years. **San hunter-gatherers** left their mark in the form of paintings and engravings at 170 sites so far discovered, the most accessible of which can be seen at the hippo pool near Crocodile Bridge gate. There is more recent evidence of farming cultures at many places in the park. Around 1000–1300 AD, centrally organized states were building stone palaces and engaging in trade that brought Chinese porcelain, jewellery and cloth into the area. The most impressive of these, overlooking the Luvuvhu River in the far north, is the **Thulamela Heritage Site**, a 16th-century stone-walled town built by the same civilization responsible for the construction of Great Zimbabwe after that larger city was abandoned.

It was the arrival of white **fortune-seekers** in the second half of the nineteenth century that made the greatest impact on the region. African farmers were kicked off their traditional lands in the early twentieth century to create the park, and hunters and poachers made their livelihoods here decimating game populations. Historical sites relating to early European explorers and Kruger's beginnings are dotted throughout the park, the most accessible being the **Albasini Ruins** (the remains of an 19th-century trading store built by its Portuguese namesake) near Phabeni Gate.

The Kruger National Park started life in 1898 as the 4600-square-kilometre Sabi Game Reserve, which was established by President **Paul Kruger** of the Zuid Afrikaansche Republiek to protect the depleted wildlife herds between the Sabi and Crocodile rivers (and included the part of present-day Kruger south of the Sabi River, as well as what is now the private Sabi Sand Game Reserve). Kruger figures as a shrewd, larger-than-life character in Afrikaner history, but while posterity credits him as having had the foresight to set aside land for wildlife conservation, it was actually **James Stevenson-Hamilton**, the first warden of the national park, who cunningly put forward Kruger's name in order to soften up Afrikaner opposition to the park's creation. In fact, Stevenson-Hamilton knew that Kruger was no conservationist and was actually an inveterate hunter; Kruger "never in his life thought of animals except as biltong", he wrote in a private letter, and it was his tenacity rather than Kruger's that saved the animals that hadn't been shot.

In 1926, Sabi and the more northerly Singwidzi Game reserves were amalgamated and gazetted as a **national park**, predating the arrival of the first three tourist cars by just one year. The park was fenced in its entirety over 1959–60, partly to prevent the transmission of diseases between livestock and wildlife, and partly to curb poaching and demarcate the border with Mozambique. Kruger attained its present-day area of 19,500 square kilometres in 1969, with the addition of the 240-square-kilometre **Pafuri Triangle**, bounded by the Luvuvhu and Limpopo rivers along the northern boundary with Zimbabwe. In keeping with the apartheid ethos of the day, the Makuleke inhabitants of the Pafuri Triangle were forcibly relocated, an injustice rectified in the 1990s when a successful land claim restored the land to its former occupants (it now forms the Makuleke Contractual Park, which is managed as part of Kruger, but hosts two private lodges on land leased from the community).

In the early 1990s, the park's effective area was further increased by dropping fences with neighbouring private conservancies such as Sabi Sand and Timbavati. In 2001, a **memorandum of understanding** was signed amalgamating Kruger with two other national parks – Gonarezhou in Zimbabwe and Limpopo in Mozambique – to form the 35,000-square-kilometre **Great Limpopo Transfrontier Park**. Two decades later, this cross-border park is still something of a work in progress, and while boundary fences have not been formally dropped, they are no longer maintained, creating more and more gaps that allow elephants and other animals to follow ancient migration routes into Mozambique. Two other important post-millennial developments have been the creation of nine concessions that function much like private reserves within the park, and the opening of two border posts linking Kruger to Mozambique's Limpopo National Park, one right at the north of the park at Pafuri near *Punda Maria Camp*, the other at Giriyondo, between *Letaba* and *Mopani* camps.

Flora and fauna

Kruger's rich mosaic of habitats encompasses mixed acacia woodland in the southwest, rocky hills in the east, open savannah in the central region, and mopane woodland in the north. Common among the three-hundred-plus **tree** species are the baobab, cluster fig, knob-thorn, Natal mahogany, monkey orange, raisin bush, tamboti, coral tree, fever tree, jackal-berry, lead-wood, marula, mopani, ilala palm and sausage tree.

Kruger is home to all the **Big Five**, and despite a high incidence of rhino poaching in recent years, it is the only African reserve of comparable size to host viable populations of all the members of this eagerly sought quintet. The most recent figures suggest the Greater Kruger supports stable populations of at least 2000 lions and 1000 leopards, while buffalo numbers have increased from 22,000 to 45,000 since the turn of the millennium, and the elephant population has soared from 8500 to more than 20,000 over the same period. White rhino, once very rare in the park, numbered around 12,000 in 2009, a figure that then represented at least half the global total. Unfortunately, a post-2009 escalation in poaching has resulted in an average loss of around 500 individual white rhinos in more recent years, though it is unclear to what extent this has been offset by fresh births (the natural annual birth rate of eight percent would theoretically mean around 1000 newborns per year in a population of that size) and/or exacerbated by the crippling drought of 2016. Kruger also supports an estimated population of 600-plus Critically Endangered black rhino, probably the largest in any one conservation area; these beasts have reputedly been less affected by poaching, since it tends to be the more secretive and aggressive of the two species.

Other large **carnivores** are well represented. Spotted hyena number 2–3000, cheetah 150–200 and African wild dog around 350. Of at least twenty further species of smaller carnivore, black-backed jackal are the most conspicuous by day, followed by slender, banded and dwarf mongoose, while the likes of small-spotted genet, large-spotted genet, African civet, white-tailed mongoose and more unusually honey-badger, serval, caracal and African wild cat are most likely to be seen or heard on guided night drives. Other conspicuous mammals, with estimated populations given where known, are as follows: impala (125,000), Burchell's zebra (20,000), blue wildebeest (10,000), greater kudu (8000), hippopotamus (7000), waterbuck (5000), warthog (3000), bushbuck, common reedbuck, steenbok, klipspringer, vervet monkey and chacma baboon.

Keep your eyes open and you'll also see a variety of **reptiles**, **amphibians** and **insects** – most rewardingly in the grounds of the restcamps themselves: there's always something to see up in the trees, in the bushes or even inside your rondavel. The Nile crocodile is the most conspicuous of the park's 114 reptile species, but if you spot a miniature ET-like reptile crawling upside down on the ceiling, don't be tempted to kill it; it's an insect-eating gecko and is doing you a good turn. The park's 34 amphibian species are seldom seen, but the ethereal communal calls of the bubbling kassina and other tree-frogs often provide a haunting aural backdrop to dusk waterhole vigils. In addition, 49 fish species have been recorded, and a cast of many thousand invertebrates includes dung beetles, which are often seen rolling balls of elephant dung along the road, and spectacular golden orb spiders perched in the centre of their giant webs. Those with

2

BUSH WALKS, GAME DRIVES AND WALKING TRAILS

Whether you're staying in Kruger or not, you can still join one of the sunrise, sunset or night **game drives** organized by the park (R258–429). These drives are one of the cheapest ways of accessing the park, but the viewing is good because of the height of the open vehicles. The drives leave from every camp in the park (book at reception or, even better, when you make your reservation) and, for those staying outside the park, from these entrance gates: Crocodile Bridge (☎013 735 6012), Malelane (☎013 735 6152), Numbi (☎013 735 5133), Paul Kruger (☎013 735 5107), Phabeni (☎013 735 5890) and Phalaborwa (☎013 735 3457).

For those staying inside the park, three-hour **game walks** (R570) are conducted every morning at dawn from each camp. Groups are restricted to eight people, so it's worth booking beforehand. Kruger also runs several three-night **wilderness trails** in different parts of the park. Undertaken with the guidance of an experienced ranger, these trails pass through landscapes of notable beauty with diverse plant and animal life. They don't bring you any nearer to game than driving, and are really about getting closer to the vegetation and smaller creatures. Groups are limited to eight people staying in the same camp, comprising four rustic, two-bed huts, served by reed-walled showers and flush toilets; simple meals are provided. You walk for five hours in the morning, return to camp for lunch and a siesta, and go walking again for an hour or two in the evening, returning to sit around a campfire. The trails are heavily subscribed; you can **book** up to eleven months in advance through SANParks (✉specialisedreservations@sanparks.org). The cost is around R5000 per person, including accommodation and meals.

In addition, there are three **backpacking trails** where you carry your own stuff on a guided, three-night walk (R2724–3128): the Olifants River Trail, following the course of the Olifants River; the Lonely Bull Trail, which leaves from Mopani; and the Mphongolo Trail, leaving from Shingwedzi. These trails offer one of the ultimate adventure wildlife experiences in Africa – sleeping out in the wild every night with no facilities.

More expensive, and easier to get a booking on, are two- or three-night walking safaris in a magnificently wild concession near Skukuza, run by Rhino Post Walking Safaris (three nights R18,760; ☺rws.co.za) with Plains Camp as its base (see page 116). These have the option of a sleep-out in a treehouse, where you spend the night cosily bedded on an elevated platform, from where you're able to see the stars and hear the sometimes chilling sounds of the night.

There are also a number of cheaper walking trails within Greater Kruger, accessed from Hoedspruit and with organized departures from Johannesburg. Transfrontiers (☎015 793 0719, ☺transfrontiers.com) offers two- to four-night walking safaris using a camp in Balule, where the Big Five roam; accommodation is in safari tents or chalets. Another recommended operator is Africa on Foot (☎021 712 5284, ☺africaonfoot.com), which runs a combination of walking and driving trails in the Klaserie area, adjoining the Timbavati Reserve (R3900 per person per night). This area is wild and lovely, and their safari camp very pleasant; you walk for two to four hours in the morning, and enjoy game drives in the afternoons and evenings – the combination of safaris should allow you to see more game.

a horror of all things creepy and crawly might want to stay away from Kruger in the rainy season (Nov–March), when insects, frogs and reptile are most active.

A staggering checklist of 517 **bird species** includes several large raptors and ground birds that are now rare outside of protected areas, for instance the lanky-limbed ostrich and macabre marabou stork, and the so-called **avian "Big Six"** of saddle-billed stork, Kori bustard, martial eagle, lappet-faced vulture, Pel's fishing owl and southern ground hornbill. You don't need to be a twitcher to appreciate some of Kruger's more colourful and conspicuous birds. The spectacular lilac-breasted roller is often seen perching openly on isolated trees, while the stunning white-fronted bee-eater, joined in the southern summer by the equally striking carmine and European bee-eaters, is often seen close to the riverbanks where it breeds communally. SANParks has a good birding page overviewing the different areas and species with details of bird hides (☺sanparks. org/groups/birders/accounts.php).

Many species are widely distributed in Kruger, but others are restricted to particular areas or niche habitats. Oribi and sable antelope, for instance, are most common in the southwest, while Sharpe's grysbok and roan antelope favour the drier mopane woodland around Letaba. The hilly country around Olifants is a good place to look for rock hyrax, klipspringer and mocking cliff-chat, while blue wildebeest and zebra are seasonally abundant in the central grasslands around Satara, also the main prowling ground for the park's small population of cheetah. Aquatic habitats form an important niche in this generally dry environment, being strongly associated with the likes of hippo, crocodile, many dozens of bird species, and to a lesser extent waterbuck and elephant. The riparian woodland that follows the series of major rivers that flows eastward though the park en route to the Indian Ocean (from south to north, the Crocodile, Sabie, Olifants, Letaba, Shingwedzi, Luvuvhu and Limpopo) is the main habitat for several striking bird species, ranging from Narina trogon, purple-crested turaco and green pigeon to African harrier-hawk, crowned eagle and crested guineafowl. Biodiversity peaks along the northerly Luvuvhu and Limpopo, which is the main stronghold for the likes of samango monkey and nyala.

2

ESSENTIALS
KRUGER NATIONAL PARK

Opening hours Daily: April, Aug & Sept 6am–6pm; May–July 6am–5.30pm; Oct & March 5.30am–6pm; Nov–Feb 5.30am–6.30pm.
Entry fee R372 per day (SA residents R93).
Internet Available at *Berg-en-Dal* and *Skukuza*. For those with a local SIM card and data bundle, there is also mobile reception at all restcamps and at many places in between.
Petrol stations At all main restcamps (petrol and diesel); legitimate petrol/fuel/garage cards are accepted, as are Visa, Mastercard and cash.

ARRIVAL AND DEPARTURE

Johannesburg is the city with the best connections to Kruger, by both land and air. An easy option if you are flying in or out of Johannesburg is to see the park as part of a tour that starts and ends in the city (see box below). Alternatively, rent a car at OR Tambo for the easy five-hour drive to the park; the airport is on the N12 motorway, which merges with the N4 to Kruger near Emalahleni (formerly Witbank).

KRUGER TOUR OPERATORS

There are many **tours** to Kruger, several of which depart from Johannesburg. Prices given below are per person unless otherwise noted, and most include park entry fees, meals and transport to and from Johannesburg. Backpacker hostels in Mbombela, Hazyview and Phalaborwa also run tours into Kruger at reasonable prices. In addition, in the Mbombela and Hazyview area are some excellent tour guides who will take you into the park or organize trips in Mpumalanga. When choosing a tour from Johannesburg, a minimum of three nights (ideally four) is advisable to allow for the long journey time (six to seven hours to get from Joburg into the park), more opportunities to view game, and more drives.

★ **Nguni Africa** ☎ 082 221 4177, ⓦ nguniafrica. co.za. An extremely knowledgeable and personable guide, Andrew Hall is based in Mbombela and can put together a package for you to see Kruger – and beyond if necessary. He has a great passion for the lowveld, where his ancestors were pioneers, and runs trips into the park in a Land Rover, where you'll be assured of spotting plenty of game, even on a day-trip (from around R7000 including meals and fees); the exclusivity of the experience, rather than being in a vehicle with several strangers, is an attractive bonus. He also offers airport or lodge transfers.
Outlook African Wildlife Safaris ☎ 079 473 2443, ⓦ outlook.co.za. Outlook has a number of options departing from Joburg, where they have a nice guesthouse not far from the airport that's ideal for before and after your safari. Options range from two to six days in duration and include camping, staying in budget huts or using superior air-conditioned chalets. To give an idea of prices, you're looking at R2300 per person for a two-day camping safari to R17,700 for a six-night safari using chalets.
Viva Safaris ☎ 071 842 5547, ⓦ vivasafaris.com. Departing from Joburg, and geared towards a price-conscious market, Viva's trips offer all you might want from a Kruger experience (and include a stop at Blyde River Canyon, too). There are 27 different packages to choose from, ranging from a cost-effective two-night lodge/tent safari to a combined Kruger Park and private reserve safari. Rates start at around R7000 for a three-day camping safari.

2

TOP 5 ACTIVITIES

Kruger has, unsurprisingly, an abundance of activities that will make your time in the park memorable. Here's our pick of the very best on offer.

Rhino gazing at Pretoriuskop Boasting the park's densest population of both white and black rhinos, the roads around this restcamp are a particularly good place to seek out these prehistoric-looking creatures. See page 115

Rhino Post Walking Safaris Head out into the wild on foot on a two- or three-day walking safari, with the option of sleeping in a treehouse. See page 108

Wildlife viewing at Sunset Dam, Lower Sabie Get close to the water for some prime hippo and crocodile spotting – great at any time of the day. See page 113

Birdwatching at Pafuri picnic site Northern Kruger at its best, with massive thorn trees and the Luvuvhu River making this the park's top birding spot. See page 122

Leopard-spotting in Sabi Sand Undoubtedly one of the best places in the world to see leopards in the wild, helpfully close to the well-connected town of Mbombela. See page 126

By plane The four local airports servicing Kruger are KMIA (see page 98) for the southern section; Skukuza (see below) in the park itself; Hoedspruit (see page 103) for the central and northern sections; and Phalaborwa (see page 103) for the northern section. Car rental is available at each airport, or you will be picked up by your safari lodge. Unfortunately, flights to airports near Kruger are pricey; all are operated by SA Airlink (⊕ flyairlink.com), SA Express (⊕ flyexpress.aero) or CemAir (⊕ flycemair.co.za)

By bus Regular buses service Mbombela, Hoedspruit and Phalaborwa from Johannesburg; from these towns, you can book on one of the many Kruger tours on offer at the backpacker lodges: the *Old Vic Inn* and *Funky Monkeys* in Mbombela and *Elephant Walk* in Phalaborwa can arrange tours.

DRIVING IN KRUGER

When driving, only approved roads should be used; don't drive on unmarked roads and never drive off-road. In heavy rainfall some roads become unusable; check ⊕ sanparks. org/parks/kruger for the latest information. Do buy a Kruger map showing all the marked roads. Roads have numbers rather than names; some are tarred, some are dirt. Speed limits are 50km/hr on tar, 40km/hr on untarred roads and 20km/hr in restcamps; speed traps operate in some parts of the park. Never leave your car (it's illegal and dangerous), except at designated sites. If you're trying to get from one part of the park to another, note that although it's far more fun driving inside, the **speed limit** makes it a slow journey – the rule of thumb is to estimate that you will be driving at 25km/h between camps – and you're bound to make frequent stops to watch animals. Bicycles and motorbikes are not allowed.

CHOOSING YOUR ROUTE

In terms of geography and travel logistics, the **public part** of Kruger can be subdivided into three rough sections – Southern, Central and Northern Kruger – which safari snobs

sometimes refer to respectively to as "the circus", "the zoo" and "the wilderness". The first two of these sobriquets are less than insightful, given that wildlife actually roams freely throughout the 20,000-plus square kilometres protected within the Kruger and neighbouring private reserves. What they do reflect, however, is that tourist development and traffic are concentrated in the south and most sparse in the more remote north.

Bounded in the north by the perennial Sabie River, **Southern Kruger** is a roughly rectangular 3500-square-kilometre block of tangled acacia bush that protrudes westward from the rest of the park like a stumpy foot. When it comes to game viewing, the far south is the best bet for a short safari (say, up to three days), since it hosts the greatest densities and variety of wildlife. That said, because the south is the most accessible part of the park coming from Johannesburg, and the main focal point for day-visits from Mbombela and Hazyview, as well as hosting five of the park's dozen main restcamps (including *Skukuza*, the largest) and five of the nine entrance gates, tourist volumes can be offputtingly high, especially during local school holidays. Less clearly defined, **Central Kruger** is a 7000-square-kilometre tract of relatively open savannah bounded by the Sabie River in the south and the Letaba River in the north. It tends to be far quieter that the south in terms of tourist traffic, while game viewing can be excellent, with the plains around Satara being a hotspot for cheetah and lion, as well as seasonal aggregations of wildebeest and zebra; for those who can spare the time, it is well worth including a couple of nights here in any itinerary of longer than three days. Central Kruger is bisected by the magnificent Olifants River, which forms the boundary between Mpumalanga and Limpopo Province, and it hosts two of the most attractive camps in the park at *Olifants* and *Letaba*.

By far the largest of the park's three sectors, **Northern Kruger** extends across 10,000 square kilometres of dry and relatively featureless bush typified by relatively low game densities and even lower tourist volumes. The dominant cover in much of the north is monotypic mopani woodland, but this is alleviated by a trio of perennial rivers – the Shingwedzi, Luvuvhu and Limpopo, the latter flowing along the border with Zimbabwe – and their fringing ribbons of riparian forest. Worth considering only if you've a week or longer to dedicate to the park, the north is emphatically unsuited to those seeking a Big Five quick fix, but it is a favourite with unhurried repeat visitors thanks to its immersive untrammelled atmosphere. It also offers perhaps the best birding in the park, particularly along the rivers.

WHEN TO VISIT

Kruger is rewarding at any time of the year, though each season has its advantages and drawbacks. If you don't like the heat, avoid **high summer** (Dec–Feb), when temperatures are in the mid- to high thirties, with short thunder showers; a lot of the accommodation is air-conditioned, however. At this time of the year, everything becomes green, the grass is high, animals are born, and birds and insects are prolific. There's little rain during the **cooler winter** months of April to August; the vegetation withers over this period, making it easier to spot game. Although daytime temperatures rise to the mid-twenties (days are invariably bright and sunny throughout winter), the nights and early mornings can be very cold, especially in June and July, when you'll definitely need a very warm jacket and woolly hat. **September and October** are the peak months for wildlife viewing.

2

ACCOMMODATION

Most overnight visitors to Kruger stay at one of the twelve main **restcamps** operated within the park by SANParks. The restcamps are pleasant, but hardly wild, and could be compared to small villages, with the sounds of the African night tending to get drowned out by air-conditioning and the merriment of braais and beer. Nearly all the camps have swimming pools, electricity, petrol stations, shops (though they don't stock much in the way of fruit or vegetables), restaurants and laundrettes. Most also have walks around the edges, complete with labelled trees to help you identify what you see on drives, and plenty of birds and smaller creatures on display. Accommodation is typically in thatched rondavels, each with an outdoor eating area, facing communally towards each other rather than out towards the views. The best rondavels are on the camp perimeters or directly facing onto rivers. Most camps have furnished permanent safari tents and huts in configurations usually sleeping two to four people.

These are fully equipped, with shared communal kitchens and ablutions. Bungalows and cottages sleep up to six people and come in several variations, with fully equipped kitchens and bathrooms. Just about all restcamps have a campsite (with shared kitchen and washing facilities), which provides the park's cheapest accommodation, but the stands are generally very close together, and you may not get shade. Sites for caravans and camper vans are available wherever there's camping and often come with a power point.

For a more rustic experience, the main restcamps are supplemented by two inexpensive **satellite camps** and around half a dozen **small bushveld camps**. These generally offer accommodation of the same standard as the main restcamps, but accommodate fewer people, and dispense with shops and restaurants, allowing for a retreat away from day-to-day trivialities and the tourist pack. If you want to stay at a bushveld camp, book as early as possible,

GAME-VIEWING TIPS

• The **best times of day for game viewing** are when it's cooler, during the early morning and late afternoon. Set out as soon as the camp gates open in the morning and go out again as the temperature starts dropping in the afternoon. Take a siesta during the midday heat, just as the animals do, when they head for deep shade where you're less likely to see them.
• It's worth investing in a **detailed map book** of Kruger (available at every gate and restcamp) in order to choose a route that includes rivers or pans where you can stop and enjoy the scenery and birdlife while you wait for game to come down to drink, especially in the late afternoon.
• **Driving really slowly** pays off, particularly if you stop often, in which case switch off your engine, open your window and use your senses. Stopping where other cars have already stopped or slowed down is probably the best strategy you could choose.
• Don't embark on overambitious drives from your restcamp. **Plan carefully**. An average distance of around 20km per hour is realistic if you regularly stop to look at game.
• **Binoculars** are a must for scanning the horizon and identifying colourful small birds.
• **Take food and drink with you**, and remember you can only use toilets and get out at the picnic sites, where there's always boiling water available, braai places powered with gas, and, at some sites, food or snacks for sale.

as demand for the bush experiences they offer is pretty high. Note that the camps are out of bounds to anyone not booked in to stay. Most offer walks, night drives and hides. Kruger's restcamps and bushveld camps are administered by SANParks (☎ 012 428 9111 or ☎ 082 233 9111, ⊛ san parks.org/tourism/reservations) – **bookings** can only be made in advance online, by email or telephone. Advance bookings are a necessity – book as early as possible, especially for school holidays and weekends, and don't turn up without a booking and expect to find accommodation. Even with advance booking, anticipate that you will most likely have to take any camp that is available, as demand far outstrips supply. Booking opens eleven months in advance.

A more exclusive option within Kruger is the dozen or more **private lodges** that now operate within individual concessions – variable in size but typically at least 100 kilometres squared – where exclusive traversing rights have been granted to a single concessionaire. These concession lodges function much like the private reserves bordering Kruger, each hosting between one and three exclusive small camps that offer guests an upmarket package inclusive of meals, guided game drives in open 4WDs, and in some cases drinks. Guiding standards are comparable to private reserves such as Sabi Sand, but the concessions are typically much larger and wildlife is less habituated to vehicles, so while there is a lot less tourist traffic, game viewing tends to be more erratic than in the best private reserves.

Southern Kruger

Incorporating much of the original **Sabi Game Reserve** as it was delineated back in 1898, **Southern Kruger** is bounded to the south by the **Crocodile River** as it flows eastward from Mbombela to Komatipoort, and in the northeast by the **Sabie River** as it courses past Paul Kruger Gate, *Skukuza* and *Lower Sable* camps. It is the widest part of the national park, measuring between thirty and sixty kilometres from north to south, and up to 85km from east to west, and also the most topographically varied, with the Sabie and Crocodile floodplains dropping to elevations of below 200m towards the Mozambican border, while the hillier country of the west mostly stands above 500m and incorporates several isolated rocky peaks of which the 891m **Sithungwane Hill** near Pretoriuskop is the highest in the park. The south receives a relatively high **rainfall**, averaging well above 500mm per annum, and supports a varied vegetation dominated by dense acacia scrub and mopane woodland in the west, more open savannah in the east, and tall riparian woodland along the Sabie River.

Serviced by five large restcamps including village-like **Skukuza**, the far south is the busiest part of Kruger when it comes both to overnight guests and to day-trippers staying outside the park. Its popularity is partly due to the exceptional game viewing – this sector of the park undoubtedly offers the best chance of seeing all the **Big Five**, in particular leopard and rhino, in a limited time frame – but is also due to its relative proximity to Gauteng, which makes it very convenient for standalone safaris out of **Johannesburg** or **Pretoria**, or for longer organized tours heading on south to Eswatini or KwaZulu-Natal. The main surfaced roads through the south generally offer the best game viewing, but they also tend to carry the densest tourist traffic.

Indeed, at peak times of year the area buzzes with vehicles jostling to get close to anywhere that big cats are sighted – events which always seem to induce bad human behaviour. If the crowds start getting to you, you can usually escape the worst of it by exploring the region's extensive network of dirt backroads.

The main centre of activities in the south, only 12km west of Paul Kruger Gate, is *Skukuza*, which is the largest restcamp in Kruger, and also houses the **research and administrative headquarters**. Criticized in some circles for being too large and impersonal, *Skukuza* has in

SOUTHERN KRUGER AT A GLANCE

South Africa's best but busiest self-drive Big Five destination still has plenty of quieter roads where you can escape the crowds.

Big Five: ****
General wildlife: *****
Birding: ****
Scenery: **
Wilderness factor: ****
Uncrowded: **
Affordability: *****
Self-drive: Y

its favour an excellent bouquet of **facilities**, a memorable view over a stretch of the Sabie River regularly visited by thirsty wildlife, and large sprawling grounds that teem with birds and small mammals. Further in its favour, *Skukuza* lies at the junction of three of the park's most reliable game-viewing roads. The pick among these is **H4-1** to Lower Sabie, which passes through a fertile mosaic of tangled riverine forest and acacia savannah that offers a good chance of spotting buffalo, leopard or elephant, and is also known for its exceptional birdlife. The **H3** south to Malelane Gate is good for lion and white rhino, as is the **H1-2** via Elephant, Jones, Leeupan and Siloweni waterholes to Tshokwane, a lovely picnic spot where you can buy meals and enjoy the attention of the resident hornbills, starlings and other birds. Lake Panic, some 7km from *Skukuza* back towards Paul Kruger Gate, has one of the best bird hides in the park, and is a good place to look for osprey, African jacana, water thick-knee and various herons, kingfishers, ducks and geese, as well as hippos and crocodiles. The area around *Skukuza* is also one of the best places to see the endangered African wild dog; worth trying is the S114 between *Skukuza* and *Berg-en-Dal*, the S1 between Phabeni Gate and Skukuza, and the H11 between Paul Kruger Gate and *Skukuza*.

Set on the north bank of a dam on the Sabie River about 45km downstream of *Skukuza*, **Lower Sabie** is a relatively small restcamp that many long-time Kruger aficionados would nominate as their favourite place to stay in the park. Elephants and hippos are plentiful around Lower Sabie, and **Sunset Dam**, a kilometre or two outside camp, is exceptional for storks, kingfishers and other water-associated birds. As with *Skukuza*, *Lower Sabie* stands at the junction of three excellent game-viewing roads. There is no better place to look for rhinos than the surfaced **H4-2** and associated dirt roads (such as the S130) running south towards Crocodile Bridge, while the **H10** north to Tshokwane Picnic Site passes several dams where hippo, lion, cheetah, elephant and rhino are regular; on the return trip be sure to divert along the S29 to the lovely

2

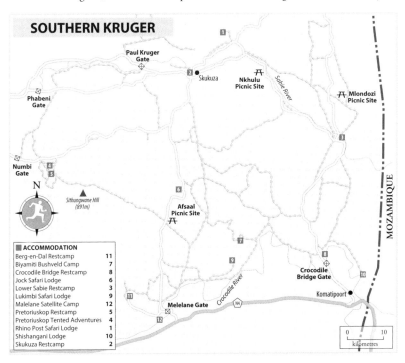

SOUTHERN KRUGER

Paul Kruger Gate

Skukuza

Nkhulu Picnic Site

Sabie River

Mlondozi Picnic Site

Phabeni Gate

Numbi Gate

N

Sithungwane Hill (891m)

Afsaal Picnic Site

MOZAMBIQUE

ACCOMMODATION	
Berg-en-Dal Restcamp	11
Biyamiti Bushveld Camp	7
Crocodile Bridge Restcamp	8
Jock Safari Lodge	6
Lower Sabie Restcamp	3
Lukimbi Safari Lodge	9
Malelane Satellite Camp	12
Pretoriuskop Restcamp	5
Pretoriuskop Tented Adventures	4
Rhino Post Safari Lodge	1
Shishangani Lodge	10
Skukuza Restcamp	2

Crocodile Bridge Gate

Komatipoort

Melelane Gate

Crocodile River

N4

0   10
kilometres

Mlondozi Picnic Spot, where a thatched lapa with some tree-shaded tables and chairs overlooks the eponymous dam. The **H4-1** to *Skukuza*, though often busy, frequently rewards with sightings of buffalo, lion and leopard, while a stop at the lushly wooded Nkhulu Picnic Site, set in riparian forest on the south bank of the Sabie River, often affords sightings of forest birds and is also a good place to look for the localized African finfoot and half-collared kingfisher.

Of the other southern camps, *Crocodile Bridge* is situated at an entrance gate, so it makes for a useful first stop if you expect to arrive late in the day. It is slightly on a limb when it comes to further exploration, though the surrounding area is known as one of the most reliable for white rhino sightings. If you're pushing north along the surfaced H4-2 north to Lower Sabie, it's worth taking the drive slowly, as this area, dotted with knob-thorn and marula trees, is known for its **herbivores**, which include giraffe, wildebeest, zebra and buffalo, as well as ostrich, warthog and the magnificent sable antelope. You should also keep your eyes peeled for predators such as lion, cheetah, hyena and jackal. The H4-2 can be combined with the more easterly S28 (Nhlowa Road), which passes through open plains inhabited by cheetah and lion, to make a great half-day loop out of the camp. Alternatively, try the dirt S25 east for elephant, rhino and buffalo, making sure to divert to the hippo pool and prehistoric rock on the Crocodile River upstream of the camp.

Venerable *Pretoriuskop*, the park's oldest (and most old-fashioned) camp, lies in a tract of thick acacia woodland that tends to offer erratic game-viewing, though the dirt H2-2 (Voortrekker Road) running east towards Afsaal Picnic Site probably offers the best chance of seeing the localized black rhino, eland and sable antelope. A decent focus for a day drive is **Transport Dam**, on the H1-1, a good place to see buffalo and elephant, and there's invariably other game to be found.

Further south, *Berg-en-Dal* is a likeable modern camp with superior accommodation and hilly well-wooded grounds overlooking a pretty dam. The focus of the camp is the Rhino Trail along the perimeter fence (with Braille facilities), meandering under riverine trees along the Matjulu Dam, where there are resident crocodiles and nesting fish eagles. Game includes white rhino, leopard and lion, and plenty of kudu. Some say this is the best camp from which to set out on a guided **morning walk** because of the likelihood of encountering white rhino, and the pretty scenery. Afsaal, one of the park's nicest picnic sites, stands alongside the H3 between *Berg-en-Dal* and *Skukuza*, and forms a good focus for a day drive from either camp. Once there, look out for the African scops owl, which sleeps in a tamboti tree nearly every day – the tree is marked so that you can try to spot the camouflaged bird. There's a shop on-site.

ACCOMMODATION
SOUTHERN KRUGER, SEE MAP PAGE 113

Apart from containing some of the largest **restcamps** and best places for seeing large quantities of game, Southern Kruger is also easily reached from Johannesburg along the N4. All Kruger's restcamps and bushveld camps must be booked in advance with SANParks (☎012 428 9111 or 082 233 9111, Mon–Fri 7.30am–5pm, Sat 8am–3pm, ⓦsanparks.org/parks/kruger). **Private concession lodges** can be booked through the concessionaire, as detailed under the individual listing.

RESTCAMPS

Berg-en-Dal In the southwest corner of the park, 12km northwest of Malelane Gate ☎013 735 6106/7. Attractively set among koppies in a shallow grassy basin, *Berg-en-Dal* overlooks the Matjulu stream and dam, and has modern, fully equipped bungalows sleeping three

people, or family cottages sleeping six, all landscaped among indigenous bushveld vegetation and widely spaced to provide privacy. Facilities include a beautifully positioned swimming pool, a shop with a good range of food, restaurants, a petrol station and a laundry. The area is known for rhinos. Camping $̄, bungalows and cottages $$–$$$

Crocodile Bridge 12km north of Komatipoort on N4 ☎013 735 6012. Positioned at the park's southeastern boundary, this is the least visually impressive of Kruger's restcamps, overlooking sugar-cane farms that do nothing to enhance the bush experience, but there is a high density of general game in the vicinity, and as good a chance of seeing the Big Five as anywhere. Moreover, it has a tranquil, low-key feel and a lovely campsite with plenty of big trees for shade. Accommodation includes camping, two-bed permanent safari tents and en-suite bungalows sleeping two to three, with cooking facilities. Amenities are limited to a laundry and filling station, and a shop selling basic supplies. Camping and safari tents $\bar{\$}$, bungalows $\bar{\$}\bar{\$}$

★ **Lower Sabie** 35km north of Crocodile Bridge ☏013 735 6056/6057. Usually fully booked, *Lower Sabie* occupies game-rich country, with an outlook over the Sabie River, which places it among the top three restcamps in the Kruger for spotting animals. One of its biggest attractions is the large wooden viewing deck outside the restaurant (open to day-visitors), where you can have a snack while often watching elephants crossing the river in front of you. Accommodation includes camping, huts using common ablutions, luxury safari tents, bungalows and guest cottages, some with river views. There's a *Mugg & Bean* restaurant, a shop, a swimming pool, a filling station and a laundry. Camping and huts using common ablutions $\bar{\$}$, standing tents and bungalows $\bar{\$}\bar{\$}$, cottages $\bar{\$}\bar{\$}\bar{\$}$

Pretoriuskop 9km east of Numbi Gate ☏013 735 5128/5132. The area surrounding *Pretoriuskop* is good for predators. However, given the dense bush, game viewing can be disappointing, and you may only see larger species such as greater kudu and giraffe. Accommodation here consists of en-suite cottages and guesthouses, bungalows and cheaper huts, and camping with shared ablution and cooking facilities. The camp has a restaurant, a snack bar, a shop, a laundry, a semi-natural rock swimming pool – one of the most beautiful in Kruger, with a surrounding garden and picnic area – and a petrol station. Around the perimeter fence at night, you're almost certain to see patrolling hyenas, waiting for scraps from braais. One feature of the camp is the tame impala that wander freely around. Camping and huts using common ablutions $\bar{\$}$, bungalows $\bar{\$}\bar{\$}$, cottages $\bar{\$}\bar{\$}\bar{\$}$

Skukuza 12km east of Paul Kruger Gate ☏013 735 4265/4196. Kruger's largest restcamp accommodates more than a thousand people and lies at the centre of the best game-viewing area in the park. Its position is a mixed blessing; although you get large amounts of game, hordes of humans aren't far behind, and cars speeding at animal sightings can chase away the very animals they are trying to see. Accommodation is in a range of en-suite guesthouses, cottages and bungalows, or more cheaply in huts, safari tents and campsites, with shared ablutions and kitchens. *Skukuza* is the hub of Kruger; with its own airport (SA Airlink, private airlines and charters) and car-rental agency, and its sprawling collection of rondavels and staff village, it resembles a small town and all the cars can be irksome. There are two swimming pools, and a deli café with internet facilities, plus a post office, a bank, a petrol station and garage, a *Cattle Baron & Bistro* steakhouse and a really good library (Mon–Fri 8.30am–4pm & 7–9pm, Sat 8.30am–12.45pm, 1.45–4pm & 7–9pm, Sun 8.30am–12.45pm & 1.45–4pm) with a collection of natural history books and exhibits. Golf at *Skukuza* is also a draw, where you'll have to sign an indemnity form in case of bumping into wildlife on

the course. There is a special area designated for day-visitors, with its own swimming pool and picnic area. Camping and standing tents $\bar{\$}$, bungalows $\bar{\$}\bar{\$}$, cottages $\bar{\$}\bar{\$}\bar{\$}$

BUSHVELD, SATELLITE AND BUDGET TENTED CAMPS

★ **Biyamiti** 41km northeast of the Malelane Gate and 26km west of Crocodile Bridge Gate ☏013 735 6171. *Biyamiti* lies on the banks of the Mbiyamiti River; its proximity is one of the main advantages of this very southerly camp, and the surrounding terrain attracts large numbers of game including lion, elephant and rhino. There are fifteen cottages, all with fully equipped kitchens. $\bar{\$}\bar{\$}–\bar{\$}\bar{\$}\bar{\$}$

Malelane 3km from Malelane Gate ☏013 735 6152. Comprising a mere five en-suite bungalows, camping space for 15 tents, and a communal dining area and ablutions, this small satellite of *Berg-en-Dal* has a pleasant tree-shaded setting on the bank of the Crocodile River but this is compromised slightly by the agricultural development on the facing bank and nocturnal hum of traffic from the N4. Camping $\bar{\$}$, bungalows $\bar{\$}\bar{\$}$

Pretoriuskop Tented Adventures Set inside Pretorius-kop Rest Camp, ☏076 146 1468, ⊛tentedadventures. com. This private tented camp within *Pretoriuskop* is a great option for those seeking fully catered budget accommodation in southern Kruger. The eight standing tents are small but comfortable, with double beds, lamps and a small private balcony facing a stretch of periphery fence where spotted hyena and elephant often stroll past at night. Guests use the common ablution blocks. Rates are inclusive of breakfast, dinner and wine, which are eaten communally around a campfire. It also offers game drives in an open 4WD with its own guides, who live on site and really know this part of the park and where best to look for wildlife. $\bar{\$}\bar{\$}\bar{\$}$

CONCESSION LODGES

★ **Jock Safari Lodge** Off the H3, 38km south of Skukuza ☏013 010 0019, ⊛jocksafarilodge.com. Fabulous location in a wildlife-rich sixty-square-kilometre concession encompassing a floodplain at the confluence of two seasonal rivers. Majestic riverine trees shade the twelve thatched luxury suites: choose a north-facing room if you can, where you can doze on the sunny daybed on your private deck above the river bank. The lodge also has a spa, a small gym and a library with internet. *Jock* also offers a two-night package of walking with a ranger and staying over at a rustic camp. $\bar{\$}\bar{\$}\bar{\$}\bar{\$}\bar{\$}$

Lukimbi Safari Lodge Off the S25 about 25km east of Malelane Gate, ☏011 792 6165, ⊛lukimbi.com. This attractive stilted lodge occupies a wonderful spot overlooking a permanent pool on the seasonal Lwakhale River. The spacious cottages are decorated in an earthy ethnic style and are reached via a raised wooden walkway which wildlife passes under unimpeded. *Lukimbi* enjoys exclusive traversing rights across a 150-square-kilometre concession dominated by acacia woodland. Good for lion, elephant, African wild dog and both types of rhino. $$$$$

★ **Rhino Post Safari Lodge** Off the S83, 15km north of Skukuza, ☎ 035 474 1473, ⊛ rhinopostsafarilodge. co.za. Situated in the magnificent, wild 120-square-kilometre Mutlumuvi concession bordering MalaMala Game Reserve, *Rhino Post* comprises two safari camps offering different experiences. *Main Lodge* has eight suites built out of stone, wood and thatch, above a sandy riverbed, while *Plains Lodge*, the base for Rhino Post Walking Safaris, comprises four super-comfy solar-powered safari tents furnished in a pioneer style in the wilderness area. For an ultimate wilderness experience, walk with a superbly informed armed guide to the tree-house overnight camp,

which has basic beds under mosquito nets set on high wooden platforms, where you hear all the African night sounds. $$$$$

Shishangeni Lodge 15km southeast of Crocodile Bridge gate, ⊛ shishangeni.com. Set on the north bank of the Crocodile River shortly before it flows across the border into Mozambique, *Shishangeni* is the centrepiece of a 150-square-kilometre concession renowned as one of the best places in Kruger to see white rhino along with lion, elephant, buffalo, hippo and – less regularly – leopard and cheetah. The concession also hosts two luxurious satellite camps comprising just five units apiece. These are *Camp Shonga*, set below the Lebombo Mountains, and *Camp Shawu*, which overlooks a dam that supports plenty of hippos and birds and is regularly visited by other wildlife. $$$$$

Central Kruger

The low-lying central plains that divide the Sabie and Letaba rivers form a good compromise between the wildlife-rich but often crowded acacia savannah of southern Kruger and the more untrammelled but less productive north. Situated in the heart of these central plains, **Satara**, Kruger's second-largest restcamp, is nobody's favourite, thanks to its rather institutional layout and lack of any memorable view. But there is no arguing with its location at the crossroads of some superb game-viewing roads. The swathes of grassland and lightly wooded savannah around *Satara* are estimated to host sixty lion prides, and it is the best part of the park for **kills**, which often also attract jackals and hyenas. It is also ideal **cheetah** territory, and these streamlined spotted cats are often seen prowling along the main H1-3 south or H1-4 north, within a 10km radius of the camp.

An excellent half-day loop from *Satara* entails following the surfaced H6 east for 20km to **N'wanetsi Picnic Site**, then continuing north for 12km along the unsurfaced S41, before returning west back along the S100. These roads pass through a variety of terrain. The open grassland that flanks the H6 hosts large seasonal concentrations of wildebeest and zebra, while the S100 follows the course of the **N'wanetsi River** and an associated strip of riverine forest where giraffes browse the canopy and buffaloes and elephants lurk in the shade. The S100 is one of the best roads to try to find lions. N'wanetsi Picnic Site, overlooking the river as it runs through a gorge in the Lebombo Mountains on the border with **Mozambique**, is a great place to stretch legs and scan the bush with binoculars.

Several good loops west of *Satara* can be undertaken by following the N7 running towards Orpen Gate. **Nsemani Pan**, only 5km from camp along the H7, frequently attracts rhinos. From here, continue west for 11km, then turn right on the S39, a reliably rewarding dirt road that follows the seasonal Timbavati River and an impressive ribbon of riparian woodland towards its confluence with the **Olifants**. Highlights of this lovely road include the Leeubron Waterhole, which as its name suggests is often frequented by lions, the Timbavati Picnic Site and the bird hide at Ratel Pan. The road follows the river for 50km before veering east to connect with the surfaced H1-4, from where it is a 35km drive back south to *Satara*.

CENTRAL KRUGER AT A GLANCE

Kruger's best compromise between quality game viewing and tranquillity is the park's central region.

Big Five: ★★★★
General wildlife: ★★★★
Birding: ★★★
Scenery: ★★★
Wilderness factor: ★★★★
Uncrowded: ★★★
Affordability: ★★★★★
Self-drive: Y

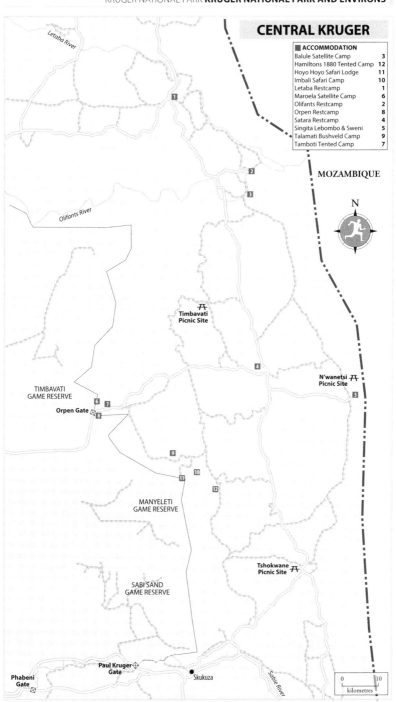

2

North of *Satara*, two of Kruger's loveliest camps, **Olifants** and **Letaba**, lie alongside the eponymous rivers, which spill out onto wide floodplains lined with shady fig and jackal-berry trees before their confluence a few kilometres west of the Mozambican border. Scenically, *Olifants* is utterly peerless, set on a clifftop offering a spectacular view over the river below (and, as often as not, abundant herds of elephant, giraffe and other game). Further north, *Letaba*, though less scenic, is a favourite of many Kruger regulars for its wonderful bush feel, and the plentiful birds and other wildlife that pass through.

Coming from further south, the area around *Olifants* and *Letaba* feels very wild and untrammelled, thanks to the relatively low tourist traffic, though game viewing is slightly less reliable than around *Satara*. Probably the best overall game-viewing loop in this part of the park is the **S44/6**, which runs east from *Olifants Camp*, following the Olifants towards the confluence, then curves northwest to follow the Letaba all the way upstream to *Letaba Camp*. Greater kudu and elephant are often seen along this road, while the immense herds of buffalo that occasionally materialize from the dense vegetation are also the favoured prey of the area's lions. Even if you are unlucky with large mammals, this road bypasses some memorable viewpoints over the river, and the birdlife is excellent, particularly around Engelhardt Dam. At the junction of the S44 and S93, the ancient **Von Wielligh's Baobab**, named after a surveyor who set up camp here in 1891, is one of the world's most southerly wild specimens of this impressive tree.

ACCOMMODATION CENTRAL KRUGER, SEE MAP PAGE 117

As with the rest of Kruger, **restcamps** and bushveld camps must be booked in advance with SANParks (☎ 012 428 9111, ⓦ sanparks.org/parks/kruger). Private **concession lodges** can be booked through the individual concessionaire.

RESTCAMPS

★ **Letaba** 52km east of Phalaborwa Gate ☎ 013 735 6636/7. *Letaba* is set in mopani shrubland along the Letaba River. Old and quite large, the camp is beautifully located on an oxbow curve, and though very few of the rondavels afford a view, the restaurant does have great vistas; you can spend a day just watching herds of buffalo mooching around, elephants drifting past and a host of other plains game. The fig trees along the river also offer fabulous birding when they are in fruit, attracting the likes of African green pigeon, purple-crested turaco and various hornbills and barbets. There is a full range of accommodation and the camp offers the usual shopping and laundry facilities, a *Mugg & Bean* restaurant, a swimming pool, a vehicle-repair workshop, and an interesting museum, Elephant Hall, with exhibits on the life of elephants, including a display on the Magnificent Seven, bulls with inordinately large tusks that once roamed the area, with six pairs of their tusks on display. Camping, standing tents and rondavels $\overline{5}$, bungalows $\overline{55}$, cottages $\overline{555}$

★ **Olifants** 80km east of Phalaborwa Gate ☎ 013 735 6606/7. With a terrific setting on cliffs overlooking the braided Olifants River, *Olifants* is reckoned by many to be the best restcamp in Kruger, and it is certainly the most scenic, which is perhaps why it lacks the campsites and other budget options found at most other restcamps. It's possible to spend hours sitting on the benches on the covered look-out terrace, gazing into the valley whose airspace is crisscrossed by Bateleur eagles and yellow-billed kites cruising the thermals, while the rushing of the water below creates a hypnotic rhythm. You can eat at the *Mugg & Bean* restaurant, and there's a shop and a laundry. This is also promising country for spotting elephant, giraffe, lion, hyena and cheetah, and you should look out for the klipspringer, a pretty medium-sized antelope that inhabits rocky terrain, which it nimbly negotiates by boulder-hopping. Bungalows $\overline{55}$, cottages $\overline{555}$

Orpen Right by Orpen Gate, 45km east of Klaserie ☎ 013 735 6355. Recommended mainly if you're arriving late and don't have time to get further into the park before the camp gates close, *Orpen* is nevertheless very good for game viewing, because the substantial Timbavati Private Game Reserve lies to the west, so you're already well into the wilderness once you get here. There's a waterhole right in front of the camp, and animals come and go all the time. Small and peaceful, the camp comprises just twelve bungalows and one cottage, all shaded by beautiful trees. Facilities include a petrol station, a shop and a swimming pool overlooking a waterhole, but there is no restaurant. Bungalows $\overline{55}$, cottages $\overline{555}$

Satara 46km due east of Orpen Gate ☎ 013 735 6306/7. *Satara* ranks second only to *Skukuza* in size, and while it commands no great views and can get very busy in season, the surrounding flat grasslands offer excellent game viewing, particularly when it comes to lions and other carnivores. Accommodation ranges from camping, through bungalows and cottages arranged around lawned areas shaded by large trees, to secluded guesthouses; besides a shop, petrol station, laundry and an AA vehicle repair workshop, there's also a swimming pool, pizzeria and café. *Satara* itself is usually good for sighting grazers such as buffalo, wildebeest, zebra, kudu, impala and elephant; the night drives are particularly recommended. Camping $\overline{S}$, bungalows $\overline{SS}$, cottages $\overline{SSS}$

BUSHVELD AND SATELLITE CAMPS

★ **Balule** On the southern bank of the Olifants River, 41km north of Satara and 87km from Phalaborwa Gate ☎013 735 6606/7. A very basic satellite to *Olifants* (11km to the north), *Balule* stands out for those seeking a genuine back-to-basics wilderness experience at a budget price. It is divided into two sections, one consisting of six rustic three-bed rondavels and another of fifteen camping and caravan sites. Each section has its own communal ablution and cooking facilities with braai places and paraffin fridge. The location on the southern floodplain of the Olifants River is rewarding for game drives, and you are bound to hear lions at night. The only electricity is in the perimeter fence, which is often patrolled by spotted hyenas after dark, though paraffin lamps are provided for lighting. Guests have to bring their own crockery, cutlery and utensils, and must report to *Olifants* at least half an hour before the gates close. $\overline{S}$

Maroela 4km from Orpen Gate and Camp, 45km east of Klaserie ☎013 735 6355. This satellite to *Orpen Camp* comprises twenty individual camping areas with power points overlooking the Timbavati River. Report to Orpen reception to check in. $\overline{S}$

Talamati On the S145 about 30km southeast of Orpen Gate ☎013 735 6343. Lying on the banks of the usually dry Nwaswitsontso stream, the mixed bush-willow woodland setting of *Talamati* attracts giraffe, kudu, wildebeest, zebra and predators like lion, hyena and jackal, as well as rhino and sable antelope. Two hides within the perimeter of the camp overlook a waterhole, where game viewing can be excellent. The camp has twenty cottages arranged in an L-shape along the river in a forest of lead-woods and russet bush-willows. $\overline{SS}$

Tamboti Turn left 2km after Orpen and continue for 1km ☎013 735 6355. Not far from Orpen Gate, *Tamboti* is Kruger's only tented camp. You sleep in tents in a tranquil position on the banks of the frequently dry Timbavati River, set among apple leaf trees, sycamore figs and jackal-berries. From the tents, elephants can often be seen just beyond the electrified fence, digging in the riverbed for moisture – hence the camp's popularity. Each walk-in tent has its own deck overlooking the river, but best of all are numbers 21 and 22, which enjoy the deep shade of large riverine trees, something you'll appreciate in the midsummer heat. The tents have fridges and electric lighting, while all kitchen, washing and toilet facilities are in two shared central blocks (bring your own cooking and eating utensils). $\overline{S}$

CONCESSION LODGES

Hamiltons 1880 Tented Camp On the S140 50km southeast of Orpen Gate ☎011 516 4367, ✆hamiltons tentedcamp.co.za. The most upmarket lodge on the Mluwati Concession, this luxury tented camp comprises six stilted canvas units set in lush riparian woodland along the seasonal Nwaswitsontso River, romantically decorated in Edwardian safari style. The tents are well spaced for privacy and linked via raised timber walkways. $\overline{SSSSS}$

Hoyo Hoyo Safari Lodge On the S140 33km southeast of Orpen Gate ☎011 516 4367, ✆hoyohoyo.com. This architecturally distinctive lodge has an innovative design based on the layout of a traditional village. Shaped like circular Tsonga huts, the six suites have tall tapered thatched roofs, and are decorated in warm earthy colours with ethnically influenced finishes. It stands on the banks of the Mluwati River in a patch of acacia savannah in the 100-square-kilometre Mluwati Concession. As a base, it offers a better-than-average chance of seeing all the Big Five over the course of 2–3 days, as well as cheetah and wild dog. $\overline{SSSSS}$

Imbali Safari Camp On the S140 40km southeast of Orpen Gate ☎011 516 4367, ✆imbali.com. *Imbali* is the largest of a trio of jointly managed lodges situated on the 100-square-kilometre Mluwati Concession, which protects an area of dense, wildlife-rich acacia savannah between *Satara* and *Skukuza*, and offers a better chance than most concessions of throwing up all the Big Five, as well as cheetah and wild dog, over the course of a few days. It consists of twelve large thatched cottages with king-size beds, walk-in nets and private wooden decks overlooking the well-wooded seasonal Nwaswitsontso River. $\overline{SSSSS}$

★ **Singita Lebombo & Sweni** 70km east of Orpen Gate via the H7 and H6 ☎021 683 3424, ✆singita. co.za. Situated in a mountainous 150-square-kilometre concession in the Lebombo foothills on the border with Mozambique, *Singita Lebombo* and *Sweni* represent what is surely the last word in boutique Kruger safari chic, hence their popularity with movie stars and others with similarly deep wallets. Elevated along a sheer cliff, the stilted open-plan units have dramatic wraparound glass walls and sliding doors that open onto a private balcony complete with outdoor shower and a double bed where you can sleep out in summer. Amenities include a spa, a state-of-the-art gymnasium, wine-tasting facilities and superb international cuisine. Such trappings aside, *Singita* also delivers where it really counts by offering possibly the best game-viewing of any of the Kruger concessions, with the added bonus that off-road driving is seldom a problem. $\overline{SSSSS}$

2

NORTHERN KRUGER AT A GLANCE

Game viewing in northern Kruger is patchier than in the south, but the wilderness feel compensates.

Big Five: **
General wildlife: ****
Birding: *****
Scenery: ***
Wilderness factor: *****
Uncrowded: *****
Affordability: *****
Self-drive: Y

Northern Kruger

Northern Kruger is different. Accounting for slightly more than half the park's area, the territory to the north of the **Letaba River** is studded with only three main restcamps and a handful of bushveld camps whose combined bed space is less than that of *Skukuza* on its own. Coming from further south, the contrast is striking. On the plus side, tourist volumes are far lower than is the case in Southern or Central Kruger, the area possesses a genuine wilderness feel that makes it a favourite with experienced safarigoers, particularly after you've crossed the **Tropic of Capricorn** north of **Mopani**, and it also provides particularly rich pickings for **birdwatchers**. Less favourably, general game viewing tends to be far slower than it is south of Letaba. Measured in crude Big Five terms, buffalo and elephant are reputedly more abundant in the north, but they are no more visible than in the south, and the odds of seeing lion, leopard or rhino are pretty slim.

Coming from the south, the first camp you reach is *Mopani*, a relatively recent creation named after the monotonous dry mopani woodland that covers the surrounding plains. A large dam below the camp attracts a fair amount of wildlife, and elephants are numerous in the vicinity, which is also the best part of the park for a chance of spotting the localized roan antelope and Sharpe's grysbok. That said, *Mopani* is probably the most poorly located of Kruger's main restcamps for general game viewing.

The more northerly and smaller *Shingwedzi Camp*, perched on the south bank of the namesake river, is one of Kruger's most underrated gems. The highlight of this area is the dirt **S134**, which tracks the river for about 10km southeast of the camp to the Kanniedood (literally "Cannot Die") Dam, passing through a tract of riparian woodland dense with elephant, buffalo, greater kudu and colourful birds, notably the exquisite broad-billed roller. Another great road loop out of *Shingwedzi* is **S32**, which follows the north bank of the river upstream for about 35km to the Silver Fish Dam, passing a striking formation known as Red Rocks en route. This is a good road for elephant sightings; if you drive it in the early morning, look out for leopards. Instead of returning the way you came, cross the river just after Silver Fish Dam and then follow the road along the south bank east until it reconnects with the surfaced H1-6.

The most northerly public restcamp in Kruger, *Punda Maria* lies on a wooded slope in an area of sandveld dominated by mopani trees and studded with craggy sandstone hills crowned with giant baobabs, some as much as 4000 years old. The real reward of *Punda* is the landscape and stunningly varied vegetation, with a remarkable nine biomes all converging in the area, making it a paradise for birdwatchers. The short **Flycatcher Trail**, which runs around the camp periphery, is named after the gorgeous African flycatcher, which is commonly seen along it, as are several other alluring birds, including purple-crested turaco, grey-hooded kingfisher, yellow-bellied greenbul, white-throated robin-chat, green-winged pytilia, blue-billed firefinch and various barbets and sunbirds. Another excellent feature of this small camp is a new game-viewing hide overlooking a waterhole that's regularly visited by lion, buffalo, elephant, various antelope and a host of different bird species. The best game-viewing road around *Punda Maria*, the 30km S99, also known as the Mahonie Loop, runs through an area of sandveld inhabited by a pair of localized small antelope, suni and Sharpe's grysbok, alongside some impressive greater kudu bulls, and it also passes a pair of

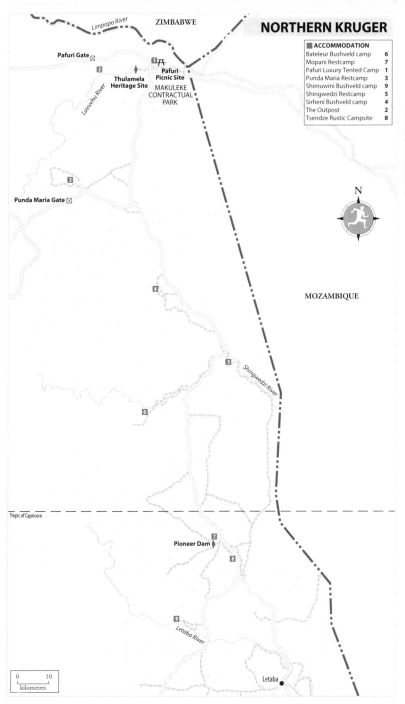

NORTHERN KRUGER

ACCOMMODATION

Bateleur Bushveld camp	6
Mopani Restcamp	7
Pafuri Luxury Tented Camp	1
Punda Maria Restcamp	3
Shimuwini Bushveld camp	9
Shingwedzi Restcamp	5
Sirheni Bushveld camp	4
The Outpost	2
Tsendze Rustic Campsite	8

ZIMBABWE

Limpopo River

Pafuri Gate

Luvuvhu River

Thulamela Heritage Site

Pafuri Picnic Site

MAKULEKE CONTRACTUAL PARK

Punda Maria Gate

N

MOZAMBIQUE

Shingwedzi River

Tropic of Capricorn

Pioneer Dam

Letaba River

Letaba

0   10
kilometres

waterholes that often attract thirsty mammals as well as the localized grey-headed parrot and Dickinson's kestrel.

Punda Maria is the closest public camp to the legendary **S63** (also known as Luvuvhu Drive) and **S64** (Nyala Drive), which runs through the lush riparian forest along the south bank of the eponymous river some 40km to the north. This is one of the park's finest game-viewing roads, notable for hosting concentrations of elephant, buffalo and nyala antelope, while the river itself is home to plenty of hippos and some seriously formidable crocodiles. The main focal point along the S63 is the **Pafuri Picnic Site**, which stands on the south bank of the Luvuvhu River under the shade of massive acacia, lead-wood and jackal-berry trees. The site is considered by many to be the park's single best spot for **birding** – possible highlights include Africa finfoot, white-crowned lapwing and half-collared kingfisher along the river; localized forest dwellers such as crested guineafowl, crowned eagle, Narina trogon, trumpeter hornbill, cinnamon dove, black-headed wattled-eye, tropical boubou, olive bush-shrike and Meves's glossy-starling; as well as the peculiar Bohm's and mottled spinetail fluttering bat-like around the baobabs where they breed. An interpretation board at the picnic site gives a fascinating account of human history in the area. There are also braai facilities, a constantly boiling kettle to make your own tea, and ice-cold canned drinks for sale. Nyala Drive terminates at the **Thulamela Heritage Site**, which protects the substantial hilltop ruins of a Zimbabwe-style stone-wall royal village that was built in the sixteenth century and can only be visited in the company of a park guide from *Punda Maria*.

The most northerly component of Kruger is **Makuleke Contractual Park**, which comprises the wedge of land sandwiched between the Luvuvhu and Limpopo rivers west of their confluence at Crooks Corner, on the tripartite border between South Africa, Zimbabwe and Mozambique. Also known as the **Pafuri Triangle**, this 236-square-kilometre area is the one part of Kruger with a truly tropical ecology, and has the highest biodiversity of any section of the park, with more than 75 percent of the park's species occurring in just one percent of its surface area. The Pafuri Triangle was incorporated into Kruger after its 1500 Makuleke residents were forcibly evicted at the hands of the apartheid government in 1969, and after being returned to its original inhabitants following a successful land claim in 1998, it now forms an encouraging example of sustainable community-based development. Wildlife and other conservation-related matters within Makuleke Contractual Park are managed by SANParks, but accommodation is restricted to two private lodges (*Pafuri Luxury Tented Camp* and *The Outpost*) leased out by the local community as a source of revenue and employment. The area is bisected by the 18km H1-9 as it runs between the Luvuvhu Bridge and Pafuri Gate, but you need to stay at one of the lodges in order to explore remote non-public sites such as the lush fever-tree forest at Crooks Corner or the spectacular Lanner Gorge, or to stand a realistic chance of ticking off avian rarities such as Pel's fishing owl, racket-tailed roller and triple-banded courser.

ACCOMMODATION   NORTHERN KRUGER, SEE MAP PAGE 121

As with the rest of Kruger, **restcamps** and bushveld camps must be booked in advance with SANParks (☎ 012 428 9111, ⓦ sanparks.org/parks/kruger). Private **concession lodges** can be booked through the individual concessionaire, as detailed under the listing.

RESTCAMPS

Mopani 42km north of Letaba ☎ 013 735 6535/6. *Mopani* overlooks the Pioneer Dam, one of the few water sources in the vicinity, which attracts animals to drink and provides an outstanding lookout for a variety of wildlife,

including elephant, buffalo and antelope. This is a sprawling place in the middle of monotonous mopani scrub, with en-suite accommodation built of rough-hewn stone and thatch, and a restaurant and a bar with a good view across to the dam. Other facilities include a shop, a laundry and a petrol station; the swimming pool, one of the best in the park, provides cool relief after a long drive. $$

★ **Punda Maria** 71km north of Shingwedzi and 5km from Punda Maria Gate ☎ 013 735 6873. Kruger's northernmost camp is also one of its smallest and least visited, an unpretentious, peaceful and relaxed tropical outpost set around a small hill about 30km south of the Zimbabwe border as the crow flies. There's less of a concentration of game up here, but this isn't to say you won't see wildlife (the Big Five all breeze through from time to time), though the main faunal hotspot, especially for birders, is the Pafuri Picnic Site and associated road circuit along the south bank of the Luvuvhu about an hour's drive to the north. Accommodation options include camping, safari tents with communal cooking and ablution areas, or en-suite fully equipped bungalows. The camp has a restaurant, a small shop, a petrol station, a swimming pool and a bird hide. Camping 5̄, bungalows and safari tents 5̄5̄, cottages 5̄5̄5̄

★ **Shingwedzi** 63km north of Mopani ☎ 013 735 6806/7. A fairly large camp featuring a campsite, brick huts and a few older, colonial-style whitewashed, thatched bungalows, as well as a cottage and a guesthouse, sited in extensive shady grounds in an area that can make rewarding wildlife viewing. From the terrace you get a long view down across the frequently dry Shingwedzi River. Look out for the weavers' nests with their long, tube-like entrances hanging from the eaves outside reception. Camping, huts and bungalows 5̄, cottages 5̄5̄

BUSHVELD CAMPS

★ **Bateleur** About 40km southwest of Shingwedzi restcamp ☎ 013 735 6843. Off the beaten track, in the remote northern section of the park on the banks of the frequently dry Mashokwe stream. The camp has a timber viewing deck, excellently placed to watch game coming to drink at a seasonally full waterhole. The nearby Silver Fish and Rooibosrand dams also attract game as well as birdlife in prodigious quantities. There are seven cottages; each has its own kitchenette and fridge, with electricity provided by solar panels. 5̄5̄

Shimuwini About 50km from Phalaborwa Gate on the Mooiplaas Rd ☎ 013 735 6683. Set in mopani and bushwillow country on the upper reaches of the Shimuwini Dam, which is filled by the Letaba River, this peaceful camp is not known for its game but is a perennial favourite among birdwatchers. It's an excellent place for spotting riverine

bird species, including fish eagles, as well as frugivores attracted to the sycamore figs along the banks of the river. Accommodation is in fifteen cottages. 5̄–5̄5̄

Sirheni Roughly 54km south of Punda Maria ☎ 013 735 6860. Set on the bank of Sirheni Dam, this is a fine spot for birdwatching, beautifully tucked into riverine forest, with some game also passing through. The big draw is its remote bushveld atmosphere in an area that sees few visitors. There are fifteen cottages, all en-suite and equipped with kitchens. The two bird hides in the camp are a great pull. 5̄5̄

Tsendze Rustic Campsite 7km south of Mopani ☎ 013 735 6535/6. Back-to-basics *Tsendze* caters to DIY campers seeking to escape the typical Kruger camp vibe. There is no electricity here – the lighting in the ablutions is from a solar battery system and hot water in the outdoor showers is from gas geysers. There are thirty camping sites (sites 14, 15 and 16 are best), but as each is surrounded by trees and scrub the atmosphere is wild and rustic. The nearest shop is at *Mopani*. 5̄

CONCESSION LODGES

★ **Pafuri Luxury Tented Camp** 20km east of Pafuri Gate ☎ 011 646 1391, ⊛ returnafrica.com. Boasting a superb location on the forested north bank of the Luvuvhu River, this is the larger of two concession lodges set in the remote Makuleke Contractual Park, comprising nineteen luxury double and family tents with stilted wooden bases, thatch roofs and private decks on the river. It is renowned among birders as the place to see Pel's fishing owl and other northern specials, and while general game viewing is erratic, it has a compelling wilderness atmosphere and can be very good for leopards. 5̄5̄5̄5̄

★ **The Outpost** 6km southeast of Pafuri Gate ☎ 011 568 0384, ⊛ rareearth.co.za. This clifftop designer lodge in Makuleke Contractual Park consists of a dozen innovatively designed rooms that are completely open to the elements except for the rock face they appear to grow out of. The unparalleled views of the Luvuvhu floodplain are spectacular at sunrise. As with *Pafuri*, wildlife viewing can be hit-and-miss, but the birding, setting and architecture are all superb. 5̄5̄5̄5̄5̄

Private reserves in Greater Kruger

Embracing such legendary properties as *MalaMala*, *Londolozi* and *Sabi Sabi*, the swathe of private reserves that shares unfenced boundaries with Kruger offers the best all-round upmarket safari experience anywhere in South Africa. Like Kruger itself, these western annexes to the national park fall within an immense self-sustaining **transfrontier ecosystem** whose populations of lion, elephant, buffalo, giraffe, white rhino and other such creatures can be measured in the thousands (or in many cases, in the tens of thousands). As is the case with most of the country's other more contained and micro-managed private sanctuaries, the cluster of reserves abutting western Kruger offer exclusive safari packages inclusive of accommodation in small luxurious lodges or tented camps, fabulous wining and dining, and twice-daily game drives in open 4WDs led by expert guides and/or trackers who are immensely skilled at locating the Big Five and permitted to drive off-road for close-up sightings. There's no finer introduction to South Africa's wildlife, but also no getting around the fact that it's a privilege for which you must be prepared to pay. Rates at these private reserves range from steep to astronomical, placing them well out of the reach of anybody on a low to middling travel budget. In all cases, you need to book ahead, and get driving instructions to your specific lodge or camp, as no pop-ins are allowed.

Running from southeast to northwest, the main private reserves sharing open borders with Kruger are **Sabi Sand**, **MalaMala**, **Manyaleti**, **Timbavati**, **Klaserie** and **Balule**. All protect a similar range of mammal species to their larger neighbour, though certain grazers and browsers might be locally scarce during the dry winter months. They are unmatched when it comes to regular close-up sightings of big cats and other carnivores. Lions are widespread in the private reserves and almost certain to be seen on any given day, and the area ranks among the very best in the world for leopards, which are very habituated and have become quite blasé about vehicles and their occupants, particularly in MalaMala and Sabi Sand, but also to a slightly lesser extent in the more northerly reserves. Other carnivores regularly seen in the private reserves include spotted hyena, cheetah, African wild dog, black-backed jackal and various mongooses, while night drives offer a chance of encounters with smaller viverrid and felid species including common genet, African civet, serval, caracal and African wild cat. The birdlife is excellent too, but game drives tend to focus mainly on mammals, which is understandable given the high price tags, and a clientele dominated by first-time safarigoers, but it does mean that dedicated birders are probably better off doing their own thing in Kruger.

With the exception of the completely autonomous MalaMala, each of the reserves listed above actually comprises a number of smaller privately owned properties that are jointly administered when it comes to conservation and wildlife management. Every individual property within each reserve is serviced by one or more lodges that operate independently from the greater reserve but must abide by its rules when it comes to tourist development and activities. Lodges on larger properties tend to have more-or-less exclusive access to that territory, while those on smaller properties usually have a complex relationship of cross-traversing rights with some but not all neighbours. Guides maintain contact by radio, alerting each other to good sightings, and limits are usually imposed on the number of vehicles that can sit with any given sighting. As a result, there tends to be more jostling for queuing space to see the likes of leopard and lion on smaller properties that share multiple cross-traversing rights than is the case on larger properties that operate more autonomously. Another odd result of this situation is that it's quite common to have to abandon a mobile sighting when it crosses onto a property to which your driver doesn't have traversing rights.

Almost all lodges and tented camps in these private reserves offer the same basic formula. Morning drives leave before or shortly after sunrise, then return in time for a late breakfast. Several lodges offer bush walks after breakfast, and most overlook waterholes, rivers or plains, so that you can look out for animals during the time you're in camp, when you're not lazing around the pool, making use of the spa or gym facilities, or perusing their collection of animal books on gigantic sofas. Then in the late afternoon, as the heat of the day starts to dissipate, you depart on a second 4WD outing, punctuated by sundowners in the bush, before continuing on a spotlit night drive to look for nocturnal specials such as leopards, genets and bushbabies. Dinners are inevitably lamplit, around a fire, in the open. In winter months you'll be given blankets on the open vehicle and possibly even hot water bottles to cope with the cold.

SPOTTED HYENA, KRUGER NATIONAL PARK

2

SABI SAND AT A GLANCE

This prestigious reserve bordering Kruger usually offers close-up sightings of all the Big Five, but parts suffer from high vehicle densities.
Big Five: *****
General wildlife: ****
Birding: ***
Scenery: **
Wilderness factor: ****
Uncrowded: ***
Affordability: *
Self-drive: N

Sabi Sand Game Reserve

Western border of Kruger and MalaMala east of Hazyview • R250 • ☎ 013 735 5102, ⓦ sabisand.co.za

South Africa's best-known and most prestigious private reserve, the **Sabi Sand Wildtuin**, as it is officially known, has been set aside for conservation almost continuously since 1898. It is named after the perennial **Sabi River**, which flows across its southern boundary with Kruger, and a near-perennial tributary called the Sand, which flows through it in an easterly direction for about 25km before crossing into MalaMala. Sabi Sand is justifiably renowned as one of the best places in the world for close-up encounters with leopards and lions, but it also reliably delivers the rest of the Big Five to the vast majority of visitors, and it is well above average when it comes to general game viewing and more challenging safari icons such as cheetah and African wild dog. Extending across 520 square kilometres, it is one of the country's largest private reserves, but while it is administered as a single conservation unit, the situation with land ownership and traversing rights is altogether more complex. And unlike, say, neighbouring MalaMala, or the more northerly Klaserie Nature Reserve, Sabi Sand supports a high density of accommodation, with at least thirty lodges and camps scattered across 25 different reserves-within-a-reserve. So, while wildlife viewing is consistently good throughout Sabi Sands, game drives from lodges in smaller properties that cross-traverse with several neighbours tend to take more of a quick-fix Big Five approach, while those that operate in larger (and generally pricier) properties are usually more relaxed and feel less packaged. Most rewarding from this point of view are a quartet of larger south-central properties, namely *Londolozi*, *Singita*, *Lion Sands* and *Sabi Sabi*, all of which are quite big and operate more-or-less autonomously when it comes to traversing rights. The cluster of relatively tiny properties in western Sabi Sands tends to suffer most from congestion associated with cross-traversing, while the cluster in the far north fall somewhere in between and also tend to be somewhat cheaper, partly since they take longer to reach coming from Gauteng or Kruger Mpumalanga International Airport.

Some history

The land now protected within Sabi Sand fell within the original boundaries of the **Sabie Game Reserve** as it was proclaimed by President Paul Kruger of the ZAR in 1898. When the Kruger National Park was gazetted with revised boundaries in 1926, the land was excised and carved up into large plots that were mostly purchased by wealthy hunters who established seasonal camps there for their private use. Sabi Sand Wildtuin came into being under its current name and in more-or-less its present form in **1948**, when a group of local landowners committed to the preservation of wilderness areas collectively created a game reserve named after the two main rivers that run through it. A game fence originally divided the eastern border of Sabi Sand from Kruger, and another 72km-long fence was erected along the reserve's western boundary in 1961 to stop wildlife straying further west into unprotected areas. **Upmarket ecotourism** was pioneered by MalaMala in the 1960s and other tourist camps established in Londolozi and Sabi Sabi in the 1970s formed an important source of revenue to support conservation and fund the reintroduction of locally extinct species such as cheetah, elephant, white rhino, sable, eland and nyala. The reserve's western fence – electrified since 1988 – remains in place, for obvious reasons, but the fence running along the eastern boundary with Kruger National Park was dropped in 1993 to allow free migration of game between the two. Today, Sabi Sand shares open borders of roughly 30km with Kruger, another 30km with MalaMala (which now operates autonomously) and 10km with Manyaleti.

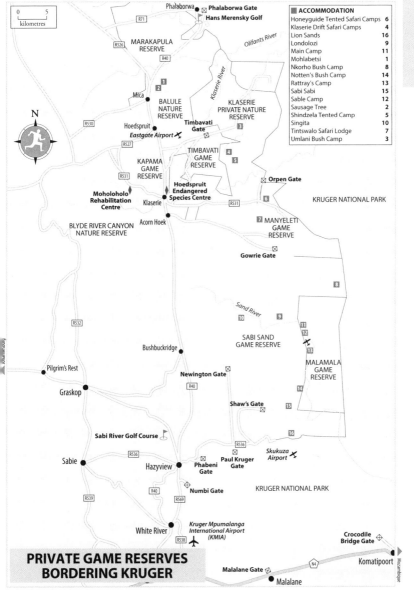

◼ ACCOMMODATION	
Honeyguide Tented Safari Camps	6
Klaserie Drift Safari Camps	4
Lion Sands	16
Londolozi	9
Main Camp	11
Mohlabetsi	1
Nkorho Bush Camp	8
Notten's Bush Camp	14
Rattray's Camp	13
Sabi Sabi	15
Sable Camp	12
Sausage Tree	2
Shindzela Tented Camp	5
Singita	10
Tintswalo Safari Lodge	7
Umlani Bush Camp	3

PRIVATE GAME RESERVES BORDERING KRUGER

ARRIVAL AND DEPARTURE
SABI SAND GAME RESERVE

By car There are three entrances to Sabi Sand: Shaw's Gate in the south, Newington Gate in the central part of the reserve, and Gowrie Gate in the north. The most convenient gate will depend on the location of your lodge or camp, which should be checked in advance. Shaw's and Newington gates are both reached from the R536 between Hazyview and the Kruger National Park's Paul Kruger Gate and are clearly signposted to the left coming from Hazyview. Both lie about 430km (6 hours) from Johannesburg's OR Tambo Airport, 100km (2.5 hours) from Kruger Mpumalanga International Airport and 35km (45 mins) from Skukuza Airport. The more remote Gowrie Gate lies 55km east of Bushbuckridge on the R40 between Hazyview and Hoedspruit.

By air Federal Air (☎ 011 395 9000, ⌨ fedair.com, R5500 one-way) operates a twice-daily shuttle service between Johannesburg and airstrips in Sabi Sand. A cheaper but less convenient option is to fly to Skukuza or Kruger Mpumalanga International Airport and arrange a transfer or car rental from there.

ACCOMMODATION
SEE MAP PAGE 127

Lion Sands ☎ 011 880 9992, ⌨ lionsands.com. Set in the far southeast of Sabi Sand, *Lion Sands* is one of the reserve's largest and most exclusive properties, so game drives tend to be as relaxed as they are productive. It is also the only reserve within Sabi Sand offering extensive frontage along the perennial Sabi River, and most of its five lodges have views onto the water. The flagship *River Lodge* comprises eighteen suites, all of which come with their own butler, and bathrooms that couldn't be more romantic. The food is top-notch, and the two swimming pools, heated in winter, are placed right next to the river so you can hang out and watch the hippos. The other lodges are smaller and even more opulent. $$$$$

★ **Londolozi** ☎ 013 735 5653, ⌨ londolozi.com. One of the first pioneers of ecotourism in Sabi Sand, *Londolozi* is renowned for its superb leopard viewing and for its association with the Varty family, which founded the first tourist lodge here in the 1970s and still manages it today. It comprises five small and ultra-luxurious camps with a classic safari style, fine food attested to by its Relais & Châteaux membership, and semi-exclusive access to around 150 square kilometres of superb game-viewing territory bisected by the Sand River. $$$$$

Nkorho Bush Camp ☎ 013 735 5367, ⌨ nkorho.com. A small, family-operated outfit in thinly wooded grassland, Nkorho scores on affordability. There are six simple chalets with showers, catering to a maximum of sixteen guests. The communal areas comprise an open-air lounge, a bar with a pool table and an African fantasy of a boma – constructed from gnarled tree trunks – where evening meals are served around an open fire. The swimming pool overlooks a productive water hole. $$$$$

★ **Notten's Bush Camp** ☎ 082 414 2711, ⌨ nottens. com. Four decades old and still resisting the temptation to expand, this family-run outfit feels as if you are staying on a sociable friend's farm and it remains a favourite with well-to-do South African bush lovers. It is the smallest property and most low-key lodge in the far south of Sabi Sand, but benefits from enjoying traversing rights with one larger and relatively exclusive neighbouring property. Meals are served around a fire, or on a massive deck that acts as a viewing platform. The camp houses just eight elegantly decorated private suites facing the plain and lit by paraffin oil lamps (with mosquito netting on windows and doors). The lack of electricity in the bedrooms is meant to bring guests into better contact with the bush. It offers very good value for a five-star game-viewing experience, and has a swimming pool where you can actually swim laps, next to the massage room. $$$$$

Sabi Sabi ☎ 011 447 7172, ⌨ sabisabi.com. Pick of the four lodges on this large property in southern Sabi Sand is *Earth Lodge*, whose thirteen innovative suites have a semi-subterranean feel like the world's most stylish and upmarket bunker – and feature individually designed furniture, a private plunge pool and a glass-fronted bathroom with indoor and outdoor shower. *Earth Lodge* is also renowned for its haute cuisine and fine wines, but isn't to everybody's taste – those seeking a more conventional safari experience are pointed to the 25-suite *Bush Lodge* or smaller *Little Bush Lodge*. Sabi Sabi has one of the larger properties in Sabi Sand but it lacks any river frontage. $$$$$

★ **Singita** ☎ 021 683 3424, ⌨ singita.com/region/singita-sabi-sand. Sharing much of their game-viewing territory with neighbouring *Londolozi* and also a member of Relais & Châteaux, award-winning *Singita Ebony* and *Boulders* lodges set the standard when it comes to innovative architecture, decor and menus. It is perhaps more overtly luxurious and has less of a bush feel than *Londolozi*, but the two vie with each other to be crowned the top pick in Sabi Sand. $$$$$

MalaMala Game Reserve

Bordering Kruger 65km east of Hazyview • R120 • ☎ 011 442 2267, ⌨ malamala.com

MalaMala is arguably the premier slice of safari real estate anywhere in Africa. As with neighbouring Sabi Sand, it fell within the original Sabie Game Reserve proclaimed by Paul Kruger in 1898, but was excluded from the area protected within the Kruger National Park as it was gazetted in 1926. The oldest and most autonomous of the private reserves that make up Greater Kruger, it started life as a seasonal hunting camp in 1930, but after being bought by the **Rattray family** in 1964, it was reinvented as a pioneering ecotourism destination offering photographic safaris to an international clientele of the rich and famous. The land remained in the Rattray

MALAMALA AT A GLANCE

A contender for South Africa's most rewarding Big Five destination.
Big Five: *****
General wildlife: ****
Birding: ***
Scenery: ***
Wilderness factor: *****
Uncrowded: *****
Affordability: *
Self-drive: N

family until 2013, when in the wake of a successful land claim, the South African government bought it and transferred ownership to the **Nwandlamhari Community**, which now manages the business in partnership with its former owners. MalaMala boasts an unusually low ratio of guests to land area, with just three small lodges sharing exclusive traversing rights to 133 square kilometres of prime game-viewing territory. This allows it to offer a uniquely exclusive safari experience underscored by the management policy of restricting the number of guests per game-drive vehicle to four or six (as opposed to the usual eight to ten) and a relaxed guiding style that focuses on making the most of good sightings rather than rushing from one thing to the next in a FOMO-ish frenzy.

Sharing an unfenced 19km eastern border with Kruger and enclosed by Sabi Sand on all other sides, MalaMala is dominated geographically by the near-perennial **Sand River**, whose wide sandy bed, fringed by a gorgeous ribbon of fig, jackal-berry and other riparian trees, runs through the reserve for a full 20km. Game drives tend to concentrate on the network of roads in and around the river, which attracts thirsty herds of elephant, buffalo, zebra and other wildlife throughout the year, as well as forming a popular winter hunting ground for the reserve's prolific lions and leopards. When it comes to leopard sightings, MalaMala possibly scores higher than any other reserve on the continent, so much so that it is quite unusual to go a day with encountering one of these enigmatic cats. Lion, elephant, white rhino, buffalo and giraffe are also usually seen on a daily basis, but black rhino, cheetah and African wild dog sightings are more sporadic, while hippos are usually present only in summer when the water level is at its highest. A striking bird commonly seen in the riverbed is the handsome saddle-billed stork.

ARRIVAL AND DEPARTURE
MALAMALA GAME RESERVE

By car Allow at least six hours for the 450km drive from Johannesburg's OR Tambo Airport. Follow the N12 and N4 east to Mbombela, then the R40 north to Hazyview, where you need to turn right at the main intersection onto the R536 towards Kruger's Paul Kruger Gate. About 37km out of Hazyview, turn left onto a dirt road signposted for Sabi Sand's Shaw's Gate and MalaMala. It is 7km from here to the gate and then another 18km or so to MalaMala, depending on which camp you are heading to.

By air Federal Air (☎ 011 395 9000, ⓦ fedair.com, R5500 one-way) operates a twice-daily shuttle service between Johannesburg and MalaMala's surfaced private airstrip, just 10 minutes' drive from the lodges. A cheaper but less convenient option is to take an Airlink flight to Skukuza Airport (twice daily from Johannesburg or once daily from Cape Town) and arrange a transfer or car rental from there.

ACCOMMODATION
SEE MAP PAGE 127

All lodges are managed by the reserve and can be booked through central reservations at ☎ 011 442 2267, ⓦ malamala.com. Direct contact numbers are given below.

★ **Main Camp** ☎ 013 735 9200. Established as a seasonal hunting camp in 1930, MalaMala's oldest and largest camp has a lovely location below luxuriant fig trees on the bank of the Sand River and is adorned with bougainvillea first planted in 1935. Most meals are taken on the wide riverside balcony, but bush dinners are often in a tree-shaded boma that also dates to the 1930s. The nineteen thatched cottages are very spacious and decorated in a warm African-themed style, and have wide balconies with river or waterhole views. Amenities include a large swimming pool, a gym and an extensive library. Game-drive vehicles carry a maximum of six guests. $$$$$

★ **Rattray's Camp** ✆ 013 735 3000. Built in 2005 and extensively renovated over 2018/9, super-luxurious *Rattray's* is the reserve's premier lodge, comprising eight modern cottages, each with four-poster bed and walk-in net, two indoor bathrooms and outside shower, air-con

and roof fan, large sitting area with DSTV discretely tucked away in a wardrobe, well-stocked mini-bar, and wide timber deck with plunge pool overlooking a stretch of the Sand River lined with jackal-berry and other riparian trees and regularly visited by all the Big Five. The buffet-style meals at this exclusive lodge are superb, drinks are included, and game drives carry a maximum of four guests per vehicle unless larger groups request to be together. $$$$$

Sable Camp ✆ 013 735 9200. Effectively an extension of *Main Camp* that operates as a separate lodge aimed at small groups, *Sable Camp* consists of seven cottages that are practically identical to those of its neighbour, but with a separate dining area and swimming pool. $$$$$

Manyeleti Game Reserve

Bordering Kruger immediately south of Orpen Gate • Gates open 6am–6pm • R30 per person, plus a community levy of R75 • ⓦ manyeleti.com

Manyeleti, a xiTsonga name that means "Place of Stars", extends across 230 square kilometres of savannah bordered by Kruger to the east and north, Sabi Sand to the south and Timbavati to the northwest. Boasting some stirring landscapes of open grasslands and rocky outcrops, it supports a similar spread of wildlife to its neighbours. Manyeleti was founded in 1963 and during the apartheid era, when Kruger was restricted to whites, it was the only reserve in the area that accepted non-whites. Today, following a successful land claim, the reserve is owned and managed by the local **Mnisi people**, who have lived in the area for many generations. The few camps within the reserve are privately owned and make use of the land, and its 200km of gravel roads, on a concession basis. General wildlife numbers are lower than in Sabi Sand due to the lack of permanent water, and leopards and lions are less conspicuous, but the open terrain is better suited to cheetahs and the relatively low number of camps means there are fewer vehicles about and it has more of a wilderness feel.

ARRIVAL AND DEPARTURE MANYALETI GAME RESERVE

By car Manyeleti lies about 480km by road from Johannesburg's OR Tambo Airport, a six-hour drive away. Follow the N12/N4 east as far as Belfast, then the R540 to Lydenberg via Dullstroom, and then the R36 and R530 to the intersection with the R40 near Acornhoek. From here,

follow the signposts to Orpen Gate for 35km, passing the South African Wildlife College, then shortly afterwards turn right to the signposted gate for Manyeleti.
By air The closest airport is at Hoedspruit, 65km to the northwest. Most camps can arrange a transfer from there.

ACCOMMODATION SEE MAP PAGE 127

MANYALETI AT A GLANCE

Top notch Big Five reserve known for its low-density family-friendly lodges.
Big Five: ****
General wildlife: ***
Birding: ***
Scenery: **
Wilderness factor: ****
Uncrowded: ***
Affordability: **
Self-drive: N

Honeyguide Tented Safari Camps 3km east of the entrance gate ✆ 015 793 1729, ⓦ honeyguidecamp. com. One of the more reasonably priced private camps in Greater Kruger, *Honeyguide* offers tented accommodation at each of its two locations: *Khoka Moya*, which is contemporary in design, and *Mantobeni*, which has more of a traditional safari-camp feel. With a lack of tended gardens, the camps maximize the bush feel, and although they don't have views of a river or a waterhole, they make up for it with attentive staff and superb rangers and trackers. Each tent is enormous and has its own bathroom with double showers and basins. These family-oriented lodges offer an imaginative kids' programme and show great tolerance of children of all ages. Meals are plated, and all beverages, including wine, are included in the price. $$$$

Tintswalo Safari Lodge 7km south of the entrance gate ☎ 011 300 8888, ⓦ tintswalo.com. This exclusive lodge comprises seven luxury suites connected by a raised wooden walkway and named after famous European explorers. The suites are individually decorated in colonial safari style, and come with a secluded deck and private plunge pool set on the bank of a seasonal river. Rates include game drives, meals and drinks. $$$$$

TIMBAVATI AT A GLANCE

Good all-round game-viewing with all the Big Five present.
Big Five: ****
General wildlife: ***
Birding: ***
Scenery: **
Wilderness factor: ****
Uncrowded: ****
Affordability: *
Self-drive: N

2

Timbavati Game Reserve

Bordering Kruger immediately north of Orpen Gate • Daily conservation levy R70 for self-catering camps and R328 for all-inclusive lodges • ☎ 015 793 2436, ⓦ timbavati.co.za

Established by an association of conservationist landowners, **Timbavati Game Reserve** was founded in 1956, dropped fences with the neighbouring Kruger National Park in 1993, and now extends over 534 square kilometres. Its xiTsonga name loosely translates as "Sacred Place" and derives from that of the Timbavati River, a wide sandy seasonal tributary of the Olifants which flows through the southern part of the reserve in a northeasterly direction before crossing into the Kruger close to Orpen Gate. The mixed bushveld of Timbavati protects a similar selection of wildlife to Central Kruger and Sabi Sand, including some large herds of buffalo, and plenty of lions, elephants, white rhino, giraffes, zebras and antelopes. It doesn't quite rank with Sabi Sand and MalaMala when it comes to all-but-guaranteed leopard encounters, but this most elusive member of the Big Five is still quite often seen here, and several individuals are very habituated to vehicles. There are fewer lodges and camps in Timbavati than in Sabi Sand, so it tends to be much quieter when it comes to tourist traffic, and it has a wilder and more untrammelled atmosphere.

WHITE LIONS OF TIMBAVATI

Timbavati Game Reserve is widely associated with the extraordinary phenomenon of **white lions**. This unusual colour morph is sometimes mistaken for albinism, but is actually caused by a recessive gene that might skip several generations and often results in piercing blue eyes. First documented in the Timbavati area in 1938, leucitic individuals have probably been a feature of the local lion population for centuries, and they have long been venerated among the local Tsonga people. The phenomenon first came to public attention in the 1970s when several white lions were born in the area, as documented in Chris McBride's 1977 bestseller *The White Lions of Timbavati*. They have since acquired something of a cult status, and they are bred selectively in several zoos worldwide, as well as being prized by trophy hunters. Oddly, while no white lions were seen in Timbavati and neighbouring parts of Kruger between 1994 and 2006, more than a dozen leucitic cubs have been recorded subsequent to that. Unfortunately, so far as can be ascertained, none of these white lions has survived to adulthood, not because they are inferior at hunting to their tawny counterparts, or otherwise less well adapted, but simply as a by-product of the high infant mortality rate amongst this most competitive of species. Still, several new litters are born every year, so there is always a chance visitors to Timbavati might be treated to a sighting of this rare phenomenon.

ARRIVAL AND DEPARTURE

By car Timbavati lies about 480km northeast of Johannesburg via Belfast, Lydenburg and Hoedspruit, and you should allow around six hours for the drive to most lodges and camps. Access is via Timbavati Control Gate, which is reached by following the R40 for about 6km south of Hoedspruit then turning left on to the

TIMBAVATI GAME RESERVE

Argyle Road, which is signposted for Hoedspruit Eastgate International Airport. You pass the airport to your left after about 5km and then it is another 12km to the control gate.

By air Most lodges can arrange a transfer from Hoedspruit Eastgate International Airport, 12km outside the reserve.

ACCOMMODATION

SEE MAP PAGE 127

There are a dozen upmarket lodges in Timbavati along with three very well-priced self-catering camps aimed at groups of family or friends; see ⓦ timbavati.co.za for a full list and links.

Shindzela Tented Camp 33km inside the reserve, accessed from Timbavati Gate ☎ 082 307 9493, ⓦ shindzela.co.za. The draws of this attractive and well-priced camp are its small size, affordability, bush atmosphere and walking opportunities. It is a twelve-bed unfenced, no-frills tented camp, with early morning walks of two to four hours, or game drives if you prefer. It also offers a daily shuttle from Johannesburg. $$$$

★ **Umlani Bush Camp** Close to Orpen Gate, accessed

from Orpen Rd ☎ 021 785 5547, ⓦ umlani.com. Eight reed-walled huts overlooking the dry Nhlaralumi River, each with an attached open-topped bush shower, heated by a wood boiler (there's no electricity). *Umlani* (meaning "place of rest") isn't fenced off, the emphasis being very much on a bush experience, and windows are covered with flimsy blinds so that you get to hear all the sounds of the night. The decor is simple, as is the food, though it's delicious and you don't end up overstuffed. Altogether, *Umlani* delivers a much more satisfying experience of the wild than many other places and is very good value. Check out their specials for some great deals. $$$$$

Klaserie Private Nature Reserve

Enclosed by Kruger, Timbavati and Balule to the east of Hoedspruit • ☎ 015 793 3051, ⓦ klaseriereserve.co.za

This lovely 600-square-kilometre nature reserve came into being in 1969 when 36 local landowners decided to drop fences with each other in the aftermath of a severe **drought** that had taken heavy toll on wildlife cut off from its traditional migration routes. Initially created as a pure conservation area rather than a tourist destination, **Klaserie** was the original site of the wilderness trails run by **Clive Walker** before he relocated his activities to the Lapalala Wilderness in 1977. Even today, it retains a wilder atmosphere and carries far lower tourist volumes than most reserves in Greater Kruger; the entire reserve is now unfenced, having dropped fences with the more easterly Kruger and Timbavati in 1993 and with Balule to the west in 2005. It is bisected by the Klaserie River, which runs from south to north through the centre of the reserve before it flows into the perennial Olifants on its northeastern border with Kruger, and is fringed by a green ribbon of riparian trees including nyala berry, jackal berry and sycamore fig. Although the Klaserie is seasonal and might stop flowing for months on end in protracted periods of drought, it is a major waterway with a wide sandy bed that almost invariably holds a few small pools in the driest of conditions, when elephants dig into the sand to access clean subterranean water. Klaserie is good for general game, though numbers drop in periods of drought, and it supports large numbers of elephant and lion, as well as some very habituated leopards. Because tourist volumes are low, game drives tend to be leisurely and focus on staying with good sightings rather than racing around to try to tick off the Big Five in one go.

KLASERIE AT A GLANCE

Scenic Klaserie probably has the wildest feeling of the private reserves in Greater Kruger, and the game viewing is very good.

Big Five: ****
General wildlife: ***
Birding: ***
Scenery: ***
Wilderness factor: *****
Uncrowded: *****
Affordability: *
Self-drive: N

ARRIVAL AND DEPARTURE

By car As with Timbavati, access is via Timbavati Control Gate, except that the lodges and camps lie to the northwest of the Argyle Road rather than the southeast.

KLASERIE NATURE RESERVE

By air Most lodges can arrange a transfer from Hoedspruit Eastgate International Airport, 12km from Timbavati Control Gate.

ACCOMMODATION

SEE MAP PAGE 127

★ **Klaserie Drift Safari Camps** ☎ 082 456 0673 or ☎ 015 793 2077, ⊛ klaseriedrift.co.za. This scenic conservancy in the remote heart of Klaserie operates two small and supremely stylish five-star camps with joint traversing rights to a 140-square-kilometre tract of undulating bushveld incised for 10km by the Klaserie River. The more established of these is *Amani Safari Camp*, a family-friendly four-room villa often booked in full by families and other groups, but also open to individuals and

couples. Better suited to couples is *Misava*, which opened in its present incarnation in 2019 but started life as a rustic private family lodge back in the 1960s. *Misava* comprises five standalone double units (the pick being the spacious and newly built riverview chalets) and boasts a superb cliffside location overlooking a stretch of riverbed that is regularly visited by elephant, giraffe and various antelope. Both lodges have a swimming pool, excellent cuisine and modern African-themed decor. $$$$$

Balule Nature Reserve

Bordering the Kruger immediately east of Hoedspruit • Daily entrance fee varies from one sector to the next

The least administratively cohesive of the private reserves bordering Kruger, **Balule** came into being in the early 1990s when a diverse group of landowners decided to drop fences between their properties. It became part of the Greater Kruger in 2005 when it dropped fences with Klaserie Nature Reserve, which borders it to the east, along with the Kruger and Timbavati, with which it shares small northern and southern borders respectively. The dominant feature of this 540-square-kilometre reserve is the perennial **Olifants River**, which flows through its northern half for about 20km before crossing into the Kruger. The river is a major magnet for thirsty wildlife in the dry season, with elephant, giraffe, greater kudu and nyala being particularly conspicuous on its banks. Balule is broken up into number of autonomous smaller conservancies, among them the Olifants West, Olifants North, Olifants East, York, Parsons and Grietjie Nature Reserves, each of which levies its own fees independently of the others. These are further subdivided into a disjointed mosaic of individual properties, and while some of the larger plots house proper lodges, many others are essentially private properties that might be smaller than one square kilometre in area. As a result, the wilderness feel of more developed parts of the reserve is undermined by a jumble of buildings, telephone lines, fences and other man-made constructions, and the situation with traversing rights can get pretty complex. That said, lodges in Balule tend to be good value, the wildlife viewing is no less rewarding than in most other parts of greater Kruger (though leopard sightings are infrequent) and the Olifants River is a truly magical presence, assuming you stay at a lodge with suitable traversing rights.

ARRIVAL AND DEPARTURE
BALULE NATURE RESERVE

By car The various camps and lodges in Balule Nature Reserve lie between 450 and 500km northeast of Johannesburg via Belfast, Lydenburg and Hoedspruit. Each of the subsidiary nature reserves within Balule has its own entrance gate set alongside or a short drive from the R40 between Hoedspruit and Phalaborwa.

By air Most lodges can arrange a transfer from Hoedspruit Eastgate International Airport, which lies about 25km from the most southerly access gate to Balule.

BALULE AT A GLANCE

This patchwork reserve in Greater Kruger offers a solid Big Five experience but feels less wild and remote than some of its neighbours.

Big Five: ★★★★
General wildlife: ★★★
Birding: ★★★
Scenery: ★★
Wilderness factor: ★★★
Uncrowded: ★★★★
Affordability: ★★
Self-drive: N

ACCOMMODATION
SEE MAP PAGE 127

Mohlabetsi York Nature Reserve ☎ 060 839 7693 or ☎ 082 503 8863, ⊕ mohlabetsi.co.za. This unpretentious and friendly eleven-room lodge feels like a smart variation on an old-style restcamp, offering accommodation in thatched rondavels with a/c, warm earthy decor, and outdoor and indoor shower. Breakfast and lunch are taken on a shady lawn where steenbok nibble at the grass and colourful birds flap around. Very good value; check the website for off-season specials. $$$$

★ **Sausage Tree** Olifants West Nature Reserve ☎ 015 793 0098, ⊕ sausagetree.co.za. The pick of the Balule's safari camps, *Sausage Tree* stands in a thick patch of woodland overlooking a small waterhole and has traversing rights to an atmospheric stretch of the nearby Olifants River. It is a small camp with very personalized attention, comprising just five comfortable standing tents with indoor tub, outdoor shower and private veranda. Meals are eaten communally on the deck, which has a plunge pool and is set high up with long views across the bushveld. Great value for money. $$$$

Eswatini

A tiny landlocked kingdom, **ESWATINI** – formerly known as Swaziland – is surrounded on three sides by South Africa, with **Mozambique** providing its eastern border along the Lebombo Mountains. Although South Africa's influence predominates, Eswatini was a British protectorate from 1903 until independence in 1968, and today the country offers an intriguing mix of colonial heritage and home-grown confidence, giving the place a friendlier, more relaxed and often safer feeling than its larger neighbour. Eswatini is traversed by the most direct road route between Kruger and northern KwaZulu-Natal, and the kingdom's outstanding scenery and commitment to wildlife conservation makes it well worth exploring for those with a car and a bit of time. A good network of national parks and other reserves exemplify the kingdom's geographical diversity. All offer good-value accommodation, and those without larger, more dangerous mammals can be explored on foot, horseback or by bike, offering an inexpensive opportunity to become truly intimate with this African landscape and her inhabitants. While not as efficiently run as South Africa's national parks, the Swazi reserves are less officious, and many people warm to their easy-going nature. Rather less compelling are the two main cities, **Mbabane** and **Manzini**, both of which can easily be bypassed by self-drivers en route to the game reserve.

ARRIVAL AND DEPARTURE
ESWATINI

BORDER CROSSINGS
Crossing the border is fairly easy – you simply show your passport and pay E50 in road tax. There are eleven border posts with South Africa and two serving Mozambique. The most convenient ones are listed below:

Ngwenya/Oshoek (7am–noon) is the most popular, the closest to Johannesburg and the easiest route to Mbabane. Can be very busy during holidays and weekends.

Sandlane/Nerston (8am–6pm) is a good alternative 35km further south, roughly 70km from Johannesburg.

Sicunusa/Houdkop (8am–6pm) is just off the N2 from Piet Retief in the southwest, which leads to the wonderfully scenic and fast MR4.

Mahamba (7am–10pm) in the south, runs lots of traffic from N2/Piet Retief and beyond.

Lavumisa/Golela (24hr) in the southeast, close to the KwaZulu-Natal coast, is the second-busiest crossing.

Mhlumeni/Goba (24hr) is a busy crossing into Mozambique and the main route for traffic from the southern half of South Africa, so expect lots of lorries.

Lomahasha/Namaacha (7am–8pm) is the second crossing into Mozambique, passing through Hlane Royal National Park and the scenic Lebombo Mountains.

Mananga (7am–6pm) leads to Kruger and the busy Lembombo border between South Africa and Mozambique.

Matsamo/Jeppe's Reef (8am–8pm) in the north, handy if you're coming in from Kruger Park and Mbombela.

Bulembu/Josefdal (8am–4pm), via Piggs Peak in the north, is the most spectacular crossing in the country, but the bad road makes it difficult in an ordinary car.

BY BUS
Several bus companies run a regular service in large, comfortable minibuses between South Africa and Eswatini. The best is TransMagnifique (☎ 24049977, ⊕ goswaziland. co.sz), which runs several buses daily between Mbabane and Johannesburg (4hr; E750 one-way), stopping at OR Tambo Airport and Sandton. TransMagnifique also runs a bus connecting Mbabane to Mbombela and Kruger National Park Airport (E600) on Fridays, Saturdays and Sundays,

and a bus connecting it to Durban (E1000) on Fridays and Sundays. Book in advance online. A cheaper option is to catch Kombi minibuses (see below), which ply the main routes into Eswatini from Johannesburg and Mbombela, and depart when they are full.

GETTING AROUND

By car Driving is the best way to see Eswatini; distances are small, the main sights are near tarred roads, and the major gravel roads are in good condition. Self-drive exploration of the Swazi game reserves is a thrilling, and affordable, alternative to guided tours. Most dirt roads are passable with an ordinary vehicle in dry months. Driving standards, however, are poor – two of the last four ministers of transport have died in road accidents. Also, the general speed limit of 80km/h outside towns is universally ignored and rarely enforced. Car rental outlets are at the airport.

By Kombi minibus Eswatini is crisscrossed by a network of cheap Kombi minibus routes that cover almost every

2

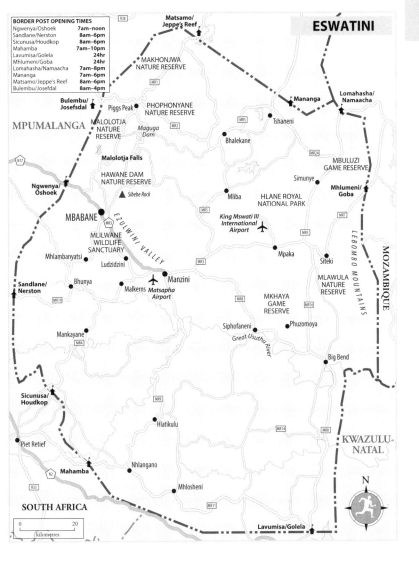

ESWATINI

BORDER POST OPENING TIMES
Ngwenya/Oshoek	7am–noon
Sandlane/Nerston	8am–6pm
Sicunusa/Houdkop	8am–6pm
Mahamba	7am–10pm
Lavumisa/Golela	24hr
Mhlumeni/Goba	24hr
Lomahasha/Namaacha	7am–8pm
Mananga	7am–6pm
Matsamo/Jeppe's Reef	8am–6pm
Bulembu/Josefdal	8am–4pm

MPUMALANGA

Matsamo/Jeppe's Reef
R38

MAKHONJWA NATURE RESERVE
MR1

Bulembu/Josefdal
Piggs Peak
PHOPHONYANE NATURE RESERVE

MALOLOTJA NATURE RESERVE
Maguga Dam
MR2

Malolotja Falls

HAWANE DAM NATURE RESERVE

Ngwenya/Oshoek
N17

Sibebe Rock

MBABANE
MR3

EZULWINI VALLEY

MLILWANE WILDLIFE SANCTUARY

Mhlambanyatsi
Ludzidzini

Sandlane/Nerston
Bhunya
MR19
Malkerns
Matsapha Airport
Manzini

Mankayane
MR4

Sicunusa/Houdkop
MR9

Piet Retief

Hlatikulu

Mahamba
N2
Nhlangano

Mhlosheni

SOUTH AFRICA
R33
MR11

Mananga
Lomahasha/Namaacha
MR5
Tshaneni
Bhalekane
MR24

MBULUZI GAME RESERVE

Simunye
Mhlumeni/Goba

Mliba
HLANE ROYAL NATIONAL PARK
MR5

King Mswati III International Airport
MR1
MR7

Mpaka
Siteki

MR3
MLAWULA NATURE RESERVE

MKHAYA GAME RESERVE
MR8
MR16

Siphofaneni
Phuzomoya
Great Usuthu River

Big Bend

LEBOMBO MOUNTAINS

MOZAMBIQUE

MR14
MR8

KWAZULU-NATAL

N

Lavumisa/Golela

0   20
kilometres

ESWATINI TRAVEL BASICS

MONEY

Currency is the **lilangeni** – plural **emalangeni** (E) – which is tied to the South African rand (1 rand = 1 lilangeni). The rand is legal tender in Eswatini, so you won't have to change any money, but note that emalangeni are not convertible outside Eswatini.

PHONES AND PHONE NUMBERS

The **country code** for Eswatini is ☎ 268, followed by the destination number (there are no area codes). The code for phoning out from Eswatini is ☎ 00, followed by the country and area codes and finally the destination number. To arrange a **collect call**, dial ☎ 94.

Eswatini has only one mobile phone network – MTN – which generally works well throughout the country. You can easily buy a chip for your phone in Mbabane.

PUBLIC HOLIDAYS

January 1
Good Friday
Easter Monday
April 19 (King Mswati III's birthday)
April 25 (National Flag Day)
May 1 (Workers' Day)
Ascension Day
July 22 (King Sobhuza II's birthday)
August/September (Umhlanga Dance Day)
September 6 (Somhlolo/Independence Day)
December/January (Incwala Day)
December 25 (Christmas Day)
December 26 (Boxing Day)

RED TAPE AND VISAS

Nationals of most Commonwealth countries (excluding Bangladesh, India, Pakistan and Sri Lanka), the US, Canada, South Africa, Australia and all EU countries are granted 30 days on entry, and may apply for a further 30-day extension. Other nationals must obtain visas before arrival. Eswatini's embassies are in Mbabane.

TOUR OPERATORS

The country's biggest **tour operator** is Swazi Trails (☎ 24162180, ⓦ swazitrails.co.sz), which offers tours to the royal village and game parks along with whitewater rafting, quad biking, caving and other activities.

WEBSITES

ⓦ **biggameparks.org** Provides information on three of the country's most visited reserves, the Hlane, Mlilwane and Mkhaya parks, with practical information about activities, and an accommodation booking site.

ⓦ **sntc.org.sz** The website of the Eswatini National Trust Commission includes detailed information about all public cultural sites and reserves not administered by Big Game Parks.

ⓦ **swazi.travel** Hosted by Swazi Trails, with an efficient online accommodation booking service, reams of information about shopping and restaurants, and details of tours and activities around Eswatini.

ⓦ **thekingdomofswaziland.com** Eswatini's official tourism website is packed with useful information, including hotel listings.

corner of the country. The Kombis leave when full from stations in the main towns, and cover the main routes linking the towns, calling at set stops along the way. Some walking to get to your final destination is likely, so make sure you're travelling light. Ask at the local bus station about the best route to get to your destination. The stations are organized by destination, so all Kombis to, say, Manzini will leave from one corner of the station, and to Big Bend from another. Although buses tend to get quite packed, they are a great way of meeting people.

Malolotja Nature Reserve

E30 • Daily 6am–6pm • ☎ 24443241, ⓦ sntc.org.sz

Eswatini's least touristy reserve, easy-going **Malolotja** offers awesome scenery, rugged nature, tranquillity, and some of the finest **hiking** in Southern Africa. Extending across 180 square kilometres, the mountains here are among the most ancient in the world, estimated to be 3.6 billion years old, and they span altitudes from 640m in the deep Nkomati River Valley to 1829m on **Ngwenya Peak**, Swaziland's second highest mountain.

MALOLOTJA AT A GLANCE

Wild mountainscapes and scenic waterfalls characterize this hiker-friendly reserve, but wildlife is patchy.

Big Five: None
General wildlife: **
Birding: ****
Scenery: *****
Wilderness factor: *****
Uncrowded: *****
Affordability: *****
Self-drive: Y

2

The reserve's montane grassland is graced by myriad streams and waterfalls, including the 95m-high **Malolotja Falls**. Nearly three hundred species of **birds** are found in Malolotja, most notably an impressive colony of the rare southern bald ibis just by the waterfalls. You'll have to look harder for game, but it supports Eswatini's only populations of black wildebeest and red hartebeest, along with blesbok, Burchell's zebra and other grazers. Leopards also lurk somewhere in the gaping tracts of mountain and valley, and elephant pass through on rare occasions. Malolotja's small network of roads passes some fine viewpoints and picnic sites, but to really savour this park's rugged wilderness and see its waterfalls you'll need to hike. Trails range from easy half-day excursions to epic seven-day marathons, with basic campsites available en route (see below). **Forbes Reef Gold Mine**, a few kilometres south of the reserve's main entrance on the main tarred road, can be visited alone, but take care on the slippery banks; you can find it using the map you get on arrival at the main entrance.

ARRIVAL AND INFORMATION

By Kombi Minibus Kombis between Mbabane and Piggs Peak stop at the main gate, which is clearly signposted on the Mbabane–Matsamo Rd.

Information and supplies Brochures and maps are available from the reserve's reception building, 500m from the main entrance gate. The reception also houses a nice

MALOLOTJA NATURE RESERVE

restaurant (daily 8am–4pm; ☎ 76606755), and there's a curio shop that sells basic provisions, but it's wiser to stock up in Piggs Peak or Mbabane.

Climate If you're on a long hike during the summer, be prepared for hot days; however, temperatures drop dramatically in winter, when the nights can be freezing.

ACCOMMODATION

Campsites ☎ 76606755, ⓦ sntc.org.sz. For those attempting longer hikes, there are 21 scenic overnight camps scattered around the reserve, all with natural water sources but few other facilities (except braai areas), so you'll need to bring all your own equipment. Camps 11 and 12 are near Malolotja Falls. Book in advance. §

Main Restcamp ☎ 76606755, ⓦ sntc.org.sz. Fifteen tent sites with hot water in a communal ablutions block, and braai areas, as well as thirteen comfortable log cabins, each sleeping up to five people and kitted out with their own fireplaces. The cabins are a short walk from the main reception so you can eat at the restaurant there if you don't fancy cooking. Book in advance and ask for a cabin in the front row for uninterrupted views. §

Sobantu Guest Farm and Backpackers ☎ 86053954, ⓦ sobantu-swaziland.net. Tucked away on a rural hillside, but with easy access to both Malolotja and Maguuga dam, this low-key backpacker hostel consists of four rondavels scattered on a grassy slope, with rocky hills leaning just behind, while the main house has several very basic double rooms and dorms. The small kitchen and comfortable lounge with a large satellite TV are decorated with a nice creative touch, and the bar area, with pool table and central fireplace, is a treat. Service can be very laidback, but the honest, friendly ambience and stunning location will make it a winner for the open-minded. Excursions are offered throughout the area. §

2

HLANE AT A GLANCE

Second-tier game reserve well-suited to self-drivers travelling between Kruger and Zululand.
Big Five: ***
General wildlife: ***
Birding: ***
Scenery: **
Wilderness factor: **
Uncrowded: ****
Affordability: *****
Self-drive: Y

Hlane Royal National Park

E50 • Daily 6am–6pm • ⓦ biggameparks.org

Some 67km northeast of Manzini, **Hlane** (Siswati for "Wilderness") is the largest conservation area in Eswatini at 220 square kilometres. Formerly a private royal hunting ground, it was proclaimed a National Park in 1967 under instruction of King Sobhuza ll. The main attraction here is the presence of big game, including elephant, rhino, lion and leopard. Hlane has a large population of easy-to-spot elephants and rhino in the northern area of the park, which you can also visit in your own vehicle, and rhino sightings are virtually guaranteed. Other animals in this section include giraffe, zebra and waterbuck. Various **southern enclosures** contain lion and leopard, along with some more elephant and rhino. Although the enclosures guarantee lion sightings, the animals are well habituated to vehicles and look completely uninterested. Hlane is also home to the largest population of tree-nesting vultures in Africa, including the white-backed vulture and the endangered Cape vulture.

ARRIVAL AND INFORMATION
HLANE ROYAL NATIONAL PARK

By car The entrance to Hlane is roughly 7km south of Simunye, off the Manzini–Lomahasha Rd.

By Kombi Kombis running between Manzini and Simunye stop 300m from the park gate.

Guided tours Birding or game tours on foot (E225 for 2hr 30min) are available any time during the day from the reception at Main Camp. You can join a guided tour in one of the park's Land Rovers (E375 for 2hr 30min), with sunrise (5.30am) and sunset (4.30pm) tours also available (E395 for 2hr 30min). The more adventurous can head out for a sunrise cycle (E300 for 2hr) or an overnight hike, fully catered and staying over at a basic bush camp (E1635). Bookings at *Main Camp* reception.

ACCOMMODATION

Bhubesi Camp 14km from Main Camp along a dirt track ☎ 23838868, ⓦ biggameparks.org. These four-person self-catering stone cottages overlook a dry river and feel much more remote than the main campsite, though they do have electricity. ⚡

Ndlovu Main Camp ☎ 23838868, ⓦ biggameparks. org. Situated near the gate, with large self-catering thatched cottages that sleep up to eight people and en-suite rondavels sleeping two. There's no electricity (paraffin lamps and gas cooker are provided), but the basic but adequate accommodation provides a relaxed setting, allowing you to focus on the wildlife. ⚡

Ndlovu Camping Area Main Camp ☎ 23838868, ⓦ biggameparks.org. Open camping ground with plenty of soft grass and trees using a communal kitchen and ablution block (with hot water) and plenty of firewood available in the braai area. ⚡

EATING

Ndlovu Restaurant Main Camp. A large thatched restaurant and lounge area, with a wide deck overlooking a nearby watering hole that attracts rhino, elephant and giraffe. There's a reliable à la carte menu offering the usual gamut of chicken and steak, as well as a buffet at dinner time. Unless there's a large group staying, the wide deck is fairly relaxed, with plenty of trees and shady spots to sit. Daily 7am–8pm.

Mbuluzi Game Reserve

E45 • Daily 6am–6pm • ☎ 2383 8861, ⓦ mbuluzigamereserve.co.sz

Privately owned and little known, **Mbuluzi** is about 1km off the Manzini–Lomahasha road in the direction of Mlawula Nature Reserve. Set in classic lowveld bush, it encompasses two perennial rivers, riverine forest and some rocky precipices, and is a quietly special landscape that has created a loyal following. It has recently been restocked with game, including giraffe, hippo, Burchell's zebra, warthog, blue wildebeest, impala, greater kudu, bushbuck and nyala, which you can view in your own vehicle – a 4WD is recommended – or on a bike. The absence of large predators in Mbuluzi also means that you can walk along a network of clearly demarcated trails.

MBULUZI AT A GLANCE

Scenic off-the-beaten-track gem ideal for self-guided walks.
Big Five: N/A
General wildlife: ***
Birding: ****
Scenery: ****
Wilderness factor: ***
Uncrowded: ****
Affordability: *****
Self-drive: Y

ARRIVAL AND DEPARTURE   MBULUZI GAME RESERVE

By car 10km past Simunye on the MR3.
By Kombi Minibus Kombis from Manzini and Simunye to the Lomahasha border stop at the Maphiveni junction, from where it's a 15min hike to the gate.

ACCOMMODATION

Campsite ⓦ mbuluzigamereserve.co.sz. The campsite is situated in the northern section of the reserve, close to the Mbuluzi River. Facilities include a shower block and the obligatory braai area. Book in advance. $̄

Lodges ⓦ mbuluzigamereserve.co.sz. Mbuluzi's accommodation consists of six privately owned self-catering lodges set well apart and located along forested riverbanks in the southern section of the reserve. They range from luxury-tented camps at *Tambuti* to a rustic stone cottage, *Leadwood Lodge*, to ultra-modern bush hideaway *Imfihlo Lodge*. Most feature creature comforts such as swimming pools, DSTV and a/c. Three of the lodges sleep eight, one sleeps six and one five, while a studio cottage sleeps two. Book well in advance. $̄$̄

Mlilwane Wildlife Sanctuary

E50 • Daily 24hr • ⓦ biggameparks.org

Set in the **eZulwini Valley** south of Mbabane, **Mlilwane Wildlife Sanctuary** is for many visitors the highlight of Eswatini, with its relaxed atmosphere and attractive, game-filled plains. The name Mlilwane refers to the "little fire" that sometimes appears when lightning strikes the granite mountains. As well as offering good game viewing and activities, Mlilwane is an easy alternative to staying in Mbabane, though given its popularity, it's wise to book ahead. The

MLILWANE AT A GLANCE

Popular and accessible backpacker-friendly sanctuary focusing on non-dangerous wildlife.
Big Five: N/A
General wildlife: ***
Birding: ***
Scenery: ***
Wilderness factor: **
Uncrowded: ****
Affordability: *****
Self-drive: Y

reserve holds a special place in the history of wildlife conservation in Eswatini; it was here that **Ted Reilly** (see page 140) first realized his dream of a sanctuary for Eswatini's fast-disappearing wildlife. Mlilwane's animals are mainly **herbivorous**, and include zebra, bountiful numbers of antelope and the sanctuary's emblem, the warthog. There's also the occasional crocodile and hippopotamus, which means you still need to be cautious if viewing the game on foot, bike or horseback.

ARRIVAL AND DEPARTURE   MLILWANE WILDLIFE SANCTUARY

By car To get to Mlilwane, take the turning from the eZulwini Valley Rd, signposted about 1km beyond the turn-off to Ludzidzini. From here it's 3.5km along a dirt road to the entrance gate, where you pay your entrance fee – if arriving after 6pm entry fees are paid at the main restcamp the following morning. Note that you'll need to show both your entry and accommodation receipts in order to leave the sanctuary again, or they may charge you twice.
By shuttle bus There is a daily shuttle bus that runs between *Sondzela* backpackers and Malandela's Homestead (a popular arts and crafts venue off the MR103), leaving *Sondzela* at 8am (see below) and Malandela's about half an hour later.

2

THE SWAZI CONSERVATION STORY

Eswatini owes the creation and survival of three of its major wildlife sanctuaries – Mlilwane, Mkhaya and Hlane – to **Ted Reilly**, who was born in Mlilwane in 1938, the son of a British Anglo-Boer War soldier who had decided to make the country his home. As Reilly was growing up, Swazi wildlife and its natural habitats were coming under serious threat from poachers and commercial farmers. In 1959 Reilly lobbied the colonial government to set aside land for parks, but was defeated by farmers who wanted the land for commercial agriculture. Undeterred, he turned his Mlilwane estate into a park anyway, and set about cultivating a relationship with **King Sobhuza II**. After Swazi independence Sobhuza became much more powerful, and Reilly's connection to him lent weight to his nature conservation efforts.

Despite rickety finances, the **Mlilwane Wildlife Sanctuary** opened in 1961, and the restocking and reintroduction of species has continued ever since. Meanwhile, Sobhuza asked Reilly to help stamp out poaching at Hlane. Reilly's tough approach resulted in shootouts with the poachers, earning him the praise of some, but the enmity of many.

Reilly's dependence on his royal links has also generated controversy, and some critics also assert that Reilly subordinates wildlife management principles to the needs of the tourist industry. Reilly's answer to his critics is simply to point to the three game parks his company runs. It's a powerful argument – without Reilly, the parks would not exist. Ted Reilly still lives at Mlilwane and remains active in Swazi conservation.

INFORMATION AND ACTIVITIES

Maps The park office, easy to spot in the middle of the main restcamp, sells maps of cycling and hiking routes in the sanctuary (E25).

Guided trails Guided walks and game drives are available through the park office at the main restcamp. There are also guided mountain-bike tours and horseback trails, both fairly relaxed ways of taking in the park's attractions. For those with a little more horseback experience, fully catered overnight trails involve camping in caves and rustic trail camps in the more remote parts of the reserve. For details, see ⓦ biggameparks.org.

Self-guided trails More than 40km of road enables you to drive through the park to view game. There are also a number of good cycling routes running throughout the park; the main restcamp rents out mountain bikes (E135/hr). The best of the self-guided walking trails is the Macobane Hill Trail, a gentle, four-hour hike through the mountains. The more adventurous can climb to the top of Nyonyane, the "Execution Rock", which rises so prominently in the north of the reserve. Whichever route you choose to take, it's important you tell a ranger of your plans before heading out; they keep track of who's out on their own and come out to find you if you're not back by dusk.

ACCOMMODATION

The reserve offers a wide variety of accommodation, which should be booked through Eswatini Big Game Parks Central Reservations (☎ 25283944, ⓦ biggameparks.org), though *Sondzela* (see below) can also be booked directly.

Main Rest Camp About 3.5km from the gate ☎ 25283992. Accommodation is basic but well kept, including a campsite, traditional beehive villages, two- and four-person rondavels and larger family cottages. A few fearless animals move freely around the camp's centre, and, slightly removed, there is a very welcome swimming pool. Self-catering and B&B options available. $̱

Reilly's Rock Hilltop Lodge On a hilltop about 30min drive from Main Rest Camp. A lovely colonial home full of antiques and hardwood furniture, and with a wrap-around veranda, situated on a hilltop surrounded by woodland and prolific birdlife. With only six rooms, it's more upmarket than a guesthouse but more rustic than a game lodge, and guests can enjoy fantastic views over the Mdzimba Mountains, and wander round the impressive gardens that surround the house. Rates include half-board. $̱$̱$̱

Sondzela Backpacker Lodge 20min walk from Main Rest Camp ☎ 25283992. A friendly place firmly established on the backpacking circuit, with dorms, doubles and comfortable adobe rondavels sleeping two overlooking the valley, all with communal ablution facilities. Camping is also an option (tents only), and there's a lush garden, bar and large swimming pool. This is a rare chance to overnight in a nature reserve at budget prices, and they offer pickups from Malandela's Homestead. $̱

EATING

You can only buy basic supplies at the Main Rest Camp, so if you've opted for self-catering accommodation it's best to stock up beforehand at the Gables Shopping Centre, which lies on the main road from Mbabane a few kilometres outside the entrance gate.

Hippo Haunt At the Main Rest Camp. The only restaurant at Mlilwane serves up some good grilled meats on the Swazi braai, a delicious chicken tikka focaccia sandwich, and buffet dinners on busy nights. There's also a well-stocked bar. The restaurant overlooks an artificially created pond, which is home to hippos, crocs and a huge variety of birds, and is a superb place to while away a few hours. Daily 6.30am–10pm.

Sondzela Backpacker Lodge A 20min walk from Main Rest Camp ☎ 25283992. Inexpensive breakfasts and dinners are available at *Sondzela*, served in front of the campfire. There's only one dish on offer – such as stewed impala prepared in cast-iron pots over an open fire – in addition to a vegetarian option. Dinner must be ordered in advance. Dinner daily 6pm.

Mkhaya Game Reserve

35km east of Manzini on the MR8, 6km past Siphofaneni • Pick-up at 10am and 4pm • ☎ 25283944, ⓦ biggameparks.org

The closest thing in Swaziland to an upmarket private reserve, **Mkhaya** is situated along a turn-off from the wonderfully named village of **Phuzumoya** ("drink the wind") in classic lowveld scrubland, filled with acacia and thorn trees. A sanctuary for the rare black rhino, Mkhaya also accommodates white rhino and numerous antelopes such as nyala, sable and eland. In 2016, the reserve's elephants were sold to US zoos to avoid almost certain death as a result of the devastating drought, but plans are in place to reintroduce new individuals. In addition, Mkhaya operates as a refuge where endangered species such as roan antelope and tsessebe are bred. Rubbing shoulders with them, in the reserve section closest to the road, are herds of **Nguni cattle**.

MKHAYA AT A GLANCE

Private breeding sanctuary for rhino and rare antelopes.
Big Five: *
General wildlife: **
Birding: ***
Scenery: **
Wilderness factor: **
Uncrowded: ****
Affordability: **
Self-drive: N

INFORMATION
MKHAYA GAME RESERVE

Essentials Book your visit to Mkhaya through Swazi Big Game Parks Central Reservations (☎ 25283944, ⓦ biggameparks.org). Day-visits cost E840 (minimum two people), including lunch. Day-visits and overnight stays at Mkhaya must be booked in advance (see above), and you can't tour Mkhaya in your own vehicle, but must arrange to be met at the gate (10am or 4pm) from where you'll drive in convoy to the reserve's ranger base and the starting point of the first game drives – Kombi buses from Manzini to Big Bend stop at the gate; ask for the Phuzumoya shop drop.

Game drives Day-visitors are taken on a game drive from the ranger base, and you'll have a high chance of encountering much of the big game. A generous lunch at the main camp is included in the price. For overnighters, morning and evening game drives are included in the accommodation price, and a sunrise walking safari can also be organized. Unlike game reserves in South Africa, Mkhaya's experienced Swazi rangers have few qualms about stopping in the middle of a game drive and inviting visitors to get out of the vehicle and walk quite close to white rhino.

ACCOMMODATION

Stone Camp ☎ 25283944, ⓦ biggameparks.org. The reserve's only camp makes up for the lack of elevation in the reserve with an atmospheric bush setting beside the dry Ngwenyane river bed. Accommodation is offered in seductively luxurious open-plan and open-sided thatched stone huts with en-suite toilets and showers, which give you a wonderful sense of sleeping right in the bush. Beautifully prepared three-course meals are served around a large campfire in the main part of the camp, under the shade of a massive sausage tree (its seed pods look like sausages). Birding within the camp is excellent. Price includes meals and three guided game drives. $$$$

KwaZulu-Natal

STUNNING SCENERY, GIANT'S CASTLE

KwaZulu-Natal

KwaZulu-Natal is South Africa's most ecologically diverse province and the most emphatically African in character. It runs inland from a lush subtropical Indian Ocean coastline to the uKhahlamba-Drakensberg, a jagged spine of 3000-plus metre peaks that's frequently blanketed in snow in winter. Best known within South Africa for the beach resorts that line its southern coast, KwaZulu-Natal is also highly alluring to wildlife enthusiasts thanks to a network of more than fifty private and provincial reserves, which include Hluhluwe-iMfolozi, famed for its rhinos, and the community-run Tembe Elephant Park. KwaZulu-Natal also hosts a pair of contrasting UNESCO World Heritage sites: the iSimangaliso Wetland Park, which protects the untrammelled and staggeringly beautiful 220km stretch of coast running south from the border with Mozambique, and the lofty uKhahlamba-Drakensberg Park, a hiker's paradise studded with prehistoric rock-art sites.

Kwazulu-Natal took its present shape in 1994, when the apartheid-era province of Natal was melded with the territorially interlocked homeland of KwaZulu (and a small section of the former Transvaal around Pongola) to become the new South Africa's second-most populous province. It is probably the country's most culturally homogenous region, and the only one to recognize a monarch, namely **King Goodwill Zwelitheni**, who is a great-great grand-nephew of King Shaka, the early nineteenth-century founder of the Zulu Nation (see page 152).

When it comes to wildlife viewing, the lush northern coastal belt of KwaZulu-Natal – a tight patchwork of wilderness and ancestral African lands unofficially but widely known as **Zululand**, or as you head further north, **Maputaland** – rivals the lowveld of Greater Kruger as South Africa's premier safari destination. True, Zululand and Maputaland lack for any single conservation area remotely comparable in geographic scale to the Kruger, but their tangled mosaic of several dozen provincial and private reserves offers visitors far more when it comes to experiential and ecological variety. Pride of place goes to **iSimangaliso Wetland Park**, a 3320-square-kilometre UNESCO World Heritage Site whose patchwork of wetland reserves, coastal forests and marine

---

PARK FEES AND BOOKINGS IN KWAZULU-NATAL

Most provincial reserves in KwaZulu-Natal are administered by **Ezemvelo KwaZulu-Natal Wildlife** (EKZNW; ☎ 033 845 1000, ⓦ kznwildlife.com), which also determines entrance fees and handles all reservation bookings for official restcamps and campsites. Two notable exceptions are **Tembe Elephant Park**, which is co-managed by EKZNW and the local community, and the various components of **iSimangaliso**, which are owned by EKZNW but managed by the Isimangaliso Wetland Park Authority (☎ 082 797 7944, ⓦ isimangaliso.com). In the case of Tembe Elephant Park, fees are determined by the park and accommodation must booked directly through it (☎ 082 651 2868, ⓦ tembe.co.za). For iSimangaliso, fees are determined by the wetland authority, but accommodation is still booked through EKZNW. A resultant quirk from this is that visitors with a **Wild Card** (see page 41) are allowed free entry to all reserves under the direct control of EKZNW, for instance Hluhluwe-iMfolozi and Ithala, but not to Tembe or iSimangaliso. A separate **Rhino Card** (R250 per person per annum; ⓦ kznwildlife.com/rhino%20card.html) allows free entrance to all provincial reserves in KwaZulu-Natal, including Tembe and iSimangaliso, but this is only available to citizens or residents of South Africa.

BOATS ON LAKE ST LUCIA

Highlights

❶ Hluhluwe-iMfolozi Park KwaZulu-Natal's most outstanding provincial game reserve is famed for black and white rhino. See page 147

❷ Lake St Lucia Most easily explored on boat trips from the eponymous village, Lake St Lucia is a firm highlight of the iSimangaliso Wetland Park. See page 153

❸ Sodwana Bay Swim with ragged-tooth sharks, sea turtles and bright tropical fish at this premier diving destination. See page 167

❹ Pongola Game Reserve Highlights of what is arguably KwaZulu-Natal's most underrated private reserve include rhino tracking and boat trips on Pongolapoort Dam. See page 174

❺ Phinda Private Game Reserve One of the finest private reserves anywhere in South Africa, this &Beyond property bordering iSimangaliso offers superb Big Five viewing as well as several localized "sand forest" specials. See page 176

❻ Zimanga Private Game Reserve A total of nine strategically located hides makes this sumptuous upmarket reserve irresistible for dedicated wildlife photographers. See page 178

❼ Giant's Castle Game Reserve The mountainous uKhahlamba-Drakensberg is renowned for its scenery, hiking and prehistoric rock art. Giant's Castle offers all this, plus a wide variety of montane wildlife. See page 188

HIGHLIGHTS ARE MARKED ON THE MAP ON PAGE 146

sanctuaries includes Lake St Lucia, Cape Vidal, Western Shores, False Bay, uMkhuze Game Reserve, Sodwana Bay, Lake Sibaya and Kosi Bay.

Zululand also contains several top-notch Big Five reserves – most legendarily **Hluhluwe-iMfolozi** and **Phinda** – known for their high densities of both white and black rhino, whilst also supporting healthy populations of lion, elephant, giraffe, buffalo, warthog and various other safari favourites. But here, far more than in Kruger, it's easy to supplement the standard safari regime of twice-daily game drives with other activities, from exploring pristine beaches lined with some of the world's tallest sand dunes or snorkelling offshore coral reefs alive with colourful fish to boating across lakes teeming with hippos and crocs and hiking through ancient forests alive with vibrant

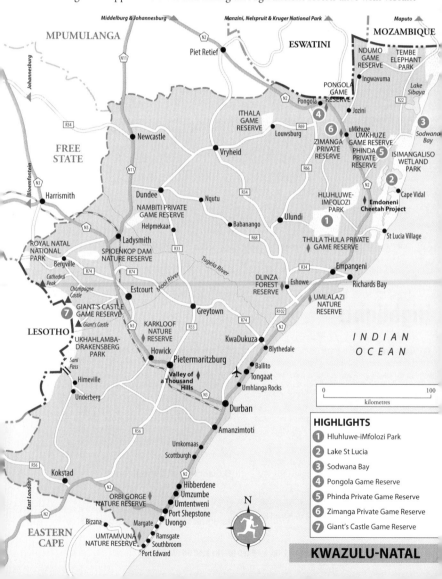

HIGHLIGHTS

1. Hluhluwe-iMfolozi Park
2. Lake St Lucia
3. Sodwana Bay
4. Pongola Game Reserve
5. Phinda Private Game Reserve
6. Zimanga Private Game Reserve
7. Giant's Castle Game Reserve

KWAZULU-NATAL

avian rarities. Indeed, for those with sufficient time and interest, it would be easy to dedicate a couple of weeks to exploring this underrated corner of South Africa without ever feeling things were becoming repetitive.

Hluhluwe-iMfolozi Park

Daily: June–Oct 6am–5pm; Nov–May 5am–6pm • R220 • ☎ 035 562 0848, Ⓦ kznwildlife.com

Often cited as Zululand's answer to the Kruger, **HLUHLUWE-IMFOLOZI** is undoubtedly the most outstanding provincially managed game reserve in KwaZulu-Natal, at least where the Big Five and other such safari heavyweights are concerned. And while it cannot match its northern rival in scale (at 960 square kilometres, it's a mere twentieth of the size), Hluhluwe-iMfolozi is hillier and more scenic than the heavily touristed southern Kruger, and it also possesses a lusher and more subtropical feel. Apart from *Hilltop Camp*, an elegant hotel-style set-up in the northern half of the park, none of the other accommodation is fenced off, and wild animals are free to wander through. The park also offers the best wilderness hiking trails in the country.

3

As the tongue-twisting double-barrelled name implies, Hluhluwe-iMfolozi actually started life as two distinct reserves which, in their original incarnations, were respectively dedicated mainly to the preservation of the **black** and **white rhino**. Even today, Hluhluwe and iMfolozi retain distinctly different characters, a situation reinforced by the public road that slices between them, but wild animals move freely between the two sectors, and they are administered jointly both in terms of conservation and when it comes to tourist access.

Hluhluwe-iMfolozi is home to almost one hundred mammal species. The Big Five are all here, and it's no exaggeration to say that this is one of the best places in the world to see rhino, both black and white, despite ongoing problems with poaching. About 160 elephants were reintroduced from Kruger between 1985 and 1991, and the present population of close to one thousand is fast approaching the park's ecological carrying capacity. Lions have also been reintroduced, and today they number around eighty, although they're not always easy to see. Other large predators include leopard, cheetah, spotted hyena and wild dog. Herbivores include blue wildebeest, buffalo, giraffe, impala, kudu, nyala and zebra.

When it comes to birds, almost 350 species have been recorded here. The most conspicuous of numerous raptors are the bateleur, white-backed vulture and African harrier-hawk, but more than a dozen species of eagle have been documented in total. Other conspicuous birds include trumpeter hornbill and purple-crested turaco (both most likely to been seen or heard in riverine forests), as well as brown-hooded kingfisher, black-crowned tchagra and the localized eastern nicator, the latter often seen trailing along behind nyala, warthog and even rhino to hawk flushed insects. Reptile species number in the sixties and include several types of venomous snake, none of which you're likely to see, but keep an eye open for crocodiles and monitor lizards along the rivers.

Brief history

One of the oldest reserves anywhere in Africa, Hluhluwe-iMfolozi is effectively an amalgamation of two disjunct conservation areas, originally proclaimed in 1895 under the names Hluhluwe (pronounced something like "shla-shloo-wee") Valley

HLUHLUWE-IMFOLOZI AT A GLANCE

Zululand's top self-drive Big Five destination.

Big Five: ★★★★
General wildlife: ★★★★
Birding: ★★★★
Scenery: ★★★★
Wilderness factor: ★★★★
Uncrowded: ★★★
Affordability: ★★★★★
Self-drive: Y

and Umfolozi ("oom-fa-low-zee") Junction game sanctuaries. Prior to that, the more southerly Umfolozi had been the private hunting preserve of the **Zulu** monarchy; what was then the most sustained campaign of hunting in the area occurred during the reign of King Shaka (1818–28). The twin reserves suffered a further series of blows that threatened their long-term viability in the decades following their establishment, most notably a rinderpest epidemic in 1898 and a debilitating drought in 1919. But these were nothing compared to the subsequent destruction caused by white farmers who undertook a campaign of game **extermination** in the mistaken belief that wild animals acted as a reservoir for the tsetse-borne blood parasite that transmits **nagana** (sleeping sickness) to cattle. The crusade undertaken by the vexed farmers resulted in the slaughter of one hundred thousand head of game comprising sixteen different species.

Umfolozi was deproclaimed twice during this period (in 1920 and 1932), and zebra and several other large herbivore species were practically extinct by the time the last mop-up campaign was conducted in 1952. That the reserves survived this onslaught is largely down to their status as the last South African stronghold for both species of rhino, which were spared during the eradication campaigns. Incredibly, every last southern white rhino on the planet today descends from a bottleneck population in Umfolozi that was estimated to stand at fewer than twenty individuals in 1916. Initiated in 1962, the celebrated **Operation Rhino** resulted in the translocation of thousands of individual rhinos from the potentially overpopulated hills of Umfolozi to other South African conservation areas, and the borders of the reserve were

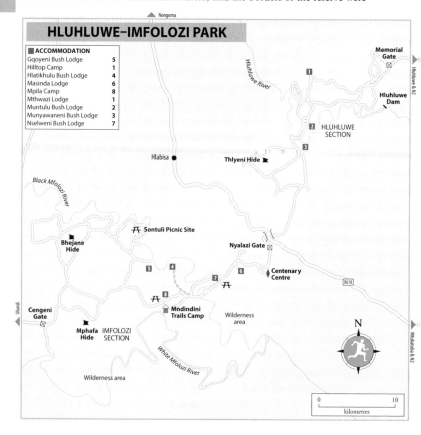

HLUHLUWE–IMFOLOZI PARK

ACCOMMODATION

Gqoyeni Bush Lodge	5
Hilltop Camp	1
Hlatikhulu Bush Lodge	4
Masinda Lodge	6
Mpila Camp	8
Mthwazi Lodge	1
Muntulu Bush Lodge	2
Munyawaneni Bush Lodge	3
Nselweni Bush Lodge	7

also extended. Hluhluwe-iMfolozi took its present shape in 1989, following the establishment of a corridor reserve between the two original areas, and the decision to manage the three contiguous properties jointly. Although the success of the rhino programme has in recent years been severely compromised by rampant poaching within the reserve – as well as in other South African parks such as Kruger – Hluhluwe-iMfolozi is still thought to support more than a thousand white rhinos and several hundred of their black brethren.

Game drives in Hluhluwe

Hluhluwe is the busier of the two sectors – particularly around Memorial Gate, the preferred point of entry for most guided day tours – with a longer network of surfaced roads. It tends to offer more reliable game viewing than iMfolozi, thanks in part to the relatively open vegetation on the slopes between Memorial Gate and *Hilltop Camp*. The grassland-loving white rhino is almost certain to be sighted on any given game drive in this area, and elephant and buffalo are readily observed here, along with giraffe, zebra, impala, warthog and vervet monkey. It is also good habitat for lion and cheetah, but you would be lucky to see either, though the high concentration of open-sided safari vehicles means there are plenty of eyes out looking for these well-camouflaged creatures.

The sector's most notable feature is the **Hluhluwe River**, a slender, slithering waterway lined with lush riparian forest and punctuated by elongated pools. The Hluhluwe rises in the mountains north of the park and passes along sandbanks, rock beds and steep cliffs in the game reserve before seeping away into Lake St Lucia to the east. The higher ground is covered by veld and dense thicket, while the well-watered ridges support the softer cover of ferns, lichens, mosses and orchids. A productive circuit for game viewing, the dirt roads that follow the river south of the main unsurfaced road pass through patches of thicket inhabited by handsome greater kudu, bushbuck and nyala antelopes, and overlook several pools where hippo congregate in the water while buffalo and elephant come down to drink. It is also here that you are most likely to catch a rare glimpse of a leopard or wild dog. This dense scrub is also ideal territory for black rhino, and the odds of seeing one here are probably about the best of any public reserve cohabited by both rhino species. In times of drought, the most easterly stretch of the riverine road can offer superb game viewing, as the Hluhluwe flows out of the park straight into an artificially dammed lake, which tends to hold water even in the driest conditions.

Also worthwhile, especially for birders, is the scenic loop that follows the Hluhluwe's main south-flowing tributary, the **Nzimane**, through a valley to the west of *Hilltop Camp*. Further west, the riverside Siwasamakhosikazi Picnic Site is frequently visited by a large male white rhino who has a midden just outside it, and the birding here can be sensational – look out, among others, for mocking cliff chat, grey-headed bush-shrike and crested barbet.

Game drives in iMfolozi

Although **iMfolozi** protects all the same species as Hluhluwe, volumes seem to be lower; as such, there's a hit-and-miss feel to game drives. The reward, especially on the network of dirt roads that runs south and west of *Mpila Rest Camp*, is that it feels far more untrammelled than the relatively busy surfaced roads closer to Memorial Gate. The topography here varies in altitude from 60m to 650m above sea level, and is characterized by wide, deep valleys incised by the Black and White Mfolozi rivers (whose name derives from *mfulawozi*, the isiZulu word for the fibrous bushes that grow along its banks). Away from the rivers, this sector is drier and more openly vegetated than Hluhluwe, and it can look pretty barren in winter, though the low vegetation makes for easy wildlife spotting. The most productive roads are those that follow the well-wooded course of the seasonal **Black Mfolozi** through the far north, and it is well worth stopping at Sontuli Picnic Site for the sweeping view to the opposite bank. It is also worth diverting to Bekapanzi Pan to look for white rhino. Close to Nyalazi Gate, the **Centenary Centre** – graced by a large bronze rhino erected in 1995 to mark the reserve's centenary – consists of a small takeaway restaurant (daily 9am–4.30pm), a craft centre, rhino museum and information centre, as well as bomas that house animals brought from other parks to be introduced here.

Overnight wilderness trails

Available from early February to mid-December, overnight **wilderness trails** through the otherwise inaccessible southern half of iMfolozi are justifiably the stuff of legend. The three-night **Base Camp Trail** (R4395) involves day walks in the **Wilderness Area**, with nights spent at the *Mndindini Trails* camp not far from Mpila; the three-night **Primitive Trail** (R2730) requires you to carry your own gear and sleep under the stars, wherever the ranger chooses, while the short two-night **Wilderness Trail** (R2670) starts from Mpila, with luggage and camping equipment carried to a bush camp by donkeys. Both the Primitive and the short Wilderness Trail can be extended by one night if you choose. All trails start at *Mpila* camp in iMfolozi. You'll be accompanied by an armed ranger; all gear – including bedding, backpacks and food – is included in the price. They must be booked through KZN Wildlife well in advance, as each excursion is limited to a maximum of eight people.

Other activities in Hluhluwe-iMfolozi

Apart from self-driving around the park, there are also self-guided **walks** near several of the restcamps, as well as both two-and-a-half-hour game drives (R350) and three-hour game walks (R300) departing each morning and evening from *Hilltop* and *Mpila* camps. In the morning, these depart at 5am (Oct–Mar) and 6am (Apr–Sept), so you must get to the park the previous night.

Emdoneni Cheetah Project

Durhlanda, off the N2 about 15km south of Hluhluwe village · Guided tours run at 10.30am daily throughout the year & 4pm May–Aug or 4.30pm Sept–Apr · R200 · ☎ 035 562 7000, 🔘 emdonenilodge.com

Established in 1994, this felid rehabilitation centre, on the same property as *Emdoneni Lodge*, is home to small numbers of cheetah, serval, caracal and African wild cat, most of which were hand-reared, orphaned or rescued from captivity. Although it started life as a rescue project, **Emdoneni** now doubles as a breeding centre for wild cats and focuses on raising the progeny in such a manner that they are fit to survive in the wild. Around forty individual cats born in the centre have now been released into iSimangaliso, uMkhuze and further afield. One-hour tours of the project offer insights into the rearing process, as well as the opportunity to see these magnificent creatures up close in spacious enclosures in which they are clearly thriving.

ARRIVAL AND INFORMATION   HLUHLUWE-IMFOLOZI PARK

By car The main urban gateways to Hluhluwe-iMfolozi are the villages of Mtubatuba and Hluhluwe, both of which lie a short distance east of the N2, some 215km and 270km northeast of Durban respectively. Self-drivers coming from Durban should allow 2–3 hours.

Access to the park itself is via three gates. The busiest is Memorial Gate, which is in the far northeast of the Hluhluwe sector and connected to the N2 and Hluhluwe village by a well-signposted 14km surfaced road. More useful if coming from

the direction of St Lucia Village, Nyalazi Gate lies about 27km inland of Mtubatuba along the R618, which then continues northwest to Hlabisa and Nongoma. The R618 actually divides the Hluhluwe and iMfolozi sectors of the park, and Nyalazi offers good access to both – turn left at the first T-junction past the gate to explore iMfolozi, or right in order to cross a tunnel below the R618 into Hluhluwe. The less widely used Cengeni Gate lies in the far west of iMfolozi and is accessible along a 30km tarred road running west from Ulundi.

By bus and minibus taxi Greyhound buses from Durban (daily; 2hr 20min), Johannesburg (daily; 9hr 45min) and Pretoria (daily; 11hr 45min) stop in Richards Bay, where regular minibuses run on to Hluhluwe, Mtubatuba or St Lucia Village – the latter being the more useful base for backpackers wanting to visit the park on an organized day tour.

By air Looking at a fly-in/self-drive option, the airport at Richards Bay (where you can also rent a car) is serviced by several daily flights from Johannesburg (1hr 15min), but it tends to be far costlier than flying into Durban and proceeding from there.

Day-trips and tours If you don't have your own car, you can take a day-trip offered by any of the accommodation options within an hour's drive of the park, or any operator in St Lucia Village.

Tourist office The friendly Elephant Coast Tourism Association information office is based at the Engen petrol station on Main St in Hluhluwe (daily 8am–4.30pm; ☎ 035 562 0966, ⓦ visitelephantcoast.co.za), providing details of numerous lodges and game farms in the vicinity.

Information Maps and information, including details of game drives and guided walks, are available at the receptions of *Hilltop* and *Mpila* camps.

ACCOMMODATION

INSIDE THE PARK   **SEE MAP PAGE 148**
Accommodation is available in both the iMfolozi and Hluhluwe sections of the park, with iMfolozi being the less developed of the two. There are no fences around the iMfolozi camps, so take care when walking around, particularly at night. There are no campsites within the park, but there is a tented safari camp at *Mpila* with pre-erected tents. Bookings are made through KZN Wildlife (☎ 033 845 1000, ⓦ kznwildlife.com).

HLUHLUWE SECTION
★ **Hilltop Camp** One of South Africa's best publicly run safari camps, *Hilltop* is set high on the edge of a slope with sweeping views across the park's hills and valleys. The camp has modern, comfortable and varied accommodation: budget two-bed rondavels that share communal ablutions and kitchen facilities; self-catering en-suite chalets sleeping two to four, with kitchenettes; and two-person en-suite chalets without kitchens. There is also a restaurant and a shop. The camp is surrounded by an electric fence, which keeps out most animals, though nyala, zebra and other herbivores still graze around the chalets. $̶–$$

Mthwazi Lodge Near Hilltop. Four luxurious en-suite rooms in the original home of the warden, set in a secluded garden. A chef is available to prepare meals. Minimum charge for six people. $$$$

Muntulu and **Munyawaneni bush lodges**. Four bedrooms with verandas at each of two upmarket lodges overlooking the Hluhluwe River. A cook is on hand to cater and a field ranger is available to take guests on walks. Minimum charge for six people. $$$$

IMFOLOZI SECTION
Gqoyeni and **Hlatikhulu bush lodges** Both of these lodges have four two-bed units elevated above the Black Mfolozi River, linked to the living area by wooden walkways. Their field ranger can conduct walks in the area, and there's a chef to cook meals. Minimum charge for six people. $$$$

Masinda Lodge Near Nyalazi Gate, this renovated

upmarket lodge has three en-suite bedrooms decorated with Zulu art, plus the services of a cook. Minimum charge for six people. $$$

Mpila Camp This camp has excellent views of the surrounding wilderness from several accommodation options: twelve one-roomed huts with two beds each, en-suite bathrooms and kitchenettes; two self-contained three-bedroom cottages for seven people (minimum charge for five); and six self-catering chalets for five people (minimum charge for four). There's also a safari camp with twelve tents that sleep two people, and two tents that sleep four. $$

Nselweni Bush Lodge Located on the banks of the Black Mfolozi River, this lodge boasts wonderful views of the river and the bushveld. Its eight two-bed chalets are self-catering and share a comfortable lounge and a picturesque elevated veranda. Minimum charge for two people. $$

OUTSIDE THE PARK   **SEE MAP PAGE 154**
Emdoneni Lodge Bushlands, off the N2 about 15km south of Hluhluwe village ☎ 035 562 7000, ⓦ emdonenilodge.com. Only thirty minutes from Memorial Gate and within easy day-tripping distance of St Lucia and uMkhuze, this likeable mid-range lodge is set in a mini-reserve crisscrossed by self-guided walking trails that stretch through sandy acacia woodland, where you are likely to see zebra, nyala, impala, vervet monkey, warthog and a wide variety of birds. The comfortable thatched chalets are set in a cool patch of shady forest and amenities include a good restaurant, spa and swimming pool. The relaxed bush feel is complemented by the friendly staff. This is also the site of the worthwhile and enjoyable Emdoneni Cheetah Project. $$

The Fever Tree Guest House 297 Koedoe Street, Hluhluwe village (300m south of the Engen petrol station) ☎ 035 562 3194 or ☎ 083 744 5261, ⓦ thefevertree. co.za. Comfy, en-suite rooms with kitchenettes opening onto an indigenous garden with a splash-pool, and there's a communal lounge/dining area. The guesthouse can arrange trips into Hluhluwe-iMfolozi Park. $

3

3

THE ZULU EMPIRE

Just one of the many small, hereditary Nguni-speaking fiefdoms that inhabited coastal KwaZulu-Natal, the **Zulu** rose to become the dominant political and military force in the region during the influential twelve-year reign of **King Shaka kaSenzangakhona**. Among the most controversial figures in African history, Shaka was born in 1787, the illegitimate son of a chief called Senzangakhona, and grew up a social outcast, his very name tinged with malicious irony (when his mother Nandi announced that she was pregnant by the chief, her claims were dismissed as an infection of ishaka, a beetle believed to suppress menstruation). As a young man, Shaka allegedly also suffered from a rash of impediments, ranging from a stutter to a deformed penis, which rather than holding him back, evidently spurred his competitive instincts when it came to games and sports.

In his twenties, Shaka rose through the ranks of King Dingiswayo's powerful Mthethwa army to become one of its most valued and innovate commanders and military tacticians. Following the death of Senzangakhona in 1816, Shaka murdered his father's appointed successor, his younger half-brother Sigujana, and was installed as chief of the Zulus under the patronage of Dingiswayo. After Dingiswayo was beheaded by the rival Ndwandwe army in 1817, Shaka became the ipso facto **King of Mthethwa**. A year later, pioneering the innovative "buffalo horn" formation he developed to trap enemies in battle, Shaka scored a decisive victory over the numerically stronger Ndwandwe, forcing them to retreat into present-day Eswatini (Swaziland). Shaka then turned his attention southward and westward, instigating an era of violent social turmoil and intertribal bloodshed remembered locally as the **Mfecane** or "Crushing".

Present-day KwaZulu-Natal was fully under Zulu rule by 1827, when Shaka's mother Nandi died – officially of dysentery, but allegedly due to a spear wound inflicted by Shaka during a heated argument. In the aftermath of Nandi's death, a grief-stricken Shaka allegedly initiated the massacre of seven thousand followers in one afternoon, then announced a year of national mourning during which it was forbidden to drink milk, grow crops or engage in sexual intercourse. The self-indulgence of this policy, and its genocidal execution, left Shaka isolated and vulnerable; in September 1828 he was stabbed to death by a triumvirate of assassins including his half-brother and successor **Dingane**.

Under Dingane, the Zulu Kingdom faced fresh pressures in the form of a newly founded British settlement at Port Natal (Durban) and the arrival of the Boers from the southwest. A series of confrontations culminated in December 1838 with the **Battle of Blood River**, where three thousand spear-wielding Zulus were mowed down by Boer guns, a defeat that shook the Zulu Empire to its core. As a result, Dingane's successor **Mpande** established diplomatic relations with Britain to secure Zulu sovereignty over the northern half of the kingdom. An uneasy truce reigned until January 1879, when Britain invaded Zululand. The first blow went to the Zulu army at Islandwana, but superior British firepower held sway thereafter: by December 1879, the Zulu royal kraal at Ondini had been razed, King **Cetshwayo** (who succeeded Mpande in 1873) was forced into hiding, and Zululand was effectively co-opted into the British empire.

Isinkwe Safaris Bush Camp Bushlands, off the N2 about 15km south of Hluhluwe village ☎ 083 338 3494 or ☎ 079 052 6529, ⊛ isinkwe.co.za. A well-run rustic hostel offering camping, dorms and a number of small chalets, some en suite. It serves reasonably priced meals (or you can self-cater) and arranges tours to Hluhluwe-iMfolozi Park and St Lucia. Camping, dorms and private doubles are available. ⑤

EATING AND DRINKING

SEE MAP PAGE 154

If you are staying inside the park, Hluhluwe's *Hilltop Camp* has a pleasant restaurant and a bar lounge, and there's an inexpensive daytime takeaway in the Centenary Centre (daily 9am–4.30pm), but all other accommodation is self-catering. Some of the bush lodges include the services of a cook to prepare your meals, but even so you'll have to provide the ingredients. *Hilltop Camp* has a small store selling a viable selection of basic supplies, and there is also a very woefully stocked store in *Mpila Camp* (beer, wine, ice and a few packaged goods), but you would be better of buying all provisions in advance at one of the well-stocked supermarkets in Hluhluwe, Mtubatuba or St Lucia villages.

Anew Hotel Hluhluwe On the R22 as you enter Hluhluwe village from the north ☎ 035 562 4000. Aside from a few chain takeaways, this recently renovated hotel is the only place to eat after dark in Hluhluwe village. It has a pleasant poolside terrace, a good wine list and a varied selection of well-priced grills, burgers and salads. Daily 8am–9pm.

Fig Tree Cafe & Deli At Ilala Weavers, 5min drive from Hluhluwe village on Ngweni Rd ☎ 082 045 1647. Serves excellent coffee, decent breakfasts and tasty lunches, including salads, curries, burgers and seafood dishes such as Thai fishcakes, on a shaded terrace. Daily 8.30am–4pm.

iSimangaliso Wetland Park

☎ 035 590 1633/1602, 🌐 isimangaliso.com

One of the most extraordinarily biodiverse conservation areas anywhere in Africa, **ISIMANGALISO** – an isiZulu name meaning "miraculous" – was inscribed as the country's first UNESCO World Heritage Site in 1999. South Africa's third largest park, it extends across 3280 square kilometres and incorporates a full 220km of largely unspoiled subtropical Indian Ocean shoreline, running north from the **St Lucia Estuary** to the **Mozambican border**. Within the park, you'll find the world's most southerly **coral reefs**, five separate Ramsar wetlands – including Africa's biggest estuarine system – and South Africa's largest natural freshwater lake, the tallest forested dunes on the planet, and a wide diversity of terrestrial habitats including grassy floodplains, acacia savannah and shady sand forest.

3

Formerly known as the Greater St Lucia Wetlands, iSimangaliso took its present shape in the early 1990s, when it was amalgamated from a dozen or more standalone reserves linking Maphelane in the south to Kosi Bay on the Mozambique border. Today, the park broadly divides into three main sections. Most accessible and best known, the **southern St Lucia sector**, which measures about 120km from south to north and has an average width of around 30km, is centred on the vast St Lucia Estuary and eponymous village at its mouth. Further north, the narrow **Maputaland sector** protects the 100km of gorgeous subtropical coastline that stretches from Sodwana Bay north to the Mozambican border via Lake Sibaya, Rocktail Bay and Kosi Bay. Further inland, the smaller **uMkhuze sector** essentially consists of the uMkhuze Game Reserve, a popular game-viewing destination known for its excellent photographic hides.

iSimangaliso's exceptional habitat diversity is reflected in its varied fauna. Nelson Mandela famously noted that it "must be the only place on the globe where the world's oldest land mammal (the rhinoceros) and the world's biggest terrestrial mammal (the elephant) share an ecosystem with the world's oldest fish (the coelacanth) and the world's biggest marine mammal (the whale)". More empirically, iSimangaliso's animal checklist – tallying roughly 130 terrestrial and aquatic mammals, 530 birds, 130 reptiles, 50 amphibians, 990 marine fish and 50 freshwater fish – means that more vertebrate species have been recorded here than in any other African conservation area.

Despite this, it feels reductive to treat iSimangaliso as a conventional safari destination in the mould of, say, Hluhluwe-iMfolozi. True, all the Big Five are present in **uMkhuze**, following the reintroduction of lions in 2013, as are the likes of cheetah and African wild dog. And the eastern and western shores of **St Lucia** also harbour a fair number of large mammals, including elephant, rhino, hippo, giraffe and zebra. But in truth there is so much more to iSimangaliso than ticking the Big Five: the truly stunning coastal scenery, the marvellous birdlife, superb offshore snorkelling and diving, seasonal excursions to see marine giants such as whales and nesting turtles, boat trips onto the lakes and estuaries, and a plethora of opportunities for exploring on foot.

Lake St Lucia and southern iSimangaliso

The most striking feature of the iSimangaliso Wetland Park is the 360-square-kilometre **Lake St Lucia**, South Africa's largest inland body of water, formed 25,000 years ago when the oceans receded. Situated in the far south of the park adjacent to **St Lucia**

3

Leveukop Gate (1km) & Johannesburg (440km)

Mbabane (160km) & Kruger National Park (230km)

Maputo (80km)

MOZAMBIQUE

Kosi Bay/Farazela

NDUMO GAME RESERVE **1**

TEMBE ELEPHANT PARK

Kwangwanase

2 Kosi Bay

3
4
5

KOSI BAY NATURE RESERVE

ESWATINI

Ephondweni **7**

6

Ingwavuma

COASTAL FOREST

Rocktail Bay

R22

Lavumisa/ Golela

PHONGOLO NATURE RESERVE

Mseleni

Lake Sibaya

8

9

Pongolapoort Dam

PONGOLA GAME RESERVE

Jozini

Mbazwana

N2

Sodwana Bay

ZIMANGA PRIVATE GAME RESERVE

Ubombo   uMkhuze River

Muzi Pan

kuMasinga Hide

uMkhuze

UMKHUZE GAME RESERVE

Yengweni Pan

Mdlanzi Pan

Lake Bhangazi (North)

MANYONI PRIVATE GAME RESERVE

Nsumo Pan

Ntshangwe Pan

N

Bayala

uMkhuze Swamps

PHINDA PRIVATE GAME RESERVE   R22

THANDA PRIVATE GAME RESERVE

10

N7

11 FALSE BAY NATURE RESERVE

12

Bird Island

13   Lake St Lucia

INDIAN OCEAN

2 **1**

Hluhluwe **14**

Emdoneni Cheetah Project **15**

16

Lane Island

Lake Bhangazi (South)

Hlabisa

Hluhluwe Dam

Hluhluwe River

R618

SEE 'SOUTHERN ISIMANGALISO' MAP FOR DETAIL

● **EATING**
Anew Hotel Hluhluwe   **2**
Fig Tree Cafe & Deli   **1**

HLUHLUWE-IMFOLOZI PARK

Nyalazi River

Khula   St Lucia Village

■ **ACCOMMODATION**
EKZNW Camp   **17**
Emdoneni Lodge   **15**
Falaza Game Park   **11**
The Fever Tree Guest House   **14**
Isinkwe Safaris Bush Camp   **16**
Kosi Bay Lodge   **2**
Kosi Bay Restcamp   **4**
Kosi Forest Lodge   **5**
Mabibi Beach Camp   **9**
Ndumo Restcamp   **1**
Ndumu River Lodge   **7**
Nibela Lake Lodge   **10**
Sand Forest Lodge   **12**
Tembe Tented Camp   **6**
Thobeka Backpackers Lodge   **3**
Thonga Beach Lodge   **8**
We Bush Camp   **13**

Mfolozi River

Mtubatuba

R618

MAPHELANE NATURE RESERVE **17** Cape St Lucia

N2

0   10
kilometres

ISIMANGALISO WETLAND PARK

Durban (190km)

KwaMbonambi

village, the lake is flanked by mountainous dunes covered by forest and grassland, whose peaks soar to an astonishing 200m above the beach to form a slender rampart against the Indian Ocean. Aside from the lake and dune ecosystems, the reserve protects a marine zone of warm tropical seas, coral reefs and endless sandy beaches; the papyrus and reed wetland of the **uMkhuze swamps**, on the north of the lake; and, on the western shore, dry savannah and thornveld. Any one of these would justify conservation, but their confluence around the lake makes this a world-class wilderness. The real prize of the area is **Cape Vidal** inside the wetland park, though the limited accommodation there may necessitate your making a day-trip from St Lucia town.

St Lucia Village

Set alongside the eponymous estuary's northeast bank and mouth, the village of **St Lucia** has undergone a gradual transformation post 1994, from a rough and remote hangout for local **angling** enthusiasts to a well-equipped travel hub that attracts eco-tourists from the world over. Linked to the rest of the country by a solitary road bridge, St Lucia is also possibly the only urban centre in South Africa whose streets are routinely patrolled by heavyweight nocturnal wildlife, most notably the hippos that bathe away the daylight hours in the adjacent estuary, but also the likes of porcupine, bushbuck, warthog, red duiker, genet and characteristically vociferous thick-tailed bushbabies. The jungle-lined roads leading down to the beach and short **iGwalaGwala Trail**, which starts at the southern end of Mackenzie Road, also offer some of South Africa's finest urban birdwatching, with African fish eagle, African goshawk, trumpeter hornbill and purple-crested turaco among the more regular specials.

The estuary mouth immediately south of the village was named Santa Lucia by Portuguese explorers when they reached it in 1576. During the second half of the eighteenth century, landlocked Boers made attempts to claim the estuary as a port, but were pipped at the post by the British, who sent HMS *Goshawk* in 1884 to annex the whole area, which then developed as a fishing resort. The estuary is today hidden behind the buildings along the main drag, and easy to miss if you drive quickly through, but well worth exploring. Otherwise, there's not much to do in St Lucia itself, but it does provide an excellent base for a number of activities (see page 158) and has a good choice of accommodation and places to eat. Other facilities include filling stations, a supermarket, self-service laundries, banks and ATMs, almost all of them concentrated along **McKenzie Street**, the main north–south drag through the village.

St Lucia Crocodile Centre

Beside the Bhangazi Gate to Cape Vidal about 2km north of town • Daily 9am–4pm • R60 • Crocodile feeding Sat 3pm • ☎ 035 590 1386

This isn't another of the exploitative wildlife freak shows common throughout South Africa, but a serious educative spin-off from KZN Wildlife's crocodile conservation campaign. Until the end of the 1960s, "flat dogs" or "travelling handbags" were regarded as pests, and a hunting free-for-all saw them facing extinction in the area. Just in time, it was realized that crocs have an important role in the ecological cycle, and KZN Wildlife began a successful **breeding programme**, returning the crocs to the wild to bolster their numbers. The **Crocodile Centre** aims to rehabilitate the reputation of these maligned creatures, with informative displays and an astonishing cross-section of species lounging around enclosed pools (only the Nile crocodile occurs in the wild in South Africa).

ARRIVAL AND INFORMATION	ST LUCIA

By car St Lucia lies around three hours' drive northeast of Durban, following the N2 for 215km as far as Mtubatuba, then turning right onto the R618, which terminates in the village after another 30km.

By bus and minibus taxi A popular option with backpackers, the North Coast Runner (☎ 084 548 4066, ⊕ northcoastrunner.co.za, R500 one-way) is a minibus shuttle that runs back and forth between selected hostels in Durban and St Lucia every Monday, Wednesday and Friday to tie in with Baz Bus arrivals and departures. In addition, minibus taxis to Mtubatuba leave from the Dolphin Centre on the corner of McKenzie St and the R618 as you enter the village.

Tourist information The most helpful place is Advantage Tours & Charters at the Dolphin Centre on the corner of McKenzie St and the R618 as you enter the village (Mon–Fri 8am–5pm, Sat 8am–2pm, Sun 8am–noon; ☎035 590 1259 ⓦadvantagetours.co.za), who can advise on accommodation and activities.

KZN Wildlife Has an office at the south end of Pelican Rd (daily 8.30am–4.30pm; ☎035 590 1340, ⓦkznwildlife.com), two blocks east of and parallel to McKenzie St.

ACCOMMODATION   SEE MAP BELOW

Elephant Lake Hotel 3 Mullet St ☎035 590 1001, ⓦelephantlake.co.za. St Lucia's only hotel, complete with a pool and a restaurant with fantastic deck for evening drinks and views of the estuary. Also runs a second property, *Elephant Lake Inn*, at 41 Flamingo St. Rates include breakfast. $

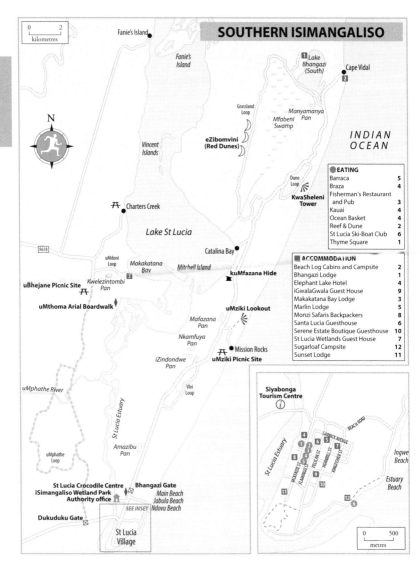

SOUTHERN ISIMANGALISO

EATING	
Barraca	5
Braza	4
Fisherman's Restaurant and Pub	3
Kauai	4
Ocean Basket	4
Reef & Dune	2
St Lucia Ski-Boat Club	6
Thyme Square	1

ACCOMMODATION	
Beach Log Cabins and Campsite	2
Bhangazi Lodge	1
Elephant Lake Hotel	4
iGwalaGwala Guest House	9
Makakatana Bay Lodge	3
Marlin Lodge	5
Monzi Safaris Backpackers	8
Santa Lucia Guesthouse	6
Serene Estate Boutique Guesthouse	10
St Lucia Wetlands Guest House	7
Sugarloaf Campsite	12
Sunset Lodge	11

iGwalaGwala Guest House 91 Pelican St ☎035 590 1069, ⓦigwalagwala.com. The spacious en-suite rooms here are simply but elegantly decorated, and the gracious hosts make you feel right at home. Some rooms open directly onto the swimming pool and quiet, leafy garden, which is often visited by the purple-crested turaco (*igwalagwala* in isiZulu). $\overline{\underline{\underline{S}}}\overline{\underline{\underline{S}}}$

Marlin Lodge 62 Garrick Ave ☎035 590 1929, ⓔinfo@ marlinlodgestlucia.co.za. A friendly and convivial guesthouse whose light-filled rooms open onto a communal patio and pool, where guests gather to braai and socialize. Some rooms accommodate families. Rates include breakfast. $\overline{\underline{\underline{S}}}$

Monzi Safaris Backpackers 81 McKenzie St ☎035 590 1697, ⓦmonzisafaris.com/backpackers. Well-managed hostel on the main road with a well-stocked kitchen, comfortable outside lounge and bar, and pool with sunbeds. Instead of dorms, there are pre-erected twin/double dome tents on wooden decks with proper camp beds and linen, plus a handful of double rooms at the back. $\overline{\underline{\underline{S}}}$

Santa Lucia Guesthouse 30 Pelican St ☎035 590 1151, ⓦsantalucia.co.za. One of the oldest lodgings in St Lucia and still managed by the same family that started it, this comfortable and personably managed guesthouse stands in a peaceful tree-shaded garden with a swimming pool and prolific birdlife. Excellent breakfast included in the room rate. $\overline{\underline{\underline{S}}}\overline{\underline{\underline{S}}}$

Serene Estate Boutique Guesthouse 119 Hornbill St ☎072 365 2450, ⓦserene-estate.com. Attractive modern architecture and minimalist ethnically inspired decor are hallmarks of this new boutique guesthouse, whose spacious rooms are offset by a leafy subtropical setting, saltwater swimming pool and roof deck offering great views over the jungly surrounds. $\overline{\underline{\underline{S}}}\overline{\underline{\underline{S}}}$

★ St Lucia Wetlands Guest House 20 Kingfisher St ☎035 590 1098, ⓦstluciawetlands.com. Six large rooms kitted out with elegant wooden furnishings, and there's a pool and a classy bar for guests. Exceptional service and the friendly atmosphere created by congenial hosts who know the area backwards make this one of the best places to stay in St Lucia. Rates include breakfast. $\overline{\underline{\underline{S}}}\overline{\underline{\underline{S}}}$

Sunset Lodge 154 McKenzie St ☎035 590 1197, ⓦsunsetstlucia.co.za. Attractive, well-appointed self-catering log cabins sleeping two, four or five, with balconies and views of the estuary. Hippos occasionally feed on the lawn in front of the wooden pool deck. Good value, and great for families. $\overline{\underline{\underline{S}}}$

CAMPSITE

Sugarloaf Campsite Sugar Loaf Rd, south of town; book through EKZNW ☎033 845 1000, or at the St Lucia office ☎035 590 1340, ⓦkznwildlife.com. A sizeable campsite on the best site in St Lucia, right on the banks of the estuary, with an on-site swimming pool and plenty of fishing and birdwatching opportunities nearby. $\overline{\underline{\underline{S}}}$

EATING AND DRINKING   SEE MAP PAGE 156

Barraca 18 McKenzie St ☎035 590 1729. Friendly Portuguese/Italian restaurant notable for its varied seafood menu, grilled chicken in spicy marinade, well-priced wine list and chilled terrace seating. Daily 8am–9pm.

Braza Georgiou Centre, 73 McKenzie St ☎035 590 1242. Portuguese specialities like *espetada* (beef skewers with peppers) and *chouriço* (pork sausage), plus plenty of grilled meat, including a "Portuguese steak" topped with a fried egg (R120). Daily 11am–10pm.

Fisherman's Restaurant and Pub 61 McKenzie St ☎035 590 1257. A good place for fresh seafood, this rough-and-ready local hangout is covered with fishing memorabilia. The owner himself is a fisherman, and it serves up good prawns and seafood baskets (R85). At night it turns into one of the few bars in town. Daily 8am–midnight.

Kauai Georgiou Centre, 73 McKenzie St ⓦkauai. co.za. Healthy wraps and salads using mostly free-range and organic ingredients, along with a tempting selection of smoothies and juices and great coffee. Daily 7am–6pm.

Ocean Basket Georgiou Centre, 73 McKenzie St ☎035 590 1241. It may be a chain, but good food and fast service make this one of the best and most reasonably priced places to eat in St Lucia. Big seafood platters and grilled fish served up in the pan are the specialities of the house, and there's a pleasant first-floor balcony. Daily 10am–10pm.

Reef & Dune 51 McKenzie St ☎035 590 1048. A casual, family-friendly eatery decked out with picnic tables and a wrap-around deck. It serves the usual seafood, along with tasty grills like steak, ribs and eisbein from around R90. Daily 10am–10pm.

St Lucia Ski-Boat Club The end of Sugar Loaf Rd ☎035 590 1376. This pub-like grill has a nice patio with pleasant views of the estuary, making it a great place for sundowners accompanied by the grunting of hippos. The food is less exciting – mainly pub fare such as burgers and fish and chips – and service is slow, but it is all very affordably priced. Daily noon–8.30pm.

Thyme Square John Dory Building, 52 McKenzie St ☎035 590 1692. It may be decorated like Barbie's dream house, but this civilized little café is a relaxing place to indulge in tea and waffles with cream (R30), or a light and healthy lunch. Mon–Sat 9am–5pm, Sun 9am–4pm.

ACTIVITIES AROUND ST LUCIA

Small as it is, St Lucia is the biggest settlement around the iSimangaliso Wetland Park, and the best place to **organize activities**. Established operators include Advantage Tours & Charters (☎ 035 590 1180/1259, ⊕ advantagetours.co.za), Heritage Tours & Safaris (☎ 035 590 1555, ⊕ heritagetoursandsafaris.com), Maputaland Tours (☎ 035 590 1041 or 082 899 7478, ⊕ maputaland.com), Monzi Safaris (☎ 035 590 1697, ⊕ monzisafaris.com) and Shaka Barker Tours (☎ 035 590 1162, ⊕ shakabarker.co.za), all of which offer a variety of activities in and around St Lucia as well as game drives to Hluhluwe-iMfolozi Park (from around R900/1200 per person half/full day).

BIKING

A knowledgeable Zulu guide can lead you on a two- to three-hour gentle **cycle** through the southern part of the estuary, along the beach and around town; the guide will teach you about flora and fauna and the use of plants in Zulu culture and medicine along the way. Book through Shaka Barker Tours (R275 including bike rental).

FISHING

Deep-sea fishing trips, with a skipper, guide, experienced fisherman, bait and tackle supplied, are available for novices and seasoned anglers. Either tag and release your game fish or take it home to cook. Advantage Tours & Charters runs six-hour trips from R1500 per person depending on numbers. Bring your own lunch and refreshments. Also enquire about charter boats at the St Lucia Ski-Boat Club.

HORSERIDING

Bhangazi Horse Safaris (☎ 083 792 7899, ⊕ bhangazihorsesafaris.com) offers **rides** through bushland, forests and lakes where you can view wildlife, or along the beach (R380/hr).

LAKE CRUISES

Probably the most popular activity in St Lucia, a **cruise** on the estuary and lake gives you a good chance of seeing crocodiles and hippos, as well as pelicans, fish eagles, kingfishers and storks. Two-hour cruises are offered by most operators in town, the cheapest being the Santa Lucia, an eighty-seater boat with a viewing deck and a bar operated by KZN Wildlife (R180; ☎ 035 590 1340). The other operators (listed at the top of the box) go out in smaller boats and provide a more personalized experience, with guides relaying information about the wildlife and birds; refreshments are included.

WETLAND WILDLIFE TOURS

An outstanding range of **tours in the wetland** is operated by Shaka Barker Tours (see above), including the full-day St Lucia World Heritage Tour (R695) to the Eastern Shores and Cape Vidal, and the interesting and unusual Night Drive (R485; 3hr), which goes out in search of jackals, leopards, nightjars, owls and the sixteen chameleon species of the St Lucia region (a staggering fourteen of which are endemic). Also recommended is the one-night, two-day Turtle Tour (Nov–March; R2650) further up the coast to see leatherback and loggerhead turtles nesting, egg-laying and hatching, and walks led by local guides to the pans, grasslands and wetlands to learn about the ecology.

WHALE-WATCHING

Humpback and southern right whales cruise along the wetland's shore, and in season (June–Nov) you can join a **whale-watching boat trip** to look for them. Book through Advantage Tours & Charters (R1190; 2hr); the trips leave from the Advantage office on McKenzie St. There's no jetty down at the beach and launching the boat into the waves is an adventure in itself – if the ocean is choppy, expect to get soaked.

Maphelane Nature Reserve

Daily: Apr–Oct 6am–6pm; Nov–Mar 6am–7pm • R45, plus R20 per vehicle • ☎ 035 590 1039

The most southerly and little-known component of iSimangaliso, **Maphelane** lies on the southeast bank of the **Mfolozi** as it empties into St Lucia estuary mouth, less than 5km from St Lucia village as the crow flies, but closer to 100km distant by road.

Ecologically, the reserve is noted for an extensive area of swampland fed by the Mfolozi River and for the tall partially forested ribbon of dunes that separate this from the ocean. The reserve supports a varied avifauna typical of the region, best explored along the two-hour self-guided **Umphafa Trail**, which leads through forest and estuarine vegetation inhabited by red duiker, crocodile, hippo and innumerable birds. A second walking trail leads to the top of the dunes, offering an expansive view over the river mouth, while other activities include swimming (low tide only), spear fishing and shore fishing. The sandy access roads require a vehicle with decent clearance, ideally with 4WD.

> ### MAPHELANE AT A GLANCE
> Maphelane offers remote seaside walking and birding.
> **Big Five:** N/A
> **General wildlife:** **
> **Birding:** *****
> **Scenery:** ****
> **Wilderness factor:** ****
> **Uncrowded:** *****
> **Affordability:** *****
> **Self-drive:** Y

ARRIVAL AND INFORMATION   MAPHELANE NATURE RESERVE

By car Maphelane is situated at the end of a sandy 50km cul-de-sac that branches northeast from the N2 at the village of KwaMbonambi 190km north of Durban and 30km south of Mtubatuba. The drive should ideally be attempted in a 4WD only, and there is no public transport.

ACCOMMODATION   SEE MAP PAGE 154

EKZNW Camp ☎ 035 590 1039, ⓦ kznwildlife.com. This no-frills camp has a beautiful waterside location. There are ten two-bedroom log cabins, all with self-catering kitchen, and forty camping spots sharing common ablutions. No provisions are available locally so bring everything you need with you. Cabins $\overline{\underline{$$}}$, camping $\overline{\underline{$}}$

Eastern Shores and Cape Vidal

Daily: Apr–Oct 6am–6pm; Nov–Mar 5am–7pm • R51, plus R61 per vehicle • ☎ 035 590 9012 • No public transport

Cape Vidal, a popular fishing, bathing and snorkelling beach set within the iSimangaliso Wetlands, is reached from St Lucia village by a 33km surfaced road that extends northwards from McKenzie Street, running past the St Lucia Crocodile Centre before entering the park at Bhangazi Gate. The road also offers access to **Eastern Shores**, the terrestrial sector of iSimangaliso which divides Lake St Lucia from the Indian Ocean. Supporting a verdant mosaic of open grassland, seasonal sand, perennial wetlands and lushly forested dunes, the Eastern Shores is populated by a fair volume of game, most conspicuously zebra, hippo, warthog, vervet monkey, waterbuck, reedbuck, impala, red duiker and common duiker, but also small numbers of elephant, white rhino, buffalo and leopard, none of which is seen with great regularity.

From the main surfaced road, a succession of dirt road loops leads to various game-viewing and scenic lookout points. Coming from the south, the first of these is **iMboma Pan**, a shallow seasonal wetland where waterbuck and various water-associated birds are usually in residence. Further north, a loop to the east leads to the rather overgrown eMakhandeni Viewpoint via thicketed dunes that look like perfect leopard territory, though a more certain attraction are roadside flocks of the localized crested guineafowl (distinguished from its commoner helmeted cousin by its shaggy black "hairdo"). It is definitely worth driving the short diversion east to the gorgeous rocky beach at **Mission Rocks** via the uMziki Picnic Site, a good spot for red duiker and also the start of a short

> ### EASTERN SHORES AT A GLANCE
> Agreeable but low-key all-rounder with a diverse marine and terrestrial fauna.
> **Big Five:** **
> **General wildlife:** ***
> **Birding:** *****
> **Scenery:** ****
> **Wilderness factor:** ****
> **Uncrowded:** ****
> **Affordability:** *****
> **Self-drive:** Y

3

walking trail to the uMziki Lookout. Just past this, kuMfazana Hide, on the west side of the main road, overlooks a forest-fringed pan that can be good for birds in summer but often dries out in winter. Further north, a short side road runs west to a viewpoint over Catalina Bay, a wide expanse of water named for the seaplane base established here during World War II; the wreck of *Catalina*, which crashed near Mitchell Island in June 1943, killing all but one of the servicemen on board, still stands in the bay. Finally, after passing the No Entry sign to the left that signals the end of the one-way Grassland Loop, it is worth diverting east along the short Dune Loop, the highlight of which is a short steep climb to the top of **KwaSheleni Tower** for panoramic views east to the ocean and back west across grassy plains to distant Lake St Lucia.

The road terminates at Cape Vidal, where a rustic camp operated by EKZNW overlooks a beautiful white-sand beach lined with invasive casuarina trees where the localized samango monkey is sometimes seen. An offshore reef shelters the coast from the high seas, making it safe for swimming and providing good opportunities for **snorkelling** – you'll see hard and soft corals, colourful fish and tiny rock pools full of snails, crabs, sea cucumbers, anemones and urchins – while **anglers** use the rocks for casting their lines. Cape Vidal is an excellent place for shore sightings of humpback whales, which, in winter, breed off Mozambique not far to the north. In October they move south, drifting on the warm **Agulhas current** with their calves. If you're lucky, you may see these and other whales from the dunes; a whale-watching tower, reached through the dune forest south of the restcamp, provides an even higher viewpoint. Eighteen-metre plankton-feeding whale sharks, the largest and gentlest of the sharks, have been sighted off this coast in schools of up to seventy at a time, and manta rays and dolphins are also common.

When you're done at Cape Vidal, it's worth returning to St Lucia along the one-way dirt loop that runs west past **Lake Bhangazi** before curving southward through an area of grassland punctuated by the red dunes of eZibomvini. This loop usually offers the best game viewing in the Eastern shores; plenty of hippos are resident in the lake, and zebra and various antelope are common on the grassland.

ACCOMMODATION **EASTERN SHORES AND CAPE VIDAL, SEE MAP PAGE 156**

Beach Log Cabins and Campsite ☎033 845 1000 or ☎035 590 1340, ☻kznwildlife.com. A collection of five and eight-bed Swiss-style log cabins, all en suite and provided with linen and cooking utensils. Minimum charge for three and four people, respectively. There is space for fifty tents in the dune forest near the beach, with ablution facilities and power points. Bookings for the campsite in particular are vital during school holidays and over long weekends; there's a minimum charge for four and maximum per site is six. A small store sells basic supplies, bait, firewood and fuel. Cabins ⬆⬆, camping ⬆

Western Shores and Charters Creek

Daily: Apr–Oct 6am–6pm; Nov–Mar 5am–7pm • R51, plus R61 per vehicle • ☎035 550 9000

The most spectacular transformation to have taken place since the creation of iSimangaliso Wetland Park is the transformation of the **Western Shores** from alien

> **WESTERN SHORES AND CHARTERS CREEK AT A GLANCE**
>
> Excellent for a two- to three-hour game drive out of St Lucia.
> **Big Five:** **
> **General wildlife:** ***
> **Birding:** *****
> **Scenery:** ***
> **Wilderness factor:** ***
> **Uncrowded:** ****
> **Affordability:** *****
> **Self-drive:** Y

forestry plantation (mostly pines) to a 250-square-kilometre game reserve dominated by grassland, interspersed with patches of palm-lined swamp, indigenous riparian forest and stands of the yellow-flowered curry bush *Helichrysum italicum*. Restocked with historically occurring game, the reserve formally opened in 2013 and now offers far more reliable terrestrial wildlife viewing than the Eastern Shores. The most easily seen large mammals are buffalo, hippo, giraffe, Burchell's zebra, blue wildebeest, waterbuck, greater kudu, nyala and bushbuck, but the reserve is also home to small numbers of elephant, white and black rhino, leopards, serval and spotted hyena. Conspicuous birds include long-crested eagle, black-chested snake-eagle, African stonechat and yellow-throated longclaw.

Western Shores can easily be explored on a half-day self-drive excursion from St Lucia village. Coming from the southerly Dukuduku Gate, after 5km you'll come to a fork in the road where it is advisable to turn left onto the **uMphathe loop**, a one-way road that can only be driven south to north. This winds westward through grassy plains, where zebra and wildebeest are common, for about 4.5km before crossing the forest-fringed **uMphathe River** on a short concrete causeway, where the jewel-like pygmy kingfisher is sometimes seen darting past. The loop then runs northwards for 10km, offering some splendid long views over the uMphathe floodplain; it's worth scanning with binoculars for grazing hippo, buffalo, southern reedbuck, greater kudu and possibly even rhino or elephant. About 2km after rejoining the main north–south road, it is worth diverting to the shady uBhejane Picnic Site to stretch your legs and look for wildlife in the seasonal marsh it overlooks.

A short distance north of this, a highlight of the Western Shores is the short (5km) but superb **uMdoni Loop**, a one-way road that runs to the east of the main road and must be driven in a clockwise direction. Be sure to stop for a few minutes at the viewpoint next to Kwelezintombi Pan, a shallow muddy waterhole that tends to be stocked even in the dry season; it's frequently visited by buffalo, greater kudu, nyala and warthog. An even more worthwhile stop is the **uMthoma Aerial Boardwalk**, a stilted wooden canopy reached along a concrete path hemmed in by dense coastal forest. The views southeast to an area of marsh, and northeast to the open lake, are lovely, and the surrounding forest is teeming with interesting birds, including trumpeter hornbill, purple-crested turaco, white-eared barbet, gorgeous bush-shrike, dark-backed weaver and various robin-chats.

From here you can either head directly back south along the main road, where you are likely to see giraffe, wildebeest, zebra and various antelope, or make a 5km diversion north to **Charters Creek**, a pretty end-of-the-road picnic site, set on a wooded bluff looking eastward over Lake St Lucia, where you are likely to see hippos along with plenty of waterbirds. Note that the 16km road running further north to Fanie's Island (once a lovely lakeshore restcamp and campsite) has been closed for some years and shows no signs of reopening.

ARRIVAL AND INFORMATION   WESTERN SHORES

By car Access is via Dukuduku Gate on the R618, only 3km from St Lucia, or Nhlozi Gate off the N2, 20km north of Mtubatuba and 32km south of Hluhluwe. It's feasible to enter through one gate and exit out the other, which takes at least 1hr 30min with stops. Many tour operators in St Lucia offer 3hr safaris in open-top vehicles, starting at around R500 per person.

ACCOMMODATION   SEE MAP PAGE 156

Bhangazi Lodge ☎ 033 845 1000 or ☎ 035 590 1340, ⓦ kznwildlife.com. Ideal for groups of up to eight, this isolated lodge lies 10km from Cape Vidal on the western shore of Lake Bhangazi. The four twin bedrooms are all en suite and are linked to a well-equipped kitchen and open-plan living area by wooden boardwalks. $$$

★ **Makatana Bay Lodge** ☎ 035 550 4189 or ☎ 079 053 3821, ⓦ makatana.com. Situated on a small enclave of private land bounded by Lake St Lucia to the east and the Western Shores on the other three sides, this stylish family-owned lodge has an agreement with iSimangaliso allowing it to offer guided game drives along a network of roads and tracks off-limits to other tourists, as well as exclusive boat trips along a stretch of the estuary flowing south from the mouth of the uMphathe River. Bright, airy and tastefully decorated, the eight chalets all have a wide private balcony and are connected by a network of boardwalks through a dense patch of riparian woodland inhabited by red duiker and a wide variety of forest birds. There's also a lakeside swimming pool and exceptional continental-style cuisine, all accompanied by the white noise of cicadas and frogs, and punctuated by scene-setting fish-eagle duets by day and grunting hippos at night. Game drives tend to be low-key compared to most private reserves outside iSimangaliso, but you've a good chance of seeing spotted hyena up close, and leopards are also a possibility. $$$$$

FALSE BAY AT A GLANCE

Pedestrian-friendly birders' paradise offering great horseback outings.

Big Five: N/A
General wildlife: **
Birding: *****
Scenery: ***
Wilderness factor: ****
Uncrowded: *****
Affordability: *****
Self-drive: Y

False Bay Nature Reserve

Daily 6am–6pm • R45, plus R20 per vehicle • ☎ 035 562 0425

This 23-square-kilometre nature reserve protects the western and northern shores of **False Bay**, a small lozenge-shaped annexe to Lake St Lucia, connected to the main body of water by a steep-sided 2km-wide channel known colourfully as "Hell's Gate". It is rather tame by comparison to uMkhuze or Hluhluwe-iMfolozi when it comes to big game viewing, but there is plenty of small wildlife, and it is one of the last parts of iSimangaliso that can be explored on foot without a guide. Two clearly marked self-guided hikes, the 8km **Dugandlovu Trail** and the 10km circular **Mpophomeni Trail**, run through the reserve, passing through a mixed terrain of woodland, open savannah, shoreline and one of the richest remaining pockets of sand forest left in South Africa. The trails offer the opportunity of seeing animals including warthog, vervet monkey, zebra, common duiker, red duiker, nyala and the rare suni antelope, but close to the lakeshore do keep a wary eye open for hippo – the only potentially dangerous large mammal. Avian attractions include rosy-throated longclaw in moist grassland, the likes of Rudd's apalis, square-tailed drongo, African broadbill and Narina trogon in woodland, and a wide selection of water-associated birds including a rare breeding colony of pink-backed pelican. If you have limited time, the Mpophomeni Trail is the better option, since it can easily be undertaken in half a day, but visitors who can spare a night should think about hiking the Dugandlovu Trail, which involves an overnight stay in one of four rustic huts offering wonderful views across the lake at sunset. There are picnic sites and a viewing platform at **Lister Point**, which overlooks the lake more-or-less opposite Hell's Gate. **Horseback** day excursions into the reserve are operated exclusively by Hluhluwe Horse Safaris (☎ 035 562 1039 or 076 029 0580, ⊕ hluhluwehorsesafaris.co.za).

ARRIVAL   FALSE BAY

By car The closest town to False Bay is Hluhluwe (see page 150), from where you need to follow the R22 northeast in the direction of Kosi Bay for 12km, then turn right onto the signposted 3km feeder road for the reserve entrance. No public transport runs into the reserve.

ACCOMMODATION   SEE MAP PAGE 154

Falaza Game Park On the D540 bordering False Bay about 12km from Hluhluwe ☎ 035 562 2319 or ☎ 072 037 9900, ⊕ falaza.co.za. This slick tented camp stands in a small private reserve and has a restaurant, swimming pool and reasonably priced spa. Activities such as guided walks around False Bay or game drives into Hluhluwe-iMfolozi Park are offered. $$$

★ **Nibela Lake Lodge** 50km from Hluhluwe along the R22 and dirt A1114 ☎ 035 562 9005 or ☎ 086 101 0347, ⊕ nibelalakelodge.co.za. This gloriously isolated eco-idyll sprawls across the densely forested 240-hectare peninsula that forms the northern part of the so-called Hell's Gate, connecting False Bay to the main body of Lake St Lucia. An extensive network of footpaths through the forested slopes makes it an ideal destination for trail runners and walkers, and there's also plenty of wildlife around, ranging from the

hippos and crocs that inhabit the lake to forest-dwellers such as nyala, red duiker and greater bushbaby. The forest birdlife is sensational, and includes the likes of trumpeter hornbill, Livingstone's turaco, Narina trogon, green malkoha, Rudd's apalis and nine species of sunbird. *Nibela Lake Lodge* also arranges boat trips onto the lake, birding trips onto the nearby floodplain, and there's a spa and restaurant. Extensively renovated in 2018–9 and connected by a wooden boardwalk through a stunning section of forest, the thatched wooden chalets are warmly decorated in bush style and have walk-in nets, air-conditioning and floor-to-ceiling windows, plus a private balcony overlooking the lake. $$$$

Sand Forest Lodge On the D540 bordering False Bay, about 11km from Hluhluwe ☎ 082 417 6484 or ☎ 083 627 7080, ⊕ sandforest.co.za. A collection of campsites and self-catering cottages, located on a small reserve with antelope,

zebra and wildebeest. Meals are available on request. $\overline{5}\overline{5}\overline{5}$
★ **We Bush Camp** On the D540 bordering False Bay, about 8km from Hluhluwe ☎ 035 562 1039, ⓦ we-bushcamp.com. The home of Hluhluwe Horse Safaris,

this comfortable Dutch-owned and managed backpacker-friendly lodge stands in a small private nature reserve and offers accommodation in brightly painted thatched rondavels, as well as a restaurant and a variety of activities. $\overline{5}$

uMkhuze Game Reserve

Daily: Apr–Oct 6am–6pm; Nov–Mar 5am–7pm • R51, plus R61 per vehicle • ☎ 035 573 9004

Situated 16km southeast of uMkhuze village by road, the 400-square-kilometre **uMkhuze Game Reserve** is the premier game-viewing destination among the mosaic of reserves that comprise iSimangaliso Wetland Park. Both the reserve and village are named after the **uMkhuze River**, and all three, rather confusingly, are also sometimes transliterated as Mkhuze, Mkuze and Mkuzi. Set in the shadow of the **Lebombo Mountains**, the reserve lies to the west and inland of the main coastal plain of iSimangaliso, to which it is connected by a slender corridor through which the forest-fringed uMkhuze River flows before it empties into Lake St Lucia. The beautiful countryside protected within uMkhuze includes tracts of dense acacia savannah and sand forest, vast swampy wetlands floating with waterlilies and reedbeds, and a cathedral-like forest of sycamore figs that can only be explored on foot. uMkhuze is widely regarded to be one of the top **birding** sites in South Africa, with an impressive 420 species on record.

uMkhuze became a Big Five reserve in 2013 following the reintroduction, after a 45-year absence, of lions from nearby Tembe Elephant Park. More lions were relocated from Tswalu in the Kalahari in 2016, and several litters have since been born in the reserve. uMkhuze also hosts good numbers of elephant, buffalo and both types of rhino, although they tend not to be seen as easily as in Hluhluwe-iMfolozi. Several types of antelope are common, including nyala, impala, greater kudu and blue wildebeest, and you also stand an excellent chance of seeing hippo, giraffe, warthog and Burchell's zebra, while baboons and vervet monkeys can generally be seen rustling around in the trees or making a nuisance of themselves on the ground. Other large predators include spotted hyena, leopard, cheetah and a pack of the endangered African wild dog; genets are also frequently seen crossing the roads towards dusk.

Game drives

Some 84km of roads traverse uMkhuze, but the bushy nature of the acacia savannah can make for challenging wildlife viewing away from the water – though it tends to be the case that just when you despair of seeing anything more exciting than another herd of nyala or impala, you'll suddenly come face to face with an elephant, rhino or giraffe in the middle of the road, a solitary leopard or pack of wild dogs crossing it, or a diminutive suni antelope traipsing warily through the sand forest. Otherwise, compensation for the slow mammal viewing away from the hides comes in the form of the wonderful birdlife, whether you're a novice blown away by a first sighting of a psychedelic lilac-breasted roller, or a dedicated twitcher searching for the obscure likes of Rudd's apalis and Neergaard's sunbird.

For those with limited time, the ideal way to construct a half-day game drive is to follow a circular loop via kuMasinga Hide to **Nsumo Pan**, then return via kuDuza Dam, stopping to stretch your legs at the various hides and observation platforms en route. More ambitiously, the little-used unsurfaced roads that run south and west from the main surfaced road

---

UMKHUZE AT A GLANCE

Underrated Big Five reserve whose hides are much loved by photographers and birders.

Big Five: ***
General wildlife: ****
Birding: *****
Scenery: **
Wilderness factor: ***
Uncrowded: ****
Affordability: *****
Self-drive: Y

loop might not necessarily offer better game viewing, but you will almost certainly have them to yourself. Before heading out on a game drive, it is well worth checking the board at Mantuma reception for recent lion and cheetah sightings, and if you're keen to see the endangered African wild dog, to ask whether and where they might be denning. Guided night drives from Mantuma cost R350.

Hides

The six **hides** and observation platforms dotted around uMkhuze are generally far more productive than the roads when it comes to game viewing, photography and birding, especially during the dry winter months, when water sources are limited.

The pick of the hides is usually **kuMasinga**, a stilted wooden construction that stands above an artificially pumped waterhole about 3km south of *Mantuma Rest Camp*. From here, there are clear views to the shore on three sides, at a distance that works well with lenses in the 200–400x range. Wildlife activity tends to be busiest here from around 8am to 2pm; small herds of nyala, impala, greater kudu, wildebeest and zebra come and go throughout the day, while other regular visitors include the vervet monkey, baboon and slender mongoose. Terrapins sunbathe on the shore, and patient visitors stand a decent chance of seeing elephant, giraffe or black or white rhino. The birdlife is fabulous too, not so much for water-associated species but more for the steady stream of colourful bushveld dwellers – among them purple-crested turaco, crested barbet, black-collared barbet, red-fronted tinkerbird, red-backed mannikin and grey waxbill – coming to drink.

Situated 2km east of Mantuma, **kuMahlahla Hide** also tends to be most productive in winter, but while there is usually some wildlife present throughout the day, it tends to be quieter and is less photogenic than kuMasinga. By contrast, **kuMalibala Hide**,

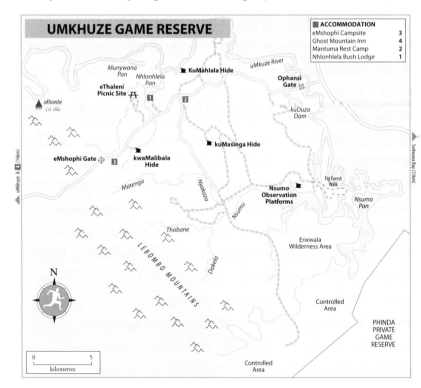

situated to the south of the surfaced road between eMshophi Gate and Mantuma, overlooks a shallow pan that tends to dry up completely in winter, but can be worth a stop in summer. For keen birders, the small hide opposite the reception in *Mantuma Camp* is also rewarding for identifying and photographing smaller seedeaters such as waxbills and canaries.

A pair of hide-like observation platforms and a picnic site overlook **Nsumo Pan**, a large and very beautiful natural lake fringed by fever trees and low hills about 18km southeast of Mantuma. Boasting a tropical African ambience that recalls the smaller Rift Valley lakes of East Africa, Nsumo is a good place to look for hippos and crocs, and the observation platforms are superbly placed for observing water-associated birds, from the raptorial African fish eagle and osprey to gorgeous small kingfishers and bee-eaters, along with large flocks of pelicans, herons, egrets, terns and spoonbills.

Fig Forest Walk

Daily by request at 6am and 2pm • R300 optionally includes a road transfer from Mantuma Rest Camp

A highlight of the reserve, especially for birdwatchers, is this relaxed guided walk along a looping trail through the beautiful forest of buttressed sycamore fig trees – some upwards of four hundred years old – that stretches eastward from the uMkhuze River a short distance past Nsumo Pan. Since it lies on a floodplain, the sycamore forest is frequently waterlogged and characterized by a very open understory, which makes it unusually easy to spot and identify forest birds. The forest echoes to the nasal shriek of trumpeter hornbills, while other specials include Pel's fishing owl, Narina trogon, African broadbill, grey cuckoo-shrike, blue-mantled crested flycatcher, gorgeous bush-shrike, pink-throated twinspot and the abundant African paradise flycatcher. Oddly, the sycamore fig has no specific fruiting season, so different trees tend to come into fruit at different times of year, and it is worth locating one and hanging out below it to look for barbets, turacos, hornbills and other frugivores, as well as the insectivores that feed on insects attracted to overripe fruit. The walk from the car-park towards the forest involves crossing the uMkhuze River on an impressive suspension bridge, and a highlight of the forest interior is a tall two-tiered wooden boardwalk that connects a series of stilted platforms offering views deep into the leafy canopy. Mammals likely to be seen in the fig forest include red duiker, vervet monkey and baboon, and the excursion is given a certain edge by the small but real possibility of bumping into lion, buffalo or elephant on foot.

Muzi Pan

One of the most underpublicized wetlands in northern KwaZulu-Natal, **Muzi Pan** is a 10km-long sliver of forest-fringed open water set on the western border of iSimangaliso, some 13km southeast of uMkhuze's Ophansi Gate by road. Home to plentiful hippos and crocs, it is renowned among birders as one of the best places in the country to see the impressive Pel's fishing owl, along with the likes of pink-backed pelican, African pygmy goose, lesser moorhen, lesser jacana, broad-billed roller, black coucal and lemon-breasted canary. Indeed, a total of 420 bird species have been recorded on this small pan alone, and serious birders frequently tick more than 120 in the course of a day. Muzi is most easily explored by canoe; try Muzi Pan Canoe Adventures (☎073 161 8189), a small locally owned company based on the southwest shore close to where the unsurfaced D820 crosses the wetlands en route between Ophansi Gate and the R22 between Hluhluwe and Kosi Bay.

ARRIVAL AND INFORMATION	UMKHUZE GAME RESERVE

By car If you're driving, the easiest way to get to the reserve is to leave the N2 at uMkhuze village and follow the signs along a good dirt road to eMshophi Gate. An alternative route to the same gate, which leaves the N2 further south, 35km north of Hluhluwe, involves a lot more driving on dirt and doesn't knock much off the distance. From Sodwana Bay and the northeast, travel south on the R22 and turn right down the D820 for 14km to the Ophansi Gate, crossing Muzi Pan after about 1km.

On a tour There's no public transport into uMkhuze, and

if you don't have your own vehicle you'll need to join one of the daytime or night-time excursions into the park from uMkhuze village. The best place to organize this is *Ghost Mountain Inn* (see below).

Information The park reception office at Mantuma, 9km from the entrance gate, provides a clear map showing all routes and distances and giving general information about the park. You can buy fuel at the entrance gate, and there's a shop selling basic supplies and books at reception, but you should stock up on provisions in uMkhuze village before heading out.

ACCOMMODATION   SEE MAP PAGE 164

Ghost Mountain Inn On Fish Eagle Rd in uMkhuze village, signposted off the N2 ☎ 035 573 1025, ⊛ ghost mountaininn.co.za. The centre of most tourist activity in and around uMkhuze, this attractive hotel has been owned by the same family since it was founded in 1962. Its selection of 74 rooms and suites combine agreeable modern decoration with good facilities. The large gardens, studded with tall sycamore figs and fever trees, support a varied birdlife, as well as small mammals like bushbaby and genet, and they run down to a pretty reed-lined dam with an island heronry in the centre. Great for a drink or meal and a dunk in the pool even if you aren't staying, the hotel also arranges a varied selection of activities for guests and non-guests. These include 4hr game drives to uMkhuze (R930 per person/two people; R685 per person/four people) or Hluhluwe-iMfolozi (R1050 per person/ two people; R920 per person/four people), boat cruises on Pongolapoort Dam (R610 per person/two people; R395 per person/four people), plus a number of other options in uMkhuze (including bird walks and night drives) and guided hikes up Ghost Mountain, an important Zulu cultural site overlooking the town of uMkhuze. $\overline{\underline{SS}}$–$\overline{\underline{SSS}}$

Mantuma Rest Camp 9km into the park in the northern section; book through KZN Wildlife ☎ 033 845 1000, ⊛ kznwildlife.com. The reserve's main restcamp and reception has a range of accommodation, the cheapest being two-bed rest huts with shared bathrooms and a kitchen. There are also larger chalets that sleep two, four or six. The most enticing units, however, are the large two- or four-person safari tents, each with its own ablutions. $\overline{\underline{S}}$

Nhlonhlela Bush Lodge Overlooking Nhlonhlela Pan between Mantuma and eMshophi Gate; book through KZN Wildlife ☎ 035 573 9004, ⊛ kznwildlife.com. Four two-bed rooms connected by wooden walkways to a communal kitchen and living area. There's a cook (you bring the ingredients) and a field ranger included in the price. Minimum charge for six. $\overline{\underline{SSS}}$

CAMPSITE

eMshophi Campsite 1km beyond eMshophi Gate; book through KZN Wildlife ☎ 033 845 1000, or direct ☎ 035 573 9004, ⊛ kznwildlife.com. A simple, fairly large campsite handily located near the reserve's main entrance, with hot showers and a swimming pool. $\overline{\underline{S}}$

Northern iSimangaliso

Running north from Sodwana Bay to the border with Mozambique, iSimangaliso's sliver-shaped **northern section** protects the most wild, remote and beautiful tract of South Africa's eastern coastline. A humid, subtropical and green wilderness area of lakes, estuaries, coastal forests, dune fields and beaches, it forms part of a region known as **Maputaland**, which is bordered by the Indian Ocean to the east and the low-lying Lebombo Mountains to the west. This stretch of coastline was once accessible only along a network of dirt roads that worked their tortuous way to the coast, but it has opened up considerably in recent years thanks to the surfacing of two different roads connecting it to the N2. Coming from the south and/or heading towards Sodwana Bay, the road of choice is the **R22**, which strikes north from Hluhluwe village, passing Sodwana Bay and Kosi Bay, before continuing on to reach the Mozambique border post after 160km. Coming from Gauteng, an alternative route is the **P522**, which departs from the N2 11km north of uMkhuze village then snakes north, via the bustling small town of **Jozini** and east past Tembe Elephant Park, to eventually connect with the R22 after 100km, some 35km southwest of Kosi Bay.

NORTHERN ISIMANGALISO AT A GLANCE

Remote coastal forests, hippo-filled lakes and top snorkelling and diving.

Big Five: N/A
General wildlife: ***
Birding: *****
Scenery: ****
Wilderness factor: ****
Uncrowded: **** (Sodwana in season *)
Affordability: *****
Self-drive: Y

Sodwana Bay

Around 80km northeast of Hluhluwe village • Daily 24hr • R28, plus R32 per vehicle • ☎ 035 571 0051/2

A tiny scoop in the Zululand Coast, **Sodwana Bay** is the only breach in an almost flawless strand extending almost 200km from St Lucia to Kosi Bay. It's the fortuitous convergence of the bay (which makes it easy to launch boats) with the world's southernmost coral reefs that makes Sodwana the most popular base in the country for **scuba diving** and the most popular resort operated by EKZNW. Because the continental shelf comes extremely close to shore (near-vertical drops are less than 1km away), it offers very deep waters, much loved by anglers who gather here for some of South Africa's best deep-sea **game fishing**, mostly tag and release. The abundance of game fish also makes for some of the best surf fly-fishing in the country.

When there's no one around, Sodwana Bay is paradise, with tepid waters, terrific sandy beaches, relaxed diving and snorkelling, and plenty of accommodation. Over weekends and during school holidays, however, fashion-conscious folk from Gauteng tear down in their 4WDs, while anglers from Free State and Mpumalanga come to drink themselves into a stupor. A gentler presence is the leatherback and loggerhead **turtles**, which have been making their way onto Sodwana's beaches for the last 60,000 years, from as far afield as Kenya and Cape Agulhas. Nesting season is usually from November to the end of February, and the hatching season is from the middle of January to the end of April each year. Meanwhile, pods of bottlenose dolphins routinely patrol up and down the coast, and, between June and November, southern right and humpback whales may be spotted beyond the breakers.

3

ARRIVAL, INFORMATION AND TOURS   SODWANA BAY

By minibus taxi Minibus taxis run to Sodwana Bay from Mbazwana (16km). If you'll be staying at *Coral Divers*, it offers a free transfer to pre-booked guests arriving at St Lucia with the North Coast Runner on Mondays, Wednesdays and Fridays at 1pm, and free transport to and from the beach to coincide with dives and meal times. Otherwise, once there, the place is so spread out that you'll have to hitchhike your way around if you haven't got your own vehicle.

Tourist facilities The park entry gate (24hr), and EKZNW office (Mon–Thurs 8am–4.30pm, Fri & Sat 7am–4.30pm, Sun 7am–3pm; ☎ 035 571 0051/2), are up the hill past the

town. A small supermarket is across the road from the office, and fuel is available at the gate.

Guided tours During the turtle nesting season from mid-November to the end of April, you can join a fascinating guided 4hr after-dark tour (R900) with Ufudu Turtle Tours (☎ 082 391 1503, ⊛ ufuduturtletours.co.za), the only operator permitted to conduct turtle tours in the Sodwana Bay area. Pre-booking is essential as spaces are limited to one vehicle per night and demand is very high. The excursion includes hot and soft drinks and a light dinner.

DIVING AND SNORKELLING IN SODWANA BAY

Unless you're a keen angler, the principal reason to come to Sodwana Bay is for the diving off the **coral reefs** that thrive here in the warm waters carried down the coast by the Agulhas current. The sea is clear, silt-free and perfect for spotting some of the 1200 varieties of **fish** that inhabit the waters off northern KwaZulu-Natal, making it second only to the Great Barrier Reef in its richness.

The closest reef to the bay, and consequently the most visited, is **Two Mile Reef**, 2km long and 900m wide, offering excellent dives. Among the others is **Five Mile Reef**, which is further north and known for its miniature staghorn corals, while beyond that, **Seven Mile Reef** is inhabited by large anemone communities and offers protection to turtles and rays, which may be found resting here.

There's excellent **snorkelling** at Jesser Point, a tiny promontory at the southern end of the bay. Just off here is **Quarter Mile Reef**, which attracts a wide variety of fish, including moray eels and rays. Low tide is the best time to venture out. You can buy competitively priced snorkels and masks (or rent them for R45 per day) from the Sodwana Bay Lodge Scuba Centre (☎ 035 571 0117, ⊛ sodwanadiving.co.za). Here you'll also find a **dive operation** offering various diving courses, diving packages and scuba equipment rental. There are also several other dive operators providing similar services.

ACCOMMODATION

Coral Divers Sodwana Main Rd ☎035 571 0290, ⓦcoraldivers.co.za. The largest dive outfit at Sodwana Bay is a basic but friendly divers' haunt with two-bed safari tents and two-bed cabins with or without their own bathrooms (those without use the KZN Wildlife ablutions); note that at least one person in each room must be planning to dive. You can self-cater or pay for half-board, and takeaways are available throughout the day. Free transport to and from the beach to coincide with dives and meal times. Self-catering. $\overline{\underline{S}}$

EKZNW accommodation Spread along behind the beach south of the gate ☎035 571 0051, ⓦkznwildlife.com. Twenty fully equipped log cabins with either four or six beds, with minimum charges for three and four people, respectively. There are also a staggering 380 campsites here (minimum charge for four), and the seasonal population explosion allegedly makes Sodwana Bay the largest campsite in South Africa. Camping $\overline{\underline{S}}$, cabins $\overline{\underline{SS}}$

Mseni Beach Lodge Right on the water's edge, south of the village ☎033 345 6531 or ☎087 803 5878, ⓦmseni.co.za. The only establishment with direct access to the beach, this comfortable lodge offers en-suite B&B log cabins or self-catering units sleeping two to eight people spread out amid thick coastal forest. There's a restaurant, bar and swimming pool. $\overline{\underline{S}}$

Natural Moments Next to Sodwana Bay Lodge, Sodwana Main Rd ☎083 236 1756, ⓦdivesodwana.com. A friendly and somewhat bohemian backpackers and dive school offering rustic but cosy cabins, most priced as dorms and some en suite, along with a couple of family units and a big communal kitchen. During the summer there's a good pizza joint out front, and campsites across the road. Camping, dorms and doubles available. $\overline{\underline{S}}$

Sodwana Bay Lodge Sodwana Main Rd, in the village ☎035 571 9101 or ☎035 571 9113, ⓦsodwanabaylodge.co.za. Simple yet comfortable reed and thatched en-suite, two-bed B&B chalets. The *Leatherbacks Seafood and Grill* and a poolside bar with sun deck attracts visitors and locals. Meal packages available. $\overline{\underline{SS}}$

EATING

Most of the lodges have bars and restaurants that are open to all, and these are the best places to join in with the post-diving camaraderie.

The Lighthouse Sodwana Main Rd ☎083 471 0868, ⓦthelighthouse-sodwana.co.za. The classiest restaurant Sodwana has to offer, with pasta, seafood and good thin-crust pizzas served on a pleasant patio strewn with fairy lights. Winter Thurs–Sun 8.30am–9pm; summer daily 8am–10pm.

Lake Sibaya and the Coastal Forest

Daily 6am–6pm • No entrance fee for Lake Sibaya, R28 for the Coastal Forest Sector plus R29 per vehicle • ☎035 592 0235

Fringed by white sandy beaches disappearing into dense forest, **Lake Sibaya**, 10km due north of Sodwana Bay, is South Africa's largest natural freshwater lake, with a surface area of 77 square kilometres. It stands at an altitude of 20 metres, about 3km inland of the Indian Ocean, and has a mean depth of 12–13 metres (and a maximum of 40 metres), which makes it deeper than Lake St Lucia, and less vulnerable to seasonal fluctuations. Sibaya was once part of the Pongola river system, connected to the ocean via a saline estuary, but today its catchment area is only ten times larger than its surface; it is fed almost entirely by subterranean springs and has no confirmed outlet. Eighteen fish species have been recorded and one, the Sibaya goby, is all but endemic to the lake.

On a windless day, the lake appears glassy, azure and flat; the waters are so transparent that when KZN Wildlife take a hippo census they just fly over and count the dark blobs clearly visible from the air (which numbered around 150 at the last count). From the margins, timid crocodiles cut the lake surface, exchanging the warmth of the sun for the safety of the water. This is not an unpopulated wilderness: the lake fringes are dotted with traditional African lands and villages. There's an exceptionally easy-going 3km circular **walk** that starts from the viewing platform behind KZN Wildlife's now-closed *Baya Camp*, but you can drive here too. **Birdwatching** can be rewarding (there are two hides), with close on three hundred species present. Long-tailed and white-breasted cormorants are very common, as is the spectacular African fish eagle, while localized specialities include rosy-throated longclaw, little bittern, pygmy goose, rufous-bellied heron and Pel's fishing owl. Needless to say, with crocs and hippos lolling about, swimming in the lake is most unwise.

Separating Sibaya from the Indian Ocean, the **Coastal Forest sector** of iSimangaliso Wetland Park protects some of the world's tallest forested dunes. The luxuriant subtropical forest harbours a rich fauna including samango monkey, greater bushbaby, large-spotted genet, porcupine and localized birds such as African broadbill, Livingstone's turaco, Neergaard's sunbird, Woodward's batis and black-throated wattle-eye. Below it, a perfect tropical beach offers **surf angling** and **snorkelling** matching that at Sodwana Bay, with a rich tropical marine life thriving on the coral reefs offshore, but none of the frenetic activity of outboard motors and 4WD vehicles found further south – indeed, outside school holidays, there's a fair chance of having it all to yourself.

ARRIVAL AND DEPARTURE

By car There are two approach roads, both very sandy and strictly 4WD only. Coming from the south, follow the R22 to Mbazwana, then turn right just north of it. Next look for the fork and follow the D1848 road left to the lake. From the north, follow directions to Mabibi via the Coastal Forest turn-off, passing Lake Sibaya to the west

LAKE SIBAYA AND THE COASTAL FOREST

en route. Alternatively, follow the R22 for 18km north of Mbazwana, then turn right at the Coastal Forest turn-off and it's 24km to the gate. If you are in non-4WD and staying at *Thonga Beach Lodge*, you can park at the Coastal Cashews office (just under 5km from the R22) and arrange a transfer from there.

ACCOMMODATION   SEE MAP PAGE 154

★ **Mabibi Beach Camp** 035 474 1504, mabibi beachcamp.co.za. One of the most peaceful spots to camp in South Africa, this forest-fringed site comprises three idyllic two-person self-catering chalets and eight camping pitches perched on a plateau on top of the dunes and sheltered from the wind. A boardwalk leads down to the sea. $

★ **Thonga Beach Lodge** 035 474 1473, thonga beachlodge.co.za. This luxury Robinson Crusoe-style lodge offers stunning thatched suites secluded in the coastal dune forest, along with a spa, dive operation, turtle-tracking tours, kayaking and sundowners at Lake Sibaya. The ultimate in barefoot beach luxury. $$$$$

Kosi Bay Nature Reserve

Kosi Mouth, 7km north of KwaNgwanase • Daily 6am–6pm • R55, plus R56 per vehicle • 035 592 0236

At the northernmost reaches of the KwaZulu-Natal coast, the 110-square-kilometre **Kosi Bay Nature Reserve** protects an enthralling area of forest-fringed waterways immediately south of the Farazela Border with Mozambique. Despite the name, it is not a bay at all, but a system of five main lakes – linked by a series of streams and channels – that drain into the Indian Ocean via a sandy estuary. This extensive wetland system is fed by a combination of subterranean groundwater seepage and precipitation (the latter averages almost 1000mm per annum) and while the three lakes closest to the estuary are almost as saline as seawater, the larger **Lake Nhlange** is intermediately brackish, and the more remote **Lake Amanzamnyama** (literally "Black Water") is essentially a freshwater body whose inky appearance is caused by peat washed in by the Sidhadla River.

Kosi Bay protects some thirty hectares of mangrove swamp and all five mangrove tree species recorded in South Africa, two at the very southern extent of their range. It also contains South Africa's largest groundwater forest and forms the southernmost extent of the natural range of the palmnut vulture, a handsome bird that nests on, and is often seen in the vicinity of, the raffia palms that flank the Sidhadla River. Canoe trips along this river also offer the opportunity to see samango monkey, Nile crocodile, some of the reserve's estimated population of sixty hippos, and other noteworthy birds such as broad-billed roller, African finfoot, osprey, pygmy goose, brown-throated weaver and Pel's fishing owl.

One of the most striking images of Kosi Bay is of mazes of reed fences in the estuary and other parts of the lake system. These are **fish traps**, or kraals, built by local **Tonga** people, a sustainable practice that has been going on for hundreds of years. The traps are passed down from father to son, and numbers are strictly controlled to ensure they capture only a small fraction of the fish that pass through. To see the fish traps – and the beach – you'll need to travel to **Kosi Mouth**, a hard-going twenty-minute drive for which you'll need 4WD. Kosi Mouth also offers superb **snorkelling** in the (usually still) waters around a large rocky reef where more than 150 fish species have been recorded and the likes of surgeonfish, damselfish, butterfly fish, moray eel, parrotfish, devil's firefish, stone bream and wrasse are all regularly seen at high tide.

ACCOMMODATION **KOSI BAY, SEE MAP PAGE 154**

Kosi Bay Lodge 2km before the Reserve gate ☎ 083 262 4865, ⓦ kosibaylodge.co.za. Popular as a place to stay overnight on the way to Mozambique, but great as a base to explore the area too, with the benefit that regular cars can reach here. There are two-, four- and six-bed rustic thatch-and-reed chalets on stilts, with kitchens, plus safari tents with shared bathrooms, a restaurant/pub and pool with sun deck. Self-catering or full board and plenty of excursions including boat rides on Lake Nhlange are available. $̄

Kosi Bay Restcamp On the western shore of Lake Nhlange; book through KZN Wildlife ☎ 033 845 1000, or camp reception ☎ 035 592 0236, ⓦ kznwildlife.com. Two-bed, four-bed (minimum charge for four people) and six-bed cabins, and a small campsite with hot showers; some sites have power points and lake views. Drinks are available from reception. The Umdoni day-visitor area is shaded and has braai facilities. Access is strictly 4WD. $̄

★ **Kosi Forest Lodge** Inside the Reserve ☎ 035 474 1473, ⓦ kosiforestlodge.co.za. Arguably the dreamiest place to stay in KwaZulu-Natal, featuring eight reed-and-thatch suites in a remote landscape of palms, lakes, sand forest and bleached white beaches. There's limited electricity, and if you don't have your own 4WD you'll be collected from KwaNgwanase. Activities include game drives, guided canoeing trips, reef snorkelling and forest walks; there's a good chance you'll see hippos, crocodiles and turtles. $̄$̄$̄$̄

★ **Thobeka Backpackers Lodge** 4km north of KwaNgwanase ☎ 035 592 3002 or ☎ 072 446 1525, ⓦ kosi.co.za. A delightfully rustic, friendly backpackers hidden away in the forest, with bush camp-style rooms connected by wooded boardwalks, family cottages, dorms and camping, plus a self-catering kitchen, bar and pool. The owners go out of their way to organize a variety of activities, including snorkelling, tours into Mozambique, trips to a colourful border market and even courses in bush cooking. $̄

The Maputaland interior

Bounded by the N2 and Eswatini (formerly Swaziland) to the west, Mozambique to the north, and the iSimangaliso Wetland Park to the east and south, the interior of **MAPUTALAND** is home to a quartet of remote game reserves, notable as much for their subtropical scenery and wilderness character as for their bountiful wildlife. The **Pongola Game Reserve** and **Phongolo Nature Reserve** both enclose the lovely Pongolapoort Dam, and together form part of the proposed Nsubane-Pongola Transfrontier Conservation Area, which extends across the border into Eswatini. Further northeast, bordering Mozambique, **Ndumo Game Reserve** and **Tembe Elephant Park** theoretically form part of the Usutu-Tembe-Futi Transfrontier Conservation Area, at least according to a protocol signed by the governments of South Africa, Mozambique and Eswatini back in 2000, but in practice both still function as self-contained entities. Pongola Game Reserve and Phongolo Nature Reserve, though little visited, are actually quite readily accessible since they lie directly alongside the N2 and/or the zippy 10km road that connects it to the Golela border post and Eswatini. Ndumo and Tembe are somewhat more remote but can be reached along the surfaced roads that connect the N2 to the northern iSimangaliso coastline. Tembe is accessible in any vehicle, however its internal roads can be explored only in a private 4WD vehicle or on guided game drives operated by the only lodge set within it.

Ndumo Game Reserve

Daily: Apr–Sept 6am–6pm; Oct–Mar 5am–7pm • R80 • ☎ 035 591 0058

One of the most lush and beautiful reserves in KwaZulu-Natal, **Ndumo** was established in 1924 to protect the floodplain of the **Usutu River** as it flows eastward along the border with Mozambique, and an associated network of seasonal waterways and perennial pans set in the shadow of the **Lebombo Mountains**. It isn't primarily a Big Five destination, but leopard and buffalo are present in small numbers, and it used to host significant populations of black and white rhino until they were airlifted to another location in 2017 following a spate of poaching incidents. Other wildlife includes an estimated three hundred hippos, giraffe, Burchell's zebra and antelope such as nyala, impala, red duiker and suni. It is also home to some of the most gigantic crocodiles you'll see anywhere south of the Zambezi.

Ndumo is regarded by many dedicated South African **birders** to be the country's single most alluring ornithological destination, with a remarkable tally of 440 species recorded in a mere 100 square kilometres, a number that includes a long list of rarities. Notable swamp- and

| **NDUMO AT A GLANCE** |
| Remote coastal forests, hippo-filled lakes and top snorkelling and diving. |
| **Big Five:** * |
| **General wildlife:** *** |
| **Birding:** ***** |
| **Scenery:** **** |
| **Wilderness factor:** **** |
| **Uncrowded:** ***** |
| **Affordability:** ***** |
| **Self-drive:** Y |

water-associated birds include Pel's fishing owl, lesser jacana, black egret, African pygmy goose and species of both flamingo and pelican. Specials associated with terrestrial habitats include African broadbill, African cuckoo-hawk, crested guineafowl, Neergaard's sunbird, pink-throated twinspot, southern brown-throated weaver and grey waxbill. A specialist bird guide is an invaluable asset if you are serious about making the most of Ndumo's birdlife; guides can usually be arranged on the spot, but it's safer to call park reception in advance.

The limited road network in Ndumo is entirely unsurfaced but sufficiently well-maintained to be tackled on all but the lowest-clearance cars. All visitors need to check in and pay fees at the restcamp **reception**, which lies about 6km east of the entrance gate, and is a great place to look for woodland birds on foot. Another must-visit, about 2.5km from the restcamp, is Ezulwini Hide, which overlooks **Nyamithi Pan**, a variable body of water lined with jaundiced fever tree forests and open floodplains. Nyamithi almost invariably hosts a good number of hippos and crocs as well as a varied selection of water-associated birds, and the fringing forest is a good place to look for giraffe and antelope. A highlight of the reserve's western road network is Red Cliffs Picnic Site, which gives soaring views across the Usutu into both Eswatini and Mozambique.

ARRIVAL AND TOURS   NDUMO GAME RESERVE

By car The most direct route to Ndumo – coming from most directions – is to branch northeast from the N2 about 11km north of uMkhuze onto the P522. Continue along it for 70km in the direction of Kosi Bay, passing en route through the often-congested town of Jozini to the junction village of Ephondweni, from where it is 17km north along a clearly signposted surfaced road to the entrance gate. Ndumo could also be approached along the R22 from Hluhluwe,

turning left at the junction with the P522 and continuing along it for 32km, past the entrance to Tembe Elephant Park, to Ephondweni.

Tours A great way to explore parts of the reserve inaccessible to self-drivers is to join one of the guided morning and evening game drives (R260) that operate out of the restcamp. Guided walks are also available (R160) and highly recommended to serious birders.

ACCOMMODATION   SEE MAP PAGE 154

Ndumo Restcamp Book through KZN Wildlife ☎ 033 845 1000, or camp reception ☎ 035 591 0058, ⓦ kznwildlife.com. Set in a park-like woodland passed through by plenty of wildlife and rustling with birds, this low-key and very likeable camp comprises a dozen recently refurbished two-bed self-catering huts with private veranda, air-conditioning and fridge. There is also a campsite with shared ablutions. A shop sells a very limited selection of basic odds and ends, but it's safer to stock up en route – there's a decent supermarket and liquor shop in

the junction village of Ephondweni and a less impressive supermarket in Ndumo village just 2km before the gate. ⑤ **Ndumu River Lodge** Ephondweni, 17km from the entrance gate ☎ 035 592 8000 or ☎ 082 759 1626, ⓦ ndumu.com. Set in lushly overgrown grounds sloping down to the Pongola River, this twenty-room lodge offers a wide range of activities including birding, fishing, canoeing and game drives, and it also makes a useful base for self-drivers seeking a catered alternative to the reserve restcamp. ⑤⑤

TEMBE ELEPHANT PARK AT A GLANCE

Underrated Big Five reserve known for its giant tuskers and offering budget-friendly guided safari packages.

Big Five: ***
General wildlife: ***
Birding: ****
Scenery: **
Wilderness factor: *****
Uncrowded: *****
Affordability: ***
Self-drive: N

Tembe Elephant Park

Daily: Apr–Sept 6am–6pm; Oct–Mar 5am–7pm • R50, plus R110 per vehicle • ☎ 082 651 2868, ⊛ tembe.co.za

Jointly managed by EKZNW and the local Tembe community, the remote **Tembe Elephant Park** extends across 300 square kilometres on the border with Mozambique, a short distance east of Ndumo. It was established in 1983 to protect what was then the last free-ranging population of elephants in South Africa, a herd of around 150 individuals that included some of the largest remaining tuskers in southern Africa, the last of which died of natural causes in 2014.

A Big Five reserve, it is now home to around 220–250 elephants, while lion, black rhino, white rhino, buffalo and giraffe have been reintroduced to supplement naturally occurring species such as hippo, nyala, impala, red duiker and suni.

Tembe supports a wide variety of habitats, including sand forest, seasonal wetlands, thick acacia savannah and open grassland. No perennial rivers run through the park, but it is liberally studded with small pans, many of which seem to hold water even in the driest conditions. Broadly speaking, the vegetation in the south, around the tented camp, is dominated by dense semi-deciduous woodland, which can make for challenging game viewing, the one exception being the open waterhole, overlooked by a photographic hide that features on the web-cam (⊛ tembe.co.za/web-cam). A striking tree associated with this habitat is the iNkehli or pod mahogany *Afzelia quanzensis*, a hardwood that stands up to 30m tall and has a wide canopy that sheds its leaves in winter, when the large flat pods are conspicuous. Game viewing tends to be far more productive in the northern part of the reserve, which supports an open floodplain-like habitat of grassland fringed by ilala and wild date palms. The varied birdlife is broadly similar to Ndumo's, albeit with a lower number of water-associated species, while crowned hornbill, African hoopoe, crested guineafowl and grey waxbill seem to be particularly common.

Access to Tembe Elephant Park is limited to those staying in its delightful community-owned tented camp, for whom guided game drives are usually included in the accommodation package, as well as up to ten private 4WD vehicles per day (by pre-arrangement only, as a guide must accompany each car). This creates an exclusive feel comparable to a private game reserve, but at a more competitive price, with all revenue helping to support local communities. Elephant and buffalo sightings are almost guaranteed, but other members of the Big Five can be more difficult to locate. Tembe is possibly the best place in South Africa to see the very localized samango monkey, while bushbabies and genets are frequently seen around the camp at night.

ARRIVAL AND ACCOMMODATION   TEMBE ELEPHANT PARK, SEE MAP PAGE 154

By car The prominently signposted entrance gate to Tembe stands on the north side of the P522, about 16km east of Ephondweni (the turn-off to Ndumo) and a similar distance west of the junction with the R22. See directions to Ndumo for further details. A 4WD is required for driving yourself within the park. If staying overnight, and your car isn't deemed suitable for the short road to the tented camp, you can leave your car at the gate – you'll be transferred in the park's own vehicle.

★ **Tembe Tented Camp** ☎ 082 651 2868, ⊛ tembe. co.za. The only accommodation in the park comprises about two dozen comfortable en-suite safari tents built on raised wooden platforms and spread across a wide area of natural bush that has been fenced off to prevent dangerous animals from entering. It employs more than fifty members of the local community, which is the largest non-government workforce in this remote region. Rates include all meals and game drives, conducted by knowledgeable guides, with traditional Tembe dancers coming to perform some evenings. Very good value. $$$

Pongolapoort Dam and environs

Focal point of one of South Africa's most historic and underrated not-quite-Big-Five safari destinations, **Pongolapoort**, also known as Lake Jozini, is an artificial freshwater body created in 1973 when an eponymous 89m-high, 450m-wide arch dam was built across the Pongola (or Phongolo) River where it flows through the narrow gorge that divides the Lebombo Mountains from the more southerly Ubombo. Made for irrigation and water-storage purposes rather than as a source of hydro-electricity, Pongolapoort was the largest dam in the country at the time of construction, and the reservoir it hems in is the fifth-largest in South African, extending across 132 square kilometres when full (which it hasn't been since the turn of the millennium). Pongolapoort is legendary with hardcore **anglers** as the southernmost refuge of the tiger fish (catch and release only), a challenging game fish more usually associated with the Zambezi Basin.

Rather less well-known is that Pongolapoort and the **Pongola Game** and **Phongolo Nature** reserves that enclose it offer some excellent and unusually affordable game-viewing opportunities in an archetypal subtropical African setting. All the Big Five except lion are present, along with the likes of giraffe, Burchell's zebra, impala, greater kudu and nyala, and while the provincially managed nature reserve is ideal for self-drivers, the adjoining private game reserve offers a thrilling range of organized activities including boat safaris, tracking white rhino on foot, and guided game drives and walks. The birding is marvellous in both reserves.

3

History

The original Pongola Game Reserve was the first reserve to be proclaimed in what is now South Africa. In August 1889, President **Paul Kruger** of the Zuid Afrikaansche Republiek (ZAR; later the Transvaal) set aside seven government-owned farms along the Pongola River as a hunting exclusion zone, in order to help boost wildlife stocks that had been depleted by indiscriminate hunting associated with an influx of white settlers over the previous two decades. The 174-square-kilometre Pongola Game Reserve was formally proclaimed in June 1894, a year before the creation of Hluhluwe, Umfolozi and St Lucia, and four years before the official proclamation of the Sabi Game Reserve (which was later extended to become the Kruger National Park). A Dutch immigrant named **Frederick van Oordt** was appointed the first warden, and his detailed report of 1895 provides valuable information about historical wildlife populations in the area. According to him, common animals included quagga (presumably Burchell's zebra), warthog, greater kudu, waterbuck, hartebeest (presumably red but possibly an outlying southern population of Lichtenstein's), tsessebe, blue wildebeest, southern reedbuck, mountain reedbuck, grey duiker, red duiker, steenbok and klipspringer, while nyala was scarce and lion, leopard, hippo and black and white rhino were sighted occasionally. Elephant were evidently all but extinct, and Van Oordt makes no mention of buffalo. Unfortunately, much of this wildlife perished in the **rinderpest** epidemic of 1897–8, and Van Oordt also reported the area experiencing a terrible malaria epidemic prior to 1899, when he was taken prisoner by the British following the outbreak of the Anglo-Boer War.

Neglected except by hunters for the next four years, Pongola Game Reserve was reproclaimed by the British in 1903 after it was found that the small populations of black rhino and elephant still persisted. However, no meaningful administrative presence was ever put in place by the British and the reserve was eventually deproclaimed in 1921 for reasons that remain unclear. Five years, later, in 1926, wildlife numbers in the area were still sufficient to provide an important source of food to construction workers on the Durban-Golela railway line and the impressive multi-arched bridge which still spans the river downstream of *Mvubu River Lodge*. In 1935, the government carved the land up into farms and inaugurated the **Pongola Irrigation Settlement** in the hope of enticing buyers, but few were prepared to brave what was then perhaps the highest-risk malaria area in South Africa, and the scheme was abandoned in 1942.

PONGOLA AT A GLANCE

Underrated and budget-friendly gem offering rhino tracking on foot and thrilling boat trips.

Big Five: **
General wildlife: ***
Birding: ****
Scenery: ****
Wilderness factor: ****
Uncrowded: *****
Affordability: ****
Self-drive: N

The area languished in obscurity prior to the construction of the **Pongolapoort Dam** in 1973, by which time malaria had been largely eliminated. In 1979, the government of the Transvaal set aside some 104 square kilometres of land enclosing the main body of Pongolapoort as a provincial nature reserve into which white rhinos were introduced in 1984. Pongola and environs were transferred to KwaZulu-Natal in the provincial shuffle that coincided with the democratic elections of 1994, and EKZNW would later rename the nature reserve Phongolo. At around the same time as the provincial reserve was created, several farms that either lay within or bordered the original 1895 reserve were bought up by the Karel Landman Trust to create the present-day Pongola Game Reserve, which flanks the widening Pongola River as it flows into the lake, and now doubles as a well-managed "ethical" hunting reserve and ecotourist destination.

It hasn't helped Pongolapoort's search for greater recognition that administration and ownership of the lake and its surrounds is somewhat confusing. The lake itself remains state property, under the authority of the Department of Water Affairs and Forestry (DWAF), while the two main reserves enclosing it are separately managed by EKZNW and a private family trust. These lines are blurred by the reality that the lake has been well under full capacity since the turn of the millennium. As a consequence, the grassy floodplains seemingly protected within the two reserves are in fact formerly submerged land technically administered by the DWAF, while the perimeter fences between the reserve no longer reach the lake, meaning that wildlife can cross freely between state, provincial and private property. Further blurring the picture, several tracts of buffering community land are administered by tribal authorities, who have reputedly made successful land claims on the provincial nature reserve as well as a strip of former military land on the southeast lakeshore. Fortunately, tentative plans do exist to amalgamate and formally drop fences between the various state, provincial, community and private possessions to create one large reserve extending over more than 300 square kilometres, including the lake. Long term, it is hoped that this this merger will eventually form part of the Nsubane-Pongola Transfrontier Conservation Area, a joint venture between South Africa and Eswatini.

Pongola Game Reserve

One of the best-priced private reserves anywhere in South Africa, **Pongola** boasts an absolutely fabulous setting, flanking the north and south banks of the Pongola River as it meanders atmospherically towards Pongolapoort Dam. It offers good game viewing, with white rhino, giraffe, hippo, warthog, Burchell's zebra, greater kudu, nyala and impala probably the most conspicuous large mammals, though elephant, buffalo and black rhino are also present, along with an elusive population of leopard, and smaller carnivores such as black-backed jackal and genet. For birders, the most eye-catching feature of Pongola is the wealth of water-associated species along the namesake river, but an interesting ecological parallel to the reserve's historic links with the former Transvaal is the conspicuous presence of the likes of African grey hornbill, grey go-away bird, Namaqua dove, Burchell's starling, magpie shrike and white-throated robin-chat – savannah dwellers one would more normally associate with the Kruger National Park than with Zululand.

A highly attractive feature of this reserve is the varied range of well-priced guided **activities**; not only game drives but also boat trips, game walks and **rhino-tracking**

excursions. A genuinely thrilling highlight are the guided white-rhino tracking excursions, which usually involve driving around until reasonably fresh tracks are found, then setting out on foot for anything from 100m to 5km until the animals are located. It often takes some time to get close to the rhinos, ideally tracking then upwind, but once you are close and they get used to you, they are surprisingly relaxed, and it is easy to get good photographs.

Another undisputed highlight of any visit to Pongola, guided **boat trips** on the river are best undertaken in the afternoon if your main interest is mammals and scenery, although the morning can be better for birds. At any time of day, you can bank on seeing a few pods of hippo, and outsized basking crocs that slither menacingly into the water when the boat approaches. There's a better than even chance of white rhino and buffalo, along with the usual antelope, and the lucky few might even encounter elephant or black rhino. Water-associated birds are varied and prolific: look out for large flocks of spur-winged goose, white-faced duck and glossy ibis, along with the more solitary likes of yellow-billed stork, purple heron, African fish-eagle, black crake and various kingfishers.

Guided game walks (good for savannah birds) and game drives are also available. No self-driving is permitted except when in transit between gate and lodge, but self-guided game drives can be undertaken in the neighbouring Phongolo Nature Reserve.

3

ARRIVAL AND ACTIVITIES

By car There are two main entrances to Pongola Game Reserve. Heading to Nkwazi, first aim for Leeukop Gate, which flanks the N2 about 35km northwest of uMkhuze and 30km east of the town of Pongola (which the local Zulu people know as uPhongolo), then allow 30 minutes to cover the rough 12km road to the lodge. For Mvubu, follow the N2 north from Leeukop for 4km, then turn onto the surfaced MR8 and continue northeast for 5km until you reach another clearly signposted entrance gate – from here, it's about 3km to the lodge on a good unsurfaced road.

Activities Boat trips, guided game walks and game drives cost R375 per person, while rhino tracking is R475. All activities leave at 7am or 2pm, last around three hours, and run with a minimum of two people. Guiding standards are high, and every effort is made to keep different parties separate to ensure a private experience.

ACCOMMODATION

In addition to the lodges listed below, the reserve is dotted with a few very reasonably priced self-catering camps aimed at small groups; check ⓦ pongolagamereserve.co.za for details. The campsite in Phongolo Nature Reserve is currently non-operational.

Mvubu River Lodge ⓣ 034 435 1123, ⓦ pongola gamereserve.co.za. This complex of standalone cottages sprawls across a lushly wooded hillside, with tremendous views over the Pongola River and its floodplain. A wide variety of birds can be seen in the lodge, along with other occasional nyala and impala, and you should see plenty of larger wildlife coming to drink at the river below. The spacious cottages are made with wood, bamboo and thatch, and come with a private balcony, fridge and large en-suite bathroom. Dinner is usually eaten communally in an outdoor boma, and an excellent breakfast is served between 8am and 11am to allow guests to complete a guided morning activity beforehand, be it rhino tracking, a boat trip or a game drive or walk. The occasional rumble of trains along the 1926 railway bridge is not so much intrusive as a historic scene setter. A good spa is attached. $$$

Nkwazi Lake Lodge ⓣ 034 435 1123, ⓦ pongola gamereserve.co.za. The larger of the two main lodges in Pongola Game Reserve has a truly breathtaking location on a wooded hillside overlooking a delta-like stretch of the river shortly before it opens up into the lake. Scan it with binoculars and you are bound to see giant crocs on the sandbanks and hippos wallowing in the shallows, along with a wide variety of water birds, grazers and possibly even a rhino or buffalo. Comfortable rather than stylish, the en-suite chalets are similar in design and feel to their counterparts at *Mvubu*, but because the lodge is larger and more hotel-like in management style, meals are not taken with other guests. Fantastic value. $$

Phongolo Nature Reserve

Daily: Apr–Sept 6am–6pm; Oct–Mar 5am–7pm • R50 • ⓣ 035 845 1394/1717

A wonderful goal for a half-day self-drive safari, the northwest portion of this provincial reserve sees few visitors other than dedicated **anglers**, so you are likely to have the small but rewarding game-viewing network of dirt roads and tracks to yourself. Most roads and tracks are fine in any vehicle with moderately high clearance during the dry winter

3

PHONGOLO AT A GLANCE
Low-key but very scenic self-drive reserve
that's great for rhino and water birds.
Big Five: **
General wildlife: ***
Birding: ****
Scenery: ****
Wilderness factor: ***
Uncrowded: *****
Affordability: *****
Self-drive: Y

months, but without 4WD you'll need to be a little cautious during the rains. Entering through the only gate, which lies 1km out of Golela, head first along the 3km road to the defunct lakeshore campsite, which doubles as a launch site for fishing boats and also offers some good waterside birding, notably breeding colonies of African darter and long-tailed cormorant in a ghost forest of semi-submerged trees, as well as a great chance of spotting hippos and possibly black or white rhino on the opposite shore.

From the campsite, a maze of tracks runs north through the grassy floodplain and bordering acacia woodland, offering some lovely lakeshore vistas backed by the forested Lebombo Mountains. Wildlife pickings are also rich, with zebra, warthog, hippo, southern reedbuck, waterbuck, impala and blue wildebeest all common on the floodplain, and the possibility of picking out a herd of elephants or buffalo drinking or foraging on the facing eastern shore. The road runs right up to the marshy lakeshore in several places, offering great aquatic birding; look out too for the savannah birds listed under Pongola Game Reserve, as well as secretary birds, perching on the acacia canopies where they nest, in the late afternoon and early morning. You could return to the gate along the 4km **Boundary Track**, which as its name suggests closely follows the reserve fence (and international border), but far nicer to return to the campsite with a snack and cold drink to enjoy the (often spectacular) sunset over the lake.

ARRIVAL, TOURS AND ACCOMMODATION

By car To reach Phongolo Nature Reserve from the N2, follow the MR8 northeast for 11km to Golela. Just before you reach the border post with Eswatini, you'll see the 1km feeder road to the only entrance gate, signposted to the right.

Tours *Ghost Mountain Inn* in uMkhuze operates game-viewing boat cruises on the south of Pongolapoort Dam (R610 per person for two people; R395 per person/four people). These come with a great chance of seeing hippos, crocs, antelope and a varied selection of water birds, but

PHONGOLO NATURE RESERVE

you'll need to make special arrangements to head further north, where you stand a better chance of encountering larger terrestrial wildlife such as elephant, rhino and buffalo.

Accommodation The campsite in Phongolo Nature Reserve is currently non-operational, but the isolated *Nkonkoni Camp* (book directly through ☎ 035 845 1394/1717), comprising four twin en-suite safari tents, and a well-equipped self-catering kitchen with adjoining lounge and dining room, offers excellent value to groups of up to eight people. $$

Private reserves near uMkhuze and Hluhluwe

A cluster of top-notch Big Five reserves sprawls across the hilly savannah country inland of southern iSimangaliso. The oldest, best known and probably most rewarding of these for general game viewing is the super-luxurious **Phinda Private Game Reserve**, while the most specialized is **Zimanga**, whose network of cleverly designed hides will have serious wildlife photographers licking their lips in anticipation. Also well worth considering is **Thanda**, which is a small notch down from Phinda in terms of both experience and price, and the more down-to-earth and relatively wallet-friendly **Manyoni**.

Phinda Private Game Reserve

Daily • Entrance fee included in room rates • ☎ 011 809 4300, 🌐 andbeyond.com

The most prestigious Big Five game-viewing destination in KwaZulu-Natal, **Phinda** (literally "Return to the Wild") is the centrepiece of the 285-square-kilometre **Munyawana Conservancy**, which ranks as both the largest private reserve in the province, and the oldest. It was established in 1991 when **&Beyond** (then CC Africa) bought up a contiguous block of neglected farmland and hunting concessions; the company initiated a massive clean-up operation in which 15,000kg of scrap metal was removed, before embarking on an even more ambitious reintroduction programme to boost resident populations of leopard, nyala, impala and other antelope. Phinda is effectively an extension of the **isimangaliso Wetland Park**, sharing a northern border with uMkhuze Game Reserve, though as things stand no plans are in place to drop fences between these Big Five reserves. The reserve supports seven distinct ecosystems, with acacia savannah and mixed woodland dominant in the south and sandveld woodland, palm savannah and floodplain grassland in the north. In addition, a few narrow ribbons of riparian forest line the **Munyawana River** and its tributaries as they run through the south of the reserve, while the central section supports more than five square kilometres of rare sand forest.

> ### PHINDA AT A GLANCE
> Phinda is among South Africa's top malaria-free private reserves.
> **Big Five:** ****
> **General wildlife:** *****
> **Birding:** *****
> **Scenery:** **
> **Wilderness factor:** ***
> **Uncrowded:** ****
> **Affordability:** *
> **Self-drive:** N

For most visitors, Phinda's main attraction is the exceptional Big Five game viewing and high standard of guiding for which it is renowned. Lion, elephant, buffalo and white rhino are almost certain sightings over the course of a two- to three-night stay, along with cheetah, which are something of a speciality in the northern grasslands and tend to be very habituated, allowing for great close-up behavioural viewing. Black rhinos are less regular, as are leopards, despite the presence of several habituated individuals. Other common wildlife includes giraffe, zebra, warthog, greater kudu, nyala and impala. More than 430 bird species have been recorded and most guides are skilled at identifying more unusual and interesting varieties. Game drives are the main activity and tend to be the most productive, assuming big game is your top priority, but guided walks can also be arranged, while seasonal boat trips on the Munyawana usually throw up hippos and several localized birds including African finfoot and purple swamphen.

The most specialized habitat in Phinda is the **sand forest**, which grows on a fossil dunefield in the centre of the reserve. The forest here is notable for its relatively open understory and the presence of several impressive trees, including the slow-growing Lebombo wattle and the tangle-trunked torch-wood (so named because it has an oily sap that burns when a wick is dipped in it). The sand forest is an important habitat for several localized mammals, notably red duiker, suni antelope and Tonga red squirrel, along with such eagerly sought birds as African broadbill, Narina trogon, Neergaard's sunbird, pink-throated twinspot and green twinspot. Visitors with a specific interest in this remarkable habitat should ask to stay at *Forest Lodge*, which lies in a patch of sand forest where several of the specials are resident.

ARRIVAL   PHINDA PRIVATE GAME RESERVE

By car Phinda lies to the east of the N2 between Hluhluwe and uMkhuze. Heading for *Forest* or *Vlei Lodge*, take the Hluhluwe off-ramp from the N2, drive east for about 4km through Hluhluwe village, then head north onto the R22 to Kosi Bay. After 28km, turn left at Mduku, then right after another 2.5km; you'll reach the eastern entrance gate to the Munyawana Conservancy after another 3.5km. Heading for *Mountain* or *Rock Lodge*, take the Phinda off-ramp (about 10km north of Hluhluwe and 40km south of uMkhuze) for the western gate to the Munyawana Conservancy. Once at the gate, all the individual lodges are signposted, and reached on unsurfaced all-weather roads.

ACCOMMODATION

Four opulent lodges in a variety of original styles are spread around the reserve. All provide hospitality of the highest standard, and game drives and walks are accompanied by well-informed expert guides as good as any you'll find in South Africa. Rates include all meals and game activities. Booking details are 📞 011 809 4300, 🌐 andbeyond.com

3

Forest Lodge A favourite with birdwatchers, this family-friendly lodge stands in an extensive patch of sand forest. The deck and infinity pool overlook a waterhole that attracts a steady trickle of nyala and other antelope. The sixteen air-conditioned glass-sided suites are attractively decorated in contemporary safari style and widely spaced along a sprawling network of forest tracks to maximize privacy. A small hide at the far end of the property is an excellent place to look for and photograph forest specials such as Narina trogon and green twinspot. $$$$

Mountain Lodge Extensively refurbished in 2019, *Mountain Lodge* is the largest and most family-oriented lodge in Phinda, standing on an aloe- and cycad-studded hill with views across to the Lebombo Mountains. The sixteen double suites and four family units are tastefully decorated with Zulu artefacts and come with well-appointed private decks, plunge pools and outdoor showers. Amenities include a freeform infinity pool, gym and spa. $$$$$

Rock Lodge Drawing inspiration from the curvaceous flat-roofed traditional homesteads of Mali's Dogon people, this exclusive lodge is the most architecturally ambitious in Phinda, comprising six air-conditioned suites with private plunge pools set into a dramatic cliff face overlooking Leopard Rock. $$$$$

Vlei Lodge Overlooking a natural wetland on the edge of the sand forest, this exclusive lodge consists of just six thatched suites, recently refurbished in the colonial style associated with the region's sugarcane and pineapple plantations. The wetland setting ensures great in-house game viewing as a steady procession of animals comes to drink, and the birdlife is great too. $$$$$

Zimanga Private Game Reserve

Daily • Entrance fee included in room rates • ☎ 074 165 4361, ⊕ zimanga.com

Offering a very different experience to any other private reserve in KwaZulu-Natal (or, for that matter, to anywhere else in Africa), **Zimanga** justifiably prides itself on being the country's top wildlife-photography destination. Owned by, managed by and catering primarily to dedicated **wildlife photographers**, this exceptional reserve extends across some 75 square kilometres of hilly acacia savannah abutting the N2 northwest of uMkhuze. It incorporates about 8km of well-wooded **uMkhuze River** frontage, as well as the 3-square-kilometre **Hlambanathi** (literally "Place where Buffalo wallow") **Dam** and an associated fever-tree forest. It is home to all the Big Five, as well as cheetah, the usual selection of ungulates, and more than four hundred bird species. It hosts a maximum of seventeen clients, and game drives are usually restricted to small groups, focus on working one subject per drive; where possible they include opportunities to get out and photograph habituated cheetah at ground level, and white rhino and other ungulates on foot. Excursions onto Hlambanathi Dam on a small boat, specially designed for low-angle photography, should be running as of 2020.

The main attraction of Zimanga is a network of **sunken hides** designed specifically for wildlife photography. Each hide has its own speciality. Mornings-only Scavenger Hide, for instance, usually attracts large flocks of white-backed vulture, allowing for dramatic action shots as they come into land and squabble, or interact with other visitors such as lappet-faced vulture, black-backed jackal and spotted hyena. By contrast, the semi-submerged Lagoon Hide, set on an extension of Hlambanathi Dam, is fabulously positioned to capture aquatic birds such as pied kingfisher, striated heron and African jacana in action, and it also sometimes attracts mammals such as hippo, elephant and various antelope. There are also two year-round, bird-bath reflection hides designed to photograph shy smaller birds such as pink-throated twinspot, green-backed pytilia and black-collared barbet. The seasonal Bee-Eater Hide is positioned to photograph a mudbank-nesting white-throated bee-eater colony, while summer-only Forest

ZIMANGA AT A GLANCE

An array of nine well-designed hides makes this one of the continent's most reliably rewarding destinations for wildlife photography.

Big Five: ****
General wildlife: *****
Birding: *****
Scenery: **
Wilderness factor: **
Uncrowded: *****
Affordability: *
Self-drive: N

Hide and Tower Hide are good for forest and woodland birds. The highlight for most photographers, however, is a catered overnight vigil at Umgodi or Tamboti Hide. These well-equipped subterranean bunkers come complete with bunk beds, flush toilet and kitchenette, and have LED floodlights installed at water level to illuminate photographic subjects as they approach the water's edge. Buffalo, warthog, scrub hares and various antelope regularly com to drink at both hides, but on a lucky night you might be visited by anything from leopard or lion to serval or spotted hyena to elephant or rhino.

Zimanga offers great photography year-round, but the hides tend to be most rewarding for mammals during the dry winter months (April to November) and better for birds in summer (November to March). All the hides are positioned to capture wildlife at a useful photographic distance (typically in the 200–400mm range), and are angled to make the most of the natural light and to ensure backgrounds are uncluttered and neutral. It is worth carefully perusing the (detailcd) website before booking to evaluate the different packages on offer, and which hides are included in them, as well as to read up on the specialities and detailed lens specifications for each one.

ARRIVAL ZIMANGA PRIVATE GAME RESERVE

By car The entrance gate to Zimanga stands on the west side of the N2 about 6km north of uMkhuze village. Guests cannot drive to the lodge unaccompanied; they will be met by their guide and can then either park at the gate and be transferred to the lodge, or drive there in convoy.

ACCOMMODATION

Zimanga Main Lodge ☎ 074 165 4361, ⊛ zimanga. com. Opened in 2018, this state-of-the-art lodge might be aimed at photographers, but it doesn't skimp when it comes to comfort and quality. The six double and three single cottages have a spacious open-plan feel, uncluttered contemporary decoration, air-conditioning, private balcony and spacious bathroom with tub and shower. The main building has a lovely deck with a swimming pool overlooking the beautiful Mkhombe valley. Food is excellent and timing is flexible to maximize photographic opportunities. $$$$$

Manyoni Private Game Reserve

Daily • R150 • ☎ 035 595 8550, ⊛ manyoni.co.za

Comprising 230 square kilometres of former farmland bisected by the **Msunduzi River**, **Manyoni** is one of the largest private reserves in KwaZulu-Natal, home to all the Big Five as well as cheetah, brown and spotted hyena, and a small pack of African wild dogs. It was created in 2004 when seventeen neighbouring landowners agreed to drop fences to create a contiguous protected area as a release site for the **WWF Black Rhino Range Expansion Project**, which established a founder population of its endangered namesake in the reserve a year later. A succession of further reintroductions followed: a matriarchal elephant herd from the Kruger National Park and a couple of heftily-tusked bulls from Tembe, along with buffalo, white rhino, cheetah and various antelope; and finally, in 2011–12, a pride of female lions from Tembe and a male coalition from Phinda, completing Manyoni's transformation from farmland to Big Five reserve. Originally known as Zululand Rhino Reserve, it later rebranded itself as **Manyoni** (isiZulu for "Place of Birds"), partly to make it a less overt target for poachers, and partly to celebrate its avian wealth, with more than four hundred species recorded. Today it is home to around eight hundred buffalo (with hundred-strong herds frequently encountered), around thirty cheetah, twenty lion, and good numbers of elephant and black and white rhino. Leopards are

MANYONI AT A GLANCE

Good and relatively affordable Big Five viewing in the scenic Msunduzi valley.
Big Five: ★★★★
General wildlife: ★★★★★
Birding: ★★★★
Scenery: ★★★
Wilderness factor: ★★★★
Uncrowded: ★★★★★
Affordability: ★★★
Self-drive: N

3

present and are occasionally encountered on night drives, which also offer a chance of seeing other nocturnal species, from side-striped and black-backed jackal to white-tailed mongoose, large-spotted genet and caracal.

The dominant vegetation type on Manyoni is acacia savannah, and since most of the land was used to ranch cattle or for low-scale agriculture such as chilli and tomatoes prior to becoming a reserve, it is generally in good ecological shape, with knob thorn and sickle thorn tending to dominate areas under regeneration. No perennial river or other natural water source runs through the reserve, but it is studded with borehole-fed waterholes, and elephants also frequently use their tusks to dig for subterranean water in the wide sandy bed of the **Msunduzi**. This attractive river, which typically flows strongest over December and January, is a scenic highlight of Manyoni, while a fringing ribbon of evergreen sycamore figs, sausage trees and fever trees is a favoured haunt of nyala and other antelope, and also attracts a rich and varied birdlife including crowned hornbill, purple-created turaco, gorgeous bush-shrike, pink-throated twinspot and the heavyweight crowned eagle and Verreaux's eagle-owl. A particularly attractive track follows the riverbed below **Buthleweni Rock**, a burnished cliff face used as a nesting site by peregrine falcons. For a panoramic view over the Msunduzi as it meanders eastward through the reserve for about 20km, ask to head up to Number II Lookout for a coffee break or sundowner.

Although Manyoni is managed as one cohesive ecological unit, it differs from most private reserves in Zululand insofar as the original farms from which it was forged are still individually owned by one or more shareholders, though they retain traversing rights across the entire conservation area. Seven of these properties now operate as small commercial lodges (none larger than fifteen rooms), but the others are essentially used by the owners to host families and friends. Tourist development is concentrated in the south, which is also where you'll find the Msunduzi River and usually the largest volumes of wildlife, but while this area is far from crowded with safari vehicles, it can be worth heading further north to experience a greater sense of wilderness. Overall, Manyoni offers some of the best-value private Big Five game viewing in Zululand.

ARRIVAL AND TOURS

By car There are two entrance gates. Most lodges are most easily accessed from the main South Gate, which stands on the west side of the N2 about 302km north of Hluhluwe and 18km south of uMkhuze town. Alternatively, North Gate lies about 2km southwest of uMkhuze town along the P234 and D240. The main internal roads are in good condition and it is permitted to self-drive to your lodge from the entrance

MANYONI PRIVATE GAME RESERVE

gate, but other tracks are closed to private vehicles.

Tours *Ghost Mountain Inn* in uMkhuze (see page 166) offers 4-hour afternoon Manyoni game drives (R1300 per person) as well as 2-hour night drives (R690pp). Within the reserve, *Bayete Zulu Lodge* operates Elephant Interaction Tours with a trio of tame elephants (☎ 035 595 8089, ⓦ bayetezulu.co.za, R550/300 per adult/child).

ACCOMMODATION

Leopard Mountain Lodge ☎ 086 111 4789, ⓦ leopard mountain.co.za. The most luxurious lodge on Manyoni, family-run *Leopard Mountain* has a stunning hillside location and panoramic views, dominated by the arcing course of the Msunduzi. Accommodation is in stone and thatch chalets with air conditioning, open-air showers with a view, and a private deck with hammock and plunge pool. Rates include meals, selected drinks and activities. $$$$

Rhino River Lodge ☎ 083 781 4924, ⓦ rhinoriverlodge. co.za. Set on the banks of the Msunduzi close to the reserve's main gate, this well-priced lodge stands in a sycamore and fever-tree forest that attracts plenty of mammal and bird activity. Accommodation is in comfortable thatched chalets with slate floor, air-conditioning and private deck, and

amenities include a swimming pool. $$$

Zebra Hills Safari Lodge ☎ 082 892 0598, ⓦ zebrahills. com. Overlooking a small waterhole in the reserve's productive southern half, this stylishly low-key lodge – fully renovated in 2019 – is divided into two sections, each with its own kitchen, boma, deck and swimming pool. The seven-bedroom *Main Lodge* sleeps up to twelve adults and five children, while the three-bedroom *Homestead* has three attached family rooms and sleeps six adults and six children. Aimed mainly at small groups, it is strictly self-catering except by prior arrangement, so guests need to bring all food and drink with them, though chefs are provided. Game drives out of the lodge are excellent and the guides are particularly strong on birds. $$

Thanda Private Game Reserve

Daily • Entrance fee included in room rates • ☎ 032 586 0149,
ⓦ thandasafari.co.za

Sharing its northern boundary with
Manyoni, **Thanda** – IsiZulu for "Love"
– is an exclusive private reserve that
protects a 145-square-kilometre tract of
undulating savannah country, into which
all the Big Five have been successfully
introduced since it was established in
2000. The western part of the reserve
was formerly used for cattle ranching,
and retains a more-or-less pristine cover

THANDA AT A GLANCE
Classy and uncrowded Big Five private reserve.
Big Five: ****
General wildlife: ****
Birding: ***
Scenery: **
Wilderness factor: ***
Uncrowded: ****
Affordability: *
Self-drive: N

of thick acacia woodland, while the east is dominated by a former cotton plantation
whose regenerating grassland is liberally studded with emergent umbrella-, sickle-
and sweet-thorn acacias. As with Manyoni, Thanda lacks for any natural source of
perennial water but it is scattered with earth dams on retentive soil that usually hold
water all year, though it occasionally has to be pumped in during times of drought.
Despite its relatively small size and proximity to the N2, the reserve retains a genuine
wilderness feel, thanks partly to the low tourist volumes – there are only two smallish
lodges on the property, both part of the luxurious **Leading Hotels of the World**
collection, and seldom more than four or five vehicles out on game drives on any
given morning or afternoon.

Following an extensive program of **reintroductions**, Thanda offers excellent overall
game viewing. Two large lion prides respectively control the north and south of
the reserve, and there are also two matriarchal elephant herds and several large
solitary bulls. Cheetah and white rhino are quite easily seen, leopard and black
rhino rather less so, while the more common stock grazers include giraffe, Burchell's
zebra, warthog, nyala, greater kudu, blue wildebeest and impala. It is also possible
to arrange cheetah and white rhino tracking excursions, which entail tracking the
subjects by radio collars in a vehicle then approaching them on foot.

3

ARRIVAL AND DEPARTURE

THANDA PRIVATE GAME RESERVE

By car The entrance gate to Thanda stands on the north side
of the D242 about 6km northwest of a signposted junction
on the N2, about 20km north of Hluhluwe and 35km south

of uMkhuze town. Guests must leave their vehicles at the
car park just inside the gate; a guide will meet you here and
provide transport to your lodge.

ACCOMMODATION

Rates at both lodges in the reserve are inclusive of meals,
select drinks and standard activities such as game drives.
Cheetah tracking (no under-13s) and white rhino tracking
(no under-16s) are billable extras. Boat trips on the St
Lucia estuary and Zulu village visits are also offered as
extras. Bookings are at ☎ 032 586 0149, ⓦ thandasafari.
co.za.

Thanda Safari Lodge This flagship lodge consists of
nine individual chalets on a hillside, with fabulous views
to the surrounding bush. Decorated in a contemporary
ethnically inspired style, each suite incorporates a
spacious master bedroom and lounge with double-
sided fireplace and an equally sumptuous bathroom

with tub and indoor and outdoor shower. Nyala and
crested guineafowl wander through the well-wooded
gardens, while the common deck overlooks a waterhole
that frequently attracts larger game. Amenities include a
swimming pool, cigar bar, wine cellar and excellent spa.
$$$$$

Thanda Tented Camp The larger, more affordable
and more family-friendly of the two lodges on Thanda
comprises fifteen luxury safari tents with private decks,
indoor tubs and outdoor showers strung out on a hillside
above a small waterhole. The common areas are focused
around a large infinity pool surrounded by aloes that
attract a variety of colourful sunbirds when in bloom. $$$$

3

ITHALA AT A GLANCE

Remote and relaxed self-drive reserve in the scenic hills bordering the Pongola River.

Big Five: **
General wildlife: ****
Birding: ****
Scenery: ****
Wilderness factor: ****
Uncrowded: *****
Affordability: ****
Self-drive: Y

Ithala Game Reserve

Daily: Mar–Oct 6am–6pm; Nov–Feb 5am–7pm • R130 • ☏ 034 983 2540

Somewhat remote from – and different in feel – to the other Zululand reserves, **Ithala** protects some 296 square kilometres of hilly acacia savannah and grassland running south from the **Pongola River**, about 50km inland of Pongolapoort Dam and Maputaland. Possibly because of its isolation, Ithala is relatively little known, and feels refreshingly uncrowded, despite being one of the most spectacularly scenic places to watch wildlife anywhere in South Africa. The terrain is mountainous, with altitudes ranging from 400m along the river to 1400m in the far south, and is characterized by numerous cliffs and rock faces contained within a protective basin. Home to prolific game prior to being carved into farmland in the late nineteenth century, the reserve was bought by the provincial conservation authority in 1973; since then, more than twenty large mammals species that once existed here have been reintroduced, notably elephant, black and white rhino, giraffe, buffalo, warthog, Burchell's zebra, tsessebe, blue wildebeest, red hartebeest, impala and eland, to supplement preexisting species such as vervet monkey, common duiker, southern reedbuck, klipspringer, nyala and greater kudu. There are no lions, but leopard occur naturally and are occasionally seen on game drives, while cheetah and brown hyena have been reintroduced. Overall, though, if ticking off the Big Five is the main objective, Ithala probably isn't for you. Instead, forget the mammal checklist, and just take a slow drive around the mountains into the valleys and along the watercourses, seeing whatever you happen to see. For those with limited time, the most rewarding drive is **Ngubhu Loop**, with a detour to Ngubhu picnic site.

ARRIVAL, INFORMATION AND TOURS   ITHALA GAME RESERVE

By car There's no public transport to the park or near it, so driving is the only option. The entrance gate is just off the R69 near the village of Louwsburg, 70km east of Vryheid and 74km southwest of Pongola on the N2.

Information The camp's reception can provide information and maps, and fuel is available.

Tours There are some self-guided trails into the wooded mountainside above *Ntshondwe Camp*, which give the chance to stretch your legs if you've spent a morning driving around. Day and night drives (R270) and game walks with snacks and drinks (R270) can be organized; both offer a good chance of close-up rhino encounters.

ACCOMMODATION AND EATING

Ithala is a little out of the way, so ensure you pre-book accommodation, all through KZN Wildlife (☏ 033 845 1000, ⓦ kznwildlife.com); otherwise try camp reception in quiet times or for cancellations (☏ 035 591 0058). If you want to self-cater, you'll need to bring supplies – the camp shop specializes in beer and frozen meat but hasn't much by way of fresh food. Louwsburg has a very small general store that's a little better.

Doornkraal Campsite Map Ithala's basic but secluded campsite lies in the west of the reserve near *Mbizo Bush Camp* and is unfenced so animals wander through. It has flushing toilets and hot bush showers in reed huts, braai pits and a communal dining area, but only accommodates twenty people in total so reservations are advised. $̱

Mbizo Bush Camp For a pared-down bush experience, you can't beat this marvellous bush camp with space for just eight people, shaded by thorn trees and ilala palms, on the banks of the Mbizo River where you can swim. There's a braai and campfire area and hot showers. Minimum charge for five people. $̱$̱

Mhlangeni and Thalu Bush Camps A wonderful choice for something a bit wilder, these camps enjoy beautiful secluded settings and have four (minimum charge for three) or ten (minimum charge for seven) beds respectively. Both are staffed by an attendant and you can arrange a ranger to take you on walks. *Thalu* (three people) $̱$̱, *Mhlangeni* (seven people) $̱$̱$̱

★ **Ntshondwe Camp** This is one of the best gamereserve restcamps in South Africa, offering comfortable two-, four- and six-bed self-catering chalets with fully equipped kitchens, lounge areas and verandas, as well as two-bed, non-self-catering units. Each chalet is surrounded by indigenous bush through which paved walkways weave their way around granite rocks and trees to the main reception area and swimming pool. If you barbecue in the evening, you might well be joined by interesting nocturnal wildlife such as greater bushbaby and genet. The camp's restaurant (daily 7.30–9.30am &

6.30–9pm) serves a surprisingly varied range of food – though meat-free meals aren't always on the menu – and takeaways can be eaten in your chalet. There's also a cosy bar whose sun deck looks out over the watering hole and across the valleys. ⬧

Ntshondwe Lodge Next to the restcamp, yet completely secluded, this luxury lodge has three beautifully decorated rooms and a small plunge pool overlooking the reserve; there's a minimum charge for five people. A cook is on hand to prepare food you bring. ⬧⬧⬧

Southern Zululand

Dominated by the industrialized port town of Richards Bay and its equally charmless inland twin Empangeni, Zululand south of the St Lucia estuary and Hluhluwe-iMfolozi is more densely settled than its northern counterpart and isn't generally regarded to be big game territory. There's plenty of smaller wildlife about, though, most notably in the peri-urban **Dlinza Forest Reserve**, which borders the historic small town of Eshowe, and the lushly subtropical coastal habitats protected in the **Umlalazi Nature Reserve** outside resorty Mtunzini. Rather less low-key is **Thula Thula Private Game Reserve**, which has become something of a cult destination thanks to its association with founder Lawrence Anthony and as the setting for the events described in his bestselling book *The Elephant Whisperer.*

3

Thula Thula Private Game Reserve

14km and clearly signposted from the R34 between Empangeni and Melmoth • Entrance fee included in day-visit or overnight rates • ☏ 087 945 5352, ⬇ thulathula.com

Comprising 45 square kilometres of undulating thornbush, some 7km south of Hluhluwe-iMfolozi as the crow flies, **Thula Thula** (an isiZulu phrase meaning "Peace and Quiet") came into being in 1999 when self-styled "elephant whisperer" **Lawrence Anthony** negotiated with local Zulu chiefs for permission to introduce a herd of nine "rogue" elephants from Mpumalanga into a fenced boma on uninhabited community land. After a couple of attempted escapes, the herd settled down in their new home, a story recounted in detail in Anthony's bestselling book *The Elephant Whisperer.* Thula Thula claims to be the oldest private game reserve in KwaZulu-Natal, since much of the land consists of a former royal hunting ground that dates back to the time of **King Shaka**, and it was accorded official protection under local chiefs in 1911. The **Nseleni River**, which runs through the reserve, is also of some historic significance as the site of the first meeting between Shaka and his father Senzangakhona, an encounter that set in motion the events that led to the creation of the **Zulu Nation**. Following the death of Thula Thula's founder in 2012, his French wife Francoise Malby-Anthony took over the running of the reserve, which is now home to 29 elephants and is earmarked for further expansion into another 35 square kilometres of uninhabited community land.

Thula Thula has a slightly cultish feel, with the vast majority of visitors being diehard fans of *The Elephant Whisperer* and Francoise's almost-as-popular 2018

THULA THULA AT A GLANCE

A mixed bag of a reserve much beloved by devotees of *The Elephant Whisperer.*
Big Five: ***
General wildlife: ***
Birding: ****
Scenery: ****
Wilderness factor: *
Uncrowded: ****
Affordability: ****
Self-drive: N

sequel *An Elephant in My Kitchen*. And for those who have read the books, it is genuinely thrilling to meet, or put a face to, so many of the pachydermal and human characters who populate their pages. Inevitably, game drives tend to focus on locating the reserve's elephants, each of which is individually named, and discussing their histories and relationships. Other wildlife likely to be seen include buffalo, giraffe, Burchell's zebra, blue wildebeest, greater kudu, nyala and impala, much of which was not reintroduced but descends from stock that has lived in the area since the time of Shaka. As for the rest of the Big Five, rhinos are represented by a couple of hand-reared individuals that rather disconcertingly like to approach safari vehicles to be scratched by the passengers, while leopards are present but predictably elusive; lions are officially absent, though it is not unknown for lone males escaping territorial pressure in Hluhluwe-iMfolozi to find their way into the reserve. Spotted hyenas are abundant and often very vocal at night, and there are plans to reintroduce cheetah. The birdlife is also excellent, with more than 350 species recorded, and the guides are very clued up on their calls.

Most visitors to Thula Thula stay overnight, and many stay on for several days, using it as a base for guided day-trips further afield. Day-trips into the reserve are also offered, starting at R1050 per person for a game drive only (see ⓦ thulathula.com/day-visitors-2 for further details).

ACCOMMODATION

The reserve is serviced by a five-star safari lodge and a slightly more low-key tented camp, both of which offer substantial discounts for longer stays including optional guided day excursions to the likes of Hluhluwe-iMfolozi and iSimangaliso. There is also a simple budget camp aimed at voluntourists at the Wildlife Rehabilitation Centre. In all cases, bookings can be made directly through reserve management (ⓘ 087 945 5352, ⓦ thulathula.com).

Elephant Safari Lodge The most exclusive accommodation on Thula Thula is this riverside lodge comprising five luxury thatched chalets with twin or queensize bed, as well as the honeymoon suite. All units are warmly decorated in colonial style and come with walk-in nets, air-conditioning, private balcony and tub and shower. A communal wooden deck overlooks park-like grounds shaded by tall trees and inhabited by a variety of smaller mammals and birds. The excellent cuisine has a distinct French influence reflecting the nationality of the reserve's hands-on owner. $$$$

THULA THULA PRIVATE GAME RESERVE

Thula Thula Luxury Tented Camp This down-to-earth camp comprises just eight comfortable and spacious standing tents with walk-in nets, open-air showers at the back and stilted wooden bases with a private terrace at the front. Tents are generously spaced out in a stretch of riverine forest that hosts plenty of nyala and a conspicuous and vociferous birdlife including purple-crested turaco, crested barbet and black-headed oriole. Tasty South African-fusion cuisine is eaten communally in the boma or on the balcony. $$$$$

Wildlife Rehabilitation Centre Set on a hilltop offering wonderful views over the surrounding bush, this simple camp is aimed at volunteers who might spend anything from three days to several weeks helping out with activities such as removing snares, clearing invasive vegetation and liaising with local communities. Simple tents with camp beds and mattresses use a common ablution block and meals are eaten communally. $$

Dlinza Forest Reserve

Off Kangela St on the southwestern side of Eshowe • Daily: May–Aug 7am–5pm; Sept–Apr 6am–5pm • R30 • ⓘ 035 474 4029

Only 250 hectares in extent and surrounded on all sides by the small town of Eshowe, **Dlinza** is the most accessible of a succession of biodiverse evergreen mist-belt forests that line the escarpment inland of the northern KwaZulu-Natal coast. It is a must for birders thanks to a wealth of localized forest species ranging from the large raptorial black sparrowhawk and crowned eagle to the smaller and more colourful Narina trogon, eastern bronze-naped pigeon, spotted ground thrush, olive woodpecker and green twinspot. It is also one of the best places in South Africa to see the blue duiker, a diminutive forest antelope, while other wildlife includes bushbuck, bushpig, vervet monkey and eighty species of butterfly. A highlight of the forest is the wheelchair-friendly **Dlinza Forest Aerial Boardwalk**, which spans 125m and is raised 10m into the air, just beneath the forest canopy, giving visitors a chance to experience a section of the woodland normally restricted to birds. The boardwalk leads to a 20m-high stainless-steel observation tower that offers stunning panoramas across the treetops to the Indian Ocean shimmering in the distance. A **visitors' centre** at the foot of the boardwalk provides information about forest ecology. From here, the 1.3km iMpunzi Trail and the 1.8km uNkonka Trail go deeper into the forest through milkwood, giant ironwood, wild plum and other trees, which are labelled with a description of their uses in traditional medicine. **Eshowe** – whose onomatopoeic Zulu name alludes to the sound of the wind rustling the forest canopy – is also of some interest as the oldest European settlement in Zululand. Picturesque **Fort Nongqayi** (Mon–Fri 7.30am–4pm, Sat & Sun 9am–4pm • R35 • ☎035 474 2281), built on the forest outskirts in 1883, is now a fascinating historical complex that houses a quartet of worthwhile museums and galleries exploring the town's rich local history, traditional Zulu culture and crafts, and contemporary Zulu art.

> ## DLINZA AT A GLANCE
> Top forest wildlife and birding from a wheelchair-friendly aerial boardwalk.
> **Big Five:** N/A
> **General wildlife:** **
> **Birding:** ****
> **Scenery:** ****
> **Wilderness factor:** **
> **Uncrowded:** ***
> **Affordability:** ****
> **Self-drive:** Y

3

ARRIVAL AND TOURS
DLINZA FOREST RESERVE

By minibus taxi Regular minibus taxis run from Eshowe to Durban and Empangeni.

★ **Zululand Eco-Adventures** Based at the George Hotel ☎035 474 2298, ⌨eshowe.com/zululand-eco-adventures. Tour company that takes an active role in the local community and runs tours that give an authentic experience of local Zulu life. They can organize visits to rural Zulu communities, where you can attend a variety of Zulu ceremonies, and unhurried trips to villages, markets and shebeens without feeling as if you're in a theme park.

ACCOMMODATION

★ **Chase Guest House** About 1.5km along John Ross Highway from KFC on Main St ☎035 474 5491, ⌨thechase.co.za. This lovely, peaceful farm has two large en-suite rooms and endless views of the surrounding sugar-cane fields. In the grounds there are also two smart self-contained units sleeping two, with the option of B&B or self-catering. A pool, tennis court and very charming hosts add to the appeal. ⒮

The George Hotel 36 Main St ☎035 474 4919, ⌨thegeorge.co.za. Something of a focal point for the town, this busy hotel in a historic 1906 building is steeped in local history. It offers renovated en-suite rooms, many with their original wooden floors, and an on-site tour operator. A good restaurant and bar are attached, too. ⒮

EATING AND DRINKING

Adam's Outpost In Fort Nongqayi ☎035 474 1787. In a converted settler house, *Adam's Outpost* dishes up healthy salads, home-made bread and good curries, plus a very popular Sunday lunch buffet. Mon–Fri 8.30am–4pm, Sun 9am–3pm.

Umlalazi Nature Reserve

Bordering Mtunzini 50km south of Richards Bay • Daily 5am–10pm • R60 • ☎035 340 1836; ⌨kznwildlife.com

Set on a near-perfect beach, this vastly underrated suburban reserve protects a remarkable habitat diversity within its compact area of just ten square kilometres. The highlight of **Umlalazi**'s bird checklist of more than three hundred species is the country's only breeding population of the striking palmnut vulture, which inhabits

> ## UMLALAZI AT A GLANCE
> South Africa's most accessible coastal mangrove habitat.
> **Big Five:** N/A
> **General wildlife:** **
> **Birding:** *****
> **Scenery:** ****
> **Wilderness factor:** ***
> **Uncrowded:** ***
> **Affordability:** *****
> **Self-drive:** Y

a raffia palm swamp that can be explored on a boardwalk. A trio of walking trails twist along the banks of a lagoon, across dunes, and into a mangrove swamp where mudskippers and hermit crabs scuttle around the mud and the localized mangrove kingfisher reveals its presence with a trademark high trilling call.

ACCOMMODATION
UMLALAZI NATURE RESERVE

Umlalazi Camp ☏ 035 340 1836, ⓦ kznwildlife. com. Set on a beach within the reserve, this rustic camp comprises twelve four-bed log cabins with fully equipped kitchens aimed at self-caters. §

uKhahlamba-Drakensberg and surrounds

Hugging the border with Lesotho, the 2428-square-kilometre **uKhahlamba-Drakensberg Park** protects a vast montane wilderness area that incorporates several dozen peaks topping the 3000m mark, the highest being the 3482m **Thaba Ntlenyana**, which lies just across the border in Lesotho. The tallest African mountain range south of Kilimanjaro, the "Dragon Mountains" (or, in isiZulu, "Barrier of Spears") is in fact an immense escarpment of burnished sandstone cliffs, set below a stratum of harder igneous basalt, that separates the high plateau country of Lesotho from the midlands of KwaZulu-Natal. In geological terms, uKhahlamba-Drakensberg is a continuation of the same escarpment that divides the Mpumalanga highveld from the game-rich lowveld of the Kruger National Park and continues into the northern section of the Eastern Cape, but when people talk of the Berg, they invariably mean the range in KwaZulu-Natal. In 2000, the park was inscribed as a UNESCO World Heritage Site, one that was later extended to incorporate the Sehlabathebe National Park in Lesotho to form the **transfrontier Maloti-Drakensberg Park**.

Wild and totally unpopulated, uKhahlamba-Drakensberg easily ranks as South Africa's premier **hiking** destination. And when it comes to elating scenery – massive spires, rock buttresses, wide grasslands, glorious waterfalls, rivers, pools and fern-carpeted forests – this vast escarpment is pretty much unrivalled. It is also one of only five mixed cultural and natural World Heritage Sites listed for Africa, thanks to its status as one if the world's richest repositories of prehistoric **rock art**. Around six hundred recorded rock-art sites, featuring more than 22,000 individual paintings, are hidden all over the mountains. That said, its claims to be a wildlife-viewing destination are rather more modest: baboons and a limited variety of antelope are frequently encountered by hikers, and the park also supports a wealth of endemic and near-endemic birds and other "small stuff", but none of the Big Five is present within the park (surprisingly, not even leopard), and most other safari favourites are also absent.

Prior to its inscription as a World Heritage Site, uKhahlamba-Drakensberg was carved up into a confusing patchwork of a couple of dozen game parks, nature reserves and state forests. Today, EKZNW manages the park as one contiguous ecological unit, but in touristic terms, the old pre-millennial reserves still retain their individual characters, amenities and access points. The all but limitless hiking opportunities within this vast wilderness area fall outside the scope of this guidebook, but we do include coverage of **Giant's Castle Game Reserve** – the best part of the range for wildlife viewing, as well as hosting perhaps its most accessible major rock-art site – as well as the singularly scenic **Royal Natal Park**. Further afield, the small **Spioenkop Dam Nature Reserve** offers some decent game-viewing in the shadow of the mountains, while the private **Nambiti Game Reserve**, outside the small town of Ladysmith, is the closest fully fledged Big Five destination to the Berg.

The park is hemmed in by rural African areas – former "homeland" territory, unsignposted and unnamed on many maps, but interesting to drive through for a slice of traditional **Zulu life** complete with beehive-shaped huts. As for the weather, summers are warm but wet; expect both dramatic thunderstorms and misty days that block out the views. Winters tend to be dry, sunny and chilly, with freezing nights and, on the high peaks, occasional snow. The best times for hiking are spring and autumn. As the weather can change rapidly at any time of year, hikers should always take sufficient clothing and food. EKZNW offices sell books on uKhahlamba-Drakensberg walks, as well as 1:50,000 trail maps they produce themselves.

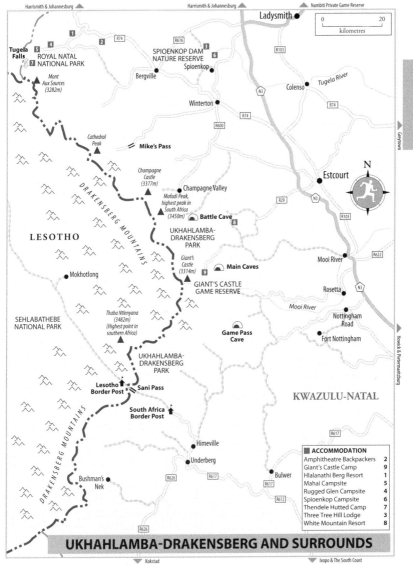

UKHAHLAMBA-DRAKENSBERG AND SURROUNDS

3

THE SAN AND THEIR ROCK PAINTINGS

Southern Africa's earliest inhabitants and the most direct descendants of the late Stone Age, the **San**, or Bushmen, lived in the caves and shelters of the uKhahlamba-Drakensberg for thousands of years before the arrival of the Nguni people and later the white farmers. Many liberal writers use the word "Bushmen" in a strictly non-pejorative sense to describe these early hunter-gatherers – though the word was originally deeply insulting. Several historians and anthropologists use "San", but as this refers to a language group and not a culture, it isn't strictly accurate. Since there is no agreed term, you'll find both words used in this book.

The San hunted and gathered on the subcontinent for a considerable period – paintings in Namibia date back 25,000 years. In the last two thousand years, the southward migration of Bantu-speaking farmers forced change upon the San, but there is evidence that the two groups lived side by side. However, tensions arose when the white settlers began to annex lands for hunting and farming. As the San started to take cattle from farmers, whites felt justified in hunting them in genocidal campaigns until they were wiped off the South African map.

San artists were also **shamans**, and their paintings of hunting, dancing and animals mostly depict religious beliefs rather than realistic narratives of everyday life. It's difficult to accurately **date** the paintings, but the oldest are likely to be at least eight hundred years old (although Bushmen lived in the area for thousands of years before that) and the most recent are believed to have been painted towards the end of the nineteenth century. The **medicine** or **trance dance** – journeying into the spiritual world to harness healing power – was the Bushmen's most important religious ritual and is depicted in much of their art. Look out for the postures the shamans adopted during the dance, including arms outstretched behind them, bending forward, kneeling, or pointing fingers. Dots along the spine depict the sensation of energy boiling upwards, while lines on faces or coming out of the nose usually refer to trance-induced nosebleeds. Other feelings experienced in trance, such as elongation, attenuation or the sensation of flight, are expressed by feathers or streamers. The depictions of horses, cattle and white settlers mark the end of the traditional way of life for the uKhahlamba-Drakensberg Bushmen, and it is possible that the settlers were painted by shamans to try to ward off their all-too-real bullets.

You'll also see the spiral-horned **eland** depicted in every cave – not because these antelope were prolific, but because they were considered to have spiritual power. Sometimes the elands are painted in layers to increase their spiritual potency. In the caves, you can see depictions of human-like figures transforming into their power animal. Besides antelope, other animals associated with trance are honeybees, felines, snakes, elephants and rhinos.

Paintings weather and fade, and many have been vandalized. People dabbing water on them to make them clearer, or touching them, has also caused them to disappear – so never be tempted. One of the best introductions to rock art is the slim **booklet** by David Lewis-Williams, Rock Paintings of the Natal Drakensberg, available from most decent bookshops in the area.

Giant's Castle Game Reserve

Daily: Apr–Sept 6am–10pm; Oct–Mar 5am–10pm • R80 • ☎ 036 353 3718, ⓦ kznwildlife.com

Extending over some three hundred square kilometres of grassland and heath, **Giant's Castle Game Reserve** was created in 1903 to protect the mountain's dwindling numbers of eland, which were numerous in the uKhahlamba-Drakensberg before the arrival of colonialists. The reserve is bordered to the west by three of the four highest peaks in South Africa: Mafadi (the highest at 3450m), Popple Peak (3325m) and **Giant's Castle** (3314m), the latter a bulky basalt-capped sandstone rampart whose isiZulu name Phosihawu ("Shield-Thrower") and Sesotho name Thaba Ikonjwa ("Mountain that Hates to be Pointed at") both refer to a legend that it brings stormy weather when piqued. It is not a traditional game park – there are no internal roads worth talking about, so the only way to see the wildlife here is by walking through the terrain. Eland are most likely to be encountered on the northern footslopes south of the restcamp (an area known locally as Mpofane, the "Place of Eland"), and the reserve is also home to other smaller montane antelope such as oribi, grey rhebok and mountain reedbuck. The checklist of 160 bird species includes several very localized highland dwellers, notably southern bald ibis, grey-winged francolin, ground woodpecker, yellow-breasted pipit, Drakensberg rockjumper, Gurney's sugarbird and Drakensberg siskin.

GIANT'S CASTLE AT A GLANCE

Magical hiking, superb rock art, and the best wildlife-viewing in the uKhahlamba-Drakensberg.

Big Five: N/A
General wildlife: ***
Birding: ****
Scenery: *****
Wilderness factor: *****
Uncrowded: *****
Affordability: *****
Self-drive: Y

The vulture hide

May–Sept • R900 for up to three people • Book as much as a year in advance through KZN Wildlife • ☎ 033 845 1000, ⓦ kznwildlife.com

One of the big attractions of Giant's Castle is a thrilling **vulture hide** where you may see the rare bearded vulture, or lammergeier, a giant, black and golden bird with massive wings and a diamond-shaped tail. A scavenger, the lammergeier is an evolutionary link between eagles and vultures and was thought extinct in Southern Africa until only a couple of decades ago. The bird is found only in mountainous areas such as the Himalayan foothills, and in South Africa only in the uKhahlamba-Drakensberg and Maloti mountains. In the locality you may also spot Cape vulture, black eagle, jackal buzzard and lanner falcon, attracted by the carcasses of animals put out by rangers during the winter.

Main Cave

Daily 9am–3pm • Guided walks from Giant's Castle Camp R50

Giant's Castle is home to one of the three major **rock-art sites** open to the public in the uKhahlamba-Drakensberg, in the form of **Main Cave**, which lies about a half-hour's easy walk up the Bushman's River Valley from the restcamp. Here, more than five hundred individual paintings depict naturalistic human figures, humanoids with animal heads, and a variety of animals ranging from the ubiquitous eland to big cats and a rare python. A rather quirky aspect of this cave, dating to the 1960s, is the replica family of life-size Bushmen intended to depict something of the artists' lifestyle.

ARRIVAL AND DEPARTURE   GIANT'S CASTLE

The most direct route to Giant's Castle from the N3 is the scenic R28, which runs west through the uKhahlamba-Drakensberg foothills, starting at the agricultural town of Mooi River, to terminate at the reserve's camp after about 65km. Coming from the north, the reserve can also be accessed from Estcourt via the R29. Public transport is limited.

ACCOMMODATION   SEE MAP PAGE 187

Giant's Castle Camp ☎ 033 845 1000, ⓦ kznwildlife. com. Situated in the heart of the reserve, *Giant's Castle Camp* offers comfortable self-contained chalets, some with wonderful picture windows looking out to the peaks. For food, there's the pleasant buffet-style restaurant *Izimbali* (daily 7.30am–9pm). You can buy frozen meat for braais and some tinned food at the reception, but stock up on other supplies beforehand. There are fabulous hiking trails from the camp, and the eight-person *Bannerman's Hut* is one of the Berg's best-located hiking huts. §–§§

White Mountain Resort Along the road to Giant's Castle hutted camp, 34km from Estcourt and 32km from the reserve ☎ 036 353 3437, ⓦ whitemountain. co.za. If the KZN Wildlife accommodation is full, try this hotel, the only one that gives access to the reserve, offering full board as well as self-catering cottages. It's located in the foothills and close to Zulu villages and farmlands, so while the area is pretty, it's neither grand nor remote. §

ROYAL NATAL AT A GLANCE

Royal Natal is home to both uKhahlamba-Drakensberg's most iconic scenic landmark and day hike.

Big Five: N/A
General wildlife: **
Birding: ***
Scenery: *****
Wilderness factor: *****
Uncrowded: ****
Affordability: *****
Self-drive: Y

Royal Natal National Park

Daily: Oct–Mar 5am–7pm; Apr–Sept 6am–6pm • R80 • ☎ 036 438 6310, Ⓦ kznwildlife.com

The most northerly protected area in uKhahlamba-Drakensberg, and the most dramatically beautiful, was established in 1916 when a quintet of farms and adjacent patches of Crown Land were set aside as the 33-square-kilometre **Natal National Park**. It earned its royal sobriquet after the British royal family (including the future Queen Elizabeth II) were hosted here by President Jan Smuts in May 1947, by which time it had been expanded to cover its present-day area of 84 square kilometres. The park's most striking geographical feature, appearing on more posters and postcards than any other single feature of uKhahlamba-Drakensberg, is the **Amphitheatre**, a 5km-long golden crescent of vertical sandstone bookended by a pair of massive rock protrusions, namely the 3165-metre Sentinel Peak and 3047-metre Eastern Buttress. The world's second-highest **waterfall** is formed by the nascent **Thukela** (or Tugela) **River** as it tumbles down the sheer escarpment of the Amphitheatre in five stages to register a total drop of 949m, just thirty metres less than Venezuela's Angel Falls. Rising behind the Amphitheatre, the 3282m **Mont Aux Sources** is the tallest point in the northern uKhahlamba-Drakensberg, and it forms the watershed from whence rise five rivers, including the Thukela and the Orange – hence its name, bestowed by French missionaries in 1878.

Royal Natal's most popular hike, and arguably the most picturesque day walk on offer anywhere in the uKhahlamba-Drakensberg, is the **Gorge Trail**, which connects *Thendele Camp* to the base of the Thukela Falls via a well-wooded boulder-strewn gorge carved by the Thukela River. The first 6.5km of the trail follows a good path and the gradients are easy, with little chance of getting lost as you walk parallel to the Thukela River. The last 1.6 kilometres, by contrast, entails three river crossings and an ascent up a chain ladder, but offers ample rewards, including superb views of the Amphitheatre with the Sentinel to your right. Allow six hours for the return walk, looking out for baboon, bushbuck, eland, grey rhebok, mountain reedbuck and a similar selection of montane birds to Giant's Castle along the way.

ARRIVAL AND DEPARTURE   ROYAL NATAL NATIONAL PARK

By car Routes to the park are surfaced all the way. Coming from the south along the N3, take the Winterton/Berg resorts turn-off onto the R74, and follow the signposts through Bergville to the park entrance, 46km away. Coming from the north, you need to depart from the N3 at Harrismith, then continue for 5km west along the N2 before turning south onto the R74, which skirts the

immense Sterkfontein Dam before descending towards the park via the spectacular Oliviershoek Pass.
By bus Using public transport, your best bet is the Baz Bus service between Durban and Joburg, which follows the R74 to stop at *Amphitheatre Backpackers*, the best place to organize budget hikes into the reserve.

ACCOMMODATION   SEE MAP PAGE 187

INSIDE THE PARK

EKZNW (Ⓦ kznwildlife.com) offers some very reasonable campsites within the park, as well as some exceptional chalets, all very well priced. Book both through their excellent online reservation system.

Mahai Campsite Along the river adjacent to the

national park ☎ 036 438 6310. With facilities for up to four hundred campers, Mahai attracts hordes of South Africans over school holidays and weekends. From here you can head straight into the mountains for some of the best walks in the Berg. Minimum charge for three. **§**

Rugged Glen Campsite Signposted 4km from Mahai

☎036 438 6310. A smaller and quieter campsite than *Mahai*, though often only open during school holidays. The views and walks here aren't as good, but horseriding is available, and the *Orion Mont-Aux-Sources Hotel* is an easy walk away – handy if you want a substantial meal. $

★ **Thendele Hutted Camp** At the end of the road into the Royal Natal National Park ☎036 438 6411. This is one of the most sought-after places to stay in the whole of South Africa, with splendid views of the Amphitheatre and excellent walks right from your front door. Accommodation is in comfortable two- and four-bed chalets, the cheapest of which have hotplates, fridges, kettles, toasters and utensils. If you opt for the more luxurious cottages or lodge, chefs are on hand to cook, though you need to bring the ingredients. There's also a good curio and supply shop. $–$$

OUTSIDE THE PARK

Amphitheatre Backpackers On the R74, 21km west of Bergville ☎082 855 9767, ⓦ amphibackpackers.co.za. A popular stop-off on the Baz Bus route between Joburg and Durban, this friendly backpacker hub is convenient for those who want to explore the Northern Drakensberg, but don't have their own transport. Accommodation is in en-suite dorms or safari tents with beds, though standard private rooms are also on offer, and camping is permitted. There's a bar and restaurant, and organized hiking trips, horseriding and mountain biking are available. $

Hlalanathi Berg Resort About 10km from the Royal Natal National Park ☎036 438 6308, ⓦ hlalanathi.co.za. A family resort with camping and self-catering thatched chalets sleeping two to six people. There's a swimming pool and trampolines, and a sit-down and takeaway restaurant serving cheap burgers, sandwiches and more substantial meals. $$

Spioenkop Dam Nature Reserve

On the R600 35km west of Ladysmith and 14km north of Winterton • Daily: Apr–Sept 6am–6pm; Oct–Mar 5am–7pm • R100 • ☎036 488 1578

Established in 1975 around an artificial lake created on the Thukela River by **Spioenkop Dam**, this scenic 60-square-kilometre nature reserve protects a tract of acacia savannah set below the burnished escarpment of the northern uKhahlamba-Drakensberg. It hosts several bushveld species that don't occur in the mountains, notably white rhinoceros, giraffe, Burchell's zebra, blue

SPIOENKOP DAM AT A GLANCE
Low-key game-viewing gem set below the uKhahlamba-Drakensberg escarpment.
Big Five: *
General wildlife: ***
Birding: ***
Scenery: ****
Wilderness factor: ***
Uncrowded: *****
Affordability: *****
Self-drive: Y

wildebeest, impala and greater kudu. And while rhinos are confined to a drive-through enclosure, the other large mammals range freely in an area that can be explored along a 3km or 6km walking trail, or on a horseback excursion, which often rewards riders with close-up views of wildlife that would be less tolerant of human pedestrians. The birding is pretty impressive too: a checklist of almost three hundred species including the likes of African fish eagle, brown snake eagle and colourful bushveld dwellers such as lilac-breasted roller, violet-backed starling and brown-hooded kingfisher.

ACCOMMODATION

SPIOENKOP, SEE MAP PAGE 187

Spioenkop Campsite Set within Spioenkop Nature Reserve ☎036 488 1578, ⓦ kznwildlife.com. This little-used lakeshore campsite, comprising thirty separate pitches with power points and slipways, is a wonderful and very affordable place for self-drivers to pitch a tent outside on weekends and school holidays, when it tends to attract hordes of local boaters as well as visitors from Gauteng. $

Three Tree Hill Lodge Adjoining the reserve, access road is off the R616 ☎036 448 1171, ⓦ threetreehill. co.za. The most stylish place to stay in the vicinity of Spioenkop and Royal Natal, this gorgeous hilltop owner-managed lodge comprises six suites, all decorated in colonial style with a private veranda overlooking a valley frequently traversed by rhino and giraffe, and there's a separate cottage for families. It offers guided game walks in the adjacent reserve, as well as battle-site tours, mountain biking, hiking and horseriding. $$$$

3

3

THE BATTLE OF SPIOENKOP

Spioenkop Dam and Nature Reserve are overlooked by and named for a prominent small mountain that rises from the lake's northern shore, whose Afrikaans name literally means "Lookout Hill". Easily distinguished from afar by the memorial cross on its summit, **Spioenkop** was the site of the bloodiest of all the **Anglo-Boer War** battles, one that took more British lives than any other and taught the British command that wars fought by means of set-piece battles were no longer viable. After this, the guerrilla-style tactics of modern warfare were increasingly adopted.

Some 1700 British troops took the hill under cover of a mist, without firing a shot, but were able to dig only shallow trenches because the surface was so hard. When the mist lifted, they discovered that they had misjudged the crest of the hill; but their real failure was one of flawed command and desperately poor intelligence. Had the British reconnoitered properly, they might have discovered that they were facing a motley collection of fewer than five hundred Boers with only seven pieces of artillery, and they could have called in their sixteen hundred reserves to relieve them. Despite holding lower ground, the Boers were able to keep the British, crammed eight men per metre into their trenches, pinned down for an entire sweltering midsummer day. Around six hundred British troops perished and were buried where they fell, on the so-called "acre of massacre".

Meanwhile, the Boers, who were aware of the British reinforcements at the base of the hill, had gradually been drifting off, and, by the end of the day, unbeknownst to the British, there were only 350 Boers left. In the evening the British withdrew, leaving the hill to the enemy. Bizarrely, three men present at the Battle of Spioenkop (one combatant and two non-combatants) were destined to become national leaders: the Boer general **Louis Botha**, a rising English journalist called **Winston Churchill**, and the Indian lawyer and part-time stretcher-bearer **Mahatma Gandhi**.

Back home, the impact on the popular consciousness of this unprecedented carnage in a remote African colony was such that three different football grounds in England contain stands whose names commemorate the dead and wounded. The best known of these is The Kop at Liverpool's Anfield Stadium, but there is also a Spioenkop Stand at Sheffield Wednesday's home ground of Hillsborough and another (recently dismantled) at Plymouth Argyle's Home Park.

Today you can stand at the summit of the rocky hill and look out over the desolate battlefield, where small plaques mark out the positions of the two sides. A mass grave marks the final resting place of hundreds of fallen British troops. **Spioenkop Battlefield** (daily 9am–4pm, R35) lies outside the nature reserve and is reached along a different road. From Bergville, follow the R616 towards Ladysmith northeast for about 24km, then turn right on to a signposted dirt feeder road that leads to the summit after about 6km.

Nambiti Private Game Reserve

Roughly 25km east of Ladysmith by road • R55 conservation fee • ☎ 036 631 9026 or ☎ 082 6520 583, ⓦ nambiti.com

An island of Big Five territory, surrounded by cattle and maize farms and community land, **Nambiti** was established in 2000 when a group of neighbouring farmers decided to convert their properties to a game reserve and went on to restock it with lion, cheetah, elephant, white rhino, black rhino, disease-free buffalo, giraffe, Burchell's zebra and a wide variety of antelope including eland, greater kudu, nyala, black and blue wildebeest, impala and blesbok. Ten years later, the reserve was bought by the government in the aftermath of a successful land claim, and handed over to neighbouring communities, which now lease out nine sites within the reserve to private-lodge owners on a renewable 35-year basis. They are in turn provided with a rich source of revenue and job opportunities – at least ninety percent of the 45-odd people employed by the reserve and its lodges hail from local communities.

Extending across roughly 100 square kilometres to the northeast of Ladysmith, Nambiti is a scenic reserve whose rounded hills and dolomitic cliffs are incised by some impressive ravines associated with the perennial **Sundays River** and its various seasonal tributaries. Ecologically, this undulating terrain supports a cover of tangled thick acacia interspersed with areas of open grassland and tracts of riparian woodland along the watercourses. Aside from the Sundays, which flows through the north of the reserve, natural sources of permanent water are scarce, so in order to prevent overgrazing around the river in times of drought, the management has installed a 15km pipeline that can be switched on in the dry season to supplement a total of fourteen dams otherwise fed by rainwater.

> **NAMBITI AT A GLANCE**
> The only Big Five reserve in the ukhahlamba-Drakensberg hinterland.
> **Big Five:** ***
> **General wildlife:** ****
> **Birding:** ***
> **Scenery:** ***
> **Wilderness factor:** *
> **Uncrowded:** ***
> **Affordability:** **
> **Self-drive:** N

Although it is not part of the ukhahlamba-Drakensberg, Nambiti offers the best general game viewing in the vicinity of the mountains, and it has more of a highveld setting than any other Big Five reserve in KwaZulu-Natal. Visitors are likely to encounter at least three of the Big Five over the course of a two- to three-night visit, as well as cheetah, giraffe and half a dozen antelope species, but leopard sightings are hit and miss, despite the presence of at least six individuals. Among the smaller wildlife, it is one of the few places in South Africa where the gorgeous serval is regularly seen and tends to be unusually habituated to vehicles. Highlights of the varied birdlife include the southern bald ibis, a large striking endemic that sometimes nests on a cliff near a waterfall within the reserve, and pretty ground dwellers such as orange-throated longclaw, African hoopoe and bokmakierie. A good variety of waterbirds is likely to be seen at the dams, but raptors are very scarce, presumably due to poisoning by local farmers and a lack of other suitable habitats in the vicinity.

Nambiti is an ideal first-time safari destination for those who want to see a wide variety of game in a short period of time, and a stay here slots easily into any itinerary that involves driving along the N3 between Gauteng and Durban or exploring the ukhahlamba-Drakensberg proper. Relatively reasonable lodge prices mean it is also a popular weekend break from Durban, Pietermaritzburg and to a lesser extent Gauteng. Overall, the relatively high number of guest beds – more than 250 spread across nine lodges – makes for a less exclusive wilderness experience than is the case in most Zululand reserves, but the guides do a good job of varying and coordinating their routes to ensure you don't find yourself tripping over other game-viewing vehicles.

ARRIVAL AND DEPARTURE   **NAMBITI PRIVATE GAME RESERVE**

By car The main urban gateway to Nambiti is Ladysmith, a substantial town situated along the N11 about 20km east of the N3 and some 55km east of Bergville, 245km northwest of Durban, and 350km southeast of Johannesburg. From Ladysmith, follow the N11 northeast in the direction of Dundee for about 10km, then turn right onto the unsurfaced D45 and follow it for another 10km to a T-junction where you need to turn right for Woodlands Gate or left for Memorial Gate, depending on which lodge you are booked into.

ACCOMMODATION

The Springbok Lodge About 2km inside Woodlands Gate, ☎ 036 637 9604 or ☎ 036 637 9612, ⊛ the springboklodge.co.za. Named not after the antelope (which doesn't occur this far east) but after the cartel of Springbok rugby players that founded it prior to its sale to another investor, this good-value family-friendly camp comprises 21 large standing tents, all with private balconies and heating to offset the chilly winter nights. A self-guided 1.2km walk through the camp offers much to birders and rates include all activities and buffet meals. $$$

Umzolozolo Private Lodge Inside Woodlands Gate, ☎ 031 579 3870, ⊛ umzolozolo.com. Among the most sumptuous properties on Nambiti, *Umzolozolo* (the isiZulu name for the African hoopoe, a bird commonly seen in the vicinity) comprises nine luxury suites, all with air-conditioning, satellite TV, private deck and jacuzzi and/or plunge pool. $$$$

The Western Cape

NATURE'S VALLEY SEEN FROM THE OTTER TRAIL

The Western Cape

The most mountainous and arguably the most beautiful of South Africa's provinces, the Western Cape also attracts more foreign tourists than any other, thanks to the beguiling presence of Cape Town, with its extraordinary seaside setting at the base of Table Mountain, and the Bacchanal delights of the nearby winelands. Ecologically, Africa's most southerly province is practically synonymous with the Cape Floristic Region, which is the smallest of the world's six floral kingdoms, dominated by a low scrubby cover of fynbos, whose exceptional level of botanical diversity and endemism includes roughly six thousand plant species found nowhere else in the world. The province is also home to a large number of endemic fynbos-associated birds and large mammals, and a rich marine fauna that includes whales, dolphins, great white sharks, seals and penguins.

Paradoxically, while Cape Town stands as possibly the busiest tourist hub in Africa, and its environs form an important centre of global biodiversity, the **WESTERN CAPE** offers little in the way of mainstream game-viewing options. True, its twenty-plus provincial reserves and half-dozen national parks incorporate some of the most **scenic** locations anywhere in the country, but none could be considered conventional safari destinations. And while a scattering of private sanctuaries now offers visitors a quick-fix Big Five experience, these tend to be rather small and to lack the wilderness feel of more expansive counterparts elsewhere in the country.

Fortunately, what the Western Cape lacks in terms of conventional safari destinations, it compensates for with some superb opportunities for more specialized wildlife watching. The **marine fauna**, for instance, is scintillating. Within easy day-tripping distance of Cape Town, you can swim with penguins at **Boulders Bay**, boat out to **Duiker Island** and its breeding colony of Cape fur seals, and enjoy what is arguably the world's best land-based **whale-watching** from the cliffs around **Hermanus**. Various antelope and other ungulates might be encountered in the Cape of Good Hope sector of **Table Mountain National Park**, as well as in the more far-flung **Karoo National Park**, **Bontebok National Park** and **De Hoop Nature Reserve**. The province is also an important centre of endemism for fynbos-associated birds, most notably the spectacular protea-loving Cape sugarbird, and a variety of reptiles and frogs unique to this habitat. And for those not heading further afield to more recognized safari regions such as the Kruger, KwaZulu-Natal or the Eastern Cape, private reserves such as **Sanbona** and **Gondwana** form a more than adequate substitute when it comes to Big Five game-viewing.

Table Mountain National Park

Tokai Manor House, Tokai Road (park admin) ☎ 021 712 0527, 🌐 sanparks.org/parks/table_mountain

Gazetted in 1998, the 220-square-kilometre **Table Mountain National Park** (TMNP) incorporates more than seventy percent of the **Cape Peninsula**, the mountainous sliver of land that extends some 60km south from Cape Town to the wave-battered cliffs of Cape Point. Inscribed as part of UNESCO's Cape Floral Region World Heritage Site in 2004, the park itself is a rather disjointed entity, interspersed as it by the numerous residential zones that make up South Africa's largest coastal city. Nevertheless, the peninsula it protects is immensely scenic, being less than 10km wide for most of its length, but rising to more than 1000m along the mountainous spine that divides its

ANTELOPE, BONTEBOK NATIONAL PARK

Highlights

❶ Table Mountain National Park
Incorporating some seventy percent of the
Cape Peninsula, this national park also protects
an African penguin colony at Boulders Beach
and typical fynbos wildlife in the dramatic Cape
of Good Hope. See page 196

❷ West Coast National Park Renowned for
the wading birds that forage on the Langebaan
Lagoon, West Coast National Park is a great
place to see gemsbok, springbok and other
wildlife set among spring-flower displays similar
to those in Namaqualand. See page 207

❸ Sanbona Wildlife Reserve The pick of a
cluster of private reserves set in the semi-arid

Karoo is home to all the Big Five and a quartet of
world-class safari lodges. See page 211

❹ De Hoop Nature Reserve Massive dunes,
spectacular whale-watching and rich fynbos-
associated wildlife make this the country's most
exciting coastal nature reserve. See page 217

❺ Bontebok National Park The star attraction
at this reserve is the bontebok, a handsome
antelope that is endemic to the Western Cape.
See page 219

❻ Gondwana Game Reserve The Garden
Route is best known for its gorgeous beaches
and forests, but is now also home to the Big Five
thanks to this private reserve. See page 222

HIGHLIGHTS ARE MARKED ON THE MAP ON PAGE 198

western and eastern seafronts. TMNP's crowning glory is **Table Mountain**, a flat-topped landmark formerly known to the local Khoikhoi as Hoerikwaggo ("Mountain in the Sea") and now often cited as one of the seven natural wonders of the world. The peninsula also incorporates some exceptionally lovely beaches, with those to the west being pummelled by the wild, chilly open Atlantic, while their eastern counterparts face out to the more sheltered and warmer waters of False Bay.

Table Mountain itself is best visited in isolation as a half-day or full-day trip out of central Cape Town, and since it is highly weather dependent, we would recommend taking the earliest suitable opportunity to do so. For wildlife enthusiasts, there are three

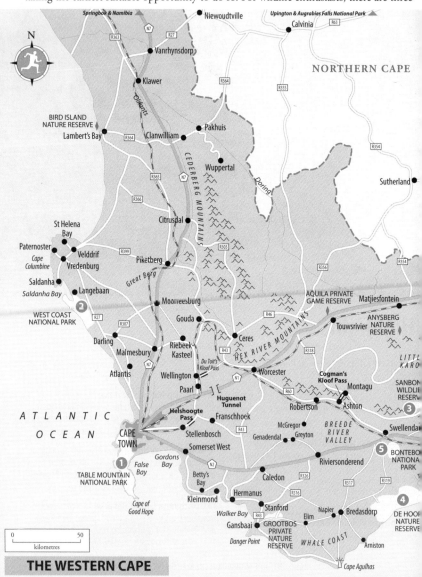

THE WESTERN CAPE

other standout sites protected within TMNP and the associated Marine Protected Area. These are penguin-crammed **Boulders Beach**, the wildlife-rich **Cape of Good Hope**, and offshore **Duiker Island** with its colony of several thousand Cape fur seals. This trio of highlights can all easily be visited over the course of a one-day self-driving or guided tour looping around the Cape Peninsula. For those who don't fancy driving, recommended operators include Cape Convoy (☎076 146 8577, ⓦcapeconvoy.com), Day Trippers (☎021 511 4766, ⓦdaytrippers.co.za) and Discovery Tours (☎021 461 9652 or ☎078 161 7818, ⓦdiscoverytours.co.za).

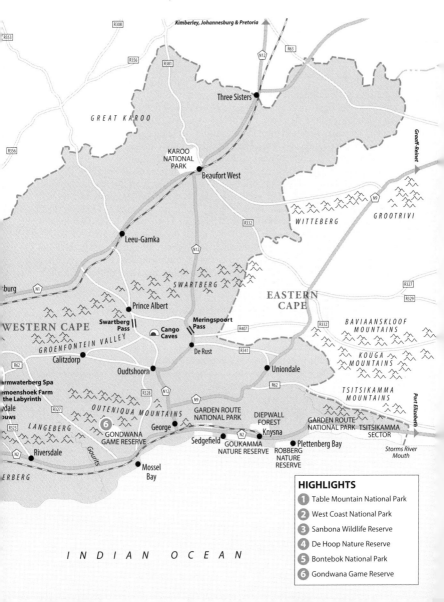

HIGHLIGHTS

1 Table Mountain National Park
2 West Coast National Park
3 Sanbona Wildlife Reserve
4 De Hoop Nature Reserve
5 Bontebok National Park
6 Gondwana Game Reserve

TABLE MOUNTAIN NATIONAL PARK AT A GLANCE

Scenic icons such as Cape Point and Table Mountain are complemented by plenty of marine and endemic wildlife.

Big Five: N/A
General wildlife: ***
Birding: ****
Scenery: *****
Wilderness factor: ***
Uncrowded: **
Affordability: ****
Self-drive: Y

Table Mountain

Table Mountain, a 1086m flat-topped massif with dramatic cliffs and eroded gorges, dominates the northern end of the Cape Peninsula. The mountain's north face overlooks central Cape Town, while the distinct formations of **Lion's Head** and **Signal Hill** lie to the west, and **Devil's Peak** rises to the east. Despite its peri-urban location, much of the mountain is a genuine wilderness area, and it boasts a floral tally of 1400 species. Wildlife is thinner on the ground, but the mountain does support a sizeable population of baboons, and visitors are almost certain to see small family groups of rock hyrax – guinea-pig lookalikes more closely related to elephants than the outsized rodents they superficially resemble. The most conspicuous bird on the plateau is the red-winged starling, but the majestic Verreaux's eagle is sometimes seen soaring about the cliffs in search of a hyrax-shaped snack, and flowering proteas and aloes often attract colourful nectar-feeders such as Cape sugarbird, lesser double-collared sunbird and malachite sunbird.

The upper plateau of Table Mountain can be reached from central Cape Town by cable car or on foot. Most visitors choose the former option in both directions, but moderately fit travellers could think about walking up via **Platteklip Gorge**, ideally with an early start to avoid the midday heat, and then catching a cable car back down. Once on the plateau, the views across the city bowl to Table Bay and the Hottentots Holland Mountains are stunning, and you can grab a meal or drink at the Table Mountain Cafe. Maclear's Beacon, which marks the 1086m summit, stands about 30 minutes' walk east from the top of the Platteklip Gorge Trail, or 40 minutes from the upper cableway station, on a clearly marked path with white squares on little yellow footsteps guiding you all the way.

Table Mountain Aerial Cableway

Lower Cableway Station, Tafelberg Rd • Daily every 10–15min: Jan–April 8am–8.30pm, Feb till 8pm, Mar till 7.30pm; May–Nov 8.30am–6pm, Sept & Oct till 7pm, Nov till 8.30pm • One-way R190, return R330; children 4–17 one-way R90, return R165; return tickets half price after 6pm Nov to mid-Dec & Jan–Feb • Last car up departs 1hr before last car down; operations can be disrupted by bad weather or maintenance work; for information contact ☏ 021 424 0015 (general queries) or ☏ 021 424 8181 (weather-related information), or check ⊕ tablemountain.net • From the Waterfront and the Civic Centre respectively, the City Sightseeing Red City Tour route and MyCiTi buses #106 & #107 serve the cableway; alternatively take an Uber or normal metered taxi to the Lower Cableway Station, where taxis wait to take you home at the end. Drivers can park along Tafelberg Rd

The least challenging, but certainly not least interesting, way up and down the mountain is via the highly popular **cable car** at the western table, which offers dizzying views across town to Table Bay and the Atlantic. The state-of-the-art Swiss system completes a 360-degree rotation during the five-minute journey, giving passengers a full panorama. At the top, if you don't want to walk far, you can wander the concrete paths stopping at the viewpoints, then grab a meal or beer in the **cafeteria** (open from 8am until 30min before the last car down). The upper-station area is of course one of the city's best spots to watch the sun go down. People start queuing early and finish late in summer, and weekends and public holidays tend to be very busy; shorten your queuing time by buying your ticket online.

Platteklip Gorge

Climbing Table Mountain will give you a greater sense of achievement than being ferried up by the cable car, but proceed with extreme caution: it may look sunny and clear when you leave, but conditions at the top could be very different. The most

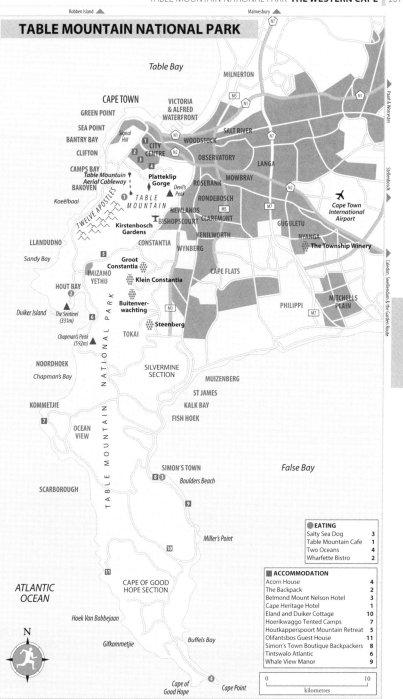

TABLE MOUNTAIN NATIONAL PARK

Robben Island

Malmesbury

Table Bay

MILNERTON

CAPE TOWN

VICTORIA & ALFRED WATERFRONT

GREEN POINT

SEA POINT

Signal Hill

SALT RIVER

BANTRY BAY

WOODSTOCK

CLIFTON

CITY CENTRE

OBSERVATORY

LANGA

CAMPS BAY

Table Mountain Aerial Cableway

MOWBRAY

BAKOVEN

Platteklip Gorge

Devil's Peak

ROSEBANK

Koeëlbaai

TABLE MOUNTAIN

RONDEBOSCH

Cape Town International Airport

TWELVE APOSTLES

NEWLANDS

BISHOPSCOURT

CLAREMONT

GUGULETU

Kirstenbosch Gardens

NYANGA

The Township Winery

LLANDUDNO

CONSTANTIA

KENILWORTH

WYNBERG

Sandy Bay

Groot Constantia

CAPE FLATS

IMIZAMO YETHU

Klein Constantia

HOUT BAY

Buitenver-wachting

Duiker Island

The Sentinel (331m)

PHILIPPI

MITCHELLS PLAIN

Steenberg

Chapman's Peak (592m)

TOKAI

NOORDHOEK

SILVERMINE SECTION

Chapman's Bay

MUIZENBERG

KOMMETJIE

ST JAMES

KALK BAY

FISH HOEK

OCEAN VIEW

TABLE MOUNTAIN NATIONAL PARK

SCARBOROUGH

SIMON'S TOWN

Boulders Beach

False Bay

Miller's Point

ATLANTIC OCEAN

CAPE OF GOOD HOPE SECTION

Hoek Van Bobbejaan

Gifkommetjie

Buffels Bay

N

Cape of Good Hope

Cape Point

● EATING	
Salty Sea Dog	3
Table Mountain Cafe	1
Two Oceans	4
Wharfette Bistro	2

■ ACCOMMODATION	
Acorn House	4
The Backpack	2
Belmond Mount Nelson Hotel	3
Cape Heritage Hotel	1
Eland and Duiker Cottage	10
Hoerikwaggo Tented Camps	7
Houtkapperspoort Mountain Retreat	5
Olifantsbos Guest House	11
Simon's Town Boutique Backpackers	8
Tintswalo Atlantic	6
Whale View Manor	9

Paarl & Worcester

Stellenbosch

Caledon, Swellendam & the Garden Route

4

0 — 10
kilometres

convenient and accessible route is the same one followed by the Portuguese captain Antonio de Saldanha in 1503 when he made the first recorded ascent to the summit. It runs through **Platteklip Gorge**, the conspicuous gap in the escarpment visible from the **front table** (the north side). The Platteklip route starts at the Lower Cableway Station and ends about ten minutes east of the upper station, so you can descend in a cable car. Consider hiring a guide, both for mountain safety and because there have been occasional random muggings of tourists.

From the lower station, walk east along Tafelberg Road until you see a sign pointing to Platteklip Gorge. A steep fifteen-minute climb brings you onto the **Upper Contour Path**. About 25m east along this, take the path indicated by a sign reading "Contour Path/Platteklip Gorge". The path zigzags from here onwards and is very clear. The gorge is the biggest chasm on the whole mountain, leading directly and safely to the top, but it's a very steep slog that will take around three hours total – provided you're reasonably fit. Once on top, turn right and ascend the last short section onto the front table for a breathtaking view of the city. A sign points to the Upper Cableway Station – a ten-minute walk along a concrete path thronging with visitors.

Boulders Beach

40km south of central Cape Town; 3km southeast of Simon's Town Station • Daily: Jan & Dec 7am–7pm; Feb, Mar, Oct & Nov 8am–6.30pm; Apr–Sept 8am–5pm • R152, child R76 • ☎ 021 786 2329 • Regular trains connect Adderley Street Station in central Cape Town to Simon's Town Station; from here it's a 30–45-minute walk to Boulders, or you can use the inexpensive taxi service run by HGTS Tours (☎ 021 703 7802, ⊕ hgtravel.co.za)

The smallest sector of TMNP is **Boulders Beach**, which lies on the False Bay coast close to the charming old naval centre of **Simon's Town**. Boulders takes its name from a set of huge granite rocks that create a cluster of little coves with sandy beaches and clear sea pools that are wonderful for swimming. The main reason people come to Boulders, however, is to visit a fenced seafront reserve that hosts a breeding colony of **African penguins** (formerly known as jackass penguins due to their distinctive bray), which first established itself here in 1983 and now comprises more than one thousand pairs. African penguins usually live on islands off the Southern African coast, including Robben Island, and the Boulders birds form one of only two mainland colonies. The reserve offers a rare opportunity to get a close look, and to hear that bray at its loudest, during the breeding season from March to May.

Access to the Boulders reserve is through two gates, one at the Boulders Beach (eastern) end, at the bottom of Bellevue Road, and the other at the **Seaforth Beach** (western) side, off Seaforth Road. Both entrances are signposted along Main Road between Simon's Town and Cape Point. At the Seaforth end, there's a small visitors' centre and deck, from which two boardwalks lead to either end of Foxy Beach where you'll see hundreds of penguins. Most people walk from Seaforth to Boulders, looking at all the penguins in the bushes along the paths, where there are masses of burrows for nesting. At Seaforth itself, there is safe swimming on the beach, which is bounded on one side by the looming grey mass of the naval base. There's also plenty of lawn shaded by palm trees, and a **restaurant** with outdoor seating and fresh fish on the menu.

Cape of Good Hope

The entrance gate lies 50km south of central Cape Town; it's another 14km from here to Cape Point • Daily: Apr–Sept 7am–5pm; Oct–Mar 6am–6pm • R303, child R152 • ☎ 021 780 9010 • No public transport but numerous tour companies offer it as part of a package of peninsula highlights that also usually includes Boulders Beach and possibly Duiker Island. Fun hiking and cycling tours are offered by Day Trippers (☎ 021 511 4766, ⊕ daytrippers.co.za; R1100 per person including entrance and picnic lunch)

Cape Point, the most remote extremity of the Cape Peninsula, is not, as many assume, the southernmost tip of Africa – that distinction belongs to Cape Agulhas, some

FURRY FELONS

Baboons may look amusing, but be warned: they can be a menace. Keep your car windows closed, as it's not uncommon for them to invade vehicles, and they're adept at swiping picnics. You should lock your car doors even if you only plan to get out for a few minutes, as baboons have opened unlocked doors while the vehicle owner's back is turned. Avoid unwrapping food or eating or drinking anything if baboons are in the vicinity. Feeding them is illegal and provocative and can incur a fine. Authorized baboon chasers are in evidence in several places, warding off the animals.

300km further southeast (see page 215) – but it is nevertheless a hugely dramatic spot, with a thrilling end-of-the-continent feel about it. It is protected in the former **Cape of Good Hope Nature Reserve**, which now forms the largest and most scenic component of part of TMNP, set atop massive sea cliffs with huge views, strong seas, and an even wilder wind that whips off caps and sunglasses as visitors gaze southwards from the old **lighthouse** buttress.

Most visitors make a beeline from the car-park to Cape Point, a windswept, swell-battered rocky promontory whose treachery has struck fear in the hearts of navigators since the Portuguese first "rounded the Cape" in the fifteenth century. A lighthouse was built here in 1860, but it was often shrouded in cloud and failed to keep ships off the rocks, so another was built lower down in 1914. A short but steep walk up a series of stairs leads to the original **lighthouse**, now a justifiably famous viewpoint, or you can save your breath by taking the **Flying Dutchman Funicular** (R65/80 one-way/return), which runs to the top (and back down again) every three minutes. You can walk to the quieter new lighthouse from the base of the first, near the lower funicular station. Try to get there as early in the morning as you can – the chances of crowding and of the wind gusting up increase as the day progresses.

A less well-known aspect of the Cape of Good Hope is that it forms an important stronghold for a wealth of endemic and rare **wildlife**. Large mammals likely to be seen along the network of roads that runs through the sector include Cape mountain zebra, eland, bontebok and red hartebeest, as well as the smaller grey rhebok and grysbok. Baboon troops lope along the rocky shoreline, while the cliffs are favoured by rock hyraxes. The angulate tortoise, bright blue-and-orange southern rock agama and black girdled lizard are the most conspicuous reptiles. For birders, the checklist of 279 species includes a conspicuous population of ostriches, as well as fynbos-dwellers such as orange-breasted sunbird, Cape siskin and Cape sugarbird. The cliffs at Cape Point are rated highly as a vantage point for pelagic wanderers, with eight albatross, six shearwater and twelve petrel species having been recorded to date. A more certain attraction on the rocky shores is the black oystercatcher jabbing limpets off the rocks with its bright red beak. You'll also see large flocks of Cape cormorants drying their outstretched wings on rocks, and white-fronted plovers, sanderlings and other waders running up and down the water's edge, probing for food between piles of shiny brown Ecklonia kelp.

Buffelsfontein Visitors' Centre (daily 9.30am–5.30pm), on the main road to Cape Point 8km past the entrance gate, has displays on the local fauna and flora as well as video screenings about the area's ecology. A popular spot for a seafood lunch is the *Two Oceans Restaurant* at Cape Point. For a picnic or braai, head to one of the beaches signposted along various side roads branching out from the main Cape Point road. The sea here is too dangerous for swimming, but there are safe tidal pools at the adjacent **Buffels Bay** and **Bordjiesrif**, midway along the east shore. Both have braai stands, but more southerly Buffels Bay is nicer, with plentiful grassy banks and some sheltered spots – but don't produce any food if there are baboons in the vicinity (see above).

4

Duiker Island

15 mins by boat from Hout Bay, 10km south of central Cape Town

A highlight of the 975-square kilometre Marine Protected Area associated with TMNP, **Duiker Island** is a tiny, wave-battered, rocky outcrop, a few hundred metres offshore from the peninsula's west coast, close to the small town of **Hout Bay**. Duiker is an Afrikaans word meaning diver, and in this instance, refers not to the small forest antelope of that name, but to the island's colony of 5000-plus **Cape fur seals**, most of which are subadult males. Numbers tend to be most impressive over the moulting season of January to March, when the seals spend less time in the water hunting. The island also supports plenty of cormorants and gulls. The island itself is off-limits to human visitors, but regular boat trips from Hout Bay harbour approach close enough to get a good view of the seals sunning themselves and flopping around on the rocks, and swimming and diving in the surrounding ocean. Of the operators running tours (45min; R100) Nauticat Charters (☎021 790 7278, ⓦnauticatcharters.co.za) is one of the best, offering five daily departures, from 8.45am to 2.45pm, in glass-bottomed boats that allow you to see the seals and kelp underwater. Departures are dependent on the weather and on a minimum group size of twenty people, so phone ahead to check the day's schedule.

ACCOMMODATION TABLE MOUNTAIN NATIONAL PARK, SEE MAP PAGE 201

Accommodation within Table Mountain National Park is limited to the few low-key options listed below. By contrast, there is no shortage of places to stay in Cape Town or on the Cape Peninsula, and all budgets and tastes are well catered for, though booking ahead is recommended, especially over the Christmas (mid-Dec to mid-Jan) and Easter holidays. A few places are listed below, and Cape Town Tourism's accommodation booking service (ⓦcapetown.travel) is a good starting point for those who want to explore other options.

WITHIN THE PARK

Eland and Duiker Cottage Cape of Good Hope ☎021 712 7471, ⓦsanparks.org/parks/table_mountain. Situated inland on a road that sees quite a bit of traffic by day, this pair of three-bedroom self-catering cottages are both fully electrified, with a kitchen and patio. A great budget base from which to explore the coastal fynbos and enjoy the wildlife. $$
Hoerikwaggo Tented Camps ☎021 712 7471, ⓦsanparks.org/parks/table_mountain. This quartet of rustic and attractively located budget-friendly tented camps was originally created to service the multi-day Hoerikwaggo Hiking Trail, but they are all now open to non-hikers and readily accessible by car. Each camp comprises five or six comfortable standing tents with wooden floors, well-equipped communal kitchens and common ablution facilities. The most comfortable of the camps is *Smitswinkel*, which has a convenient location near the entrance to the Cape of Good Hope sector and is the only one with en-suite tents. The most beautiful is arguably *Slangkop*, which stands in a forest of indigenous milkwood trees less than 100m from the sea, near the quaint West Coast village of Kommetjie. The other two camps are at *Orangekloof* and *Silvermine*. $

★ **Olifantsbos Guest House** Cape of Good Hope, 13km inside the entrance gate ☎021 712 7471, ⓦsanparks.org/parks/table_mountain. This isolated self-catering getaway overlooks what is effectively a private beach in the heart of TMNP's Cape of Good Hope sector. The main cottage, powered by solar and gas, comprises three double rooms, an equipped kitchen, a shared bathroom and an open-plan lounge/dining area, and patio braai area with a boardwalk to the beach. $$$
★ **Tintswalo Atlantic** Chapman's Peak Drive, Hout Bay ☎011 300 8888, ⓦtintswalo.com/atlantic. Perched on the rocks below Chapman's Peak, with a dramatic view of Hout Bay and the Sentinel peak, this stunning five-star luxury lodge is the only hotel in Table Mountain National Park. The large bedrooms are lavishly furnished with tropical beach-house chic, each with ocean views and unique in style, and you might spot whales from the wooden deck as you wander to the pool, lounge, bar and restaurant. $$$$$

OUTSIDE THE PARK

★ **Acorn House** 1 Montrose Ave, Oranjezicht ☎021 461 1782, ⓦacornhouse.co.za. High on the slopes of Table Mountain, this century-old residence has maintained its grandeur with a sweeping lawn, colonial furnishings and elegant lounge, with added comforts such as the pool and sun-loungers. Each room is unique; those at the front of the house offer great city views, while the back shows off Table Mountain. $$
The Backpack 74 New Church St, Tamboerskloof ☎021 423 4530, ⓦbackpackers.co.za. An excellent and long-serving backpackers made up of four interconnected houses, where the interior has a spacious maze-like effect. *The Backpack* has some of the best communal and

outdoor spaces in town, including a pool terrace, lounge area, restaurant, bar, courtyard, travel desk and craft shop. Choose between three- to eight-bed mixed and female-only dorms, including an en-suite option, as well as private rooms and self-catering studios. $\overline{\underline{S}}$

Belmond Mount Nelson Hotel 76 Orange St (rear entrance on Kloof St) ☎ 021 483 1000, ⓦ mountnelson. co.za. Cape Town's *grande dame*: a fine and famous high-colonial Victorian hotel, built in the shadow of Table Mountain in 1899 (and extended in the late 1990s). Perfectly located, the building is set in extensive gardens with a majestic palm-lined driveway leading to the main entrance. Behind its jolly pink facade, the *Nellie* reflects its historical clout in the rates for its rooms, suites and garden cottages. $\overline{\underline{S}}\overline{\underline{S}}\overline{\underline{S}}\overline{\underline{S}}$

★ **Cape Heritage Hotel** 90 Bree St, Cape Town ☎ 021 424 4646, ⓦ capeheritage.co.za. An exceptionally stylish, elegant and tastefully restored boutique hotel with a central location in the redeveloped eighteenth-century complex at Heritage Square, where a walkway shaded by South Africa's oldest fruit-bearing grapevine links the hotel and central courtyard. The spacious rooms are decorated with contemporary handcrafted objects and original paintings. The service is charming and there's also a roof terrace and jacuzzi. $\overline{\underline{S}}\overline{\underline{S}}\overline{\underline{S}}$

Houtkapperspoort Mountain Retreat Hout Bay Main Rd, Constantia Nek, around 4km from Hout Bay and 17km from the city centre ☎ 021 795 0189, ⓦ houtkapperspoortresort.co.za. These rustic one- to three-bedroom, stone-and-brick self-catering cottages are set right alongside Table Mountain National Park in the valley between Hout Bay and Constantia, so they offer excellent access to hiking trails through the fynbos and forest. $\overline{\underline{S}}$

Simon's Town Boutique Backpackers 66 St George's St, Simon's Town ☎ 021 786 1964, ⓦ capepax.co.za. Conveniently located in the heart of historic Simon's Town, 1km south of the railway station and 2km from Boulders Beach, this boutique backpacker joint offers bunk-bed dorms and fairly spacious doubles, plus there's a large balcony with a view of the waterfront. Rent bicycles to ride to the Cape of Good Hope or arrange a kayak tour to paddle past the Boulders penguin colony. $\overline{\underline{S}}$

Whale View Manor 402 Main Road, Murdock Valley ☎ 021 786 3291, ⓦ whaleviewmanor.co.za. This imposing white villa, 1km south of Boulders Beach, houses a four-star boutique hotel and spa with sunny, relaxing and contemporary public spaces. It's right next to the surf, just 10–15 minutes' walk from the penguin colony, and only 8km by road from the Cape of Good Hope. $\overline{\underline{S}}\overline{\underline{S}}$

EATING

SEE MAP PAGE 201

Cape Town is a world-class culinary destination whose Mediterranean climate nurtures farms, vineyards and small producers galore. Prices are inexpensive compared with Western countries; for the cost of an unmemorable meal back home, you can eat innovative dishes by outstanding chefs in an upmarket restaurant. This is the place to splash out on whatever takes your fancy, and you'll find the quality of meat, from steaks to springbok, is high, whilst seafood is abundant, and many vegetarian options are available too. The options listed below are restricted to a handful of eateries that service the sites in TMNP described above, but the city centre and peninsula coastline offers a bottomless selection of relaxed and convivial restaurants serving imaginative food of a high standard.

Salty Sea Dog 2 Wharf St, Waterfront, Simon's Town ☎ 021 786 1918. There's nothing fancy about this small restaurant on Simon's Town's wharf, but the plain old fish and chips are tasty and well-priced, and it also serves beer and wine. With indoor and alfresco seating 2km northwest of Boulders Beach, *Salty Sea Dog* makes a great lunch stop, possibly on a day outing to Cape Point. Mon–Sat 8.30am–9pm, Sun 8.30am–4.30pm.

Table Mountain Cafe Table Mountain Upper Cableway ☎ 021 424 0015, ⓦ tablemountain.net. Catering to a captive market of non-repeat visitors, the only restaurant on the summit of Table Mountain has a bit

of a canteen-like feel, and the food is on the ordinary side, but the splendid view, resident hyraxes, realistic prices and eco-friendly ethos go a long way to compensating, as – on a chilly day – does the opportunity to warm up with a steaming coffee or hot chocolate. Daily 9am–1pm, weather permitting.

Two Oceans Cape Point ☎ 021 780 9200, ⓦ twooceans.co.za. This touristic restaurant set in TMNP's Cape of Good Hope sector should really be called "Two Ocean Currents", as it's the Benguela and Agulhas currents that meet hereabouts, rather than the Atlantic and Indian oceans. Still, this quibble seems irrelevant when you reach the stunning clifftop deck that overlooks the ocean, taking in the whole of False Bay and its mountains. It's also a great place to see whales in season. As well as seafood including fish and sushi, they serve some meaty options, plus gourmet breakfasts. Daily 9am–11am & noon–4.30pm.

Wharfette Bistro Mariner's Wharf, Harbour Rd, Hout Bay ☎ 021 790 1100, ⓦ marinerswharf.com. This relaxed and popular seafood restaurant is decorated with nostalgic passenger-liner photographs and memorabilia. The harbour views from the terrace seating outshine the food, but it's a fine spot to eat inexpensive hake 'n' chips (R75) while sipping a cold beer after an outing to Duiker Island. Daily 10am–8.30pm.

West Coast

Remote, windswept and bordered by the cold Atlantic, the **West Coast** that runs north from Cape Town is neither resorty in a conventional sense, nor particularly rewarding when it comes to big game viewing, but it does offer much to keen **botanists** and **birders**. The sandy soil and dunes harbour a distinctive coastal fynbos vegetation, one that looks unremarkable for much of the year, but which – like Namaqualand to the north – erupts into a riot of colourful spring wildflowers over August and September. Birding is good throughout the year, with a reliable highlight being Lambert's Bay's **Bird Island**, where a sunken hide provides a fantastic view of a garrulous breeding colony of Cape gannets. Elsewhere, avian activity peaks over the summer months of October to March, when some 750,000 Palaearctic migrants – mostly waders – descend upon the region to fatten up on delicacies from the mudflats before undertaking their arduous journey back to their breeding grounds in the Arctic Circle or elsewhere in the northern hemisphere. The most important of these feeding grounds are protected within **West Coast National Park**, which is also the best place in the region to look for large mammals.

> ### WEST COAST NATIONAL PARK AT A GLANCE
>
> A birdwatcher's paradise known for its spring wildflowers and lovely seascapes.
> **Big Five:** N/A
> **General wildlife:** ***
> **Birding:** *****
> **Scenery:** ****
> **Wilderness factor:** ***
> **Uncrowded:** ****
> **Affordability:** ****
> **Self-drive:** Y

4

West Coast National Park

Daily: Apr–Aug 7am–6pm; Sept–Mar 7am–7pm • R87 (outside flower season), R186 (in flower season Aug & Sept) • ☎ 022 772 2144 • ⓦ sanparks.org/parks/west_coast

Protecting more than forty percent of South Africa's remaining pristine strandveld and 35 percent of its salt marshes, the 363-square-kilometre **West Coast National Park** is centred on the vast **Langebaan Lagoon**, which was listed as a Ramsar Wetland of International Importance in 1988. The sheltered lagoon serves as a nursery for juvenile large **fish** such as skates, rays and sharks, while its intertidal zone and shallows serve as an important feeding ground not only for resident **shorebirds** such as African black oystercatcher, greater and lesser flamingo and various plovers, but also for an annual influx of more than 50,000 migrant **waders**, most numerously curlew sandpiper, grey plover, knot, turnstone and sanderling. A fair variety of naturally occurring and reintroduced large mammals includes Cape mountain zebra, eland, greater kudu, red hartebeest, bontebok, Cape grysbok, steenbok, bat-eared fox, caracal, yellow mongoose and small grey mongoose. Most of these species are present throughout the park, but larger ungulates are most highly concentrated in the Postberg sector, which is open only during the spring flower season, which is the best time to visit. A number of interpretive walking trails lead through the dunes to the long, smooth, wave-beaten Atlantic coastline, offering plenty of opportunity to look for birds and to learn about the hardy fynbos vegetation that so defines the look and feel of the region.

ARRIVAL AND INFORMATION

WEST COAST NATIONAL PARK

By car The park is 90km from Cape Town, and there are two entrance gates to the park: one on the R27, roughly 10km north of the turning to Yzerfontein, and the other south of Langebaan. The park isn't huge – if you're driving, you'll cover the extent of the roads in a couple of hours.

Information The Geelbek Information Centre (Mon–Fri 8.30am–4pm, Sat & Sun 9am–1pm; ☎ 022 772 2144), set in the same Cape Dutch house as the namesake restaurant, can direct you to the bird hides nearby, or provide åinformation about walks in the area.

ACCOMMODATION

SEE MAP BELOW

Duinepos Chalets 1km from Geelbek (signposted) ☎ 022 707 9900, ⓦ duinepos.co.za. Converted from former staff houses as part of a community-based ecotourism project, this low-key complex comprises eleven self-catering chalets designed to have a low environmental impact by using minimal water and electricity. Boasting a lovely fynbos setting within the national park, it has a swimming pool on-site, and there's lagoon swimming at Priekstool or Kraalbaai some 12–15km away. Very good value. ⑤

EATING

SEE MAP BELOW

Geelbek Restaurant Geelbek ☎ 084 406 7434, ⓦ geelbek.net. Magnificent setting in a graceful Cape Dutch building that dates back to 1744 and is listed as a national monument. The deck overlooks the lagoon, so you can sit outside and watch flamingos – if you are lucky. South African dishes, such as bobotie, ostrich burgers, snoek salad and Cape Malay curries, are the speciality. Booking essential during flower season. Tues–Fri 9am–4pm, Sat 9am–5pm, Sun 8.30am–5pm.

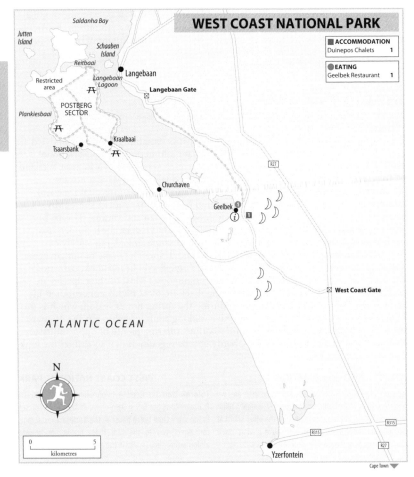

Bird Island Nature Reserve

Daily 8am–6pm • R50 • ☎ 071 657 5651, ⓦ capenature.co.za/
reserves/bird-island-nature-reserve

Situated one hundred metres offshore of the sleepy port town of **Lambert's Bay**, this small rocky island is one of only six breeding sites worldwide for the **Cape gannet**, a striking marine bird distinguished by its bulky appearance and combination of yellow crown and neck, black eye mask, and pale blue bill. A walkable causeway leads from the port to the island, where a strategically located

BIRD ISLAND AT A GLANCE

Bird Island is famed for its impressive gannet colony and other marine wildlife.

Big Five: N/A
General wildlife: *
Birding: *****
Scenery: ***
Wilderness factor: **
Uncrowded: ****
Affordability: *****
Self-drive: Y

hide offers a close-up look at the tightly packed, ear-piercing mass of thousands of petulant gannets, along with a few disapproving-looking penguins and cormorants, though viewing is not always guaranteed outside of the breeding season. Cape fur seals also inhabit the island, while the bay hosts a small breeding pod of **humpback whales** over July to November. Lambert's Bay is also the southernmost area ranged by **Heaviside's dolphin** – a small, friendly marine mammal with wedge-shaped beak and white, striped patterning reminiscent of killer whales. You may well be lucky and see the cavorting dolphins on trips from the fishing port.

ARRIVAL AND INFORMATION   **BIRD ISLAND NATURE RESERVE**

By car Lambert's Bay and Bird Island lie about 260km north of Cape Town via the N7 and R365, or 160km north of West Coast National Park via the R27 and R356.

Information The Lambert's Bay tourist office is in the Medical Centre on Main Rd (Mon–Fri 9am–5pm, Sat 9am–12.30pm; ☎ 027 432 1000, ⓦ lambertsbay.co.za).

ACCOMMODATION

Grootvlei Guest Farm On the R365, 6km south of Lambert's Bay ☎ 027 432 2716 or ☎ 076 592 6541, ⓦ grootvleiguestfarm.co.za. There are two venues to choose from at *Grootvlei*: a luxurious guesthouse in a two-storey homestead or, for something very different, one of the shell-shaped rooms in an elegant, eco-friendly B&B set amid the dunes and just a step away from the ocean. No children or pets allowed. $$

Lambert's Bay Hotel Voortrekker St ☎ 027 432 1126, ⓦ lambertsbayhotel.co.za. Smack in the centre of town, this conventional and rather old-fashioned hotel offers neat and reasonably priced rooms, a swimming pool at the back, and help with organizing activities such as boat trips, birding, beach riding or spring flower trips. There is a restaurant open for breakfast, lunch and dinner, and a ladies' bar. $

Western Karoo

Although the Western Cape is best known for the beautiful beaches and graceful wine estates along the bountiful and relatively well-watered coastal belt, the province's interior is dominated by the vast semi-arid region known as the **Karoo**, a name that derives from a local Khoisan term that loosely translates as "Thirstland". Characterized by ancient rock strata, low rainfall (typically below 250mm per annum), and a sparse cover of succulents and other xerophytic plants, the Karoo formed a daunting barrier to European exploration of the deep interior until the nineteenth century, when it was opened up to settlers by the **Great Trek** inland from Cape Town. Back then, the region was renowned for the prodigious seasonal herds of springbok, quagga and other ungulates that migrated across its plains, but by the start of the twentieth century most of the indigenous large game had been shot out to make way for sheep farms and other livestock. That has changed to some extent in recent years, and while the part of the Karoo set within the Western Cape could hardly be punted as a major safari destination, it is home to the vast **Karoo National**

Park as well as a scattering of private and provincial sanctuaries including the popular but rather contrived **Aquila Private Game Reserve** (the closest Big Five reserve to Cape Town), the larger and more exclusive **Sanbona Wildlife Reserve**, and the remote and little-known **Anysberg Nature Reserve**.

Aquila Private Game Reserve

Off the N1, 175km northeast of Cape Town • Entrance fee included in room or game-drive rates • ☎ 021 430 7260, ⓦ aquilasafari.com.

The closest Big Five reserve to **Cape Town** is also South Africa's ultimate quick-fix safari package destination, offering first-timers a near certainty of seeing lion, elephant, buffalo and white rhino over the course of any given two-hour game drive, as well as an outside chance of black rhino. Established in 1995, the reserve protects around one hundred square kilometres of semi-arid Karoo scrub, overshadowed by seriously impressive rocky mountains and graced by a network of pans fed by the **Touws River** (also the name of the closest town, which straddles the N1 about 10km to the northeast). Naturally occurring wildlife includes a few of the secretive leopards that inhabit the mountains of the Western Cape, as well as chacma baboon, black-backed jackal, caracal, klipspringer (sometimes seen silhouetted on the rocky slopes), the cliff-nesting Verreaux's eagle *Aquila verreauxii* for which the reserve is named, and water-associated birds such as South African shelduck and pied avocet. Introduced wildlife includes Burchell's zebra, giraffe, hippo and a selection of antelope with a confirmed historical presence in the area, for instance springbok, eland and black wildebeest. The stands of exotic *Eucalyptus* in and around the lodge and main entrance notwithstanding, most of **Aquila** seems to be in good ecological shape, with a low ground cover dominated by the succulents and fynbos-like scrub typical of the Karoo.

As a safari experience, however, it is unabashedly populist, closer in spirit to a European safari park or overgrown zoo than to a typical African game reserve. Game drives are conducted in packed 25-seater open-sided trucks, half a dozen of which might leave in convoy on a busy afternoon, creating something of a treadmill atmosphere. In addition, several of the reserve's more iconic species are rescue animals unable to fend for themselves. Lions, for instance, are kept in a drive-through enclosure that houses half a dozen declawed individuals rescued from a hunting operation, while the reserve's two elephant bulls, both saved from culls, are free to roam by day, but are herded back into an overnight boma at dusk. None of which should be an issue to Cape Town-based tourists whose objective is to tick off a good selection of African wildlife in as short a space of time as possible, but for those seeking a full-blown safari experience, it is likely to feel a bit contrived.

Half-day safaris to Aquila, inclusive of a game drive, welcome drinks, and snacks or a meal, range in price from R995 to R1550 per person, depending on time of day and season. Full-day combo safaris including a horseback or quad-bike excursion are pricier. An overnight package is preferable to a day-trip, as the two game drives included leave in the late afternoon and first thing in the morning, the most rewarding hours for wildlife viewing and photography. An overnight package also includes all meals, and (weather permitting) it allows you to experience the typically dazzling Karoo night sky to a backdrop of grunting hippos and yelping jackals.

AQUILA AT A GLANCE

The closest Big Five reserve to Cape Town is unabashedly packaged but offers a near certainty of seeing lion, elephant, buffalo and rhino.

Big Five: ****
General wildlife: ****
Birding: **
Scenery: ****
Wilderness factor: *
Uncrowded: *
Affordability: ***
Self-drive: N

ARRIVAL AND DEPARTURE

By car and transfer To get to Aquila, follow the N1 northeast of Cape Town towards Touws River for around 170km, then turn left on to the R46 towards Ceres, where you'll see the reception and lodge to your left after another

AQUILA PRIVATE GAME RESERVE

3km. Self-drivers should allow at least two hours in either direction. Aquila also offers road transfers from Cape Town (R890 per person return).

ACCOMMODATION

Aquila Lodge On the R46 adjacent to the entrance gate ☎ 021 430 7260, ⓦ aquilasafari.com. This three-storey lodge comprises 22 standard rooms without a view, and another 22 premier semi-suites with wide balconies overlooking the reserve and a waterhole. Comfortable and well-equipped, rooms are decorated in a blandly inoffensive modern style. Rates include lunch and dinner on the day of arrival, breakfast on the day of departure, and early morning and late afternoon game drives. $̶$̶$̶

Sanbona Wildlife Reserve

Main entrance 30km west of Barrydale off the R62 • No day-visitors • ☎ 021 010 0028, ⓦ sanbona.com

The largest private reserve in the Western Cape, **Sanbona** lies three hours' drive inland of Cape Town, just off the Route 62, an increasingly popular back-route connecting the Cape winelands to Oudtshoorn and the Garden Route. Originally called the Cape Wildlife Reserve, it was established in 2000 from what was formerly low-yield farmland, and has since been expanded to protect a gorgeous 580-square-kilometre Karoo landscape of rocky outcrops, towering mountains and semi-desert. Sanbona is now home to a wealth of large mammals including all the Big Five, but unlike most South African private reserves, the wildlife is arguably less of an attraction than the expansive **scenery** and exclusive wilderness atmosphere. The reserve also houses a wealth of prehistoric **rock art**, including some exquisite bushman paintings dating back more than 3500 years, and more recent and cruder white finger paintings attributed to the Khoikhoi.

Sanbona is dominated geographically by the towering 350-million-year old crags of the **Warmwaterberg** (Hot Water Mountains), an ancient range whose name refers to the springs that erupt from its slopes outside the reserve boundaries. Cut through by a spectacular gorge that flanks the rutted main road connecting the entrance gate to the two main lodges, the Warmwaterberg is a watershed that divides Sanbona into two distinct biomes. The mountain's southern rain shadow supports a cover of relatively well-watered renosterveld fynbos, bisected by the seasonal Klein Kalkoenshoek (Little Turkey Corner) River. By contrast, the drought-prone badlands to the north of the mountains form part of the succulent Karoo and host a wealth of dwarf *Mesembryanthemum*, *Crassula* and other shrubs that erupt into flower after spring rains.

Sanbona's two main lodges and most rewarding game-viewing circuit lie in the north of the reserve, where the **Brak** (Brackish) **River**, a seasonal waterway whose wide bed of overgrown white pebbles sometimes goes years without flowing properly, is flanked by a ribbon of spiky sweet-thorns and other relatively tall shrubs browsed upon by the likes of giraffe and elephant. The Brak also feeds the Bellair Dam, which was originally built in 1922 but was reconstructed and reinforced in 2006 after being destroyed by floods three years earlier. The associated reservoir extends over more than one square kilometre when full, and although it has been greatly reduced in recent years due to ongoing **droughts**, it remains an important source of year-round drinking water for the reserve's wildlife.

> **SANBONA AT A GLANCE**
>
> Encounter white lions and vast desert Karoo landscapes in the Western Cape's largest Big Five reserve.
> **Big Five:** ****
> **General wildlife:** ****
> **Birding:** ***
> **Scenery:** *****
> **Wilderness factor:** ****
> **Uncrowded:** ****
> **Affordability:** *
> **Self-drive:** N

4

Sanbona is one of the few reserves in the Western Cape to support free-roaming lion, cheetah, elephant and white rhino, all of which are likely to be seen over the course of a two-night visit, and although other game is relatively sparse, it is also home to reintroduced giraffe, Cape mountain zebra, gemsbok, springbok and eland, as well as naturally occurring populations of greater kudu, Cape grysbok, steenbok, chacma baboon, black-backed jackal, bat-eared fox, caracal and (seldom seen) leopard. A small herd of buffalo is kept in a separate enclosure to protect it from the reserve's rapacious lions, and there are plans to reintroduce black rhino when the current drought ends. Sanbona is one of the few reserves anywhere where the recessive "**white lion**" gene is prevalent; at the time of writing, is it home to two adult lions that sport this striking and unusual colouration. Sanbona is an important refuge for the **riverine rabbit**, which was first recorded in the renosterveld south of the Warmwaterberg in 2005, a sighting that represented a significant range extension for a Critically Endangered species previously thought to be endemic to the Karoo.

Sanbona supports an interesting **birdlife**, too. Typical dry-country species found here include ostrich, Karoo korhaan, Karoo eremomela, Karoo prinia, Karoo thrush, pririt batis, Layard's tit-babbler and Namaqua warbler. The most majestic of the raptors that nest on the reserve's cliffs is Verreaux's eagle, which is often seen perched on high or soaring overhead, while other conspicuous species include jackal buzzard and southern pale chanting goshawk. Despite the arid surrounds, **Bellair Dam** supports a surprisingly varied array of water-associated birds including black-winged stilt, pied avocet and various ducks, while the secretive black-capped night heron is resident on a nearby waterhole fed by piped water from the dam.

ARRIVAL AND DEPARTURE   SANBONA WILDLIFE RESERVE

By car The most direct route to Sanbona, coming from Cape Town, is to follow the N1 northeast for 110km to Worcester then turn right on to the R60 and continue east through Robertson and Ashton where it becomes the R62. Roughly 115km past Worcester, you'll see a signposted junction to the left, about 20km before the small town of Barrydale. It's 7km from this junction to the main entrance gate, where all visitors need to sign in, then another 15km to the Welcome Lounge, from where you can either drive on to your accommodation (about 30km to *Gondwana Lodge* and almost 40km to *Dwyka* on corrugated but otherwise good dirt roads) or by prior arrangement hop on the free shuttle that leaves at 12.30pm and 4pm. Allow at least four hours for the full drive from Cape Town to your lodge.

An alternative route coming from Hermanus or anywhere along the N2 east of Cape Town is to cut inland onto the R324 about 12km east of Swellendam and follow it northeast for 33km through the spectacular Tradouw Pass to connect with the R62 at Barrydale, 20km east of the junction for Sanbona.

Coming from or heading on elsewhere, there are two other relatively little-used gates, both of which lie significantly closer to the lodges than the main gate. These are the Western Gate, which is connected to Touws River on the N1 by a well-maintained and clearly signposted unsurfaced road, and the Eastern Gate, which lies 20km along a dirt road running west from the R62 about 25km northeast of Barrydale and 50km southwest of Ladismith.

ACCOMMODATION

All accommodation in the reserve can be booked through central reservations (☎021 010 0028, ⊛sanbona.com). Rates include all meals and activities but not drinks.

★**Dwyka Tented Lodge** Set in a secluded ravine enclosed by cliffs of twisted and buckled ancient rock strata, Sanbona's flagship lodge comprises nine luxurious canvas-and-stone suites arranged in a wide semi-circle around a central building whose state-of-the-art architecture is offset by reproductions of prehistoric rock art and a fabulous collection of artworks from all around the continent. All suites have a/c, a private deck with a jacuzzi, outdoor and indoor shower, and a mini-bar. Other amenities include an infinity pool, walk-in wine cellar and spa. $$$$$

Explorer Camp The option that gets you closest to nature, this luxury seasonal tented camp offers more adventurous guests an opportunity to explore the Karoo and see the Big Five on foot on two-day wilderness trails that leave every Friday over October to April. Limited to those aged 16–60. $$$$$

Gondwana Family Lodge This child-friendly lodge consists of a dozen ample and well-equipped suites, all with wide balconies facing a waterhole and the more distant Bellair Dam and Anysberg Mountains, split across two double-storey thatched buildings. In addition to a swimming pool for adults, there's a kiddies' pool, children's play area, and short educational interpretive trail set within the small compound. $$$$$

Anysberg Nature Reserve

Daily 8am–6pm • R50 • ☎ 021 483 0190, ⓦ capenature.co.za/
reserves/anysberg-nature-reserve

Established in 1988, this remote and
ruggedly scenic 800-square-kilometre
provincial reserve is effectively a northern
extension of **Sanbona**, since the two
protected areas are less than 5km apart
and plans reputedly exist to link them
with a game corridor on private land. The
reserve protects the **Anysberg** (Aniseed)
Mountains, whose name refers to a type
of anise *Pimpinella spp* that grows wild
here. As with the more southerly Sanbona, Anysberg forms part of the succulent Karoo,
but the protea-rich stands of mountain fynbos on its upper slopes led to it being
incorporated into UNESCO's Cape Floral Kingdom World Heritage Site in 2015.
Naturally occurring and reintroduced wildlife includes the endemic riverine rabbit and
Cape mountain zebra, as well as leopard, caracal, brown hyena, black-backed jackal,
gemsbok, red hartebeest, steenbok and common duiker. Anysberg is also notable for its
dry-country birdlife (a checklist of 180 species includes several Karoo endemics) and for
the wealth of prehistoric **rock art** on its slopes. Activities include guided and unguided
hiking, 4WD trails, visits to rock-art sites and horseback safaris. The reserve was
temporarily closed in 2019 due to a local **drought** but will hopefully reopen in 2020.

> **ANYSBERG AT A GLANCE**
>
> Remote hiker-friendly gem in the scenic
> heart of the Karoo.
> **Big Five:** None
> **General wildlife:** **
> **Birding:** ***
> **Scenery:** *****
> **Wilderness factor:** ****
> **Uncrowded:** *****
> **Affordability:** *****
> **Self-drive:** Y

4

ARRIVAL AND DEPARTURE   ANYSBERG NATURE RESERVE

By car Coming from the direction of Cape Town, take
the N1 to Laingsburg (about 260km northeast of the
city), then turn right onto the R323 and follow it south
for 25km before turning right again onto a dirt road that
leads to the main entrance gate after another 25km. The
accommodation and campsite at *Vrede* is another 20km

past the entrance gate. The main entrance gate can also
be approached from the southeast, along a 50km road
that leaves the R62 at Ladismith. Both approaches involve
some rough stretches and 4WD is recommended (though
not essential, provided your vehicle has reasonably high
clearance).

ACCOMMODATION

Vrede ☎ 021 483 0190, ⓦ capenature.co.za. This remote
and rustic restcamp comprises five cottages, sleeping a total
of up to 21 people, with private bathrooms, solar lighting

and fridges, and gas stoves and braai places. There are also
five campsites that use a communal ablution block and
kitchen with a gas stove, fridge and freezer. $\overline{\underline{\$}}$

Karoo National Park

Entrance gate 2km south of Beaufort West • R218 • **Gate** daily:
summer 6am–7pm, winter 7am–6pm; **Reception** daily
7am–7pm • ☎ 023 415 2828, ⓦ sanparks.org/parks/karoo

The main attraction of the 831-square-
kilometre **Karoo National Park** is the starkly
mountainous **landscape**, studded with
magnificent rock formations. This serene
park also scores highly as a place to break
the long drive between Gauteng and Cape
Town. There's an environmental **education
centre** near the main restcamp, along
with an imaginative self-guided fossil trail
(designed to accommodate wheelchairs
and incorporating Braille boards) which
tells the fascinating 250-million-year

> **KAROO NATIONAL PARK AT A
> GLANCE**
>
> Scenic and low-key game-viewing to break
> up the long drive between Cape Town and
> Gauteng.
> **Big Five:** *
> **General wildlife:** ***
> **Birding:** ****
> **Scenery:** *****
> **Wilderness factor:** ****
> **Uncrowded:** ****
> **Affordability:** *****
> **Self-drive:** Y

4

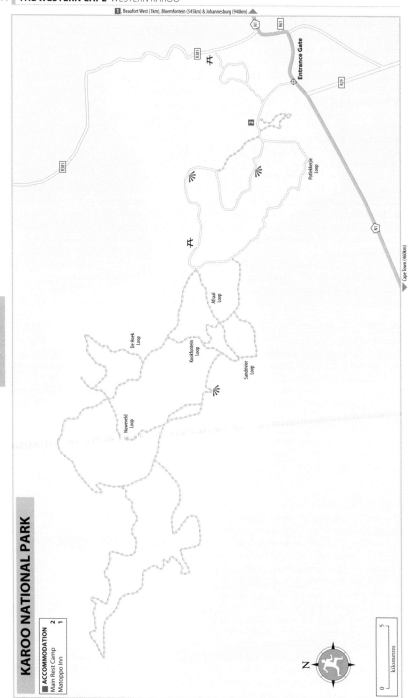

KAROO NATIONAL PARK

■ ACCOMMODATION
Main Rest Camp 2
Matoppo Inn 1

1 , Beaufort West (1km), Bloemfontein (545km) & Johannesburg (940km)

N1
R61

Entrance Gate

R29

R381

R381

Cape Town (460km)

N1

Potlekkerjie Loop

Afsaal Loop

De Hoek Loop

Kookfonteim Loop

Sandrivier Loop

Nuweveld Loop

N

0   kilometres   5

geological history of the area and shows fossils of the unusual animals that lived when the Karoo was a vast inland sea. Large mammals are sparsely distributed, but species that might be seen along the 60km of all-weather game-viewing roads include lion, leopard, black rhino, Cape mountain zebra, red hartebeest, gemsbok, springbok, eland, greater kudu, klipspringer, mountain reedbuck and grey rhebok. The rich reptilian fauna includes five species of tortoise, while the birdlife is strong on dry-country and Karoo endemics, notably Karoo korhaan, Ludwig's bustard, Karoo scrub-robin, chestnut-vented tit-babbler, Layard's tit-babbler, dusky sunbird and redheaded finch, many of which might be seen from the bird hide in the restcamp. The park also has a high concentration of raptors including Verreaux's eagle. Guided game drives (from R932 per person) and walks (R233 per person) are also offered and are best booked a day in advance.

ARRIVAL AND DEPARTURE · KAROO NATIONAL PARK

By car The entrance gate to Karoo National Park is on north side of the N1, about 2km south of Beaufort West, a large town that straddles the N1 some 460km northeast of Cape Town, 545km southwest of Bloemfontein, and 940km from Johannesburg. The park reception and adjacent *Rest Camp* lies about 10km inside the park.

ACCOMMODATION · SEE MAP PAGE 214

★ **Main Rest Camp** 10km into park ☎ 023 415 2828, ⓦ sanparks.org/parks/karoo. Thirty fully equipped chalets and cottages are strung out on either side of the main complex, all with lovely outlooks onto the Karoo landscape. There's a pool nearby, a shop selling basic foodstuffs and a restaurant (daily breakfast is included in the rate, but you need to book dinner in advance). The campsite is hidden away over a rise. Camping ‾S‾, doubles ‾SS‾

Matoppo Inn 7 Bird St, Beaufort West ☎ 023 415 1055, ⓦ matoppoinn.co.za. Elegant rooms with brass beds and antique furniture, as well as standard rooms with more modern furnishings, in the town's old *drostdy*, or magistrate's house. The gardens are beautiful – a green oasis in the desert-like Karoo – and there's a pool, good food all day, and a tranquil atmosphere. ‾SS‾

The Overberg

An Afrikaans name that translates as "Over the Mountain", the **Overberg** runs for about 200km east of Cape Town and False Bay as far as the historic old town of **Swellendam**. Though rather loosely delineated, the region is bounded by the **N2** highway to the north, while its long and rugged coastline – renowned for offering some of the world's finest land-based **whale-watching** between June and October – terminates at **Cape Agulhas**, the most southerly headland on the African continent. **Hermanus**, the main town in the area, has good swimming beaches and plentiful accommodation, but owes its fame to its status as the whale-watching capital of South Africa. The region also boasts two relatively low-key game parks in the form of **Bontebok National Park**, which stands on the southwestern outskirts of Swellendam, and the **De Hoop Nature Reserve**, which protects a coastal wilderness of craggy rockscapes and bleached dunes to the east of Agulhas.

Hermanus

On the edge of rocky cliffs and backed by mountains, **HERMANUS**, 112km east of Cape Town, sits at the northernmost end of Walker Bay, a crescent-shaped inlet whose protective curve slides south more than 20km to a craggy promontory called Danger Point. Walker Bay is perhaps the most important of several warmer sheltered bays in the Western Cape that form calving grounds for large numbers of **southern right whales** between July and November (with some annual variation in movement from one year to the next). The whales sometimes enter Hermanus's harbour – when this happens, there's nowhere better to base yourself for a spot of whale-watching than

WHALE-WATCHING BY LAND, SEA AND AIR

The Southern Cape coast offers some of the world's easiest **whale-watching** opportunities – you don't even need to rent a boat or take a pricey tour to see them. Arrive in season, and whales are often easily visible from shore, although a good pair of binoculars will still come in useful. The best vantage points include the cliff paths above **Hermanus**, **De Kelders** some 39km further east, and **Koppie Alleen** in De Hoop Nature Reserve, but whales are often seen at other locations too, among them False Bay on the east side of the Cape Peninsula.

The most commonly seen of the nine great whale species that pass by South Africa's shores is the **southern right whale**, whose name derives from it being the "right" one for whalers to kill, thanks to a high oil and bone yield, and the fact that it floats when dead. Southern right whales are easily recognized by the callosities (patches of raised, roughened, pale brown skin on their snouts and heads) whose distinct pattern helps scientists keep track of different individuals. The female whales come inshore to calve in sheltered bays and stay to nurse their young for up to three months. July to October is the best time to see them, but they start appearing in June and some stay around until December. When the calves are big enough, the whales return to colder, stormier, more southerly waters, where they feed on enormous quantities of plankton, making up for the nursing months when the females don't eat at all.

What gives away the presence of a whale is the blow or **spout**, a tall smoky plume which disperses after a few seconds and is actually the whale breathing out before it surfaces. Though you're most likely to see females and young, you may see males early in the season boisterously flopping about the females, though they neither help rear the calves nor form lasting bonds with females. If luck is on your side, you may see whales **breaching** – the movement when they thrust high out of the water and fall back with a great splash.

Several **operators** run boat trips from Hermanus, all essentially offering the same service. Boats must give a 50m berth to whales, but if a whale approaches a boat, the boat may stop and watch it for up to twenty minutes. Recommended outfits include Hermanus Whale Cruises (☎028 313 2722, ⊛hermanus-whale-cruises.co.za, R800) and Dyer Island Cruises (☎082 801 8014 or ☎076 555 5520, ⊛whalewatchsa.com, from R1290); book in advance. To see whales from the air, African Wings (☎081 761 2411, ⊛africanwings.co.za) flies a maximum of three people in a small plane over the bay to see whales, dolphins, sharks and other sea life.

The Gecko (see opposite) – but a more reliable place to spot these charismatic marine behemoths is the almost continuous 5km **cliff path** that hugs the coastline connecting the harbour to the more easterly Grotto Beach.

ARRIVAL AND INFORMATION HERMANUS

By car The most direct route to Hermanus, 125km from Cape Town, is to take the N2 then head south onto the R43 at Bot River (a 1hr 30min drive), though the winding road that leaves the N2 just before Sir Lowry's Pass hugs the coast from Strand and is one of the most scenic coastal drives in South Africa (2hr).

By bus The Baz Bus (☎021 422 5202, ⊛bazbus.com) between Cape Town and Port Elizabeth drops off at Bot River 34km northeast of Hermanus on the R43, from where you can arrange to be collected by your hostel. The Bernadus Shuttle (☎028 316 1093 or ☎083 658 7848, ⊛bernardustransfershermanus.co.za) also plies the route

between Hermanus and Cape Town (1hr 30min). This is effectively a taxi service, operating on demand, so you need to book in advance.

Tourist information The tourist office, at the old station building in Mitchell St (May–Aug Mon–Sat 9am–5pm & Sun 9am–2pm; Sept–Apr Mon–Sat 8am–6pm; ☎028 312 2629, ⊛hermanustourism.info), provides maps and brochures about the area, and can book accommodation and whale-watching trips.

Festival During the last week in September, the town puts on a lively show of almost anything with a whale connection, however tenuous (⊛hermanuswhalefestival.co.za).

ACCOMMODATION

Auberge Burgundy 16 Harbour Rd ☎028 313 1201, ⊛auberge.co.za. A Provençal-style country house in the town centre, close to the water, with a stylish Mediterranean atmosphere and a lavender garden. The

rooms are light and airy and decorated with imported French fabrics. $\overline{\underline{S}}\overline{\underline{S}}$

House on Westcliff 96 Westcliff Rd ☎028 313 2388, ⊛westcliffhouse.co.za. This homely B&B is situated just out of the centre near the new harbour, and boasts six bedrooms in a classic Cape-style house with a protected, tranquil garden and swimming pool. All rooms are en suite and have their own entrance off the garden. $\overline{\underline{5}}$

Windsor Hotel 49 Marine Drive ☎ 028 312 3727, ⓦwindsorhotel.co.za. This old, but popular, seafront hotel offers a full range of accommodation right on the cliff edge. It's ideally situated in the centre of town and guests can enjoy sea views from the dining room, lounges and almost half of the bedrooms. $\overline{\underline{55}}$

Zoete Inval Traveller's Lodge 23 Main Rd ☎ 028 312 1242 or ☎ 078 583 4101, ⓦzoeteinval.co.za. A quiet and relaxing hostel, with a distinct lack of party vibe, comprising dorms, doubles and family suites, with extras like good coffee, a jacuzzi and a fireplace. They can organize tours and outings in the area. $\overline{\underline{5}}$

EATING

Dutchies 10th Ave, Grotto Beach, Voelklip ☎ 028 314 1392, ⓦdutchies.co.za. The only place to eat on the beach, with sparkling management and service. Prices are reasonable – a "health" breakfast (hot drink, fresh orange juice, fruit salad, Greek yoghurt and muesli) will set you back just R75, while a Dutch cheese and ham ciabatta is R85. Book ahead, especially to get outdoor seating. Daily 9am–9pm.

The Gecko 24a Still St, New Harbour ☎ 028 312 4665, ⓦgeckohermanus.co.za. With great harbour views that offer prime in-house whale-watching, this packed bar has excellent cocktails, along with pizzas, burgers and pub grub. It's an ideal spot for a sundowner and a regular venue for live music, showcasing local artists. Daily 11am–2am.

★ **Lizette's Bar & Restaurant** 20 8th St, Voelklip ☎ 028 314 0308, ⓦlizetteskitchen.com. Named after its well-known chef, this spacious restored house has a cosy interior, plenty of outdoor seating and a play area for kids. The menu ranges from Vietnamese street food (R100–125) and Moroccan dishes to burgers and South African favourites with a twist. Mon–Thurs 11.30am–9pm, Fri–Sun 9am–9pm.

De Hoop Nature Reserve

4

140km west of Hermanus via Bredasdorp and 50km south of Swellendam on the N2 • Daily 7am–6pm • R50 • ☎ 087 087 8250, ⓦcapenature.co.za/reserves/de-hoop-nature-reserve

De Hoop is a provincially managed reserve best known for its **coastal scenery** and for rivalling Hermanus as one of the top places in the world for land-based **whale-watching**. Comprising a 240-square-kilometre marine and 360-square-kilometre terrestrial sector, the reserve protects a breathtaking coastline edged by bleached sand dunes – standing 90m high in places – and rocky formations that at one point open to the sea in a massive craggy arch. Whale-watching in De Hoop is strictly seasonal: more than one hundred southern right whales take residence in the offshore calving grounds over July to October, with the greatest numbers likely to be seen in August and September. And there's no need to take a boat or use binoculars; in season you'll often see them close to shore blowing or breaching – leaping clear of the water – or perhaps slapping a giant tail.

The **terrestrial sector** of De Hoop comprises one of the region's best-preserved tracts of coastal fynbos and renosterveld, with 1500 floral species recorded. Eland, bontebok, Cape mountain zebra and baboon are the most conspicuous large mammals, but look out too for smaller antelope such as grey rhebok, Cape grysbok and klipspringer. As for the Big Five, the only species recorded is the leopard, and it is probably a transient visitor rather than a resident, but small carnivores are well represented and include caracal, Cape clawless otter and several types of mongoose of which the most common is the yellow mongoose, which often reveals its presence by standing upright, meerkat-like, balanced on its hind legs and tail. The reserve incorporates the Western Cape's only breeding colony of the Cape vulture, which is often seen soaring overhead, as

DE HOOP AT A GLANCE

Fynbos endemics and marine wildlife abound in this scenic coastal wilderness.
Big Five: None
General wildlife: ***
Birding: ****
Scenery: *****
Wilderness factor: ****
Uncrowded: *****
Affordability: *****
Self-drive: Y

is African fish eagle, jackal buzzard and black harrier. The **De Hoop Vlei** is a seasonally fluctuating 19km wetland that often hosts large numbers of waterfowl, including Cape shoveller and southern pochard, and it also serves as an occasional breeding ground for greater flamingo. The coastline attracts a wide variety of marine birds and waders, while conspicuous fynbos species include Denham's bustard, Cape spurfowl, Cape rockjumper and Cape grassbird.

De Hoop could technically be visited as a day-trip from Agulhas, Bredasdorp or Swellendam, but it is far more rewarding to spend a night or more in the reserve. The only part of the reserve that can be explored by car is the far west, where the roads around the De Hoop Vlei offer good birding and a high chance of spotting Cape mountain zebra and various antelope; **Koppie Alleen** (literally "Hillock Alone") is a great vantage point for seasonal whale-watching and marine birding. A second road leads to the **Potberg Educational Centre**, starting point of the six-day, 55km Whale Trail (porterage optional; book at ☎087 087 8250, ⓦcapenature.co.za), which ranks among South Africa's best coastal walks, looping through the reserve's eastern sector via a series of commodious overnight huts to emerge on the last day at Koppie Alleen.

ARRIVAL AND INFORMATION

DE HOOP NATURE RESERVE

By car The quickest route from Cape Town is along the N2; De Hoop is signposted off it, 13km west of Swellendam. Alternatively, if you are in the Overberg, take the signposted dirt road that spurs off the R319 as it heads out of Bredasdorp, 50km to its west.

Tourist information The information office (daily 7am–

6pm; ☎028 542 1114) is at De Opstel, which stands in the western sector overlooking De Hoop Vlei, a 20min drive from the coast. Next door is the reserve's only restaurant and a small shop selling basics, so stock up in Swellendam or Bredasdorp before you come.

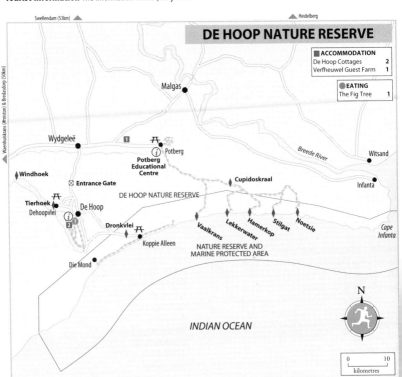

DE HOOP NATURE RESERVE

ACCOMMODATION
De Hoop Cottages	2
Verfheuwel Guest Farm	1

EATING
The Fig Tree	1

Swellendam (53km) · Heidelberg · Malgas · Breede River · Witsand · Wydgeleë · Potberg · Potberg Educational Centre · Windhoek · Entrance Gate · DE HOOP NATURE RESERVE · Cupidoskraal · Infanta · Tierhoek · Dehoopvlei · De Hoop · Dronkvlei · Vaalkrans · Lekkerwater · Hamerkop · Stilgat · Noetsie · Cape Infanta · Koppie Alleen · NATURE RESERVE AND MARINE PROTECTED AREA · Die Mond · Waenhuiskrans (Arniston) & Bredasdorp (50km) · INDIAN OCEAN · N · 0 10 kilometres

ACCOMMODATION   SEE MAP PAGE 218

★**De Hoop Cottages** ☎021 422 4522, �🌐dehoop collection.co.za. You'll find an array of accommodation at this privately managed restcamp, which overlooks the vlei in the far west of De Hoop Nature Reserve. At the top end, you can enjoy a bed and breakfast stay, with dinner included, in the converted manor house. Camping is the cheapest way to visit the reserve, and there are also a number of appealing self-catering properties of varying sizes – from basic rondavels with outdoor showers to a fully equipped cottage. None of it is especially cheap, but it's all appealing and comfortable.

Camping and rondavels $\overline{\underline{S}}$, cottages $\overline{\underline{SS}}$, manor house $\overline{\underline{SSS}}$
Verfheuwel Guest Farm Potberg Rd, in the direction of Malgas ☎028 542 1038 or ☎082 767 0148, �🌐verfheuwel guestfarm.co.za. This cottage accommodation, attached to the main farmhouse, is run by hospitable Afrikaner farming folk, with dinner brought to your cottage if you ask in advance. It accommodates a couple, with beds in the living area for children, and there's a beautiful garden with a swimming pool. If *Verfheuwel* is full, the owner will direct you to others in the area offering farm accommodation. $\overline{\underline{S}}$

EATING   SEE MAP PAGE 218

The Fig Tree On the reserve, close to reception ☎021 422 4522, ⍟dehoopcollection.com/restaurant. De Hoop's only restaurant uses local ingredients complementing the Elim wines, with good-value set-menu dinners, usually

including fish, plus a children's menu. Reservations are required. Picnic baskets can be ordered, and there is a lovely spot outside that is ideal for sundowners after a good day at the beach. Daily 8am–9pm.

Bontebok National Park

Entrance gate just off the N2, 215km east of Cape Town and 4km south of Swellendam • Daily: May–Oct 7am–6pm; Nov–Apr 7am–7pm • R100 • ☎028 514 3206, ⍟sanparks.org/parks/bontebok

An excellent goal for an overnight stop between Cape Town and the Garden Route, the 28-square-kilometre **Bontebok National Park**, set at the foot of the **Langeberg** (Long Mountain), is bordered to the south by the aptly named Breede ("Wide") River and to the north by South Africa's third-oldest town, **Swellendam**. The park was established in 1931 to protect the **bontebok**, an attractive fynbos-endemic antelope which was hunted to within seventeen individuals by Dutch and British settlers. Following the creation of the national park, bontebok numbers quickly increased, but the original location proved to be ecologically unsuitable, and after half the population was wiped out by worm infestations and mineral deficiencies, the survivors were relocated to their present-day location in 1961. Since then, the bontebok population has increased steadily: the national park maintains a population of two to three hundred individuals, which is its maximum carrying capacity, but the rest of the global population of 3000-odd descendants have been translocated to other suitable national parks and reserves.

The main attraction of the park remains the bontebok, which resembles a hartebeest in shape, but is smaller and more strikingly marked, with a distinctive cappuccino, chocolate-brown coat offset by bold white markings on the face, belly, lower legs and hindquarters. Other mammals likely to be encountered include the reintroduced Cape mountain zebra and red hartebeest, alongside naturally occurring smaller antelope such as grey rhebok, steenbok and common duiker. The largest carnivore is the caracal, but yellow mongoose, small grey mongoose and – if you are very lucky – the endemic Cape fox are more likely to be sighted on game drives. More than two hundred bird species have been recorded, too; southern black korhaan, Denham's bustard, black harrier, blue crane and the very localized Agulhas long-billed lark are likely to be seen in open fynbos, which

BONTEBOK AT A GLANCE
Beautiful bontebok and other endemic wildlife in a compact but pretty fynbos reserve well suited to self-drive and walking.
Big Five: N/A
General wildlife: ***
Birding: ****
Scenery: ***
Wilderness factor: ***
Uncrowded: *****
Affordability: *****
Self-drive: Y

is the predominant biome, with nearly five hundred plant species present, including various *Erica* heathers, gladioli and proteas. The more densely wooded vegetation around the restcamp and trails following the **Breede River** supports thicket species such as bokmakierie, southern boubou, southern tchagra, chestnut-vented tit-babbler and African paradise flycatcher. Look out too for the localized angulate and parrot-beaked tortoises.

The park's small but well-maintained network of game-viewing roads can be explored over two to three hours, with **Skilpad** (Tortoise) **Dam** being a good spot to park for a while and wait for thirsty bontebok and other antelope to come to drink. For walkers and bikers, there are five nature trails, ranging in length from the 1.6km Acacia Trail to the 9.2km Cobra Mountain Bike Trail. The 3.2km Blue Crane Trail passes Skilpad Dam and is recommended if you hope to encounter large mammals on foot, while the 3.3km Aloe Hill Trail offers good birding and great views over the Breede River to the Langeberg. Other activities include swimming, kayaking and fishing in the river, through you need your own gear for the latter two.

ARRIVAL AND DEPARTURE — BONTEBOK NATIONAL PARK

By car The national park stands on the outskirts of Swellendam, an attractive, small town established in 1745 by Baron Gustav van Imhoff and now dotted with historic Cape Dutch buildings, despite having been partially razed by fire in 1865. Coming from Cape Town, the straightforward 210km drive along the N2 to Swellendam takes about 2.5 hours and any coach heading east to George or Port Elizabeth can drop you there. Coming from elsewhere in the Overberg, Swellendam is 135km northeast of Hermanus on the R326 and N2, or 50km north of De Hoop.

4

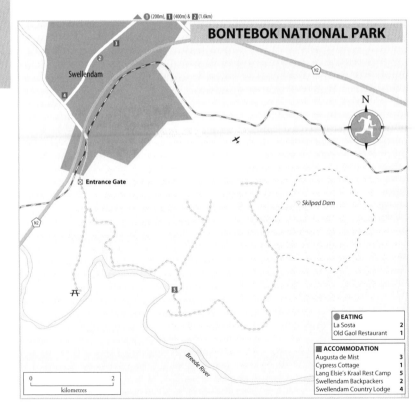

▲ ❶ (200m), ❶ (400m) & ❷ (1.6km)

BONTEBOK NATIONAL PARK

3

2

Swellendam

4

N2

N

⊠ **Entrance Gate**

N2

♢ *Skilpad Dam*

5

Breede River

0	2
kilometres	

● EATING	
La Sosta	2
Old Gaol Restaurant	1

■ ACCOMMODATION	
Augusta de Mist	3
Cypress Cottage	1
Lang Elsie's Kraal Rest Camp	5
Swellendam Backpackers	2
Swellendam Country Lodge	4

ACCOMMODATION

SEE MAP PAGE 220

★ **Augusta de Mist** 3 Human St, Swellendam ☎ 028 514 2425, ⓦ augustademist.com. This two hundred-year-old homestead has three beautifully renovated cottages, two garden suites and a family unit. All are luxurious and stylish, with percale linen. There's a rambling terraced garden and pool, plus a good restaurant on-site, though you need to book meals in advance. $$

★ **Cypress Cottage** 3 Voortrek St, Swellendam ☎ 028 514 3296, ⓦ cypress-cottage.co.za. This charming and well-priced B&B includes two rooms in the old homestead – one of the oldest in town and decorated with antiques – and five in the converted stables. The friendly owner-manager is a brilliant gardener. $

★ **Lang Elsie's Kraal Rest Camp** ☎ 012 428 9111 (central reservations) or ☎ 028 514 3206, ⓦ sanparks. org/parks/bontebok. Named after a female Khoikhoi leader who lived in the area in the late eighteenth century, this idyllic self-catering camp is the only accommodation set within the park itself. It comprises ten fully equipped chalets, the best of which have river views. There are lovely grassy areas, plenty of birds, and bontebok and other antelope wandering about grazing. There is also a campsite with good washing facilities – the pitches without electricity are cheaper. $

Swellendam Backpackers 5 Lichtenstein St, Swellendam ☎ 028 514 2648, ⓦ swellendambackpackers.co.za. Centrally situated hostel with a large campsite, and decent twins and doubles. No dorms, so if you are on your own, you can have a room to yourself. Friendly staff can arrange activities including horseriding. $

Swellendam Country Lodge 237 Voortrek St, Swellendam ☎ 028 514 3629, ⓦ swellendamlodge.com. Six garden rooms with separate entrances, reed ceilings and elegant, uncluttered decor in muted hues. There's a veranda for summer days, as well as a swimming pool and well-kept garden. $$

EATING

SEE MAP PAGE 220

Note that if you stay overnight in the national park, all accommodation there is self-catering, and there is no restaurant, so stock up with ingredients in Swellendam before you arrive.

★ **La Sosta** 145 Voortrek St, Swellendam ☎ 028 514 1470, ⓦ lasostaswellendam.com. Set in a thatched and whitewashed Cape Dutch homestead dating from 1838, this elegant establishment is one of the best restaurants in the Western Cape and needs advance booking. Serving contemporary Italian food, it offers three set menus: one for fish eaters (R510), one for carnivores (R490) and one (named *Garden*) for vegetarians (R440). Tues–Sat 6.30–10pm.

Old Gaol Restaurant Church Square, 8A Voortrek St, Swellendam ☎ 028 514 3847, ⓦ oldgaolrestaurant. co.za. Committed to serving wholesome country food, this is a great place where you can try an imaginative selection of quiches, sandwiches, burgers, soups and salads by day, and a more cosmopolitan menu of tapas and mains in the evening. The outdoor play area makes it an ideal choice for anyone travelling with kids. Wed–Sat 8am–late, Sun–Tues 8am–5pm.

4

The Garden Route

Widely referred to as the **Garden Route**, the slender coastal plain that stretches for 200km between **Mossel Bay** and **Storms River Mouth** has an idyllic reputation reflected in local names such as Outeniqua (a Khoi word meaning "place of honey"), Garden of Eden, Nature's Valley and Wilderness. In most respects, this lovely region is a true paradise for outdoor enthusiasts, offering up a smorgasbord of gorgeous sandy beaches, tiny craggy coves, dense indigenous forests, assailable fynbos-covered peaks and myriad adventure and family-friendly activities. It is also punctuated by a string of unusually agreeable towns, of which the most important, starting in the west, are the semi-industrialized port of Mossel Bay, the inland metropolis of **George** (the unofficial regional capital and site of its main airport), lovely lagoonside **Knysna** and resort-like **Plettenberg Bay** with its postcard-perfect swimming beach. Paradoxically, however, while the Garden Route lends its name to one of South Africa's largest national parks, which together with a scattering of scenic smaller reserves harbours a rich birdlife and conspicuous marine fauna, the region actually offers very little in the way of conventional game viewing, the one truly worthwhile exception being the private **Gondwana Game Reserve**, a genuine Big Five safari destination situated in the hills inland of Mossel Bay.

GONDWANA AT A GLANCE

The Garden Route's premier private reserve is the only place where the Big Five thrive in a fynbos habitat.

Big Five: ****
General wildlife: ****
Birding: ****
Scenery: ****
Wilderness factor: ***
Uncrowded: ****
Affordability: **
Self-drive: N

Gondwana Game Reserve

Off the R327, 25km northwest of Mossel Bay • R300 per stay • ☎ 021 555 0807, ⓦ gondwanagr.co.za.

Rivalling Sanbona as the most rewarding safari destination in the Western Cape, **Gondwana Game Reserve** protects a scenic 120-square-kilometre tract of montane fynbos and regenerating farmland set in the shadow of the Langeberg (Long Mountains), the range that separates the fynbos biome from the Little Karoo. Less than 30 minutes' drive inland of the busy industrial port of **Mossel Bay**, this gorgeous reserve is characterized by sheer sandstone mountains and stands of around a dozen protea species, including the spectacular King protea, shrub-like suikerbos (sugarbush) and localized Mossel Bay pincushion. The reserve was forged from old farmland between 2004 and 2008, when it first opened its gates to tourists, and more than twenty species of large mammal have been introduced – including lion, elephant, buffalo, white rhino, hippo, giraffe, Burchell's zebra, greater kudu, eland and red hartebeest. It is now the only place in South Africa where the Big Five – all of which roamed the area in historic times – can be seen in a fynbos habitat, along with naturally occurring species such as leopard, caracal, black-backed jackal, bat-eared fox, large grey mongoose and Cape grysbok.

While endemic **fynbos** dominates the reserve, it is interspersed with stands of invasive flora, most conspicuously the pervasive black wattle, but the management is making great efforts to eradicate such species. A good introduction to both the indigenous fynbos and invasive aliens that have partially displaced it is provided by the guided **flora walks**, led by a botanist specializing in the flora of the Western Cape. For greater insight into the behind-the-scenes running of the reserve and its ecosystem, the three- or five-night packages out of **Gondwana Eco Camp** are highly recommended. For birders, Gondwana is an excellent place to look for fynbos endemics and other localized species such as black harrier, jackal buzzard, secretary bird, Cape sugarbird, Cape grassbird, Karoo prinia, Cape rock thrush, orange-breasted sunbird and yellow bishop.

The main activity in the reserve is guided game drives, and these come with a near certainty of encountering all the Big Five except leopard in the course of a two- to three-day visit. Active guests and those with specific interest in rare wildlife should make the effort to visit the 12-square-kilometre **Protected Endangered Species Area**, which is fenced off from the rest of the reserve to protect the likes of Cape mountain zebra, bontebok and sable antelope from the attention of lions. Five self-guided trails run through this part of the reserve, ranging in length from 2.2km to 12.5km, and are ideal for walking, trail running or cycling (mountain bikes are available from the Activity Shed at the start of the trails).

ARRIVAL AND DEPARTURE

GONDWANA GAME RESERVE

By car Coming from the west, follow the N2 east from Cape Town for about 375km to reach the R327 to Mossdustria/Herbertsdale signposted to your left. Follow the R327 for about 125km until you see the reserve signposted to your right. Fork to the right shortly afterwards and you'll reach the entrance gate after another 3km. Allow at least four hours, better five, for the drive from Cape Town.

Coming from George, follow the N2 west for about 60km, bypassing all turn-offs for Mossel Bay, and you will see the junction for the R327 to Mossdustria/Herbertsdale to your right shortly after passing an Engen One Stop to the left and Total Petroport to the right.

By air The reserve entrance gate is less than an hour's drive from George International Airport, which is serviced by several inexpensive daily flights to and from Johannesburg and Cape Town. All the major car-rental companies are represented at the airport, and the reservation office for Gondwana can also arrange chauffeured transfers.

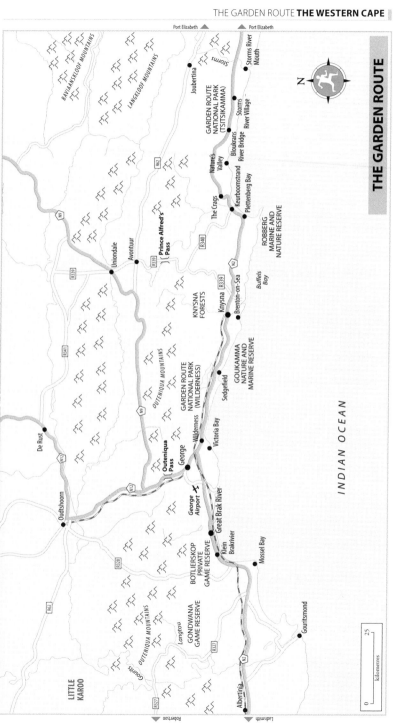

THE GARDEN ROUTE

N

Port Elizabeth

Port Elizabeth

BAVIAANSKLOOF MOUNTAINS

LANGKLOOF MOUNTAINS

Joubertina

Storms

Storms River Mouth

R62

GARDEN ROUTE NATIONAL PARK (TSITSIKAMMA)

Nature's Valley

Bloukrans River Bridge

Storms River Village

W

Keurboomstrand

The Crags

Plettenberg Bay

R340

Prince Alfred's Pass

ROBBERG MARINE AND NATURE RESERVE

Uniondale

Avontuur

R339

R340

R339

KNYSNA FORESTS

Knysna

Brenton-on-Sea

N2

Buffels Bay

R341

OUTENIQUA MOUNTAINS

W

GARDEN ROUTE NATIONAL PARK (WILDERNESS)

Sedgefield

GOUKAMMA NATURE AND MARINE RESERVE

De Rust

V112

Wilderness

Victoria Bay

Oudtshoorn

Outeniqua Pass

George

George Airport

Great Brak River

INDIAN OCEAN

Klein Brakrivier

Mossel Bay

4

R328

BOTLIERSKOP PRIVATE GAME RESERVE

Gouritsmond

Langtou

GONDWANA GAME RESERVE

R327

OUTENIQUA MOUNTAINS

Gourits

R62

LITTLE KAROO

N2

Albertinia

Robertson

Ladismith

0   25
kilometres

ACCOMMODATION

In addition to the lodges described below, several private bush and fynbos villas are scattered around the reserve. All accommodation can be booked through central reservations at ☎ 021 5550807, ✆ gondwanagr.co.za.

Gondwana Tented Eco Camp This small camp comprises five unpretentious standing tents set in a remote valley in the west of the reserve, some 30 minutes' drive on bumpy roads from the main lodge. It offers a unique participatory conservation experience that mixes conventional game drives with more specialized activities such as guided fynbos walks, excursions to clear invasive vegetation, and tracking, counting and feeding wildlife as required. Three- and five-night packages are available, all starting on a Thursday, ensuring that all guests arrive on the same day and get an opportunity to bond over activities and group meals. Although not luxurious, the standing tents are very comfortable and all come with solar-powered lighting, gas-heated showers and private deck, while communal amenities include a small swimming pool surrounded by hammocks. Rates include meals and activities. $$$$

Kwena Lodge Gondwana's flagship lodge comprises fourteen thatch-roof cottages whose unusual architecture is a modern take on traditional domed huts built by the Khoikhoi pastoralists who once inhabited the area. Arranged in a semi-circle overlooking a large, sparkling freeform swimming pool and a waterhole that regularly attracts thirsty animals, each chalet is an open-plan semi-suite with warm decor, en-suite bathroom with tub and shower, and private deck with a view. Rates include meals and activities. $$$$

GOUKAMMA AT A GLANCE

Low-key and oft-overlooked coastal gem in the heart of the Garden Route.
Big Five: N/A
General wildlife: *
Birding: *****
Scenery: ****
Wilderness factor: ***
Uncrowded: *****
Affordability: *****
Self-drive: Y

Goukamma Nature Reserve

Access from Platbank Car Park, 3km south of the N2 outside Sedgefield • Daily 7.30am–4pm • R40, free entry for overnight visitors • ☎ 044 383 0042

Goukamma Nature Reserve is an unassuming 220-square-kilometre sanctuary that protects a 14km stretch of coastline that starts near Sedgefield and stretches east to Buffels (Buffalo) Bay. The reserve's boundaries take in the freshwater Groenvlei Lake and approximately 18km of beach frontage, as well as some of the highest vegetated dunes in the country. The landscape is good for walking, as it's covered with coastal fynbos and dense thickets of milkwood, yellowwood and candlewood trees. Because of the diversity of coastal and wetland habitats, over 220 different kinds of birds have been recorded in the reserve, including African fish eagle, Knysna turaco, African black oystercatcher and several types of kingfisher. Mammals include bushbuck, Cape grysbok, mongoose, vervet monkeys, caracals and otters. Several day trails enable you to explore the reserve's different habitats on foot. They include a beach walk (4hrs one-way) traversing the 14km of crumbling cliffs and sands between Platbank on the west side of the reserve and Rowwehoek on the east; alternatively, you can go from one end of the reserve to the other via a slightly longer inland trek across the dunes. There's also a shorter circular walk from the reserve office through a milkwood forest.

DIEPWALLE AT A GLANCE

Stunning hiker-friendly forest inhabited by the Cape's last free-roaming elephant.
Big Five: None
General wildlife: *
Birding: ****
Scenery: ****
Wilderness factor: ****
Uncrowded: *****
Affordability: *****
Self-drive: Y

Diepwalle Forest

Around 20km northeast of Knysna • Daily 6am–6pm • R100 • Follow the N2 east towards Plettenberg Bay, turning left onto the R339 after 7km. Continue towards Avontuur and Uniondale for 17km until the signposted turn-off to the Diepwalle Forest Station

The best reason to come to **Knysna** – the hub town of the Garden Route – is for its **forests**, shreds of a once magnificent woodland that was home to Khoi clans and harboured a thrilling variety of wildlife, including large herds of elephants. In the early nineteenth century, the forests started to attract European explorers and naturalists, and in their wake woodcutters, gold-diggers and businessmen, all bent on making their fortunes. Two hundred years later, all that's left of the Khoi people are a few local place names, while the legendary elephants have fared little better, with recent DNA tests on dung samples collected in **Diepwalle Forest**, their last confirmed haunt, confirming it is all the excrement of one last surviving female. Despite this, Diepwalle ("deep walls") is one of the highlights of the Garden Route, renowned for its impressive density of huge trees, especially Outeniqua yellowwoods, and prolific birdlife. As for mammals, elephant sightings are very infrequent, but if you're quiet and alert, you stand a chance of seeing vervet monkeys, bushbuck and blue duiker. The best way to explore the forest is on the Elephant Walk Trail, which consists of three looped hiking routes that all start and end at **Diepwalle Forest Station**, and take about three to four hours each.

Robberg Nature Reserve

Robberg Rd, 8km southeast of central Plettenberg Bay •
Daily 8am–5pm • R50 • ⓦ capenature.co.za/reserves/robberg-nature-reserve

One of the Garden Route's nicest walks is the four-hour, 9km circular route around the sheer cliffs of **Robberg**, a spectacular peninsula that rises some 150m above the waves that crash at its rocky base. Literally translating as "Mountain of Seals", Robberg supports a 6000-strong breeding colony of **Cape fur seals** that can be seen sunning themselves on the rocks below the cliff paths, or swimming in the ocean,

ROBBERG AT A GLANCE

Cavorting seals and stunning clifftop vistas are the main draw of the country's prettiest coastal ramble.
Big Five: N/A
General wildlife: **
Birding: ***
Scenery: *****
Wilderness factor: ****
Uncrowded: ****
Affordability: *****
Self-drive: Y

sometimes alongside the **great white sharks** that feed on them. Other marine wildlife often seen from the cliffs includes dolphins Wolfberg ing through the water, Southern right whales further out in the bay (only during the breeding and calving months of June to November) and gulls, African black oystercatchers and various pelagic birds soaring overhead. If you don't have time for the full circular walk, there is a shorter two-hour hike and a thirty-minute ramble – a map is provided at the entrance gate. There is one rustic cottage, *Fountain Shack*, in which to overnight (see page 227).

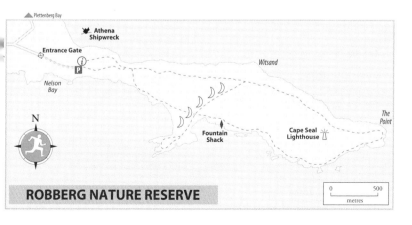

ROBBERG NATURE RESERVE

STORMS RIVER MOUTH AT A GLANCE
Stunning coastal reserve offering limited wildlife viewing but lovely walking.
Big Five: N/A
General wildlife: *
Birding: ***
Scenery: *****
Wilderness factor: *****
Uncrowded: ***
Affordability: *****
Self-drive: Y

Storms River Mouth

65km east of Plettenberg Bay • Daily 7am–7.30pm • R235 • ☎ 042 281 1607, ⊛ sanparks.org

The most dramatic estuary on this exhilarating piece of coast, **Storms River Mouth** is the focal point of Garden Route National Park's **Tsitsikamma sector**, which extends for 68km along a narrow belt of rocky coast incised by deep river gorges where ancient hardwood forests cling to the edge of tangled, green cliffs. Established in 1962, Tsitsikamma also incorporates South Africa's oldest **marine reserve**, stretching 5.5km out to sea, with an underwater trail open to snorkellers and licensed scuba divers. Storms River Mouth presents the elemental face of the Garden Route, with the dark **Storms River** surging through a tall narrow gorge to battle with the surf. Walking is the main activity here and the visitors' office at the restcamp will sort you out with maps of short, waymarked coastal trails that leave from here. Most rewarding is the 3km hike west from the restcamp, along the start of the legendary overnight **Otter Trail**, to a fantastic pool at the base of 5m-high falls. Less demanding is the kilometre-long boardwalk stroll from the restaurant to the suspension bridge to see the river mouth. On your way to the bridge, don't miss the dank strandloper (beachcomber) cave, which was frequented by hunter-gatherers between five thousand and two thousand years ago. Swimming is restricted to a safe and pristine little sandy bay below the restaurant, with a changing hut, though conditions can be cold in summer if there are easterly winds and cold upwellings of deep water from the continental shelf.

GETTING AROUND

THE GARDEN ROUTE

By air George International Airport, set on the outskirts of the Garden Route's largest town, is served by around ten daily scheduled flights from Johannesburg (2hr), as well as a couple from Cape Town (1hr). Flights from Johannesburg, operated by Kulula (⊛ kulula.com) and Mango (⊛ flymango.com), are generally very good value, but flights from Cape Town tend to be pricier. All the major car-rental companies are represented at the airport, and taxis are also available.

CeMair also runs direct flights to Plettenberg Bay's tiny airport from Johannesburg (2hr 30min) and Cape Town (1hr 15min).

By Baz Bus The Baz Bus (☎ 086 122 9287, ⊛ bazbus. com) runs between Cape Town and Port Elizabeth five times per week, and can drop passengers at any of several backpacker hostels in the region. It will carry outdoor gear, such as surfboards or mountain bikes. Although the buses take standby passengers if space permits, you should book ahead to secure a seat.

By intercity bus Intercape, Greyhound and Translux intercity buses from Cape Town and Port Elizabeth stop at Mossel Bay, George, Wilderness, Sedgefield, Knysna and Storms River (the village, not the river mouth). They are better and cheaper than the Baz Bus for more direct journeys, though buses often don't go into the towns, letting passengers off at petrol stations on the highway instead.

ACCOMMODATION

For accommodation in Gondwana, see page 224.

Botlierskop Private Game Reserve 22km from Mossel Bay ☎ 044 696 6055, ⊛ botlierskop.co.za. While there is nothing wild about it, the tented accommodation in this small reserve has a real safari atmosphere, with decks and outdoor seating from which to admire the lovely views. There's a good chance of spotting lion, rhino, elephant, giraffe and various antelope. $$$$$
Buffelsdrift Game Lodge 7km from Oudtshoorn ☎ 044 272 0106, ⊛ buffelsdrift.com. Luxurious en-suite

safari tents overlook a large dam where hippo can be seen. Breakfast – served in the grand thatched dining space – is included. Game drives or horseback rides to view rhino, buffalo, elephant, giraffe and various antelope can be added to a package or paid for separately. There are lions, too, but they are tame and live within a small enclosure. $$$
Fairy Knowe Backpackers 6km from Wilderness ☎ 044 877 1285, ⊛ wildernessbackpackers.com. Built in 1897, this is the oldest home in the area, and it features a wraparound balcony. It's set in quiet woodlands on the

THE OTTER AND DOLPHIN TRAILS

South Africa's flagship hike, the **Otter Trail** is a simply magnificent five-day, 42km trail that follows a pristine stretch of coastline and forest – there's no habitation or vehicle access – through the Tsitsikamma sector of Garden Route National Park. It starts at Storms River Mouth and ends at Nature's Valley, and the maximum number of people on the trail is twelve. It is geared to locals in a group, but if you're desperate to do it and have been told it is full, keep checking the website for cancellations. You need to be fit for the steep sections, and an experienced hiker – you carry everything from hut to hut and have to be able to manage river crossings. Book through South African National Parks at least twelve months in advance (R302 per person; ☎012 428 911, ⓦsanparks.org).

The luxury portered counterpart to the Otter Trail, the **Dolphin Trail** uses comfortable accommodation and is suited to those holidaying solo without their own gear. It passes through breathtaking terrain in the Tsitsikamma Sector, and habitats incorporate forest as well as coast. It starts at Storms River Mouth and ends at Sandrif River Mouth, covering a distance of 20km over three and a half days. The price (R7050 per person) includes food, accommodation and permits, a guide, a boat trip up the Storms River Gorge and a 4WD through the Storms River Pass: book through the Fernery (☎042 280 3588, ⓦdolphintrail.co.za).

Touw River lagoon, and makes a great base for forest walks, despite being some distance from the sea. Note that during peak season it gets busy and can be very noisy at the bar. The Baz Bus drops off here. $\overline{\underline{S}}$

★ **Forest Edge Cottages** Rheenendal turn-off, 16km west of Knysna on the N2 ☎082 456 1338, ⓦforest edge.co.za. Ideal if you want to be close to the forest, these traditional two-bedroom woodcutters' cottages have verandas built in the vernacular tin-roofed style. Both cottages are private and romantic, with interiors that have been upgraded for extra comfort with good linen and fittings. Forest walks and cycling trails start from the cottages, from where you can walk to rock pools and waterfalls. A minimum stay of two nights is required. $\overline{\underline{S}}$–$\overline{\underline{SS}}$

Fountain Shack Robberg Nature Reserve ☎021 483 0190, ⓦcapenature.co.za/reserves/robberg-nature-reserve. A remote bungalow sleeping eight; there is no electricity but the setting by the ocean is beautiful. *Fountain Shack* is the only accommodation in the reserve with no vehicle access – it's a 2hr walk to get here. Linen, cooking facilities and cutlery are provided, so just bring your own food. $\overline{\underline{S}}$

Goukamma Nature Reserve There are two fully equipped bush camps on the Groenvlei side of Goukamma reserve, and three thatched rondavels on the east side; all can be booked through CapeNature (☎021 483 0000, ⓦcapenature.co.za). $\overline{\underline{S}}$

Knysna Backpackers 42 Queen St, Knysna ☎044 382 2554, ⓦknysnabackpackers.co.za. Spotless, well-organized hostel in a large, rambling and centrally located Victorian house that has been declared a National Monument. This tranquil establishment has five rooms rented as doubles (but able to sleep up to four people) and a dorm that sleeps eight. It's also on the Baz Bus route. $\overline{\underline{S}}$

Old Trading Post 1km off the N2 east of Wilderness ☎044 882 1207, ⓦoldtradingpost.co.za. Boasting an attractive location close to Island Lake, this characterful owner-managed lodge offers great birdwatching and occupies a wide-balconied century-old building that started life as a general dealer store until it closed in the 1970s. There are three double rooms in the main building as well as a separate cottage and a lovely rustic tented camp, both sleeping up to four. Great value. $\overline{\underline{S}}$

★ **Storms River Mouth Restcamp** ☎042 281 1607, ⓦsanparks.org. Sited on tended lawns, this restcamp is poised between a craggy shoreline of black rocks, pounded by foamy white surf, and steeply raking forested cliffs. It has a variety of accommodation options, none outstanding, but all with sea views and the ever-present sound of the surging surf. Two units have disabled access. Advance booking is essential. The restaurant (daily 8.30am–10pm) has such startling views that it can be forgiven for its mediocre fare and its indifferent service. Camping and forest hut $\overline{\underline{S}}$, chalet $\overline{\underline{SS}}$

★ **Teniqua Treetops** 23km northeast of Sedgefield ☎044 356 2868, ⓦteniquatreetops.co.za. Well positioned for exploring Goukamma Nature Reserve, this retreat stands beneath boughs of virgin forest between Sedgefield and Knysna, on a property with 4km of woodland walks and a river with pools for swimming. Luxury tents are raised on timber decks, and one unit is wheelchair accessible. As well as being a chilled-out hideout, this is a great example of sustainable living in practice: no trees were felled to build *Teniqua*; recycled materials were used where possible; water is gravity fed; showers are solar-heated; and toilets use a dry composting system. $\overline{\underline{SS}}$

Wilderness Bushcamp Heights Rd, Wilderness ☎044 877 1168, ⓦwildernessbushcamp.co.za. Six self-catering timber units with loft bedrooms, thatched roofs and ocean views. The camp, set on a hillside amid fynbos wilderness, is part of a conservation estate where you're free to roam around. $\overline{\underline{S}}$

The Eastern Cape

DIE TUISHUISE, CRADOCK

5 The Eastern Cape

Sandwiched between the Western Cape and KwaZulu-Natal (South Africa's two most popular coastal provinces), the Eastern Cape is relatively neglected by international visitors. For anyone wanting to get off the beaten track, however, this underrated province – South Africa's second largest – offers a diverse array of rewarding travel opportunities. The 1000km coastline alone, sweeping back inland in immense undulations of vegetated dunefields, justifies a visit. More pertinently, the Eastern Cape also now ranks as one of the country's key malaria-free safari destinations, supporting a trio of national parks and a burgeoning collection of private reserves at the eastern terminus of the popular self-drive route between Cape Town and Port Elizabeth via the Garden Route.

An amalgamation of what were formerly the Xhosa homelands of the Transkei and Ciskei with the eastern part of the Cape Province, the **EASTERN CAPE** came into being in April 1994 (the same month that saw its most famous son, Transkei-born Nelson Mandela, swept to power in South Africa's first democratic election). Few then would have thought of the newly created province as a budding safari destination. Admittedly, it housed two of South Africa's oldest national parks in the form of Addo Elephant and Mountain Zebra, both then focused mainly on the conservation of a single eponymous species, while the pioneering **Shamwari Private Game Reserve** had opened its doors to visitors two years earlier. Elsewhere, however, the massive herds of black wildebeest, springbok and quagga (an extinct subspecies of plains zebra) that once roamed the plains south of the Orange River had long since been hunted out by European settlers, partly as sport, partly to make way for livestock. Indeed, the most recent reports of several iconic large mammals in the Eastern Cape dated back longer than a century – the last documented wild lion was shot in 1879, the last cheetah in 1889, the last black rhino in 1885, and so on.

All that has changed. **Addo Elephant National Park**, vastly expanded since 1994, is now a fully fledged Big Five self-drive safari destination. **Mountain Zebra National Park**, another great self-drive destination, is also home to reintroduced lion and cheetah, the latter the subject of thrilling daily tracking excursions with experienced rangers. Furthermore, following the ecological and commercial success of Shamwari, large swathes of former farmland have been bought up by conservation-minded souls and converted to private reserves such as **Kwandwe**, **Samara**, **Amakhala** and **Kariega**. Today, these private sanctuaries offer visitors an all-inclusive five-star guided safari experience that offers a good chance of spotting lion, rhino, buffalo, elephant, cheetah, giraffe, warthog, zebra and up to a dozen antelope including the hefty eland, the endemic black wildebeest and the incomparably graceful greater kudu.

Of all South Africa's key wildlife-viewing regions, the Eastern Cape is by far the most convenient, time-efficient and cost-effective to first-time safarigoers whose itinerary is otherwise focused on **Cape Town** and the Western Cape. Coming from the **Garden Route**, you can drive through to any of the Eastern Cape's national parks or main private reserves in a long half-day, then – once your safari is complete – fly directly out of the provincial capital Port Elizabeth to connect with your international flight in Cape Town or Johannesburg. The Eastern Cape is also more **family friendly** than most safari destinations, and totally free of malaria. In summer, the main tourist season, its relatively temperate climate is also more agreeable than the searing heat that tends to characterize more northerly safari destinations such as the Kruger, Madikwe and northern KwaZulu-Natal.

BROWN HOODED KINGFISHER, KARIEGA GAME RESERVE

Highlights

❶ Addo Elephant National Park The premier public reserve in the southern half of the country offers self-drivers the opportunity to see elephants and the rest of the Big Five in malaria-free surrounds. See page 235

❷ Shamwari Private Game Reserve Opened in 1992, this pioneering reserve still offers the best general game viewing in the Eastern Cape, and the setting is lovely. See page 246

❸ Sibuya Game Reserve Reached by a magical boat trip, this spectacular reserve is notable as much for its verdant mountainous scenery and insanely good birding as for the opportunity to see the Big Five. See page 251

❹ Kwandwe Private Game Reserve Of all the region's private reserves, Kwandwe offers the best compromise between Big Five sightings and a genuine wilderness feel. See page 254

❺ Mountain Zebra National Park Another great self-drive destination, this small national park preserves a wide range of regional endemics, from the Cape mountain zebra to the comical black wildebeest. See page 258

❻ Samara Private Game Reserve Close-up cheetah encounters, all the Big Five and unusually low tourist volumes in the panoramic landscape of the Karoo semi-desert that sweeps across South Africa's interior. See page 266

HIGHLIGHTS ARE MARKED ON THE MAP ON PAGE 232

5

Negatives? Well, in the core winter months of June to August, the Eastern Cape does tend to be rather chilly, with temperatures often dropping below freezing after dark, making for pretty arduous night drives. This might justifiably put off cold-blooded visitors seeking a fix of tropical sunshine, but for repeat safarigoers who pack plenty of warm clothing, the cold weather also coerces nocturnal creatures such as aardwolf, aardvark, bat-eared fox and porcupine into a more crepuscular foraging routine, greatly increasing the odds of spotting these oddities on late afternoon and early morning drives. For those seeking a full hand of the Big Five, the Cape leopard, though widespread, tends to be very furtive and is far less likely to be seen than its habituated counterparts in the Greater Kruger. Finally, the relatively recent conversion of most of

the region's reserves from farmland means that evidence of human activity – fences, telephone lines, trunk roads and so on – is seldom far out of eyeshot, and most lack the deep wilderness feel associated with larger and older conservation areas.

When it comes to planning your time in the region, Addo Elephant National Park should be the focal point for budget-conscious travellers, whether they explore it on an organized day-trip from a nearby backpackers or lodge, or they drive themselves around the main game-viewing circuit. Two nights would be sufficient to explore the main circuit, but a longer stay would increase the odds of seeing more elusive species such as black rhino, lion and leopard, or you could use it to explore the park's more far-flung sectors. For visitors with a more generous budget, we would recommend either a

HIGHLIGHTS

1 Addo Elephant National Park
2 Shamwari Game Reserve
3 Sibuya Game Reserve
4 Kwandwe Private Game Reserve
5 Mountain Zebra National Park
6 Samara Private Game Reserve

5

ALBANY THICKET

All but unique to the Eastern Cape, the **Albany thicket** ecoregion comprises a dense cover of low spiny scrubland associated with deep and well-drained sandy soils in the Great Fish, Sundays and Gamtoos river valleys, all of which are characterized by high daytime and annual temperature ranges, and low and sporadic non-seasonal rainfall (around 300–450mm per annum). The name Albany thicket dates to the early nineteenth century and refers to an obsolete administrative district centred on the city of **Makhanda** (Grahamstown); prior to this the earliest Dutch visitors named it Zuurveld (sour bush) and it is also known as Spekboom succulent thicket after its most characteristic plant. Together with the fynbos biome concentrated in the Western Cape, Albany thicket forms part of the **Cape Floristic Region**, which is by far the smallest and most vulnerable of the world's six floral kingdoms.

Albany thicket boasts a high level of **floral endemism**. It supports more than sixty plant species found in no other ecoregion, with Euphorbias (cactus-like succulents that secrete a sticky milky latex and often attain tree-like dimensions) being particularly well represented, along with geophytes (bulbed plants) of the genera *Cyrtanthus*, *Albuca* and *Ornithogallum*. By contrast, Albany thicket supports a relatively low faunal diversity and few endemic animals. Six reptile species are known to be endemic to the ecoregion, which also forms the core range of two types of bird (orange-breasted sunbird and Cape siskin) and the near-endemic Duthie's golden mole. Typical larger wildlife includes medium-small antelope such as bushbuck, grey rhebok, mountain reedbuck, cape grysbok and common duiker, and it also provides ideal conditions for greater kudu and to a lesser extent eland, buffalo and elephant.

The dominant shrub in Albany thicket is the **spekboom** *Portulacuria afra*, a soft-wooded evergreen succulent that typically stands around 2–2.5 metres high but can grow slightly taller. The plump waxy leaves of the spekboom form an important component in the diet of Addo's elephants, greater kudus and other browsers, since they are highly nutritious and store a high volume of water. The leaf is also edible to humans, and it can be used as a salad ingredient, though contrary to the Afrikaans name (literally "bacon tree") it has a sour lemony flavour. The spekboom is notable for its high carbon-storage capability. Indeed, despite its scrubby appearance and arid living conditions, a spekboom thicket can sequester atmospheric carbon at a rate similar to an equivalent-sized bloc of moist subtropical forest. In addition, the spekboom's ability to sprout a new plant from fallen pieces, without irrigation or other human interference, makes it ideally suited to the restoration of former farmland and other areas of degraded bush.

Since the early nineteenth century, roughly fifty percent of the Eastern Cape's original cover of Albany thicket has been **cleared** to make way for stock farming or agriculture. Elsewhere, it is often badly degraded, with spekboom in particular being highly vulnerable to goats, which (unlike most wild browsers) tend to forage on the basal strata, negating the plant's capacity to regenerate itself from fallen or trampled branches. The most significant surviving Albany thicket is protected within Addo Elephant National Park, and much of this remains in near-pristine condition. Most of the region's private reserves, despite having been converted from farmland during or since the 1990s, still incorporate significant stands of thicket, usually on steep hillsides or in riverine valleys. Nevertheless, this small ecoregion is regarded to be **highly endangered**, thanks to ongoing land pressure exerted by farmers, and the fact that it would take several hundred years for cleared land to be restored to a mature thicket community.

three-night stay at one of the region's many worthwhile private reserves, or a four-night stay split evenly between Addo and a private reserve. As for which private reserve to choose, that will depend greatly on your individual budget and priorities, but all those covered in this chapter have their merits.

Addo Elephant National Park

Entrance gate to Addo Main Camp 70km north of Port Elizabeth off the R335; Mathyolweni entrance to Colchester sector (at the southern end of the game-viewing circuit) only 40km northeast of Port Elizabeth off the N2 • Daily 7am–7pm • R307 • ☎ 042 233 8600 (reception), ⓦ sanparks.org/parks/addo

The Eastern Cape's most popular wildlife attraction, **Addo Elephant National Park** is South Africa's third-largest national park, running inland for 1642 square kilometres from the Indian Ocean east of Port Elizabeth to the Zuurberg Mountains and southern Karoo. Its biodiversity encompasses five of South Africa's seven terrestrial biomes (most importantly subtropical thicket, but also forest, grassland, fynbos and Nama-Karoo) along with the southern hemisphere's largest and least degraded coastal dunefields, extending over 158 square kilometres, at Alexandria. For most casual visitors, the main attraction of this **malaria-free** park is the presence of all the Big Five, with elephant and to a lesser extent buffalo and lion being particularly conspicuous. It also supports a wide variety of antelope and small carnivores, along with a total of around 420 bird species. Serviced by several affordable restcamps and lodges, it also boasts a well-maintained and extensive network of surfaced and unsurfaced game-viewing roads ideally suited to self-drive safaris.

Elephants are the star attraction of Addo. Arguably the most fascinating of the sociable large mammals, these charismatic heavyweights can be easily observed at close quarters. You might stumble across a pair of youngsters playing push-me-pull-you in the road metres in front of your car, a giant bull stretching its trunk across the bonnet to reach a juicy branch, or a large breeding herd filling the air with its distinctive earthy and somewhat flatulent elephantine aroma as it slakes its thirst at a waterhole. Addo's elephants are reliably entertaining, and exceptionally habituated, but do take note that they should always be treated with due respect – overstep the boundaries of a male in musth, or a protective mother with a newborn calf, and it is fully capable of overturning a car. Elephants and other Big Fivers aside, the statuesque greater kudu is abundant, while other mammal species to look out for on the main game-viewing circuit include eland, bushbuck, red hartebeest, Burchell's zebra, warthog and predators such as spotted hyena, black-backed jackal and the delightful yellow mongoose and meerkat.

Tourist development in Addo is largely focused on the **Main Game Viewing Area**, comprising the original pre-1997 elephant enclosure (now known as Addo Main Camp) and adjacent Colchester Sector (with which fences were dropped in 2010). These conjoined sectors account for slightly less than one-third of the park's terrestrial area but contain almost all its public roads. But while the vast majority of visitors confine their exploration of Addo to this Main Game Viewing Area, the more rugged and northwesterly Nyathi, Zuurberg, Kabouga and Darlington Dam sectors also offer some intriguing opportunities to adventurous hikers and 4WD-enthusiasts. Further southeast, the disjunct Woody Cape Sector protects a combination of lush coastal forest and tall dunefields traversed by the legendary Alexandria Hiking Trail. Finally, the marine sector offers fine whale-watching, while a trio of offshore islands host the world's largest breeding colony of Cape gannets (120,000 birds), as well as significant numbers of Cape fur seal, African penguin and other marine species.

Brief history

Middens in the Alexandria Dunefields containing fragments of shellfish, pottery and Stone-age tools indicate that the area has been inhabited by small **strandloper** (beachcomber) hunter-gatherer

---

ADDO AT A GLANCE

Elephants are the stars of Addo, but plenty of other wildlife inhabits the south coast's top self-drive Big Five destination.

Big Five: ***
General wildlife: ****
Birding: ***
Scenery: ***
Wilderness factor: **
Uncrowded: ***
Affordability: *****
Self-drive: Y

5

communities for at least five thousand years. More recent middens containing cattle bones suggest that the pastoralist Khoikhoi arrived here at least two thousand years back and were probably the dominant inhabitants of the coastal belt prior to the outbreak of a killer **smallpox epidemic** in 1713. This opened the way for some settlement by the Xhosa, who traditionally lived further east, but the main long-term beneficiaries were Dutch and later English settlers. When William Paterson crossed the Sundays River only 10km from present-day Addo in 1779, he reported "great numbers of quadrupeds, such as lions, panthers, elephants, rhinoceroses, buffaloes, springbucks, etc." A century later, the wildlife was practically all gone, and the fertile Sundays River around Addo supported a thriving **agricultural industry** dominated by oranges and other citrus fruits.

Following a largely successful campaign to eradicate what was then South Africa's largest surviving elephant population from the dense Addo thicket east of the Sundays River, a small municipal **sanctuary** to protect the last dozen individual survivors was set aside in 1921 and gazetted as a 22-square-kilometre **national park** ten years later (see page 239). The national park was gradually expanded through the acquisition of private farmland to accommodate the growing elephant population, and the first self-drive tourists were permitted to explore it as recently as 1980. At this time, however, Addo – like the nearby Mountain Zebra and Bontebok national parks – still existed primarily to conserve a single endangered species that had been driven close to local extinction in the early twentieth century.

That all changed in 1997, when SANParks accepted a visionary proposal to create a **Greater Addo Elephant National Park** (GAENP) linking the arid northern Karoo to the Indian Ocean coastline. The initial rate of progress in realizing this vision was little short of astonishing. Within a decade, the national park boundaries were extended to embrace a not-quite-contiguous 1642-square-kilometre tract of land stretching southeast from the Karoo around Darlington Dam to a 46km stretch of coast that incorporated the immense Alexandria dunefields. It is hoped that future acquisitions of thinly populated

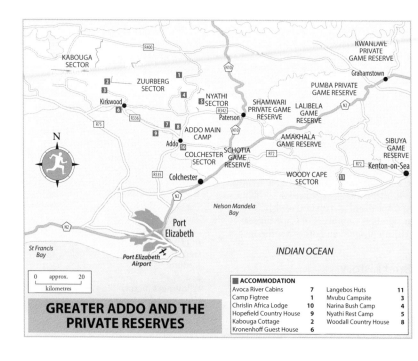

■ ACCOMMODATION			
Avoca River Cabins	7	Langebos Huts	11
Camp Figtree	1	Mvubu Campsite	3
Chrislin Africa Lodge	10	Narina Bush Camp	4
Hopefield Country House	9	Nyathi Rest Camp	5
Kabouga Cottage	2	Woodall Country House	8
Kronenhoff Guest House	6		

GREATER ADDO AND THE PRIVATE RESERVES

Karoo ranches, together with the formal incorporation of an already proclaimed offshore Marine Protected Area running east from Port Elizabeth to Alexandria, will increase the total area of the GAENP to between 3500 and 5000 square kilometres.

The **expansion** of Addo's boundaries solved an overpopulation problem that would have been inconceivable in 1931. By the late 1990s, the elephant density within the main fenced reserve stood at three individuals per square kilometre, and without intervention this figure might easily have doubled by now. Instead, the authorities have undertaken a series of territory-expanding relocations, the first being the removal of 56 elephants from the Nyathi Sector in 2003 and the most recent the transfer of 27 elephants to the Darlington Dam sector in 2018. In addition, the size of the core game-viewing area doubled in 2010 when fences between Addo Main Camp and the more southerly 240-square-kilometre Colchester section were dropped, bringing their range to within a tantalising five kilometres of the beach.

In addition to elephants, Addo has always contained a healthy population of buffalo (some thirty individuals were fenced in together with the elephants back in 1931) and small numbers of typically secretive leopard. Black rhinos, once common in the Addo thicket, were introduced to the park in 1961, but since these first individuals belonged to the larger East African subspecies, they were replaced with a South African-sourced population in 1977, in keeping with SANParks policy of limiting introductions in national parks to naturally occurring taxa. In October 2003, Addo became a fully fledged **Big Five** reserve following the translocation of two prides of three lions apiece from the Kgalagadi Transfrontier Park. Predator diversity was further boosted by the reintroduction of spotted hyenas from Madikwe and Kruger over 2003–4. And while the reintroduction of lions in particular might be perceived to be a sop to tourism, the reality is that Addo had long been ecologically compromised by the low ratio of large predator to ungulates, and the presence of lions and hyenas has restored the natural balance.

Game drives and activities

Addo Rest Camp

A good place to start your exploration of the park, especially if you arrive in the middle of a hot summer day, is the **Ulwazi Interpretive Centre** opposite the *Rest Camp*'s restaurant and shop. Opened in 2010, this facility includes informative displays about the park's geology, the area's original Khoikhoi and Xhosa inhabitants, and unusual wildlife such as the flightless dung beetle, all overlooked by a cast of the head of Hapoor (the dominant elephant bull over 1944–68) and accompanied by noises emanating from a booth where you can listen to various animal calls. Next to the interpretive centre, a shady picnic site and viewing deck overlooks a small waterhole that is usually attended by a few greater kudus and more occasionally attracts elephants. Opposite this, a photographic hide stands alongside a reedy wetland where brightly coloured red bishops nest in summer. Also situated within the *Rest Camp*, the wheelchair-friendly PPC Discovery Trail – 1.8 kilometres long, but with shorter variations – provides an excellent open-air introduction to the park's vegetation, with display panels illustrating some common species, as well as a good opportunity to spot birds and possibly small antelope.

Game drives

The most popular and rewarding game-viewing roads traverse the far north of **Addo Main Camp**, running south or southeast of *Addo Rest Camp* as far as Spekboom Hide and Jack's Picnic Site. For those with limited time, the most reliable route for elephant sightings, easily covered in two to three hours, runs east from the restcamp to **Domkrag Dam** then south along the **Gorah Loop** and back north via **Carol's Rest Waterhole**. It is worth stopping at the viewpoint over Domkrag Dam, as it often supports a wide variety of waterfowl (look out for South African shelduck, red-knobbed coot, common

5

THE ELEPHANTS OF ADDO

In June 1919, a local municipality contracted the veteran hunter **Major P.J. Pretorius** to undertake what must surely rank among the most ambitious **vermin-eradication** schemes of all time: the extermination of the small, relict population of elephants in the Addo thicket inland of Port Elizabeth. The task came with a substantial element of risk, as Pretorius regularly followed panicked herds or wounded individuals deep into the dense bush. But by late 1920, when the job was declared done, the future of Addo's elephants looked very bleak. More than 115 elephants fell to Pretorius's gun in the space of fourteen months, and the survivors numbered fewer than twenty, many seriously wounded. The cull undertaken by Pretorius is often cited as the beginning of the story of **Addo Elephant National Park**, but it might as easily be remembered as the closing act in another unhappier saga – one in which South Africa's formerly prodigious elephant population was hunted to within a tusk's length of extinction.

Elephants were first documented on South African soil by the Portuguese navigator Vasco da Gama on his pioneering 1497 voyage around the Cape. We can only guess at how many elephants would have roamed what later became the Cape Province in Da Gama's day, but estimates climb as high as 100,000. These numbers went into a steady but undramatic decline following the European settlement of the Cape in 1652, mostly as a result of casual hunting in the vicinity of new habitations. The subsequent and more dramatic decline in elephant numbers is attributable to an insatiable international **demand for ivory**. In the early nineteenth century, export figures suggest that professional hunters operating to the south of the Zambezi were shooting elephants at an astonishing rate of up to 50,000 individuals annually. By 1919, South Africa harboured just four vestigial elephant populations – a paltry tally of at most two hundred individuals – of which only the 25-strong herd that ranged between the Shingwedzi and Olifants rivers (incorporated into the Kruger National Park in 1926) and the estimated 130 individuals in the Addo area could be regarded as viable.

That an isolated elephant population survived in Addo into the twentieth century pays ample testament to the impenetrability of its natural cover, which in non-degraded form comprises a 2.5m high tangle of thorny thicket dominated by the **spekboom**. Unfortunately, from the elephants' perspective, a contributory factor to the inhospitality of the Addo bush is its semi-arid character, unpredictable rainfall and lack of perennial water sources. So it was that in times of **drought**, the elephants of Addo were forced to leave the thicket at night and range out onto the nearby Sundays River valley to quench their thirst. And much to the ire of local citrus farmers, these parched nocturnal visitors also took the opportunity to supplement their leafy diet with oranges and tasty agricultural titbits.

Elephant-caused crop damage precipitated the **cull of 1919–20**, which having come close

---

moorhen and black crake) and has a reputation for being a popular watering point for lions. Scan the plains to its southeast with binoculars and you might well also pick up some of the spotted hyena and black-backed jackal that den in this part of the park, or an elephant herd or solitary bull foraging in the distance. Domkrag, incidentally, is the Afrikaans word for a car jack, the nickname of a now-deceased 60kg leopard tortoise that lived in the area and habitually crawled underneath vehicles (his shell is now on display in the interpretive centre).

Elephants can be surprisingly difficult to locate in the dense, dry, prickly thicket that covers much of the main game-viewing circuit, especially after rain, when they tend to stick to the thickest bush, and you might go an entire game drive without seeing one. Most days, however, you can expect to encounter several herds along the Gorah Loop, sometimes recognizable only as large grey backs moving quietly through the thicket, at other times marching openly across tracts of grassland, or congregating at waterholes to drink. The Gorah Loop passes through a few areas of grassland where you can expect to see large grazers such as Burchell's zebra, red hartebeest and eland, and with a bit more luck might even encounter a black rhino. Look out, too, for warthogs trotting off with tails held stiffly erect, yellow mongooses surveying their surrounds on their hind legs, and grassland birds such as Denham's bustard, black-headed heron, pied starling and Cape longclaw.

to eliminating what was then South Africa's largest remaining elephant population, came with a neat little twist insofar as it was none other than Major Pretorius who in 1921 persuaded the local authorities to set aside a small area of farmland as a sanctuary for the few remaining elephants. The unfenced reserve had little meaning except on paper prior to 1931, when it was gazetted as Addo Elephant National Park, and the new warden **Stephen Trollope** created a permanent waterhole within its boundaries, then used fires and beaters to herd the last eleven survivors – a twelfth had to be shot during the operation – into their officially sanctioned home.

For the first two decades of its existence, the national park's future hung in the balance. No fence, electric or otherwise, was adequate to contain Addo's elephants, nor for that matter did daily feeding sessions of oranges and oats, introduced in 1933, dissuade them from the occasional foray onto neighbouring farmland, where several individuals were shot. Only in 1954, following the completion of an elephant-proof fence designed by warden **Graham Armstrong**, was the original 22-square-kilometre elephant enclosure more-or-less secure.

In 1954, Addo's elephant population stood at twenty, a modest increase on the 1931 figure. Since then, however, it has maintained a steady annual growth rate of around six percent. In 1979, the population finally topped the century mark, and by 2003 it stood at 415. Up until the late 1960s, Addo's elephants – led by a legendarily misanthropic bull nicknamed Hapoor (literally "Nicked Ear", in reference to a minor injury caused by a misdirected bullet) – were notoriously elusive and aggressive towards the humans that had persecuted them for generations. By 1980, however, Addo's inhabitants were sufficiently dedramatized for their enclosure to be opened to private game drives – today, they must rank as among most relaxed and habituated elephants anywhere in Africa.

Noted for their relatively small stature and tuskless females, the elephants of Addo were once thought to belong to a different subspecies to their more northerly kin, while their relative hairiness led some researchers to postulate a closer genetic affiliation to the west-central African forest race than the more widespread savannah race. Recent genetic studies have demonstrated that neither theory is accurate, which perhaps shouldn't have come as a surprise, bearing in mind that the isolation of Addo's elephants is a modern phenomenon. In fact, the population, which has increased forty-fold in seventy years, is bound to be consistently bottom-heavy with younger and smaller individuals, while the dozen survivors of two centuries of ivory hunting might be expected to be less than spectacularly endowed in the tusk department. These genetic affiliations established, Addo's elephants were joined by eight bulls introduced from the Kruger National Park in 2003 in an attempt to broaden a gene pool bottlenecked through a mere six sexually active individuals in the 1930s. The reintroduced bulls have settled in splendidly and the park's burgeoning elephant population now stands at more than seven hundred individuals.

With time to spare, you could extend a half-day game drive west to loop past Janwal Pan, Hapoor Dam, Rooi Dam and Gwarrie Pan. The thicket in this area supports a dense population of greater kudu, including some impressively horned old males, as well as the less conspicuous bushbuck and common duiker. Lions and elephants might be seen around any of the pans and waterholes, and the area is a favoured haunt of buffalo. There's no better place to see the bokmakierie, an endemic species of bush-shrike with predominantly yellow feathering and a habit of calling loudly from open perches, while other common birds include pale chanting goshawk, common fiscal, southern tchagra and southern boubou. Often encountered crossing the road pushing a ball of dung several times its own body weight, the flightless dung beetle is an Eastern Cape endemic whose life cycle is dependent on the availability of the elephant (and to a lesser extent rhino or buffalo) dung in which it lays its eggs.

Just south of Hapoor Dam, Spekboom Hide (next to the eponymous tented camp), reached via a short footpath through a tangle of spekboom thicket, overlooks a small waterhole that often attracts a good variety of birds. The nearby Jack's Picnic Site is an agreeable place to stop for a leg stretch and toilet break. The picnic site is named after the first black rhino to be introduced to the national park, a male from Kenya that arrived in 1961, and often frequented the clearing where it now stands. The site now sits within a 5-square-kilometre experimental botanical reserve that has been fenced off to help monitor the impact of elephants on similar subtropical thicket in the rest of the park.

Most visitors confine their exploration of Addo to the northern circuit described above, but it is worth continuing south past Jack's Picnic Site onto the **Colchester Sector**. True, game viewing here tends to be more hit and miss than it is further north, but the wilderness feel and lovely scenery – capped by occasional oceanic views to Algoa Bay – do much to compensate. The steep thicketed slopes of Colchester are studded with impressive giant euphorbia trees and smoothly rounded termite hills, while the grassy valleys support herds of grazing Burchell's zebra and red hartebeest, along with large ground birds such as ostrich, secretary bird and blue crane.

For self-drivers who'd like some assistance with navigating around the park, "hop-on" local **guides** (R240 per two hours) are available at *Addo Rest Camp* reception to direct visitors to the best places to find game. *Addo Rest Camp* is also the booking and start point for two-hour guided game drives (R389/person) by open 4WD, which stand higher off the ground than a normal sedan to improve viewing opportunities. These depart at 6am (summer only), 7am (winter only), 9am, noon and 3pm. Sundowner drives (R535/person, including drinks & snacks) depart at 4pm in winter and 6pm in summer. Guided night drives (R414/person) are particularly worthwhile for the opportunity to spot nocturnal carnivores; these leave at 6pm in winter and 8pm in summer. For those staying outside the park, most lodges listed (see page 244) offer full-day excursions including a picnic or braai lunch; rates are typically around R1250–1550 per person.

Other sectors

Nyathi

Home to all the Big Five, **Nyathi** lies on the north side of the R335, more-or-less directly opposite *Addo Main Camp*. Road access is limited, but it is home to a four-star restcamp and upmarket concession lodge. Escorted horserides into Nyathi are offered at *Addo Rest Camp* at extremely low prices (R535–575/person), but only to experienced riders – you need to be able to gallop in case of danger from wildlife. The horseback excursions set out daily at 8.30am and 2pm and advance booking by phone is required (☎042 233 8621).

Zuurberg

Protecting a mountainous wilderness area that rises to an elevation of 936 metres, the beautiful **Zuurberg** sector supports a diverse mosaic of grassland, thicket and forested ravines run through by babbling streams. Endemic plants include the glossy-leaved, purple-flowered Zuurberg hunchback and the prehistoric-looking Zuurberg cycad, which stands up to 3m tall and boasts the largest cones (up to 35kg) of any species in the genus, while flowering aloes and proteas attract the lovely malachite sunbird and endemic Cape sugarbird. Zuurberg is only accessible on foot or horseback, and large mammals are relatively thin on the ground, but eland, red hartebeest and Cape mountain zebra are all likely to be seen. Because there's no dangerous wildlife, novices as well as experienced riders can take one- to five-hour horseback excursions into Zuurberg (R535–575/person), or the overnight horse trail that ends at *Narina Bush Camp* (R660), though you'll need a head for heights on the longer trails and advance booking by phone is required (☎042 233 8621). Two self-guided circular day hikes, the 2.4km Cycad Trail and 12km Doringnek Trail, lead into the mountains from the entrance gate, which lies about 20km north of *Addo Rest Camp* right alongside the R335.

Kabouga

As with Zuurberg, this mountainous sector is notable more for its scenery than large numbers of wildlife. The only road traversing **Kabouga** is a ruggedly beautiful 4WD trail that can be explored from *Mvubu Campsite* or *Kabouga Cottage*, with the option of

5

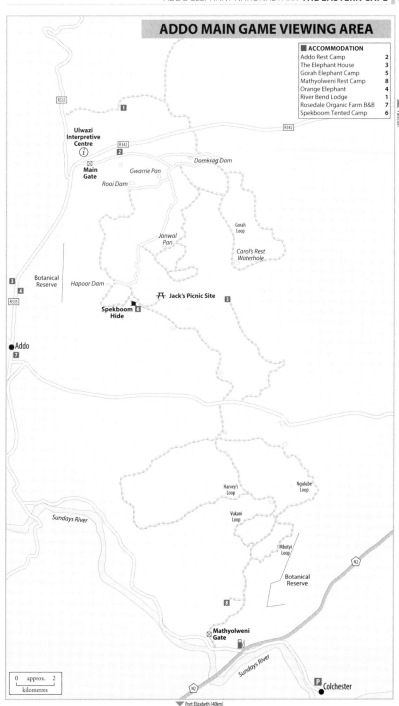

ADDO MAIN GAME VIEWING AREA

ACCOMMODATION

Addo Rest Camp	2
The Elephant House	3
Gorah Elephant Camp	5
Mathyolweni Rest Camp	8
Orange Elephant	4
River Bend Lodge	1
Rosedale Organic Farm B&B	7
Spekboom Tented Camp	6

5

continuing all the way to Darlington Dam. The entrance gate stands outside the small town of Kirkwood, 40km west of *Addo Rest Camp* on the R336.

Darlington Dam

Incorporated into Addo in 2000, **Darlington Dam** is the park's largest sector at 450 square kilometres, and it protects a tract of semi-arid Karoo scrub centred on a large irrigation dam constructed on the Sundays River shortly after World War I. Typical Karoo wildlife includes black wildebeest, springbok and gemsbok, and the sector – which supports Addo's only cheetah population – became a Big Five area following the translocation of a 27-strong elephant herd in the summer of 2018. The entrance gate lies 135km from *Addo Rest Camp* via the R335 and R400, but the limited internal road network is only really suited to 4WDs and forms an extension of the 4WD Trail through the Kabouga sector.

Woody Cape

Originally protected as the Alexandria State Forest in 1896, Addo's breathtakingly beautiful **Woody Cape** sector incorporates a 50km tract of deserted Eastern Cape beachfront flanked by the largest and most pristine **dunefield** in the southern hemisphere, with a magnificent swathe of evergreen indigenous forest set on fossil dunes further inland. The tallest of the golden dunes rises to 140 metres, while the forested relics set within Alexandria Forest attain a maximum altitude of 350 metres. Notable for its giant Outeniqua yellowwoods and scarlet-flowered coral trees, the forest supports a rich fauna including bushbuck, blue duiker, bushpig, vervet monkey, the nocturnally vociferous but visually elusive tree hyrax, and stellar forest birds such as Knysna turaco and crowned eagle. The dunefield is rather more impoverished in terms of wildlife, but it forms an important breeding site for marine birds such as African black oystercatcher, Damara tern and white-fronted plover. Woody Cape can only be explored on foot by following one of the trails that lead into it from the park office and *Langebos Huts*. For dedicated hikes, the circular two-day, 35km **Alexandria Hiking Trail** (☎041 468 0916, R140/person) ranks as one of South Africa's finest coastal walks, winding through the forest before it crosses a landscape of great hulking sand dunes to the ocean. The less demanding Tree Dassie Trail is a 7km day walk that can be completed in two to three hours.

Addo Marine Protected Area

Extending over 1200 square kilometres, this offshore reserve runs from Algoa Bay east past Woody Cape, and incorporates a trio of small islands used as breeding sites by marine birds. **Bird Island**, offshore of Woody Cape, supports the world's largest **gannet colony**, with almost 100,000 pairs of Cape Gannet present, as well as the entire Indian Ocean breeding population of Antarctic tern, while the smaller **St Croix Island** in Algoa Bay is an important breeding site for African penguin, African black oystercatcher and roseate tern. The marine reserve also houses the most easterly breeding colony of Cape fur seal, large numbers of bottleneck dolphin and seasonal influxes of humpback and southern right whale. Placed under the management of SANParks in 2002, the marine protected area has yet to be fully incorporated into the eponymous national park, and there are no facilities for tourists at present – but do watch this space.

ARRIVAL AND DEPARTURE	ADDO ELEPHANT NATIONAL PARK

By car The most popular point of access is the entrance gate to *Addo Rest Camp* and the main park reception office, which lies just off the R335 about 70km north of Port Elizabeth. To get here, follow the N2 northeast towards Makhanda (Grahamstown), then 5km past Port Elizabeth to branch left at the Addo/Motherwell/Markman signpost, continuing north along the R335 through the scruffy junction of Addo village, which stands about 13km before the gate. Alternatively, Addo's southern Mathyolweni Gate is accessed off the N2 near the village of Colchester, only 40km northeast of Port Elizabeth. From Mathyolweni Gate it is only a few minutes' drive to Mathyolweni Camp, or you can take you can take a slow, scenic drive north through the park to *Addo Rest Camp*, a journey of at least an hour along well-maintained tarred roads. Most of the listed accommodation outside the park lies close alongside or close to the R335 within a few kilometres of the main entrance gate. To get to the Zuurberg sector, including *Narina Bush Camp* and the

Zuurberg horse trails, turn off 1km before you reach *Main Camp*, and travel for 21km along a good gravel road. The access point to the Woody Cape sector, the park office is situated 9km south of the village of Alexandra, which lies 100km east of Port Elizabeth following the N2 via Colchester to Nanaga, then branching right onto the R72.

INFORMATION AND TOURS

Eating The restaurant at *Main Camp* is open for three meals a day (daily 7.30am–10pm), while the shop is well stocked with food and drink.

Guided tours For those without a vehicle, Calabash Tours (🖥 calabashtours.co.za) runs all-inclusive day-trips to Addo out of Port Elizabeth (R1700/person), as do most of the city's backpacker hostels. Full-day tours booked locally through

Orange Elephant and other lodges close to Addo tend to be cheaper and to incorporate more game-viewing time due their proximity to the park. Two-hour guided game drives and night drives can be booked out of *Addo Rest Camp* (see below).

Maps A good road map of the park, indicating the location of dams, hides, picnic and braai sites, is handed out to all visitors when they pay their park fees at reception.

ACCOMMODATION   SEE MAPS PAGES 236 AND 241

ADDO MAIN CAMP AND COLCHESTER SECTORS

Reservations for accommodation within the national park are essential in high season. This can be done through SANParks (☎ 012 428 9111, 🖥 sanparks.org/parks/addo) or directly with Addo if it's less than 72 hours in advance (☎ 042 233 8600). You are likely to have to take whatever is available, as it's a highly popular destination. There is a well-stocked shop selling a fair range of groceries at *Addo Rest Camp*, but you might prefer to stock up on self-catering supplies at a supermarket in Port Elizabeth or Colchester.

Addo Rest Camp Situated just inside the entrance gate to *Addo Main Camp*, this is the oldest and largest of the National Parks camps. In addition to camping facilities, there are forest cabins that sleep two people and share cooking facilities in communal kitchens, and more luxurious two-person chalets with their own kitchenettes. Some units sleep up to four people (minimum charge is for two occupants). The cheapest accommodation is in well-designed, spacious safari tents, perfect during the summer months, with decks right next to the perimeter fence. Amenities include a well-stocked supermarket, a good steakhouse-style restaurant, a waterhole that regularly attracts wildlife, and a site museum and bird hide. Camping & standing safari tent $\overline{\underline{S}}$, cabins & chalets $\overline{\underline{SS}}$

★ **Gorah Elephant Camp** 33km southeast of Addo Rest Camp by road, or 25km north of Mathyolweni Gate ☎ 044 501 1111, 🖥 gorah.hunterhotels.com. The only concession lodge in the park's main sector, this ultra-luxurious outfit is focused on a restored nineteenth-century farmhouse adorned with appropriate paraphernalia including mounted antelope skulls above the fireplace. Accommodation is in eleven beautifully decorated tented suites that evoke the Edwardian era. There's a landscaped pool, and meals and guided game drives are included in the rack rate. $\overline{\underline{SSSSS}}$

Mathyolweni Rest Camp Situated inside Mathyolweni Gate along the relatively untrammelled southern part of the main game-viewing circuit, this attractive small camp comprises a dozen fully equipped self-catering chalets, each of which sleeps two to four people, and has a shower and viewing deck. The chalets are set in a secluded valley surrounded by thicket that supports a wealth of birdlife. $\overline{\underline{SS}}$

★ **Spekboom Tented Camp** The most rustic accommodation along the main game-viewing circuit, this bush camp consists of five fixed tents on decks with twin beds. Each tent is equipped with camp chairs, a table and solar light, with communal showers and toilets within a short walking distance. There is no electricity, so you'll need to bring a torch; barbecue facilities and a communal gas fridge and stove plates are available. $\overline{\underline{S}}$

OTHER SECTORS

As with *Addo Main Camp*, all accommodation in other sectors of the park should be booked ahead through the numbers or website listed above.

Kabouga Cottage Sleeping a maximum of six, this converted old two-bedroom farmhouse in the Kabouga sector lies along the 4WD trail and has an open-plan self-catering kitchen with gas cooker and fridge, and a reservoir where you can swim. $\overline{\underline{S}}$

Langebos Huts This pair of four-bedroom huts in the Woody Cape sector each has a well-equipped kitchen, a dining room and lounge, and a wide veranda with braai facilities. $\overline{\underline{S}}$

Mvubu Campsite This small rustic campsite stands on the bank of the Sundays River as it flows through the remote Kabouga sector. There are braai places and basic ablution facilities. Ideal for self-sufficient birders or anglers, or 4WD enthusiasts wanting to explore the sector's 4WD trail. $\overline{\underline{S}}$

Narina Bush Camp *Narina* is a small, very attractive bush camp with a riverside location in the mountainous Zuurberg sector. The four safari tents each sleep four people and

5

there are shared washing and cooking facilities. There is no restaurant, so bring your own provisions. $\overline{\$\$}$

Nyathi Rest Camp Set in the wild Nyathi sector immediately north of *Addo Main Camp*, this relatively new four-star camp at the base of the Zuurberg Mountains offers spectacular views over a pristine floodplain. There are eleven self-catering, domed cottages on offer – eight two-bed, one four-bed and two six-bed units – all of them rather luxurious, with individual plunge pools and a braai area. $\overline{\$\$}$

★ **River Bend Lodge** ☎ 042 233 8000, ⓦ riverbend lodge.co.za. Opened in 2017, this luxury concession lodge stands on a hilltop overlooking the Coerney River floodplain in the park's Nyathi sector, directly opposite the main entrance gate. The eight suites all have air-conditioning, satellite television, private plunge pools and splendid views. Rates include meals and guided game drives in the untrammelled Nyathi Sector, which is now home to all the Big Five. $\overline{\$\$\$\$\$}$

OUTSIDE THE PARK

Outside the park, but within easy striking distance of the popular game-viewing road circuit through *Addo Main Camp* and Colchester sectors, you'll find an abundance of B&Bs and guesthouses, especially among the citrus groves of the Sundays River Valley. Many offer day and night drives in the game reserve.

Avoca River Cabins 13km northwest of Addo village on the R336 ☎ 074 248 3940 or ☎ 082 677 9920, ⓦ avocarivercabins.co.za. Reasonably priced B&B and self-catering accommodation on a farm in the Sundays River Valley. The self-catering accommodation ranges from budget cabins (sleeping four/five) to more comfortable thatched huts (some on the banks of the river). There is a swimming pool, some pleasant walks to be had on the citrus farm, plus a treetop course for kids, and canoes are available to rent. $\overline{\$}$

★ **Camp Figtree** 30km northwest of Addo village on the R335 ☎ 082 611 3603, ⓦ campfigtree.co.za. Luxury mountain lodge, on the Zuurberg slopes with glorious views, and built to satisfy every dream of romantic Africa. The rates include excellent food, and the packages on offer include a three-hour game drive into the park. It scores high on hilly scenery and total relaxation, though it is not near enough to nip in and out of the main part of the park, and the drive there involves 15km on a gravel road as you twist up the mountain. $\overline{\$\$\$}$

Chrislin Africa Lodge 12km south of Addo main gate, off the R336 ☎ 082 783 3553, ⓦ chrislin.co.za. This quirky B&B offers accommodation in thatched huts that have been built using traditional Xhosa construction techniques. There's also a lovely *lapa* (courtyard) and pool, and they serve up hearty country breakfasts, as well as dinners, though these are on request. $\overline{\$\$}$

★ **The Elephant House** 5km north of Addo village

on the R335 ☎ 042 233 2462 or ☎ 083 799 5671, ⓦ elephanthouse.co.za. Just minutes from Addo, this stunning thatched lodge, filled with Persian rugs and antique furniture, perfectly balances luxury with a supremely relaxed atmosphere. The eight bedrooms and six garden cottages (ideal for families, and half the price) open onto a lawned courtyard where tall fever trees shade a tempting swimming pool. Candlelit dinners are available, as are game drives (R1250/person) into Addo and the surrounding reserves. Main house $\overline{\$\$\$}$, stable cottage $\overline{\$\$}$

Hopefield Country House 20km southwest of Addo main gate ☎ 042 234 0333, ⓦ hopefield.co.za. An atmospheric 1930s farmhouse set in beautiful English-style gardens on a citrus farm. The nine bedrooms are imaginatively furnished with period pieces in a style the owners – a pair of classical musicians who sometimes organize concerts for guests – describe as "farmhouse eclectic". $\overline{\$\$}$

Kronenhoff Guest House On the R336 as you enter Kirkwood ☎ 042 230 1448, ⓦ kronenhoff.co.za. Situated in a small farming town, this is a hospitable, high-ceilinged Cape Dutch-style home, with five spacious suites, polished wooden floors, large leather sofas and a reasonable restaurant. In summer the scent of orange blossom carries from the surrounding citrus groves. $\overline{\$\$}$

Orange Elephant On the R335, 8km from the National Park gate ☎ 042 233 0023 or ☎ 074 179 6715, ⓦ addobackpackers.com. Budget accommodation at a comfortable hostel, whose management will help you organize outings into the surrounding game reserves – an Addo full-day tour including a braai in the park, with an excellent guide, costs R1550. The lively bar is well known for its large portions of pub grub. Dorms and doubles are available. $\overline{\$}$

★ **Rosedale Organic Farm B&B** On the R335, 1km north of Addo village ☎ 042 233 0404, ⓦ rosedalebnb. co.za. Very reasonably priced accommodation in eight brightly decorated cottages on a certified organic farm that exports citrus fruits to the EU. Hosts Keith and Nondumiso Finnemore are seriously committed to sustainable farming and tourism – water for the cottages is solar-heated, and you can enjoy organic oranges and juice at breakfast. Keith offers a free one-hour walking tour of the farm to guests. There is also a kitchen available for guests who prefer to self-cater. $\overline{\$}$

★ **Woodall Country House** About 7km west of Addo main gate ☎ 042 233 0128, ⓦ woodall-addo.co.za. Excellent luxury guesthouse on a working citrus farm with eleven self-contained suites and rooms. There's a swimming pool, gymnasium, spa and sauna (massages are available, and there's a resident beautician). A lovely sundowner deck overlooks a small lake full of waterfowl. Addo day tours cost R1220/person all-inclusive. Renowned for its outstanding country cuisine, the restaurant offers three- to six-course dinners. $\overline{\$\$\$}$

East of Addo

Given over almost entirely to livestock farming for most of the twentieth century, the coastal belt east of **Port Elizabeth** is now fast developing as a prime international safari destination thanks to a spate of recently established **private wildlife sanctuaries**. The trendsetter among these is **Shamwari Private Game Reserve**, a five-star facility that first opened its doors to tourists in 1992. This has since been joined by maybe a dozen other private reserves of varying ambition and quality, the pick among them being **Amakhala**, **Kariega**, **Kwandwe** and **Sibuya**. Ecologically, these reserves typically protect a cover of Albany thicket interspersed with small patches of fynbos and larger swathes of grassland and savannah (the latter two biomes being to a large extent associated with areas where naturally occurring vegetation was cleared to make way for farmland). They all cater to a relatively upmarket clientele and are usually visited as an alternative or add-on to Addo Elephant National Park. All offer overnight packages inclusive of expertly guided game drives in an open vehicle, with the focus being on locating reintroduced populations of the Big Five. Some, most notably **Schotia**, also offer guided safaris to day visitors.

The main urban focus in this region, the university town of **Makhanda** was founded as a colonial frontier outpost in 1812, and was known as Grahamstown until as recently as June 2018. The new name of Makhanda honours the eponymous Xhosa warrior and prophet who was captured in an attack on the British garrison here in April 1819 and drowned in December the same year whilst trying to escape incarceration on Robben Island. Individual reserves in the region are described below as if coming from Port Elizabeth or the Garden Route, starting with Schotia, which stands on the eastern border of Addo Elephant National Park, and running in an easterly direction from there. The last place covered, the anomalous **Great Fish River Nature Reserve**, 35km northeast of Makhanda, is a scenic, provincially managed conservation area whose densely thicketed slopes host impressive numbers of rhino, buffalo and various antelope, and whose super-affordable accommodation is ideal for budget-conscious and independent-minded self-drivers.

Schotia Game Reserve

On the N10, 55km northeast of Port Elizabeth or 40km southeast of Addo Rest Camp • ☎ 042 235 1436, ⌨ schotiasafaris.co.za

Abutting the eastern flank of Addo Elephant National Park, **Schotia** is one of the oldest and smallest private reserves in the Eastern Cape, extending over 23 square kilometres. It is divided into two large enclosures, the **south** being home to buffalo, elephant and hippo, while the **north** houses a population of white rhino. A variety of ungulates including giraffe, Burchell's zebra, blesbok, mountain reedbuck, red hartebeest, sable antelope, springbok, impala, eland, bushbuck, nyala and greater kudu is protected in both enclosures; meanwhile, a lion pride is moved between the two on a regular basis in order to allow populations in one to recover while they hunt in the other. Other large carnivores such as leopard, brown hyena and caracal are present but seldom seem. Schotia is the busiest of the province's reserves, since it stands so close to Port Elizabeth and Addo, offers relatively good value, and is geared towards day-trippers, but it lacks the wilderness character of larger sanctuaries and can feel a bit contrived. Still, the near certainty of seeing three or four of the Big Five on one game drive makes it a good bet for those

> ### SCHOTIA AT A GLANCE
>
> Quick-fix Big Five viewing in a small and rather contrived private reserve.
> **Big Five:** ★★★★
> **General wildlife:** ★★★★
> **Birding:** ★★
> **Scenery:** ★★
> **Wilderness factor:** ★
> **Uncrowded:** ★
> **Affordability:** ★★★
> **Self-drive:** N

5

with limited time or a tight budget. Full-day safaris (R3500/person) involve a morning game drive through Addo and an evening game drive with lunch and dinner, or you can just opt for the afternoon game drive and dinner (R2000/person).

ARRIVAL   SCHOTIA GAME RESERVE

By car Schotia's entrance gate and reception is clearly signposted on the west side of the N10 about 5km north of Nanaga on the junction with the N2, 50km northeast of Port Elizabeth. The best route coming from Addo is to follow the R342 east to Paterson, then turn right onto the N10 and continue south for 18km. Alternatively, full-day visitors can be collected from Port Elizabeth or anywhere in the Addo vicinity.

ACCOMMODATION

Schotia is one of the cheapest private reserves for an overnight stay and rates include a game drive into Addo. It is quite pricey in any other context, however, and we would recommend either sleeping elsewhere and sticking to a day-trip, or paying the extra for an overnight in one of the larger private reserves further east. $$$$

Shamwari Private Game Reserve

75km north of Port Elizabeth and 65km west of Makhanda (Grahamstown) • ☎ 042 203 1111, ⓦ shamwari.com

The oldest and justifiably the most famous of the Eastern Cape's major private reserves, **Shamwari** was established in 1990, subjected to a massive clean-up operation to remove fences and other redundant structures, then stocked with lions from Madikwe and Pilanesberg, elephants from Kruger and a host of other wildlife; it opened its doors to the public just two years later. Since then the reserve has cultivated a jetsetter fan base, having hosted such celebrities as Brad Pitt, Tiger Woods and John Travolta, and won a cartload of awards including Africa's Leading Conservation Company at the World Travel Awards for eight successive years starting in 2008. With its diverse landscapes and high standards of game viewing, Shamwari certainly deserves all the accolades it gets, and the eight intimate lodges and camps scattered across its 250 square kilometres offer the last word in safari luxury, and are priced accordingly, but a total of 71 rooms and suites means it tends to carry a larger volume of safari vehicles than the likes of Kwandwe or Samara.

As is the case with other reserves in the Eastern Cape, Shamwari supports a dominant cover of dense Albany thicket, particularly on the dry hilly slopes that characterize the northern half, where is its punctuated by flaming stands of Aloe ferox. Of the five other biomes represented, grassland and sweet-thorn savannah are predominant in the south, which is much flatter than the north, and suffered from greater ecological degradation during the farming era. These two sectors are separated by the **Bushman's River**, which forms a series of sweeping oxbows and supports a ribbon of riparian forest as it meanders through the reserve in a broadly easterly direction. When it comes to game drives, the southern plains tend to be more productive for large mammals, but game drives in the north offer perhaps your best chance anywhere in the Eastern Cape of encountering the thicket-loving **black rhino**, and the scenery and birding are sensational.

All the Big Five are present and correct in Shamwari, and sightings are usually excellent. Roughly twenty lions live on the reserve, split between rival "north" and "south" prides, and it is also home to around eighty elephants, several herds of buffalo, significant populations of black and white rhino, and a naturally occurring but typically elusive population

---

SHAMWARI AT A GLANCE

Celebrity-endorsed five-star operation that reliably delivers close-up encounters with lion, elephant and both rhino species.
Big Five: ★★★★
General wildlife: ★★★★
Birding: ★★
Scenery: ★★★★
Wilderness factor: ★★
Uncrowded: ★★
Affordability: ★
Self-drive: N

5

of leopards. Other conspicuous large mammals include cheetah, giraffe, hippo, Burchell's zebra and a full seventeen species of antelope, including some seriously impressive eland and greater kudu bulls and near-endemics and endemics such as black wildebeest, red hartebeest and springbok. Yellow mongoose is the commonest diurnal carnivore, while the likes of aardwolf, brown hyena, caracal, porcupine and very occasionally aardvark – all of which occur naturally – are sometimes seen on night drives.

Although the reintroduction programme at Shamwari in the 1990s focused mainly on large mammals, it also included two lower-profile species that had become locally extinct a century earlier. These are the **flightless dung beetle**, an Eastern Cape endemic whose dependence on elephant, rhino and buffalo dung had resulted in a range reduction that left it practically restricted to Addo Elephant National Park for most of the twentieth century, and the **red-billed oxpecker**, a small but pretty bird that plays an important natural role in tick control but which disappeared from the Eastern Cape in the 1890s as a result of the arsenic then used in cattle dips. The reintroduced oxpecker is now one of the most conspicuous of the reserve's 275 bird species, with small chattering flocks often to be seen hitching a lift on the back of ungulates such as buffalo, giraffe and wildebeest. Other common savannah-dwelling birds include pale chanting goshawk, southern black korhaan, Cape glossy starling, bokmakierie and Karoo prinia, while the hillier and more densely wooded areas support the likes of jackal buzzard, Verreaux's eagle, crowned hornbill, green woodhoopoe and African paradise flycatcher.

Shamwari is also home to a pair of **Big Cat Rescue and Education Centres**, one in the north and one in the south, designed in collaboration with the **Born Free Foundation** to provide a home to rescued lions and leopards from around the world. A separate **Wildlife Rehabilitation Centre** provides sanctuary to injured or orphaned animals (both from within the reserve and outside it) whilst rehabilitating them for release back into the wild. Guests can ask for an educational visit to one of these facilities to be incorporated into their safari.

ARRIVAL   SHAMWARI PRIVATE GAME RESERVE

By car The main entrance gate, which provides access to Long Lee Manor, Riverdene, Sarili, Sindile and Explorer Camp, is on the R342 about 9km southeast of Paterson and 7km north of the junction with the N2 between Port Elizabeth and Makhanda (Grahamstown). Allow about one hour for the 75km drive from Port Elizabeth or 65km drive from Makhanda. Coming from Addo, it's a 35km drive along the R342 from Addo Rest Camp.

The best route to Eagles Crag and Bayethe is the unsurfaced Sidbury Road, which runs north from the N2 about 11km past the junction with the R342.

For Lobengula, follow the N10 north from its junction with the N2 at Nanaga for 33km, passing through Paterson, then turn right onto the Alicedale road and follow it for another 12km until you see the gate for Lobengula to your right.

ACCOMMODATION

Eight luxury lodges and camps with a combined 71 rooms, standing tents and suites are dotted around the reserve. Of these, only Long Lee, Riverdene and Sarili accept children under 12, while Explorer Camp is limited to people aged 16 to 65. All have some sort of swimming or plunge pool and Explorer Camp is the only one without air-conditioning or spa facilities. Bookings can be made directly through 📞 042 203 1111 or 🌐 shamwari.com.

Bayethe Twelve-unit camp whose comfortable and classically decorated standing safari tents have an intimate bush setting. $$$$$

★ **Eagles Crag** Shamwari's flagship lodge, Eagles Crag, with its eyrie-like location in the north of the reserve, is a four-time winner of the World's Leading Eco-lodge category

at the World Travel Awards. The nine super-stylish suites all have a private deck with a heated plunge pool. $$$$$

★ **Explorer Camp** This relatively basic camp is aimed at those seeking a deeper bush experience than is offered by any conventional lodge. It comprises just three double tents with a common deck and plunge pool, and is used as a base for two-night trails from October to April, when it operates on Tues and Wed, then again on Fri and Sat with an optional third night on Sun. $$$$

Lobengula Named after a nineteenth-century Ndebele king, Lobengula started life as a hunting lodge before the reserve's creation, but has since been reinvented as an intimate and tranquil six-suite lodge whose African village theme is reflected in the thatch roofs and whitewashed exteriors. The luxurious air-conditioned suites are very spacious and have an indoor and outdoor shower, while the property itself is nestled in a near-pristine patch of thicket teeming with birds and small wildlife such as bushbuck and vervet monkey. $$$$$

★ **Long Lee Manor** Set in a farm homestead that was built in 1910 and underwent lavish renovations in 2019, this family-friendly lodge is the largest on the property, with eighteen rooms and suites in total. It is furnished in Edwardian style with every conceivable comfort and amenities include a fabulous infinity pool, a spa, a fitness cente, a teen play zone, and a boma overlooking a waterhole. $$$$$

Riverdene This family-friendly nine-room lodge has a special "Kids on Safari" educational programme and offers sweeping view across plains teeming with wildlife. $$$$$

Sarili This child-friendly five-suite lodge is aimed mainly at private parties of families and friends. and offers a wonderful view over the Bushman's River. $$$$$

Sindile Constructed in 2019, Shamwari's newest and most prestigious lodge shares its name (an isiXhosa word meaning survivor) with the famous leopard Sindile, who survived numerous lion attacks on the reserve to raise five cub litters. The nine low-impact luxury tented suites are elevated to allow uninhibited views over the Bushman's River, unsullied by other artificial structures or lights. $$$$$

Amakhala Game Reserve

75km northeast of Port Elizabeth on the N2 ☎ 041 450 5658 or ☎ 082 659 1796, Ⓦ amakhala.co.za

Created in 1999 in the aftermath of a crippling **drought** that had gripped the region for several years, good-value **Amakhala** – an isiXhosa name meaning "Place of Aloes" – is a joint conservation venture that amalgamated six separate livestock farms (owned by six families with 1820 settler roots) into one contiguous 85-square-kilometre wildlife conservancy. Much of the reserve protects the original cover of dense spekboom-dominated zuurveld or Albany thicket, while areas cleared for livestock grazing and agriculture have been rehabilitated as tracts of grassland and sweet-thorn acacia savannah, and there are also some significant patches of renosterbos. The hilly reserve is flowed through by a near-perennial stretch of the **Bushman's River**, and its main game-viewing circuit is towered over by a magnificent amphitheatre of undulating mountains whose sandstone cliffs glow golden in the morning and evening sun.

Following an extensive **restocking programme**, Amakhala is now home to all the Big Five. Visitors can be reasonably confident of seeing lion, elephant, white rhino and buffalo in the course of a two- to three-night stay, but the resident leopard population is characteristically shy and elusive. Other wildlife likely to be seen over the course of an ordinary visit includes cheetah, giraffe, Burchell's zebra, hippo, black wildebeest, red hartebeest, springbok, gemsbok, common waterbuck, eland, greater kudu and bushbuck. Black-backed jackal and yellow mongoose are the most conspicuous small carnivores, but lucky visitors might also see bat-eared fox, aardwolf, meerkat and various felids. Among the more common and interesting birds are ostrich, secretary bird, Denham's bustard, jackal buzzard, pale chanting goshawk, pied starling, bokmakierie and stonechat.

Unusually for a private reserve, accommodation in Amakhala is not centrally managed, but instead comprises eleven **individual-owned lodges**, many still run by one or other of the founding families, and each with strict restriction on room numbers. This means that when all the lodges are full, there are quite a number of vehicles out on game drives, and it tends feel far busier than, say, Shamwari or Kwandwe. It should also be noted that the **N2**, which runs along the reserve's northern boundary and also through a section of the park itself, is an unavoidable presence, and while it is less intrusive than might be expected, you'll often see cars speeding past when on a game drive, and may hear the traffic rumble past when you

---

AMAKHALA AT A GLANCE

Affordable Big Five experience in a rather busy private reserve edged and bisected by the N2 highway.

Big Five: ★★★★
General wildlife: ★★★★
Birding: ★★★
Scenery: ★★★
Wilderness factor: ★
Uncrowded: ★★
Affordability: ★★★
Self-drive: N

5

THE (RE)INTRODUCTION GAME

A significant difference between the reserves of the Eastern Cape and most of their counterparts further north in Africa is that almost all the large mammals you'll see at the former are descended from **relocated stock** from further afield since 1990. There are exceptions – the elephants of Addo, for instance, are naturally occurring, as are most populations of leopard, greater kudu, bushbuck and various smaller antelope – but the reality is that for most of the twentieth century there were no wild lions in the region now referred to as the Eastern Cape, nor any rhinos (black nor white), nor many of the other large mammals that now furnish its national parks and reserves.

In most respects, the conversion of old livestock farms into a patchwork of **small private reserves** is an unambiguously positive development. Indigenous grazers and browsers place far less strain on the environment than domestic livestock, and they potentially form a much healthier and more eco-friendly meat source. The widespread introduction of endemic and endangered large mammals, from black rhinos to black wildebeest, helps bolster global populations of these **vulnerable species**. Ecologically minded landowners, meanwhile, are highly motivated to eradicate the invasive plants that tend to thrive on farmland. There are economic benefits insofar as the tourist sector tends to create more employment opportunities, and to offer better pay, than farming. And while many reserves in the eastern Cape are too small to represent viable ecosystems, one can take the long-term view that they might one day be the building blocks from which a much larger mega-reserve, running from the coast deep inland to the Karoo, could be crafted.

All the same, in conservation terms, there is a significant distinction between reintroducing species that once occurred naturally in an area and introducing those that didn't. **SANParks**, being first and foremost a conservation body, adheres to the purist line, refusing to introduce species into Addo Elephant or Mountain Zebra National Park without some historical precedent. Many private reserves, by contrast, take a more **laissez-faire approach** and will stock any creature that is likely to survive and to please paying clients. And while it is certainly the case that all the Big Five roamed widely across the Eastern Cape into historic times, there's no reason to think that white rhino, giraffe or cheetah would have existed naturally in certain reserves into which they have been introduced, while some now-common antelope – impala, nyala and blue wildebeest, for instance – never occurred in the province at all.

Some situations are ambiguous. Burchell's zebra, for instance, is not known to have occurred to the south of the Orange River, but another subspecies of plains zebra, the quagga, was numerous prior to being hunted to extinction by settlers. Likewise, the Cape lion and Cape warthog, both now extinct, are thought to have been taxonomically distinct from more northerly populations (though the latter, oddly enough, was probably a subspecies of the desert warthog *Phacochoerus aethiopicus*, which is otherwise restricted to the Horn of Africa). In such cases, it would seem bloody minded rather than constructive to refuse to introduce a species because it represented a different race (though with Burchell's zebra, the risk of hybridizing with the rarer Cape mountain zebra might be a consideration).

A strong argument against limiting **introduction programmes** to species that formerly occurred in the Eastern Cape relates to the ecological impact of humans over the past couple of centuries. Along much of the coastal belt, for instance, the naturally occurring cover of Albany thicket was cleared by settlers to make way for grazing or agricultural land, with the result that many of the region's reserves now incorporate tracts of savannah and grassland that are essentially artificial but would require several centuries to restore to their original state. Cheetah, for instance, would have struggled to hunt in the dense thicket vegetation that once blanketed the slopes between Addo and the Great Fish River, and white rhino might have struggled find suitable grazing there, but the reality is that this area now contains plenty of habitat suited to both animals. So why not introduce them?

bed down at night. Guided game drives are the main activity, but most lodges also offer canoe safaris and riverboat sundowner cruises (good for birds and small mammals) when the level of the Bushman's River is sufficient, entertaining and expertly guided bush walks with the owner of *Quatermain's* (from R600/person), and horseback safaris with Amakhala Horse Trails (under the same management as *Woodbury Tented Lodge*; from R850/person).

ARRIVAL AND DEPARTURE

By car Access is from the N2 as it runs northeast from Port Elizabeth towards Makhanda (Grahamstown). It is a

AMAKHALA GAME RESERVE

70–80km drive, depending on where you are staying and which of several entrance gates you need to use.

ACCOMMODATION

Rates of all the lodges listed below are full board and include game drives and most drinks.

★ **Hillsnek Safari Camp** ☎ 082 324 3484, ⓦ hillsnek safaris.com. Attractively integrated into the riverine thicket bordering the Bushman's River, below a striking, burnished sandstone cliff, this intimate camp comprises four large and stylishly furnished standing tents set on stilted wooden platforms with private decks that offer a fine view over the plains. The management style is relaxed, down-to-earth and friendly, excellent meals are eaten communally with other guests, and there's a small plunge pool that regularly attracts thirsty elephants. It is well-equipped for honeymooners and for children, while energetic travellers can stretch their legs on a free guided walk on a neighbouring property that harbours plenty of non-dangerous wildlife. It is far enough from the N2 that traffic noise isn't usually an issue. $$$$$

Leeuwenbosch Country House ☎ 042 235 1252, ⓦ leeuwenbosch.co.za. This four-bedroom lodge flanking the N2 comprises a gracious 1908 settler homestead; it's attached to a nineteenth-century chapel and small, intimate pub where you can enjoy a drink with the owners or staff. Guest rooms are all in the old house and come with original tall ceilings, hardwood floors and characterful period decor. The wide wraparound balcony is a lovely spot

to enjoy a coffee or glass of wine and admire the beautifully tended gardens. $$$$

★ **Quatermain's 1920s Safari Camp** ☎ 079 307 6640, ⓦ quatermainscamp.co.za. This delightful small owner-managed camp espouses a welcome back-to-basics ethos, comprising just three standing tents whose simple settler-style decor evokes the *Out of Africa* feel of an Edwardian safari. There's no electricity, no Wi-Fi, dinners are eaten by gaslight in a communal boma, and outward signs of the twenty-first century are few, though on a still night the "deep bush" experience can be undermined by the distant rumble of traffic. The camp lies in a tract of lush riparian woodland within a separate enclave of the reserve that hosts no dangerous wildlife, which means you can walk freely in the vicinity. $$$$

★ **Woodbury Tented Camp** ☎ 042 235 1109, ⓦ wood burytentedcamp.co.za. One of the best-value safari camps in the Eastern Cape, this well-run and unpretentious spot comprises ten double and family standing tents widely spaced in a dense spekboom thicket close to the central conservation centre. Set on stilted wooden platforms with a private balcony, the en-suite tents are very comfortable, and buffet meals are eaten communally on a deck with a great view over the reserve. $$$$

Lalibela Game Reserve

90km northeast of Port Elizabeth ☎ 041 581 8170, ⓦ lalibela.net

This 105-square kilometre private reserve borders the N2 east of Amakhala and supports a grassland-dominated tract of former farmland now better suited to lion and other savannah species than animals historically associated with Albany thicket. It is home to introduced populations of all the Big Five (though leopards are coy as ever), along with the likes of cheetah, giraffe, hippo, Burchell's zebra, impala, red hartebeest, blesbok and eland. Game drives are included in the accommodation rate, along with all meals and drinks – you can dine on terrific contemporary Eastern Cape cuisine.

LALIBELA AT A GLANCE

Smallish reserve hosting all the Big Five and some exceptional lodges.

Big Five: ★★★★
General wildlife: ★★★★
Birding: ★★
Scenery: ★★
Wilderness factor: ★
Uncrowded: ★★
Affordability: ★
Self-drive: N

ARRIVAL   LALIBELA GAME RESERVE

By car The reserve lies 90km (1hr) from Port Elizabeth along the N2 in the direction of Makhanda (Grahamstown).

ACCOMMODATION

There are five lodges on the property, all air-conditioned with Wi-Fi, which are bookable through the central reservations office (☎ 041 581 8170, ⓦ lalibela.net).

Kichaka Lodge This five-star lodge overlooks a waterhole that attracts plenty of game. The ten rooms have stone-clad exterior walls, thatched roofs, private plunge pools and indoor and outdoor showers. $$$$$

Lentaba Lodge Set on a hillside overlooking a waterhole, this lodge is a step down from *Kichaka* in terms of luxury, but it also has ten rooms with stone-clad exterior walls, thatched roofs and a private viewing deck. $$$$$

Mark's Camp Completely renovated in 2018, this family-friendly lodge is the only one on the property that welcomes under-12s. It has four double and four family units sleeping up to eighteen adults and eight children in total. $$$$$

Mills Manor This converted Edwardian mansion is an exclusive-use villa that sleeps up to ten and is aimed at private groups of family and friends. $$$$$

Tree Tops Tented Camp This luxury tented camp stands on raised wooden walkways above a forested valley. All units have private viewing decks and there is a swimming pool to boot. $$$$$

Sibuya Game Reserve

39 Eastbourne Rd, Kenton-on-Sea (reception) • Conservation fee R150/night • ☎ 046 648 1040, ⓦ sibuya.co.za

Arguably the most scenic of the Eastern Cape's private reserves, and certainly the most rewarding to birders, **Sibuya** protects a stirring landscape of evergreen hills flanking a 10km stretch of the **Kariega River** downstream of the pretty coastal town of Kenton-on-Sea. Established from partially degraded farmland in 2003 and extended to cover a total area of fifty square kilometres in 2019, the reserve has since been restored as closely as possible to its natural state through the clearance of invasive stands of eucalyptus, cactus and other exotic trees, and the dismantling of internal cattle fences and other redundant artificial structures. As with most other reserves in the Eastern Cape, Sibuya supports a dominant cover of Albany thicket, but here it tends to be lush and green year-round due to the relatively high rainfall and regular sea mists. Other biomes include the band of riparian forest that follows the river, and some extensive tracts of grassland.

Undoubtedly the dominant feature of Sibuya, the Kariega is a compelling and memorable presence as it meanders wide and calm through a setting of steep, wooded hills studded with prehistoric-looking euphorbias and cycads. The reserve also offers fabulous game viewing. When it comes to the Big Five, it is home to one breeding herd of elephant and a trio of bulls, all of which regularly cross the river, as well as a decent number of buffalo and several white (but no black) rhinos. At least three leopards are resident on the reserve, but they are very shy and sightings are infrequent. Lions have been reintroduced, but a municipal restriction on allowing them access to the public waterway means they are confined to a fenced part of the reserve that is currently being extended to twenty square kilometres in area. Other commonly seen wildlife includes giraffe, blue wildebeest, greater kudu, nyala, bushbuck and impala.

A notable feature of Sibuya is its exceptionally varied **birdlife**. Almost four hundred species have been recorded, and it is particularly rewarding for forest and water-associated specials not normally associated with this part of the Eastern Cape. On the river, look out for African finfoot, African fish eagle, osprey, mountain wagtail, six types of kingfisher (including giant, pygmy and the localised half-collared) and marine species such as gulls and terns.

Forest-dwellers include African crowned eagle, red-breasted sparrowhawk, Narina trogon, Knysna turaco, crowned hornbill, olive bush-shrike and dark-backed weaver. Most of the guides are pretty clued-up on birds and specialist guides can be requested in advance.

Sibuya is serviced by a trio of intimate all-inclusive camps, and a two- or better three-night stay is recommended to explore it properly and enjoy activities such as guided game drives, guided walks, fishing and canoeing (all included in the

---

SIBUYA AT A GLANCE

Riverside private reserve that combines decent Big Five viewing and a magnificent location with truly outstanding birdlife.

Big Five: ****
General wildlife: ****
Birding: *****
Scenery: *****
Wilderness factor: ****
Uncrowded: *****
Affordability: **
Self-drive: N

5

rack rate). Pre-booked day-visits are also offered and range from a river cruise with lunch (R920/person) to full-day safaris incorporating a morning and afternoon game drive and lunch (R2055/person). Whether you are an overnight guest or day-tripper, public access to Sibuya is **by boat** only, and the meandering hour-long trip upriver from Kenton-on-Sea provides a truly magical introduction to a safari.

ARRIVAL AND DEPARTURE   SIBUYA GAME RESERVE

By car and boat All visitors are transferred by boat from the reserve's reception office, which stands on the west bank of the Kariega Estuary in Kenton-on-Sea, at the junction of the R72 and R343, about 130km east of Port Elizabeth, 60km south of Makhanda (Grahamstown) and 155km southwest of East London. The scheduled boat departure for overnight visitors leaves Kenton-on-Sea at noon daily, while the return trip usually starts at around 10am, but late transfers (on arrival) and early transfers (on departure) can be booked in advance at an additional cost. For day-trippers, morning and full-day tours leave Kenton-on-Sea at 9am, and afternoon packages including lunch leave at noon. Visitors are requested to be at reception thirty minutes before the transfer departs. Most visitors drive themselves to reception, but transfers from Port Elizabeth, East London and points in-between can be arranged.

ACCOMMODATION

Bookings can be made directly through the reserve (☏ 046 648 1040, ⓦ sibuya.co.za). Rates are inclusive of all meals, most drinks and game activities, as well as canoeing, fishing and walking.

Bush Lodge The most luxurious option on Sibuya, *Bush Lodge* comprises four stylish thatched cottages set on a forested slope overlooking the river. Spacious viewing decks offer great birdwatching and there's a wonderfully sited freeform swimming pool. All units have air-conditioning and grid-powered lighting. $$$$$

Forest Camp Comprising eight standing tents similar in quality to *River Camp* (see below), with an equally lovely riverside setting, this eco-camp is aimed mainly at couples rather than families, and no under-12s are permitted. The tents are widely spaced and connected by wooden walkways that run through a patch of riparian forest teeming with birds. In keeping with *River Camp's* ethos, it runs on borehole water and solar power, and there is no Wi-Fi, television, air conditioning or electric fans. $$$$

★ **River Camp** Stunningly located in a lush forest on a bend in the river, this family-friendly eco-camp comprises just four spacious and well-equipped tents, all of which have a private river-facing balcony with seating and hammock, and sleep up to two adults and two children. A range of engaging activities, suited to children of all ages, includes a junior ranger programme – the idea is that parents can leave younger kids in safe hands while they head off on game drives or walks and other activities. In keeping with Sibuya's eco-friendly ethos, it runs borehole water and solar power (with gas backup) and there is no Wi-Fi, television, air conditioning or electric fans. $$$$

Kariega Game Reserve

Main entrance 14km north of Kenton-on-Sea on the R343 • Conservation & Community Levy R150/night • ☏ 046 636 7904, ⓦ kariega.co.za

Sharing a southern border with Sibuya, this wonderfully scenic and uncrowded Big Five reserve protects a tract of undulating hills and grassy plains bounded to the east and west by the Kariega and Bushman's rivers. Founded in 1989 and first opened to tourists ten years later, it originally comprised fewer than twenty square kilometres of former farmland running east from the R343 to the **Kariega River**, but it has since been extended to 110 square kilometres through the acquisition of more than a dozen farms, mostly to the west of the R343. The older and relatively small **eastern sector**, comprising a flat grassy plain enclosed by a spectacular amphitheatre of thicketed hills, supports high densities of grazers such as white rhino, giraffe,

KARIEGA AT A GLANCE

Excellent upmarket Big Five reserve notable for its attractive hilly setting.
Big Five: ★★★★
General wildlife: ★★★★
Birding: ★★★
Scenery: ★★★★
Wilderness factor: ★★★
Uncrowded: ★★★
Affordability: ★
Self-drive: N

5

eland, blue wildebeest and blesbok, while a population of hippo has been introduced to the Kariega upstream of the boundary with Sibuya. To see the Big Five, you need to explore the more extensive and ecologically diverse **western sector**, which supports tracts of fynbos, grassland and savannah incised by a succession of deep and wild-feeling riverine valleys whose thicketed slopes are punctuated by skeletal euphorbia trees and draped in old-man's-beard lichen. Elephants were reintroduced into this western sector in 2004, and the population now stands at more than fifty, split between four breeding herds, together with a few solitary bulls. Lion, black rhino and buffalo have also been reintroduced to this sector, and are regularly seen on game drives, while leopards still occur naturally, and are closely monitored by management, but seldom seen by tourists.

Kariega is closed to day-visits. Overnight guests have the choice of five lodges, all of which operate on an all-inclusive basis. Twice-daily game drives are the main activity, and while the relaxed guiding style and breathtaking scenery means that these are seldom reduced to a single-minded hunt for the Big Five, odds are that you will encounter all but leopard over the course of a three-night stay. Other activities included in the rack rates are motorized boat cruises on the Kariega and Bushman's River (a must for birders), canoeing on both rivers (in the case of the Kariega, downstream of the area where hippos have been introduced), fishing, and guided game walks in the eastern sector.

ARRIVAL KARIEGA GAME RESERVE

By car Kariega straddles the R343 between Kenton-on-Sea and Makhanda (Grahamstown), roughly 140km east of Port Elizabeth. The entrance gate for *Main* and *Ukhozi* lodges is actually on the R343, 45km south of Makhanda and 14km north of Kenton-on-Sea. The entrances for *Settler's Drift* and *River Lodge* are on the north side of the R72, and respectively lie 10km and 15km past the small village of Alexandria coming from the direction of Addo or Port Elizabeth. For those staying at *Settlers Drift*, a 20-minute boat transfer to the lodge departs from the jetty next to the entrance gate at 1.30pm daily, weather permitting.

ACCOMMODATION

Bookings for all five lodges on Kariega can be made through the central reservation office by calling ☏ 046 636 7904 or online at ⓦ kariega.co.za. Rates at all lodges include guided activities and meals, and the only one that doesn't include drinks is *Main Lodge*.

The Homestead Catering to families and small tour groups, this renovated and stylishly decorated nineteenth-century farmhouse is centred on a green courtyard with a swimming pool. The entire seven-bedroom homestead is rented out as one unit, sleeping a total of fourteen, with two game drive vehicles allocated to it. $$$$$

Main Lodge The original self-catering lodge that opened on the property in 1999 comprises 24 cosy one- to three-bedroom log chalets with air conditioning, lounge, private viewing deck and in some cases a plunge pool. It has a massive boma where visitors eat outdoors on alternate nights (weather permitting), a large dining room overlooking a beautiful euphorbia-clad gorge, and a well-organized children's centre offering special activities to under-12s. It is significantly cheaper than the reserve's other lodges, but is better suited to families with children or tour groups than to couples. $$$$$

River Lodge A good base for more active travellers, *River Lodge* stands in a 7-square-kilometre enclave that is ideal for guided game walks (plenty of giraffe, zebra and antelope but no dangerous wildlife). It stands alongside a tidal stretch of the Bushman's River that's ideal for kayaking or boat trips to a nearby swimming beach. A huge open deck over the river offers good birding and amenities include a boma and riverfront spa. Decoration throughout is tastefully colourful and the air-conditioned rooms are spacious, light and airy. $$$$$

★ **Settlers Drift** Opened in 2014, this five-star "barefoot luxury" tented camp, set on a euphorbia-studded slope overlooking the Bushman's River, is the most upmarket option on Kariega, comprising nine gorgeous canvas-and-glass units that take the term tented accommodation to its luxurious extreme. All units come with air conditioning, fireplace, hardwood floor, standing tub, outdoor shower, colourful minimalist decor and a private veranda. $$$$$

Ukhozi Lodge Fully refurbished and modernized after being partially destroyed by fire in 2017, the ten cottages here have a contemporary bush feel – clean lines, pale woods, treated concrete floor, dry-stacked stone walls – that makes it popular with young couples. The expansive view over a plain teeming with wildlife makes for great in-house game-viewing. $$$$$

5

KWANDWE AT A GLANCE

Low tourist volumes and open vistas make this the Eastern Cape's wildest Big Five reserve.

Big Five: ****
General wildlife: ****
Birding: ****
Scenery: ***
Wilderness factor: *****
Uncrowded: *****
Affordability: *
Self-drive: N

Kwandwe Private Game Reserve

On the R67, 41km north of Makhanda (Grahamstown) and 160km from Port Elizabeth • Conservation Fee R350/night • ☎ 046 603 3400, Ⓦ kwandwe.com

One of the Eastern Cape's top Big Five destinations, **Kwandwe** extends over 220 square kilometres of semi-arid scrubland inland of Makhanda, yet the two lodges and three villas that scatter the property have a maximum capacity of just 52. The main biome is Albany thicket, with some forty percent of the reserve's cover being dominated by spekboom, but the scrub here tends to have a lower canopy and is less green than it is around Addo. Areas of stonier ground associated with Ecca shales support a sparse-looking but diverse succulent flora typical of the Karoo, and there are also patches of grassland (usually associated with former cultivation), sweet-thorn savannah and fynbos. Kwandwe possesses a more remote and pristine feel than most other private reserves elsewhere in the Eastern Cape, but like them it was converted from farmland in the 1990s, a task that involved removing an astonishing 2000km of fencing and other relicts of the agricultural infrastructure to clear the way for a massive **wildlife reintroduction programme** that entailed the relocation of seven thousand individual animals historically associated with the region.

The dominant geographic feature of this vast reserve is the **Great Fish River**, which courses for 30km through its parched plains. In times past, this near-perennial river was prone to dry up in years of low rainfall, but these days it runs throughout the year thanks to the implementation of an ambitious project to supplement its natural flow with water from the Orange River via a tunnel constructed at Oviston in 1971. The increased reliability of the Great Fish has been a boon to farmers whose land lies alongside it, but it also had a negative ecological impact, insofar as much of its aquatic ecosystem is now dominated by invasive species from the Orange. Despite this, the ample river frontage does provide the wildlife at Kwandwe with a reliable source of drinking water, and it has also attracted several previously unrecorded water-associated bird species, most notably the dashing white-fronted bee-eaters that now nest colonially in holes on its muddy banks.

Kwandwe offers excellent Big Five viewing. The reserve has a total population of roughly 75 elephants, split between two large breeding herds and a few solitary bulls, and visitors can also expect to see buffalo, lion and white rhino, as well as cheetah. Black rhinos are somewhat more elusive, and you'd need a hefty dose of luck to see a leopard. Also easily spotted are giraffe, plains zebra, warthog and dry-country antelope such as eland, greater kudu, red hartebeest, black wildebeest, gemsbok, springbok and steenbok. The most conspicuous smaller predators are black-backed jackal, yellow mongoose and meerkat, but night drives also sometimes throw up sightings of aardwolf, brown hyena, bat-eared fox and various felids. Birdlife is also varied; conspicuous species include South Africa's national bird, the exquisite blue crane – the isiXhosa name Kwandwe actually translates as "Place of the Blue Crane" – as well as ostrich, Kori bustard, spur-winged goose, pale chanting goshawk, bokmakierie and malachite sunbird, the latter often associated with flowering aloes.

Kwandwe is not open to day-visitors and it has one of the lowest bed-to-land area ratios of any private reserve in South Africa, thus ensuring that overnight guests have a genuinely exclusive experience. Activities included in the rack rate are twice-daily game drives, which offer the best chance of good Big Five sightings, as well as guided big game walks (no under-16s), guided interpretative walks that focus on birds,

plants and other small stuff (no under-12s) and fishing. At least two nights, better three, is recommended for a decent chance of spotting a good selection of iconic safari favourites.

ARRIVAL   KWANDWE PRIVATE GAME RESERVE

By car Coming from Port Elizabeth, site of the closest major airport, allow at least two hours for the 160km drive to Kwandwe. Follow the N2 out of town east for about 135km, then shortly after bypassing Makhanda (Grahamstown), turn left on R67 to Fort Beaufort. Follow the R67 north through Ecca Pass for 19km, then turn left onto a gravel road signposted for Kwandwe and Kranzdrift. It is 5km from here to Kwandwe gate, then another 6km to the reception at Heatherton Towers, from where you'll be transferred to your lodge. It is also possible to arrange a road transfer from Port Elizabeth or a charter flight from there or any other airport in South Africa.

ACCOMMODATION

In addition to the two lodges listed below, three private three- or four-bedroom villas are available to parties of six to eight people. All accommodation on the reserve is inclusive of activities, meals and drinks, and can be booked directly (☎ 046 603 3400, ⊛ kwandwe.com).

Ecca Lodge Vibrant colours and contemporary African decor are the hallmarks of this trendy boutique hotel in the bush. The six standalone double and family suites are ingeniously designed with glass walls that allow you to lie on your bed and feel you're totally alone in the middle of the wilderness, and all have a deck with private plunge pool. $$$$$

★ **Great Fish River Lodge** This luxurious lodge consists of nine stylish and super-spacious thatched suites strung out along a well-wooded ridge overlooking the Great Fish River. Ceiling-high glass doors open out to a private wooden deck with a plunge pool offering panoramic views. Stunning. $$$$$

GREAT FISH RIVER AT A GLANCE

The Eastern Cape's wildest self-drive retreat supports high densities of buffalo and rhino.

Big Five: **
General wildlife: ***
Birding: ****
Scenery: ****
Wilderness factor: *****
Uncrowded: *****
Affordability: *****
Self-drive: Y

Great Fish River Nature Reserve

On the R67, 34km north of Makhanda (Grahamstown) • office daily 8am–4.30pm • day-visitors R20 ☎ 087 286 6545, ⊛ visiteasterncape.co.za

This scenic 450-square-kilometre reserve spans what, from the late eighteenth to late nineteenth century, was the fiercely contested border between the Cape Colony and the Xhosa territory to its east. It was created in 1994 as an amalgamation of a trio of older conservation areas: Andries Vosloo Kudu Reserve and Sam Knott Nature Reserve in the former Cape Province, and the Ciskei's Double Drift Nature Reserve. Centred upon the **Great Fish River** and a trio of major tributaries, the terrain is rather mountainous, with altitudes ranging from below 100m to above 500m, and the slopes are swathed in dense evergreen Albany thicket. Accessed by rough dirt roads, the reserve supports plenty of wildlife, including the Eastern Cape's largest populations of black rhino and buffalo, as well as greater kudu, eland, red hartebeest and a few elusive leopards and brown hyenas. Wildlife is generally quite difficult to see in the thicket, so the reserve is not suited to those seeking a quick-fix Big Five safari, but the wilderness atmosphere and affordable accommodation will make it rather attractive to budget-conscious self-drivers with a high-clearance vehicle.

ARRIVAL AND DEPARTURE   GREAT FISH RIVER NATURE RESERVE

By car The main entrance gate is in the north on the R345, 30km south of Alice. There is also a more southerly entrance gate on the R345, 35km north of Peddie (which lies on the N2 east of Makhanda/Grahamstown), and an eastern entrance gate off the R67 between Makhanda (Grahamstown) and Fort Beaufort.

Fort Beaufort

GREAT FISH RIVER NATURE RESERVE

5

■ **ACCOMMODATION**
Mvubu Chalets   1

Main Gate
(northern entrance)

Keiskamma River

Koonap River

R67

Sam Knott
Memorial Gate

R345

1

Secondary Gate
(southern entrance)

Great Fish River

N

Kamadole
Gate

0   5
kilometres

Grahamstown

| ACCOMMODATION | SEE MAP ABOVE |

Mvubu Chalets ☎ 043 492 0881, 🌐 bookonline.ecpta. co.za. Situated in the southwestern section, closest to Makhanda (Grahamstown), this small self-catering camp comprises six double chalets offering breathtaking views of the Great Fish River. Amenities include a swimming pool and wooden deck. Superb value. $\overline{\underline{5}}$

The Eastern Karoo

Situated about 150km inland of Port Elizabeth, the **Eastern Karoo**, centred on the historic towns of **Graaff-Reinet** and **Cradock**, is an emergent Big Five game-viewing destination that sees relatively few visitors by comparison to Greater Addo. Like much of the Karoo, it has long been given over to sheep farming, and the countryside has a distinct outback feel, punctuated by the occasional dorp rising against the horizon, offering the experience of an archetypal one-horse outpost. The quiet roads through this vast emptiness run through rocky plain and hills where dun-coloured sheep, angora goats, the occasional herd of springbok and groups of charcoal-and-grey ostriches graze on brown stubble. For more focused game viewing, the scenic **Mountain Zebra** and **Camdeboo** national parks support a diverse Karoo-associated fauna including the endemic mountain zebra, black wildebeest and springbok. Mountain Zebra National Park is also home to reintroduced lion and cheetah, both seen with increasing ease these days, along with more elusive populations of Cape buffalo and black rhino. In addition, several tracts of the scrubby farmland that divides the two national parks is now given over to private reserves, some aimed mainly at hunters, while others – most notably **Samara**, which became a bona fide Big Five destination in 2019 – cater solely to the photographic safari market. Long-term plans include the linking of the two national parks, which lie about 70km apart as the crow flies, via a wildlife corridor that

5

will also incorporate existing private reserves such as Samara to create a 5000-square-kilometre mega-reserve that will rank among South Africa's five largest conservation areas. This plan was first mooted in 2003 and implementation began in 2012, but it will most likely take many more years to come to full fruition, partly because of the divergent conservation policies of SANParks and various private reserves.

MOUNTAIN ZEBRA AT A GLANCE

Relaxed and low-key self-drive reserve notable for its endemic wildlife and for offering cheetah-tracking on foot.

Big Five: **
General wildlife: ***
Birding: ***
Scenery: ****
Wilderness factor: ***
Uncrowded: ****
Affordability: *****
Self-drive: Y

Mountain Zebra National Park

13km west of Cradock • Daily: Apr–Sept 7am–6pm; Oct–Mar 7am–7pm • Adults R218, children R109, SA citizens R55 • T 048 801 5700/5701, W sanparks.org/parks/mountain_zebra

One of South Africa's most beautiful but least-known protected areas, **Mountain Zebra National Park** safeguards a mountainous semi-arid Karoo landscape of rolling grassland, low scrubby succulents, and acacia woodland dominated by sweet thorn. Bisected by the Wilgerboom ("Willow") River, it receives an annual rainfall of around 400mm and mostly stands at an altitude of 1200–1500 metres, but the uplands rise to 1957 metres at **Bakenkop** ("Beacon Head") on the southern border. As its name suggests, the park was originally created to protect the Cape mountain zebra, a Cape endemic, but it is also now one of the best places to see the original megafauna of South Africa's dry interior – antelope such as gemsbok, red hartebeest, black wildebeest, blesbok, springbok, greater kudu and grey rhebok – undiluted by the more whimsically introduced species associated with many private reserves in the Eastern Cape. Cheetah were reintroduced to the national park in 2007 and can now be tracked on foot as a guided activity. Lion were reintroduced in 2013 and the population is now estimated at twenty individuals, including a couple of magnificently maned males. Of the rest of the Big Five, buffalo and black rhino have also been introduced, but both tend to stick to thickets along the Wilgerboom River and neither is commonly seen. Among the smaller predators, the black-backed jackal is most conspicuous, while yellow mongoose and meerkat both tend to reveal their presence by standing tall on their hind legs, and the park has a reputation for regular sightings of aardwolf and bat-eared fox in winter. The birdlife seems rather subdued by South African standards, but 277 species have been recorded. Regularly seen highlights include blue crane, Ludwig's bustard, pale chanting goshawk, jackal buzzard and Verreaux's eagle. The gorgeous malachite sunbird is often seen feeding on aloes in the restcamp.

Brief history

Not much is known about the territory around Mountain Zebra National Park prior to the establishment of a nearby administrative and military outpost at Cradock in 1812 (named after General John Cradock, then Governor of the Cape). But late Stone Age pottery and stone artefacts dating back more than 10,000 years have been discovered along the banks of the Wilgerboom River as it runs through the park, while **rock art** attributed to San hunter-gatherers is at least three hundred years old. The area also supported prolific wildlife – in particular **Cape mountain zebra**, black wildebeest, eland and the now-extinct quagga – prior to being carved up into farmland by Dutch and British settlers in the mid- to late-nineteenth century, when Cradock emerged as a major sheep ranching centre.

The original 65-square-kilometre Mount Zebra National Park came into being in 1937 when the farm **Babylonstoren** (literally Tower of Babel) was set aside as a sanctuary to protect the Cape mountain zebra, a once-abundant equid that had been hunted close to extinction by settlers. The park's original population of one female and four male zebras fared poorly, however, and it had died out completely by 1950. Fortunately, the park's raison d'être was revived a few months later when local farmer Hans Lombard agreed to donate the herd of eleven mountain zebras that roamed his nearby farm Waterval. Supplemented by another small herd in 1964, the reintroduced zebras thrived and by 1988 the park supported a population of around 280 individuals.

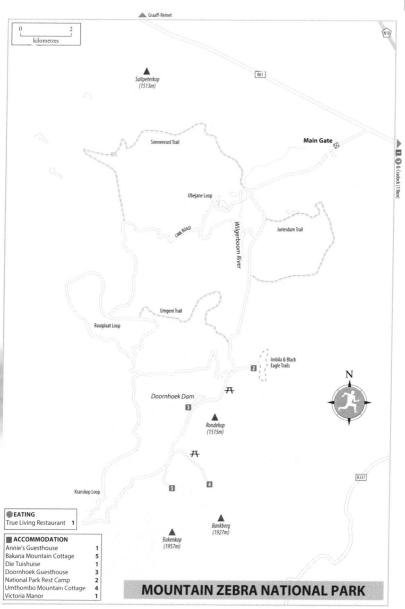

MOUNTAIN ZEBRA NATIONAL PARK

● EATING
True Living Restaurant   1

■ ACCOMMODATION
Annie's Guesthouse   1
Bakana Mountain Cottage   5
Die Tuishuise   1
Doornhoek Guesthouse   3
National Park Rest Camp   2
Umthombo Mountain Cottage   4
Victoria Manor   1

5

In the late 1970s, it was recognized that the zebra population was in danger of outgrowing the park, so excess stock was relocated to what are now the Camdeboo, Karoo and Table Mountain national parks. In 1998, the original park was expanded to cover its present area of 284 square kilometres. The park's mountain zebra population has since increased to more than one thousand individuals, which represents roughly one-third of the global population. The expansion of the national park also paved the way for the reintroduction of lion, cheetah, buffalo, black rhino and gemsbok, all of which have done well in their adopted home. Long-term plans include the creation of a **wildlife corridor** to Camdeboo National Park.

Game drives

The park has two main game-viewing routes, both predominately unsurfaced but asphalted at a few steep or potentially tricky sections. Either can be covered quite comfortably in around two hours, depending to some extent on how often you stop to look and photograph wildlife. The roads are suited to the most low-slung of saloon cars, so there is no obstacle to driving yourself around, but the park also offers guided morning and evening drives in an open-sided 4WD, as well as night drives in search of unusual nocturnal species (from R258/127 per adult/child).

The **more northerly route** links the entrance gate to the restcamp via the 12km main road or a highly recommended and largely circuitous 30km route via Ubejane Loop, Link Road and Rooiplaat Loop. Coming from the entrance gate, the main road crosses a few drainage ditches where small groups of the delightful meerkat are regularly seen. After 4km, turn right onto the Ubejane Loop, and almost immediately afterwards, you'll see a few sandy burrows either side of the road that house a colony of Cape ground squirrels. This is also a good area to look for blue korhaan, a handsome 50cm tall ground bird that's endemic to the South African interior and IUCN red-listed as Near Threatened. On cold winter mornings and evenings, bat-eared fox and aardvark are also occasionally seen in daylight along the 4km stretch of the loop that leads past a large (usually dry) dam to Link Road, which can be productive for lions and antelope such as eland, red hartebeest and black wildebeest, and passes through several patches of acacias where you should look out for the characteristically scruffy nests of white-browed sparrow-weaver and scaly feathered finch. Link Road connects to the 12km Rooiplaat Loop, which runs through a plateau of open grassland that usually provides the best general game viewing in the park, including plentiful mountain zebra, springbok and blesbok, as well as offering a fair chance of spotting lion or cheetah.

The **Kranskop Loop**, a 25km circuit running southwest from the restcamp, tends to be less productive for game viewing, but it passes through some truly spectacular scenery. The more westerly leg of the loop follows a high grass- and fynbos-swathed ridge that offers splendid views into a series of rolling valleys outside the park's eastern border. Wildlife sometimes seen in this area includes buffalo, greater kudu and mountain reedbuck, while grey rheboks sometimes reveal their presence with a high nasal alarm call. The road then descends dramatically to the Wilgerboom River and follows its east bank north through a well-wooded landscape punctuated by some spectacular dolerite domes and outcrops, often inhabited by rock hyrax, klipspringer and mocking cliff-chat. Doornhoek Dam, to your left as you return to the restcamp, supports a good selection of water-associated birds, including African fish eagle, African black duck and giant kingfisher.

Three **4WD-only trails** offer visitors with suitable vehicles and driving experience the opportunity to escape the relatively busy all-weather road circuits. The 9.5km Juriesdam Trail, which runs east from the main road between the entrance gate and restcamp, ascends steeply to a vast grassy plateau where large herds of mountain zebra, black wildebeest and other antelope can be seen alongside the bulky (up to 80cm high) Ludwig's bustard and various larks. The 14km Sonnenrust Trail, a northern extension

5

of Ubejane Loop and Link Road, passes through denser and scrubbier vegetation inhabited by greater kudu, eland and red hartebeest. The more challenging Umgeni Trail, which follows the main road north of the restcamp west to emerge on to the Rooiplaat Plateau, follows a series of spectacular vertigo-inducing ridges more notable for their scenic qualities than for wildlife viewing.

Other activities

Mountain Zebra is the only national park in South Africa to offer guided **cheetah tracking** on foot (7am summer, 8.30am winter; R429 per person). Trips entail tracking one of the park's GPS-collared cheetahs from a vehicle using VHF telemetry, then once you have located an animal, following it on foot at enough distance that you don't interfere with its hunting or other activities. The success rate for this exhilarating activity is around 85 percent, and it usually takes anything from two to five hours. Cheetahs are essentially harmless to people, but one might conceivably go for a child, so a minimum age restriction of 12 is imposed, while the rough terrain means that people aged 65 or above require a medical certificate stating they are sufficiently fit to undertake the walk.

Several **rock art sites** lie within the park, the most impressive being **Boesmanskloof**, which depicts a human figure and several animals, including a cheetah, and can only be visited with an armed ranger (R227/111 per adult/child). A more extensive site is **Saltpeterkop**, a small rocky hill that rises to 1513 metres in the far north, and can only be visited on a guided hike accompanied by a park ranger (R399 per person). In addition to some prehistoric paintings of hunters and antelope, Saltpeterkop houses some rock engravings depicting a shamanic trance and a white rhino, a (relatively modern) engraved chess board carved by British soldiers during the Anglo-Boer War of 1899–1902, and a stone cattle kraal presumably built by local sheep farmers.

Two self-guided walking trails lie within the fenced restcamp. The 2.5km Black Eagle Trail leads uphill to a rocky summit where you might encounter baboons, rock hyrax, various lizards and rock-associated birds including the spectacular Verreaux's (aka black) eagle. The 1km Imbila Trail is flatter and less demanding, but it can be rewarding for thicket and grassland birds.

ARRIVAL AND SERVICES

MOUNTAIN ZEBRA NATIONAL PARK

By car The closest town to Mountain Zebra National Park is Cradock, which straddles the N10 about 250km north of Port Elizabeth, 175km northwest of Grahamstown and 200km south of Colesburg (at the junction with the N1 between Cape Town and Johannesburg). Notable for its nineteenth-century colonial architecture and as a hotbed of resistance during the apartheid era, Cradock today possesses a slightly down-at-heel atmosphere, but it makes a useful base for exploring the national park if the restcamp is full or you don't fancy staying there. The park entrance gate lies 13km west of town and can be reached by following the N10 northwest for around 5km, then turning left onto the R61

and after another 6km left again onto a well-signposted and well-maintained dirt feeder road. From the entrance gate it is another 12km, with game viewing all the way, to the restcamp and reception, where entrance fees must be paid in order to obtain an exit permit to show at the gate as you leave.

Services A small shop at the park reception and restcamp sells basics, souvenirs, alcohol and soft drinks, but if you're staying for a few days you should stock up in Cradock, which has a fair selection of supermarkets. The restcamp also has a reasonable licensed à la carte restaurant (daily 11am–9pm), a post office, a filling station and a swimming pool.

ACCOMMODATION

SEE MAP PAGE 259

Annie's Guest House 112 Adderley St, Cradock ☎ 048 881 5241, ⓦ anniesguesthouse.co.za. Reliable, clean and well-run B&B guesthouse in a Victorian house with fourteen brightly coloured rooms, a swimming pool and a garden. Transportation is provided to and from the bus stop, if you need it. ‾s‾

★ **Die Tuishuise** Market St, Cradock ☎ 048 881 1322, ⓦ tuishuise.co.za. Staying in this street of comfortable and stylish one- to four-bedroomed Victorian craftsmen's houses, with their candy-striped veranda roofs, gives an authentic sense of colonial domestic life in the 1850s. Prices are very reasonable, given that you get what amounts to

5

a mini-museum to yourself, each house kitted out with antique furniture and crockery. Breakfast is included; for other meals you can either self-cater or eat in the affiliated Victoria Manor on the same road. $\overline{\underline{SS}}$

★ **Doornhoek Guesthouse** Booking details as for national park restcamp. Overlooking Doornhoek Dam about 5km south of the main restcamp, this restored Cape Dutch farm cottage dates to 1838 and was used as a set for the 2004 film The Story of an African Farm. Complete with original yellowwood floors, wide balcony and period decor, it sleeps up to six people in three en-suite double and twin rooms, making it ideal for small self-catering parties. $\overline{\underline{SSS}}$

National Park Rest Camp ☎ 012 428 9111 (central reservations) or ☎ 048 8015700/1, ⊛ sanparks.org/parks/mountain_zebra. Set in a large, fenced area 12km from the entrance gate, the park's restcamp offers the choice of comfy one- and two-bedroom cottages, and smarter and more modern rock chalets, all with outstanding mountain views and their own kitchens and bathrooms. There is also a campsite. All units have self-catering facilities. Camping $\overline{\underline{S}}$, cottages $\overline{\underline{SS}}$, rock chalets $\overline{\underline{SSS}}$

Umthombo and Bakana Mountain Cottages Booking details as for national park restcamp. Accessible by 4WD only, this isolated pair of stone cottages, set a few kilometres apart in the park's mountainous far south, offers a genuine back-to-basics self-catering experience with gas stove and fridge as well as a braai area. $\overline{\underline{S}}$

Victoria Manor 36 Market St, Cradock ☎ 048 881 1650, ⊛ tuishuise.co.za. Step back in time at this effortlessly gracious, old-fashioned hotel built in 1848, with excellent service, bags of character and period fittings. The dining room and bar are bursting with period character and it's about the only place in town that's open every evening for dinner. $\overline{\underline{S}}$

EATING SEE MAP PAGE 259

If you are staying in the park, the only options are self-catering (all units have kitchens and braai facilities, and there's a reasonably well-stocked shop) or the adequate and inexpensive restaurant in the reception building.

★ **True Living Restaurant** 44 J A Calata St, Cradock ☎ 048 881 3288. A restaurant, deli and bakery where everything is made, produced or hunted on the owners' farm outside Cradock. It serves a varied selection of salads, toasted sandwiches and Karoo favourites in a shady courtyard at the back of the house, or you could stock up with locally grown goodies for a picnic at the national park. All meals are prepared from scratch so be prepared for a wait. Mon–Fri 8am–5pm, Sat 8am–1pm.

Camdeboo National Park

Park headquarters and Lakeview Entrance Gate on the N9 4km north of Graaff-Reinet, entrance to Valley of Desolation 5km northwest of Graaff-Reinet along the R63 • R113 • Daily 6am–7pm (winter), 6am–8pm (summer) • ☎ 049 892 3453, ⊛ sanparks.org/parks/camdeboo

One of South Africa's newest national parks, 194-square-kilometre **Camdeboo** was established in 1979 as the provincially owned Karoo Nature Reserve, and upgraded to its present status under the management of SANParks in 2005. Carved into three sectors by the N9 and R63, the park practically surrounds South Africa's fourth-oldest town, **Graaff-Reinet**, which was founded in 1786 and was later the birthplace of **Robert Sobukwe** (1923–78), charismatic founder of the Pan Africanist Congress (PAC). Camdeboo – the name derives from a Khoi-khoi word meaning "Green Valley" – stands at a slightly lower elevation than Mountain Zebra National Park, but it also protects a mountainous semi-arid Karoo landscape of wiry tussocked grassland, shrubby sweet-thorn savannah and succulent spekboom-dominated thicket punctuated by spike-flowered aloes. Around 45 mammal species are present, with the largest concentrations to be found in a designated game-viewing area flanked by the N9 and R63. This central sector is also the site of **Nqweba Dam**, a municipal water source and prime birdwatching spot fed by the **Sundays River**, a wide and fast-flowing waterway that rises further north in the Sneeuberg Mountains and which used to be known by the Khoi-khoi name *Nukakamma* (Grassy Water) in reference to its perennially green reed-lined banks.

CAMDEBOO AT A GLANCE
This peri-urban gem in the heart of the Karoo is stronger on scenery than wildlife.
Big Five: *
General wildlife: **
Birding: ***
Scenery: *****
Wilderness factor: ****
Uncrowded: ****
Affordability: *****
Self-drive: Y

5

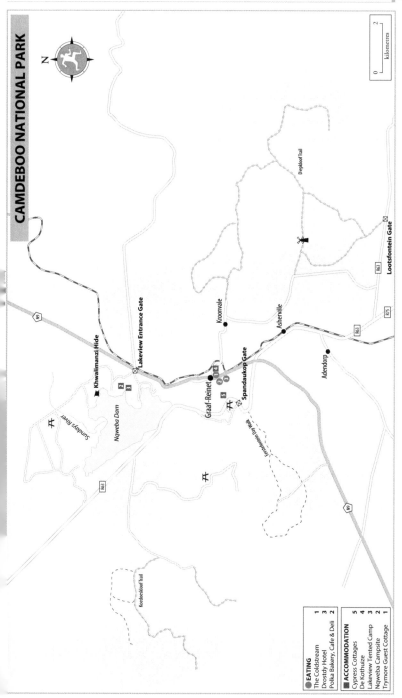

CAMDEBOO NATIONAL PARK

N

0 2
kilometres

Sundays River

Koedoeskloof Trail

N9

Nqweba Dam

Khwalimanzi Hide

Lakeview Entrance Gate

R63

Graaf-Reinet

Spandaukop Gate

Spandaukop Walk

Kroonvale

Asherville

Adendorp

Depskloof Trail

Lootsfontein Gate

R63

R75

R63

N9

● **EATING**
The Coldstream	1
Drostdy Hotel	3
Polka Bakery, Cafe & Deli	2

■ **ACCOMMODATION**
Cypress Cottages	5
De Kothuize	4
Lakeview Tented Camp	3
Nqweba Campsite	2
Trymore Guest Cottage	1

5

The park's best-known feature is the magnificent **Valley of Desolation**, which lies to the west of the R63 and is easily accessible in a saloon car. East of the N9, a hilly sector currently given over to a few little-used 4WD trails is the one earmarked eventually to form the western component of a Big Five mega-reserve running all the way east to Mountain Zebra National Park. Camdeboo can be explored from a rustic restcamp and campsite overlooking Nqweba Dam, but most visitors prefer to visit as a day-trip from Graaff-Reinet, an attractive and gracious town whose period feel is underscored by the presence of more than two hundred **national monuments**, most dating to the eighteenth and nineteenth century.

Game drives and other activities

The highlight of Camdeboo National Park, attracting 50–100,000 visitors annually, is the strikingly deep **Valley of Desolation**, which lies in the most westerly sector, 8.5km southwest of the entrance gate on the west side of the R63. A narrow, tarred road ascends the bush-flecked mountainside, passing a series of viewpoints up to the cliffs overlooking the valley. The views from the lip of the canyon, across intricately carved dolerite columns that rise 120m from the valley floor and deep into the plains of Camdeboo, are truly thrilling. Listen out for the echoing bird calls of the many raptors that breed in the cliffs; it's especially exciting when pairs of Verreaux's eagle – jet black with a prominent white rump and V-shape on the back – circle the dolomite towers, scanning the crevices for prey.

If you are reasonably sure-footed, don't miss out on the 1.5km circular **Crag Lizard Trail**, which leads from the Valley of Desolation car park to a beacon at the western end of the cliff, taking in some spectacular viewpoints and offering the chance to spot wildlife such as greater kudu, mountain reedbuck, klipspringer, troops of baboons, smaller families of rock hyrax and Cape crag lizards sunning themselves on the rocks.

For more serious hikers, the park's western sector is also traversed by the **Eerstefontein Day Walk** – 5km, 11km and 14km variants of which all start and end at Spandaukop Gate, on the N9 southwest of Graaf-Reinet. The walk runs through a spectacular dolerite landscape where greater kudu, Cape Mountain zebra, springbok and bat-eared fox might be encountered.

For dedicated wildlife-watching, a 20km road network runs through the main game-viewing area, which constitutes the park's **central sector** and is accessed from the Lakeview Gate on the west side of the N9. The only member of the Big Five present here is the Cape buffalo, but endemic large mammals are well represented and include Cape mountain zebra, black wildebeest, springbok, gemsbok, grey rhebok and blesbok. Other large mammals likely to be seen here include eland, greater kudu and steenbok, while Cape ground squirrel is also common. The most conspicuous of the park's thirteen carnivores is black-blacked jackal, yellow mongoose, large grey mongoose and meerkat, but lucky visitors might also encounter aardwolf, bat-eared fox, Cape fox, genet and caracal, especially in the chilly winter mornings and late afternoons.

The central sector is rewarding for **birders**, too. Patches of acacia woodland host Karoo specials such as chestnut-vented tit-babbler, Acacia pied barbet, Karoo prinia and fairy flycatcher, while species associated with more open territory include Ludwig's bustard, Karoo korhaan, blue crane, secretary bird and various larks and chats. Nqweba Dam, which also lies in the central sector, is a magnet for water-associated birds, most notably greater and lesser flamingo (whose presence is dependent on water levels), great crested grebe and half-a-dozen species of duck.

Two relatively straightforward 4WD-only trails run through the park, both often offering good but low-density wildlife viewing. The Koedoeskloof in the far west is only 7km long and leads up the Winterhoek Mountains to a peak offering a back view into the Valley of Desolation, while the much longer **Diepkloof Trail** provides the only road access to the park's wild and little-visited Eastern sector.

ARRIVAL AND SERVICES — CAMDEBOO NATIONAL PARK

By car Enclosed by the national park on 3.5 sides, Graaff-Reinet stands at the junction of the N9, R75 and R63, about 260km north of Port Elizabeth, 140km west of Cradock and around 200km respectively east of Beaufort West and south of Hanover (both of which are on a junction with the N1 between Cape Town and Johannesburg). Using public transport, Translux buses between Johannesburg and Port Elizabeth, and Intercape buses connecting Joburg with the Garden Route towns, pull in daily at Graaff-Reinet at the Engen garage on Church St. For bus tickets and timetables, check the bus company websites.

Guided tours Karoo Connections (T 049 892 3978, W karooconnections.co.za) offers a variety of recommended and reasonably priced tours to Camdeboo National Park, including game drives in an open 4WD, nature walks, the Driekoppe 4WD Trail and the Valley of Desolation.

Services The restcamp in Camdeboo National Park is self-catering and has no restaurant or shop. Graaff-Reinet, by contrast, is well equipped with supermarkets and has no shortage of good places to eat, and there is nothing preventing those staying at the restcamp from driving through to town for dinner.

ACCOMMODATION

SEE MAP PAGE 263

Cypress Cottages 76 Donkin St, Graaff-Reinet T 049 892 3965 or T 083 456 1795, W cypresscottage.co.za. Two restored Karoo cottages each with three double en-suite rooms and a communal lounge and dining room. In addition, there are four self-catering units at *River Bend*, also housed in renovated historical cottages. All the cottages are tastefully furnished with antiques and natural fabrics, and there is a swimming pool to boot. $$

De Kothuize 6 Parsonage St, Graaff-Reinet T 049 892 3469 or T 082 339 1680, W dekothuize.co.za. *De Kothuize* comprises seven beautifully restored Karoo cottages – most of them National Monuments – in three of the oldest streets in the centre of town. Five are on Parsonage St, two on Cradock St and one on Middle St. All are self-catering, comfortably furnished with a/c, and an easy walk from the museums and restaurants. $

Lakeview Tented Camp T 012 428 9111 (central reservations), W sanparks.org/parks/camdeboo. Set attractively within the national park's game-viewing area, this rustic camp comprises four standing tents set on stilted platforms and furnished with twin beds and an outdoor table and chairs. There are braai places, a communal kitchen and common showers/toilets. $

★ **Trymore Guest Cottage** Wellwood Farm, off the N9, 30km north of Graaff-Reinet T 049 840 0302, W wellwood.co.za. A self-catering, comfortable, four-bedroom house on a beautiful, long-established 100-square-kilometre Karoo sheep farm. Braai packs are available and evening dinners can be arranged, with Karoo lamb or venison on the menu. An added bonus is the outstanding collection of Karoo reptile fossils, which is available to guests to look at. $$

CAMPING

Nqweba Campsite T 012 428 9111 (central reservations), W sanparks.org/parks/camdeboo. Situated within the national park's game-viewing area close to *Lakeview Tented Camp*, this small acacia-shaded campsite comprises 15 individual sites equipped each with a braai place and powerpoint. The communal kitchen has a deep freeze, stove top and microwave facilities. $

SIBELLA THE CHEETAH

The first wild cheetah to be reintroduced to the Eastern Karoo after an absence of longer than a century, **Sibella** went on to become something of an icon in South African conservation circles. Born in Northwest Province circa 2000, she would almost certainly have died at the age of two from wounds inflicted by a hunter's dogs had she not been rescued by the **De Wildt Cheetah Trust**, and then undergone five hours of surgery followed by a dedicated programme of rehabilitation. In December 2003, by then fully recovered, Sibella was released into **Samara**, where she proved to be an exemplary mother, successfully raising a total of nineteen cubs in four litters over the next dozen years. The grand matriarch, Samara died in 2015 after a clash with an antelope left her with a hole in her abdomen, but her legacy remains considerable. Astonishingly, Sibella's genes are present in fifteen different cheetah populations across South Africa, and are carried by an estimated three percent of individuals countrywide. For visitors to Samara, Sibella's complete trust of people has been carried over to grown-up cubs such as **Chilli**, and their offspring, which makes this private reserve a particularly rewarding place to watch these engaging spotted felids go about their daily business.

EATING   **SEE MAP PAGE 263**

The Coldstream 3 Church Square, Graaff-Reinet ☎ 087 285 4587. In a wing of the former colonial *Graaff-Reinet Club*, with veranda seating overlooking the garden, this restaurant serves Karoo lamb chops, a considerable variety of local meats, plus generous snack platters. Mon–Sat 9am–9pm.

Drostdy Hotel 30 Church St, Graaff-Reinet ☎ 049 892 216. The town's premier historical building has a good – and very upmarket – indoor restaurant, and the best garden

setting for a tranquil drink, coffee or light lunch. If it's too cold outside, the indoor bar is a snug place to sip your gin and tonic. Daily 11am–11pm.

Polka Bakery, Cafe & Deli 52 Somerset St, Graaff-Reinet ☎ 087 550 1363. A cottage restaurant on a quiet, leafy side street serving well-presented and delicious Karoo cuisine, such as lamb shanks (R130) and bobotie with unusual touches. Mon–Sat 7.30am–9pm.

Samara Private Game Reserve

20km along a dirt road north of the R63 between Graaff-Reinet and Somerset East • Conservation fee R150/night • ☎ 031 262 0324 (reservations) or ☎ 049 891 0880 (reception), ⓦ samara.co.za

The largest and most impressive private reserve in the Eastern Karoo, **Samara** extends across 283 square kilometres of semi-arid plains and mountains less than 10km south of Camdeboo National Park as the crow flies. Established in 1997 by **Mark and Sarah Tompkins**, the reserve was assembled from eleven partly degraded livestock farms. The landscape is still in the process of being restored to its historic, pristine state through the eradication of invasive species such as cacti and sisal, the planting of indigenous species such as the carbon-sequestering spekboom, and reducing and reversing water erosion associated with farming. Over its first two decades, Samara also undertook a slow and considered **reintroduction programme** concentrating at first on endemic Karoo ungulates such as black wildebeest, gemsbok and springbok, then on more iconic species such as black rhino, white rhino, giraffe and buffalo. Following the reintroduction of elephants in 2017 and a pair of lions in 2019, Samara now ranks among South Africa's newest Big Five reserves, but management and guides remain dedicated to upholding a broader conservation ethic and offering a holistic wilderness experience to guests. Samara is also looking into medium-term plans to create a corridor reserve with the nearby Camdeboo National Park by buying up the farmland that divides them.

Samara is a very scenic reserve. The sandy red plains, set at an altitude of around 900m, support a natural cover of acacia, spike thorn and spekboom thicket interspersed with isolated white-barked shepherd's trees and oddly shaped cabbage trees. The plains also sport areas of grassland, whose presence is usually associated with former cultivation. These are enclosed by a horseshoe of tall mountains, some of which rise to well above 2000m, most impressively the **Tandjiesberg** (literally "Teeth Mountain"), which comprises a sequence of about a dozen small jagged peaks that resemble a lower jaw. Forbidding as these mountains look from the base, their upper slopes support a vast, gorgeous plateau of undulating golden Afromontane grassland locally referred to as the **Samara Mara**, a reference to Kenya's legendary Masai Mara. Coming from the dry plains, these unexpectedly beautiful highlands feel like another world entirely, an ecological shift emphasized by the fact that Samara is one of the few reserves, if not the only one, where Burchell's zebra and Cape mountain zebra coexist with little danger of hybridization, since the former species sticks almost entirely to the low-lying plains while the latter is restricted to the high montane meadows.

SAMARA AT A GLANCE

Stirring Karoo scenery in a vast Big Five private reserve hosting the lowest tourist volumes in the Eastern Cape.
Big Five: ***
General wildlife: ****
Birding: ***
Scenery: *****
Wilderness factor: *****
Uncrowded: *****
Affordability: *
Self-drive: N

5

Game drives in Samara have a refreshingly different feel to those in most private reserves. With a maximum of 26 guests and only three game-viewing vehicles heading out on any given day, the guides tend to place greater emphasis on the broad wilderness experience and less on ticking off the Big Five. An unusual and rather thrilling aspect of game drives here is that the armed guides will often disembark to track species such as giraffe, white rhino and cheetah on foot (but not, for obvious reasons of safety, more dangerous wildlife such as lion, elephant and black rhino). Most game drives take place on the plains in the south of the reserve, where you can expect to see large numbers of eland, black wildebeest, red hartebeest, greater kudu, springbok, steenbok, Burchell's zebra and giraffe. White rhinos and black-backed jackals are also plentiful in this area, and there's a good chance of spotting elephant and cheetah. Conspicuous birds include Kori bustard, southern black korhaan, blue crane, pale chanting goshawk and Karoo robin. It is worth doing at least one night drive, especially in winter, when you can expect to see a few bat-eared foxes, plenty of springhares hopping about like miniature kangaroos, and with a bit of luck, one of the **aardvarks** for which Samara is renowned (they are quite often seen by daylight in the chilliest months of July and August). Also recommended is an early start for a morning drive into the highlands, which are particularly beautiful around sunrise and support plenty of Cape mountain zebra and capricious black wildebeest herds, as well as being the favoured hunting ground of the reserve's recently reintroduced lions.

ARRIVAL AND DEPARTURE   SAMARA PRIVATE GAME RESERVE

By car Allow at least 45 minutes from Graaff-Reinet, following the R63 southeast out of town for 32km then turning left at the signposted junction for Petersburg on to a dirt road that leads to the two lodges after about 20km. Coming from Port Elizabeth, site of the closest major airport, allow three hours for the drive. More detailed directions and gate codes can be supplied when you book. Although most visitors self-drive to the lodges, transfers can be arranged at the time of booking. Accommodation packages are inclusive of all activities, meals and non-alcoholic beverages. No day-visitors are permitted.

ACCOMMODATION

★ **Karoo Lodge** ☎ 031 262 0324 (reservations), ⓦ samara.co.za/lodges/karoo-lodge. This main lodge on Samara is centred on a nineteenth-century farm homestead, complete with wide wraparound balcony, period furniture, family heirlooms and other vintage paraphernalia. Of nine luxurious suites (sleeping a maximum of eighteen), four are in the main house while the remainder are in standalone cottages. Exceptional food and service are complemented by a large tree-shaded swimming pool area and a short walking trail to a waterhole that attracts plenty of birdlife. $$$$
The Manor ☎ 031 262 0324 (reservations), ⓦ samara.co.za/lodges/the-manor. This five-star villa comprises just four rooms and is well suited to small parties of family and friends. The contemporary classic decor is Africa-themed and a long infinity pool overlooks a waterhole regularly visited by buffalo and other wildlife.

The
Northern
Cape

SUNSET OVER AUGRABIES FALLS NATIONAL PARK

The Northern Cape

The vast Northern Cape, the largest, most dispersed and least populated of South Africa's provinces, is not an easy region for a visitor to tackle. From the lonely Atlantic coast to the provincial capital Kimberley set deep in the interior, it covers over one-third of the nation's landmass, an area dominated by heat, aridity, empty spaces and huge travelling distances, but supports a mere two percent of the population. Under great cloudless skies, it's the miracles of the desert that provide the main attraction of the Northern Cape – the wild animals resident in the peach-coloured dunes and golden grasses of the Kalahari, and the swathes of spring flowers that transform the rocky plains of Namaqualand into a sensational riot of colour over August and September.

When it comes to wildlife viewing, the **NORTHERN CAPE** is a bit of a mixed bag. The South African portion of the **Kgalagadi Transfrontier Park**, protecting a wild and scenic **Kalahari** dunescape wedged in between the borders with Botswana and Namibia, is the country's second-largest national park after Kruger, and one of the finest for big cat sightings, but the other members of the Big Five are absent, making it better suited to wildlife connoisseurs than to first-time safarigoers. Indeed, so far as we can ascertain, there are no elephants at all in the province, while buffalo and rhino are present only in the superb (but, for most, dauntingly pricey) **Tswalu Kalahari Reserve** and the low-key **Mokala National Park** outside Kimberley. Most other national parks and reserves in the Northern Cape are primarily of interest either for their untrammelled scenery and wilderness feel, or else for their improbably wealthy succulent flora and associated spring flowers.

Overall, then, the Northern Cape lacks the uncomplicated popular appeal of, say, the Kruger or Cape Town. Equally, many dedicated nature lovers would regard this thinly populated and starkly beautiful province – and Kgalagadi in particular – to be South Africa's best-kept secret. A big factor in deciding whether to visit would be the **season**. The days can be uncomfortably hot in summer, while winter nights tend to be characterized by sub-zero temperatures. Climatically, it tends to be a lot less extreme and far more pleasant in the autumn (late March to May), while spring has the added advantage of the multihued wildflower displays for which **Namaqualand** is famed. Another factor is timing: realistically you'd need to set aside the best part of two weeks to do this vast province justice, ideally driving between Cape Town and Johannesburg with a diversion of at least four days to Kgalagadi Transfrontier Park. It isn't for everybody. But for self-drivers who are able to travel in the August/September flower season, and who have sufficient time and interest, this is arguably South Africa's most rewarding road trip.

Namaqualand

Conjuring up images of desolation and magic, **NAMAQUALAND** (spelt Namakwaland in Afrikaans) is the land of the Khoikhoi herders called the **Nama** – the Little Nama, who lived south of the Orange River, and the Great Nama who lived north of the river in what is now Namibia. Sparsely populated, the region stretches east from the **Atlantic coast** inland to the edge of the **Great Karoo**, and north from Vanrhynsdorp all the way to the Orange as it flows along the border with Namibia. Above all, Namaqualand is synonymous with one of South Africa's most compelling spectacles, namely the incredible annual display of brightly coloured **wild flowers** that carpet the landscape in August and September. Even outside flower season, swathes of orange, purple and white

Highlights

❶ **Namaqua National Park** In August and September, much of Namaqualand, including its only national park and several lesser reserves, bursts into colour with a superb natural floral display. A fascinating variety of unusual succulents are present all year round. See page 276

❷ **Ai-Ais Richtersveld Transfrontier Park** South Africa's only true desert, a hot, dry and forbidding place whose mountainous slopes can only be explored by 4WD or by drifting down the Orange River in an inflatable canoe. See page 279

❸ **Augrabies Falls** Marvel at South Africa's most powerful waterfall, where the Orange River thunders into an echoing gorge carved into a semi-desert, which also hosts plenty of wildlife. See page 282

❹ **Kgalagadi Transfrontier Park** Discover lion, gemsbok and meerkat among the parched red sand dunes of the Kalahari in the most off-the-beaten-track of all South Africa's major self-drive game parks. See page 285

❺ **Tswalu Kalahari Reserve** South Africa's largest privately owned game reserve protects a vast tract of Kalahari savannah, accessible only to overnight guests at its stylish but pricey lodge. See page 290

HIGHLIGHTS ARE MARKED ON THE MAP ON PAGE 272

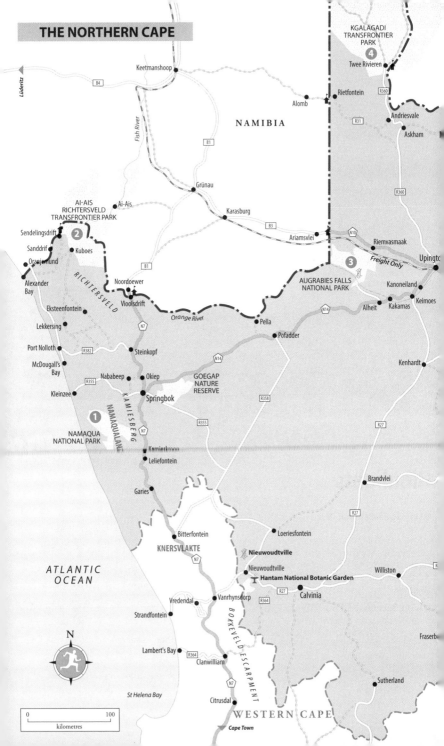

THE NORTHERN CAPE

Lüderitz

Keetmanshoop

B4

NAMIBIA

Fish River

B1

Alomb

Rietfontein

KGALAGADI
TRANSFRONTIER
PARK

Twee Rivieren **4**

R360

Andriesvale

Askham

R31

Grünau

Karasburg

B3

Ariamsvlei

N10

R360

AI-AIS
RICHTERSVELD
TRANSFRONTIER
PARK

Ai-Ais

Sendelingsdrift **2**

Sanddrif

Kuboes

Oranjemund

Alexander
Bay

RICHTERSVELD

Noordoewer

B1

Vioolsdrift

Orange River

Pella

Pofadder

Riemvasmaak

Upingtc

Freight Only **3**

AUGRABIES FALLS
NATIONAL PARK

Kanoneiland

Keimoes

Kakamas

Alheit

N14

Eksteenfontein

Lekkersing

Port Nolloth

R382

Steinkopf

N14

Kenhardt

McDougall's
Bay

R355

Nababeep

Okiep

KAMIESBERG

Springbok

GOEGAP
NATURE
RESERVE

R358

R27

Kleinzee

NAMAQUALAND

1

NAMAQUA
NATIONAL PARK

N7

R355

Kamieskroon

Leliefontein

Garies

Brandvlei

R27

ATLANTIC
OCEAN

Bitterfontein

KNERSVLAKTE

N7

Loeriesfontein

Nieuwoudtville

Nieuwoudtville

Hantam National Botanic Garden

Williston

R

Vredendal

Vanrhynsdorp

R364

R27

Calvinia

Strandfontein

BOKKEVELD ESCARPMENT

Fraserb

Lambert's Bay

R364

Clanwilliam

Sutherland

N7

St Helena Bay

Citrusdal

WESTERN CAPE

N

0   100
kilometres

Cape Town

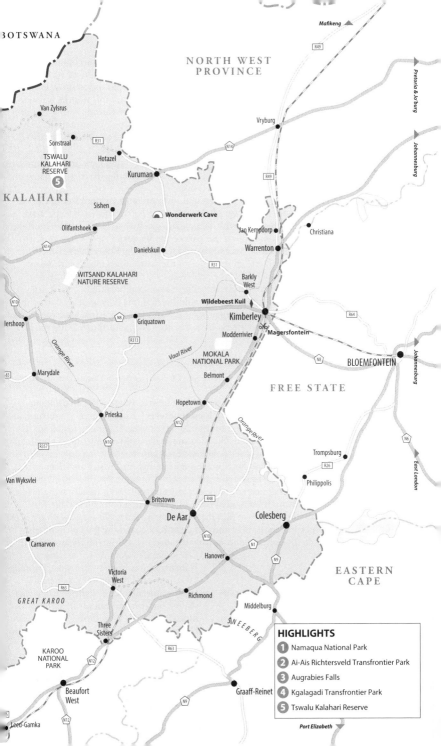

6

daisies emerge, and this dry, empty landscape of mountain deserts, mineral-bearing granite hills and drought-defiant succulents retains a stark but tenacious beauty.

Namaqualand is bisected by the **N7** highway as its runs north for almost 700km from Cape Town to Namibia, offering one of the most scenic drives in the country. Close to its northern end, at the junction with the dusty **N14** from Upington and the Kalahari, lies the region's capital, **Springbok**. This is an excellent base for viewing spring-flower displays. Nearby **Namaqua National Park** is reliable even in years of low rainfall, when displays elsewhere may be muted, while the more northerly **Goegap Nature Reserve** also supports a fair variety of dry-country wildlife. Springbok is also the springboard for visits to the harsh but spectacular **Ai-Ais Richtersveld Transfrontier Park**, which stands in the province's remote northwest corner, bisected by the Orange River – canoeing on which ranks high among the region's attractions.

Coming from the south, the small agricultural town of **Vanrhynsdorp**, set in the lee of the spectacular flat-topped Maskam Mountain, some 300km north of Cape Town at the crossroads of the N7 and the R27, is the main gateway to Namaqualand and the Northern Cape, despite its official status as part of the Western Cape. Vanrhynsdorp stands in a typically bleak part of Namaqualand known as the **Knersvlakte**, which means "Plains of Gnashing Teeth" in reference to the sound once made by wooden wagon-wheels as they toiled across its the pebble-strewn terrain. Vanrhynsdorp is a good place for northbound travellers to refuel or take a meal break, but there's little reason to stop for longer, at least in terms of wildlife, and it is only another two to three hours' drive north along the N7 to Namaqualand National Park, while **Nieuwoudtville**, another popular seasonal flower-viewing base, lies only 50km northeast along the R27.

Hantam National Botanic Garden

Oorlogskloof Rd • During flower season (usually Aug–Oct) daily 8am–5pm • R20 • Rest of year Mon–Fri 7.30am–4.30pm • Free • ☎ 027 218 1200, Ⓦ sanbi.org/gardens/hantam

One of the best places in the country for seeing wild flowers, **Hantam National Botanic Garden** stands on the southern outskirts of **Nieuwoudtville** ("Knee-voet-vil"), a picturesque *dorp* of tin-roofed honey-coloured sandstone buildings situated 350km by road from Cape Town. The area around Hantam and Nieuwoudtville receives unusually high rainfall thanks to its location at the edge of the **Bokkeveld Escarpment**, and it consequently boasts more than three hundred different floral species, around eighty of which are endemic to the immediate vicinity. The 60-square-kilometre botanical garden was established under its present name in 2007, having first hosted flower tours back in 1960, when it was a private family farm called Glenlyon. It was visited twice by David Attenborough and the BBC Natural History Unit in the 1990s to film the documentary series *The Private Life of Plants*. The dominant biomes are renosterveld and succulent Karoo, and the flora includes most species endemic to the Bokkeveld, most notably the lovely blue Pride-of-Nieuwoudtville

Geissorhiza splendidissima. The name Hantam derives from a Khoi phase meaning "Where the red bulbs grow", a reference to the candelabra lily *Brunsvigia bosmaniae* that blooms here prolifically in autumn. Indeed, while spring is the best time to visit Hantam, it is almost as rewarding to be here in autumn, the so-called "secret season", thanks not only to the brilliant pink displays of the candelabra lily but also to the firework-like yellow-and-red inflorescences of *Crossyne flava*. You'll also find a number of early blooming flowers in winter. Belying its name, the Bokkeveld (literally "Antelope

HANTAM AT A GLANCE

Pretty walks and some wildlife are on offer at this reserve, known mainly for spring wildflower displays.

Big Five: N/A
General wildlife: *
Birding: ***
Scenery: ****
Wilderness factor: ***
Uncrowded: ***
Affordability: *****
Self-drive: Y

QUIVER TREES

Also known locally as the kokerboom, the characteristic **quiver tree** (Aloe dichotoma) is broadly distributed throughout the Northern Cape and Namibia. Because it can store water in its trunk, it is known to live up to four hundred years and is perfectly adapted to the region's arid conditions. Discovered in 1685, during Governor Simon van der Stel's expedition to Namaqualand in search of copper, it is not actually a tree but an aloe, with greyish-green leaves and bright yellow flowers. Plants can grow as high as 9m and their smooth trunks can be up to 1m in diameter at ground level. Quiver trees are often encountered growing at the most precarious positions, such as on the edges of canyons where the rocks anchor the plants' spread-root system. The name comes from the San practice of making quivers for their poison arrows from the dried-out hollow branches. The best time to photograph these sculptural trees is when they produce flowers, usually from May to July. The largest quiver tree "forest" in South Africa is situated on Gannabos Farm, 35km north of Nieuwoudtville, off the R357 towards Loeriesfontein; see page 275. There's no charge to visit the forest.

6

Field") no longer supports much in the way of indigenous large ungulates, but a fair variety of dry-country wildlife can also be seen from the nine different walking trails that run through the garden. Among the more conspicuous species are steenbok, baboon, bat-eared fox, black-backed jackal, Cape rock elephant-shrew, the endemic angulate tortoise and more than 150 birds including Ludwig's Bustard, black korhaan, black harrier, secretary bird, blue crane and Cape clapper lark.

ARRIVAL AND INFORMATION

By car The botanical garden stands on the southern outskirts of Nieuwoudtville, which lies 50km northeast of Vanrhynsdorp along the R27. Allow four hours for the 350km drive from Cape Town, two hours to cover the 150km from Lambert's Bay, or 45 minutes coming directly from Vanrhynsdorp.

By bus or taxi Using public transport, Intercape buses (reservations ☎ 021 380 4400, ⊚ intercape.co.za) and taxis running to and from Cape Town, Springbok or Upington stop in Vanrhynsdorp at either the Shell or Caltex garages at the start of Van Riebeeck St after turning off the N7 highway.

HANTAM NATIONAL BOTANIC GARDEN

Public transport from Vanrhynsdorp on to Nieuwoudtville is limited to occasional minibus taxis, which drop off and pick up on Kerk St, 700m east of the tourist office.

Tourist information The tourist office operates out of the church hall on Kerk St (mid-July–Sept Mon–Sat 9am–5pm, Sun 9am–2pm; Oct–mid-July Mon, Wed & Fri 9am–2pm; ☎ 027 218 1336, ⊚ nieuwoudtville.com). It can provide maps and information about the best local flower routes, which tend to vary greatly from one week to the next during season.

ACCOMMODATION

Gannabos Guest Houses 35km north of Nieuwoudtville, off the R357 towards Loeriesfontein ☎ 027 218 1249 or ☎ 087 150 8101, ⊚ gannabos.co.za. Situated on the same farm as South Africa's largest quiver tree "forest", this pair of self-catering cottages are ideal for photographing the trees in silhouette at dawn or dusk. $

Papkuilsfontein Guest Farm 23km south of Nieuwoudtville, off the dirt road to Clanwilliam ☎ 027 218 1246, ⊚ papkuilsfontein.com. Six lovingly restored whitewashed, self-catering cottages spread around the farm – some date back to the 1800s and are hugely atmospheric. Tasty home-cooked light lunches, cakes and coffee are

available at the farm restaurant, *Die Waenhuis* (daily 10am–4pm), with dinners by prior arrangement. Activities include hiking, birding and swimming in the farm dams. $$

Van Zijl Guesthouses and Caravan Park 1 Neethling St ☎ 027 218 1535, ⊚ nieuwoudtville.co.za. A collection of six attractive self-catering houses, sleeping two to six, clustered around the Smidswinkel Restaurant. Most are in restored traditional sandstone buildings, complete with fireplaces and cosy old furniture. The pleasant caravan park and campsite is on Kerk St. All the pitches have electricity and hot-water showers and there's a large thatched braai area. $$

EATING

Smidswinkel Restaurant 1 Neethling St ☎ 027 218 1535. You can't do better than this excellent restaurant at the *Van Zijl Guesthouses*; the leg of lamb is famously good, especially when washed down with the local wine. For less

common Afrikaner specialities like baked sheep's heads and stuffed heart, give them a day's notice. Main courses average around R100, and light meals and teas are served in the garden. Daily 7am–10pm.

6

NAMAQUA AT A GLANCE

Low-key national park whose coastal landscapes and varied marine and dry-country wildlife are enhanced by spectacular wild flowers in spring.

Big Five: N/A
General wildlife: ***
Birding: ***
Scenery: ****
Wilderness factor: *****
Uncrowded: *****
Affordability: *****
Self-drive: Y

Namaqua National Park

21km northwest of Kamieskroon, which lies 70km south of Springbok on the N7 • Daily 8am–5pm • R85 • ☎ 027 672 1948, ⓦ sanparks.org/parks/namaqua

Gazetted in 1999, **Namaqua National Park** started life in 1988 as the 10-square-kilometre World Wildlife Fund-sponsored Skilpad Wildflower Reserve; it was extended to its present area of 1410 square kilometres in 2008. The park is well worth visiting in flower season, even if you're just passing through on the highway, with the Skilpad sector in the southern half still being the main attraction. Access is along a signposted gravel road from the village of **Kamieskroon**, itself a useful stop on the N7 for its filling station, small shops and hotel. Once in the park, the floral displays, featuring great swathes of orange, tend to be more reliable than elsewhere, even in years with low rainfall. Butterfly fanatics and twitchers should be in for a treat too, and there are plenty of mammals to be seen, including springbok, gemsbok, red hartebeest, klipspringer, steenbok, common duiker and baboon, along with the elusive Smiths red rock hare, and a variety of secretive small carnivores. The bird checklist of 150 species includes several dry-country endemics. As indicated by its name (skilpad translates literally as "tortoise"), the Skilpad Wildlife Reserve is also a good place to see two endemic chelonids, the angulate tortoise and much smaller and more localized speckled padloper. There's a circular 5km drive around the reserve, two short walking trails and a scenic picnic site. More ambitiously, a network of walking and biking trails slopes to the wildly scenic 40km coastline running between Groen and Sproeg river mouths. Just outside the park, the coast south of the Groen River mouth is home to a breeding colony of thousands of Cape fur seals.

ACCOMMODATION

WITHIN THE NATIONAL PARK

All accommodation and campsites within the park should be booked through central reservations (☎ 012 428 9111, ⓦ sanparks.org); for camping and late bookings, contact reception directly (☎ 027 672 1948).

Campsites SANParks operates ten wilderness campsites in the park, most of them dotted along the remote but wildly beautiful coast, each of which is restricted to one party comprising a maximum of six people and two vehicles. Enviro toilets are provided but otherwise campers must be totally self-sufficient, as there is no water, electricity or ablution block at any of the sites.

Namaqua Flowers Beach and Skilpad camps During flower season (August and September) SANParks operates two of these "flower camps", with accommodation in dome tents and all meals provided. ₹₹₹

Skilpad Rest Camp In the Skilpad section of the park are four three-bed chalets set in the park's rocky hills, all comfortably equipped with fireplaces, cooking equipment and enclosed verandas. You can also camp here but there is no electricity or showers and only simple toilets. Bring all supplies including firewood. ₹

KAMIESKROON

Kamieskroon Hotel To the right as you come off the N7 at Kamieskroon ☎ 027 672 1614, ⓦ kamieskroonhotel. com. A good option on the way to the park or as a stopover on the N7, with comfortable rooms, some of them with self-catering facilities, and a caravan and camping park. The restaurant offers generous farm-style breakfasts and dinners on request, there's a swimming pool and the owners run photographic tours during flower season. ₹₹

VIEWING THE FLOWERS OF NAMAQUALAND

The seeds of the spectacular **flowers of Namaqualand** – daisies, aloes, gladioli and lilies – lie dormant under the soil through the droughts of summer, waiting for the rain that sometimes takes years to materialize. About four thousand floral species are found in the area, a quarter of which are found nowhere else on Earth. Although it's difficult to predict where the best displays will occur, for more or less guaranteed flowers you can head for the Skilpad section of **Namaqua National Park** (see page 276) or to the **Ai-Ais Richtersveld Transfrontier Park** (see page 279), with its ocean mist-fed succulents.

One indication of where the displays will occur is **winter rainfall**; flowers follow the rain, so early in the season they will be out near the coast, moving steadily inland.

PRACTICALITIES

Viewing flowers in Namaqualand involves a lot of driving, simply because the distances are so great. Book **accommodation** well in advance, either on a farm (ideal if you don't have your own transport, as you can walk around the farm's own flower fields) or in a town like Springbok. Note that accommodation rates can increase substantially during flower season. The following tactics are worth keeping in mind:

• Plan your route before heading out – your hosts may have inside information about the best spots on a particular day.
• Flowers open only in sunshine in a minimum temperature of 18°C, and do not open on rainy or overcast days. Because they turn to face the sun, it's best to drive westwards in the morning and eastwards in the afternoon.
• The flowers only open up from around 11am to 3pm, so you have time for a good breakfast.
• Take lots of pictures, but don't pick the flowers.

FURTHER INFORMATION

TOURIST INFORMATION

Springbok's helpful Namakwa Tourism office (Mon–Fri 8am–4.45pm, during flower season Sat & Sun 8.30am–4pm; ☎ 027 712 8034/5, ⓦ namakwa-dm.gov.za) is at 40 Voortrekker St, 700m south of the taxi rank. It operates the Namakwa Flower Line during spring (daily 8am–8pm, ☎ 079 294 7260) for pre-recorded information about flower "sightings" and related information, and is also a good source of accommodation recommendations during the busy flower season. Another source of local wisdom is the *Springbok Lodge & Restaurant* at 37 Voortrekker St on the corner of Kerk St. A hub for travellers and locals, the shop in the main reception (daily 7am–10pm) sells souvenirs and an excellent selection of books, including plenty of titles on Namaqualand and its flowers, the

history of copper mining and the Nama, the Richtersveld and rock art.

FLOWER TOUR OPERATORS

Several tour operators offer three- to five-day tours from Cape Town to Namaqualand during flower season and can make arrangements to pick up locally, and some also stop at selected fishing villages on the West Coast. Expect to pay around R7000 per person for a three-night/four-day tour from Cape Town staying in B&B accommodation, but not including dinners.
Namaqualand Flower Tours Stellenbosch ☎ 083 272 2233, ⓦ flower-tours.co.za.
Namaqua Tours Based at *Namaqualand Lodge* ☎ 027 219 1377, ⓦ namaquatours.com.

Goegap Nature Reserve

Entrance on the R355, 10km southeast of Springbok • Daily 8am–4.30pm • R30 • ☎ 027 718 9906

One of the most reliable places to see wildflowers in season, the **Goegap Nature Reserve** extends across 148 square kilometres of boulder-strewn semi-desert to the east of **Springbok**, the main commercial and administrative centre of Namaqualand. Set in the **Klein Koperberge** (Small Copper Mountains), its highest point is the 1344m Carolusberg, upon whose slopes Commander Simon Van der Stel sank a shaft in 1685 to discover what was then the world's largest known copper deposit. The main attractions of the reserve, which proclaims itself to be "Namaqualand in miniature", are undoubtedly its spectacular scenery of granite outcrops and inselbergs, and a diverse flora that embraces close to six hundred indigenous species. Its focal point is the **Hester Malan Wild Flower Garden**, which forms a popular destination during flower season, but is worth visiting all year round to see

6

GOEGAP AT A GLANCE

Self-drive, hike or bike through the scenic semi-arid landscape at Goegap, known for its prolific spring blooms.

Big Five: N/A
General wildlife: ***
Birding: ***
Scenery: ****
Wilderness factor: ****
Uncrowded: ****
Affordability: *****
Self-drive: Y

the quiver trees and other unusual-looking endemic succulents showcased here. Around 45 mammal species are present, most conspicuously gemsbok, eland, springbok, klipspringer, yellow mongoose and meerkat. It is also home to one of South Africa's only populations of Hartmann's mountain zebra, a subspecies whose range is otherwise confined to Namibia. More secretive wildlife includes bat-eared fox and aardwolf. Around one hundred bird species have been recorded, notably Verreaux's eagle, Ludwig's bustard, Namaqua sandgrouse, cinnamon-breasted warbler, dusky sunbird, Layard's tit-babbler and a variety of inconspicuous but localized larks. The reserve can be explored along a 17km gravel road suitable to all cars, as well as 35km of 4WD tracks (also great for mountain biking) and a number of short walking trails. Horseback trails into Goegap are offered by Namaqua Horse Trails (☎ 082 877 5764, ⓦ namaquahorsetrails.co.za).

ARRIVAL AND DEPARTURE   GOEGAP NATURE RESERVE

By car Springbok stands at the junction of the N7 and N14 some 560km (6 hours) north of Cape Town and 380km (4 hours) west of Upington, making it a convenient place to break up the road trip between the two. Coming from Upington, the N14 eventually becomes Voortrekker St, the town's main drag, and veers south at the taxi rank to rejoin the N7 for Cape Town. The entrance to Goegap is on the R355, 10 minutes' drive southeast of Springbok.
By bus Intercape buses pick up and drop off next to the Engen

Garage on Voortrekker St (reservations ☎ 021 380 4400, ⓦ intercape.co.za, or buy tickets at Shoprite supermarket, 200m back towards town).
Destinations: Cape Town (daily; 9hr); Upington (daily; 4hr 40min); Windhoek, Namibia (daily; 14hr 15min).
By minibus Most minibuses leave Springbok from the taxi rank at Klipkoppie, and run to Cape Town (6–8hr) at around 11am every day except Saturdays and go via other towns on the N7.

ACCOMMODATION

Accommodation within the reserve is limited but good value. There's a far greater choice of rooms in Springbok. Either way, you're advised to book ahead in flower season (Aug–Sept) when room rates may be slightly higher.
★ **Annie's Cottage** 4 King St, Springbok ☎ 027 712 1451, ⓦ anniescottage.co.za. Extremely stylish, comfortable and colourful B&B rooms in a restored colonial house decorated with local artwork, with a swimming pool under jacaranda trees. There are hiking trails nearby, and the gregarious owner is a good source of information about where to see the best flowers. 5̄
Goegap Nature Reserve ☎ 027 718 9906. The main camp near reception has two well-equipped three-bedroom chalets with a lounge, self-catering kitchen, braai on the terrace, and solar lighting. There are also four-bed bush huts using a common ablution, and a campsite for those with their own tents. 5̄
Mountain View Guest House 2 Overberg Ave, Springbok (turn-off is 100m south of the tourist office, from where it's another 1km along Overberg Ave) ☎ 027 712 1438, ⓦ mountview.co.za. Ten colourful but tasteful African-themed rooms (two self-catering) in this stylish guesthouse, pleasantly situated on the fringe of the town,

right by a short trail with views over Springbok. 5̄
Naries Namakwa Retreat 27km west of town along the Kleinzee Rd (R355) ☎ 021 872 0398, ⓦ naries.co.za. A homely, comfortable place to stay, with stylish rooms in an atmospheric Cape Dutch farmhouse, plus a self-catering cottage and three luxurious dome-shaped suites nestled among the boulders nearby. No under-12s allowed in the main farmhouse or the suites. The candlelight dinners are a big draw, and hiking and horseriding can be arranged. Rates are for half-board. 5̄5̄5̄
Springbok Caravan Park 2km southeast of town along the R355 ☎ 027 718 1584, ⓦ springbokcaravanpark. co.za. Convenient for the N7, the park is well maintained and attractively surrounded by quiver trees; along with tent sites, it offers two-bed rondavels sharing kitchen and bathrooms with campers, self-catering chalets and a swimming pool. 5̄
Springbok Lodge 37 Voortrekker St, entrance on Kerk St ☎ 027 718 1832, ⓦ springboklodge.com. Simple but characterful and good value, offering 48 rooms with or without kitchens, all in distinctive white and yellow buildings within walking distance of the reception office/ curio shop. The reliable restaurant offers the usual range of fish and chips, burgers and pizzas. 5̄

EATING

Herb Garden Voortrekker St, corner of Kruis Rd ☎ 027 712 1247 or ☎ 027 848 1163. On the same property as a plant nursery, an airy coffee shop by day offering build-your-own breakfasts, pizzas, sandwiches and desserts like malva pudding. More sophisticated meals such as lamb chops or steaks in the evening. Mon–Sat 8am–9pm, Sun 8am–3pm.

Pot & Barrel 39 Voortrekker St, just south of Springbok Lodge ☎ 027 718 1475. This no-frills pub and occasional venue for local Afrikaans live music serves pizzas and meaty dishes such as pork chops or lamb curry. Mon–Sat 8am–2am, Sun 11am–2pm, 5–10pm.

Springbok Lodge Restaurant 37 Voortrekker St, entrance on Kerk St ☎ 027 712 1321. Vaguely reminiscent of an American diner from the 1950s, serving a large selection of steak, fish and burger meals, plus local favourites like Karoo lamb and beef bobotie (mains R50–100). Or you could just stop for a coffee, milkshake or a big serving of "slap-chips" (fries). Mon–Sat 7am–10pm, Sun 8am–10pm.

6

Ai-Ais Richtersveld Transfrontier Park

Daily May–September 7am–6pm, Oct–April 7am–7pm, reception 8am–4pm • R243 • ☎ 027 831 1506, ⬮ sanparks.org/parks/richtersveld

Realistically accessible only in a high-clearance vehicle, preferably with 4WD, the **Ai-Ais Richtersveld Transfrontier Park** in northwest Namaqualand – commonly known as **the Richtersveld** – covers an area roughly bounded by the Orange River to the north, the N7 to the east, and the R382 to Port Nolloth to the south. The starkly beautiful park was formed in 2003 by the merger of South Africa's Richtersveld National Park (by which name the new park is still often known in South Africa) and Namibia's former Ai-Ais Hot Springs Game Park. Tucked along either side of a loop in the Orange, the landscape is fierce and rugged; names such as Hellskloof, Skeleton Gorge, Devil's Tooth and Gorgon's Head indicate the austerity of the inhospitable brown mountainscape, tempered only by a broad range of hardy succulents, mighty rock formations, the magnificence of the light cast at dawn and dusk, and the glittering canopy of stars at night. Annual rainfall in parts of the park is under 50mm, making this the only true **desert** – and mountain desert at that – in South Africa. In summer the daytime heat can be unbearable, with temperatures over 50°C recorded, while on winter nights the temperature drops below freezing.

The **best time to visit** is August and September, when the area's succulents – representing almost one-third of South Africa's species – burst into flower. Whenever you visit, a striking feature of the landscape is the bizarre **halfmensboom** (half-human tree), a succulent whose unbranched northward-leaning cylindric stem can grow up to four metres tall and is topped with a tuft of branches, and which is revered by the Nama people as a half-human embodiment of their mourning ancestors. Large mammals subsist at low volumes in this parched environment, but you can expect to see the localized Hartmann's mountain zebra along with gemsbok, springbok and steenbok in the denser vegetation around the Orange River. Rockier areas are home to klipspringer, grey rhebok, baboon and rock hyrax. A wide variety of carnivores – most seldom seen by casual visitors – includes leopard, brown hyena, bat-eared fox, yellow mongoose and meerkat. A checklist of 210 bird species includes large raptors such as Verreaux's eagle, martial eagle and black-breasted snake-eagle, and a variety of dry-country specials with a localized distribution in South Africa, most notably the gorgeous rosy-faced lovebird and somewhat drabber Barlow's lark.

AI-AIS RICHTERSVELD AT A GLANCE

Hemmed in by the Orange River and populated by weird succulents and dry-country wildlife, this is a firm favourite with 4WD enthusiasts.

Big Five: N/A
General wildlife: **
Birding: ****
Scenery: *****
Wilderness factor: *****
Uncrowded: *****
Affordability: ***
Self-drive: Y

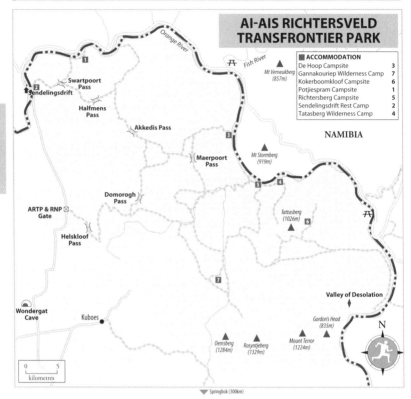

AI-AIS RICHTERSVELD TRANSFRONTIER PARK

ACCOMMODATION

De Hoop Campsite	3
Gannakouriep Wilderness Camp	7
Kokerboomkloof Campsite	6
Potjiespram Campsite	1
Richtersberg Campsite	5
Sendelingsdrift Rest Camp	2
Tatasberg Wilderness Camp	4

Springbok (300km)

ARRIVAL AND DEPARTURE

Given its remoteness, this is not the place for a day visit, and there's no public transport. Unless you're a skilled driver with a 4WD or solid high-clearance pick-up, the best way of seeing the park is as part of a tour (see page 282).

By car The park lies about 310km from Springbok by road. Allow five hours for the drive; given you are required to be at the park office before 4pm in order to reach the campsites before dark, in practice this means leaving before 11am. The most direct route from Springbok is to drive north along the N7 to Steinkopf (49km). From here, follow the R382 via the Annenous Pass to Port Nolloth and then Alexander Bay, from where the park is signposted. It is 93km on a gravel road from Alexander Bay to the park office at Sendelingsdrift. Those coming from Namibia can take the 140km road from the Vioolsdrift border on the N7, via Kotzehoop, Eksteenfontein, and then take the Sendelingsdrift pontoon (daily 8am–4pm)

AI-AIS RICHTERSVELD TRANSFRONTIER PARK

across the Orange River, which marks the boundary between South Africa and its neighbour (with immigration facilities). In high-water season from December to April, you should phone the park in advance to find out if it is operating.

GETTING AROUND

By car Ordinary cars are not allowed inside the park; the only way to explore is in a 4WD or a pick-up with a high enough clearance to handle the sandy river beds and rough mountain passes between the designated campsites. Pay particular attention along the track linking the Richtersberg and De Hoop campsites, which is covered with thick sand and treacherously jagged rocks. It is recommended that you travel in a group of two vehicles; single vehicles must sign an agreement to report back to park headquarters on departure. No driving is allowed at night.

ACCOMMODATION

SEE MAP ABOVE

It's advisable to prebook accommodation; reservations should be made through SANParks in Pretoria (☎ 012 428 9111, ⊛ sanparks.org). For camping and late bookings, contact reception directly (☎ 027 831 1506). There is no

shop or restaurant in the park, but fuel is available at the park headquarters at Sendelingsdrift (daily 8am–4pm), 93km from Alexander Bay. The nearest shops are at Alexander Bay, but there is far greater choice in the large

ACTIVITIES IN THE RICHTERSVELD

Between April and September it's possible to take **guided hikes** along three designated trails in the park, although note that these trails are pretty tough going and should only be attempted by experienced wilderness hikers. They are: the Vensterval Trail (four days, three nights), the Lelieshoek–Oemsberg Trail (three days, two nights) and the Kodaspiek Trail (two days, one night). Most overnights on the trails are in the Hiking Trails Base Camp in the Ganakouriep Valley within the park, which has bunks, gas stoves, fridges and hot showers. For more information and reservations contact South African National Parks in Pretoria (T 012 428 9111, W sanparks.org).

Several companies on both the South African and Namibian sides of the Orange River offer multiday **canoeing trips**; two-person inflatable rafts or fibreglass canoes are used and nights are spent camping under the stars on the riverbanks. These trips are a gentle and relaxing jaunt and are not too physically challenging; children over the age of six can join. Expect to pay from R450 for a day-trip to R3500 per person for a three-night/four-day trip. A recommended South African canoeing company is **Bushwhacked Outdoor Adventure** (T 027 761 8953, W bushwhacked.co.za), based at the riverside *Fiddler's Creek* campsite, which stands on the south bank of the river 12km from the Namibian border post at Vioolsdrif. You can camp here; alternatively, there are inexpensive pre-erected dome tents under reed shelters ($), with a bar and all meals available. Transfer from the border can be arranged for R300 for up to four people. A similar set-up is offered by Cape Town-based **Umkulu Adventures** (T 082 082 6715, W umkuluadventures.com), based at *Growcery Camp* on the river 22km from the border, which has budget huts and camping ($). Again, all meals and border transfers are available.

supermarkets in Springbok.

Campsites Spread throughout the park at Kokerboomkloof, Potjiespram, Richtersberg and De Hoop. These are four very basic wilderness campsites; all have cold showers except for *Kokerboomkloof*, which doesn't have any showers. You will need to bring all drinking water, and jerry cans should be filled at Sendelingsdrift. $

Gannakouriep Wilderness Camp Set among dramatic boulders in the south of the park. At *Gannakouriep* there are four picturesque, two-person reed cabins that come with cooking facilities and showers, but you should bring your own drinking water. There is a resident caretaker on-site. $

Sendelingsdrift Rest Camp By the gate at Sendelingsdrift. Ten decent chalets sleeping between two and four people, each equipped with a/c, fridges and stoves. There are views over the Orange River from the front porches, and a swimming pool as well as a campsite. $

Tatasberg Wilderness Camp Overlooking the Orange River. With views across to the mountains on the Namibian side, this is a similar set-up to *Gannakouriep*, with four two-person reed cabins and an on-site caretaker. $

The Kalahari

While the Northern Cape has no shortage of dry, endless expanses, the most emotive by far is the **Kalahari**. The very name holds a resonance of sun-bleached, faraway spaces and the unknown vastness of the African interior, both harsh and magical. The name derives from the word *kgalagadi* (saltpans, or thirsty land), and describes the semi-desert stretching north from the Orange River to the Okavango Delta in northern Botswana, west into Namibia and east until the bushveld begins to dominate in the catchment areas of the Vaal and Limpopo rivers.

The Kalahari in the Northern Cape is characterized by surprisingly high, thinly vegetated red or orange sand dunes, scored with dry riverbeds and large, shimmering saltpans. Although this is, strictly speaking, semi-desert, daytime temperatures are searingly hot in summer and nights are numbingly cold in winter. North of the Orange, South Africa's longest river, the land is populated by tough, hard-working farmers and communities largely descended from the indigenous San hunter-gatherers and nomadic Khoi herders. For many land-users, there is an increasing realization that **eco-tourism** may be the only viable option on huge areas where stock farming and hunting provide at best a marginal living.

6

KALAHARI AND RICHTERSVELD TOURS

To save yourself driving the vast distances of the Kalahari region – and to take advantage of specialized knowledge of the area's distinctive flora, fauna, landscapes and climate – it's worth considering joining a **guided tour**. The following is a list of reliable, knowledgeable and well-organized tour operators offering a range of Kalahari-based trips, which incorporate a visit to **Augrabies Falls** and the **Kgalagadi Transfrontier Park**, although customized itineraries are also available. Prices start at around R5000–7500 per person for a three-night camping safari depending on numbers and what's included. These operators can also organize tours to the Ai-Ais Richtersveld Transfrontier Park (see page 279).

Kalahari Outventures Augrabies Village ☏ 082 476 8213, ⊛ kalahari-adventures.co.za.

Kalahari Safaris Upington ☏ 082 435 0007, ⊛ kalaharisafaris.co.za.

Kalahari Tours & Travel Upington ☏ 054 338 0375, ⊛ kalahari-tours.co.za.

Tata Ma Tata Tours Upington ☏ 054 339 1112, ⊛ tatamatata.co.za.

It's well worth the long trek to get to the **Kgalagadi Transfrontier Park**, which is the undoubted highlight of this area, a vast desert sanctuary whose magnificent landscape of redder-than-red dunes and hardy vegetation is also surprisingly rich in game. The other main regional highlight is **Augrabies Falls National Park**, where the Orange River – South Africa's largest – froths and tumbles into a huge granite gorge. The main town in the area, **Upington** stands on the northern bank of the Orange about an hour's drive east of Augrabies, at the opposite end of a corridor of wine-producing vineyards and wheat and cotton farms whose existence depends on an ambitious irrigation scheme extending either side of the river.

Augrabies Falls National Park

40km from Kakamas • Daily 7am–6.30pm • R210 • ☏ 054 452 9200, ⊛ sanparks.org/parks/augrabies

One of the undoubted highlights of any trip to the Northern Cape, the 510-square-kilometre **Augrabies Falls National Park** stands some 30km north of the N14 about 300km east of Springbok and 120km west of Upington. Roaring out of the barren semi-desert, sending great plumes of spray up above the brown horizon, the falls – still known by their Khoikhoi name, *Aukoerabis*, "the place of great noise" – are the most spectacular moment in the two-thousand-kilometre progress of the **Orange River**. At peak flow, the huge volume of water plunging through the narrow channel actually compares with the more docile periods at Victoria Falls and Niagara, although Augrabies lacks both the height and the soul-wrenching grandeur of its larger rivals. But in its eerie desert setting under an azure evening sky, the falls provide a moving and absorbing experience.

AUGRABIES FALLS AT A GLANCE

South Africa's mightiest waterfall punctuates a scenic semi-arid rockscape with great walking opportunities.

Big Five: None
General wildlife: ***
Birding: ****
Scenery: *****
Wilderness factor: ****
Uncrowded: ****
Affordability: *****
Self-drive: Y

The **falls** are viewed from behind a large fence, while a boardwalk allows wheelchair access to the viewpoint. To see more of the **gorge**, walk the short distance to **Arrow Point** or drive on the link roads round to Ararat or Echo Corner. The atmosphere is at its best near **sunset**, when the sun shines straight into the west-facing part of the gorge. Be careful, though: the sides of the canyon are shaped like a smooth parabola, and there are many tales of curious visitors venturing too far to peer at the falls and sliding helplessly into the seething maelstrom below. Despite the

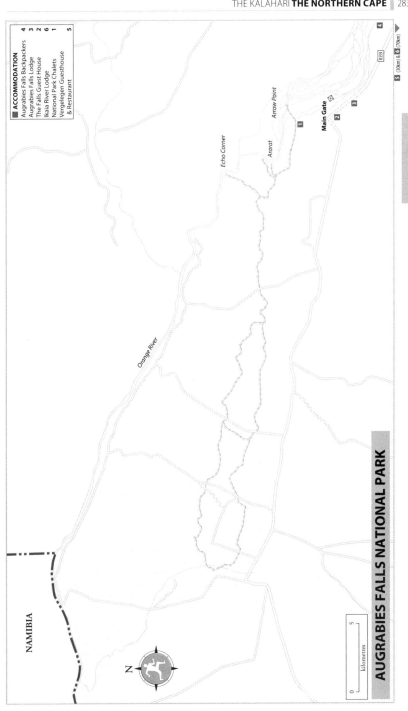

AUGRABIES FALLS NATIONAL PARK

ACCOMMODATION	
Augrabies Falls Backpackers	4
Augrabies Falls Lodge	3
The Falls Guest House	2
Ikaia River Lodge	6
National Park Chalets	1
Vergelegen Guesthouse & Restaurant	5

NAMIBIA

Orange River

Echo Corner

Ararat

Arrow Point

Main Gate

R359

S [30km] & G [70km]

6

N

0   5
kilometres

6

ACTIVITIES AT AUGRABIES FALLS

The circular **Dassie nature trail** is an easy 5km hike out from the main restcamp along the river and to Moon Rock; reception can provide maps. More challenging is the three-day **Klipspringer trail** (Apr 1 to Sept 30), which involves two overnight stops at simple huts; advance booking is essential. **Night game drives** can also be booked at reception, and there's a 94km **self-drive route** (4WD only) in the park's northwestern section for viewing plains game that takes about six hours to complete.

Perhaps more instantly gratifying is the "**Augrabies Rush**", a half-day trip on small rafts down 9km of increasingly swift river immediately above the falls. This is by Kalahari Outventures (see page 282), which also runs an overnight rafting trip, and the four-day Augrabies Canoe Trail, which takes you deep into the empty country upriver of the falls with simple camps set up on the riverbank.

---

odd miraculous survival, several dozen people have died here since the national park was created in 1966.

Receiving an annual rainfall of 100–150mm, the park is dry and harsh away from the river, with sparse plants typical of arid areas, such as kokerboom (quiver tree), camelthorn and Namaqua fig. The landscape is punctuated by various striking rock formations, notably **Moon Rock**, a huge dome of smooth, flaking granite rising out of the flat plains. If you drive on the (unsurfaced) roads in the park you'll probably spot some of the resident ungulates, which include eland, klipspringer, springbok and reintroduced Hartmann's mountain zebra and giraffe, the latter paler than it tends to be in more well-wooded habitats, and often seen unusually stoop-necked to browse on the low trees. Black rhinos are also present but confined to the park's **northern section**, which covers 184 square kilometres on both sides of the river and is accessible only in a 4WD. Guided night drives offer an opportunity to see nocturnal hunters such as bat-eared fox, small-spotted genet, caracal, aardwolf and possibly even leopard.

Smaller wildlife is better looked for on foot. Rock hyrax, southern ground squirrel, yellow mongoose and meerkat are often seen around the camp, while the main viewpoint over the falls is renowned as the place to see the brightly coloured Broadley's flat lizard, whose range is restricted to within 100km of the site, and a trio of different agama lizards. Augrabies is also an excellent place for birders to seek out dry-country species such as Namaqua warbler, cinnamon-breasted warbler, pririt batis, Layard's tit-babbler, dusky sunbird, pale-winged and various larks, bustards, sandgrouse and coursers. The gorge is a breeding site for raptors such as Verreaux's eagle, peregrine falcon and rock kestrel.

The **best time to visit** Augrabies is from March to May, when the temperatures are slightly cooler, and the river is at its maximum flow after summer rainfall up in the Lesotho catchment areas. The water is lower in August and September, but the climate is also comfortable at this time of year, and it ties in with the spring flower season in Namaqualand. With your own transport, the falls are easily visited as a day-trip from Upington, but there's plenty of reasonable accommodation both in the park itself and nearby.

ARRIVAL AND INFORMATION   AUGRABIES FALLS NATIONAL PARK

By car The signposted turn-off to the park is at Alheit on the N14, 10km west of Kakamas. From here, it is about 40km to the park along the R359. Allow three to four hours coming from Springbok or 90 minutes coming from Upington. There is no public transport, but most of the Kalahari tours in the

Northern Cape (see page 282) include a visit to the falls.

Information The park's reception, just up the road from the entrance gate (daily 7am–7pm), has a shop, a self-service snack bar and a restaurant with views towards the gorge.

ACCOMMODATION   SEE MAP PAGE 283

The park accommodation is perfectly adequate, and has the advantage of being in the heart of it, but there are other good choices within 10–20 kilometres, all very reasonably

priced. Given that the falls are the main attraction, there's little need to be there at the crack of dawn for game viewing.

Augrabies Falls Backpackers Augrabies village, 11km before the park gate ⓣ072 515 6079, ⓔaugrabiesbackpackers@gmail.com. Rustic, laidback country house 2km down a dirt road (follow the signs from the main road to the falls). The six rooms are simple, only one is en suite, others share bathrooms, but the owner is full of tips on local activities. There's a kitchen, outdoor bar and braai facilities, and you can swim in a dam on the property. $

Augrabies Falls Lodge 3km before the gate ⓣ054 451 7203, ⓦaugfallslodge.co.za. This revamped lodge, set in an early nineteenth-century homestead close to the falls, offers a/c double rooms and self-catering chalets set among palm trees, and with a swimming pool. There's also a campsite where each site has its own bathroom, and a decent bar and restaurant. $

The Falls Guest House On the R359, 2km before the gate ⓣ082 928 7938, ⓦthefallsaugrabies.com. One of the more upmarket options in the area, this renovated farmhouse has four big, cool rooms and one family cottage, with nice furnishings and a generous veranda overlooking rows of vines. English breakfast is included and dinners or braais can be arranged. $

Ikaia River Lodge Off the R27 on the south side of the bridge over the Orange River, 2km from Keimoes ⓣ082 331 1353, ⓦikaia.co.za. Superbly sited on the banks of the Orange, this tranquil spot has spectacular views and is excellent for watching fish eagles, goliath herons and other birds. There are comfortable rooms, self-catering chalets and four camping sites with private bathrooms. The restaurant serves breakfast and has a short but adequate menu for dinner. $

National Park Chalets At the park reception, reservations through SANParks in Pretoria ⓣ012 428 9111, ⓦsanparks.org; for camping and late bookings, contact reception directly ⓣ054 452 9200. A large camp with a number of comfortable brick chalets and family cottages (three of which are wheelchair accessible), all located within walking distance of the falls and with access to three swimming pools. There is also a campsite. You can either self-cater (the nearest supermarket is in Kakamas) or eat at the restaurant. Camping $, chalets $$

Vergelegen Guesthouse & Restaurant On the N14 about 3km east of Kakamas ⓣ054 431 0976, ⓦaugrabiesfalls.co.za. Located on a farm by the main road, this is one of the most attractive guesthouses in the region, with sixteen neat rooms, two of which are self-catering, and a swimming pool. The restaurant is excellent, with a menu of interesting local dishes like lamb shank, biltong soup and springbok carpaccio. Rates include breakfast. $

6

Kgalagadi Transfrontier Park

Opening hours vary from month to month, roughly sunrise–sunset • R356 • ⓣ054 561 2000, ⓦsanparks.org/parks/kgalagadi

Named after the ancient San name for the Kalahari, the vast, remote and compellingly wild **Kgalagadi Transfrontier Park** (pronounced "kha-la-khadi", the kh as in the Scottish "loch") is almost twice the size of the Kruger National Park, covering an area of roughly 38,000 square kilometres divided between South Africa and Botswana. The South African section, formerly known as the Kalahari Gemsbok, is far smaller than its counterpart in Botswana, but it is still the country's second-largest national park, encompassing some 9590 square kilometres, making it almost six times larger than third-placed Addo Elephant. It occupies a near-triangular wedge of sandy South African soil bordered by Botswana and the meandering path of the Nossob River to the east, and a clinical straight line with Namibia to the west, while its southwestern boundary runs a few kilometres south of the near-parallel course followed by the Auob River. The park entrance, headquarters and largest restcamp stand in the extreme south at **Twee Rivieren**, which as its name suggests, stands at the confluence of the Nossob and Auob, a full 250km by road from Upington, the nearest settlement of any substance.

No fences exist along the border with Botswana, allowing the wildlife undisturbed access to the ancient migration routes so necessary for survival in the desert. The main roads follow the river beds, and this is where the game – and their predators – are most

KGALAGADI AT A GLANCE

Magnificent dunescapes and great carnivore- and bird-viewing in the heart of the Kalahari.

Big Five: **
General wildlife: ****
Birding: *****
Scenery: *****
Wilderness factor: *****
Uncrowded: ****
Affordability: ****
Self-drive: Y

likely to be. Water flows very rarely in the two rivers, but frequent boreholes have been drilled to provide a reliable year-round source of drinking water. Larger trees such as the camelthorn acacia and witgat (shepherd's tree) offer a degree of shade and nutrition, and desert-adapted plants, including types of melon and cucumber, are a source of moisture for the animals. Much of the park is dominated by **red sand dunes**, which, when seen from the air, lie strung out in long, wave-like bands. From a car, the perspective is different, as you are in the valley of the river bed, but this doesn't prevent the path from offering one of the finest **game-viewing** experiences in South Africa – not only for the animals, but for the setting, with its broad landscapes, the crisp light of morning and the huge open skies. The clear viewing and wonderful light are ideal for **photography**, as shown by the exhibition at the visitor centre at *Twee Rivieren Rest Camp*.

Visitors to Kgalagadi should be prepared to clock up some serious mileage; the game drive between the park entrance at **Twee Rivieren** and the **Mata-Mata restcamp** on the western edge of the reserve takes about two-and-a-half hours. But while many visitors only encounter the South African section, where most of the established tourist facilities are found, three-quarters of the park lies within Botswana territory. If you are in a 4WD, the option is to go over from *Twee Rivieren* – Botswana park fees are P20, plus P4 per vehicle (the Botswana Pula is worth about R1.30). Immigration and customs facilities allow travellers to enter the park in one country and depart in the other. You can also enter for a few days and stay at one of the campsites without having to go through border procedures, just as long as you return to South Africa through *Twee Rivieren*.

Brief history

Ecologically, the South African portion of Kgalagadi is an extension of the 580,000-square-kilometre **Kalahari Desert**, a vast sandy depression of rippling dunes and scrubby acacia savannah set mostly within Botswana. Despite the aridity of the climate, the area has been inhabited by people for at least 200,000 years, as evidenced by the discovery of Stone Age hand axes and

KGALAGADI TRANSFRONTIER PARK

Kaa Gate
Union's End
Nossob River
Mabuasehube Gate & ⓘ
BOTSWANA
Nossob
SOUTH AFRICA
NAMIBIA
Mata-Mata
Mata-Mata Gate
Auob River
Nossob River
Pulai
N
Twee Rivieren ⊠ Two Rivers Gate
ⓘ Twee Rivieren
Van Zylsrus & Kuruman
Nossob River
Askham
Andriesvale
R360
Upington

0   25
kilometres

■ ACCOMMODATION	
Askham Post Office Guesthouse	15
Bitterpan Wilderness Camp	7
Gharagab Wilderness Camp	2
Grootkolk Wilderness Camp	1
Kalahari Tented Camp	8
Kieliekrankie Wilderness Camp	10
Mabuasehube Campsite	4
Mata-Mata Rest Camp	6
Molopo Kalahari Lodge	14
Nossob Rest Camp	5
Polentswa Campsite	3
Rooiputs Campsite	11
Twee Rivieren Rest Camp	12
Two Rivers Campsite	13
Urikaruus Wilderness Camp	9

other similar artefacts at several sites. The oldest modern inhabitants of the area are the **Khoe-speaking bushmen** who practised a hunter-gatherer lifestyle here into the colonial era, and semi-nomadic **Kgalagadi pastoralists** who speak a language similar to seTswana and seSotho.

In 1891, in the wake of the so-called "**Scramble for Africa**", the remote and then all-but-uninhabited area that now comprises the South African portion of Kgalagadi was formally annexed to the British protectorate of Bechuanaland (now Botswana). A few years later, it was briefly occupied by troops from South West Africa (present-day Namibia). It effectively fell under its modern sphere of influence at the start of **World War I**, when the South African military, viewing the area as a potential springboard from which to invade its German-ruled neighbour, drilled a series of boreholes along the Auob and left them under the watch of locally recruited guards who were permitted to settle there with their families and livestock. Further settlement took place shortly after World War I, when the land either side of the Auob was carved up into a mosaic of large plots, some of which were sold to commercial farmers, while others were zoned for low-density settlement by rural Coloured communities.

This human influx sent the area's once-prolific wildlife into rapid decline. As a result, the influential Minister of Land, **Piet Grobler** (the prime mover behind the passing of the 1926 National Parks Act), was invited up on a hunting trip to assess the situation by a group of conservationist-minded farmers. Grobler was persuaded to strike a deal with the Coloured settlers to relocate to more fertile land further south, opening the way for the proclamation of the **Kalahari Gemsbok National Park** in 1931. Seven years later, the Gemsbok National Park was proclaimed in neighbouring Botswana, and an informal verbal agreement to treat the two contiguous reserves as a single conservation area followed in 1948. The first tourist amenities in Kalahari Gemsbok were a cluster of three basic huts constructed close to the entrance gate in 1950. By 1966, the national park supported a trio of restcamps at *Twee Rivieren*, *Mata Mata* and *Nossob*.

In 2000, the signature of a historic **bilateral agreement** between the governments of South Africa and Botswana formalized the joint management of the parks and led to Kgalagadi becoming Africa's first official **transfrontier park**. While the park is run as a single ecological unit, and gate receipts are shared, tourist facilities either side of the international border are still run autonomously by SANParks and its counterpart in Botswana. In 2002, following a successful land claim on part of the park's South African territory by the Khomani San and Mier communities, both of which had been dispossessed of community land during the apartheid era, SANParks set aside an area of 580 square kilometres to be managed jointly with the claimants, who were also provided with funding to construct *!Xaus Lodge* as a source of community revenue.

Game-viewing

The truth of Kgalagadi's claims of being a top-rung game-viewing destination depend to some extent on the individual visitor's expectations. For first-time safarigoers seeking a quick Big-Five fix, it will be something of a washout. There are no rhinos in Kgalagadi, and the park is too dry to support elephants or buffalos, while other high-profile absentees include zebra, impala and – as might be expected – hippo and crocodile. Yet despite this, the game viewing can be scintillating. A wide diversity of carnivores is present and unusually conspicuous. **Black-maned Kalahari lions** are often seen lazing under the camelthorns that shade the riverbank, and cheetah and leopard are also more easily seen here than in the majority of non-private parks. Black-backed jackal, suricate and yellow mongoose are common, the bat-eared fox is most visible in winter when it tends to be more diurnal, and fortunate visitors might even encounter Cape fox, caracal, small-spotted cat and African wild cat towards dusk. The most visible antelope are springbok, red hartebeest, blue wildebeest, eland, steenbok and the rapier-horned gemsbok for which the park used to be named. Giraffes, reintroduced to the park in the late 1990s after an absence of several decades, can

6

wrap their long prehensile tongues around the thorny camelthorn branches and strip the leaves with seeming immunity to their cruel spikes.

The park's 280 bird species include a high density of raptors, with bateleur, pale chanting goshawk and gabar goshawk among the most conspicuous. The most prominent dry-country endemics are the sociable weavers whose immense, labyrinthine communal nests look like scruffy tan lollipops perched precariously on the top of dead trees. Many sociable weaver nests are attended by a pair of pygmy falcons, South Africa's smallest raptor, likely to be mistaken for an unusual shrike by the novice birder. Other striking birds whose South African range is more-or-less restricted to the Kalahari are the swallow-tailed bee-eater, crimson-breasted shrike, pied babbler, black-faced waxbill and violet-eared waxbill.

ARRIVAL AND DEPARTURE   KGALAGADI TRANSFRONTIER PARK

By car Coming from Gauteng, the shorter but slower approach to the park is by taking the R31 off the N14 at Kuruman, which is surfaced only as far as Hotazel – the remainder is a long, bleak dirt road which should only be tackled in a sturdy vehicle, as beyond Vanzylsrus it is badly corrugated. Alternatively, you can drive further along the N14 to Upington and turn onto the R360, which is surfaced along the 265km to the park entrance at *Twee Rivieren*. You can also access the park from Namibia through the Mata-Mata Gate and from Botswana through the Two Rivers, Mabuasehube and Kaa gates. Visitors wanting to exit the park via a different country from the one they entered from should note that all immigration controls must be done at *Twee Rivieren* and that a two-night stay in the park is compulsory. Whichever way you get there, the journey is a hot and weary one, but

you'll see plenty of the classic red dunes of the Kalahari on the way. Fuel is available at Andriesvale and Askham on the R360 before *Twee Rivieren*, and at *Twee Rivieren*, *Nossob* and *Mata-Mata* camps, but note it is more expensive within the park than at the filling stations outside.

By plane and tour The two alternatives to making the long drive to Kgalagadi from Gauteng or the Cape are to go on a package tour (see page 282), or to fly to Upington Airport from where you can pick up a rental car; there are also companies in Upington that rent out 4WDs with camping equipment, which can be an affordable way to explore the park; try Desert 4x4 Rental (☎054 332 1183 or ☎082 334 2243, ⊚desert4x4.co.za) or Kalahari 4x4 Hire (☎054 332 3099/8 or ☎082 490 1937, ⊚kalahari4x4hire. co.za).

INFORMATION AND ACTIVITIES

Tourist information *Twee Rivieren* is the largest restcamp and administrative headquarters, and has the main reception, plus a shop, fuel, an ATM, immigration facilities, restaurant and swimming pool. It is the only restcamp with mobile-phone reception. The visitors' centre (☎054 561 2000) has exhibitions and slide shows that are worth checking out.

Activities The focus in Kgalagadi Transfrontier Park is on self-guided game drives, but night and day game drives and day walks can be booked on arrival at *Twee Rivieren*, *Mata Mata* and *Nossob* restcamps. Look out for details posted at the restcamp offices about what's happening on any given day. Rates are R240–400 per person depending on number and duration.

GETTING AROUND

By car The park roads are gravel. While you can travel in a normal car, bear in mind that the higher the clearance the better – a car packed with four adults might struggle. It's also a good idea to reduce the pressure in your tyres by about half a bar before setting off and to play the steering to maintain traction. You might find it's often easier to drive either side

of the "road" along tracks left by other drivers. If you're in a rental car, check the small print as it may exclude cover for damaged wheels, undercarriage and paintwork. In the event of a breakdown you just have to sit it out until someone else passes; a park vehicle patrols most roads each day. Entry to the Botswana side of Kgalagadi is only allowed by 4WD.

ACCOMMODATION

SEE MAP PAGE 286

INSIDE THE PARK

It's vital to book park accommodation, even for campsites, as early as you can through South African National Parks in Pretoria (☎012 428 9111, ⓦsanparks.org). The park has a choice of cottages and camping in two broad types of site: fenced restcamps at *Twee Rivieren*, *Mata-Mata* and *Nossob*, which have electricity (even in the campsites) and creature comforts such as kitchens, fans or air conditioning, braai areas and shops, with some of the units wheelchair accessible; and six far more basic and remote unfenced wilderness camps, for which you need to be completely self-sufficient. It's worth staying at least a night at a park restcamp away from *Twee Rivieren* to taste the raw flavour of the desert. If time is limited, an excursion to *Mata-Mata* makes sense, but *Nossob,* although further off, is better for atmosphere and game viewing: as well as hearing the lions roaring at night, you'll probably have your best chance of seeing them in this area. The roads to *Nossob* and *Mata-Mata* follow river beds, and so are good for spotting game. On the Botswana side, facilities are limited but include campsites run by the Botswana Department of Wildlife and National Parks at *Mabuasehube*, *Two Rivers*, *Rooiputs* and *Polentswa*; visitors need to be completely self-sufficient. For reservations, contact the Botswana Department of Wildlife and National Parks office in Gaborone (☎09 267 318 0774, ⓔdwnp@gov.bw). There are also several campsites in the north and east of the Botswana section run by private operators.

Bitterpan Wilderness Camp A peaceful spot near the centre of the park on a 4WD trail between *Nossob* and *Mata-Mata* (4WD access only), with four reed cabins perched on the edge of a saltpan. $\overline{\underline{\$\$}}$

Gharagab Wilderness Camp Four log cabins in an unfenced area in the far north, a 4hr drive from *Nossob* (access by 4WD), with elevated views onto a landscape of dunes and thornveld savannah. $\overline{\underline{\$\$}}$

Grootkolk Wilderness Camp This unfenced desert camp near Union's End at the very northern tip of the South African section is in prime predator country; its four chalets come fully equipped with cooking supplies, linen and fans, and they're usually solidly booked months in advance. $\overline{\underline{\$\$}}$

★ **Kalahari Tented Camp** Guarded by an armed guide, this unfenced site has comfortable, fully equipped, self-catering tents built of sandbags and canvas (including one luxurious "honeymoon tent"), all decorated in desert tones with views over the Auob River. $\overline{\underline{\$\$}}$

Kieliekrankie Wilderness Camp This is the closest wilderness camp to *Twee Rivieren* (41km), and is accessible to ordinary vehicles; it offers four unfenced cabins sunk into a red sand dune, providing lovely panoramic views of the desert. $\overline{\underline{\$\$}}$

Mata-Mata Rest Camp This fenced restcamp is 120km northwest of *Twee Rivieren* on the Namibian border at the end of the road that follows the course of the Auob River. There are fully equipped family cottages (sleeping six), comfortable two-person chalets and a campsite. Other amenities include a waterhole lit up at night and a shop. Camping $\overline{\underline{\$}}$, chalets $\overline{\underline{\$\$}}$

Nossob Rest Camp On the Botswana border, 160km north of *Twee Rivieren* along the Nossob River Rd, this is the most remote of the three fenced restcamps, and a 4WD is advisable. It has fifteen simple chalets, better family-size guesthouses (sleeping four), a cottage and campsites (the premium one has sites with their own bathrooms and kitchens; R600 for two people). There's also a supply shop, fuel, plus a predator information centre (the place is famed for nocturnal visits by lions). Camping $\overline{\underline{\$}}$, chalets $\overline{\underline{\$}}$

Twee Rivieren Rest Camp The most developed of the three fenced restcamps, right by the entrance, offering over thirty pleasant self-catering chalets with thatched roofs and nice patio areas, a sizeable campsite (with or without electricity), a mediocre restaurant, pool, fuel, and a shop selling souvenirs and simple foodstuffs. Camping $\overline{\underline{\$}}$, chalets $\overline{\underline{\$\$}}$

Urikaruus Wilderness Camp Roughly halfway between *Twee Rivieren* and *Mata-Mata*, with an attractive setting among camelthorn trees overlooking the Auob River; the four two-person cabins, all equipped with solar power and kitchen supplies, are built on stilts and connected by a plank walkway. $\overline{\underline{\$\$}}$

OUTSIDE THE PARK

On the approach road to Kgalagadi there are a couple of places to stay. However, with morning being the best time for game viewing, staying en route to the park isn't really an option if you're on a tight schedule.

Askham Post Office Guesthouse 52 Kameeldoring Ave, Askham, 72km from Twee Rivieren ☎082 494 4520, ⓔaskhamk@mweb.co.za. This B&B offers three spacious and neat en-suite rooms and a self-catering flat for four on the site of the old post office. There's also a small coffee shop and craft shop; overnight guests can pre-order evening meals. $\overline{\underline{\$}}$

Molopo Kalahari Lodge 55km from Twee Rivieren, in Andriesvale ☎054 511 0008, ⓦmolopo.ncfamous lodges.com. A smart, well-run place with more than fifty comfortable chalets set around a pool, as well as luxury bush tents, campsites, a bar and a decent restaurant. It also has a filling station and a small shop selling drinks, ice and meat for braais, and you can stop for coffee when driving towards the park. All rates (even camping) include a simple tea/coffee and toast breakfast. $\overline{\underline{\$}}$

6

6

TSWALU AT A GLANCE

Top dry-country game viewing in a vast
private reserve.
Big Five: ***
General wildlife: ****
Birding: ****
Scenery: ***
Wilderness factor: ****
Uncrowded: *****
Affordability: *
Self-drive: N

Tswalu Kalahari Reserve

On the R31, 100km northwest of Kuruman • ☎ 053 781 9311,
reservations ☎ 011 274 2299, ⓦ tswalu.com

Extending across an astonishing 1140
square kilometres of dry savannah tucked
under the 1500m-high Korannaberg
Mountains to the northwest of Kuruman,
Tswalu is the largest and arguably most
exclusive private reserve anywhere in
South Africa, and the only one of genuine
substance set in the Kalahari. Some R50
million was spent bringing over nine
thousand head of game to this desert
setting, including the endangered desert-adapted black rhino, sable antelope, roan
antelope and cheetah. A total of eighty mammal species includes all the Big Five except
elephant, along with dry-country specialists such as aardvark, aardwolf and brown
hyena, which are quite often seen on night drives. The reserve is accessible only to
overnight guests at a pair of small and impeccably stylish game lodges; accommodation
rates ($$$$$) include expertly guided game drives, horseriding and full board.

Mokala National Park

N12 70km southwest of Kimberley • Daily May–Aug 6am–5.30pm, Sept–April 6am–7pm • R178 • ☎ 053 204 8000, ⓦ sanparks.org/
parks/mokala

The 196-square-kilometre **Mokala National Park** was proclaimed in 2007 as a new
home for more than eight hundred head of game that had to be relocated from the
defunct Vaalbos National Park after a successful land claim necessitated its closure.
Makola is somewhat remote from any major game-viewing circuit, and the absence
of such charismatic safari favourites as lion, leopard and elephant means that few
would view it as a destination in its own right. That said, its location on the N12
only 70km southwest from Kimberley makes it worth consideration as a one- or two-night stopover travelling between Cape Town and Gauteng. The park is traversed by
70km of gravel game-viewing roads, which are normally fine in a standard car, but
might require a 4WD after heavy rain. Guided tours to a 2000-year-old **rock-art site**
are offered.

Makola is the Setswana name for the gnarly camelthorn acacia that dominates
the park's hilly, sandy landscape, which rises to a maximum altitude of 1306m
at **Bakenskop**. The vegetation ranges from transitional zone to the dry Kalahari
savannah and the Nama Karoo, making the park well suited to a wide variety of
plains game. Introduced species include
black and white rhino, buffalo, tsessebe,
roan, eland, gemsbok, sable, giraffe,
Burchell's zebra, and blue and black
wildebeest. There are no elephants or
large cats, but smaller carnivores include
brown hyena, aardwolf, bat-eared fox,
black-backed jackal, caracal and four
species of mongoose. For birders, the
dolerite outcrops and riverine vegetation
of Makola attract a prolific number of
raptors, notably pale chanting goshawk,
martial eagle and lappet-faced, white-backed and Cape vulture. A hide

---

MOKALA AT A GLANCE

Good second-tier game reserve ideally
located for breaking up the drive between
Cape Town and Gauteng.
Big Five: **
General wildlife: ****
Birding: ***
Scenery: ***
Wilderness factor: ***
Uncrowded: ****
Affordability: ****
Self-drive: N

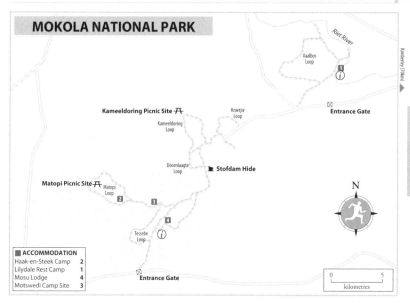

6

overlooking Stofdam is a good place to look for the colourful crimson-breasted shrike and various kingfishers. At night, with the Kalahari sky full of stars, keep an eye open for Cape eagle owls in the camelthorns.

ARRIVAL AND INFORMATION

MOKALA NATIONAL PARK

By car The park lies roughly 70km southwest of Kimberley. There are two entrances off the N12 towards Cape Town; the first turn-off is 37km from Kimberley and leads 16km to *Lilydale Rest Camp*; the second turn-off is 57km from Kimberley at the Heuningneskloof Crossing and goes 21km to the main reception and *Mosu Lodge*. The closest fuel station is at Modderrivier on the N12, 36km south of Kimberley.

Information Both *Lilydale* and *Mosu* are 6km from the park entrance gates. There are no shops, but there is a restaurant at *Mosu Lodge* (daily 8–10am, noon–2pm & 6–9pm). Guided morning, sunset and night drives can be arranged at *Mosu* (R240).

ACCOMMODATION

SEE MAP ABOVE

Reservations for all accommodation should be made through South African National Parks in Pretoria (☎ 012 428 9111, ⊛ sanparks.org). For late bookings (under 48 hours) and camping contact the park direct (☎ 053 204 8000). Wheelchairs are accommodated in all the camps.

Haak-en-Steek Camp This isolated private cottage overlooks a waterhole and accommodates a maximum of four guests. Though somewhat rustic, it has a gas stove and geyser, solar lighting and an outside braai. $\overline{S}\overline{S}$

Lilydale Rest Camp The more rustic option in the park, with twelve self-catering thatched chalets, some with mattresses in the loft for children, and a shared swimming pool, in a picturesque location on the Riet River in the north of the park, which will particularly appeal to birders. $\overline{S}$

Mosu Lodge Comfortable, smart and well designed, Mokala's main camp has low stone and thatched bungalows; some are family-sized with kitchens, while others are two-person units with fridge and kettle, and facilities include a pool, communal lounge with fireplace, and a restaurant and bar. $\overline{S}\overline{S}$

Motswedi Camp Site About 10km from *Mosu* in the south of the park, *Motswedi* offers attractive camping sites, arranged in a half-moon around a waterhole and each with its own ablution and cooking facilities. You can eat at the *Mosu* restaurant but must pre-book dinner. Camping $\overline{S}$

SAN ROCK ART, UKHAHLAMBA-DRAKENSBERG

Contexts

History

Recent fossil finds show that *Homo sapiens* existed along Africa's southern coast over fifty thousand years ago. The descendants of these nomadic Stone Age people – ochre-skinned San hunter-gatherers and Khoikhoi herders (see below) – still inhabited the Western Cape when Europeans arrived in the fifteenth century. By the time of the Dutch settlement at the Cape in the mid-seventeenth century, much of the eastern half of the country was occupied by people who had begun crossing the Limpopo around the time of Christ's birth.

The stage was now set for the complex drama of South Africa's modern history, which in crude terms was a battle for the control of scarce resources between the various indigenous people, African states and the European colonizers. The twentieth century alone saw the endurance of colonialism, the unification of South Africa and the attempts by the white minority to keep at bay the black population's demands for civil rights, culminating in the implementation of South Africa's most notorious social invention – **apartheid**. Ultimately, multiracialism has been victorious and, despite numerous problems, South Africa's lively elections are proof that democracy is still alive.

The first South Africans

Rock art provides evidence of human culture in the subcontinent dating back nearly 30,000 years and represents Southern Africa's oldest and most enduring artistic tradition. The artists were hunter-gatherers, sometimes called Bushmen, but more commonly **San**. The most direct descendants of the late Stone Age, San people have survived in tiny pockets, mostly in Namibia and Botswana, making theirs the longest-spanning culture in the subcontinent. At one time they probably spread throughout sub-Saharan Africa, having pretty well perfected their **nomadic lifestyle**, which involved an enviable twenty-hour working week spent by the men hunting and the women gathering. This left considerable time for artistic and religious pursuits. People lived in small, loosely connected bands comprising family units and were free to leave and join up with other groups. The concept of private property had little meaning because everything required for survival could be obtained from the environment.

About two thousand years ago, this changed when some groups in present-day northern Botswana laid their hands on fat-tailed sheep and cattle from Northern Africa, thus transforming themselves into herding communities. The introduction of livestock revolutionized social organization, creating the idea of ownership and accumulation. Social divisions developed, and political units became larger and centred around a chief, who had important powers, such as the allocation of pasturage.

These were the first South Africans encountered by Portuguese mariners, who landed along the Cape coast in the fifteenth century. Known as **Khoikhoi** (meaning "men of men"), they were not ethnically distinct from the San, as many anthropologists once believed, but simply represented a distinct social organization. According to current thinking, it was possible for Khoi who lost their livestock to revert to being San, and for San to acquire animals to become Khoi, giving rise to the collective term "Khoisan".

30,000 BC	500 BC	500 AD	1488
Hunter-gatherers occupy Cape Peninsula	Khoikhoi sheep herders drift southwards into South Africa, eventually reaching the southern coast	Tall Bantu-speaking farmers cross Limpopo River and begin dispersing down South Africa's east coast	Bartholomeu Dias becomes the first European to set foot on South African soil at Mossel Bay

Farms and crafts

Around two thousand years ago, tall, dark-skinned people who practised mixed farming – raising both crops and livestock – crossed the Limpopo River into what is today South Africa. These **Bantu-speaking** farmers were the ancestors of South Africa's majority African population, who gradually drifted south to occupy the entire eastern half of the subcontinent as far as the Eastern Cape, where they first encountered Europeans in the sixteenth century.

Apart from having highly developed farming know-how and a far more sedentary life than the Khoisan, the early Bantu speakers were skilled craft workers and knew about mining and smelting metals, including gold, copper and iron, which became an important factor in the extensive network of trade that developed.

The Cape goes Dutch

In the late fifteenth century, Portuguese mariners led by **Bartholomeu Dias** first rounded the Cape of Good Hope, but it was another 170 years before any European settlement was established here. In 1652, *De Goede Hoop* and two other vessels of the **Dutch East India Company**, trading between the Netherlands and the East Indies, pulled into Table Bay to set up a refreshment station to resupply company ships.

Despite the view of station commander Jan van Riebeeck that the indigenous Khoi were savages "living without conscience", from the start the Dutch were dependent on them to provide livestock, which were traded for trinkets. As the settlement developed, Van Riebeeck needed more labour to keep the show going. Much to his annoyance, the bosses back in Amsterdam had forbidden him from enslaving the locals, and refused his request for slaves from elsewhere in the company's empire.

This kicked off the process of colonization of the lands around the fort, when a number of Dutch men were released in 1657 from their contracts to farm as free burghers on land granted by the company. The idea was that they would sell their produce to the company at a fixed price, thereby overcoming the labour shortage. The move sparked the first of a series of Khoikhoi–Dutch wars. Although the first campaign ended in stalemate, the Khoikhoi were ultimately no match for the Dutch, who had the advantage of superior mobility and firepower in horses and guns.

Meanwhile, in 1658, Van Riebeeck established **slavery** at the Cape via the back door, when he purloined a shipload of slaves from West Africa. The Dutch East India Company itself became the biggest slaveholder at the Cape and continued importing slaves, mostly from the East Indies, at such a pace that by 1711 there were more slaves than burghers in the colony. With the help of this ready workforce, the embryonic Cape Colony expanded outwards, displacing the Peninsula Khoikhoi, who by 1713 had lost everything. Most of their livestock (nearly fifty thousand head) and most of their land west of the Hottentots Holland Mountains (90km southeast of present-day Cape Town) had been swallowed by the Dutch East India Company. Dispossession and diseases like smallpox, previously unknown in South Africa, decimated their numbers and shattered their social system. By the middle of the eighteenth century, those who remained had been reduced to a condition of miserable servitude to the colonists.

1652	1657	1658	1679
Dutch East India Company establishes a supply station at Cape for trade ships sailing to Indies	Company releases indentured labourers to farm as free settlers	First slaves introduced at Cape and within fifty years slaves outnumber settlers	Castle of Good Hope completed

THE TREKBOERS

Like the Khoikhoi, impoverished white people living at the fringes of colonial society had limited options. Many just packed up their wagons and rolled out into the interior, where they lived by the gun, either hunting game or taking cattle from the Khoi by force. Beyond the control of the Dutch East India Company, these nomadic **trekboers** began to assume a pastoral niche previously occupied by the Khoi. By the beginning of the nineteenth century, trekboers had penetrated well into the Eastern Cape, pushing back the Khoi and San in the process.

As their lives became disrupted and living by **traditional** means became impossible, the Khoi and San began to prey on the cattle and sheep of the trekboers. The trekboers responded by hunting down the Khoi and San as vermin, killing the men and often taking women and children as slaves. After the British occupation of the Cape in 1795, the trekboer migration from the Cape accelerated.

Rise of the Zulus

While in the west of the country trekboers were migrating from the Cape Colony, in the east equally significant movements were under way. Throughout the seventeenth and eighteenth centuries, descendants of the first Bantu-speakers to penetrate into South Africa had been swelling their numbers and had expanded right across the eastern half of the country.

Nowhere was this more marked than in **KwaZulu-Natal**, where, prompted by pressures on grazing land, chiefdoms survived by subduing and absorbing their neighbours. By the early nineteenth century, two chiefdoms, the Ndwandwe and the Mthethwa, dominated eastern South Africa around the Tugela River. During the late 1810s a major confrontation between them ended in the defeat of the Mthethwa. Out of their ruins emerged the **Zulus**, who were to become one of the most powerful polities in Southern Africa. Around 1816, **Shaka** assumed the chieftaincy of the Zulus, whose fighting tactics he quickly transformed.

By 1820, the Zulus had become the dominant regional power and by the middle of the century had established a centralized military state with a forty-thousand-strong standing army. One of the strengths of the system lay in its ability to absorb the survivors of conflict, who became members of the expanding Zulu state. Throughout the 1820s, Shaka sent his armies to invade neighbouring territory. But in 1828 he was stabbed to death by two of his half-brothers, one of whom, Dingane, succeeded him. Dingane continued with his brother's ruthless but devastatingly successful policies and tactics.

The rise of the Zulu state reverberated across Southern Africa and led to the creation of a series of **centralized Nguni states** as well as paving the way for **Boer expansion** into the interior. In a movement of forced migrations known as the **mfecane**, or **difaqane**, instigated by Zulu expansion, huge areas of the country were laid waste and people across eastern South Africa were driven off their lands. They attempted to survive either in small groups or by banding together to form larger political organizations.

To the north of the Zulu kingdom another Nguni group with strong cultural and linguistic affinities with the Zulus came together under **Sobhuza I** and his son Mswati II, after whom their new state **Swaziland** took its name. In North West Province,

1713	1795	1816–1828	1820s
Khoikhoi dispossessed of livestock by settlers and reduced to servitude	Company goes bust and English becomes official language when British take over	Shaka assumes chieftainship of Zulus and forges militarized regional power in southeast	As defence against Shaka, Nguni states form in Swaziland, Lesotho and Matabeleland

a few hundred Zulus under **Mzilikazi** were displaced by Shaka and relocated to Matabeleland, now southwestern Zimbabwe, where they re-established themselves as the **Matabele** kingdom. In the Drakensberg, on the west flank of KwaZulu-Natal, **Moshoeshoe I** used diplomacy and cunning to establish the territory that became the modern state of **Lesotho**.

The Great Trek

Back in the Cape, many Afrikaners were becoming fed up with British rule. Their principal grievance was the way in which the colonial authorities were tampering with labour relations and destroying what they saw as a divine distinction between blacks and whites. In 1828 a proclamation gave Khoi residents and free blacks equality with whites before the law. The **abolition of slavery** in 1834 was the last straw.

Fifteen thousand Afrikaners (one out of ten living in the colony) left the Cape to escape the meddlesome British. When they arrived in the eastern half of the country, they were delighted to find vast tracts of apparently unoccupied land. In fact, they were merely stumbling into the eye of the **mfecane** storm – areas that had been temporarily cleared either by war parties or by fearful refugees hiding out to escape detection. As they fanned out further, they encountered the Nguni states and a series of battles followed. By the middle of the nineteenth century, descendants of the Dutch had consolidated control and established the two Boer states of the **South African Republic**, aka the Transvaal (now Gauteng, Mpumalanga, North West Province and Limpopo) and the **Orange Free State** (now Free State). Britain recognized the independence of both of these states in the 1850s.

The Anglo-Boer War

Despite the benefits it brought, the discovery of gold (see page 297) was also one of the principal causes of the **Anglo-Boer War** (more often referred to locally as the South African War, in recognition of the fact that South Africans of all colours took part). Gold-mining had shifted the economic centre of South Africa from the British-controlled Cape to the South African Republic, while at the same time Britain's European rival, Germany, was beginning to make political and economic inroads in the Boer republics. Britain feared losing its strategic Cape naval base, but perhaps even more important were questions of international finance and the substantial British investment in the mines. London was at the heart of world trade and was eager to see a flourishing gold-mining industry in South Africa, but the Boers seemed rather sluggish about modernizing their infrastructure to assist the exploitation of the mines.

In any case, a number of Britons had for some time seen the unification of South Africa as the key to securing British interests in the subcontinent. To this end, under a wafer-thin pretext, Britain had declared war and subdued the last of the independent African kingdoms by means of the **Zulu War of 1879**. This secured KwaZulu-Natal, bringing all the coastal territories of South Africa under British control. To control the entire subcontinent south of the Limpopo, Britain needed to bring the two Boer republics under the Union flag.

1820s	1834	1843	1860s
British settlers arrive at Port Elizabeth as bulwark against Xhosa on eastern frontier	Abolition of slavery causes many Boers to leave Cape and establish two republics	British annex Natal, settlers arrive and indentured Indian labourers brought to work cane fields	Discovery of world's biggest diamond deposit at Kimberley

> **GOLD AND DIAMONDS**
>
> In the 1850s Britain wasn't too concerned about the interior of South Africa. Its strategic position aside, South Africa was a chaotic backwater at the butt-end of the empire. Things changed in the 1860s, with the discovery of **diamonds** (the world's largest deposit) around modern-day Kimberley, and even more significantly in the 1880s, with the discovery of **gold** on the Witwatersrand (now Gauteng). Together, these finds were the catalyst that transformed South Africa from a down-at-heel rural society into an urbanized industrial one. In the process great fortunes were made by capitalists like Cecil Rhodes, traditional African society was crushed and the independence of the Boer republics ended.

During the closing years of the nineteenth century, Britain demanded that the South African Republic grant voting rights to British miners living there – a demand that, if met, would have meant the end of Boer political control over their own state, since they were outnumbered by the foreigners. The Boers turned down the request and war broke out in October 1899. The British command believed they were looking at a walkover: in the words of **Lord Kitchener**, a "teatime war" that would get the troops home by Christmas.

In fact, the campaign turned into Britain's most expensive since the Napoleonic Wars. During the early stages, the Boers took the imperial power by surprise and penetrated into British-controlled KwaZulu-Natal and the Northern Cape, inflicting a series of humiliating defeats. By June, a reinforced British army was pushing the Boers back, but the Boers fought on for another two years. Lord Kitchener responded with a **scorched-earth policy** that left the countryside a wasteland and thousands of women and children homeless. To house them, the British invented the **concentration camps**, in which 26,370 Boer women and children died. For some Afrikaners, this episode remains a source of bitterness against the British even today. Less widely publicized were the **African concentration camps** which took 14,000 lives. By 1902, the Boers were demoralized, and in May the Afrikaner republics surrendered their independence in exchange for British promises of reconstruction. By the end of the so-called teatime war, Britain had committed nearly half a million men to the field and lost 22,000 of them. Of the 88,000 Boers who fought, seven thousand died in combat. With the two Boer republics and the two British colonies under imperial control, the way was clear for the federation of the **Union of South Africa** in 1910.

Migrant labour and the Bambatha Rebellion

Between the conclusion of the Anglo-Boer War and the unification of South Africa, the mines suffered a **shortage of unskilled labour**. Most Africans still lived by agriculture: to counter this, the government took measures to compel them to supply their labour to the mines. One method was the imposition of **taxes** that had to be paid in coin, thus forcing Africans from subsistence farming and into the cash economy. Responding to one such tax, in 1906 a group of Zulus refused to pay. The authorities declared martial law and dealt mercilessly with the protesters, burning their homes and seizing their possessions. This provoked a full-blown rebellion led by Chief Bambatha, which was

1879	1886	1899–1901	1910
Britain declares war on Zulus, suffers humiliating defeat at Isandlwana, but eventually wins	Discovery of gold around Johannesburg	Britain defeats Afrikaners in Anglo-Boer War to gain total hegemony over South Africa	Boer republics and British colonies merge into Union of South Africa

ruthlessly put down, at a cost of four thousand rebel lives. Armed resistance by Africans was thus ended for over half a century. After the defeat of the **Bambatha Rebellion**, the number of African men from Zululand working in the Gauteng mines shot up by sixty percent. By 1909, eighty percent of adult males in the territory were away from home, working as migrant labourers. **Migrant labour**, with its shattering effects on family life, became one of the foundations of South Africa's economic and social system, and a basic cornerstone of apartheid.

Kick-starting Afrikanerdom

In a parallel development, large numbers of **Afrikaners** were forced to leave rural areas in the early part of the twentieth century. This was partly a result of the war, but also of overcrowding, drought and pestilence. Many Afrikaners joined the ranks of a swelling poor **white working class** whose members often felt despised by the English-speaking capitalists who commanded the economy, and threatened by lower-paid Africans competing for their jobs.

In 1918 a group of Afrikaners formed the **Broederbond** ("the brotherhood"), a secret society to promote the interest of Afrikaners. It aimed to uplift impoverished members of the **volk** ("people") and to develop a sense of pride in their language, religion and culture (see page 299). The Broederbond would come to dominate every aspect of the way the country was run for half a century.

During the early twentieth century, a number of young Afrikaner intellectuals travelled to Europe, where they were inspired by fascism. It was around this time that Afrikaner intellectuals began using the term **apartheid** (pronounced "apart-hate"). Among those kicking their heels in Germany in the 1920s and 30s were **Nico Diederichs**, who became a minister of finance under the Afrikaner Nationalist Party; **Hendrik Frensch Verwoerd**, apartheid's leading theorist and prime minister from 1958 to 1966; and **Piet Meyer**, controller of the state broadcasting service, who named his son Izan ("Nazi" spelled backwards – he later claimed this was sheer coincidence).

In 1939, the Broederbond introduced a scheme that, in the space of a decade, launched ten thousand Afrikaner businesses, some of which are still among the leading players in South Africa's economy.

Africans' claims

Despite having relied on African cooperation for their victory in the South African War and having hinted at enhanced rights for black people after the war, the British excluded them from the cosy federal deal between themselves and the Afrikaners. It wasn't long, in fact, before the white Union government began eroding African rights. In response, a group of middle-class mission-educated Africans formed the **South African Native National Congress** (later to become the ANC) in 1912 to campaign for universal suffrage. In 1914, the leaders went to London to protest against the 1913 **Natives' Land Act**, which confined the black majority to less than ten percent of the land. The trip failed and the Land Act became the foundation for apartheid some 35 years later.

Through the early half of the twentieth century, the ANC remained conservative, unwilling to engage in active protest. In response, a number of alternative mass

1912	1913	1918	1920s
ANC forms to fight for universal suffrage	Land Act gives white South Africans (20 percent of population) 92 percent of the land	Afrikaner secret society, Broederbond, forms and Nelson Mandela born	Agatha Christie surfs at Muizenberg, Cape Town

---

NEW WORD ORDER

In the late nineteenth century, white Afrikaans-speakers, fighting for an identity, sought to create a "racially pure" culture by driving a wedge between themselves and coloured Afrikaans-speakers. They reinvented **Afrikaans** as a "white man's language", eradicating the supposed stigma of its coloured ties by substituting Dutch words for those with Asian or African roots. In 1925, the dialect of Afrikaans spoken by upper-crust white people became an official language alongside English, and the dialects spoken by coloured people were treated as inferior deviations from correct usage.

For Afrikaner nationalists this wasn't enough, and after the introduction of apartheid in 1948, they attempted to codify perceived racial differences. Under the **Population Registration Act**, all South Africans were classified as white, coloured or African. These classifications became fundamental to what kind of life you could expect. There are numerous cases of families in which one sibling was classified coloured with limited rights and another white with the right to live in comfortable white areas, enjoy superior job opportunities, and be able to send their children to better schools and universities.

With the demise of apartheid, the make-up of residential areas is slowly (very slowly) shifting – and so is the thinking on ethnic terminology. Some people now reject the term "coloured" because of its apartheid associations, and refuse any racial definitions; others proudly embrace the term as a means of acknowledging their distinct culture, with its slave, East Indies and Khoikhoi roots.

---

organizations arose, among them the **Industrial and Commercial Union**, an African trade union founded in 1919, which at its peak in 1928 had gathered an impressive 150,000 members. But in the 1930s it ran out of steam. The first political movement in the country not organized along ethnic lines was the South African Communist Party, founded in 1921 with a multiracial executive. While it never gained widespread membership itself, it became an important force inside the ANC.

Throughout the 1930s, the ANC plodded on with speeches, petitions and pleas, which proved completely fruitless.

Young Turks and striking miners

In 1944, a passionate young student named **Nelson Mandela** formed the **ANC Youth League** with friends **Oliver Tambo**, **Walter Sisulu** and **Anton Lembede**. The League's founding manifesto criticized the ANC leadership for being "gentlemen with clean hands". The 1945 annual conference of the ANC adopted a document called "**Africans' Claims in South Africa**", which reflected an emerging politicization. The document demanded **universal franchise** and an end to the **colour bar**, which reserved most skilled jobs for white people.

In 1946 the African Mineworkers' Union launched one of the biggest strikes in the country's history in protest against falling living standards. Virtually the entire Gauteng gold-mining region came to a standstill as one hundred thousand workers downed tools. Prime Minister Jan Smuts sent in police who forced the workers back down the shafts at gunpoint.

The following year Nelson Mandela took his first step into public life when he was elected general secretary of the ANC.

1930s	1939	1948	1949
Orlando township, the nucleus of Soweto, begins evolving	World War II splits Afrikaners, with future prime minister John Vorster among those supporting Germany	National Party wins election and goes full throttle on segregation	Government bans inter-racial marriage and sex, followed by slew of other discriminatory laws

Winds of change

For years, the white government had been hinting at easing up on segregation, and even Smuts himself, no soft liberal, had reckoned that it would have to end at some point. The relentless influx of Africans into the urban areas was breaking the stereotype of them as rural tribespeople. The government appointed the **Fagan Commission** to look into the question of the **pass laws**, which controlled the movement of Africans and sought to keep them out of the white cities unless they had a job.

When the Fagan Commission reported its findings in 1948, it concluded that "the trend to urbanization is irreversible and the pass laws should be eased". While some blacks may have felt heartened by this whiff of reform, this was the last thing many whites wanted to hear. Afrikaner farmers were alarmed by the idea of a labour shortage caused by Africans leaving the rural areas for better prospects in the cities, while white workers feared the prospect of losing jobs to lower-paid African workers.

The National Party comes to power

Against this background of black aspiration and white fears, the Smuts government called a **general election**. The opposition **National Party**, which promoted Afrikaner nationalism, campaigned on a *swart gevaar* or "black peril" ticket, playing on white insecurity and fear. With an eye on the vote of Afrikaner workers and farmers, they promised to reverse the tide of Africans into the cities and to send them all back to the reserves. For white business they made the conflicting promise to bring black workers into the cities as a cheap and plentiful supply of labour.

On Friday May 28, 1948, South Africa awoke to a National Party victory at the polls. Party leader **D.F. Malan** told a group of ecstatic supporters: "For the first time, South Africa is our own. May God grant that it always remains our own. It is to us that millions of semi-barbarous blacks look for guidance, justice and the Christian way of life."

Meanwhile, the **ANC** was driven by its own power struggle. Fed up with the ineffectiveness of the old guard, the Youth League staged a coup, voted in its own leadership with Nelson Mandela on the executive and adopted the League's radical Programme of Action, with an arsenal of tactics that Mandela explained would include "the new weapons of boycott, strike, civil disobedience and non-cooperation".

The 1950s: peaceful protest

During the 1950s, the National Party began putting in place a barrage of laws that would eventually constitute the structure of apartheid. Some early onslaughts on black civil rights included the **Bantu Authorities Act**, which set up puppet authorities to govern Africans in the reserves; the **Population Registration Act**, which classified every South African at birth as "white, native or coloured" (see page 299); the **Group Areas Act**, which divided South Africa into ethnically distinct areas; and the **Suppression of Communism Act**, which made any anti-apartheid opposition (Communist or not) a criminal offence.

The ANC responded in 1952 with the **Defiance Campaign**, aimed at achieving full civil rights for blacks. During the campaign, eight thousand volunteers deliberately broke the apartheid laws and were jailed. The campaign rolled on through 1952 until the police provoked violence in November by firing on a prayer meeting in East

1952	1955	1958	1960
Mandela leads Defiance Campaign against apartheid legislation	Mass non-racial meeting drafts the Freedom Charter, which becomes policy of ANC	New prime minister Verwoerd creates ten ethnic "homelands", the cornerstone of Grand Apartheid	Sixty-nine Africans shot dead at anti-pass law protest; government bans anti-apartheid opposition

London. A riot followed in which two white people were killed, thus appearing to discredit claims that the campaign was non-violent. The government used this pretext to swoop on the homes of the ANC leadership, resulting in the detention and then **banning** of more than one hundred ANC organizers. Bannings restricted a person's movement and political activities: a banned person was prohibited from seeing more than one person at a time or talking to any other banned person; prohibited from entering certain buildings; kept under surveillance; required to report regularly to the police; and could not be quoted or published.

> ### THE FREEDOM CHARTER
> - The people shall govern.
> - All national groups shall have equal rights.
> - The people shall share the nation's wealth.
> - The land shall be shared by those who work it.
> - All shall be equal before the law.
> - All shall enjoy equal human rights.
> - There shall be work and security for all.
> - The doors of learning and culture shall be opened.
> - There shall be houses, security and comfort.
> - There shall be peace and friendship.

The most far-reaching event of the decade was the **Congress of the People**, held near Johannesburg in 1955. At a mass meeting of three thousand delegates, four organizations, representing Africans, coloureds, whites and Indians, formed a strategic partnership called the Congress Alliance. ANC leader **Chief Albert Luthuli** explained that "for the first time in the history of our multiracial nation its people will meet as equals, irrespective of race, colour and creed, to formulate a freedom charter for all the people of our country". Adopted at the Congress of the People, the **Freedom Charter** (see box above) became the principal document defining ANC policy.

The government rounded up 156 opposition leaders and charged them with treason. Evidence at the Treason Trial was based on the Freedom Charter, described as a "blueprint for violent Communist revolution". Although all the defendants were acquitted, the four-year trial disrupted the ANC and splits began to emerge. In 1958 a group of Africanists led by the charismatic **Robert Mangaliso Sobukwe** (see page 299) broke away from the ANC to form the **Pan Africanist Congress (PAC)**, arguing that cooperation with white activists was not in the interests of black liberation.

Sharpeville

On March 21, 1960, Sobukwe and thousands of followers presented themselves without passes to police stations across Gauteng and the Western Cape. At **Sharpeville** police station, south of Johannesburg, the police opened fire, killing 69 and injuring nearly two hundred. Most were shot in the back.

Demonstrations swept the country on March 27. The next day Africans staged a total stay-away from work and thousands joined a public pass-burning demonstration. The day after that, the government declared a **state of emergency**, rounded up 22,000 people and banned the ANC and PAC. White South Africa panicked as the value of the rand slipped and shares slid. Some feared an imminent and bloody revolution.

Later that month, Prime Minister Hendrik Verwoerd was shot in the head by a half-crazed white farmer. Many hoped that, if he died, apartheid would be ditched. But Dr Verwoerd survived, his appetite for apartheid stronger than ever. More than

1961	1962	1966–1970s
South Africa leaves Commonwealth and becomes republic; ANC launches armed struggle	ANC leadership jailed for treason on Robben Island	3.5 million black Africans and coloured people forcibly removed from "white" areas

anyone, Verwoerd made apartheid his own and formulated the system of **Bantustans** – notionally independent statelets in which Africans were to exercise their political rights away from the white areas. The aim was to dismantle the black majority into several separate "tribal" minorities, none of which on its own could outnumber whites.

In 1961 Nelson Mandela called for a national convention "to determine a non-racial democratic constitution". Instead, Verwoerd appointed one-time neo-Nazi John Vorster as justice minister. A trained lawyer, Vorster eagerly set about passing repressive legislation that circumvented the rule of law.

Nelson Mandela saw the writing on the wall. "The time comes in the life of any nation when there remain only two choices: submit or fight. That time has now come to South Africa. We shall not submit," he told the BBC, before going underground as commander in chief of **Umkhonto we Sizwe** (Spear of the Nation, aka MK), the newly formed armed wing of the ANC. The organization was dedicated to economic and symbolic acts of sabotage and was under strict orders not to kill or injure people. In August 1962 Mandela was captured, tried and with nine other ANC leaders he was handed a **life sentence**.

Apartheid: everything going white

With the leadership of the liberation movement behind bars, the 1960s was the decade in which everything seemed to be going the white government's way. Resistance was stifled, the state grew more powerful, and for white South Africans, businessmen and foreign investors life seemed perfect. For black South Africans, poverty deepened – a state of affairs enforced by apartheid legislation and repressive measures that included bannings, detentions without trial, house arrests and murders of political prisoners.

The ANC was impotent, and resistance by its armed wing MK was virtually nonexistent. But as South Africa swung into the 1970s, the uneasy peace began to fray, prompted at first by deteriorating black living standards, which reawakened industrial action. Trade unions came to fill the vacuum left by the ANC.

The **Soweto uprising** of June 16, 1976, signalled the transfer of protest from the workplace to the townships, as black youths took to the streets in protest against the imposition of Afrikaans as a medium of instruction in their schools. The protest spread across the country and by the following February, 575 people (nearly a quarter of them children) had been killed in the rolling series of revolts that followed.

The government relied increasingly on armed police to impose order. Even this was unable to stop the mushrooming of new liberation organizations, many of them part of the broadly based **Black Consciousness Movement**. As the unrest rumbled on into 1977, the government responded by banning all the new black organizations and detaining their leadership. In September 1977, **Steve Biko** (one of the detained) became the 46th political prisoner to die in police custody.

The banned organizations were rapidly replaced by new movements and the government never again successfully put the lid on opposition. By the late 1970s business was complaining that apartheid wasn't working any more, and even the government was having its doubts. The growth of the black population was outstripping that of the white; from a peak of 21 percent of the population in 1910, white people now made up only 16 percent. This proportion was set to fall to ten percent by the end of the century. The sums just didn't add up.

1970	1976	1978
Black Africans stripped of SA citizenship and assigned to impoverished ethnic "homelands"	Police shoot dead over 600 during countrywide protests, which start in Soweto schools	Hawkish former defence minister P.W. Botha becomes president

Total Strategy

It was becoming clear that the deployment of the police couldn't solve South Africa's problems, and in 1978 defence minister **Pieter Willem (P.W.) Botha** became prime minister in a palace coup. Botha adopted a two-handed strategy, of reform accompanied by unprecedented repression. He devised his so-called **Total Strategy**, which aimed to draw every facet of white society into the fight against the opponents of apartheid. This included military training programmes in white schools, propaganda campaigns, the extension of conscription, and political reforms aimed at co-opting Indians and coloured people.

Despite this, the 1980s saw the growing use of sabotage against the apartheid state. Botha began contemplating reform and moved Nelson Mandela and other ANC leaders from **Robben Island** to Pollsmoor Prison in Tokai, Cape Town. But he also poured ever-increasing numbers of troops into African townships to stop unrest, while intimidating neighbouring countries. Between 1981 and 1983, the army launched operations into every one of the country's black-ruled neighbours: Angola, Mozambique, Botswana, Zimbabwe, Swaziland and Lesotho.

In 1983 Botha came up with another scheme to shore up apartheid: the so-called New Constitution in which coloured people and Indians would be granted the vote for their own racially segregated – and powerless – chambers. For Africans, apartheid was to continue as usual.

Around the same time, fifteen thousand **anti-apartheid** delegates met at Mitchell's Plain in Cape Town to form the **United Democratic Front** (UDF), a multiracial umbrella for 575 opposition organizations. The UDF became a proxy for the ANC as two years of strikes, protest and boycotts followed.

Towards the end of the decade, the world watched as apartheid troops and police were regularly shown on TV beating up and shooting unarmed Africans. The Commonwealth condemned the apartheid government, the United States and Australia severed air links and the US Congress passed legislation promoting disinvestment. An increasingly desperate Botha offered to release Mandela "if he renounces violence".

Mandela replied: "I am surprised by the conditions the government wants to impose. I am not a violent man. It was only when all other forms of resistance were no longer open to us that we turned to armed struggle. Let Botha … renounce violence."

As events unfolded, a subtle shift became palpable: Botha was the prisoner and Mandela held the keys. While black resistance wasn't abating, Botha was now also facing a white right-wing backlash. The ultra-right Conservative Party was winning electoral support and the neo-Nazi Afrikaner Weerstandsbeweging (Afrikaner Resistance Movement, aka AWB) was darkly muttering about civil war.

Crisis

In 1986, Botha declared yet another **state of emergency** accompanied by assassinations, mass arrests, detentions, treason trials and torture. Alarmed by the violence engulfing the country, a group of South African businessmen, mostly Afrikaners, flew to Senegal in 1987 to meet an ANC delegation headed by **Thabo Mbeki**. A joint statement pressed for unequivocal support for a negotiated settlement.

1980s	**1983**	**1989**
Botha floods townships with troops and sends army into neighbouring countries	Government cracks down further on opposition after formation of ANC-proxy, United Democratic Front	Botha rebuffs Mandela's appeal from prison for negotiations "to avert civil war"

In 1988 Mandela was rushed to Tygerberg Hospital in Cape Town, suffering from tuberculosis. Although he was better by October, the government announced that he wouldn't be returning to Pollsmoor **Prison**. Instead he was moved to a prison warder's cottage at **Victor Verster** (now Drakenstein) Prison just outside Paarl. Outside the prison walls, Botha's policies had collapsed and the army top brass were telling him that there could be no decisive military victory over the anti-apartheid opposition – and that South Africa's undeclared war in Angola was bleeding the treasury dry.

At the beginning of 1989, Mandela wrote to Botha from Victor Verster calling for negotiations. The intransigent Botha found himself with little room to manoeuvre. When he suffered a stroke, his party colleagues moved swiftly to oust him and replaced him with **Frederik Willem (F.W.) De Klerk**.

De Klerk made it clear that he was opposed to majority rule. But he inherited a massive pile of problems that could no longer be ignored: the economy was in trouble and the cost of maintaining apartheid prohibitive; the illegal influx of Africans from the country to the city had become unstoppable; blacks hadn't been taken in by Botha's constitutional reforms; and even South Africa's friends were losing patience. In September 1989, US President George Bush (the elder) told De Klerk that if there wasn't progress on releasing Mandela within six months, he would extend US sanctions.

De Klerk gambled on his ability to outmanoeuvre the opposition. In February 1990, he announced the unbanning of the ANC, the PAC, the Communist Party and 33 other organizations, as well as the **release of Mandela**. On Sunday February 11, at around 4pm, Mandela stepped out of Victor Verster Prison and was driven to City Hall in Cape Town, from where he spoke publicly for the first time in three decades. That May, Mandela and De Klerk signed an agreement in which the government undertook to repeal repressive laws and release political prisoners, while the ANC agreed to suspend the armed struggle. As events moved towards full-blown negotiations it became clear that De Klerk still clung to race-based notions for a settlement: "Majority rule is not suitable for South Africa," he said, "because it will lead to the domination of minorities."

Negotiations

The **negotiating** process, from 1990 to 1994, was fragile, and at many points a descent into chaos looked likely. Obstacles included violence linked to a sinister element in the apartheid security forces who were working behind the scenes to destabilize the ANC; **threats of civil war** from heavily armed right-wingers; and a low-key war of attrition in KwaZulu-Natal between Zulu nationalists of the **Inkatha Freedom Party** (IFP) and ANC supporters, which had already claimed three thousand lives between 1987 and 1990.

In April 1993 it looked as if it would all fall apart with the **assassination** of Chris Hani, the most popular ANC leader after Mandela. Hani's slaying by a right-wing gunman touched deep fears among all South Africans. A descent into civil war loomed, and for three consecutive nights the nation watched as Mandela appeared on prime-time television appealing for calm. This marked the decisive turning point as it became obvious that only the ANC president could stave off chaos, while De Klerk kept his head down. Pushing his strategic advantage, Mandela called for the immediate setting of an election date. Shortly afterwards the date for elections was set for April 27, 1994.

1989	1990	1994	1999
Botha suffers stroke and is replaced by F.W. De Klerk, who unbans ANC	Mandela walks to freedom	Mandela votes in election for first time and becomes president when ANC wins	Thabo Mbeki succeeds Mandela

The 1994 election

The election passed peacefully. At the age of 76, Nelson Mandela, along with millions of his fellow citizens, voted for the first time in his life in a national election. On May 2, De Klerk conceded defeat after an ANC landslide, in which they took 62.7 percent of the vote. Of the remaining significant parties, the National Party fared best with 20.4 percent, followed by the Inkatha Freedom Party with 10.5 percent. The ANC was dominant in all of the provinces apart from **Western Cape** and **KwaZulu-Natal**. One of the disappointments for the ANC was its inability to appeal broadly to non-Africans.

For the ANC, the real struggle was only beginning. It inherited a country of 38 million people. Of these it was estimated that six million were unemployed, nine million were destitute, ten million had no access to running water, and twenty million had no electricity. Among black adults, sixty percent were illiterate and fewer than fifty percent of black children under 14 went to school. Infant mortality ran at eighty deaths per thousand among Africans, compared with just seven among white children.

The Mandela era

Few people in recorded history have been the subject of such high expectations; still fewer have matched them; Mandela has exceeded them. We knew of his fortitude before he left jail; we have since experienced his extraordinary reserves of goodwill, his sense of fun and the depth of his maturity. As others' prisoner, he very nearly decided the date of his own release; as president, he has wisely chosen the moment of his going. Any other nation would consider itself privileged to have his equal as its leader. His last full year in power provides us with an occasion again to consider his achievement in bringing and holding our fractious land together. Mail & Guardian, December 24, 1998

South Africa's first five years of democracy are inextricably linked to the towering figure of **Nelson Mandela**. On the one hand, he had to temper the impatience of a black majority that, having finally achieved civil rights, found it hard to understand why economic advancement wasn't following quickly. And on the other, he had to mollify many fearful white citizens. The achievements of the government, however, were more uneven than those of its leader.

The overriding theme of the Mandela presidency was that of **reconciliation**. Perhaps the highlight of this policy was in May and June 1995, when the rugby union World Cup was staged in South Africa. **The Springboks**, for many years international pariahs due to their whites-only membership, won, watched by Mandela, sporting Springbok colours – events portrayed in Clint Eastwood's 2009 film *Invictus* (based on a book by John Carlin).

The most significant sideshow of the period was the **Truth and Reconciliation Commission**, set up to examine gross human rights abuses in South Africa between 1960 and 1993 (see page 306).

The **New Constitution**, approved in May 1996, ensured that South Africa would remain a parliamentary democracy with an executive president. One of the most progressive constitutions in the world, it incorporated an extensive bill of rights.

Despite the victory of liberal democratic principles, South Africa still displayed a singular lack of the trappings associated with civil society. Crime, sensationalized daily in the media, continued to dog the country. In the closing stages of the ANC's first five years, the police were reporting an average of 52 murders a day, a rape every half-hour (including a frightening rise in child rape), and one car theft every nine minutes.

2007	2009	2010
Mbeki replaced as president by Jacob Zuma, at the time facing bribery and racketeering charges	Charges against Zuma dropped on eve of general election; ANC wins by a landslide	SA stages successful football World Cup and unleashes vuvuzela on unsuspecting planet

THE TRUTH AND RECONCILIATION COMMISSION

As you type, you don't know you are crying until you feel and see the tears on your hands.

Chief typist of the transcripts of the TRC hearings as told to Archbishop Tutu

By the time South Africa achieved **democracy** in 1994, it was internationally accepted that apartheid was, in the words of a UN resolution, "a crime against humanity", and that atrocities had been committed in its name. But no one could have imagined how systematic and horrific these atrocities had been. This emerged at the hearings of the **Truth and Reconciliation Commission** (TRC), set up to investigate gross abuses of human rights under apartheid. Under the chairmanship of Nobel Peace laureate, Archbishop Desmond Tutu, the commission examined acts committed between March 1960, the date of the Sharpeville massacre, and May 10, 1994, the day of Mandela's inauguration as president.

Evidence was heard from victims and perpetrators under a provision that amnesty would be given in exchange for "full disclosure of all the relevant facts". Unsurprisingly, the commission found that "the South African government was the primary perpetrator of gross human rights abuses in South Africa". It confirmed that from the 1970s to the 1990s the state had been involved in criminal activities including "extra-judicial killings of political opponents". Among the violations it listed were torture, abduction, sexual abuse, incursions across South Africa's borders to kill opponents in exile, and the deployment of hit squads. It also found that the ANC (and a number of other organizations, including the PAC and IFP) was guilty of human-rights violations.

There was considerable criticism of the TRC from all quarters. Many felt that justice would have been better served by a Nuremberg-style trial of those guilty of gross violations, but Tutu argued that this would have been impossible in South Africa, given that neither side had won a military victory.

Mr Delivery doesn't

In 1999 **Thabo Mbeki** succeeded Mandela as president of South Africa. A hopeful media dubbed Mbeki "Mr Delivery", believing that this clever, well-educated technocrat would confront poverty and build schools, hospitals and houses – and at the same time create badly needed jobs. Mbeki's business-friendly policies produced healthy **economic growth**, expanded the black middle class and created a small coterie of mega-rich black entrepreneurs. But it did little for the poor fifty percent of the population, and the gulf of inequality became wider than ever.

The poor also bore the brunt of Mbeki's misguided policies on **AIDS**. Holding the view that there was no link between HIV and AIDS, he blocked the provision of **anti-retrovirals** in state hospitals, causing over 330,000 deaths and the birth of 35,000 HIV-infected babies.

And like the virus, **corruption** seemed to be infecting society, the most far-reaching example being the arms deal, in which the ANC government bought military equipment that South Africa's own defence force deemed unsuitable and too expensive. Newspapers alleged that the defence minister at the time was bribed and that a massive donation was paid to the ANC.

While money was squandered on arms, a raft of **social problems** festered. At the beginning of 2007, eight years after Mbeki assumed power, eight million people

2011	2012	2013
South Africa joins BRIC (Brazil, Russia, India and China), club of the most important developing nations	Forty-four striking miners are shot in the back by police in the Marikana Massacre	South Africa and the world mourn the passing of Nelson Mandela – and of an era

were living in shacks, millions had no water-borne sewerage and unemployment was running at forty percent. Disquiet at the slow pace of change was growing, and **protests** erupted on the streets of the townships. In 2005 alone, there were six thousand protests, and at the end of 2007 Mbeki was unseated by his party.

His replacement was the controversial former deputy president, **Jacob Zuma**, who was facing charges of bribery, fraud, racketeering, money laundering and tax evasion. A supreme populist, he portrayed himself as the people's president fighting off a conspiracy by a Mbeki-led elite. Miraculously, just two weeks before the April 2009 elections, top-secret recordings surfaced, purporting to prove that former president Mbeki had interfered in the Zuma case and charges against Zuma were dropped.

As expected, the Zuma-led ANC **won by a landslide**, while the Democratic Alliance (DA), the official opposition, increased its proportion of the vote. Support for the two main parties split down broadly racial lines, with the ANC getting most of its support from Africans and the DA from white and coloured voters. Given the ANC's overwhelming dominance of South African politics, it perhaps comes as no surprise that South Africa's most significant post-Mandela politics has taken place away from parliament – inside the ANC itself or on the streets.

After the vuvuzelas

For a brief period during 2010, South Africans united in a fever of vuvuzela-blowing euphoria, during the highly successful staging of the **Fifa World Cup**. But there was a return to politics as usual once the visitors had left and the country had returned to work – or not, as in the case of a million public-sector workers who staged a three-week strike in August over pay increases and housing allowances. Trade union leader **Zwelinzima Vavi** attacked the ANC for leading South Africa on the path to becoming "a predator state" in which an "elite of political hyenas increasingly controls the state as a vehicle for accumulation". These have turned out to be prescient words, following revelations of "state capture" by the Guptas, a powerful trio of Indian brothers with a high level of influence over Zuma.

Vavi's views represented the feelings of millions of South Africa's poor and dispossessed, who, nearly two decades after winning democracy, were still waiting for its economic fruits to be delivered. During Zuma's first two years of tenure, frustration with the ruling party accelerated. There were twice as many service-delivery protests in just 2009 and 2010 than there had been in the previous five Mbeki years.

By 2011, forty percent of South Africa's municipalities had been hit by popular street protests and there were attacks on Zuma from inside his own party. ANC Youth League leader **Julius Malema**, who had helped replace Mbeki with Zuma, now viciously attacked the president as being "worse than Mbeki", leading to Malema's expulsion from the ANC and his formation of a new populist party the **Economic Freedom Fighters** (EFF).

Meanwhile, dissatisfaction festered in the platinum mines, with workers staging a **wildcat strike** at the Marikana mine in 2012. In an echo of the 1960 Sharpeville massacre (see page 301), one of apartheid's darkest hours, police fired on and killed 44 strikers at Marikana and wounded many more. Most of those killed in the **Marikana Massacre** were shot in the back – just as they had been at Sharpeville – delivering

2014	2014	2015
Public Protector orders President Zuma to repay some of the R200m of taxpayers' money spent on upgrading his private residence	ANC wins general election by a landslide	Aiming to "decolonize" education, #RhodesMustFall movement topples Cape Town University's prominent statue of Cecil Rhodes

massive political capital to Julius Malema, who made a point of appearing at Marikana and proffering his support to the miners following the bloodshed. Malema traded on his working-class credentials all the way to the 2014 general election.

While mineworkers were dying in the cause of decent living conditions and millions of citizens were struggling to make ends meet, President Zuma was using taxpayers' money – over R200m of it – to refurbish his private residence at **Nkandla** in rural KwaZulu-Natal. With **Nelson Mandela's death** on 5 December 2013, the nation – and the world – mourned, not just because it had lost one of the country's greatest statesmen, but also because his passing symbolized the passing of an idealistic era that had promised a new dawn for South Africa. When President Zuma took the podium during the ten-day state memorial service, he was booed by sections of the crowd, in reaction to the dark clouds of corruption hanging over him.

These clouds proved to have a silver lining, however, when South Africa's political system demonstrated an encouraging robustness. The **Nkandla scandal** was widely reported by the independent media, and, perhaps more importantly, it was referred to the Office of the Public Protector, a constitutional watchdog that protects citizens against abuses of state power. Despite official attempts to derail her investigations, the fiercely courageous Public Protector, **Thuli Madonsela**, delivered a measured report in 2014, in which she found, among other things, serious flaws in the tendering process for the upgrade of Zuma's home and numerous violations of the government's ethics code. She ordered Zuma to pay back millions of rands.

Strangely, the Nkandla scandal did little to dent the ANC's performance in the **2014 general election**. Despite losing some support, much of it to Julius Malema's EFF which won 25 seats, the ANC still managed to win the poll by a very healthy 62 percent majority. Nonetheless, many in the party realized that if the ANC was to retain its support, it needed to be more responsive to the country's workers, the disenchanted and the dispossessed, as well as avoiding the allegations of corruption associated with Zuma, who was increasingly perceived as a liability to his party and the country, and as a leader trampling on the principles championed by Mandela.

These concerns were reflected in the **local elections of 2016**, which saw the ANC losing Johannesburg, Pretoria and Port Elizabeth to the DA. The following year, Zuma fired the well-respected finance minister, Pravhin Gordhan, prompting discontent in ANC ranks and nationwide demonstrations as two credit-rating agencies downgraded South Africa to "junk" status. In December 2017, the increasingly unpopular Zuma was replaced as ANC president by **Cyril Ramaphosa**, a former Secretary General of the party who had headed up the team that negotiated the transition to democracy with the apartheid government before retiring from politics to pursue a career in business in 1997. The embattled Zuma finally resigned as president of South Africa in February 2018, to be replaced by Ramaphosa.

Ramaphosa takes the reigns

Although Ramaphosa had served as deputy president of both party and country under Zuma since 2014, he was widely perceived to be the candidate most likely to reverse the damage done by his predecessor. Within a month of assuming office, he appointed Deputy Chief Justice Zondo to head up a far-reaching **commission of**

2016	2018
The Democratic Alliance (DA) retains Cape Town in local elections, led in the Western Cape by former party leader Helen Zille	The scandal-ridden Jacob Zuma resigns as president, and is replaced by Cyril Ramaphosa, who initiates a commission of inquiry into state capture under his predecessor

inquiry into state capture that exposed the staggering extent of corruption under the Zuma administration. Long-standing charges of corruption against Zuma that had been dropped during his presidency were also reinstated in 2018, though it remains to be seen whether the former president – who turned 78 in April 2020 – will ever stand trial for these charges, or whether they will simply be postponed on an indefinite basis.

Some of the harm caused to the ANC's standing under Zuma has been eased by Ramaphosa's verbal commitment to fighting **corruption**, to accelerating the process of **land redistribution** without comprising agricultural production, and to large-scale job creation coupled with economic growth. The incumbent party's cause is further aided by the reality that, a full 25 years after the heady 1994 election, it faces no truly credible opposition. The DA's image of being an old white party persisted under Mmusi Maimane, a Soweto-born Tswana who was only 34 years of age when he became the party leader in 2015; Maimane resigned in October 2019 stating that he no longer believed his party was "the vehicle best suited to take forward the vision of building One South Africa for All". The next largest party after the DA, the more populist EFF, has probably been too tainted by the antics of its firebrand leader Julius Malema to have mass appeal.

As a result, by the time the **general election of May 2019** rolled around, Ramaphosa and the ANC cruised home with 57.5 percent of the vote, admittedly the lowest in the six elections the party had contested, but still far ahead of the DA (20.77 percent), EFF (10.79 percent) and a veritable legion of lesser parties. The provincial breakdown remained unchanged too, with the DA holding onto the Western Cape, while the ANC prevailed in the other eight, albeit with a majority of less than 51 percent in Gauteng, the country's most diverse and economically powerful province. Despite this apparent political stability, the South African economy is poised on a knife edge, with recent year-on-year growth figures hovering at or below one percent, unemployment standing at 27.6 percent and rising, and a host of parastatal organizations – the electricity supplier Eskom, the national carrier SAA and national broadcaster SABC – looking increasingly dysfunctional as a result of corruption and mismanagement. If anybody can rescue South Africa, it is probably Ramaphosa – but he has his work cut out.

2019	**2019**
The ANC wins its sixth successive general election, garnering almost three times as many votes as the DA, its closest rival	South Africa wins the rugby union World Cup for the third time

Geology and geography

The most southerly and ninth-largest of the 48 countries that comprise mainland Africa, South Africa extends over an area of 1,221,037 square kilometres, making it roughly five times the size of the United Kingdom, or slightly larger than Texas and California combined. It has a 2850km coastline battered by the **Atlantic Ocean** to the west and lapped more gently by the **Indian Ocean** to the east. The two oceans meet at **Cape Agulhas**, a hazardous rocky headland that stands at the southern tip of Africa at 34°49'58". Most of South Africa is **subtropical** and has a temperate climate, but the **Tropic of Capricorn** runs through the north of Limpopo Province, meaning that the likes of Mapungubwe National Park, the northern Kruger National Park and the towns of Louis Trichardt and Musina lie within the tropics. **Seasons** are opposite to those in the northern hemisphere, with summer falling between October and March, and winter from May to August.

The contrasting nature of the prevailing currents in the two oceans that border South Africa has a strong influence on climate patterns. The **Benguela Current**, a north-flowing upwell of cold water from the depths of the Atlantic, tends to retain moisture and thus to inhibit rain, whereas the Indian Ocean's south-flowing **Agulhas** (Mozambique) **Current** brings warm water from the tropics and experiences high levels of evaporation that induce rain. As a result, South Africa's eastern coastal belt is the wettest part of the country; **rainfall** decreases as you head further west, with semi-arid and desert conditions prevailing in much of the Western Cape interior and the Northern Cape. Most of South Africa has a strongly defined summer rainfall pattern, with many areas going several months without rain in winter. This is reversed in Cape Town and much of the Western Cape, which is a winter rainfall area with a Mediterranean climate, while the Garden Route and coastal belt running east to Port Elizabeth are less seasonal and receive some rain throughout the year.

South Africa's most important topographical feature is the tall escarpment that follows the coastline in a rough crescent, typically rising between 50km and 250km inland to divide the country into three broad altitudinal regions. These are the low-lying **coastal belt**, the narrow **escarpment**, and the **central plateau** or highveld above it. Altitude is another important factor in determining climate, with the coastal plateau tending to be far warmer than the highveld, and less prone to nocturnal winter frosts – though this is also influenced by **latitude**, with the north of the country tending to be far warmer than the south.

South Africa provides us with a unique and almost complete overview of the earth's geological and evolutionary history. The northeast hosts some of the world's most ancient rocks, with early **Precambrian formations** such as the Archaean Basement and Barberton Greenstone Belt estimated to be about 3.5 billion years old. The greenstones hold the fossilized relics of the very earliest micro-organisms to have inhabited the earth, whilst the somewhat younger **Karoo Basin** of the southwest has yielded the world's largest collection of proto-mammalian reptiles, a unique fossil record documenting the emergence of early mammals over a period of fifty million years. At the other end of the evolutionary continuum, the dolomitic caves and limestone sinkholes of Gauteng's **Cradle of Humankind** – a UNESCO World Heritage site since 1999 – have yielded the world's richest collection of early hominid fossils, providing us with a unique and near-complete paleoanthropological record stretching back roughly 3.5 million years.

Compared to the Precambrian formations of the northeast, South Africa's most significant mountain range, the **uKhahlamba-Drakensberg**, is something of a geological infant. Essentially the stretch of the escarpment that runs along the border between KwaZulu-Natal and the Kingdom of Lesotho, this formidable range took recognizable shape over the past 5–10 million years, and its 200-plus kilometre-long basaltic cliffs are breached by just one solitary road, the 4WD-only **Sani Pass**. The uKhahlamba-

Drakensberg is the tallest African mountain range south of Kilimanjaro, boasting several dozen peaks that top the 3000-metre mark. These include the 3450-metre **Mafedi**, which ranks as the highest peak in South Africa, but is surpassed in elevation by the 3482-metre Thabana Ntlenyana across the border in Lesotho. The best-known peak in the uKhahlamba-Drakensberg, **Mont Aux Sources** rises to a relatively modest 3282 metres, but as its name suggests, it forms the country's most important watershed, being the source of five different rivers, including the east-flowing **Thukela** and west-flowing **Orange**.

South Africa is a rather dry country, receiving a national average rainfall of just below 500mm, about half the global average, and even its moister regions are prone to periods of extended **drought**. The country's most important arid ecosystem is the **Karoo**, a 400,000-square-kilometre basin that dominates the southwestern interior. The Karoo has been in place for around 250 million years, through periods of glaciation, flooding and intense volcanic activity, and is rich in dinosaur and other fossils dating back to before the break-up of the supercontinent of **Gondwanaland**.

South Africa's low rainfall is reflected in a serious paucity of large freshwater bodies. Indeed, the country's most extensive natural lake is **Sibaya**, which has a surface area of 64 square kilometres and is protected within the iSimangaliso Westland Park. South Africa is also traversed by relatively few large rivers, the two major exceptions being the **Orange** or Gariep, which rises in the uKhahlamba-Drakensberg and flows west for 2200 kilometres before emptying into the Atlantic on the border with Namibia, and the 1750-kilometre-long **Limpopo**, which runs along the border with Botswana and Zimbabwe before crossing into Mozambique in the north of the Kruger Park. Other important rivers include the Vaal, which is the most important tributary of the Orange, the Tugela or Thukela, which flows for 500km east from its source in the uKhahlamba-Drakensberg to its mouth on the Indian Ocean north of Durban, and the Great Fish and Kei in the Eastern Cape. South Africa's low rainfall and lack of natural lakes has led to the construction of an extensive network of **reservoirs**, most notably the 352-square-kilometre Gariep Dam on the Orange River and the 322-square-kilometre Vaal Dam on the Vaal, the former being an important hydroelectric site and the latter the main source of tap water for drought-prone Gauteng.

Habitats and flora

From the weird succulents of the dry **Kalahari** to the brilliantly coloured blossoms which transform the semi-desert plains of **Namaqualand** in spring, South Africa is endowed with some impressively spectacular **plant life**. Indeed, South Africa's inclusion as one of the world's seventeen **megadiverse** countries is primarily down to its flora. More than 22,000 species of vascular plant have been described for the country – roughly one-tenth of the global total – and something like sixty percent of these occur nowhere else in the world. The most enticing region for botanists, particular in terms of endemics, is the **Cape Floristic Region**, which enjoys a special status as the smallest of the world's six floral kingdoms, and the one with the richest species diversity. Set entirely within South Africa, this small area, centred on Cape Town and the Western Cape, is dominated by a unique heath-like vegetation known as **fynbos**. Other endemic-rich regions include the succulent-dominated semi-arid badlands of the Karoo, and the lofty plateaus and well-watered slopes of the central uKhahlamba-Drakensberg.

As one measure of South Africa's floral wealth, the country is the original home of a great number of spectacular flowering plants that were introduced into European botanical gardens and private collections in the eighteenth century and are now a familiar sight in gardens around the world. These popular exports include the bird-of-paradise or crane flower of the near-endemic genus *Strelitzia*, the arum lily *Zantedeschia aethiopica*, and the so-called African lilies of the near-endemic genus *Agapanthus*. South

Africa is also the main centre of global diversity for the gladioli of the genus *Gladiolus* (260 of the world's 300-odd species), the red-hot pokers of the Africa-specific genus *Kniphofia* (roughly two-thirds of the world's 70-odd species), the sweet-scented blooms of the genus *Freesia*, and the richly coloured daisy-like flowering plants of the hardy drought-tolerant genera *Gazania* and *Osteospermum*, which open their petals only when the sun shines.

Two terms are commonly used when describing the ecology of any given place. The first is "**biome**", which refers to a large naturally occurring biotic community characterized by certain typical plant species and associated animals. Most authorities recognize seven major biomes in South Africa, namely Forest, Thicket, Savannah, Grassland, Fynbos, Nama Karoo and Succulent Karoo. The second term is "**habitat**", which denotes the environment preferred by any given species of plant or animal, and which might or might not correspond with one or more of the above biomes. This is because some species have very contained and easily identifiable habitats that are not particularly linked to a specific biome (reed-lined pools, for instance), while others are strongly associated with one particular biome, and a few are so habitat tolerant they might occur almost anywhere. Overall, though, visitors who learn to recognize the different biomes in any given national park or game reserve, and are conscious of various species' habitat preferences, will be better placed not only to predict what wildlife might be seen in a given locality, but also to distinguish similar-looking species based partly on their environment.

Forest biome

Forest differs from any form of wooded savannah in that it has a **closed canopy** and often comprises several vertically layered sub-canopies that cast a permanent shadow over a jungle-like tangle of undergrowth, epiphytes and vines. Thanks partly to extensive deforestation since the nineteenth century, indigenous forest now accounts for less than 0.25 percent of South Africa's surface area. Despite this, it supports an exceptionally diverse fauna, and is of particular interest to **birdwatchers** as the main habitat of localized species such as the hefty, conspicuous and noisy *Bycanistes* hornbills, the colourful turacos and trogons, various forest barbet and tinkerbirds, and a miscellany of inconspicuous and secretive warblers, thrushes and bulbuls. The invertebrate diversity of the forests is incalculable, with **butterflies** in particular being very well represented.

Several different forest types are recognized in South Africa. The Afro-montane "mistbelt" forests inland of the eastern coastal belt and the coastal forests of Zululand and the Garden Route are distinguished by the presence of large **hardwood trees** such as black stinkwood *Ocotea bullata* (named for its unpleasant odour when freshly cut) and Outeniqua yellowwood *Podocarpus falcatus* (which can grow to be forty metres tall). Elsewhere, many watercourses and other wetland habitats sustain a ribbon of riparian (or riverine) forest, often dominated by the fever tree and various leafy *Ficus* species, to provide a corridor supporting forest wildlife in non-forested habitats. Accessible examples of this important niche habitat are the Kruger Park's **Sabie and Luvuvhu rivers**, whose forested banks provide refuge to the likes of bushbuck, nyala and various forest birds, as well as attracting dense numbers of elephant.

Thicket biome

The main natural climax vegetation on the coastal belt of the Eastern Cape and southern KwaZulu-Natal, **subtropical thicket** is a cover of closed-canopy shrub that is too low and lacking in substrata to be considered true forest, but also lacks the grassy ground layer that characterizes savannah. It accounts for just 2.5 percent of South Africa's surface area and is typically associated with sloping areas that are neither prone to fire nor receive enough rainfall to support a proper forest community. Transitional in nature and rather dense and impenetrable to humans, the subtropical thicket of

South Africa is dominated by **evergreen succulents** such as the waxen-leafed spekboom *Portulacuria afra* and various cactus-like *Euphorbia* species. The main stronghold of this biome is the Eastern Cape's **Albany thicket** (see page 234), and although much of this was cleared to make way for livestock farming in the nineteenth and early twentieth century, large tracts are still protected in Addo Elephant National Park, Great Fish River Nature Reserve and various nearby private sanctuaries.

Savannah biome

Savannah is a loosely defined term that in sub-Saharan Africa denotes any area characterized by a ground cover of **grass** and a higher layer of **fire-resistant shrubs or trees** that is insufficiently dense to create a closed canopy. Savannah accounts for some 46 percent of South Africa's surface area, and it is typically associated with medium-precipitation areas that have clearly defined rainy and dry seasons and are set at an altitude of below 2000m. This includes most of KwaZulu-Natal, Limpopo and North West provinces, as well as eastern Mpumalanga, the northeast of the Northern Cape, and parts of the Eastern Cape. It also includes the Kalahari, even the tall red dunefields protected within Kgalagadi Transfrontier Park, which though desert-like in appearance are classified as semi-desert and form part of the savannah biome.

Savannah is the dominant biome in most of South Africa's main game parks, but that doesn't necessarily mean it is the natural climax vegetation type. In parts of the Eastern Cape, the present-day cover of savannah has replaced thicket cut down in the nineteenth century by European settlers. Elsewhere, some ecologists think it is result of centuries of deliberate burning by pastoralists seeking to stimulate fresh growth to feed their cattle, aided and abetted by the tree-shredding activities of elephants.

Highly characteristic of the African savannah are thorn-trees still widely known as **Acacias**, even though they were recently split from their Australian counterparts and controversially reassigned from the genus *Acacia* to the genera *Senegalia* and *Vachellia*. These include large trees such as the flat-topped umbrella-thorn *V. tortilis* (known in Afrikaans as *haak-en-steek* – hook and stab), the camel-thorn *V. erioloba*, the monkey-thorn *S. galpinii* (the tallest species, growing up to 30m tall) and the common hook-thorn *S. caffra*. A distinctive acacia of marshes and lake verges is the fever tree *V. xanthophloea*, a groundwater-loving, jaundice-barked species thought by the earliest settlers to be responsible for the spread of malaria. Other savannah trees include the sausage tree *Kigelia africana*, which has a thick evergreen canopy and gigantic sausage-shaped pods eaten by elephants and used by locals as gourds. Often associated with rocky slopes in savannah settings, the candelabra tree *Euphorbia candelabra* is a superficially cactus-like succulent with an inverted umbrella shape that grows to more than 10m in height.

In the northern **Kruger Park**, the mixed acacia savannah of the south is replaced by a near-monospecific cover of **mopane woodland**. This is dominated by the mopane *Colophospermum mopane*, a medium-sized tree noted for its hard termite-resistant wood and diagnostic butterfly-shaped leaves whose green summery hues transform into autumnal yellows and greens as winter approaches. The mopane is a major food source for the so-called mopane worm *Gonimbrasia belina*, a colourful caterpillar (of a type of emperor moth) which is roasted and eaten as a protein-rich delicacy by locals in many parts of sub-equatorial Africa. The bizarre baobab *Adansonia digitata*, with its mighty trunk which often attains a diameter of several feet, can also be found in the extreme north, along with the marula *Sclerocarya birrea*, whose yellow-skinned, white-fleshed fruit is used to make the popular cream-liqueur Amarula.

The Africa savannah can support immense herds of **grazing ungulates**, including mixed herds of wildebeest, zebra and antelope such as still occur in the central Kruger. Other large grazers associated with lightly wooded savannah include eland, red hartebeest, tsessebe, reedbuck and oribi, while more thickly wooded areas are favoured by impala, buffalo, giraffe and warthog. Predator populations are proportionately dense, particularly lion, spotted hyena and black-backed jackal. Open savannah is often notable for the presence of heavyweights such as ostrich, kori bustard, secretary bird and southern ground hornbill alongside ground-dwelling plovers, larks, longclaws and waxbills. More densely wooded savannah supports a greater avian variety, with conspicuous hawkers such as rollers, shrikes, bee-eaters and raptors occurring alongside the more active sunbirds, parrots, hornbills, starlings, helmet-shrikes and relatively secretive bush-shrikes, owls, woodpeckers, cuckoos and batises. Several bird species associated mostly with the "**miombo**" **woodland** of Zimbabwe and areas further north occur in the mopane savannah of northern Kruger.

Grassland biome

The second most extensive biome in South Africa is **grassland**, which covers about 28 percent of the country and is typically associated with medium- to high-altitude areas that regularly experience subzero temperatures on winter nights. It is the dominant biome on the **highveld** of the Free State, Gauteng, western Mpumalanga and the interior of KwaZulu-Natal and the Eastern Cape, and an estimated ten percent of the world's ten thousand **grass species** are indigenous to the area. The grasses of the west are generally designated "**sweet**" or "**white**", while the eastern, moister region produces "**sour**" or "**purple**" grasses – farming terms that refer to their value as fodder. Also present are geophytes and other small plants that are resistant to both fire and frost, and many areas now are planted with *Eucalyptus spp* and other non-indigenous trees. The grassy highveld of South Africa naturally supports large herds of grazers such as Burchell's zebra, black wildebeest and blesbok, but much of it is now given over to livestock farming, agriculture, industry and urban development.

Set within South Africa's grassland biome, the **uKhahlamba-Drakensberg** and bordering parts of Lesotho comprise a 40,000-square-kilometre hub of Afromontane floral diversity known as the **Drakensberg Alpine Centre** (DAC). This comprises three main altitudinal vegetation zones: moist montane grassland interspersed with stands of fire-resistant suikerbossie (sugarbush) proteas below the 2000m contour; a subalpine zone of open or bushed grassland interspersed with patches of heath-like scrub; and finally, above 2800m, an alpine zone whose undulating windswept plateau supports a low sparse cover of snow-resistant tussock grasses and pastel-shaded *Erica* and *Helichrysum* shrubs. Of more than two thousand plant species identified within the uKhahlamba-Drakensberg Park, almost thirty percent are DAC endemics, and more than one hundred are listed as globally threatened, the most localized being the cloud protea *Protea nubigena*, whose known range extends over less than one hectare of the Royal Natal Park. The uKhahlamba-Drakensberg is not a game park as such, though it does support fair variety of antelope including eland and the endemic grey rhebok, but it is an important site for avian endemics, providing refuge to about half of the bird species whose natural range is restricted to South Africa (and/or Lesotho and/or Eswatini).

Fynbos biome

The coastal belt extending east from Cape Town is something of an ecological island thanks to its so-called **Mediterranean climate**, which is characterized by dry summers and rainy winters, a reversal of the trend elsewhere in southern Africa. The borders of this winter rainfall region coincide with – indeed, define – those of the smallest of the world's six floristic regions, which extends over a mere 90,000 square kilometres but supports at least nine thousand **flowering plant species**, two-thirds of which occur nowhere else on earth. As some measure of this region's extraordinary floral diversity, a greater number of indigenous plant species have been identified in the Cape of Good Hope sector of Table Mountain National Park than on the whole of the British Isles. Renowned for its proteas and heathers, the Cape Peninsula is also where you'll find South Africa's most famous orchid, the red disa *Disa uniflora*, whose showy scarlet and pink flower, which comes into bloom over January to March, has been dubbed "The Pride of Table Mountain". Sadly, as many as 1326 fynbos plant species are on the endangered list, including the white-coned snow protea *Protea cryophilla*, which only grows above the snow line in the Cederberg and defies cultivation.

The region's predominant vegetation is a low, heath-like ground cover known as **fynbos** (an Afrikaans word meaning "fine bush" in reference to the small narrow leaves, which are often protected by hairs). It can appear rather drab at first glance, but on closer inspection fynbos reveals a rich sprinkling of subtle pastel hues that explode into flamboyant colour during the spring wildflower season. The three most common fynbos families are the striking winter-flowering Proteaceae (including the King protea *Protea cynaroides*, the national flower), the heath-like Ericaceae and the reedy Restionaceae. Fynbos grows in some extremely diverse habitats – from arid salt marshes and sand dunes to mountain slopes and crags up in the cloud zone, but the best time to see it is during the spring (September and October), when it blooms into kaleidoscopic colour. High levels of endemism are noted among fynbos invertebrates and cold-blooded vertebrates, and eight bird species are more-or-less unique to fynbos habitats, including the emblematic Cape Sugarbird, whose long, curved bill is designed to drink protea nectar.

Set within the fynbos biome, **Renosterveld** is a unique cover named after its most conspicuous component *Elytropappus rhinocerotis*, a shrubby drought-resistant member of the daisy family known as Renosterbos (literally "rhinoceros bush", and more likely a reference to the plant's grey leathery foliage than to any former abundance of rhinos). Unlike true fynbos, renosterveld incorporates an abundance of grasses that once provided grazing to a wide variety of ungulates, including the extinct bluebuck and quagga.

Nama Karoo biome

More or less confined to South Africa, the semi-arid **Nama Karoo** is the country's third largest biome, extending across most of the Northern Cape, as well as parts of the Free State and Eastern and Western Cape interior, to account for some twenty percent of the national surface area. It typically stands at medium altitudes (around 1000m) and is characterized by low rainfall (below 400mm), stony or sandy ground, and high seasonal temperature fluctuations with regular subzero temperatures and frost on winter nights. The typical vegetation of the Nama Karoo is a deciduous dwarf scrubland, which usually has a grassy understory where the soil is sufficiently sandy. Larger trees include the sweet-thorn acacia *V. karroo*, whose fearsomely long and thick thorns are often used as a nesting site by wasps or ants. Floral biodiversity and levels of endemism are rather low, but succulents, in particular the genus *Euphorbia*, are well represented. Invasive drought-resistant aliens such as the prickly pear cactus *Opuntia aurantiaca* and honey mesquite *Prosopis glandulosa* are a problem in some areas.

The Nama Karoo was once grazed by large nomadic herds of springbok and other ungulates, but these days it is mostly given over to **sheep and goat farming**, and it supports few indigenous large mammals, though smaller species such as bay-eared fox, aardvark, springhare and the riverine rabbit (a Critically Endangered endemic), are still present. Birdlife includes a wide variety of larks, pipits and other ground birds including the ostrich, which is farmed commercially in certain areas such as Oudtshoorn. Much of the Nama Karoo was unprotected until recent times, but that has changed with the creation of the likes of Karoo and Camdeboo National Park and private reserves such as Kwandwe and Sanbona.

Succulent Karoo biome

The **Succulent Karoo** is the smaller, more westerly and more arid of South Africa's two dry-country biomes, covering around seven percent of the country, though it also extends northwards into Namibia. It is the world's most florally diverse arid area, hosting almost four thousand plant species of which some seventy percent occur nowhere else in the world. As its name suggests, the biome is particularly rich in **succulents** (plants that store water in their fleshy leaves and/or stems), with something like thirty percent of the world's species present. These include several large and strikingly bizarre endemics, notably the quiver tree *Aloe dichotoma*, giant aloe tree *Aloe pillansii* and halfmensboom (half-human tree) *Pachypodium namaquanum*. The Succulent Karoo is also renowned for the peerless displays of Mesembryanthemums ("vygies" in Afrikaans) and other daisy-like spring flowers that transform the stony plains of **Namaqualand** into a shimmering sea of colour –from metallic red and copper to violet, yellow and white – over August and September.

The Succulent Karoo biome embraces South Africa's only true desert, which forms part of the Orange River Valley as it runs along the remote Namibian border. Known as the **Springbokvlakte** (Springbok Plain), this parched border region receives an annual rainfall of around 20mm and daytime temperatures frequently soar above 40°C. Part of the desert is protected in the remote Ai-Ais/Richtersveld Transfrontier Park, while the remainder was inscribed by UNESCO as the community-managed Richtersveld Cultural and Botanical Landscape World Heritage Site in 2007.

Wildlife tends to be thinly distributed and it is dominated by **desert-adapted creatures** such as gemsbok, springbok, Hartmann's mountain zebra and ground squirrel. The biome is rich in small predators, particularly brown hyena, aardwolf, bat-eared fox, black-backed jackal, black-footed cat, meerkat and yellow mongoose. **Reptiles** are well represented and display a high level of endemism, with fifteen lizard species, for instance, being endemic to the Karoo, among them the peculiar armadillo girdled lizard *Cordylus cataphractus*, which has a heavily armoured body and spiny tail, and rolls into a tight ball when threatened. The arid west is a stronghold for dozens of bird species endemic to Southern Africa, among them white-backed mousebird, Ludwig's bustard, Karoo korhaan, Karoo eremomela, Namaqua warbler, cinnamon-breasted warbler, Karoo scrub-robin, Karoo chat, dusky sunbird and numerous species of lark.

Niche habitats

Certain habitats might occur in any biome and tend to create a niche for various species that are non-biome specific. The most obvious of these is **freshwater wetlands**, a term that embraces any habitat that combines terrestrial and aquatic features. The most important habitat of this type in South Africa is KwaZulu-Natal's **iSimangaliso Wetland Park**, a vast protected area that incorporates Lake Sibaya (the country's largest natural freshwater body) and three other Ramsar sites. The significance of these wetlands is almost impossible to overstate, both as self-sustaining ecosystems supporting fish, amphibians and other water-associated birds and mammals, and as a source of vital drinking water to most terrestrial creatures – including humans.

Mammals exclusive to wetlands include **hippo**, marsh mongoose and Cape clawless otter. Elephant and buffalo also regularly take to water, and most other large mammals need to drink daily. More than one hundred **bird species** indigenous to South Africa are strongly associated with one or other wetland habitat, ranging from the swallows and martins that feed above lakes, to aerial anglers such as the pied kingfisher and African fish eagle, to the waders that peck in the shallows. And while a few water-associated birds, such as the Egyptian goose or cattle egret, might inhabit almost any aquatic habitat, others have more specific requirements. African finfoot and white-backed night heron, for instance, favour still or sluggish waters with overhanging vegetation, whereas many lapwings and migrant waders are associated with exposed sandbanks; quiet lily-covered pools, meanwhile, are the haunt of the African jacana and pygmy goose.

Sadly, wetlands, more than any other habitat, are frequently **threatened by development**, whether by swamp drainage, industrial pollution, the disruption of riverine habitats to feed reservoirs or hydroelectric schemes, or the introduction of exotic species – though it is equally true, in the case of a relatively dry country such as South Africa, that man's need for reservoirs and dams has created an enormous number of artificial wetlands that are highly beneficial to wildlife.

Another important niche habitat comprises isolated rocky hills called **koppies** (meaning "little heads") and the **tall cliffs** associated with parts of the escarpment. Both possess something of an island ecology, offering permanent or part-time refuge to a range of rock- and thicket-loving plants and animals that couldn't easily survive on surrounding plains. Koppies and cliffs are favoured by baboons, which seem to be more skittish and vocal in this rocky environment than on the open plains. It is also the main niche utilized by the rock-hopping klipspringer antelope. **Bush and rock hyraxes** often live alongside each other on koppies, with the former grazing around rocks and the latter feeding mainly on acacia and other trees, which it climbs readily. An important part of the koppie food chain, hyraxes are the main dietary constituent of the mighty Verreaux's eagle that nest on the pinnacles, and they are also taken by other raptors, as well as by leopards and smaller felids that take daytime refuge in the rocks, and the cobras and puff adders that live in the crevices between the giant granite slabs.

Mammals

For most visitors, the primary attraction of South Africa's game parks is the so-called Big Five (lion, leopard, buffalo, elephant and rhino), which can be seen in larger parks such as Kruger, Kgalagadi, Hluhluwe-iMfolozi, Addo, Madikwe and the Pilanesberg, as well as in a burgeoning number of private reserves. But these and more than a hundred other small reserves also host a wide variety of smaller predators and herbivores, including many endangered and/or endemic species, in invariably beautiful settings.

This field guide provides a quick reference to help you identify some of the **mammals** most likely to be encountered in South Africa. It includes species found throughout the country as well a number whose range is more restricted. The photos show easily identified markings and features. The notes give pointers about the kind of habitat in which you are likely to see each mammal; its daily rhythm; the kind of social groups it usually forms; and some of the reserves you're most likely to find it in.

PRIMATES

Southern Africa has the lowest diversity of primates on the continent, with a mere five species recorded, excluding Homo sapiens. In addition to one species of baboon – the largest and most formidable of the country's primates – there are two other species of monkey and two nocturnal galagos (also known as bushbabies). Great apes such as gorillas and chimpanzees don't occur naturally in Southern Africa.

CHACMA BABOON (PAPIO URSINUS)

Apart from humans, baboons are the primates most widely found in South Africa. Males can be intimidating and when sufficiently habituated are sometimes bold enough to raid vehicles or accommodation in search of food, undeterred by the presence of people. Troops are led by a dominant male and are governed by complex social relations in which gender, precedence, physical strength and family ties determine status. Every adult male enjoys dominance over every female. Grooming forms part of the social glue and you'll commonly see baboons lolling about while performing this massage-like activity. Baboons are highly opportunistic omnivores and will tuck into a scorpion or a newborn antelope as readily as raid a citrus farm for oranges.

Reserves Addo, Garden Route (Tsitsikamma), Kruger, Marakele, Mkhuze, Mountain Zebra, Pilanesberg, Table Mountain (Cape of Good Hope), uKhahlamba-Drakensberg.

Habitat Open country with trees and cliffs; adaptable, but always near water; sometimes venture close to human habitation.

Daily rhythm Diurnal.

Social life Troops of 15–100.

VERVET MONKEY (CERCOPITHECUS AETHIOPS)

A widespread primate you may see outside reserves, living around nearby farms and even on suburban fringes, where opportunities for scavenging are promising. Vervet monkeys are principally vegetarian but are not averse to eating invertebrates, small lizards, nestlings and eggs, as well as biscuits and sweets. Vervet society is made up of family groups of females and young, defended by associate males, and is highly caste-ridden. A mother's rank determines that of her daughter from infancy, and lower-ranking

adult females risk being castigated if they fail to show due respect to these "upper-crust" youngsters.

Reserves Eastern half of South Africa: virtually every game reserve in KwaZulu-Natal, Limpopo, Mpumalanga and North West Province, as well as along the coast from Mossel Bay to northern KwaZulu-Natal.

Habitat Will forage in grasslands, but rarely far from woodland; particularly along river courses; arboreal and terrestrial.

Daily rhythm Diurnal.

Social life Troops.

SAMANGO (OR BLUE) MONKEY (CERCOPITHECUS MITIS)

In striking contrast with the bolder vervet, the rarer samango monkey is shy and troops may only reveal their presence through their explosive call or the breaking of branches as they go about their business. The samango monkey is larger than the vervet and has long cheek hair. Like the vervet, it is highly social and lives in troops of females under the proprietorship of a dominant male, but unlike its relatives they are more inclined to fan out when looking for food.

Reserves Hluhluwe-iMfolozi, iSimangaliso Wetland, Ndumo and Tembe.

Habitat Prefer higher reaches of gallery forest; occasionally venture into the open to forage.

Daily rhythm Diurnal.

Social life Troops.

SOUTHERN LESSER GALAGO (GALAGO MOHOLI)

With their large, soft, fluffy pelts, huge saucer-like eyes, large rounded ears and superficially cat-like appearance, the galagos (or bushbabies) are the ultimate in cute, cuddly-looking primates. Of the two dozen or so species endemic to Africa, only two are found to the south of the Limpopo. The more widespread of these is the southern lesser galago, whose range includes the northeast and extends across the north of the country into North West Province. Strictly nocturnal, it is often seen on night drives in the Kruger, bordering private reserves, and elsewhere.

Reserves Kruger and Pilanesberg.

Habitat Woodland savannah and riverine woodland.

Daily rhythm Nocturnal.

Social life Small family groups.

THICK-TAILED GALAGO (OTOLEMUR CRASSICAUDATUS)

By far the larger of the two bushbaby species found in South Africa is the thick-tailed or brown greater galago, which is confined to the country's eastern fringes. If you're staying at any of the KwaZulu-Natal reserves, you stand a fair chance of seeing one after dark as it emerges from the dense forest canopy, where it rests in small groups, to forage for tree gum and fruit. Unlike other bushbabies, which leap with ease and speed, the thick-tailed is a slow mover that hops or walks along branches, often with considerable stealth. Even if you don't see one, you're bound to hear their piercing scream cut through the sounds of the night. Bushbabies habituate easily to humans and will sometimes come into lodge dining rooms, scavenging for titbits.

Reserves Hluhluwe-iMfolozi, iSimangaliso Wetland, Kruger.

Habitat Dry and riverine woodland; arboreal.

Daily rhythm Nocturnal.

Social life Small groups of a mating pair or one or two females with young; males territorial with ranges that overlap several female ranges.

DOGS

Five species of canid occur in South Africa. The African wild dog, listed as Endangered on the IUCN Red List, is now more-or-less confined to a few national parks and reserves, but the others are more widespread outside conservation areas. These include two jackal species, which are placed in the same genus as wolves and domestic dogs, as well as one true fox and the oddball bat-eared fox, a dry-country insectivore placed in the monospecific genus Otocyon. Unlike most other carnivores, canids are typically very sociable, either living in large hierarchical packs or in pairs and small family groups.

AFRICAN WILD DOG (LYCAON PICTUS)

Once among the most numerous hunters of the African plains, the wild dog – also known as the painted dog or Cape hunting dog – has been brought to the edge of extinction as a result of persecution by humans. It is the world's second rarest canid, and the South African population consists of just five hundred individuals, half of which are in the Greater Kruger. For many years, wild dogs were shot on sight, having gained an unjustified reputation as cruel and wanton killers of cattle and sheep. More recent scientific evidence reveals them to be economical and efficient hunters – and more successful at it than any other African species. Capable of sustaining high speeds (up to 50km/h) over long distances, wild dogs lunge at their prey en masse, tearing it to pieces – a gruesome finish, but no more grisly than the suffocating muzzle-bite of a lion. The entire pack of ten to fifteen adult animals participates in looking after the pups, bringing back food and regurgitating it for them.

Reserves Kruger and Madikwe (best places) as well as Hluhluwe-iMfolozi, Waterberg Biosphere Reserve, Pilanesberg and Tswalu.
Habitat Open savannah in the vicinity of grazing herds.
Daily rhythm Diurnal.
Social life Nomadic packs.

BLACK-BACKED JACKAL (CANIS MESOMELAS)

The member of the dog family you're most likely to see is the black-backed jackal, which naturally occurs throughout South Africa, living on unprotected farmland as well as in most reserves. It bears a strong resemblance to a small, skinny German Shepherd, but with a muzzle more like that of a fox, and is distinguished from the grey, side-striped jackal (see below) by the white-flecked black saddle on its back, to which it owes its name. Jackals are omnivorous scavenger-hunters, who get most of their food from catching small creatures such as insects, lizards, snakes or birds, but will also tackle baby antelope and larger birds, and they are cheeky enough to steal pieces of prey from under the noses of lions or hyenas at a kill. The high-pitched yelping of the black-backed jackal is a characteristic crepuscular and nocturnal sound in many game reserves, but it tends to be silent in unprotected areas, where it is persecuted by farmers.

Reserves Addo, Hluhluwe-iMfolozi, Karoo, Kgalagadi, Kruger, Mkhuze, Mountain Zebra, Pilanesberg and most others.
Habitat Broad range, from moist mountain regions to desert; avoids dense woodland.

Daily rhythm Normally nocturnal, but diurnal in safety of game reserves.
Social life Mostly monogamous pairs, but also seen singly and in small family groups.

SIDE-STRIPED JACKAL (CANIS ADUSTUS)

Like its black-backed relative, the side-striped jackal is omnivorous, with a diet that takes in carrion, small animals, reptiles, birds and insects, as well as wild fruit and berries. The fact that the black-backed jackal seeks a drier habitat, in contrast to the side-striped's preference for well-watered woodland, is an identification pointer. In South Africa, its range is confined to the extreme northeast where it is less common and conspicuous than the black-backed jackal.

Reserves iSimangaliso Wetland, Kruger.
Habitat Well-watered woodland.
Daily rhythm Mainly nocturnal.
Social life Solitary or pairs.

CAPE FOX (VULPES CHAMA)

A regional endemic restricted to arid and semi-arid habitats in South Africa, Botswana, Namibia and Southern Angola, this is the smallest of South Africa's canids and the country's only true fox. It is distinguished from other dogs by its bushy tail, and combination of grey back and russet belly with few distinctive markings. It is a strictly nocturnal forager whose main diet comprises invertebrates and rodents. Common and widespread but seldom observed.

Reserves Addo, Augrabies, Karoo, Kgalagadi, Madikwe and Pilanesberg.
Habitat Open countryside; scrubland; grassland.
Daily rhythm Nocturnal.
Social life Pairs and small family groups.

BAT-EARED FOX (OTOCYON MEGALOTIS)

The bat-eared fox can easily be distinguished from the other canids by its black Zorro mask, outsized ears, shorter, pointier muzzle and smaller size. Like other dogs, the bat-eared fox is an omnivore, but it favours termites and larvae, which is where its large radar-like ears come in handy. With these it can triangulate the precise position of dung-beetle larvae up to 30cm underground and dig them out.

Reserves Addo, Bontebok, Karoo, Kgalagadi, Mountain Zebra and Pilanesberg.
Habitat Open countryside; scrubland; lightly forested areas.
Daily rhythm Nocturnal and diurnal.
Social life Family groups of 2–6.

HYENAS

Maligned by the ancients as hermaphroditic (due to the false scrotum and penis that covers the female's vagina) and in contemporary popular culture as cowardly scavengers, hyenas are in fact fascinating and highly successful carnivores whose rather doglike appearance belies their far closer evolutionary kinship to cats and mongooses. Three of the world's four hyena species occur in South Africa.

SPOTTED HYENA (CROCUTA CROCUTA)

The spotted hyena is Africa's second-largest carnivore after the lions. A scavenger *par excellence*, the spotted hyena is also a formidable hunter, most often found where antelope and zebra are present. Exceptionally efficient consumers, with immensely strong teeth and jaws, spotted hyenas eat virtually every part of their prey, including bones and hide, and, where accustomed to humans, often steal shoes, unwashed pans and refuse from tents. They are most active at night, when they issue their unnerving whooping cries. Clans of twenty or so are dominated by females, who are larger than the males and compete with each other for rank. The spotted hyena is probably the most commonly seen large carnivore in Kruger.

Reserves Addo, Hluhluwe-iMfolozi, Kgalagadi and Kruger.
Habitat Wide variety of habitat apart from dense forest.
Daily rhythm Generally nocturnal from dusk, but diurnal in many parks.
Social life Usually seen singly, but in fact highly social, usually living in extended matrilineal clans.

BROWN HYENA (HYAENA BRUNNEA)

With a range restricted to western South Africa, Botswana, Namibia and Southern Angola, this regional endemic is a nocturnal scavenger associated mainly with semi-arid and arid savannah habitats. Though its repertoire of far-carrying whoops and chuckles is similar to that of the more familiar spotted hyena, the brown hyena is far scarcer and more secretive. It is also smaller and shaggier in appearance, and boasts a distinctive ruff-like cream mane.

Reserves Addo, Kgalagadi, Kruger, Madikwe and Pilanesberg.
Habitat Most open habitats and light woodland.
Daily rhythm Nocturnal.
Social life Solitary.

AARDWOLF (PROTELES CRISTATUS)

The most atypical of hyenas, the aardwolf (literally earth-wolf) is distinguished from other species by its smaller size, lighter build, vertically striped tawny body, and insectivorous diet. It has a particular preference for harvester termites, which it laps up en masse (up to 200,000 in one night) with its broad sticky tongue. Though mostly associated with semi-arid habitats, it is widely distributed in South Africa, but shy and nocturnal, so seldom seen.

Reserves Addo, Bontebok, Kruger, Madikwe and Pilanesberg.
Habitat Most open habitats.
Daily rhythm Nocturnal; sometimes active in the cooler hours just before dusk or after dawn.
Social life Solitary.

CATS

Apart from lions, which notably live in social groups, cats are solitary carnivores. With the exception of the cheetah, which is anatomically distinct from the other cats, the remaining members of the family are so similar, says mammal ecologist Richard Estes, that big cats are just "jumbo versions" of the domestic cat, "distinguished mainly by a modification of the larynx that enables them to roar". Despite this, the seven species of cat resident in South Africa are split across five different genera.

LION (PANTHERA LEO)

The largest of the cats, and most compelling for most safari-goers, are lions. Fortunately, despite having the most limited distribution of any cat in South Africa, lions are also the ones you're most likely to see. Lazy, gregarious and sizeable, lions rarely attempt to hide, making them relatively easy to find, especially if someone else has already found them – a gathering of stationary vehicles frequently signals lions. Their fabled reputation as cold, efficient hunters is ill-founded, as lions are only successful around thirty percent of the time, and only if operating as a group. Males don't hunt at all if they can help it and will happily enjoy a free lunch courtesy of the females of the pride.

Reserves Addo, Kgalagadi, Kruger and adjoining private reserves (best place), Hluhluwe-iMfolozi, Marakele and Pilanesberg.
Habitat Wherever there's water and shade except thick forest.
Daily rhythm Diurnal and nocturnal.
Social life Prides of three to forty, more usually around twelve.

LEOPARD (PANTHERA PARDUS)

The lion may be king, but most successful and arguably most beautiful of the large cats is the leopard, which survives from the southern coastal strip of Africa all the way to China. Highly adaptable, they can subsist in extremes of aridity or cold, as well as in proximity to human habitation, where they happily prey on domestic animals – which accounts for their absence in the sheep-farming regions of central South Africa, due to extermination by farmers. Powerfully built, they can bring down prey twice their weight and drag an impala (see page 333) their own weight up a tree. The chase is not part of the leopard's tactical repertoire; they hunt by stealth, getting to within 2m of their target before pouncing.

Reserves Kruger, Hluhluwe-iMfolozi, Marakele and Pilanesberg; best places are the private reserves abutting Kruger, in particular MalaMala and Sabi Sands, which trade on their leopards being highly accustomed to humans; also present in rugged, mountainous southern Western Cape, but secretive and rarely seen.
Habitat Highly adaptable; frequently arboreal.
Daily rhythm Nocturnal; also cooler daylight hours.
Social life Solitary.

CHEETAH (ACINONYX JUBATUS)

Africa's third-largest cat species after lion and leopard, the cheetah is the felid counterpart to a greyhound, with its small head, streamlined torso and long legs designed for sprinting on the open plains. Though both the leopard and cheetah have a spotted coat, the two are so different in the flesh that it's hard to see how there could ever be any confusion between them. Unlike leopards, cheetahs never climb high in trees, though they do occasionally perch on a dead branch or termite mound to survey their surrounds. Hunting is normally a solitary activity, down to keen eyesight and an incredible burst of speed that can take the animal up to 100km/h for a few seconds. Because they're lighter than lions and less powerful than leopards, cheetahs can't rely on strength to bring down their prey. Instead they resort to tripping or knocking the victim off balance by striking its hindquarters, and then pouncing.

Reserves Addo, Kgalagadi, Kruger, Mountain Zebra as well as Phinda and most private reserves in the Eastern Cape, Mpumalanga and KwaZulu-Natal.
Habitat Savannah in the vicinity of plains game.
Daily rhythm Diurnal.
Social life Solitary or temporary nuclear family groups.

SERVAL (FELIS SERVAL)

Long legged and spotted, servals bear some resemblance to cheetahs, but are far smaller and less often seen. Efficient hunters, servals use their large rounded ears to pinpoint prey (usually small rodents, birds or reptiles), which they pounce on with both front paws after performing impressive athletic leaps.

Reserves Hluhluwe-iMfolozi, Ithala, Kruger, Pilanesberg, uKhahlamba-Drakensberg.
Habitat Reed beds or tall grasslands near water.
Daily rhythm Normally nocturnal, but can be seen during daylight hours.
Social life Usually solitary.

CARACAL (CARACAL CARACAL)

Although classified as a small cat, the caracal is a fairly substantial animal. An unmistakable and awesome hunter, it has long tufted ears that resemble those of a lynx, a light fawn coat, and great climbing agility. It is able to take prey, such as adult impala and sheep, which far exceed its own weight of 8–18kg. More common it will feed on birds, which it pounces on, sometimes while still in flight, as well as smaller mammals, including hyraxes.

Reserves Addo, Karoo, Kgalagadi, Kruger, Mountain Zebra (one of the best places), Table Mountain (Cape of Good Hope).
Habitat Open bush and plains; occasionally arboreal.
Daily rhythm Mainly nocturnal.
Social life Solitary.

AFRICAN WILD CAT (FELIS LYBICA)

Officially split from its European counterpart *Felis sylvestris* by an IUCN task force in 2017, the African wild cat is thought to be ancestral to the domestic cat (with which it often hybridises near human settlements) and it strongly resembles a common tabby with its grey-buff coat, and striped legs and tail. It typically has longer legs and looks higher on its feet than any domestic cat, and has a distinctive ginger back to the ears. A solitary nocturnal hunter, it feeds on small mammals and birds, and occurs throughout South Africa, but is seldom seen due to its shy nocturnal habits.

Reserves Addo, Kgalagadi, Kruger, Madikwe and Pilanesberg

Habitat Very habitat tolerant but prefers relatively open country.

Daily rhythm Nocturnal.

Social life Highly solitary.

BLACK-FOOTED CAT (FELIS NIGRIPES)

The world's second-smallest felid (after the Asian rusty-spotted cat), the black-footed or small spotted cat is a dry-country specialist whose global range barely extends beyond the borders of South Africa and Namibia. Listed as Vulnerable on the IUCN Red List, it is still quite common in the country's arid west, and is easily distinguished from the wild cat by its more densely spotted coat and black paw pads. It is a shy nocturnal hunter that feeds mainly on birds, invertebrates and small rodents.

Reserves Kgalagadi, Madikwe, Tswalu and Pilanesberg.

Habitat Dry country.

Daily rhythm Nocturnal.

Social life Highly solitary.

MONGOOSES

Mongooses rank among the most prolific and diverse of carnivore families, with 34 species recognised worldwide, one-third of which occur in South Africa. Certain Asian species feed mainly on venomous snakes (hence the Latin name *Herpestes*), but most South African mongooses are foragers who'll root for anything edible – mostly crabs and amphibians, but also invertebrates, eggs, lizards and small rodents. Mongooses are common both inside and outside national parks and reserves; keep your eyes peeled when driving on the open road, and you'll often see one darting across your path. Social arrangements differ from species to species, some being solitary while others live in packs. They are often relatively tolerant of humans and, even when disturbed, can often be observed for some time. The nine species described below are all likely to be seen in suitable habitat within their range; not so two other species whose ranges nudge into South Africa, namely Meller's mongoose *Rhynchogale melleri* and Selous's mongoose *Paracynictis selousi*.

SURICATE (SURICATA SURICATTA)

South Africa's least typical but best-known mongoose, the suricate (or meerkat) is famed for its endearing habit of standing upright. Closely knit gangs of around twenty individuals live colonially in old ground-squirrel burrows. Pale grey in colour, it has unique monkey-like fingers with long claws used for digging, grooming and foraging, and often stands sentry on its hind legs, particularly when curious or disturbed. A southern African dry-country endemic whose range extends from southern Angola to the Western and Eastern Cape, the suricate is particularly common in Kgalagadi Transfrontier Park.

Reserves Addo, Karoo, Kgalagadi, Tswalu.
Habitat Dry habitats such as the sandy Kalahari or stonier Karoo.
Daily rhythm Diurnal.
Social life Highly gregarious.

YELLOW MONGOOSE (CYNICTIS PENCILLATA)

Also endemic to southwest Africa, common in Kgalagadi, and prone to standing upright on its hind legs, this distinctive mongoose can be differentiated from the suricate by its plain yellow-orange (as opposed to brownish with black stripes) coat and uniquely white-tipped tail. It favours sandy environments where it lives in sprawling burrows with dozens of entrance holes.

Reserves Addo, Karoo, Kgalagadi, Tswalu.
Habitat Dry habitats such as the sandy Kalahari or stonier Karoo.
Daily rhythm Diurnal.
Social life Highly gregarious.

BANDED MONGOOSE (MUNGOS MUNGO)

One of the most conspicuous, sociable and diurnally active mongooses within its range, the banded mongoose is named for the dozen or so faint black stripes that run across the back of its otherwise dark brown-grey coat. It typically occurs in family bands of up to twenty members, and might be seen in any savannah or wooded habitat in the northeast.

Reserves Kruger, Madikwe, Pilanesberg.
Habitat Savannah.

Daily rhythm Diurnal.
Social life Highly sociable.

DWARF MONGOOSE (HELOGALE PARVULA)

Another gregarious species whose range is confined to the northeast, this diminutive (shoulder height 7cm) light brown mongoose is often seen in the vicinity of the hollow tree stumps and termite mounds it uses as communal dens.

Reserves Kruger, Madikwe, Pilanesberg.
Habitat Savannah.
Daily rhythm Diurnal.
Social life Highly sociable.

SLENDER MONGOOSE (GALERELLA SANGUINEA)

This widespread and solitary diurnal savannah species has a reddish-brown coat and distinctive tail that curves back towards the torso, ending in a black tip. It occurs in most parts of the country north of Lesotho.

Reserves Hluhluwe-iMfolozi, Kgalagadi, Kruger, Madikwe, Mkhuze, Pilanesberg.
Habitat Well-watered areas, such as alongside streams, rivers and lakes.
Daily rhythm Mainly nocturnal, but also active at dusk and dawn
Social life Solitary.

CAPE GREY MONGOOSE (GALERELLA PULVERULENTA)

The southern counterpart to the slender mongoose is this near-endemic whose range is centred on the Northern and Western Cape but also extends into southern Namibia and western Lesotho. It has a white-on-black flecked coat that looks uniform grey from a distance, and no obvious distinguishing features.

Reserves Addo, Bontebok, Table Mountain, West Coast.
Habitat Fynbos and other scrubby habitats.
Daily rhythm Diurnal.
Social life Solitary.

EGYPTIAN MONGOOSE (HERPESTES ICHNEUMON)

Also known as the large grey mongoose, this is one of the world's most widespread carnivores, with a range that extends from the Cape to Turkey and the Iberian Peninsula. A distinct black tail tip could cause it to be mistaken for a slender mongoose, but it is much heftier (weighing up to 3.5kg) and has a very shaggy grey coat. It is usually found close to rivers and other freshwater habitats. Within South Africa, its range is restricted to the coastal belt running northeast from Cape Town to Kosi Bay on the Mozambique border.

Reserves Addo, iSimangaliso Wetland.
Habitat Riverbanks, marshes and other water margins.
Daily rhythm Diurnal.
Social life Solitary.

WATER MONGOOSE (ATILAX PALUDINOSUS)

Also known as the marsh mongoose, this widely distributed species vaguely resembles an otter, but is a lot smaller and lighter, and has a shaggier coat. It is found in a deep swathe across Southern Africa, sweeping down from Mpumalanga in the northeast to the Cape Peninsula in the southwest.

Reserves Bontebok, Hluhluwe-iMfolozi, Karoo, Kruger, Mkhuze, Table Mountain (Cape of Good Hope).
Habitat Well-watered areas, such as alongside streams, rivers and lakes.
Daily rhythm Mainly nocturnal, but also active at dusk and dawn.
Social life Solitary.

WHITE-TAILED MONGOOSE (ICHNEUMIA ALBICAUDA)

Africa's largest mongoose, weighing in at up to 4.5kg, this badger-sized nocturnal species is a solitary hunter whose bushy white tail renders it unmistakable. It is often observed by spotlight on night drives in the Kruger and associated private reserves.

Reserves Hluhluwe-iMfolozi, iSimangaliso, Kruger, Pilanesberg.
Habitat Savannah.
Daily rhythm Nocturnal.
Social life Solitary.

OTHER SMALL CARNIVORES

GENETS (GENETTA SPP)

Reminiscent of slender spotted cats with elongated torsos and very long striped tails, genets are actually classified as viverrids, and thus more related to mongooses than to felids. They were once domesticated around the Mediterranean (but cats turned out to be better mouse hunters) and even today they are frequently seen after dark around lodges, where some live a semi-domesticated existence. Three equally beautiful and difficult-to-tell-apart species occur in South Africa. The common or small-spotted genet *G. genetta*, the only species with a white tail tip, is widespread in the west and central part of the country, while the rusty-spotted genet *G. maculata* inhabits the northeast interior and the eastern coastal belt north of Lesotho, and the large-spotted or Cape genet *G. tigrina* is a South African endemic confined to the coastal belt of the Eastern and Western Cape.

Reserves Addo, Bontebok, Karoo, Kgalagadi, Kruger, Mountain Zebra, Pilanesberg, Table Mountain (Cape of Good Hope).
Habitat Wide range: light bush country, even arid areas; partly arboreal.
Daily rhythm Nocturnal. But becomes active at dusk.
Social life Solitary.

CIVET (CIVETTICTIS CIVETTA)

The civet (or African civet) is a stocky animal resembling a large, terrestrial genet. Civets were formerly kept in captivity for their musk (once an ingredient in perfume), which is secreted from glands near the tail. Civets aren't often seen, but they're predictable creatures, wending their way along the same path at the same time, night after night. Civets are omnivores that will scavenge for carrion and feed on small rodents, birds, reptiles and even fruit. Found in northern South Africa, Mpumalanga and extreme north of KwaZulu-Natal.

Reserves Kruger and Pilanesberg.
Habitat Open, especially riverine, woodland.
Daily rhythm Nocturnal.
Social life Solitary.

HONEY BADGER (MELLIVORA CAPENSIS)

The unusual honey badger, related to the European badger, has a reputation for defending itself extremely fiercely. Primarily an omnivorous forager, it will tear open bees' nests (to which it is led by a small bird, the honey guide), its thick, loose hide rendering it impervious to stings.

Reserves Addo, Hluhluwe-iMfolozi, Karoo, Kgalagadi, Kruger and Pilanesberg.
Habitat Wide range except forest.
Daily rhythm Mainly nocturnal.
Social life Solitary, sometimes pairs.

CAPE CLAWLESS OTTER (AONYX CAPENSIS)

Weighing in at up to 18kg, this large aquatic carnivore might be encountered in almost any freshwater habitat, and is distributed throughout the country – with the exception of the arid Karoo and Kalahari (though its range does follow the Orange River along the border with Namibia all the way to the West Coast). It has a uniform grey coat with a distinctive white neck and throat.

Reserves Addo, Augrabies, Garden Route, iSimangaliso, Kruger, Mapungubwe.
Habitat All freshwater habitats.
Daily rhythm Diurnal.
Social life Solitary, pairs or family groups.

SPOTTED-NECKED OTTER (LUTRA MACULICOLLIS)

The spotted-necked otter is more strictly aquatic than its Cape clawless cousin, and far less common. It is relatively lightly built, weighing in at below 5kg, as well as being darker in colour (in fact it appears to be black when wet). It is named for the creamy blotches that typically adorn its throat and neck.

Reserves iSimangaliso, Kruger.
Habitat All freshwater habitats.
Daily rhythm Diurnal.
Social life Solitary, pairs or family groups.

STRIPED POLECAT (ICTONYX STRIATUS)

Also known as the zorilla, the striped polecat is a small weasel-like creature whose black coat is offset by four white stripes that run from scalp to tail. It is most likely to be seen darting hump-backed through the grass with stripes prominent on its back. It is probably South Africa's most widespread carnivore, and highly habitat tolerant, though it does seem to favour grasslands.

Reserves iSimangaliso, Kruger, Pilanesberg, uKhahlamba-Drakensberg.
Habitat Prefers open grassland and savannah.
Daily rhythm Highly nocturnal.
Social life Solitary.

ANTELOPE

The antelopes are the most frequently seen animal family in South Africa's game reserves. You'll even sometimes spot them on farmland in the extensive open stretches that separate interior towns. Roughly one-third of all Africa's antelope species occur in South Africa, and they are subdivided into a number of tribes. Like buffalo, domestic cattle, sheep and deer, they are ruminants – animals that have four stomachs and chew the cud. Though the terms are often used interchangeably, antelope are distinguished from deer by having permanent horns rather than seasonal antlers. In an evolutionary sense, the term antelope has no real meaning: the spiral-horned antelope of the genera *Taurotragus* and *Tragelaphus* (represented in South Africa by the common eland, greater kudu, nyala and bushbuck) are now known to be more closely related to buffalo, cattle and other true bovines than they are to any other group of antelopes, which in turn are more closely related to sheep and goats than to spiral-horned antelope.

COMMON ELAND (TAUROTRAGUS ORYX)

The common eland vies with the related Derby's eland, its West African counterpart, as the world's largest living antelope. Betraying its taxonomic affinity to cattle, it is not only built like an ox, but it also habitually moves with slow bovine deliberation, though it's also a superb jumper. The male has moderately sized spiralled horns and a large cow-like dewlap. Once widely distributed, the eland now survives only in pockets of northeast South Africa and protected areas of the uKhahlamba-Drakensberg, where it was also the most revered and popular subject of the Shamanic hunter-gatherer artists responsible for the region's unique wealth of prehistoric rock paintings. Small introduced populations occur in numerous other reserves.

Reserves Addo, Ithala, Karoo, Kgalagadi, Kruger, Marakele, Mountain Zebra, Pilanesberg and Table Mountain (Cape of Good Hope).

Habitat Highly adaptable; semi-desert to mountains, but prefers scrubby plains.

Daily rhythm Nocturnal and diurnal.

Social life Non-territorial herds of up to sixty.

GREATER KUDU (TRAGELAPHUS STREPSICEROS)

The magnificent greater kudu is more elegantly built than the eland, to which it is quite closely related, and males are adorned with sensational spiralled horns that can reach well over 1.5m in length. Known for its athleticism, the greater kudu can easily vault a 2m fence. Usually associated with rather dense bush, it is closely related to the lesser kudu, a smaller East African species not found in South Africa.

Reserves Northern Limpopo and North West Province reserves, and those in Mpumalanga and northeastern KwaZulu-Natal; Addo, Ithala, Hluhluwe-iMfolozi, Karoo, Kgalagadi, Kruger, Marakele, Mountain Zebra and Pilanesberg.

Habitat Semi-arid, hilly or undulating bush country; tolerant of drought.

Daily rhythm Diurnal when secure, otherwise nocturnal.

Social life Males usually solitary or in small transient groups; females in small groups with young.

BUSHBUCK (TRAGELAPHUS SYLVATICUS)

Despite a distinct family resemblance, you could never confuse a bushbuck with a kudu, since the former is considerably shorter and the male has a single twist to its horns, in contrast to the kudu's two or three. They also differ in being the only solitary members of the tribe, one reason you're less likely to spot them. Often seen in thickets or heard crashing through them. Not to be confused with the larger nyala. Until recently, the southern bushbuck was lumped together with the harnessed bushbuck of West-central Africa as *T. scriptus*, but DNA testing has revealed the two to be distinct species.

Reserves Addo, Garden Route (Wilderness and Knysna), iSimangaliso Wetland, Kruger, Mapungubwe, Pilanesberg; also most reserves (even minor ones) in KwaZulu-Natal.

Habitat Thick bush and woodland near water.

Daily rhythm Mainly nocturnal, but also active during the day when cool.

Social life Solitary, but casually sociable; sometimes grazes in small groups.

NYALA (TRAGELAPHUS ANGASII)

Nyalas are midway in size between the kudu and bushbuck, with which they could be confused at first glance. Telling pointers are their size, the sharp vertical white stripes on the side of the nyala (up to fourteen on the male, eighteen on the female), orange legs, and, in the males, a short stiff mane from neck to shoulder. Females tend to group with their two last offspring and gather with other females in small herds, rarely exceeding ten. Males become more solitary the older they get.

Reserves Kruger and around three dozen reserves in KwaZulu-Natal, of which Hluhluwe-iMfolozi, Mkhuze and Ndumo have the largest populations.

Habitat Dense woodland near water.

Daily rhythm Mainly nocturnal with some diurnal activity.

Social life Non-territorial; basic unit is female and two offspring.

BLUE WILDEBEEST (CONNOCHAETES TAURINUS)

Both wildebeest species are sociable, but the exemplar of this is the blue wildebeest (sometimes known as the brindled gnu), which,

in East Africa, gathers in hundreds of thousands for the annual Serengeti migration. You won't see these numbers in South Africa, but you'll still see substantial herds in some areas. Blue wildebeest are often seen in association with zebra.
Reserves Hluhluwe-iMfolozi, Ithala, Kgalagadi, Kruger, Mapungubwe and Mkhuze.
Habitat Grasslands.
Daily rhythm Diurnal, occasionally nocturnal.
Social life Intensely gregarious in a wide variety of associations from small groups to sizeable herds.

BLACK WILDEBEEST (CONNOCHAETES GNOU)

Black wildebeest were brought to the edge of extinction in the nineteenth century and now number around ten thousand in South Africa, though many are stocked semi-domestically on farmland rather than in bona fide reserves. You can tell them apart from their blue relatives by their darker colour (brown rather than the black suggested by their name) and long white tail. Black wildebeest (1–1.2m high at the shoulder; 160–180kg) are also significantly shorter and lighter than their blue cousins (1.7m; 380kg). The black and blue wildebeest don't naturally occur alongside each other, and most parks in South Africa now avoid stocking both, since they can interbreed and produce fertile hybrids, which could cause the rarer of the two species to be bred out of existence.

Reserves Karoo, Mountain Zebra and uKhahlamba-Drakensberg.
Habitat Low scrub and open grassland.
Daily rhythm Diurnal.
Social life Cows and offspring wander freely through bull territories; during rutting bulls try to keep females within their territory.

RED HARTEBEEST (ALCELAPHUS BUSELAPHUS CAAMA)

Closely related to wildebeests, the hartebeest is a large antelope with high shoulders, backward sloping back, heart-shaped horns (for which is named), and an elongated face that gives it a somewhat hangdog demeanour. There are around ten distinct subspecies, best distinguished from each other by geographical distribution and horn shape; the one indigenous to South Africa is the red hartebeest, which has a pale red-brown coat and is most associated with the dry northwest of the country.
Reserves Kgalagadi, Madikwe, Pilanesberg, Tswalu.
Habitat Dry grassland and light woodland.
Daily rhythm Diurnal.
Social life Very sociable, almost always seen in herds, often mingling with zebra or other antelope.

TSESSEBE (DAMALISCUS LUNATUS)

Somewhat ungainly in appearance because, according to legend, it arrived late when the Creator was dishing out the goodies, the

tsessebe turns out to be a thoroughbred when it comes to speed. One of the fastest antelope on the African plains, a fleeing tsessebe can reach 70km/h. Males often stand sentry on termite hills, marking territory against rivals (rather than defending it against predators). Tricky customers, tsessebe bulls will sometimes falsely give an alarm signal to deter females from wandering out of their territory.

Reserves Restricted to northern extremities of South Africa; best place is Kruger NP; also present in Ithala, Marakele and Pilanesberg.

Habitat Savannah woodland.

Daily rhythm Diurnal.

Social life Females and young form permanent herds usually of about half a dozen, but up to thirty individuals with a territorial bull.

BONTEBOK AND BLESBOK (DAMALISCUS DORCAS DORCAS)

Better-looking version of the tsessebe, from which it's distinguished by its smaller size, chocolate-brown colouring and white facial and rump markings. The bontebok *D. d. dorcas*, a subspecies historically limited to a small range in the southern Cape, teetered on the edge of extinction in the early twentieth century, but its survival is now secured on several reserves and farms. The commoner and somewhat drabber blesbok *D. d. phillipsi* is a subspecies found in the Free State and northern Eastern Cape.

Reserves Bontebok, De Hoop, Table Mountain (Cape of Good Hope), West Coast.

Habitat Coastal plain where Cape fynbos occurs.

Daily rhythm Diurnal.

Social life Rams hold territories; ewe and lamb herds numbering up to ten wander freely between territories.

SABLE ANTELOPE (HIPPOTRAGUS NIGER)

The magnificent sable has a sleek, black upper body set in sharp counterpoint to its white underparts and facial markings, as well as its massive backwardly curving horns, making it the thoroughbred of the ruminants, particularly when galloping majestically across the savannah.

Reserves Kruger, Waterberg.

Habitat Open woodland with medium to tall grass near water.

Daily rhythm Nocturnal and diurnal.

Social life Highly hierarchical female herds of up to three dozen; territorial bulls divide into sub-territories, through which cows roam.

ROAN ANTELOPE (HIPPOTRAGUS EQUINUS)

The roan looks very similar to but is larger than a sable (it's Africa's second-largest antelope), with less impressive horns and lighter colouring. You're more likely to see it in open savannah than the sable.

Reserves Kruger NP.

Habitat Tall grassland near water.

Daily rhythm Nocturnal and diurnal; peak afternoon feeding.

Social life Small herds led by dominant bull; herds of immature males; sometimes pairs in season.

GEMSBOK (OR ORYX) (ORYX GAZELLA)

If you encounter a herd of these highly gregarious grazers, you should be left in no doubt as to what they are. Gemsbok are highly adapted for survival in the arid country they inhabit, able to go for long periods without water, relying instead on melons and vegetation for moisture. They tolerate temperatures above 40°C by raising their normal body temperature of 35°C above that of the surrounding air, losing heat by conduction and radiation; their brains are kept cool by a supply of blood from their noses.

Reserves Addo, Augrabies, Karoo, Kgalagadi, Mokala, Pilanesberg and Tankwa Karoo.

Habitat Open grasslands; waterless wastelands; tolerant of prolonged drought.

Daily rhythm Nocturnal and diurnal.

Social life Highly hierarchical mixed herds of up to fifteen, led by a dominant male.

WATERBUCK (KOBUS ELLIPSIPRYMNUS)

The waterbuck is the largest species in the Kob tribe, most members of which live in marshy areas or close to water. They are sturdy animals – 1.3m at the shoulder, and with a distinctive white horseshoe marking on their rump. Only the males have horns. Unable to reach or sustain significant speed, they rely on cover to evade predators. It is also claimed that the oily, musky secretion and powerful odour waterbuck emit from their hair is distasteful to predators and acts as a deterrent. They are common and rather tame where they occur, predominantly in KwaZulu-Natal, Limpopo and Mpumalanga.

Reserves Hluhluwe-iMfolozi, iSimangaliso Wetland, Ithala, Kruger, Mapungubwe, Marakele and Mkhuze.

Habitat Open woodland and savannah, near permanent water.

Daily rhythm Nocturnal and diurnal.

Social life Sociable animals, they usually gather in small herds of up to ten, and occasionally up to thirty.

SOUTHERN REEDBUCK (REDUNCA ARUNDINUM)

This nondescript medium-sized antelope has fawn to grey upperparts, a white belly and inner legs, curved horns (male only) and is distinguished by the black lines that run down its front legs and (if you get close enough) the bare patches found behind each ear.

Reserves Hluhluwe-iMfolozi, Kruger, Ithala, iSimangaliso Wetland.

Habitat Reedbeds and moist grassland.

Daily rhythm Diurnal.

Social life Pairs and small family groups.

MOUNTAIN REEDBUCK (REDUNCA FULVORUFULA)

Associated with high-altitude grasslands, the mountain reedbuck is more widespread than the similar-looking southern reedbuck in a continental context, but more localized within South Africa. Darker in colour than the southern reedbuck, with a more grizzled coat, it

also displays a more distinct separation between grey upperparts and white belly and has a black patch behind the ears. The male has small forward-curving horns.
Reserves uKhahlamba-Drakensberg.
Habitat Reedbeds and moist grassland.
Daily rhythm Diurnal.
Social life Pairs and small family groups.

IMPALA (AEPYCEROS MELAMPUS)

By far the most abundant large mammal in the Kruger National Park and environs, the impala is an elegant and athletic antelope that frequently lives in herds comprising several hundred individuals. It has a complex social structure that involves plenty of fighting between rival males. Prodigious jumpers, impala have been recorded leaping distances of 11m and heights of 3m. Only the males carry the distinctive lyre-shaped pair of horns. They are so common in the reserves of the northeast and of KwaZulu-Natal that some jaded rangers look on them as the goats of the savannah – a perception that carries more than a germ of truth, as these flexible feeders are both browsers and grazers.
Reserves Hluhluwe-iMfolozi, Ithala, Kruger, Mapungubwe, Marakele, Mkhuze and Pilanesberg.
Habitat Open savannah, near light woodland cover.
Daily rhythm Diurnal.

Social life Large herds of females overlap with several male territories; during the rut (first five months of the year) dominant males will cut out harem herds of around twenty and expend considerable amounts of effort driving off any potential rivals.

SPRINGBOK (ANTIDORCAS MARSUPIALIS)

South Africa's national animal, the springbok is also the only species of gazelle found in southern Africa. It superficially resembles the impala, but is smaller and lighter, and prefers drier and more open habitats. Its characteristic horns and dark horizontal side patch separating the reddish tawny upper body from the white underparts are definitive identifiers. Springboks are recorded as having reached nearly 90km/h and are noted for "pronking", a movement in which they arch their backs and straighten their legs as they leap into the air. Indigenous to the (often arid) northern reaches of South Africa, where they were once seen in their hundreds, they are now more widespread in reserves and on farms where they are raised for their venison and hides.
Reserves Addo, Augrabies, Golden Gate, Karoo, Kgalagadi, Mountain Zebra, Pilanesberg, Tankwa Karoo and West Coast.
Habitat Wide range of open country, from deserts to wetter savannah.
Daily rhythm Seasonally variable, but usually cooler times of day.

Social life Highly gregarious, sometimes in huge herds of hundreds or even thousands; various herding combinations of males, females and young.

ORIBI (OUREBIA OUREBI)

A widespread and locally common small antelope associated with open grassland, where it tends to draw attention to itself with a sneeze-like alarm call. With a range limited to moister eastern parts of the country, it has uniform sandy upperparts, a white belly, small straight horns (both sexes) and a distinctive black gland below the ears.

Reserves Ithala, uKhahlamba-Drakensberg.
Habitat Moist grassland, often associated with slopes.
Daily rhythm Diurnal.
Social life Almost always seen in pairs or small family groups.

KLIPSPRINGER (OREOTRAGUS OREOTRAGUS)

Another dwarf antelope (about 60cm at the shoulder) you might see is the stocky klipspringer, whose Afrikaans name (meaning "rock hopper") reflects its goat-like adaptation to living on *koppies* and cliffs – the only antelope to do so, making it unmistakable. It's also the only one to walk on the tips of its hooves. They occur sporadically throughout South Africa where there are rocky outcrops.

Reserves Addo, Augrabies, Garden Route (Tsitsikamma), Karoo, Kruger, Mapungubwe, Mkhuze, Mountain Zebra, Pilanesberg and Table Mountain (Cape of Good Hope).
Habitat Rocky terrain.
Daily rhythm Diurnal; most active in morning and late afternoon.
Social life Monogamous pairs or small family groups.

STEENBOK (RAPHICERUS CAMPESTRIS)

One of the most widespread and common antelopes in South Africa, the steenbok can be found in most relatively open habitats, from grassland to patchy thicket. It tends to lie low when disturbed, then to bound off suddenly following a zigzag route to try to confuse pursuers. A small antelope with a fawn-brown torso, white underparts and small straight horns, it possesses few features to distinguish it from other similarly sized antelope, but is less grizzled in appearance than the closely related grysboks, and has a straighter back than the duikers.

Reserves Hluhluwe-iMfolozi, Kruger, Mapungubwe, Marakele, Mkhuze, Pilanesberg, uKhahlamba-Drakensberg.
Habitat Thicket and grassland.
Daily rhythm Mainly nocturnal but often seen by day.
Social life Singly or sometimes in pairs.

CAPE GRYSBOK (RAPHICERUS MELANOTIS)

Endemic to South Africa, this chunky small antelope has a range focused on the fynbos biome of the Western Cape, though it also extends into the semi-arid Karoo and grassy slopes of the Drakensberg. It has a white-flecked sandy-red coat, while distinguishing features include a black mark on the nose, narrow white eye-rings, large rabbit-like ears and a tailless appearance. Males also have short straight horns.

Reserves Karoo, Table Mountain, uKhahlamba-Drakensberg.
Habitat Thicket and grassland.
Daily rhythm Mainly diurnal.
Social life Usually seen singly or in pairs.

SHARPE'S GRYSBOK (RAPHICERUS SHARPEI)

This close relative of the Cape grysbok is a subtropical species whose range nudges into the far northeast of South Africa. It has a similar fleck-coated appearance to the Cape grysbok and habitually raises its rump.

Reserves Kruger (in particular the Lebombo Concession), Waterberg.
Habitat Low-altitude thicket.
Daily rhythm Mainly diurnal.
Social life Single or in pairs.

SUNI (NEOTRAGUS MOSCHATUS)

Within South Africa, this tiny antelope of eastern coastal forest and thickets is more-or-less restricted to northern KwaZulu-Natal. Also known as Livingstone's suni, it is red-brown in colour, with a sloping back, and could be mistaken for a duiker, but for its rabbit-like ears and customary tail-flicking behaviour. Unlike duikers, only the male suni has horns, and these are backward-curving rather than straight.

Reserves Hluhluwe-iMfolozi, iSimangaliso Wetland, Ndumo, Phinda, Tembe.
Habitat Coastal thicket.
Daily rhythm Diurnal.
Social life Solitary or in pairs.

COMMON (OR GREY) DUIKER (SYLVICAPRA GRIMMIA)

Of three duikers recorded in South Africa, the one you're most likely to see is the common duiker (sometimes called the grey duiker, reflecting its colouring), which occurs all over the country and is relatively tolerant of human habitation. When under threat it freezes in the undergrowth, but if chased will dart off in an erratic zigzagging run designed to throw pursuers off balance. The common duiker has a characteristic rounded back, is about 50cm high at the shoulder, and rams have short, straight horns.

Reserves Addo, Bontebok, Hluhluwe-iMfolozi, Ithala, Karoo, Kruger, Mkhuze, Mountain Zebra, Pilanesberg and Table Mountain (Cape of Good Hope).
Habitat Adaptable; prefers scrub and bush.
Daily rhythm Nocturnal and diurnal.
Social life Mostly solitary, but sometimes in pairs.

RED DUIKER (CEPHALOPHUS NATALENSIS)

Sometimes referred to as the Natal duiker to distinguish it from similar-looking species that occur outside South Africa, the red duiker is a secretive slope-backed denizen of evergreen forest and coastal thickets in the east of the country. Both sexes are deep chestnut-red in colour and have small straight horns separated by a darker tuft of hair. They often emerge from the deep forest and thickets to graze in grassy clearings towards dusk.

Reserves Hluhluwe-iMfolozi, iSimangaliso Wetland, Ndumo, Phinda, Tembe.

Habitat Forest, coastal thicket and associated clearings.

Daily rhythm Mainly but not strictly nocturnal.

Social life Solitary or in pairs.

BLUE DUIKER (PHILANTOMBA MONTICOLA)

The smallest South African antelope, the blue duiker weighs in at around 4kg, has an arched back and stands 35cm at the shoulder (roughly the height of a domestic cat). Pairs stick together and remain vigilant as a defence against predators, which can include leopards, baboons and even large birds of prey. Duiker are found in the forested areas of the coastal strip from George in the Western Cape to northern KwaZulu-Natal, but are extremely shy and seldom seen.

Reserves Garden Route (Knysna), iSimangaliso Wetland and Ndumo.

Habitat Forests and dense bushland.

Daily rhythm Mainly diurnal.

Social life Monogamous couples.

OTHER HOOFED RUMINANTS

Alongside cattle, sheep, goats and antelope, buffalo and giraffe are also hoofed ruminants. Bacteria in their digestive systems process plant matter into carbohydrates, while the dead bacteria are absorbed as protein – a highly efficient arrangement that makes them economical consumers, far more so than non-ruminants such as elephants, which pass vast quantities of what they eat as unutilized fibre. Species that concentrate on grasses are grazers; those eating leaves are browsers.

BUFFALO (SYNCERUS CAFFER)

You won't have to be in the Kruger or most of the other reserves in South Africa for long to see buffalo, a common safari animal that, as one of the Big Five, appears on every hunter's shopping list. Don't let the resemblance to domestic cattle or water buffalo, or their apparent docility, lull you into complacency; lone bulls, in particular, are noted and feared even by hardened hunters as dangerous and relentless killers. Herds consist of clans and you'll be able to spot distinct units within the group: at rest, clan members often cuddle up close to each other. There are separate pecking orders among females and males, the latter being forced to leave the herd during adolescence (at about three years) or once they're over the hill, to form bachelor herds, which you can recognize by their small numbers. To distinguish males from females, look for their heavier horns bisected by a distinct boss, or furrow. Once found throughout South Africa, natural populations survive in the Eastern Cape, KwaZulu-Natal and Mpumalanga and have been widely reintroduced elsewhere.

Reserves Addo, Hluhluwe-iMfolozi, iSimangaliso Wetland, Karoo, Kruger and Mountain Zebra.

Habitat Wide range of habitats, always near water.

Daily rhythm Nocturnal and diurnal, but inactive during heat of the day.

Social life Buffalo are non-territorial and gather in large herds of hundreds or even sometimes thousands. Herds under one or more dominant bulls consist of clans of a dozen or so related females under a leading cow.

GIRAFFE (GIRAFFA CAMELOPARDALIS)

Giraffe are among the easiest animals to spot because their long necks make them visible above the low scrub. The tallest mammals on earth, they spend their daylight hours browsing on the leaves of trees too high up for other species; combretum and acacias are favourites. Their highly flexible lips and prehensile tongues give them almost hand-like agility and enable them to select the most nutritious leaves while avoiding deadly sharp acacia thorns. At night they lie down and spend the evening ruminating. If you encounter a bachelor herd, look out for young males testing their strength with neck wrestling. When the female comes into oestrus, which can happen at any time of year, the dominant male mates with her. She will give birth after a fourteen-month gestation. Over half of all young, however, fall prey to lions or hyenas in their early years.

Reserves Hluhluwe-iMfolozi, Ithala, Kgalagadi, Kruger, Mapungubwe, Mkhuze and Pilanesberg.

Habitat Wooded savannah and thorn country.

Daily rhythm Diurnal.

Social life Loose, non-territorial, leaderless herds.

NON-RUMINANTS

Non-ruminating mammals have more primitive digestive systems than animals that chew the cud. Although both have bacteria in their gut that convert vegetable matter into carbohydrates, the less efficient system of the non-ruminants means they have to consume more raw material and process it faster. The upside is they can handle food that's far more fibrous.

AFRICAN ELEPHANT (LOXODONTA AFRICANA)

Elephants were once found throughout South Africa. Now you'll only see them in a handful of reserves. When encountered in the flesh, elephants seem even bigger than you would imagine. You'll need little persuasion from those flapping warning ears to back off if you're too close, but they are at the same time amazingly graceful. In a matter of moments a large herd can merge into the trees and disappear, silent on their padded, carefully placed feet, their presence betrayed only by the noisy cracking of branches as they strip trees and uproot saplings. Elephants are the most engaging of animals to watch, perhaps because their interactions, behaviour patterns and personality have so many human parallels. Like people, they lead complex, interdependent social lives, growing from helpless infancy through self-conscious adolescence to adulthood. Babies are born with other cows in close attendance, after a 22-month gestation. Calves suckle for two to three years. Basic family units are composed of a group of related females, tightly protecting their young and led by a venerable matriarch. Bush mythology has it that elephants become ashamed after killing a human, covering the body with sticks and grass. They certainly pay much attention to the disposal of their own dead relatives, often dispersing the bones and spending time near the remains. Old animals die in their 70s or 80s, when their last set of teeth wears out so that they are no longer able to feed themselves. **Reserves** Addo (the only population to survive naturally in the southern two-thirds of the country), Hluhluwe-iMfolozi, Ithala, Kruger, Mkhuze, Pilanesberg and Tembe.

Habitat Wide range of habitats, wherever there are trees or water.
Daily rhythm Nocturnal and diurnal; sleeps as little as four hours a day.
Social life Highly complex; cows and offspring in herds headed by matriarch; bulls solitary or in bachelor herds.

ROCK HYRAX (PROCAVIA CAPENSIS)

Associated with mountainous habitats, hyraxes look like they ought to be rodents but, amazingly, despite being fluffy and rabbit-sized, their closest living relatives (admittedly from some way back) are elephants, dugongs and manatees. Their local name, *dassie* (pronounced like "dusty" without the "t"), is the Afrikaans version of *dasje*, meaning "little badger", as given to them by the first Dutch settlers. Like reptiles, hyraxes have poor body control systems and rely on shelter against both the cold and hot sunlight. They wake up sluggish and seek out rocks to catch the early morning sun – this is one of the best times to look out for them. One adult stands sentry against predators and issues a low-pitched warning cry in response to a threat. They are found throughout South Africa and are frequently sighted.
Reserves Bontebok, Garden Route (Tsitsikamma), Karoo, Kruger, Mountain Zebra, Pilanesberg, Table Mountain (Cape of Good Hope), uKhahlamba-Drakensberg.
Habitat Rocky areas, from mountains to isolated outcrops and coastal cliffs.
Daily rhythm Diurnal.
Social life Colonies of a dominant male and eight or more related females and their offspring.

RHINOS AND HIPPOS

"Square-lipped" and "hook-lipped" are technically more accurate terms for Africa's two species of rhino than "white" or "black", since both are a greyish muddy colour. The more common names are often said to be based on a linguistic misunderstanding (the German "*weid*", which refers to the square-lipped's wide mouth, was misheard by English-speakers as "white"), but there is absolutely no documentary evidence to support this oft-repeated legend. True or not, the different shape of the two species' mouths is highly significant, as it indicates their respective diets and consequently their favoured habitat. Rhinos give birth to a single calf after a gestation period of fifteen to eighteen months, and the baby is not weaned until it is at least a year old, sometimes two. Their population grows slowly compared with most animals, another factor contributing to their predicament.

BLACK RHINO (DICEROS BICORNIS)

The smaller, more cantankerous and rarer of Africa's two species, the black rhino is IUCN-listed as Critically Endangered; South Africa's estimated two thousand individuals comprise forty percent of the global population. It has the narrow prehensile lips of a browser, suited to picking leaves off trees and bushes. A solitary animal, it relies on the camouflage of dense thickets, which is why it is so much more difficult to see than the white rhino.

Reserves Addo, Augrabies, Hluhluwe-iMfolozi, iSimangaliso Wetland, Ithala, Karoo, Kruger, Marakele, Mkhuze and Pilanesberg.

Habitat Thick bush.

Daily rhythm Active day and night, resting between periods of activity.

Social life Solitary.

WHITE RHINO (CERATOTHERIUM SIMUM)

Twice as bulky as its black counterpart, the white rhino is Africa's second-heaviest non-marine animal, with adult males often tipping the scales at above 2000kg. Unlike the black rhino, it is not generally aggressive towards people, though rival males have often been known to fight each other to the death. Diet and habitat account for the greater sociability of the white rhino, which relies on safety in numbers under the exposure of open grassland, while its wide, flatter mouth is well suited to chomping away at grasses like a lawnmower. Two geographically disjunct subspecies of white rhino are recognized. These are the southern white rhino, whose natural range is concentrated to the south of the Zambezi River, and the northern white rhino, which once inhabited parts of Uganda, South Sudan, the Central African Republic and the Democratic Republic of the Congo. By the end of the nineteenth century, the only place the southern white rhino survived was in the Hluhluwe-iMfolozi reserve (where it still thrives), but it has since been introduced to a number of national parks and other reserves in South Africa, and is quite easily seen in most. The southern white rhino is IUCN listed as Near-threatened, with a global population estimated to be at least twenty thousand, some ninety percent of it resident in South Africa. By contrast, the northern white rhino is listed as functionally extinct as of March 2018, when the last male died, leaving just two surviving individual semi-captive females protected in Kenya's Ol Pejeta Sanctuary.

Reserves Hluhluwe-iMfolozi, Ithala, Kruger, Marakele, Mkhuze, Ndumo, Pilanesberg and Tembe.

Habitat Savannah.

Daily rhythm Active day and night, resting between periods of activity.

Social life Mother/s and calves, or small same-sex herds of immature animals; old males solitary.

HIPPOPOTAMUS (HIPPOPOTAMUS AMPHIBIUS)

Hippos are highly adaptable animals that once inhabited South African waterways from the Limpopo in the north to the marshes of the Cape Peninsula in the south. Today they're far more restricted, but you'll see them elsewhere, in places where they've been reintroduced. Hippos need fresh water deep enough to submerge themselves, with a surrounding of suitable grazing grass. By day, they need to spend most of their time in water to protect their thin, hairless skin. After dark, hippos leave the water to spend the whole night grazing, often walking up to 10km in one session. Their grunting and jostling in the water may give the impression of loveable buffoons, but throughout Africa they are feared, and rightly so, as they are reckoned to be responsible for more human deaths on the continent than any other animal. When disturbed, lone bulls and cows with calves can become extremely aggressive. Their fearsomely long incisors can slash through a canoe with ease; on land they can charge at speeds of up to 30km/h, with a tight turning circle.

Reserves Addo, iSimangaliso Wetland, Kruger and Pilanesberg.

Habitat Slow-flowing rivers, dams and lakes.

Daily rhythm Principally nocturnal, leaving the water to graze at night.

Social life Bulls solitary; others live in family groups known as pods, headed by a matriarch.

ZEBRAS

Zebras are closely related to horses and, together with them, donkeys and wild asses, form the equidae family. Of the three species of zebra, two live in South Africa. Zebras congregate in family herds of a breeding stallion and two mares (or more) and their foals. Unattached males will often form bachelor herds. Among plains zebras, offspring leave the family group after between one and two years, while mountain zebras are far more tolerant in allowing adolescents to remain in the family.

PLAINS (BURCHELL'S) ZEBRA (EQUUS QUAGGA)

A highly successful herbivore that can survive in a variety of grassland habitats, the plains zebra has small ears and thick, black stripes, with lighter "shadows". Half a dozen subspecies are widely recognized, ranging north and west to southern Ethiopia and southern Angola. The subspecies present in South Africa is Burchell's zebra (*E. q. burchellii*), which is distinguished from other variants by its distinctive shadow stripes. The quagga (*E. q. quagga*) is an extinct partially striped subspecies of plains zebra that proliferated to the south of the Orange River prior to the arrival of European settlers and their guns; the last known individual was a captive specimen that died in Amsterdam Zoo in 1883. A century later, the Quagga Project started its attempt to recreate the extinct subspecies by selective breeding of Burchell's zebra that resemble it; over several generations it has produced about six individuals that fit the bill.

Reserves Addo, Hluhluwe-iMfolozi, iSimangaliso Wetland, Ithala, Kruger, Mapungubwe, Mkhuze, Pilanesberg.

Habitat Savannah, with or without trees.

Daily rhythm Active day and night, resting intermittently.

Social life Harems of several mares and foals, led by a dominant stallion, usually group together in large herds; harems highly stable and harem mares typically remain with the same male for life.

MOUNTAIN ZEBRA (EQUUS ZEBRA)

Once abundant in much of the Western and Eastern Cape, the Cape mountain zebra (*E. z. zebra*) is a South African endemic that narrowly escaped the fate of its extinct relative the quagga, with the global population of around just eighty individuals in the 1950s. It now survives in healthy if limited numbers in several reserves in the southern half of South Africa, wherever there is suitably mountainous terrain, and its IUCN red list status was since upgraded from Endangered to Vulnerable. A second subspecies, Hartmann's mountain zebra (*E. z. hartmannae*), is concentrated in Namibia but its range extends into the Northern Cape, where a few hundred individuals live in a handful of protected areas. Characteristics that distinguish mountain zebras from other species within South Africa include its relatively small size, the slight dewlap on its lower neck (most clearly seen in profile), the absence of shadow stripes, the larger ears, and stripes that go all the way down to the hooves rather than fading out as they progress down the legs.

Reserves Bontebok, De Hoop, Karoo, Mountain Zebra, Table Mountain (Cape of Good Hope) and Augrabies.

Habitat Mountainous areas and their immediate surrounds.

Daily rhythm Active by day.

Social life Harems of stallions with four or five mares and their foals.

OTHER MAMMALS

AARDVARK (ORYCTEROPUS AFER)

One of Africa's – indeed the world's – strangest animals, a solitary mammal weighing up to 70kg. Its name, Afrikaans for "earth pig", is an apt description, as it holes up during the day in large burrows that are excavated with remarkable speed and energy. It emerges at night to visit termite mounds within a radius of up to 5km, digging for its main diet. It's most likely to be common in bush country that's well scattered with termite mounds. Found throughout South Africa, but rarely seen.

Reserves Addo, Karoo, Kgalagadi, Kruger, Mapungubwe and Mountain Zebra; Samara and Kwandwe private reserves have a good reputation for producing aardvark sightings, especially in winter.

Habitat Open or wooded termite country; softer soil preferred.
Daily rhythm Nocturnal.
Social life Solitary.

PANGOLIN (MANIS TEMMINCKII)

Equally unusual – scale-covered mammals, resembling armadillos and feeding on ants and termites. Under attack they roll themselves into a ball. Pangolins occur widely in South Africa, north of the Orange River.

Reserves Kgalagadi and Kruger.
Habitat Wide range apart from desert and forest.
Daily rhythm Nocturnal.
Social life Solitary.

PORCUPINE (HYSTRIX AFRICAEAUSTRALIS)

The most singular and largest (up to 90cm) of the African rodents is the porcupine, which is quite unmistakable with its coat of many quills. Porcupines are widespread and present in most reserves but, because they're nocturnal, you may only see shed quills. Rarely seen, but common away from croplands, where it is hunted as a pest.

Reserves Virtually all.
Habitat Adaptable to a wide range of habitats.
Daily rhythm Nocturnal; sometimes active at dusk.
Social life Family groups.

SPRINGHARE (PEDETES CAPENSIS)

If you go on a night drive in the Kruger or one of several other reserves in the north of the country, you'd be most unlucky not to see the glinting eyes of springhares which, despite their resemblance to rabbit-sized kangaroos, are in fact true rodents.

Reserves Kgalagadi, Kruger, Mountain Zebra and Pilanesberg.
Habitat Savannah; softer soil areas preferred.
Daily rhythm Nocturnal.

Social life Burrows, usually with a pair and their young; often linked into a network, almost like a colony.

WARTHOG (PHACOCHOERUS AETHIOPICUS)

If you're visiting the Kruger, Pilanesberg or the KwaZulu-Natal parks, families of warthogs will become a familiar sight, trotting across the savannah with their tails erect like communications antennae. Boars join family groups only to mate; they're distinguished from sows by their prominent face warts, which are thought to be defensive pads protecting their heads during often violent fights.

Reserves Addo, Hluhluwe-iMfolozi, iSimangaliso Wetland, Ithala, Kruger, Mkhuze and Pilanesberg.
Habitat Savannah.
Daily rhythm Diurnal.
Social life Family groups usually consist of a mother and her litter of two to four piglets, or occasionally two or three females and their young.

BUSHPIG (POTOMOCHOERUS LARVATUS)

The secretive bushpig is bulkier and hairier than the warthog, and reddish-brown rather than grey in colour, with a distinctive hair ridge on its back. Quite possibly the more widespread and commoner of South Africa's two swine species, at least in the moister east, it is infrequently seen due to its nocturnal habits and preference for dense vegetation.

Reserves Hluhluwe-iMfolozi, iSimangaliso Wetland, Kruger, Mkhuze.
Habitat Riverine and other forests.
Daily rhythm Nocturnal.
Social life Solitary or in pairs or family groups.

CAPE GROUND SQUIRREL (XERUS INAURIS)

The most distinctive of several squirrel species found in South Africa, and the only one that is almost wholly terrestrial, this charismatic and entertaining creature lives in sociable subterranean colonies of twenty-plus individuals. Associated with the sandy soils in the dry northwest, it is particularly common in the Kalahari, where semi-habituated groups can be observed busying themselves in the restcamps of Kgalagadi. Light grey-brown in colour with a pronounced side-stripe, it is replaced in the north and east by various arboreal bush squirrel species.

Reserves Augrabies Falls, Addo Elephant, Mountain Zebra, Kgalagadi.
Habitat Arid and semi-arid areas with sandy soil.
Daily rhythm Diurnal.
Social life Highly sociable, living in colonies of twenty or more.

Cats (drawn to scale)

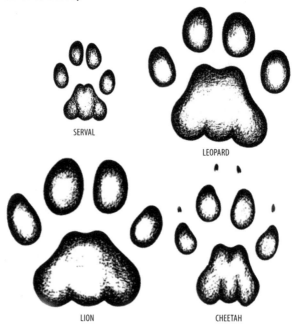

SERVAL

LEOPARD

LION

CHEETAH

Dogs and hyenas (drawn to scale)

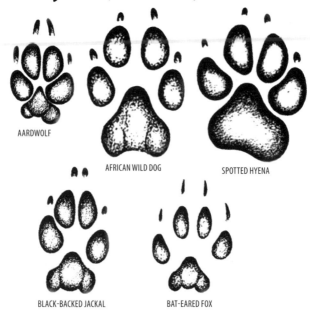

AARDWOLF

AFRICAN WILD DOG

SPOTTED HYENA

BLACK-BACKED JACKAL

BAT-EARED FOX

Large antelopes (drawn to scale)

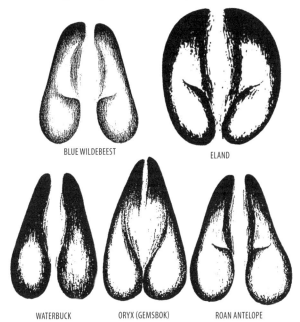

BLUE WILDEBEEST

ELAND

WATERBUCK

ORYX (GEMSBOK)

ROAN ANTELOPE

Small antelope (drawn to scale)

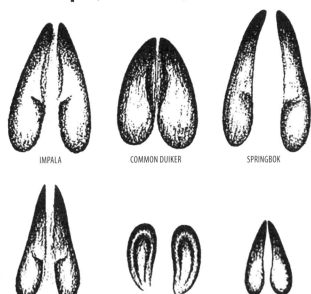

IMPALA

COMMON DUIKER

SPRINGBOK

STEENBOK

KLIPSPRINGER

DAMARA DIK-DIK

Primates (drawn to scale)

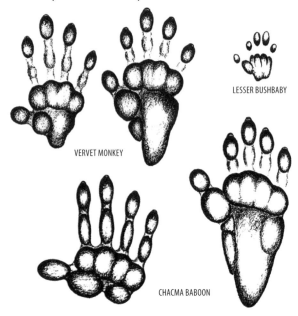

LESSER BUSHBABY

VERVET MONKEY

CHACMA BABOON

Small carnivores (drawn to scale)

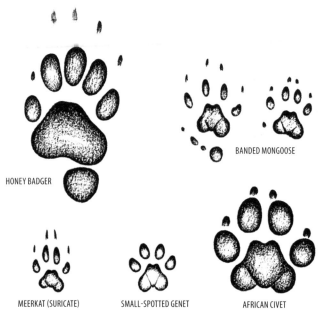

HONEY BADGER

BANDED MONGOOSE

MEERKAT (SURICATE)

SMALL-SPOTTED GENET

AFRICAN CIVET

Other large mammals (not drawn to scale)

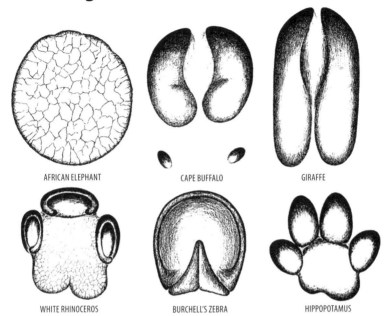

AFRICAN ELEPHANT

CAPE BUFFALO

GIRAFFE

WHITE RHINOCEROS

BURCHELL'S ZEBRA

HIPPOPOTAMUS

Other small mammals (drawn to scale)

PANGOLIN

PORCUPINE

ROCK HYRAX

WARTHOG

Birds

Most first-time visitors to South Africa are struck by its colourful and conspicuous **birdlife**. And for dedicated birdwatchers, the country ranks as one of the world's most important and enjoyable ornithological destinations. The numbers alone are impressive. South Africa's national checklist of roughly **850 species** represents eight percent of the global total, and places it in the top thirty worldwide in terms of avian diversity. For serious birders, South Africa is home to a full thirty **endemics**, species that occur nowhere else in the world, or whose range extends only into the Kingdoms of Lesotho and/or Eswatini (respectively enclosed by South Africa entirely and on three sides). South Africa also forms the core territory of most of the 160 species regarded to be endemic or near-endemic to Africa south of the Zambezi. Put plainly, not only does South Africa host an immense diversity of birds, but it is also the only or best place in the world to see a large number of range-restricted species.

These statistics only tell half the story. South Africa's birdlife is not merely prolific, it is also utterly captivating. Be it the dazzling bee-eaters and rollers that hawk from the thorn-trees of the northern savannah; the boldly-marked fish eagles whose unforgettable duets resound along the country's wooded waterways; the green-and-red turacos that creep along evergreen forest boughs; or improbable oddities such as the outsized ostriches of Oudtshoorn and scolding mobs of guineafowl that flock along the roadsides, South Africa's more conspicuous birds tend to possess a charisma that enchants even the most avi-sceptical of visitors.

Birds are a significant presence almost wherever you go in South Africa, even in the cities. But the best starting point for visitors hoping to see a good selection of the country's avian diversity is the game parks. The **Kruger National Park** and adjoining private reserves, for instance, protect more than five hundred species, and are particularly good for eagles, vultures, storks, ground hornbills and other heavyweights whose existence is increasingly tenuous outside protected areas. Most other major game parks are equally rewarding for birds: **iSimangaliso Wetland** tops the list when it comes to aquatic and tropical marine species, the reserves of northeast **KwaZulu-Natal** are strong on savannah dwellers, **Madikwe** and **Pilanesberg** protect a host of range-restricted Kalahari specials at the most easterly extent of their range, **Kgalagadi** is excellent for dry-country specialists and raptors, while the private reserves of the **Eastern Cape** are good for southern endemics.

South Africa offers excellent birdwatching throughout the year, but avian variety and activity peaks during the **southern summer** (October to March), which also doubles as the rainy season in most parts of the country. There are three reasons why these months form the prime birding season. The first and most obvious is that resident bird populations are boosted by an influx of **migrants**, some from elsewhere in Africa, but the vast majority being Palaearctic species that spend the northern hemisphere winter in equatorial or southern Africa. An estimated six billion individual birds undertake this trans-Sahara migration annually, ranging in size from the diminutive willow warbler to the bulky white stork, along with innumerable flocks of European (barn) swallow, several types of raptor and various waders, wagtails and waterfowl. The second reason is that the southern summer is when the males of several resident species – various weavers, whydahs and widowbirds, for instance – shed their drab eclipse plumage in favour of bright yellow, black and red **breeding colours**. Finally, since it is also the main breeding season for most species, the summer is also when secretive forest birds tend to **vocalize** the most, and are easiest to track down by call.

Serious birders might think about joining a dedicating **birdwatching tour**. These tours are designed to visit the best birding spots at the most productive times of the day, to maximize chances of seeing localized endemics and other **unusual species**. Trips are led by specialist ornithological **guides** who will help locate and identify difficult species.

A GROUP OF BIRDERS, POLOKWANE NATURE RESERVE

More casual birders will find that most local guides, especially those in private reserves, are very knowledgeable about birds and keen to spend time with clients whose interest extends beyond ticking off the Big Five and other large mammals, though it is always a good idea to specify your interest when you make a booking at a reserve to ensure you are allocated a guide who knowns his stuff. Meanwhile, those who prefer a more DIY approach will find that South Africa is served by an excellent selection of field guides, apps, and other useful literature (see page 389).

It's worth buying a comprehensive **field guide** to the birds of Southern Africa (or an equivalent app version). This will describe all species ever recorded in the country, as well as highlighting important **field characters** and providing **distribution details**. Most field guides also illustrate all common and some uncommon plumages for all species (in some cases, males and females look very different, as do juveniles, then there are also subspecific regional variations or other morphs). Counterintuitively, perhaps, field guides with drawn or painted plates are more reliable than those with photographs when it comes to identifying tricky lookalike species; this is because the **illustrations** will be rendered to highlight each bird's key field characters, and to reflect true colours untainted by random variations in ambient light. For serious birders, the introductory section that follows is no substitute for a full field guide, but for the less dedicated, it does provide an overview of the main bird families and some more common and noteworthy species.

Aquatic birds

Although South Africa is a relatively dry country, its inland waters and 2850km coastline form an important avian habitat. So much so that more than 25 percent of the bird species recorded here are non-passerine **waterbirds**, ranging from gulls and terns to ducks and herons, together with such oddities as pelicans, flamingos and spoonbills. Most freshwater-associated birds are quite easy to see and identify, since they tend to forage in the open throughout the day. By contrast, the identification of marine species such as gulls, terns and petrels can be challenging even to expert birders, since they tend to be quite similar in appearance and are normally only seen in flight.

Marine birds

Of the roughly one hundred species of gull, tern, petrel, albatross, skua and other marine birds recorded along and off the shores of South Africa, many are rare vagrants or oceanic wanderers whose inclusion is based almost exclusively on sightings made at sea. And even those marine species which are regularly observed on the mainland are unlikely to be seen in the country's game parks, most of which lie inland. The main exceptions are the grey-headed gull *Larus cirrocephalus,* white-winged tern *Chlidonias leucopterus* and whiskered tern *Chlidonias hybridus*, all of which regularly frequent inland waters. Another – now very rare in South Africa – is the African skimmer *Rhynchops flavirostris*, which is basically an anomalous tern that habitually flies low above rivers and lakes with its elongated red bill, slicing the surface looking for suitable morsels.

Marine birds of interest to casual visitors include the near-endemic African black oystercatcher *Haematopus moquini* (often seen on beaches and rocky stretches of coast in the Western Cape), the endangered Cape gannet *Morus capensis* (breeds in large numbers at Lambert's Bay) and comical African penguin *Spheniscus demersus* (most easily seen at Boulders Beach on the Cape Peninsula). Recommended sites for visitors with a strong interest in marine birds include West Coast National Park, the Cape of Good Hope, and to a lesser extent iSimangaliso Wetland Park.

Waterfowl

Eighteen species of anatid (ducks and geese) are naturally resident in or migrant to South Africa. You're almost certain to encounter the Egyptian goose *Alopochen aegyptiacus,* a hefty, noisy and thuggishly territorial rufous-brown waterfowl that occurs on most freshwater habitats. The more uncommon and less pugnacious spur-winged goose *Plectopterus gambensis* is Africa's bulkiest waterfowl, weighing in at up to 6kg. Other waterfowl often seen in Kruger and other game parks include the pretty yellow-billed duck *Anas undulata,* the gregarious white-faced duck *Dendocygna viduata* and the bulkier knob-billed duck *Sarkidiornis melanotus*, all whose names reflect their most prominent field character. South Africa also forms the core range for two regional endemics: South African shelduck *Tadorna cana* and Cape shoveller *Spatula smithii.*

Though quite duck-like in appearance, grebes have a longer neck, a more arrow-like bill, and are less likely to be seen out of the water. Three species occur in South Africa. The little grebe *Tachybaptus ruficollis*, often referred to locally as the dabchick, is the region's smallest duck lookalike, and quite possibly the most common. The inconspicuous black-necked grebe *Podiceps nigricollis* and striking great crested grebe *P. cristatus* are both quite localized but most likely to be seen on lakes and other open waterbodies in the Western Cape.

Midway in appearance between ducks and quails, rallids are a diverse group of mostly water-associated birds characterized by a rather dumpy stance and short upturned tail. Of the twelve species resident in South Africa, the most likely to be seen are the familiar Eurasian moorhen *Gallinula cholorpus,* the gregarious red-knobbed coot *Fulica cristata*, the stunning African purple gallinule *Porphyrio madagascariensis* and the diminutive black crake *Amaurornis flavirostris*. Most other species are scarcer, more secretive, or both. Closely allied to the rails, but smaller and even more furtive, are five colourful very seldom-seem species of forest- or swamp-dwelling flufftail.

Cormorants are long-necked, short-legged diving birds specialized in catching fish underwater. Of the five species that occur in South Africa, three are near-endemics with a range restricted to the coast. The other two – the large, boldly marked and sociable white-breasted cormorant *Phalacrocorax lucidus* and the smaller, duller and more solitary reed cormorant *P. africanus* – are regularly seen in freshwater habitats in game parks and elsewhere. Easily mistaken for a cormorant, the African darter *Anhinga rufa* has a long, kinked neck alluded to in its nickname "snakebird"; it is usually seen perched on bare branches overhanging inland waters. By contrast, the secretive and eagerly sought African finfoot *Podiceps senegalensis, a* long-necked bird distinguished from similar species by its bold red bill, tends to swim low in the water close to the banks of forest-fringed rivers.

Herons, egrets, storks and cranes

Herons belong to the Ardeidae, a family of long-legged and long-necked birds that fly with their neck retracted and typically spend long periods of time standing in or close to water patiently waiting to impale fish, frogs and other prey on their long sharp bills. Of the 21 species recorded in South Africa, the grey heron *Ardea cinerea* is one of the most common and will be the most familiar to European visitors. Other typical herons are the hulking 1.4m-high Goliath heron *A. goliath*, the swamp-loving purple heron *A. purpurea*, and the less water-dependent black-headed heron *A. melanocephala*.

A monochrome variation on herons, egrets typically have all-white feathering, but some species are all grey or all black. The great white egret *Casmerodius albus*, which stands almost a metre tall, can be distinguished by its height alone, while the black egret *Egretta ardesiaca* is known as the "umbrella bird" due to its habit of spreading its wings above its head to form a canopy that blocks the sun's reflection when it fishes. The smaller cattle egret *Bulbulcus ibis* is a common and gregarious, medium-sized white bird that often feeds on insects disturbed by grazing cattle or buffalo herds. Most other heron and bittern species are squatter, more secretive and more cryptically marked than egrets and typical herons.

Striking long-legged birds that stand between 80cm and 1.5m tall, storks bear a superficial similarity to herons, but are mostly stockier and more boldly coloured. Eight species occur in South Africa. This includes the European white stork *Ciconia ciconia*, black stork *C. nigra* and Abdim's stork *C. Abdimii*, a trio of migrants that are usually present only from October to March and which often aggregate together near recently burned grass and insect irruptions. Resident water-associated species are the saddle-billed stork *Ephippiorhynchus senegalensis*, yellow-billed stork *Mycteria ibis*, African open-billed stork *Anastomus lemelligerus* and woolly necked stork *Ciconia episcopus*. Then there is the rather macabre marabou *Leptoptilos crumeniferus*, a 1.5-metre tall omnivore with a scabby bald head, flesh-coloured neck pouch, hunched back and propensity for hanging out alongside vultures at kills. Like many large birds, the country's resident stork species are now largely confined to game parks such as Kruger, but the migrants are quite commonly seen in farmland too.

Standing up to 1.5m tall with a similar lanky appearance to storks, the trio of crane species that occurs in South Africa are all listed as Vulnerable or Endangered by the IUCN. The blue crane *Grus paradisea*, South Africa's national bird, is a near-endemic with a uniform slate-blue colouring, a white forehead, and trailing feathers that almost touch the ground. The wattled crane *G. carunculata* is a more widespread but patchily distributed bird with an overall dark grey coloration offset by a contrasting white neck. The gorgeous grey crowned crane *Balearica regulorum*, easily distinguished by its unique golden crown, is also known as "the mayhem" in reference to its far-carrying low-pitched booming call. All three species are less likely to be seen near open water than they are in moist grassland or marshy habitats, and are probably most common in the vicinity of the uKhahlamba-Drakensberg foothills.

Waders, plovers and other small upright waterbirds

The *Scolopacidae* is a diverse family of small to medium-sized shorebirds often referred to as waders. More than 35 species have been recorded in South Africa, but around half of these are accidental vagrants, and most others are seasonal Palaearctic migrants that breed in the northern hemisphere and tend to be very nondescript in the non-breeding plumage they sport whilst in Africa. Wader identification away from the coast is easiest during the southern winter, when the possibilities are restricted to a handful of resident species including common sandpiper *Actitis hypoleucus*, wood sandpiper *Tringa glareola* and common greenshank *T. nebularia*. South Africa is also home to two striking and easily identified wader-like species in the form of the black-winged stilt *Himantopus himantopus* (a slender black-and-white bird with a long black bill and red legs) and pied avocet *Recurvirostra avosetta* (a tall black-and-white shorebird with a distinctive upward curving bill).

Similar in build to waders but typically more terrestrial and more boldly marked, plovers are well represented in South Africa, with 21 species recorded. This includes eight lapwing plovers of the genus *Vanellus,* the most visible being the blacksmith lapwing *V. spinosis,* which is usually found close to water and is named after its clinking call, and the crowned lapwing *V. coronatus*, which is one of the more visible roadside birds in many game reserves. The smaller "sand plovers" of the genus *Charadrius* are represented by ten species, the most widespread and common in game parks being the handsome three-banded plover *C. tricollaris*.

Similar in overall appearance to the *Vanellus* plovers, coursers (*Rhinoptilus* and *Cursorius* spp) are crepuscular, fast-running ground birds associated with waterside habitats or arid and recently burnt grassland. Also rather plover-like, but more heavyset and cryptically marked, South Africa's two species of thick-knee (also known as a dikkop – "thickhead") have yellow legs and eyes, and tend to be most active at night. The spotted thick-knee *Burhimus capensis* inhabits a variety of savannah habitats and is often seen at night in game park restcamps, while the water thick-knee *B. vermiculatus* favours riverbank and lakeshore habitats.

The African jacana *Actophilornis africanus* is one of South Africa's most striking small waterbirds, and is totally unmistakable with its rich chestnut torso and wings, blue

bill and frontal shield, and long spreading toes that allow it to walk on lily pads and other floating vegetation. The related greater painted snipe *Rostratula benghalensis* is a beautiful shorebird with cryptically marked wings, white breast, orange head and bold white eye ring.

Other waterbirds

Weighing in at up to 10kg, pelicans are piscivores that forage in synchronised flotillas and are famed for their capacity to store uneaten prey in their massive and improbably shaped bill. The great white pelican *Pelecanus onocrotalus*, the region's bulkiest waterbird, is predominantly white with black underwings and a large yellow bill pouch, while the smaller and rather misleadingly named pink-backed pelican *P. rufescans* is greyer in colour and lacks for distinguishing features. Both are essentially tropical species whose range extends into the northeast of South Africa, where they are most likely to be seen in iSimangaliso Wetland Park. The great white pelican also occurs along and immediately inland of the west coast.

A genuine one-off whose closest living relative is probably the pelican, the hamerkop *Scopus umbretta* is a medium-large rusty-brown bird whose long, flattened bill and angular crest combine to create the hammer-like appearance referred to in its Afrikaans name (literally "hammer head"). The hamerkop might be seen in any freshwater habitat, provided that it's sufficiently well-wooded to support its unmistakable nest: an untidy two-metre-high construction that is built using pretty much anything the bird can lay its beak on, and that often attracts a fearsome community of predatorial squatters including snakes, monitor lizards and owls.

Flamingos are distinctively shaped pink-tinged birds with unusual downward-pointing bills adapted for filter-feeding on algae and microscopic fauna, and a habit of standing on one leg. Two species, the greater flamingo *Phoenicopterus ruber* and lesser flamingo *Phoeniconaias minor,* are present in South Africa. Both are highly nomadic, tending to aggregate temporarily in large flocks in shallow pans with high algae concentrations, only to relocate elsewhere when conditions change.

Ibises are a family of robust medium-large water-associated birds whose most conspicuous member is the hadeda *Bostrychia hagedash,* a grey-black species named for its harsh explosive cackle, a characteristic sound of grassy wetlands and suburban hotel gardens. Dull from a distance, it actually has quite beautiful iridescent reflective feathers in its wings, and a long decurved bill it uses to probe the soil in search of snails. The more subdued glossy ibis *Plegadis falcinellus* is a green-brown wetland specialist, while the sacred ibis *Threskiornis aethiopicus* is a striking and quite common black-and-white bird whose name reflects its exalted status in ancient Egypt (where it is now extinct). Listed as vulnerable by the IUCN, the endemic southern bald ibis *Geronticus calvus* is a large white-headed, red-billed cliff-nester most likely to be seen in the vicinity of the uKhahlamba-Drakensberg or the Mpumalanga escarpment west of Kruger.

Placed in the same family as ibises, the widespread African spoonbill *Platalea alba* is an all-white bird with a red face and legs, and a spatulate bill it sweeps through the water sideways in search of small fish and invertebrates.

Raptors

Renowned for their intelligence, keen eyesight, alert demeanour and soaring wings, **raptors** (birds of prey) are perhaps the birds that most excite casual safarigoers. Fortunate, then, that South Africa truly excels when it comes to raptors, with more than seventy diurnal species present. The majority of these are **Accipitriformes**, a divers order of small to large raptors that includes eagles, kites, hawks, buzzards, old-world vultures and the anomalous secretary bird. The "typical raptors" hawk the countryside alongside fifteen species of **Falconiformes**, an order of relatively small raptors that includes falcons and kestrels. Once thought to be closely related to each other, the Accipitriformes and Falconiformes are now known to be quite distinct in evolutionary terms. An important difference between the two is that accipiters are adapted to kill their prey with their heavy clawed talons, while falcons use their sharp beaks.

Outside of game parks, the extensive loss of natural habitat and reduction in prey numbers, together with direct persecution by farmers, has resulted in a significant recent **population decline** amongst eagles, vultures and other large raptors. Fortunately, however, these magnificent aerial hunters still thrive in larger parks such as Kruger and Kgalagadi, and they also remain reasonably common in some smaller protected areas. Note, however, that the very abundance of raptors in game parks can be frustrating when it comes to the identification of "difficult" birds – a decent field guide is essential to identify confusingly marked species.

Eagles

The archetypal large raptors, eagles are swift and powerful in flight, as keen of sight as "eagle-eyed" suggests, and impressively bulky when perched. Sixteen species occur in South Africa, most of them resident. The largest savannah species is the martial eagle *Polemaetus bellicosis*, a powerfully built off-black bird that can weigh more than 4kg, has a distinct occipital crest and a lightly speckled white breast, and is capable of downing antelopes double its weight. Where the martial eagle often perches openly in tall trees, the similarly sized crowned eagle *Stephanoartus coronatus* is an elusive species confined to riparian woodland and forest interiors where it preys mainly on smallish mammals such as tree hyraxes and monkeys.

South Africa's most typical eagles are the seven species placed in the genera *Aquila* and *Hieraaetus*. Most of these are dark brown in colour and can be difficult for an inexperienced birder to tell apart. An exception is the spectacular Verreaux's (or black) eagle *A. verreauxii*, which weighs up to 4.5kg, has a 2.8m wingspan and is dark black in colour with a diagnostic white V on its back and bold yellow beak and legs. Verreaux's eagle is normally observed soaring effortlessly in the vicinity of the rocky mountains and cliffs where it nests and feeds primarily on hyraxes. Fortunate observers might witness the male's cartwheeling courtship display, during which it might ascend or descend several hundred of metres in one powerful swoop.

A common resident in most larger game parks, the tawny eagle *A. rapax* is a large bird with a uniform brown plumage whose tone ranges from dirty blond through tawny-buff to dark brown. The tawny eagle is generally paler than the migrant steppe eagle *A. nipalensis*, but the best way to distinguish between these lookalike species is to establish whether the yellow gape terminates below the eye (tawny) or extends behind it (steppe). The steppe eagle is also more insectivorous and large numbers sometimes aggregate at termite and other insect emergences. Other all-brown eagles include Wahlberg's eagle *H. wahlbergi*, an intra-African migrant that's even more variable in colour than the tawny eagle, and the booted eagle *H. pennatus*, a Palaearctic migrant with a small occipital crest. The localized African hawk-eagle *A. spilogaster* and Ayres's hawk-eagle *H. ayresii* are streamlined medium-sized eagles with black upperparts, black-on-white streaked underparts and yellow feet.

Snake-eagles are solitary medium-large raptors that tend to perch conspicuously on a bare branch and possess a distinctive upright stance, slight occipital crest and piercing yellow eyes. Three species are present and, as their name suggests, they all feed to a greater or lesser extent on snakes, though lizards, small birds and mammals are also taken. The brown snake-eagle *Circaetus cinereus* is a conspicuous savannah resident distinguished from other large all-brown raptors by the combination of yellow eyes and a lack of yellow on the cere, bill or legs. The less common black-chested snake-eagle *C. pectoralis* is a distinctive black bird with a plain white belly, while the eastern banded snake eagle *C. fasciolatus* is a dark grey-brown forest-edge species whose South African range is restricted to northeast KwaZulu-Natal.

The spectacular bateleur *Terathopius ecaudatus* is named for its unique tilting flight pattern (reminiscent of a tightrope walker wobbling along a suspended line) but it is also unmistakable at rest thanks to the combination of all black feathering with orange (or occasionally white) back or bright red face mask, beak and legs. Equally distinctive is the long-crested eagle *Lophaetus occipitalis*, a large dark brown raptor with bold yellow eyes and a long windblown occipital crest that gives it regular bad hair days. Today, the bateleur is almost entirely restricted to game parks, where it is often the most conspicuous eagle, whereas the long-crested eagle tends to be most common in moist farmland with tall trees.

The first bird that many first-time safarigoers learn to identify, the African fish eagle *Haliaeetus vocifer* is a bulky black-and-white raptor with a rich chestnut belly and yellow base to its large hooked bill. Conspicuous along the shore of most wooded rivers and lakes, it is often seen perched in a waterside tree, in soaring flight or sweeping down to scoop up a fish in its large talons. One of the most evocative sounds of the African bush is the far-carrying duet delivered by monogamous pairs of fish eagle.

Vultures

The sight of several dozen vultures amassed around a fresh carcass, squabbling and squawking in their characteristically undignified manner, is among the most memorable the African bush has to offer. Many people also find it rather repulsive, so it's worth pointing out that vultures play the important ecological role of clearing away carcasses that might otherwise rot away over weeks or months. Vultures also rank among the most powerful of fliers, capable of soaring on thermals for hours on end, and they also possess incredibly good long-distance vision, and are fastidious about cleaning themselves after a no-holds-barred feed.

Six carrion-eating vulture species have been recorded in South Africa, and it isn't unusual to see several on the same carcass. Easiest to identify is the lappet-faced vulture *Torgus tracheliotus*, a truly massive bird – Africa's bulkiest raptor, weighing up to 6.5kg – with a bald pink head, massive blue and ivory bill, and heavy black wings that it spreads open like a vampire's cape. Smaller than the above, but still larger than most eagles, the white-backed griffon *Gryps africanus* often comprises more than ninety percent of the headcount at any given kill, but is rather nondescript plumage-wise aside from the diagnostic off-white mark on its back. The affiliated Cape griffon *G. coprotheres* is a pale near-endemic most likely to be seen within a day's flying range of the cliffs where it breeds colonially, while Rüppell's griffon *G. rueppellii* is a rare vagrant distinguished by its horn-coloured (as opposed to black) bill.

The smaller white-backed vulture *Trigonoceps occipitalis*, though relatively uncommon, can be distinguished from all other species by its white crest and heavy red bill. Even smaller is the hooded vulture *Necrosyrtes monachus*, an all-brown bird with a bald red face and a strikingly long and narrow bill. The **palmnut vulture** *Gypohierax angolensis*, which looks like a whiter variation on the African fish eagle, but with a distinctive red face mask, is dependent on the raffia palms whose fruit form the core of its diet, and in South Africa it is restricted to a couple of sites in northeast KwaZulu-Natal (Kosi Bay and Umlalazi) where these plants occur. The distinctive Egyptian vulture *Neophron percnopterus*, off-white with a bald yellow face mask, was once a common breeding resident in South Africa, but is now a scarce vagrant. Also very rare in South Africa, the massive (up to 5.5kg) cliff-dwelling lammergeier or bearded vulture *Gypaetus barbatus* is the only bird whose main dietary component is bone marrow (which it sometimes obtains by throwing the bone to the ground to crack it open) and is most likely to be seen in the vicinity of the uKhahlamba-Drakensberg.

Medium/small accipiters

Buzzards are similar in shape and size to a small eagle, but stockier in appearance when perched, and relatively short-tailed in flight. Likely to be encountered by casual visitors at any time of year, the jackal buzzard *Buteo rufofuscus* is a handsome grassland and hill-country species with a black back and orange-red breast and tail. By contrast, the steppe buzzard *B. buteo* is a seasonally abundant Palaearctic migrant whose nondescript brown feathering is usually broken by an indistinct pale chest band. Three other buzzards have been recorded but all are quite localized and/or rare.

Once regarded to be races of the same species, the black kite *Milvus migrans* and yellow-billed kite *M. parasitus* are both seasonal migrants that tend to be the commonest medium-large raptor in urban areas in season. The much smaller black-shouldered kite *Elanus caeruleus* has a rather dove-like appearance when perched, but it is also sometimes seen hovering low for several minutes before swooping to capture a rodent or small bird. The near-endemic black harrier *Circus maurus*, its range focused mainly on fynbos, farmland and scrub of the Western Cape, is the most spectacular of South Africa's five species of harrier, a group of medium-sized raptors whose elegant streamlined build is designed for flying low and fast over open country or wetlands looking for prey.

Sparrowhawks and goshawks are small to medium-large raptors characterized by slender, plain dark grey or brown wings, paler streaked or barred underparts and long barred tails. Common species include the forest-dwelling African goshawk *Accipiter tachiro,* the tiny shikra *A. badius*, and the even smaller **little sparrowhawk** *A. minullus*. The spectacular black sparrowhawk *A. melanoleucus,* a buzzard-sized bird with bold black-and-white plumage, is less common – but represents one of the few raptors whose population is actually growing – due to its unique proclivity for exotic pine and eucalyptus plantation forests.

The pale chanting-goshawk *Melierax canorus* and dark chanting-goshawk *M. metabates* are striking buzzard-sized goshawks with distinctive upright stances, grey backs, finely barred bellies and red bills and legs. The first species has a more easterly range than the second, and as its names suggests, is pale grey as opposed to dark grey. The Gabar goshawk *Micronisus gabar* looks like a scaled-down dark chanting-goshawk, though it is occasionally seen in all-black morph, as is the misleadingly named lizard buzzard *Kaupifalco monogrammaticus,* which can be distinguished from all other hawks by the bold black vertical stripe on its white throat. The African harrier-hawk or gymnogene *Polyboroides typus* is a common and adaptable goshawk-like nest-raider with a yellow mask and long flexible legs adapted to climbing trees in search of eggs and chicks. The crepuscular bat hawk *Machieramphus alcinus* is a brown hawk-like species most likely to be seen flying at dusk between trees roosted in by the bats that form its main prey.

Placed in a separate family to all other Accipiters due to the overlapping scales that cover its tarsi, the osprey *Pandion haliaetus* ranks among the most widely distributed of raptors in global terms, but in South Africa it is a thinly distributed Palaearctic migrant, and far from common. A dedicated piscivore, it is quieter and more solitary than the African fish eagle, and it tends to favour still well-wooded freshwater lakes.

Secretary bird

The weirdest of all raptors is the secretary bird *Sagittarius serpentarius,* an utterly unmistakable bird that stands up to 1.5m tall and has long skinny legs, a slender grey torso and a bare red face mask. Some say its name alludes to the resemblance between its flaccid black crest and the quills used by Victorian secretaries, others that it is a corruption of an Arabic phrase meaning hunting bird. Distributed throughout South Africa, it might be seen striding purposefully through any light wooded habitat, in search of its favoured prey of snakes, which it stamps to death in a bizarre flailing dance ritual, but it is most common in larger protected areas such as Kruger. Primarily terrestrial, it does roost and nest in trees, and has a long take-off and landing that recalls an aeroplane on a runway.

Falcons and kestrels

South Africa is home to fifteen species of falcon and kestrel, a family of small, slim and rather similar raptors characterized by their direct flight. All but one of the species is assigned to the genus *Falco*, the exception being the peculiar pygmy falcon *Polihierax semitorquatus*, a pretty dry-country raptor often seen in Kgalagadi where its diminutive size means it might easily be mistaken for a shrike. Other falcon species tend to be uncommon or inconspicuous. Most spectacular are the lanner *F. biarmicus* and peregrine *F. peregrinus*, but neither is as common as the smaller common kestrel *F. tinnunculus* and lesser kestrel *F. neumanni*.

Large ground birds

The world's largest bird, the common ostrich *Struthio camelus* is a slightly preposterous-looking creature that stands up to 2m tall, weighs in at around 70kg, and compensates for its inability to fly with its speed on the ground (up to 50km/hour). It is totally unmistakable, despite displaying strong sexual dimorphism, with the handsome male boasting a striking black-and-white plumage, while the female is scruffier and dowdier. Widely distributed but now quite scarce in the wild, the ostrich is quite likely to be seen in most large game parks, where it favours short grassland and other open habitats. In stony semi-arid habitats such as the Karoo around Oudtshoorn, it is also widely farmed for its meat, which makes for a very eco-friendly and low-cholesterol free-range alternative to beef.

With ten of the world's 25 species represented, including two national endemics, South Africa is an important centre of diversity for bustards, a family of large terrestrial omnivores characterized by their long necks and legs, plumper body, and habit of walking stealthily in open habitats. Most striking is the kori bustard *Ardeotis kori*, which can weigh in at more than 20kg, making it the world's heaviest bird. Often seen in the Kruger Park and other savannah reserves, it is also renowned for its far-carrying booming call and spectacular courtship dance. The endemic southern black korhaan *Afrotis afra* is associated with fynbos and semi-arid habitats in the Western, Eastern and Northern Cape, while the handsome blue korhaan *Eupodotis caerulescens* prefers higher-altitude grassland in the Eastern Cape and Free State. South Africa is also home to four near-endemic bustard species whose range extends into Namibia and/or Botswana.

The most characteristic African ground birds are the chicken-like fowls of the order *Galliformes*. Fifteen species occur naturally in South Africa. Most conspicuous is the highly gregarious, archetypically birdbrained and perennially overwrought helmeted guinea-fowl *Numida meleagris*, a near-ubiquitous species with white-on-grey feathering and a bare blue head capped by an ivory-coloured helmet. In northeast KwaZulu-Natal and parts of the Kruger, it lives alongside the more localized crested guinea-fowl *Guttera pucherani,* a forest-dweller with striking shaggy mop-top. Also present are eleven species of francolin, several of which are quite common in many game parks, most notably **Natal francolin** *Pternistis natalensis*, **red-billed francolin** *P. afer,* **Swainson's francolin** *P. swainsonii* and the smaller cock-tailed **crested francolin** *Dendroperdix sephaena*. Two species of **quail** are also indigenous.

Similar in appearance to pigeons but more closely related to waders, sandgrouse are plump and sociable ground birds associated with open grasslands and arid country. Large flocks tend to congregate at pools and lakes once or twice daily, but they can also be seen scurrying singly or in pairs alongside game. The four species resident in South Africa are all golden-brown in general colour but with distinctive markings that allow for easy identification. Three species are regional endemics, with Namaqua sandgrouse *Pterocles namaqua* being by far the most widespread in South Africa.

Near-passerines

The catch-all term "**near-passerine**" traditionally describes a disparate array of non-aquatic birds that resemble the perching birds of the order Passeriformes but lack their trademark characteristic of three toes pointing forward and one back. Recent DNA testing has established the term near-passerines to be all but meaningless in evolutionary and taxonomic terms, but it remains a convenient way of grouping together non-passerines such as turacos, doves, parrots, cuckoos, owls, nightjars, swifts, kingfishers, hornbills, rollers, woodpeckers and barbets.

Honeyguides

These inconspicuous and nondescript hole-nesting relatives of the woodpeckers are represented in South Africa by four species. Best known and most common is the **greater honeyguide**, which has a rather sparrow-like appearance offset by a heavy pink bill, and whose far-carrying persistent two-note trilling call is a characteristic sound of riparian woodland. It is also the only species of honeyguide that actually performs the eponymous trick of guiding people (and honey-badgers) to beehives in order to feed on discarded scraps of honeycomb.

Woodpeckers

Seven species of woodpecker occur in South Africa. Most are almost exclusively arboreal, feeding on insects bored out from below the bark of a tree while the bird clings upright to a trunk or branch. African woodpeckers tend to be rather inconspicuous and similar in appearance, with green backs, pale underparts, and red and/or black markings on their face, and none matches the most spectacular species from the Americas and Asia. The most common and widespread species are the sparrow-sized **cardinal woodpecker** *Dendropicos fuscescens* and the bulkier **bearded woodpecker** *D. namaquus*. Rather atypical insofar as they have grey or green unmarked bellies, the **olive woodpecker** *D. griseocephalus* and **ground woodpecker** *D. olivaceous* are associated with evergreen forest and with boulder-strewn slopes respectively. The ground woodpecker is endemic to South Africa, as is the **Knysna woodpecker** *Campethera notata*, which inhabits forests along the southern Cape coast.

Barbets and tinkerbirds

South Africa is home to nine species of barbet, a group of stocky and colourful hole-nesting relatives of the woodpeckers. Among the most familiar is the **crested barbet** *Trachyphonus vaillantii*, a striking yellow, black, red and white-specked bird whose persistent high-pitched trill is a characteristic sound of wooded habitats – from suburbia to the bushveld – northeast of Lesotho. The **black-collared barbet** *Lybius torquatus* has a similar distribution to the crested barbet and is equally vociferous, but its call is very different (a piping three-note duet repeated a dozen or more times) and it has a distinctive bold red face. Far smaller, the finch-sized **tinkerbirds** of the genus *Pogonolius* are often heard but very difficult to see as they perch high in the canopy tirelessly repeating a one-note "poop" call.

Hornbills

Among the most characterful inhabitants of South Africa's game parks, hornbills are conspicuous medium-to-large birds distinguished by their heavy decurved bills and the rather comical demeanour that has earned them the nickname "clowns of the bush". Most hornbills are hole-nesters: the female will seal herself in a hole in a tree trunk by plastering closed the entrance, and she depends on the male to feed her through a small slit until the eggs have hatched. Of six species present in South Africa, three are medium-sized savannah dwellers likely to be seen on a daily basis in the Kruger Park, where they tend to scavenge in picnic sites and restcamps. Easily told apart by their bill colour, these are the **southern yellow-billed hornbill** *Tockus* *leucomelas*, the **southern red-billed hornbill** *T. rufirostris* and the **African grey hornbill** *Lophoceros nasutus.*

The larger **crowned hornbill** *L. alboterminatus* is a widespread woodland bird with a large casqued red bill, while the **trumpeter hornbill** *Bycanistes bucinator* is heftier still and has a red eye mask and truly massive casqued bill. Bulkier again is the **southern ground hornbill** *Bucorvus leadbeateri*, a rather improbable turkey lookalike that weighs up to 3.8kg and has black feathering with white underwings, a large casqued bill, conspicuous red throat and eye wattles, and long fluttering eyelashes. Typically seen marching through the savannah in parties of up to five, this predatorial hulk is often assumed to be strictly terrestrial, but it is a surprisingly strong flier, and might occasionally be seen roosting on a thick bare branch.

Hoopoes and allies

The **African hoopoe** *Upupa africana* is a distinctive and widespread orange, black and white bird with a prominent erectile crest and a habit of walking sedately through open habitats such as savannah and hotel or suburban gardens. Very different in appearance, the **green wood-hoopoe** *Phoeniculus purpureus* is a gregarious glossy-black woodland bird with a heavy decurved red bill and cacophonous, cackling call. The similar-looking **common scimitarbill** *Rhinopomastus cyanomelas* is smaller, more solitary, and has a black decurved bill.

Trogons

A predominantly South American and Asian family of colourful forest-dwelling insectivores, trogons are represented in South Africa by a solitary species that stands close to the top of many local birders' wish list. This is the stunning **Narina trogon** *Apaloderma narina*, which boasts a lustrous green back and wings, rich crimson breast, yellow bill and plain tail, but is difficult to locate as it perches motionless on a horizontal branch in riparian woodland and forest interiors.

Rollers

Rollers are brightly coloured pigeon-sized insectivores that perch openly in savannah country and are known for their agile aerial displays. The **lilac-breasted roller** *Coracias caudata,* whose purple chest, sky-blue underparts and golden-brown back vaguely resemble a jay, ranks among the most popular and instantly recognizable residents of the Kruger Park and many other reserves. Almost as handsome, the **European roller** *C. garrulous* is locally common during the Palaearctic winter, while the unmistakable **racket-tailed roller** *C. spatulatus* is a central African miombo species whose range extends into the far north of Kruger. Also largely confined to northern Kruger, the squatter **broad-billed roller** *Eurystormus glaucurus* is a dark purple, blue and brown forest-dweller with a bright yellow bill.

Kingfishers

South Africa's ten species of kingfisher – many of them actually insectivores, with no particular affinity for aquatic habitats – are a characterful and variable bunch split across three different families, but can all be recognized by their spear-like bills and robust profile. They range in size from the giant kingfisher *Megaceryle maxima*, a pied chestnut-breasted bird that reaches a length of 45cm and is generally associated with tree-lined rivers and lakes, to the sparrow-sized African pygmy kingfisher *Ispidina picta*, an orange, blue and pink inhabitant of well-wooded savannah.

The most visible water-associated species is the pied kingfisher *Ceryle rudis*, an unmistakable medium-sized black-and-white bird whose unique hunting modus operandi involves hovering above open water then diving down to spear a fish with its sharp bill. The localized and unobtrusive half-collared kingfisher *Alcedo semitorquata* strongly resembles its European namesake, as to a lesser extent does the commoner and smaller malachite kingfisher *Alcedo cristata*, which is most often observed perched gemlike on waterside reeds and shrubs, typically less than one metre above the surface.

The most characteristic African kingfishers, members of the genus *Halcyon*, mostly have blue and/or brown backs, pale underparts and strong, sharp black and/or red bills. Aside from the coastal mangrove kingfisher *H. senegaloides*, the Halcyon kingfishers are insectivorous and are often seen some distance from water. Other species – all pretty common in the Kruger and other game parks within their range – are the widespread brown-hooded kingfisher *H. albiventris*, chestnut-bellied grey-headed kingfisher *H. leucocephala*, dumpier striped kingfisher *H. chelicuti*, and the light blue woodland kingfisher *H. senegalensis*, the latter an intra-African migrant whose explosive rattling call is a characteristic sound of the northeastern bush in the southern summer.

Bee-eaters

Bee-eaters are dashingly colourful insectivores recognizable by their sleek profile, upright stance, long wings and tail, long slightly decurved bills, and habit of hawking openly from a bare branch a metre or two above the ground. Generally associated with wooded savannah and riverine habitats, most species are sociable hole-nesters, and are capable of eating stinging insects, which they disarm by banging or scraping them against a branch. Eight of the world's 25 species have been recorded in South Africa, two as vagrants, and most are common and conspicuous in suitable habitats within their range. Most widespread in South Africa, the European bee-eater *Merops apiaster* is a Palaearctic migrant that sometimes overwinters here and has a distinctive combination of golden-brown back, yellow throat and blue breast. The little bee-eater *M. pusillus* is a smallish species usually seen in pairs perched on lake margins and/or close to watercourses. The stunning white-fronted bee-eater *M. bullockoides*, a common resident of the Kruger Park, is a rainbow-coloured species with a diagnostic red throat. Another stunner is the southern carmine bee-eater *M. nubicus*, a hefty bright red, blue-crowned intra-African migrant that is seasonally common in Kruger. By contrast, the descriptively named swallow-tailed bee-eater *M. hirundineus* is most common in the northwest.

Mousebirds

Mousebirds are long-tailed, prominently crested frugivores whose name alludes to their habit of shuffling nimbly along branches – but it also describes their dull coloration. Endemic to Africa, they are represented in South Africa by three species, of which the aptly named **red-faced mousebird** *Urocolius indicus* is most widespread, but the scruffy and more nondescript **speckled mousebird** *Colius striatus* is commoner in game parks on the east side of the country.

Cuckoos and coucals

South Africa is home to thirteen species of cuckoo, brood parasites that lay their eggs in the nest of another bird species and leave it to the unwitting foster parents to raise the hatchling. Most of the country's cuckoos are intra-African migrants and highly vocal in season, but difficult to see due to their habit of perching motionless as they emit a ventriloquial call. Despite this, the red-chested cuckoo *Cuculus solitarius*, which parasitizes robin-chats and scrub-robins, is among the region's best-known birds thanks to its persistent three-note descending call, often transcribed as *piet-my-vrou*. Almost as well-known and vocally persistent, especially around colonies of nesting weavers (which it parasitizes), the Dideric cuckoo *Chrysococcyx caprius* is a pretty green bird whose clamorous *dee-dee-dee-Dideric* call is often repeated again and again until it finally reaches a hysterical crescendo. The similar-looking Klaas's cuckoo *Chrysococcyx klaas* has a soft but distinctive two-note call reflected in its Afrikaans name, *meitjie*. More elusive than the above trio of savannah-dwellers is the emerald cuckoo *Chrysococcyx cupreus*, a stunning green-and-yellow forest species that has driven many a birdwatcher to distraction as they scan the canopy in vain in search of the source of a ventriloquial four-note *you-can't-find-me.*

Closely related to cuckoos but non-parasitic and more visually conspicuous, coucals are large, clumsy birds associated with rank grassland, marsh and riverine vegetation. The most widespread of three South African species, Burchell's coucal *Centropus burchellii* (sometimes given as a subspecies of **white-browed coucal** *Centropus superciliosus*) has chestnut upperparts and wings, creamy white underparts, a black cap and an attractive dove-like bubbling call said to be predictive of rain (indeed, it is nicknamed the rainbird). Also related to cuckoos, the green malkoha *Ceuthmochares australis*, also known as the yellowbill or green coucal, is a secretive green-grey thicket dweller with a long bold yellow bill.

Parrots and lovebirds

Visitors from Australia or South America are likely to find South Africa's parrots a disappointing bunch. A mere five of the world's 360 *Psittacidae* species range into the country, and most have a very limited distribution and are rather dull in colour when compared to their most outrageous extralimital cousins. Of these, **Meyer's parrot** *Poicephalus meyeri*, **brown-headed parrot** *P. cryptoxanthus* and **grey-headed parrot** *P. fuscicollis* are largely confined to the game reserves in the northeast, while the smaller **rosy-faced lovebird** *Agapornis roseicollis* is a regional endemic restricted to the semi-arid northeast. The **Cape parrot** *P. robustus* is a vulnerable endemic of the forest (mostly in the Eastern Cape, where it is feared it may now number fewer than a thousand individuals in the wild).

Swifts

The most aerially specialized of birds, more so even than the similar-looking but unrelated swallows, swifts feed, mate and in some cases even sleep while in flight. Mixed flocks are often seen circling rapidly in the vicinity of cliffs, bridges and tall buildings, sometimes mingling with various swallows, from which they can be distinguished by their narrower crescent-shaped wings. Most swifts are dull grey-brown in colour and short on diagnostic field characters. Exceptions include the supersized Alpine swift *Apus melba*, which is usually seen near cliffs or mountains, the narrow-tailed African palm swift *Cypsiurus parvus,* which is almost invariably seen flying around the trees for which it is named, and the baobab-associated bat-like spinetail *Neafrapus boehmi.*

Turacos

Also known as loeries, turacos are medium-to-large fruit-eating birds whose elongated shape is exaggerated by a long crest and tail. Turacos are endemic to Africa and most of the 23 species are confined to the tropics, but four are represented in South Africa. Of these, the one most associated with game parks is the grey go-away bird *Corythaixoides concolor*, a characterful all-grey bird that perches openly in small flocks emitting the nasal onomatopoeic call for which it is named from the treetops. The country's other three turaco species are all exceptionally beautiful, with predominantly green feathering offset by some purple on the wings, bright scarlet underwings (seen to best effect in flight) and prominent white or purple crests. They also tend to be quite secretive, creeping through the boughs in search of fruit, and usually only flying short distances, but often draw attention to themselves with explosive guttural calls. Best-known is the Knysna turaco *Tauraco corythaix*, a South African endemic of coastal and escarpment forest that has practically been adopted as the avian emblem of the Garden Route. It is replaced in northeast KwaZulu-Natal by Livingstone's turaco *T. livingstonii* and in the Kruger Park and lowveld by purple-crested loerie *T. porphyreolophus.*

Owls

Specialized nocturnal predators known for their exceptional night vision, owls are represented in South Africa by a dozen species ranging from the thrush-sized scops-owls to the gigantic eagle-owls. Widespread and common species include the familiar **barn owl** *Tyto alba* and the larger **spotted eagle-owl** *Bubo lacteus* and **Cape eagle owl** *B. capensis*. Of the smaller owls, the most frequently observed are the delicate **pearl-spotted owlet** *Glaucidium perlatum*, a partially diurnal hunter that is frequently mobbed by other small birds, and the **African scops-owl** *Otus senegalensis*. Two gigantic owls most likely to be seen in the Kruger Park and adjoining reserves are **Verreaux's eagle-owl** *Bubo lacteus* and the eagerly sought **Pel's fishing owl** *Scotopelia peli*, both of which can weigh more than 2kg. Demonized by many African cultures as harbingers of death, owls are occasionally flushed or chanced upon in daylight, but they are most likely to be seen on night drives in private reserves.

Nightjars

Most likely to be seen perched on dirt roads in private reserves after dark, nightjars are beautiful but cryptically marked dove-sized nocturnal birds that present a serious identification challenge to all but the most experienced of ornithologists. Of seven species recorded in South Africa, the most visually distinctive, at least when in breeding plumage, is the male pennant-winged nightjar *Macrodipteryx vexillarius*, which might be seen flying above water at dusk, trailing a pair of elongated second primaries twice as long as its body. Other species are most likely to be recognized by call, none more so than the fiery-necked nightjar *Caprimulgus pectoralis*, whose deliberate song, often rendered as *Good-lord-deliver-us,* is a characteristic sound of the bush at night, and might be repeated more than one hundred times in close succession.

Doves and pigeons

Doves are conspicuous and vocal in most parts of the world, and South Africa is no exception. The bubbling five- or six-note coo of the **laughing dove** *Streptopelia senegalensis*, the harsher "work harder" command of the **Cape turtle dove** *S. capicola,* and the prosaic "I am a red-eyed dove" of the **red-eyed dove** all rank among the definitive sounds of the South African bush. Commonly seen on game drives in woodland habitats is the **emerald-spotted wood-dove** *Turtus chalcospilos*, while the **Namaqua dove** *Oena capensis* – small, with a long graduating tail and, in the case of the male, distinctive black face and red-and-yellow bill – tends to prefer semi-arid habitats. Pigeons are associated with more forested habitats, the main exceptions being the **speckled pigeon** *Columba guinea*, with its distinctive red eye-mask, and the ubiquitous **feral pigeon** *C. Livia*, an introduced species. The African **green pigeon** *Treron calva* is a brightly coloured frugivore often seen in the vicinity of fruiting ficus trees in the Kruger Park and the reserves of northern KwaZulu-Natal.

Passerines

With more than 6500 species and 140 families recognized worldwide, Passeriformes is perhaps the most diverse and successful of vertebrate orders and accounts for well over fifty percent of the global avifauna. **Passerines** are generally quite small, the main exception being the crows and ravens, and they are distinguished from all other birds by the design of their feet, which invariably incorporate one backward- and three forward-facing toes, an arrangement that allows them to perch tightly on small branches or grass and reeds. The diversity of South Africa's passerines means that the descriptions below deal mainly with the more conspicuous families and genera as opposed to individual species.

Pittas
Pittas are relatively large short-tailed passerines represented in South Africa by one species, the rainbow-coloured **African pitta** *Pitta angolensis*, an eagerly sought but localized and secretive migrant that sometimes reveals its presence with its frog-like single-note call.

Broadbills
Broadbills are also represented locally by one species. This is the **African broadbill** *Smithornis capensis*, an unobtrusive bird with a rattling call most likely to be seen in coastal bush in northern KwaZulu-Natal.

Orioles
The three oriole species recorded in South Africa resemble larger versions of weavers, being bright yellow with bold black face or wing markings, and a red eye and beak. The most widespread species is the **black-headed oriole** *Oriolus larvatus*, a woodland-dweller with an attractive liquid call.

Drongos
A characteristic bird of savannah and woodland habitats, the **fork-tailed drongo** *Discrurus adsimilis* is an all-black bird with a deeply forked tail that tends to perch openly like a large shrike and emits a wide array of nasal calls. Intelligent and characterful birds, they are known to imitate the alarm calls of other birds to scare them into dropping recently caught prey. They also frequently dive-bomb larger raptors.

Monarch flycatchers
Monarch flycatchers are busy insectivores that combine hawking with leaf-gleaning. Best known is the **African paradise flycatcher** *Terpsiphone viridis*, a popular woodland and garden bird with a crested blue head and an orange back and tail (with vastly extended central feathers in the case of the male).

Bush-shrikes and allies
Endemic to mainland Africa, and represented in South Africa by 25 species, the Malaconotidae is a family of medium to small shrike-like birds with strong hooked bills and striking colour patterns. Many are quite secretive and would easily be overlooked were it not for their distinctive and far-carrying calls. The best-known members of the family are the boubous of the genus *Laniarius*, whose tightly synchronized duets typically involve the male singing a short series of loud antiphonal notes and the female replying with a harsh clicking or chirring sound. The black, white and buff **southern boubou** *L. ferrugineus* is a common garden bird in eastern parts of South Africa, but it is replaced in the northwest by the **crimson-breasted shrike** *L. atrococcineus*, a striking boubou with bright red underparts. More skulking even than the boubous, the typical bush-shrikes of the genus *Malaconotus* are brilliantly coloured birds of savannah and forest, typically with green backs, yellow underparts, some grey on the head, and in several cases a black mask and/or bib and red or orange throat. Other members of the family include the helmet-shrike *Prionops spp*, a group of medium-small black or pied birds that tend to move around in small busy flocks, and the smaller batises *Batis spp*, boldly marked leaf-gleaners that move warbler-like through the canopy. The most atypical of bush-shrikes is the **bokmakierie** *Telophorus zeylonus*, a southern African endemic with bold yellow, black and grey markings, and a preference for grassland and other relatively open habitats.

Corvids
Bulky black passerines that spend much of their time on the wing, crows and ravens are regarded to be among the most intelligent and adaptable of all birds. Three

species are indigenous to South Africa, among them the **white-necked raven** *Corvus albicollis*, which is the world's second-largest passerine (outranked only by the closely related thick-billed raven of Ethiopia). The smaller **Indian house crow** *C. splendens* is an invasive species first recorded in the country in 1972 and now quite common in several port cities.

Shrikes

True shrikes are conspicuous and boldly marked carnivores with a characteristic upright stance, a heavy hooked bill, a longish tail and a habit of impaling items of prey on a thorn or barbed wire fence (hence the nickname butcher bird). The **common fiscal** *L. collaris* is by far the most widespread species in South Africa, but visitors to the Kruger Park are also likely to encounter the striking floppy-tailed **magpie shrike** *Corvinella melanoleuca*.

Cuckoo-shrikes

These inconspicuous woodland and forest birds show an unusually high level of sexual dimorphism and are represented in South Africa by three species.

Rock-jumpers

Thrush-like birds with bright orange or red underparts and upright white-tipped tails, rock-jumpers are placed in a unique family that is endemic to South Africa and Lesotho. As their name suggests, they favour mountainous habitats and are usually seen on or in the vicinity of boulders. Two species are recognized, with the **Cape rockjumper** *Chaetus frenatus* being more-or-less endemic to the Western Cape, while the **Drakensberg rockjumper** *C. aurantius* inhabits the upper slopes of the Drakensberg and Lesotho.

Tits

Tits are sparrow-sized woodland and savannah birds that spend much of their time working their way along tree trunks gleaning insects. The most conspicuous species in most of South Africa's game parks is the **southern black tit** *Parus niger*.

Swallows and martins

From September to April, the **barn swallow** *Hirundo rustica*, a Palaearctic migrant that will be familiar to European visitors, is by far the most conspicuous of South Africa's seventeen species of swallow and martin – a family of highly aerial passerines that broadly resemble swifts but tend to be more distinctively marked. Other notable species include the endemic **South African cliff swallow** *H. spilodera*, the **blue swallow** *H. atrocaerulea* (an intra-African migrant listed as Vulnerable by the IUCN) and the forest-associated **black saw-wing** *Psalidoprocne pristoptera*.

Bulbuls and allies

Among the first birds likely to be encountered by visitors, South Africa's habitat-tolerant trio of bulbul species *Pycnonotus spp* all have black crests, pale bellies, yellow vents and busy cheerful calls, but can be distinguished from each other by geographic distribution and eye colour. Also present are six more localized and secretive species of forest- and woodland-dwelling greenbul, brownbul and nicator.

Warblers and babblers

One of the most radical recent revisions of avian taxonomy was the split of the warblers formerly assigned to the Sylviidae into two separate families, and the incorporation of two genera once considered to be unrelated to warblers into one of these families. The new family created was the Cisticolidae, or African warblers, which are represented

in South Africa by around thirty species. Roughly half of these are small, dull-brown grassland birds belonging to the genus *Cisticola*, while the remainder include several long-tailed and mostly quite strikingly marked species of the genera *Prinia* and *Apalis*, the vociferous "bleating warblers" of the genus *Cameroptera*, and the bar-chested wren-warblers of the genus *Calamonastes*. Meanwhile, some 35 South African bird species are now embraced by the family Sylviidae, a varied bunch that includes the graceful small "flycatchers" of the genus *Elminia*, the babblers of the genus *Turdoides* (robust thrush-sized birds that habitually travel through the undergrowth in noisy parties of 5–10 individuals), and the pretty and near-tailless crombecs of the genus *Sylvietta*. It also includes several Palaearctic migrants familiar to European visitors, for instance the **willow warbler** *Phylloscopus trochilus*, **great reed-warbler** *Acrocephalus arundinaceus* and **olive-tree warbler** *Hippolais olivetorum*.

White-eyes
South Africa is home to three species of white-eye, a family of small, pretty and often rather confiding green-yellow birds that have bold white eye-rings and typically move through the foliage in busy parties of 5–10 individuals.

Larks
Associated mainly with short grassland and semi-arid habitats, larks and sparrow-larks are easily overlooked brownish ground birds that tend to be difficult to distinguish from each other in the field, though many species have distinctive songs. South Africa is an important centre of lark speciation, with five of its twenty species being endemic and another nine near-endemic, but most of these have very limited distributions and are likely to be seen only by those who actively seek them.

Thrushes and relatives
The Muscicapidae is a diverse group of colourful medium-to-small insectivores represented in South Africa by some 45 species. One of the most familiar to European visitors will be the three species of thrushes *Turdus*, which look much like their European counterparts and are often to be seen in gardens and on hotel lawns. Even more common in gardens are the robin-chats of the genus *Cossypha*, which typically have bright orange underparts and darker wings and back. The most common countrywide is the **Cape robin-chat** *C. caffra*, but you might also see the larger and more boldly marked **white-browed robin** *C. heuglinii* and the very pretty **red-capped robin-chat** *C. natalensis* in game parks in the east of the country.

Muscicapidae also includes the Old World flycatchers, a group of rather dull and inconspicuous birds that hawk insects from static perches, the grassland-dwelling wheatears of the genus *Oenanthe*, and the rather inconspicuous wing-flicking chats of the genus *Cercomela*. Associated with rocky slopes, the **mocking cliff-chat** *M. cinnamomeiventris* is a spectacular black bird with a bright red breast, while the **African stonechat** *Saxicola torquatus*, a neat little pied chat with a bold chestnut chest, is a common resident of open grassland, where it tends to perch upright in low trees. The **white-browed scrub-robin** *Cercotrichas leucophrys* is a common resident of acacia woodland in the Kruger Park.

Starlings and oxpeckers
Most of South Africa's thirteen indigenous and two introduced starling species are instantly recognizable due to their distinctive semi-upright stance and strong pointed bills. The near-ubiquitous **Cape starling** *Lamprotornis nitens* is the most widespread of five closely related species of "glossy starling", all of which have beautiful iridescent blue-green plumages. Also noteworthy are the rather large cliff-dwelling **red-winged starling** *Onychognathus morio*, the widespread and sensationally colourful **violet-backed starling** *Cinnyricinclus leucogaster*, and the endemic **pied starling** *Spreo bicolor*.

Closely related to the starlings, the red-billed and yellow-billed oxpeckers of the genus *Buphagus* spend much of their time picking ticks off ungulates such as buffalo, antelope and giraffe, but for obvious reasons they are now quite rare outside of game reserves. By contrast, the **European starling** *Sturnus vulgaris* and **common myna** *Acridotheres tristis* are introduced species that often outnumber their indigenous counterparts in the (mostly urban) areas they've colonized.

Sunbirds

Resembling hummingbirds both in their appearance (long decurved bill and iridescent feathering) and their nectarivore diet, sunbirds are in fact unrelated to their American lookalikes and the two families represent a perfect example of convergent evolution. Seventeen species of these restless small passerines are present in South Africa, and most display a high degree of sexual dimorphism, with males being larger and more brightly coloured than females. Most species have iridescent green backs, pale or black bellies and some red on the chest, while others – for instance, the aptly named **malachite sunbird** *Nectarinia famosa* and **coppery sunbird** *Cinnyris cupreus*, or the mostly black **amethyst sunbird** *Chalcomitra amethystina* and **scarlet-chested sunbird** *C. senegalensis* – are more distinctive.

Sugarbirds

Endemic to Southern Africa, the family Promeropidae comprises just two species that bear some resemblance to sunbirds, with their long decurved bills and nectarivorous habits, but they are duller in colour and significantly larger. Largely confined to the Western Cape, the **Cape sugarbird** *Promerops cafer* is a yellow-vented bird whose tail can extend more than three times longer than the body. **Gurney's sugarbird** *P. gurneyi* also has a yellow vent, but it is smaller, has a bold russet breast, and is resident in the Drakensberg and Mpumalanga escarpment. Both species are strongly associated with flowering proteas and aloes.

Weavers and allies

Most members of the family Ploceidae are sexually dimorphic sparrow-like seedeaters notable both for the male's bright plumages in the breeding season and their ability to weave intricate ball-shaped nests from grass and twigs. An integral feature of Africa's avian landscape, the true weavers of the genus *Ploceus* are represented in South Africa by nine species, all predominantly yellow in colour, and most with black facial masks or spectacles. It is *Ploceus* males who build the nest, then allow it to be inspected by their chosen partner, who will tear it apart if the result is unsatisfactory. Many weaver species are colonial and build relatively plain oval nests with an unadorned entrance hole. Other more solitary weavers tend to construct elaborate entrances to protect their eggs against snakes and other predators. The most striking of all weaver nests is the improbably neat dome built by the reedbed-dwelling **thick-billed weaver** *Amblyospiza albifrons*. Reedbeds are also the favoured nesting site of many of South Africa's seven species of the genus *Euplectes*, a group of striking black, red and yellow birds that include the spectacular **long-tailed widowbird** *E. progne* and the gorgeous **southern red bishop** *E. orix* and **yellow-crowned bishop** *E. afer*, the latter given to puffing out its feathers like an oversized bumblebee.

Waxbills and whydahs

South Africa is home to 26 species of the seed-eating family Estrildidae, most of which are small and easily missed ground-feeding birds distinguished by their spectacularly colourful plumages. Species likely to be seen in game parks include the **blue waxbill** *Uraeginthus angolensis*, **African firefinch** *Lagonosticta rubricata,* water-loving **common waxbill** *Estrilda astrild* and (in the drier northwest) **violet-eared waxbill** *Granatina*

granatina. The mannikin species of the genus *Lonchura* are brightly marked black-white and chestnut finches associated with wetlands, forest fringes and suburban gardens. Arguably the most brilliantly coloured of all waxbills, however, are the forest-dwelling twinspots *Hypargos spp*. Closely related to waxbills, which they brood parasitize, the whydahs of the genus *Vidua* are small colourful savannah birds most notable for the oddly shaped and very long tails (in some cases 3–4 times the body length) that the males sport in breeding season. Most common is the **pin-tailed whydah** *V. macroura*, the fiercely territorial male of which is known for its pugnacious attitude to rival males and other birds – not to mention to its own reflection.

Sparrows
These familiar small seedeaters are represented in South Africa by four indigenous species, all of which are quite nondescript and unobtrusive, as well as the introduced **house sparrow** *Passer domesticus*, which is now common throughout the country.

Wagtails, pipits and longclaws
Wagtails are water-associated birds whose slender appearance is emphasized by their long perpetually bobbing tail and narrow bill. Of three resident species, the most widespread and common is the greyish **Cape wagtail** *Motacilla capensis*, but it is replaced by the more boldly marked **African pied wagtail** *M. aguimp* in the northeast. The **yellow wagtail** *M. flava* is the most common of three migrant species. Related to wagtails, pipits *Anthus spp* are superficially lark-like species that tend to be difficult to identify on a specific level. Far more striking, the country's three species of longclaw *Macronyx spp* are pipit-like grassland birds with black bibs and striking yellow, orange or pink throats.

Canaries and buntings
South Africa is home to thirteen species of canary (also known as seedeaters or siskins) and four of bunting. Most of the canaries are unobtrusive and have unmemorable songs, but many are endemic or near-endemics, among them the **Cape canary** *Serinus canicollis*, **black-headed canary** *S. alario*, **forest canary** *Crithagra scotops,* **protea seedeater** *C. leucoptera*, **Cape siskin** *C. totta* and **Drakensberg siskin** *C. symonsi*. The lovely **golden-breasted bunting** *Emberiza flaviventris* is common in some game reserves, while the **cinnamon-breasted bunting** *E. tahapisi* is often associated with rocky slopes and cliffs.

Reptiles, amphibians and invertebrates

Reptiles

South Africa boasts one of the world's highest levels of **reptile** diversity. More than 350 species have been described (a higher tally than the USA or the whole of Europe) and at least one-third of these are endemic to the region that also includes the tiny kingdoms of Lesotho and Eswatini. Despite the negative connotations many people associate with reptiles, most species are totally harmless to humans – the major exceptions in South Africa being the fearsomely predatorial Nile crocodile and a dozen or so snakes with potentially fatal bites – and many play an important ecological role. Crocodiles are the aquatic counterpart of vultures, devouring carrion that might otherwise fester in Africa's waterways, while snakes help to prevent plague-like outbreaks of rats, and the lizards that frequent game park lodges and restcamps help to keep down mosquito numbers.

Nile crocodile

The **Nile crocodile**, the only member of the world's twenty-odd crocodilian species to occur in South Africa, is a rapacious freshwater predator, making for a formidably primeval and sinister sight as it lies on the water's edge with its long jagged-toothed mouth agape. Africa's largest and longest-lived predator, it typically grows to a length of at least five metres, weighs up to 1000kg, and has a lifespan comparable to that of a human. It occurs naturally in lower-lying tropical and subtropical rivers and lakes, but numbers have declined as a result of human persecution, and its range within South Africa is now more-or-less restricted to national parks and other protected areas in North West Province, Mpumalanga, Limpopo and northern KwaZulu-Natal. In common with other crocodiles and alligators, the Nile crocodile is placed in the order **Crocodilia**, which is more closely related to birds than it is to all other living reptiles. It also represents something of a "living fossil" insofar as it is placed in the same family as ancestral stock that lived alongside dinosaurs more than 65 million years ago.

Where fish densities are sufficient, the Nile crocodile is a piscivore that occasionally supplements its diet with aquatic birds, terrapins, other small swimming creatures and submerged carrion. Less often and more opportunistically, it will attack a drinking or swimming mammal, dragging it underwater with its powerful jaw until it drowns. The Nile crocodile is capable of killing a lion or wildebeest, and it's been known to attack animals as large as an adult rhino or giraffe. It is also responsible for more human fatalities than any other African predator. Which means – bearing in mind that a Nile crocodile can submerge without drawing breath for 45–60 minutes, and it might easily be mistaken for a floating log when it surfaces – it is wise to assume that any river or waterhole in a game park is unsafe for swimming, unless you have reliable local information to the contrary. Crocodiles seldom attack outside of their normal aquatic hunting environment, so if you keep a few metres from shore, you are at no appreciable risk.

Snakes

Possibly the most feared and vilified of all animals, **snakes** are legless reptilian carnivores whose long backbones can in some cases comprise more than four hundred vertebrae. Of the 130-odd species recorded in South Africa, the overwhelming majority are non-venomous, and only fifteen have been known to inflict a fatal bite on a person. Most snakes are very shy, and when they sense the seismic vibration of approaching

human footsteps, will usually slither away unseen – hardly surprising when you consider that in Africa they have evolved alongside, and presumably been persecuted by, our hominin ancestors for literally millions of years. All the same, when walking in the bush, it is advisable to wear sealed shoes, socks and long trousers in order to reduce the risk of a bite. Keep a watchful eye on the path ahead and, in the unlikely event you do see a snake, freeze and then retreat slowly. Fortunately, the dangers of snakebite have been greatly reduced by the excellent quality of modern antivenins, and fatal bites are very rare. For further information, the African Snakebite Institute (ⓦafricansnakebiteinstitute.com) is a great online resource with a downloadable app that includes snake-identification features, first-aid information and more.

South Africa's bulkiest snake, and one of the half-dozen largest found anywhere in the world, is the **southern rock python** *Python natalensis*, which typically attains a length of around 3.5m, but might sometimes reach 5m. Like all pythons, it is non-venomous and kills by strangulation, wrapping its muscular body around its prey, and coiling tighter every time it exhales. It is an opportunistic feeder and might take anything from a hyrax, monkey or small antelope to fruit bats and livestock. Generally associated with savannah habitats, it is among the more commonly seen snakes in the game parks of the north and east, and easily recognized by its length, thick muscular body, and blotched brown, black and gold scale pattern. It is absent from most parts of the semi-arid west.

The most common and widespread of South Africa's **vipers** is the **puff adder** *Bitis arietans*, a medium-length (typically about 1m) snake with a stocky muscular appearance and variable blotched scaling. It is widely considered to be Africa's most dangerous snake, not because it is especially venomous, but because it has a rather sluggish disposition that means it is less likely than other species to slither away unnoticed by walkers, and it is also quick to strike when cornered. The puff adder is commonest in thinly inhabited savannah and rocky habitats, but it is highly habitat-tolerant and might be seen almost anywhere in the country. By contrast, eight of the country's other fourteen viper species are very localized endemics.

Probably the most feared of all African snakes, the **black mamba** *Dendroaspis polylepis* is the world's second-largest venomous species. It can be recognized by its streamlined length (up to 4.3m long in exceptional cases), coffin-shaped head and uniform olive-brown colour. The black mamba's reputation for overt aggression towards people is probably exaggerated, but it is quick to strike when cornered, and the venom is highly toxic. The related **green mamba** *D. augusticeps* is greener, smaller, less aggressive and has less toxic venom, but it is still dangerous. Both mamba species are essentially confined to bush habitats in the northeast.

South Africa's five species of **cobra** *Naja spp* and the closely related **rinkhals** *Hemachatus haemachatus* are long (1–2m) venomous snakes that have a conspicuous hood when they raise their head in warning or to strike. All cobras might bite when threatened, but some species' first line of defence is to spit venom in a perceived attacker's eyes. The arboreal and unobtrusive **boomslang** *Dispholidus typus*, which has large eyes and variable plain green or yellow-black speckled scaling, is reputed to have the most toxic venom of any of Africa's snakes, but since it is back-fanged and very unaggressive, fatalities are almost unknown except among snake handlers.

One of South Africa's most common non-venomous snakes, the **spotted bush snake** and other species of the genus *Philothamnus* are slender, large-eyed and green snakes, and their colouration and arboreal habits mean they are often mistaken for the green mamba or boomslang. The **rhombic egg-eater** *Dasypeltis scabra* is unusual, and popular with snake-keepers because it feeds exclusively on bird's eggs, which it swallows whole, then punctures internally to extract the liquid, before regurgitating the shell in one neat package. Two of the most important species for vermin control are the **mole snake** *Pseudaspis cana* and **brown house snake** *Boaedon capensis*, both of which are large (more than 1m), non-venomous, and feed mainly on rats and other rodents.

Lizards

Lizards account for about seventy percent of South Africa's reptile species, and they are far more numerous and conspicuous than snakes. None is venomous, and the only species that could conceivably be considered as dangerous are the **rock monitor** *Varanus albigularis* and **water monitor** *V. niloticus,* which can grow to a length of more than 2m and could inflict a nasty bite when cornered (but seldom do). The water monitor is common in aquatic habitats, mostly in the north and east of the country, where it is sometimes mistaken for a small crocodile. The habitat-tolerant rock monitor is more widespread, but most common in savannah or rocky areas.

The most diverse lizard family, **geckoes** have unique adhesive toes that enable them to run upside-down on smooth surfaces. Often associated with restcamps and lodges in game parks, the **tropical house gecko** *Hemidactylus mabouia* is an endearing bug-eyed, translucent white lizard that scampers up walls and ceilings in voracious pursuit of insects attracted to the lights. The **common barking gecko** *Ptenopus garrulus* is a small dry-country lizard whose distinctive clicking call is often heard at sunset or on cool mornings in parts of the Karoo and Kalahari.

South Africa is home to six species of **agama** *Agama* and *Acanthocercus* spp, a group of striking, plump and relatively large (typically 20–30cm long) lizards that typically have bright blue, purple, orange or red scaling, with the flattened head a different colour to the torso. Not closely related but rather similar in shape and colouration are the flat lizards of the genus *Platysaurus*, a dozen of which occur in South Africa, all but two being endemic to the country. Both agamas and flat lizards tend to occur on rocks, where they alternate between darting around manically and standing still with their heads raised prominently. Another conspicuous group is the girdled lizards of the genus *Cordylus*, which is represented by some twenty species, almost all endemic, most notably the prehistoric-looking giant girdled lizard or sungazer *C. giganteus.*

Venerated as sacred by some rural communities, **chameleons** are known for their abrupt colour changes (a trait that tends to be exaggerated in popular literature), but are no less remarkable for their protuberant eyes, which offer 180-degree vision and swivel independently of each other. The swaying gait of the chameleons, and the crests or horns on their heads, are also distinctive, while their exceptionally long extrudable tongues, which have a sticky pad on the end, are shot out at lightning speed to snare their prey. South Africa lacks the giant chameleons found in the forests of East Africa and Madagascar, but is an important centre of speciation for **dwarf chameleons** *Bradypodoin spp*, with some fifteen species recognized, all very localized endemics that clock in at between 4cm and 8cm long. The species most likely to be seen on safari is the larger (up to 15cm) and very widespread **flap-necked chameleon** *Chamaeleo dilepis*, which occurs in savannah and woodland habitats in the north and east, but is replaced by the similarly sized **Namaqua chameleon** *C. namaquensis* in the semi-arid west.

Chelonians

The **tortoises**, **terrapins** and **turtles** of the order **Chelonia**, unique among vertebrates in possessing an armoured exoskeleton that protects adults against most predators, are very well represented in South Africa. A full fourteen species of land tortoise is the highest tally for any one country, and all but four of these species are endemic, many being associated with fynbos or semi-arid Karoo habitats in the southwest. Some are also IUCN listed as Endangered, with the uniquely shelled **geometric tortoise** *Psammobates geometricus*, which occurs on the Cape Flats, regarded to be South Africa's most threatened reptile species. Also notable are the tiny **parrot-beaked tortoise** *Homopus areolatus* and **speckled padloper** *H. signatus*, neither of which reaches 10cm in length, even when fully grown – the latter is regarded to be the world's smallest chelonian.

The most visible chelonian in most South African game parks is undoubtedly the **leopard tortoise** *Geochelone pardalis*, a very widespread species distinguished by its large size (adults range from 35–70cm in length and occasionally weigh as much as 40kg) and the tall domed gold-and-black mottled shell alluded to in its name. Known to live for more than fifty years in captivity, the adult has few natural enemies other than humans, but its lack of mobility makes it highly susceptible to fast-spreading bush fires.

Flatter and plainer brown than terrestrial tortoises are the freshwater chelonians known as **terrapins**. Of three species recorded in South Africa, by far the most common and widespread is the **marsh terrapin** *Pelomedusa subrufa*, which inhabits waterholes, puddles and other stagnant bodies in non-arid savannah habitats. The marsh terrapin often wanders considerable distances between suitable pools in rainy weather, and will usually aestivate during the dry season, burying itself deep in mud or sand, only to re-emerge after the first rains as if from nowhere – giving rise to a local legend that terrapins drop from the sky during storms.

The marine turtle species recorded off the coast of South Africa are all much larger than any of the region's indigenous tortoises or terrapins and differ from them in being unable to retract their heads or flippers into their shell for protection. The immense **leatherback** *Dermchelys coriacea*, which can weigh up to 800kg, regularly comes ashore on the beaches of iSimangaliso Wetland to lay eggs over November to January. Three other species have been recorded, namely the **green turtle** *Chelonia mydas*, **hawksbill** *Eretmochelys imbricata* and **olive ridley turtle** *Lepidochelys olivacea*, but none breeds regularly on the South Africa coast. All these turtle species are in numeric decline as a result of trapping, habitat destruction and pollution, and are listed as Endangered or Critically Endangered on the IUCN Red Data List.

Amphibians

Roughly 135 **frog** species are known from southern Africa – south of the Zambezi – and a full eighty percent of these are national endemics. Since most frogs are nocturnal, it can be hard to spot them unless you head out into wetlands after dark with a head torch, but the mating calls emitted by male frogs to attract potential partners are unique to each species, and often provide the most reliable clue to identification. Calling is most vigorous after rain during spring and early summer, when safarigoers are often treated to an unforgettable evening chorus of guttural croaks and ethereal whistles. Indeed, one of the most wondrous sounds of the African night is the spectral popping chorus of the **bubbling kassina** *Kassina Senegalensis*, a small and colourful but seldom-seen frog of marshes and moist grassland whose range extends across much of sub-Saharan Africa.

One of the most common indigenous amphibians is the **African clawed frog** or **platanna** *Xenopus laevis*, whose name is a corruption of the Afrikaans phrase "plat-hander" (flat-handed one). The platanna uses its fingers to cram food such as fish and dead animals into its mouth; it also has short claws on the inner toes of its webbed hind legs to help it dissect its prey before swallowing. It is rarely heard, for it lives, feeds and breeds underwater, but is quite often seen suspended below the surface of ponds, front legs akimbo. It is replaced in the Western Cape by the **Cape platanna** *X. gilli*, a very localized fynbos-associated endemic, and in the Kruger and surrounds by the **tropical platanna** *X. muelleri.*

Another widespread but far more vocal species, the **guttural toad** *Sclerophrys gutturalis* is an adaptable heavyweight that frequently aggregates around waterholes and riverbanks in large male choruses issuing the loud and repetitive rasping call for which it is named. Larger still, the hulking great **African bullfrog** *Pyxicephalus adspersus* is the continent's largest amphibian, sometimes weighing up to 2kg. It feeds on everything from small rodents and birds to its own tadpoles, and is generally associated with seasonal pools in the western half of the country.

At the other extreme, **tree frogs** *Hyperolius spp* are a diverse group of small and distinctively patterned frogs with long broad-tipped toes adapted for climbing vegetation in the forest woodland and reedy habitats with which they are associated. Southern Africa is also home to around fifteen species of **rain frog** *Breviceps spp*, whose Afrikaans name *blaasop* (blow up) refers to their ability to inflate their bodies with air when alarmed. Rain frogs can live independently of water, even for reproductive purposes, since they nest underground, where larval development takes place.

Invertebrates

South Africa is home to a staggering diversity of **invertebrates**, a term that includes all animals lacking the backbone common to the mammals, birds, reptiles, amphibians and fish of the subphyla Vertebrata. The term is actually something of a catch-all, one with no real taxonomic meaning, since it includes all nine animal phyla other than chordates, as well as two chordate subphyla more closely related to vertebrates than to other invertebrates. Nevertheless, while invertebrates tend to go largely unnoticed on a South African safari, they probably account for more than 97 percent of the world's animal species, a great many still undescribed by scientists. The most numerous and familiar of invertebrates, accounting for eighty percent of species worldwide, are the **arthropods**, a phylum that includes **insects**, **arachnids**, **crustaceans** and **myriapods** (centipedes and millipedes), all of which have a segmented body, an external skeleton and multiple pairs of jointed legs. Of the other invertebrate phyla, many are predominantly marine and aquatic, but those with a strong terrestrial presence include the **annelids** (earthworm and leeches) and **molluscs** (snails and slugs).

Insects

South Africa has much to excite entomological enthusiasts and photographers, with 80–100,000 species of **insect** estimated to inhabit the country. Ranging from dragonflies and mantises to mosquitoes and silverfish, these insects come in a diversity of shape and sizes, but all species have three pairs of jointed legs, a chitinous exoskeleton, a body divided into three segments (head, thorax and abdomen), compound eyes and a single pair of antennae. With a few exceptions (fleas and lice, for instance), almost all insects also have two sets of wings, which unlike those of birds are not adapted limbs but separate adult appendages that grow out from the thorax.

Among the best known and certainly the most attractive of insects, the **butterflies** and **moths** of the order Lepidoptera are represented in South Africa by around seven thousand species. Most butterflies are diurnal and many species are very colourful, meaning they are conspicuous all over the country, with activity tending to peak on summer mid-mornings. Some species such as the **African monarch** *Danaus chrysippus* (orange wings with white tips), **African clouded yellow** *Colias electo* (small orange-yellow wings) and **citrus swallowtail** *Papilio demodocus* (large yellow and brown wings) have a very cosmopolitan distribution and might be seen almost anywhere in South Africa. Most are somewhat more localized, however, and many are endemics associated with one particular plant on which the larvae feed. Among the most beautiful of South Africa's butterflies are the **Christmas forester** *Celaenorrhinus mokeezi* (iridescent multihued purple and pink wings) of the coastal and montane forests in the east, the **Table Mountain beauty** *Aeropetes tulbaghia* (brown wings with yellow patches and mauve spots), found on rocky slopes throughout the country, and the **black swallowtail** *Graphium colonna* (large black wings with broken stripes of vivid turquoise), located in northern KwaZulu-Natal. Unlike butterflies, moths tend to be nocturnal and most species are rather dull, but there are exceptions, for instance the **silver-spotted ghost moth** *Leto venus* (massive maroon wings spotted silver), which occurs in forests along the Garden Route, and the various **emperor**

moths of the family Saturniidae, many of which have large colourful wings marked with eye-like spots. Also notable is the **sundowner moth** *Sphingomorpha chlorea*, a fruit-eating species whose name refers to its attraction to the smell of alcoholic drinks, in particular wine.

Many other spectacular insects might be seen in South Africa's game parks. The **dung beetles** of the family Scarabaeidae are mostly dependent on dung of large animals as a source of food, and while some species simply live in the dung or bury it, others roll it into large round balls which they push along with their hind legs to a suitable spot as a breeding chamber. One nocturnal species of dung beetle *Scarabaeus satyrus* was discovered in 2013 to be the only known invertebrate capable of navigating on moonless nights using the Milky Way to orientate itself.

The **stick insects** of the family Phasmatidae are large slow-moving insects with cleverly camouflaged elongated bodies that resemble sticks and can in some cases grow up to 25cm in length. Then there are the beautiful **praying mantises** of the order Mantodea, a group of large but delicate and slow-moving insects that have green leaf-like wings and frequently practise sexual cannibalism (i.e. the females eat their mate after copulation). Named for their habit of standing still with forelimbs clasped together in front of the face as of praying, mantises were venerated by the San/Bushmen hunter-gatherers who once inhabited much of the country, and they are much loved by gardeners for their role as pest controllers.

Most of South Africa's game parks provide an important refuge for colonies of ground-nesting **termites**, many of which construct massive subterranean termitaria capped by solid mounds that protrude up to a few metres above ground and are pockmarked with sealable tunnels that can be opened and closed to control the internal temperature. Termites are the main prey of several nocturnal mammals, including aardvark, aardwolf and bat-eared fox, and the nuptial flights of "flying ants" (actually winged alates) that irrupt from the termitaria after rain often attract large flocks of raptors and other carnivorous birds, as well as being a popular local snack (lightly fried like peanuts) in many parts of Africa. The colonial nesters of the Hymenoptera, an order that includes **wasps**, **bees** and **ants**, are also well represented in South Africa. Many bees and wasps have nasty stings, while army-like columns of the 2cm-long **Matabele ant** *Megaponera analis* – off to stage raiding parties on neighbouring termite nests before they themselves are waylaid by robber flies – can inflict a ferocious bite on any person that gets in their way.

The unique Cape Floral Kingdom supports some fascinating endemic insects. All seventeen species of **Cape stag beetle** *Colophon spp* are Endangered endemic with a range confined to one or another mountain peak in the Western Cape, with some species being so rare and localized that they are known only from the fragments of a solitary dead individual. The protea, South Africa's national flower, plays host to a variety of beautiful beetles including the metallic emerald-green **protea chafer** *Trichostetha fascicularis*. Forests here are home to Africa's only few species of **velvet worm** *Peripatopsis spp*, a group of terrestrial predators that has survived almost unchanged in anatomy for four hundred million years and is thought to be ancestral to modern Arthropods, as well as being notable for their strange breeding habits – both sexes have gonads and testes, and the females are unusual among invertebrates insofar as they bear live young rather than laying eggs.

Arachnids

Distinguished from insects by having eight legs rather than six, **Arachnids** are a class of mostly terrestrial and predatory invertebrates that includes **spiders**, **scorpions** and **ticks**. Spiders are particularly well represented in South Africa, with more than three thousand species identified to date, among them the spectacular **golden orbs** whose huge webs are often seen in the game parks of the lowveld, and the scarily hairy

THE LITTLE FIVE

Everybody has heard of the Big Five, but fewer know about the **Little Five**, a quintet of easily overlooked namesakes assembled by wildlife enthusiasts to emphasize that there is far more to be seen on an African safari than many people imagine. Gimmicky as the concept of the Little Five might be, you'd do well to see all five of the fascinating creatures described below during your time in South Africa.

Elephant shrew Also known as sengis or jumping shrews, elephant shrews are small and largely nocturnal insectivorous mammals which, as their name suggests, look like shrews upon which some prankster has attached a twitchy elephant-like trunk. In fact, their closest living relative is probably the aardvark. Around half-a-dozen species have been recorded in South Africa, and two – the Cape elephant shrew *Elephantulus edwardii* and Karoo rock elephant shrew *E. pilicaudus* – are endemic to the country.

Red-billed buffalo-weaver *Bubalornis niger* Confined to dry savannah habitats in the far north, this distinctive colonial-nesting bird is dark black with a white shoulder patch and bright red bill, and is often seen in the vicinity of the scruffy nests it builds in acacia and baobab trees.

Rhinoceros beetle Named for their large backward curving horns, the rhinoceros beetles of the subfamily Dynastinae also resemble their mammalian namesakes in their bulky armoured appearance. Several species occur in South Africa and although most are nocturnal, they are often attracted to lodges in game parks by the artificial lights.

Leopard tortoise This large and widespread tortoise, the most likely of the Little Five to be seen on safari in most parts of South Africa, is named for its gold-on-black mottled shell.

Ant-lion Associated with the sandy soils where they dig pits to trap their main prey of ants, the ant-lions of the family Myrmeleontidae are actually rapacious larvae that later grow into nocturnal flyers that somewhat resemble dragonflies.

baboon spiders that are sometime seen in developed residential gardens. These large spiders are essentially harmless to people, but it's wise to give a wide berth to any small shiny, spherical spiders you might encounter – they could be members of the genus Latrodectus – the **button spider**. The poisonous black variety is most commonly found in the wheatfields of the Western Cape; you should be able to recognize it by a red stripe or spot on the tip of the abdomen.

Well-known for their stinging tails, **scorpions** are mainly confined to drier parts of the country and are seldom seen unless sought for by turning over rocks or dead logs. Many species are quite docile and their sting, though painful, is essentially harmless. Others, however, are strongly venomous, and could potentially kill a child if they go untreated.

Tick-bite fever may be transmitted by the bite of the **red-legged tick** as well as the common **dog tick**. The disease is most widespread during the summer, when humans spend most time outdoors in grassy or wooded areas.

Conservation past and present

Included on a shortlist of seventeen **megadiverse** countries identified by **Conservation International** in 1998, South Africa supports a remarkable wealth of endemic plant and animal species. The country is also deeply committed to conserving these natural assets. A network of 21 **national parks**, protecting everything from the sweltering savannah of the lowveld to the rarified fynbos of Table Mountain, is supplemented by literally hundreds of **provincial and municipal reserves**, along with a burgeoning selection of **private reserves**. Tourism and conservation in South Africa are deeply intertwined. Most national parks and public reserves provide affordable facilities to self-drivers or hikers, while private reserves offer an exclusive guided safari experience aimed at a more well-heeled market. But while the Big Five and other iconic safari favourites are now conspicuous in South Africa's major game parks, it hasn't always been this way. During the course of the seventeenth to nineteenth centuries, most of the country's large fauna was shot out by European settlers, and it is only through the concerted efforts of **conservationists** – catalyzed by the proclamation of the 20,000-square-kilometre Kruger National Park in 1926 – that so much has been restored over the past one hundred years.

Early days

Traditional **African cultures** tend to possess a strong conservationist ethic, one that is steeped in respect for the environment and the wildlife that inhabits it. Hunting is condoned – whether for the pot, or for ritual purposes – as a sporadic activity to be undertaken only when necessary. Indeed, considering that **palaeontological records** show humans and wildlife to have coexisted in South Africa for literally millions of years, it is remarkable that the first European mariners to reach the country's shores in the 1490s were greeted by a diverse, prolific and all but pristine **megafauna**. In November 1497, when Vasco da Gama landed at Mossel Bay, for instance, he noted that **gazelles**, **birds** and **elephants** were plentiful. Da Gama's crew then turned its attention to the thousands of **Cape fur seals** and **African penguins** that inhabited an island in the bay, firing cannonballs at the former for amusement, and slaying as many of the latter as they could for sport – an interaction that set the trend for much of what would follow.

In 1652, when Jan van Riebeeck, the founder of Cape Town, landed at Table Bay, the area still supported plenty of wildlife. Greater kudu, eland, Cape mountain zebra and a host of other **large ungulates** browsed and grazed on the slopes of Table Mountain, while **hippos** wallowed in the peninsula's lakes and rivers, and the likes of **lion**, **leopard**, **buffalo**, **elephant** and **black rhino** roamed the nearby hinterland. Early Dutch and British forays deeper into the interior revealed even greater concentrations of wildlife. In the eighteenth and early nineteenth centuries, herds of **trekbokke** (migratory springbok) – numbering in the hundreds of thousands – were regularly encountered in the Karoo and Namaqualand, often accompanied by large numbers of **quagga**, **blesbok** and **black wildebeest**. One of the last such migrations, as documented by Sir John Fraser in 1849, "took about three days" as it passed through Beaufort West, and the hungry antelope "left the country as if a fire had raged over it".

The demise of the Cape's megafauna was a direct result of persecution by **Dutch** and later **British settlers**. The **bluebuck**, a graceful roan-like antelope more-or-less endemic to the Western Cape, had been blasted to extinction prior to 1800. The once-prolific **quagga**, a distinctive subspecies of plains zebra with unstriped hindquarters, followed it into oblivion in the nineteenth century. Other local variants such as the **Cape warthog** and **black-maned Cape lion** (both regarded by some authorities to have been distinct subspecies) are also long gone. The likes of **bontebok** and **Cape mountain zebra** only escaped the same fate through the creation of national parks set aside specifically to protect barely viable bottleneck populations in the 1930s. The **elephants** that inhabited the indigenous forests of the Garden Route, once found to be so plentiful by Da Gama, are now reduced to one lonely individual, a mature female, that roams the forests around Knysna. The **spotted hyena** and **black-backed jackals** that scavenged the periphery of Cape Town were **poisoned** by settlers, also inadvertently causing the demise of the **Cape vultures** that once nested on the cliffs of Table Mountain. Many other iconic species – from white and black rhino to hippo and giraffe – were also eliminated from the Cape in the nineteenth century, and only exist there today because they have been reintroduced from elsewhere in the country.

A similar pattern emerged as the **Voortrekkers** and other European settlers expanded northwards into what are today Free State, KwaZulu-Natal, Gauteng, Mpumalanga, North West and Limpopo provinces. Great swathes of natural grassland and bush were cleared to make way for **agriculture and livestock**, while antelope and other ungulates were hunted for the pot or because they competed for fodder with domestic sheep and cattle. Elephants were butchered for their valuable **tusks**; rhinos, buffalos and lions as **sport**; hippos and crocodiles for the **threat they posed** to people at rivers, lake and other water sources. Carnivores great and small were persecuted as **vermin**, often by leaving out poisoned food, a non-discriminatory practice that took a severe incidental toll on local populations of vultures, eagles and other large raptors.

The late nineteenth and early twentieth centuries

Ironically, the earliest attempts to conserve South Africa's diminishing wildlife were initiated mainly by hunters concerned at the potential loss of sport. An unexpected pioneer in this respect was the **King Shaka Zulu**, who forbade excessive hunting in his private hunting ground in the Umfolozi River Valley during his reign (1816–28). The same tract of land served as a protected royal hunting ground under Shaka's successors and it was later set aside as one of the first two protected areas in Britain's Natal Colony. This was the **Umfolozi Junction Game Sanctuary**, which was proclaimed in 1895 together with the nearby **Hluhluwe Valley Game Sanctuary** (the two now form the core of the Hluhluwe-iMfolozi Park).

An important conservationist pioneer motivated primarily by his love of hunting was **President Paul Kruger** of the Zuid Afrikaansche Republiek. Kruger set aside a hunting exclusion zone along the Pongola River in 1889 and formally upgraded it in 1894 to become the **Pongola Game Reserve**, the oldest such entity in South Africa. It was also Kruger who, in 1898, proclaimed the 10,364-square-kilometre **Sabi Game Reserve**, which comprised what is now the southern part of the Kruger National Park as well as land now protected in neighbouring private reserves such as MalaMala and Sabi Sands.

Concurrent with this early bout of conservationist action, a devastating **rinderpest epidemic** swept southward from Ethiopia and East Africa in the late 1890s, killing at least five million head of cattle in southern Africa, along with untold numbers of buffalo, giraffe, blue wildebeest, greater kudu and other ungulates. The epidemic was followed in close succession by the profoundly disruptive **Anglo-Boer War** (1899–1902), as well as a series of debilitating **droughts**, while sporadic outbreaks of **nagana** (a lethal tsetse-borne form of trypanosomiasis that affects livestock) prompted farmers in affected areas to eradicate the wildlife they mistakenly believed acted as a reservoir for the disease. So it was that by 1910, when the British colonies of the Cape and Natal amalgamated with the Boer republics of the Transvaal and Orange Free State to form the **Union of South Africa**, the prolific wildlife that once roamed the newly created country had been marginalized to such an extent that several iconic species – including lion, cheetah and both rhino species – were tottering on the **brink of extinction** within its borders.

The modern era of conservation in South Africa arguably started in 1926 with the creation of the **National Parks Board** (now **SANParks**) and the simultaneous creation of the **Kruger National Park**, which amalgamated the eastern portion of the original Sabi Game Reserve with the more northerly Singwidzi Game Reserve (originally proclaimed in 1903) and a connecting triangle of land between the Olifants and Letaba rivers. Four new national parks were created over the course of the 1930s, all primarily focused on the conservation of one species. These were **Addo Elephant**, set aside to protect the last few surviving elephants in the dense Albany thicket north of Port Elizabeth; **Kalahari Gemsbok**, which now forms the South African component of the Kgalagadi Transfrontier Park; and the **Bontebok and Mountain Zebra National Parks**, both of which went on to play a crucial role in preventing the extinction of the endemic ungulates for which they are named. Another early milestone in the history of conservation in South Africa was the formation in 1947 of the Natal Parks, Game and Fish Preservation Board (now **Ezemvelo KwaZulu-Natal Wildlife**), the dynamic provincial authority responsible for rescuing the white rhino (and South Africa's then-dwindling population of black rhino) from the verge of extinction in what is now Hluhluwe-iMfolozi Park.

Tourism and conservation

As early as 1916, a provincially appointed commission, established to investigate the advisability of altering the boundaries of the Sabi and Singwidzi game reserves, recognized that it would "be increasingly difficult to maintain... so large an area... merely for the preservation of the fauna". For conservation to be a success, it required public interest and support. Ecotourism of a sort arrived as early as 1923, when the first warden, **James Stevenson-Hamilton**, persuaded South African Railways to include an overnight stop at Sabi Bridge (now Skukuza) and short guided bush walk on its popular "Round in Nine" rail-package tour, which travelled from Pretoria to the Mozambican port of Lourenço Marques (now Maputo) via an 80km stretch of the Selati Railway that ran through the Sabi Game Reserve.

In 1927, only a year after it had been gazetted, the re-delineated **Kruger National Park** formally opened to the public, attracting just three tourist cars in its first year of operation. By 1929, more than 600km of dirt roads had been constructed through the park, and tourist arrivals had increased to 850 cars. The high public interest in Kruger's wildlife led to the construction of the first **restcamp** at Pretoriuskop in 1930 and to the opening of the private **Sabi River Bungalows** (with thirteen en-suite rondavels and six more basic ones for chauffeurs) outside Numbi Gate in 1932. Meanwhile, much of the westerly land excised from the Sabi Game Reserve in 1926 was bought up by wealthy hunting enthusiasts, who preserved them as seasonal **hunting camps** that eventually mutated into private game reserves such as MalaMala and Sabi Sands.

An impetus for conservation post-World War II was the growing popularity of game reserves and birdwatching as a **leisure pursuit** among middle-class white South Africans (it is widely held that Austin Roberts's eponymous bird field guide, first published in 1940 and still in print several editions and eighty years later, is the country's bestselling book after the Bible). By 1955, Kruger was attracting more than 100,000 (mostly domestic) tourists annually; in 1968 the number of annual arrivals topped 300,000 for the first time. It was also during the 1960s that **MalaMala**, which shares a 19km border with Kruger, reinvented itself as an **exclusive private game reserve** on which so many others later modelled themselves. Away from the lowveld, SANParks expanded its portfolio by gazetting eight new national parks between 1963 and 1986. This period also saw the establishment of a diverse array of provincial and municipal reserves. Some, such as Ithala and Tembe in KwaZulu-Natal, or Pilanesberg in what was then the nominally independent homeland of Bophuthatswana, were primarily designed as **big game sanctuaries**. Many others, however, were set aside with the broader and arguably more important ecological goal of protecting pristine tracts of fynbos, grassland, forest, succulent Karoo and other **vulnerable habitats**.

Persisting problems

It is often assumed that **hunting**, whether legal or illegal, is the biggest threat to South Africa's wildlife. But a far greater concern – and one that affects not only the charismatic large mammals that woo safarigoers, but also an untold diversity of less conspicuous and loveable species, from butterflies and birds to snakes and spiders – is the rampant **habitat destruction** that has taken place since European settlement. The moist savannah and grassland that once swathed the eastern highveld and lowveld has largely been replaced by **cultivated monocultures** and **subsistence farms**. The indigenous evergreen forests that grew on the slopes of the escarpment and coastal mountains have been chopped down to make way for sterile plantations of fast-growing softwoods. Large tracts of the endemic fynbos that once dominated the Western Cape are gone, while much of the Karoo and other semi-arid habitats of the west has been eroded, denuded or otherwise damaged by **overgrazing livestock**.

A related and more insidious threat to the ecological integrity of any given ecosystem is the inadvertent **spread of exotics** (i.e. species that don't occur there naturally). These might sometimes be animals, such as the Indian mynas and house sparrows that breed profusely in an increasing number of urban centres. More often, however, they are plants introduced deliberately for cropping, plantation or hedging purposes. Most such plants are poorly adapted to local conditions and cannot survive long or propagate without human intervention, but a small proportion will find local conditions to their liking, and these adaptable aliens – referred to as **invasive species** – often spread like wildfire because they aren't controlled by any of the natural predators that occur in their country of origin.

The spread of invasive exotics and associated loss of biodiversity has become a major global concern over the past century. And while South Africa is less compromised than much of the world in this respect (which is why so much wildlife still remains) it is no exception. Of an estimated eight thousand alien plant species planted since the arrival of European settlers, at least 160 are regarded as invasive, and collectively they cover around ten percent of the country's surface area. Worryingly, the most heavily affected province, with an invader cover estimated at thirty percent, is the **Western Cape**, whose unique fynbos and succulent habitats account for the majority of South Africa's 16,000 plus endemic plant species. Indeed, while South Africa does support one of the world's most extensive networks of national parks and other reserves, these protected areas increasingly function as enclaves of near-pristine biodiversity in a country otherwise dominated by artificial or degraded habitats.

According to a study undertaken by the Endangered Wildlife Trust in 2016, there are now around nine thousand privately owned **wildlife ranches** in South Africa, most of which specialize in breeding wildlife for **auctions**, **hunting** and **venison production** (or a combination of these). Collectively these ranches extend across more than 170,000 square kilometres, which accounts for fifteen percent of the country's surface area, and is fivefold larger than all its national parks combined – as well as accounting for a far larger area than private reserves dedicated purely to conservation and ecotourism. These ranches generate an annual revenue of around US$500 million from hunting, meat sales and wildlife auctions, and form an important source of employment and impetus for **economic growth** in poor rural areas. They typically occupy marginal land not only unsuited to agriculture but also better served ecologically by indigenous wildlife than by domestic livestock, whose overgrazing of vulnerable habitats often creates openings for invasive species. South Africa's ranches support an estimated six million individual large ungulates, and since many lie close to national parks or other reserves, they have become an important buffer zone for small carnivores and other wildlife that can move freely through game fences.

Conservation in the post-apartheid era

The post-apartheid era has been an exciting time for conservation in South Africa. Changing global perceptions and an unprecedented influx of **international tourism** has transformed conservation into a **profitable concern**, with mostly positive results. Seven new national parks have been gazetted since 1994, but a more important development has arguably been the establishment of dozens of new **private reserves** on what was formerly farmland. True, on one level, these private reserves might appear to be little more than commercial enterprises offering well-heeled punters an ever-growing choice of luxury Big Five safari packages in artificially stocked, tightly managed and relatively contained reserves. But the bigger picture, in most cases, is that the conservation-minded landowners will direct income from the luxury lodges towards funding the preservation of vulnerable habitats and/or the rehabilitation of degraded former farmland. Furthermore, while most individual private reserves are too small to support viable numbers of large carnivores such as lion and cheetah, they have come to play a vital collective role in the conservation of these and other vulnerable species by hosting an **intra-reserve metapopulation** where the genetic diversity and integrity of relocated individuals is tightly regulated by the likes of Endangered Wildlife Trust's Cheetah Metapopulation Project.

Another important post-apartheid development has been the trend towards the **amalgamation of bordering conservation areas**. The best example of this is the dropping of fences between Kruger and several neighbouring private reserves between 1993 and 2005. Elsewhere, KwaZulu-Natal's vast and biodiverse iSimangaliso Wetland Park and uKhahlamba-Drakensberg Park were forged from numerous smaller reserves following their inscription as UNESCO World Heritage sites at the turn of the millennium, while Table Mountain, Greater Addo and Garden Route National Parks have all been created by joining several smaller reserves since the late 1990s. The trend to amalgamation has traversed international boundaries, too. In 2001, Kruger combined with Zimbabwe's Gonarezhou and Mozambique's Limpopo National Park to form the 35,000-square-kilometre Great Limpopo Transfrontier Park. Other important transfrontier parks include Kgalagadi (which extends into Botswana), Ai-Ais Richtersveld (Namibia) and Maloti-Drakensberg (Lesotho). Looking ahead, there is plenty of room for further dropping of fences between neighbouring public and private reserves, be it uMkhuze and Phinda in KwaZulu-Natal, Marakele and Welgevonden in the Waterberg, or Camdeboo and Samara in the Eastern Cape.

Much of Africa has suffered a precipitous decline in large wildlife populations over the past century, while the reverse has happened in South Africa. Admittedly, this is largely because **intensive hunting** prior to the twentieth century had left the country's wildlife stocks so abjectly depleted by comparison to most other parts of equatorial and southern Africa. When the first wildlife estimates for the Sabi Game Reserve were published in 1918, the buffalo, giraffe, elephant, black rhino and white rhino populations stood at 250, 210, 65, six and zero respectively. Indeed, it is more than likely that the total countrywide total tally of elephant, lion or rhino, for instance, would then have been measurable in the hundreds rather than the thousands. A century later, the Kruger National Park alone supports around 45,000 buffalos, 8000 giraffes and 20,000 elephants, while populations of white and black rhino, last seen in the area in 1896 and 1936 prior to be being reintroduced in the 1960s, stood at 12,000 and 600 respectively.

It isn't all rosy, by any means. **Deforestation** and colonization by **invasive plants** continue apace. **Rhino poaching** has hit unprecedented highs since 2010, while **poisoning** by farmers and the use of **pesticides** has resulted in a tragic recent decline in numbers of predators, from spiders and snakes to vultures and hyenas. The unchecked growth of **Kruger's elephant population**, from around 8000 in 1994, when a moratorium was placed on culling, to more than 20,000 today, is seen by some as an ecological disaster in the making. Many wildlife areas face long-term pressure from fast-growing **neighbouring communities** where unemployment and poverty are rife. Writing in late 2019, several of the country's top wildlife regions are in the grip of an extended **drought** that threatens their long-term viability. Yet despite all this, South Africa today is estimated to harbour ten times as many individual large mammals as it did in the 1960s, and populations of most vulnerable species are spread across many dozens of reserves that work together to protect the integrity of their gene pool. For all the disasters of the past and concerns of the present, the future of conservation in South Africa appears to be in good hands.

RHINOS: LAST CHANCE TO SEE?

Two species of **rhinoceros** are found in Africa: the hook-lipped or black rhino and the much heavier square-lipped or white rhino. Both have come close to extinction in the past century or so. The global population of southern white rhino bottlenecked at fewer than twenty individuals, all resident in Hluhluwe-iMfolozi, back in 1916, but it is now thought to stand at more than 20,000. An outbreak of commercial poaching in the 1970s and 1980s reduced the black rhino population from around 70,000 in 1970 to a nadir of below 2500 in 1995. Today, South Africa supports around eighty percent of the world's individual rhinos of all species (including the three Asian ones), with more than 18,000 white and roughly 2000 black rhinos being protected in various reserves, making it the best place on earth to view these ancient mammals.

Sadly, **rhino poaching** in South Africa – almost non-existent as recently as 2007, when just thirteen incidents were documented – has since escalated to worrying proportions, with more than a thousand animals falling to poachers every year from 2013 to 2017. The main market for rhino horn is Asia, where it is used as an ingredient in traditional medicine. Here, a single 3kg horn can fetch up to US$300,000, making it more expensive per kilo than gold. So lucrative is the trade that sophisticated **criminal syndicates** have moved in, using helicopters and night-vision equipment to slaughter the mammals under cover of night.

Efforts are being made to **protect the rhinos** – 2017 saw the arrest of more than 350 poachers, who risk shoot-outs with anti-poaching units – but this is insufficient to save the animals, who are now being killed faster than they can reproduce. Tactics such as removing the rhinos' horns have proved unsuccessful, because even the remaining stumps are hugely valuable, and some conservationists argue that more resources need to be thrown at the problem. Others maintain that the only real solution is to legalize the trade in rhino horn and to harvest it commercially (like human fingernails, the horn is made of keratin and it will regrow over a couple of years, though never to its original length).

Meanwhile, ongoing **conservation programmes** have included the relocation of large numbers of white rhino and smaller numbers of black rhino to numerous national parks, provincial reserves and private sanctuaries countrywide, thereby spreading the risk and making it easier to monitor individuals. Further afield, one hundred rhinos have been relocated from South Africa into **Botswana**, whose vast and remote wildernesses, it is hoped, will prove inaccessible to poachers. Indeed, there is reason to be positive about such projects – since its creation 25 years ago, Botswana's community-based **Khama Rhino Sanctuary** has relocated sixteen rhinos to different parts of the country from a foundation population of four animals, thanks to protection from anti-poaching units and the military.

In South Africa, the increase in **poacher arrests** brought down rhino losses from a 2014 peak of over 1214 individuals of both species down to 769 in 2018. Worrying as these figures are, the overwhelming majority of individuals poached are white rhinos, whose birth rate of around six percent per annum means that the population is still regarded by the IUCN to be on the increase. Indeed, where the white rhino was once IUCN-listed as Critically Endangered, then more recently as Endangered and Vulnerable, it is now listed as Near-threatened, a lower level of concern than is accorded to, for instance, the African elephant, lion or cheetah. The prognosis for the Critically Endangered black rhino is bleaker, but even so the global population now stands at more than 5000 individuals, more than double its all-time low in 1995.

Books

For a country with a proportionately small reading and book-buying public, South Africa generates a substantial amount of literature, particularly on wildlife and the uncomfortable subjects of politics and history. Titles marked ★ are particularly recommended.

FIELD GUIDES AND WILDLIFE

GENERAL

Peter Allison *Don't Run, Whatever You Do: My Adventures as a Safari Guide*. Though it is set in Botswana, this amusing and informative set of hair-raising tales gives some insight into the life of a safari guide.

Lawrence Anthony *The Elephant Whisperer*. Subtitled "Learning About Life, Loyalty and Freedom From a Remarkable Herd of Elephants", this feel-good true-life story recounts the introduction of a herd of "rogue" elephants on the Thula Thula Game Reserve.

★ **George Branch and Charles Griffiths** *Two Oceans: A Guide to the Marine Life of Southern Africa*. Don't be put off by the coffee-table format; this stalwart – now in its third edition – is a comprehensive guide to Southern Africa's marine life, with more than 2000 species described and illustrated.

Vincent Carruthers *Wildlife of Southern Africa: A Field Guide to the Animals and Plants of the Region*. Handy all-round identification guide that packs a huge amount of information into its 360 pages but inevitably lacks detail on more uncommon flora and fauna.

Richard Cowling and Dave Richardson *Fynbos: South Africa's Unique Floral Kingdom*. Lavishly illustrated book which offers a fascinating portrait of the *fynbos* ecosystem.

★ **Jeff Gordon** *101 Kruger Tales: Extraordinary Stories from Ordinary Visitors to the Kruger National Park*. A fabulous appetite-whetter for a visit to South Africa's premier safari destination, jam-packed with accounts of exciting and occasionally terrifying wildlife encounters.

John Manning *Field Guide to Wild Flowers of South Africa*. More than 1000 of the region's more common, conspicuous and/or striking flowering plants are introduced in this user-friendly 400-plus pager.

J. McMahon and M. Fraser *A Fynbos Year*. Exquisitely illustrated and well-written book about South Africa's unique floral kingdom.

Ingrid van den Berg *Kruger Self Drive: Routes, Roads & Sightings*. The hardback format is less than ideal, but there's no better handbook for those who want to spend an extended period exploring Kruger. Includes coverage of every road in this vast national park, and what to expect from them.

Piet and Braam van Wyk *Field Guide to Trees of Southern Africa*. More than 1000 species are described and illustrated in this definitive guide to the region's trees.

MAMMALS

Richard D. Estes *Safari Companion: A Guide to Watching African Mammals*. A vital handbook on African wildlife, with fascinating information on the behaviour and social structures of the major species. Highly recommended for anyone wanting to go beyond the checklists.

★ **Jonathan Kingdon** *Kingdon Field Guide to African Mammals*. The most comprehensive one-volume book to the mammals of Africa serves as a more-than-useful field guide, but it is far more than that – a true labour of love that's also very strong on taxonomic and behavioural detail.

Jonathan Kingdon *Kingdon Pocket Field Guide to African Mammals*. Aimed more at casual mammal-watchers, this is basically a condensed version of the full Kingdon guide.

Chris and Mathilde Stuart *Stuarts' Field Guide to the Mammals of Southern Africa*. The leading field guide on this subject, providing excellent background and clear illustrations to help you recognize species.

Chris and Mathilde Stuart *Pocket Guide Mammals of Southern Africa*. Handy pocket guide by the always authoritative Stuarts.

Clive Walker *Signs of the Wild*. This field guide to the footprints and other spoor of South Africa's mammals will add a whole new dimension to any walking safari.

BIRDS

★ **Hugh Chittenden** (ed) *Roberts Bird Guide*. This condensed version of the full *Roberts Birds of Southern Africa* is arguably the preeminent field guide to the 950-plus avian species recorded in Africa south of the Zambezi. Even better still is the app version, which can be bought from the likes of Ⓦ play.google.com/store and Ⓦ apple.com/ios/app-store.

Phil Hockey, WRJ Dean and Peter Ryan (ed) *Roberts Birds of Southern Africa 7th edition*. The definitive reference work on the avifauna of Africa south of the Zambezi contains superb plates, and immensely detailed species accounts, but a weighty 1300 coffee-table size pages, it's emphatically more reference work than field guide.

Kenneth Newman *Newman's Birds of Southern Africa*. The late Kenneth Newman is South Africa's most loved bird illustrator and this revamped commemorative edition still leads the field-guide pack when it comes to lifelike plates.

Ian Sinclair, Phil Hockey and Warwick Tarboton

Sasol Birds of Southern Africa. Now in its 4th edition, this comprehensive field guide illustrates all species recorded in the region and has useful pointers to aid quick identification.

Ian Sinclair *Pocket Guide to the Birds of Southern Africa*. Handy and highly portable entry-level field guide illustrating and describing 500 of the region's more conspicuous bird species.

OTHER WILDLIFE

Bill Branch *Field Guide to Snakes and Other Reptiles of Southern Africa*. An ophiophobe's nightmare of a book, this is an invaluable guide to the region's snakes, lizards and tortoises, written by the country's leading herpetologist.

Louis du Preez and Vincent Carruthers *Field Guide to the Frogs of Southern Africa*. This comprehensive guide comes with a useful CD of frog calls.

Mike Picker, Alan Weaving and Charles Griffiths *Field Guide to Insects of South Africa*. An impossible subject to cover definitely, but with photos of more than 1200 species, this colourful book gives it a good shot.

HISTORY, SOCIETY AND ANTHROPOLOGY

Ian Berry *Living Apart*. Superbly evocative and moving photographs spanning the 1950s to 1990s, which chart a compelling vision of the politics of the nation.

John Carlin *Playing the Enemy: Nelson Mandela and the Game that made a Nation*. Gripping account of Nelson Mandela's use of the 1995 rugby World Cup to unite a fractious nation in danger of collapsing into civil war. Also published as *Invictus*, the title of the Clint Eastwood film, which starred Matt Damon and Morgan Freeman.

Paul Faber *Group Portrait South Africa: Nine Family Histories*. Fascinating account revealing the complexities of South Africa past and present, through the histories of nine South African families of different races, backgrounds and aspirations. Includes photos and illustrations.

★ **Douglas Foster** *After Mandela: The Struggle for Freedom in Post-Apartheid South Africa*. Former editor of *Mother Jones*, Foster brings together political analysis and street-level accounts based on interviews recorded over six years to create one of the past decade's most interesting and penetrating accounts of a country poised between liberation and decline.

Hermann Giliomee and Bernard Mbenga *A New History of South Africa*. A comprehensive, reliable and entertaining account of South Africa's history.

★ **Peter Harris** *In a Different Time: The Inside Story of the Delmas Four*. Brilliantly told true historical drama about four young South Africans sent on a mission by the ANC-in-exile, which ultimately led them to Death Row. As their defence lawyer, Harris had unique and sympathetic insight into their personalities and motivations. Also published as *A Just Defiance: The Bombmakers, the Insurgents and a Legendary Treason Trial*.

★ **Antjie Krog** *Country of My Skull*. A deeply personal and gripping account of the hearings of the Truth and Reconciliation Commission. Krog, an Afrikaner former-SABC radio journalist and poet, reveals the complexity of horrors committed by apartheid.

★ **J.D. Lewis-Williams** *Discovering Southern African Rock Art* and *Images of Power: Understanding Bushman Rock Art*. Concise books written by an expert in the field, full of drawings and photos.

Greg Marinovich *Murder at Small Koppie*. A meticulously researched account of the Marikana Massacre and its ongoing repercussions.

★ **Noel Mostert** *Frontiers: The Epic of South Africa's Creation and the Tragedy of the Xhosa People*. An academically solid, brilliantly written history of the Xhosa of the Eastern Cape, and their tragic fate in the frontier wars against the British.

★ **Pieter-Louis Myburgh** *The Republic of Gupta: A Story of State Capture*. A page-turning exposé of the dodgy deals that have gone on behind the scenes during Zuma's presidency, covering the Gupta family's influence on the governing party.

★ **Thomas Pakenham** *The Boer War*. The definitive liberal history of the Anglo-Boer War that reads grippingly like a novel.

Ralf-Peter Seippel *South African Photography: 1950–2010*. South Africa's history has provided a rich vein of material for photographers and this volume covers the work of some of the country's most celebrated lensmen, whose work is divided into three periods: apartheid, struggle and freedom.

Charlene Smith *Robben Island*. Comprehensive and well-written account of Robben Island from prehistoric times to the present, including coverage of its most notorious period – as a prison for opponents of apartheid.

Desmond Tutu *No Future Without Forgiveness*. The Truth and Reconciliation Commission as described by its chairman. The book offers essential insight into one of South Africa's most unlikely heroes.

Paul Weinberg *Then & Now*. Collection by eight photographers, tracing the changes in their subjects and approaches as South Africa moved from apartheid into the present democratic era.

Frank Welsh *A History of South Africa*. Solid scholarship and a strong sense of overall narrative mark this publication as a much-needed addition to South African historiography.

Sue Williamson *South African Art Now*. A survey of South African art from the "Resistance Art" of the 1960s to the present, covering movements, genres and leading artists such as Marlene Dumas and William Kentridge, by one of the country's most influential commentators and a accomplished artist in her own right.

Francis Wilson *Dinosaurs, Diamonds & Democracy: Short, Short History of South Africa*. Brilliant account that packs two billion years into 128 pages, making it the perfect bluffer's guide to South Africa's history.

★**Zapiro** A series of annual cartoon collections by South Africa's leading, and always excellent, political cartoonist. Jonathan Shapiro, aka Zapiro, consistently reveals what needs to be exposed in satirical, hard-hitting and shocking cartoons (🖰 zapiro.com).

AUTOBIOGRAPHY AND BIOGRAPHY

★**Sindiwe Magoma** *To My Children's Children*. A fascinating autobiography – initially started so that her family would never forget their roots – that traces Magoma's life from the rural Transkei to the hard townships of Cape Town, and from political innocence to wisdom born of bitter experience.

★**Nelson Mandela** *Long Walk to Freedom*. The superb bestselling autobiography of the former South African president. Mandela's generosity of spirit and tremendous understanding of the delicate balance between principle and tactics come through very strongly, and the book is wonderfully evocative of his early years and intensely moving about his long years in prison.

★**Greg Marinovich and João Silva** *The Bang Bang Club*. Compelling account of the photographers who covered the bloody unrest in the townships at the end of apartheid, including the late Kevin Carter.

★**Benjamin Pogrund** *How Can Man Die Better? The Life of Robert Sobukwe*. The story of one of the most important anti-apartheid liberation heroes. The late leader of the Pan Africanist Congress and a contemporary of Nelson Mandela, Sobukwe was so feared by the white government that they passed a special law – The Sobukwe Clause – to keep him in solitary confinement on Robben Island after he'd served his sentence.

Anthony Sampson *Mandela, The Authorised Biography*. Released to coincide with Mandela's retirement from the presidency in 1999, Sampson's authoritative volume competes favourably with *Long Walk to Freedom*, offering a broader perspective and sharper analysis than the autobiography.

TRAVEL WRITING AND PHOTOGRAPHY

Richard Dobson *Karoo Moons: A Photographic Journey*. If you need encouragement to explore the desert interior of South Africa, these enticing images should do the trick.

Sihle Khumalo *Dark Continent, My Black Arse*. Insightful and witty account by a black South African who quit his well-paid job to realize a dream of travelling from the Cape to Cairo by public transport.

Julia Martin *A Millimetre of Dust: Visiting Ancestral Sites*. Sensitively crafted narrative that begins on the Cape Peninsula and takes the author, her husband and two children on a journey to important archeological sites in the Northern Cape, raising ethical, ecological and philosophical questions along the way.

Dervla Murphy *South from the Limpopo: Travels Through South Africa*. A fascinating and intrepid journey – by bicycle – through the new South Africa. The author isn't afraid to explore the complexities and paradoxes of this country.

★**Paul Theroux** *Dark Star Safari*. Theroux's powerful account of his overland trip from Cairo to Cape Town, with a couple of chapters on South Africa, including an account of meeting writer Nadine Gordimer (see page 392).

SPECIALIST GUIDES

★**Mike Lundy** *Best Walks in the Cape Peninsula*. Handy, solidly researched guide to some of the peninsula's many walks, and small enough to fit comfortably in a backpack.

Willie and Sandra Olivier *Hiking Trails of Southern Africa*. Guide to major hikes, from strolls to expeditions lasting several days, throughout South Africa with information and where to get permits.

Colin Paterson-Jones *Best Walks of the Garden Route*. Handy for accessing some of South Africa's premier coastline and forests along the Garden Route.

Steve Pike *Surfing in South Africa: Swells, Spots and Surf African Culture*. The essential guide to everything you need to know about riding the waves along the country's 3000km coastline, written by veteran journalist, surfing aficionado and founder of the definitive surfing website 🖰 wavescape.co.za.

★**Philip van Zyl** (ed) *Platter's South African Wine Guide*. One of the bestselling titles in South Africa – an annually updated pocket book that rates virtually every wine produced in the country.

FICTION

Tatamkhulu Afrika *The Innocents*. Set in the struggle years, this novel examines the moral and ethical issues of the time from a Muslim perspective.

Mark Behr *The Smell of Apples*. Behr's powerful first novel set in the 1970s recounts the gradual falling of the scales from the eyes of an eleven-year-old Afrikaner boy, whose father is a major-general in the apartheid army.

★**Lauren Beukes** *Zoo City*. Winner in 2011 of the Arthur C. Clarke award for science fiction, this cyberpunk-style novel is set in an alternative Johannesburg where convicts are sentenced to be "animalled" – to have an animal familiar attached to them.

Herman Charles Bosman *Unto Dust*. A superb collection of short stories from South Africa's master of the genre, all set in the tiny Afrikaner farming district of Groot Marico in the 1930s. The tales share a narrator who, with delicious irony, reveals the passions and foibles of his community.

André Brink *A Chain of Voices*. This hugely evocative tale of eighteenth-century Cape life explores the impact of slavery on one farming family.

★ **Michael Chapman** *Omnibus of a Century of South African Short Stories*. Comprehensive collection of South African tale-telling, starting with San oral stories and working up to twenty-first-century writing, including work by Olive Schreiner, Alan Paton, Es'kia Mphahlele and Ivan Vladislavic.

★ **J.M. Coetzee** *Age of Iron* and *Disgrace*. In a *Mail & Guardian* poll of writers, *Age of Iron* emerged as the finest South African novel of the 1990s. The book depicts a white female classics professor dying from cancer during the political craziness of the 1980s. She is joined by a tramp who sets up home in her garden, and thus evolves a curious and fascinating relationship. But even better is *Disgrace*, a disturbing story of a university professor's fall from grace, set in the Eastern Cape. No writer better portrays the ever-present undercurrents of violence and unease in South Africa.

Achmat Dangor *The Z Town Trilogy*. A well-respected South African Indian writer once shortlisted for the Booker Prize, Dangor sets this novel during one of apartheid South Africa's many states of emergency, which is burrowing in intricate ways into the psyches of his characters.

Tracey Farren *Whiplash*. Powerful, acclaimed, and by turns relentless and funny, debut novel written in the voice of a Cape Town prostitute coming to terms with her past and present on her own personal walk to freedom.

Nadine Gordimer *July's People*. This controversial work by Nobel Literature Prize winner Gordimer was first banned by the apartheid regime for being subversive and later temporarily removed from schools by the ANC-governed Gauteng education department for being "deeply racist superior and patronizing". Published in the 1980s when revolution in South Africa looked increasingly possible, it tells the story of a liberal white family rescued by its gardener July from a political deluge, and taken to his home village for safety.

Lily Herne *Deadlands*. South Africa's street-smart answer to *Twilight* follows the adventures and romance of 17-year-old Lele as she navigates the shattered, dystopian and zombie-infested suburbs of a post-apocalyptic Cape Town.

Pamela Jooste *Dance with a Poor Man's Daughter*. The fragile world of a young coloured girl during the early apartheid years is sensitively imagined in this hugely successful first novel.

★ **Alex La Guma** *A Walk in the Night and Other Stories*. An evocative collection of short stories by this talented political activist/author, set in District Six, the ethnically mixed quarter of Cape Town razed by the apartheid government.

Anne Landsman *The Devil's Chimney*. A stylish and entertaining piece of magical realism set in the Karoo town of Oudtshoorn in the days of the ostrich-feather boom.

Sindiwe Magona *Mother to Mother*. Magona adopts the narrative voice of the mother of the killer of Amy Biehl, an American student murdered in a Cape Town township in 1993. The novel is a trenchant and lyrical meditation on the traumas of the past.

Songeziwe Mahlangu *Penumbra*. Semi-autobiographical debut novel that etches a unique vision of Cape Town through the eyes of a young man employed by a large insurance company. Torn by turns between mindless web-surfing, drug-induced mania and charismatic Christianity, Manga charts his course through the Mother City.

★ **Dalene Matthee** *Circles in a Forest*. A descendant of Sir Walter Scott, Matthee powerfully evokes the bygone world of woodcutters dodging wild elephants in the forests of the Garden Route.

Zakes Mda *Ways of Dying*, *His Madonna of Excelsior* and *The Heart of Redness*. The first is a brilliant tale of a professional mourner, full of sly insights into the culture of black South Africa; *Madonna* focuses on a family at the heart of the scandalous case in the Free State in which nineteen people from the small town of Excelsior were charged with sex across the races; while *Heart*, which won the *Sunday Times* Fiction Prize, weaves the historical story of the Eastern Cape cattle killings with a contemporary narrative.

★ **Es'kia Mphahlele** *Down Second Avenue*. A classic autobiographical novel set in the 1940s in the impoverished township of Alexandra, where Mphahlele grew up as part of a large extended family battling daily to survive.

★ **Alan Paton** *Cry, The Beloved Country*. Classic 1948 novel encapsulating the deep injustices of the country, by one of South Africa's great liberals. With tremendous lyricism, the book describes the journey of a black pastor from rural Natal to Johannesburg to rescue his missing son from the city's clutches.

Sol Plaatje *Mhudi*. The first English novel by a black South African writer, *Mhudi* is set in the 1830s, at a time when the Afrikaner Great Trek had just begun. It's the epic tale of a young rural woman who saves her future husband from the raids of the Ndebele, who were then a powerful state in the Marico region.

★ **Olive Schreiner** *Story of an African Farm*. The first-ever South African novel, written in 1883. Though subject to the ideologies of the era, the book nonetheless explores with a genuinely open vision the tale of two female cousins living on a remote Karoo farm.

★ **Ivan Vladislavic** *The Restless Supermarket*, *The Exploded View* and *Portrait with Keys: Joburg and What What*. *The Restless Supermarket* is a dark and intricate urban satire from the exciting Croatian–South African writer, about Johannesburg's notorious Hillbrow district during the last days of apartheid. *The Exploded View* is collection of four interlinked pieces, a great follow-up from a writer who's unrivalled at evoking the contradictions and fascinations of Joburg, while *Portrait* is not so much a novel as an account, in a series of numbered texts, of the city that inspires Vladislavic's imagination.

Language

South Africa has eleven official languages, all of which have equal status under the law. In practice, however, **English** is the lingua franca that dominates politics, commerce and the media. If you're staying in the main cities and national parks you'll rarely, if ever, need to use any other language. **Afrikaans**, although a language you seldom need to speak, nevertheless remains very much in evidence and you will certainly encounter it on official forms and countless signs, particularly on the road; for this reason we give a comprehensive list of written Afrikaans terms you could come across (see opposite).

Unless you're planning on staying a very long time, there's little point trying to get to grips with the whole gamut of **indigenous African languages**, of which there are nine official ones and several unofficial ones. Having said that, it's always useful to know a few phrases of the local indigenous language, especially greetings – the use of which will always be appreciated even if you aren't able to carry your foray through to a proper conversation.

The nine official African languages are split into four groups: **Nguni**, which consists of Zulu, Xhosa, siSwati and Ndebele; **Sotho**, which comprises Northern Sotho, Southern Sotho (or Sesotho) and Tswana; **Venda** and **Tsonga**. Most black people speak languages in the first two groups. In common with all indigenous southern African languages, these operate under very different principles from European languages in that their sentences are dominated by the noun, with which the other words, such as verbs and adjectives, must agree in person, gender, number or case. Known as concordal agreement, this is achieved by supplementing word stems – the basic element of each word – with prefixes and suffixes to change meaning.

The Nguni group, and Southern Sotho, both contain a few **clicks** adopted from San languages, which are difficult for speakers of European languages. In practice, most English-speaking South Africans sidestep the issue altogether and pronounce African names in ways that are often only approximations.

English

South African English is a mixed bag, one language with many variants. Around thirty-five percent of white people are mother-tongue English-speakers, and South African English has its own distinct character, as different from the Queen's English as is Australian. Its most notable characteristic is its huge and rich vocabulary, with unique words and usages, some drawn from Afrikaans and the African languages. The hefty *Oxford Dictionary of South African English* makes an interesting browse.

As a language used widely by non-native speakers, there is great **variation in pronunciation** and usage – largely a result of mother-tongue interference from other languages. Take, for example, the sentence "The bad bird sat on the bed", which speakers of some African languages (which don't distinguish between some of the vowel sounds of English) might pronounce as "The bed bed set on the bed". While some English-speaking purists may feel that their language is being mangled and misused, linguists argue that it is simply being transformed.

Afrikaans

Recognized as a language in 1925, **Afrikaans** is a dialect of Dutch, which became modified on the Cape frontier through its encounter with French, German and English settlers, and is peppered with words and phrases from indigenous tongues as well as African and Asian languages used by slaves. Some historians argue, very plausibly, that Afrikaans was first written in Arabic script in the early nineteenth century by Cape Muslims.

Despite this heritage, the language was used by Afrikaners from the late nineteenth century onwards as a key element in the construction of their racially exclusive ethnic identity. The attempt, in 1976, by the apartheid government to make Afrikaans the medium of instruction in black schools, which led to the Soweto uprising, confirmed the hated status of the language for many urban Africans, which persists to this day.

Contrary to popular belief outside South Africa, the majority of Afrikaans-speakers are not white but coloured, and the language, far from dying out, is in fact understood by more South Africans than any other language. It's the predominant tongue in the Western and Northern Cape provinces, and in the Free State it is the language of the media.

Afrikaans signs

Bed en Ontbyt Bed and breakfast
Dankie Thank you
Derde Third
Doeane Customs
Drankwinkel Liquor shop
Droe vrugte Dry fruit
Eerste First
Geen ingang No entry
Gevaar Danger
Grens Border
Hoof Main
Hoog High
Ingang Entry
Inligting Information
Kantoor Office
Kerk Church
Kort Short
Links Left
Lughawe Airport
Mans Men
Mark Market
Ompad Detour
Pad Road
Padwerke voor Roadworks ahead
Pastorie Parsonage

Perron Platform (train station)
Plaas Farm
Poskantoor Post office
Regs Right
Ry Go
Sentrum Centre
Singel Crescent
Slaghuis Butcher
Stad City
Stadig Slow
Stad sentrum City/town centre
Stasie Station
Straat Street
Strand Beach
Swembad Swimming pool
Toegang Admission
Tweede Second
Verbode Prohibited
Verkeer Traffic
Versigtig Carefully
Vierde Fourth
Vrouens Women
Vrugte Fruit
Vyfde Fifth

BASIC GREETINGS AND FAREWELLS

ENGLISH	AFRIKAANS	NORTHERN SOTHO
Yes	Ja	Ee
No	Nee	Aowa
Please	Asseblief	Hle…/…hle
Thank you	Dankie	Ke a leboga
Excuse me	Verskoon my	Tshwarelo
Good morning	Goiemore	Thobela/dumela
Good afternoon	Goeiemiddag	Thobela/dumela
Good evening	Goeinaand	Thobela/dumela
Goodbye	Totsiens	Sala gabotse/sepele gabotse
See you later	Sien jou later	Re tla bonana
Until we meet again	Totsiens	Go fihla re kopana gape
How do you do?	Aangename kennis?	Ke leboga go le tseba?
How are you?	Hoe gaan dit?	Le kae?

The Nguni group

Zulu (or isiZulu), the most widely spoken black African language in South Africa, is understood by around sixteen million people. It's the mother tongue of residents of the southeastern parts of the country, including the whole of KwaZulu-Natal, the eastern Free State, southern Mpumalanga and eastern Gauteng – as well as South Africa's president, Jacob Zuma. Some linguists believe that Zulu's broad reach could make it an alternative to English as a South African lingua franca. Don't confuse Zulu with **Fanakalo**, which is a pidgin Zulu mixed with other languages. Still sometimes spoken in the mines, it is not popular with most Zulu-speakers, though many white South Africans tend to believe it is.

For all practical purposes, **siSwati**, the language spoken in Swaziland, is almost identical to Zulu, but for historical reasons has developed its own identity. The same applies to **Ndebele**, which shares around 95 percent in common with Zulu. It broke off from Zulu (around the same time as siSwati) when a group of Zulu-speakers fled north to escape the expansionism of the Zulu chief Shaka. Ndebele is now spoken in pockets of Gauteng, Mpumalanga, Limpopo and North West Province, as well as throughout southern Zimbabwe.

Xhosa (itself an example of a word beginning with a click sound) was Nelson Mandela's mother tongue. Today it is spoken by some eight million South Africans, predominantly in the Eastern Cape, though with some speakers in the Western Cape, most of whom are concentrated in Cape Town.

The Sotho group

Northern Sotho dialects, which are numerous and diverse, are spoken by around 2.5 million people in a huge chunk of South Africa that takes in the country around the Kruger National Park, across Limpopo to the Botswana border and south from there to Pretoria. **Southern Sotho**, one of the first African languages to be written, is spoken in the Free State and parts of Gauteng, as well as Lesotho and the areas of the Eastern Cape bordering it.

Tswana, also characterized by a great diversity of dialects, is geographically the most widespread language in Southern Africa, and is the principal language of Botswana. In South Africa its dialects are dispersed through the Northern Cape, the Free State and North West Province.

As with the Nguni languages, the distinctions between the languages in the Sotho group owe more to history, politics and geography than to pure linguistic factors; speakers of some Northern Sotho dialects can understand some dialects of Tswana more readily than they can other Northern Sotho dialects.

SESOTHO	TSWANA	XHOSA	ZULU
E!	Ee	Ewe	Yebo
Tjhe	Nnyaa	Hayi	Cha
(Ka kopo) hle	Tsweetswee	Nceda	Uxolo
Ke a leboha	Ke a leboga	Enkosi	Ngiyabonga
Ntshwaerele	Intshwarele	Uxolo	Uxolo
Dumela (ng)	Dumela	Molo/bhota	Sawubona
Dumela (ng)	Dumela	Molo/bhoto	Sawubona
Fonaneng	Dumela	Molo/bhota	Sawubona
Sala(ng) hantle	Sala sentle	Nisale kakuhle	Sala kahle
Re tla bonana	Ke tla go bona	Sobe sibonane	Sizobonana
Ho fihlela re bonana	Go fitlhelela re bonana gape	De sibonane kwakhona	Size sibonane
Ke thabela ho o tseba?	O tsogile jang?	Kunjani?	Ninjani?
O/le sa phela?	O tsogile jang?	Kunjani?	Ninjani?

Pronouncing place names

The largest number of unfamiliar **place names** that visitors are likely to encounter in South Africa are of Afrikaans origin, followed by names with origins in the Nguni group of languages. Afrikaans and English names are found across the country, while African names tend to be more localized, according to the predominant language in that area. Nguni group pronunciations generally apply in the Eastern Cape, KwaZulu-Natal, parts of Mpumalanga and Swaziland, while Sotho group names will be found in North West Province, Limpopo, the Northern Cape, Free State and parts of Gauteng. Sometimes you'll encounter names with Khoisan derivations, such as "Tsitsikamma" (in which the ts is pronounced as in "tsunami"). The pronunciation tips below are intended as a guide and are neither comprehensive nor definitive.

Afrikaans

In common with other Germanic languages, Afrikaans has a number of consonants that are **guttural**. Apart from these, most consonant sounds will be unproblematic for English-speakers. However, Afrikaans has numerous vowels and diphthongs, which have rough English equivalents but which are frequently spelled in an unfamiliar way – take, for example, the variation in the pronunciation of the letter "e" in the list below.

Vowels and diphthongs

a as in Kakam*a*s	u as in p*u*p
aa as in Br*aa*mfontein	a as in c*a*r
ae as in H*ae*nertsburg	a as in c*a*r but slightly lengthened
aai as in Smitswinkelb*aai*	y as in dr*y*
au as in *Au*grabies	o as in bl*o*w
ar as in G*ar*ies	u as in b*u*rrow
e as in Bontebok	er as in rubb*er*, but clipped
e as in Clar*e*ns	e as in ang*e*l
ee as in Rieb*ee*ck	ee as in b*ee*r
ei as in Bloemfont*ei*n	ai as in p*ai*n
eu as in K*eu*rboomstrand	u as in c*u*re
i as in Cal*i*tzdorp	e as in ang*e*l
ie as in D*ie*pwalle	i as in p*i*ck
o as in B*o*ntebok	o as in c*o*rk, but clipped
oe as in Bl*oe*mfontein	oo as in b*oo*k
oo as in Kl*oo*f	oo as in b*oo*r
ou as in *Ou*drif	o as in wr*o*te
u as in W*u*ppertaal	i as in p*i*ck
ui as in Nelspr*ui*t	a as in g*a*te
uu as in S*uu*rbraak	o as in wr*o*te
y as in Vanrhynsdorp	ai as in p*ai*n

Consonants

d as in Suikerbosran*d*	t as in run*t*
g as in Ma*g*ersfontein	guttural ch as in the Scottish lo*ch*
tj as in Ma*tj*iesfontein	k as in *k*ey
v as in Nys*lv*lei	f as in *f*ig
w as in *W*aterkant	v as in *v*ase

Nguni group

The clicks in Nguni languages are the most unfamiliar and difficult sounds for English speakers to pronounce. The three basic clicks – which, as it happens, occur in the names of three places featured in the Wild Coast of the Eastern Cape – are: the **dental click** (transliterated using "c", as in the Cwebe Nature Reserve), made by pulling the tongue away from the front teeth as one would when expressing disapproval in "tsk tsk"; the **palatal click** (transliterated "q", as in Qholorha Mouth), made by pulling the tongue away from the palate as you would when trying to replicate the sound of a bubbly cork being popped; and the **lateral click** (transliterated "x", as in Nxaxo Mouth), made by pulling away the tongue from the side teeth. To complicate matters, each click can be pronounced in one of three ways (aspirated, nasalized or delayed) and may change when spoken in combination with other consonants.

Vowels

a as in Kwa*Zulu*   a as in f*a*ther
e as in Cwebe   e as in b*e*nd
i as in Kwambonamb*i*   ee as in fl*ee*
o as in Umkomaas   a as in t*a*ll
u as in Hl*u*hl*u*we   u as in p*u*t

Consonants

dl as in *Dl*inza   hard g as in hu*g*
g as in Ha*g*a-Ha*g*a   aspirated ll as in the Welsh *Ll*ewellyn (though often
hl as in *Hl*uh*l*uwe   pronounced like the shl in *shl*emiel by English-
ph as in M*ph*ep*h*u   speakers)
r as in Q*h*olorha   p as in *p*ass followed by a rapid rush of air
ty as in Idu*ty*wa   guttural ch as in the Scottish lo*ch*
aspirated ll as in the Welsh *Ll*ewellyn   approximately the initial sound in *tu*be

Sotho group

Vowels

a as in Th*a*ba   a as in f*a*ther
e as in Mots*e*kuoa   e as in h*e*
o as in Mantseb*o*   o as in b*o*re, but curtailed
u as in B*u*tha   u as in f*u*ll

Consonants

j as in Ha-Le*j*one   aspirated ll as in the Welsh *Ll*ewellyn (often
hl as in *Hl*otse   pronounced like the shl in *shl*emiel by English-
ph as in Ma*ph*utseng   speakers)
th as in *Th*aba   p as in *p*ool
y as in *y*es   t as in *t*ar

Glossary

Words whose spelling makes it hard to guess how to render them have their approximate pronunciation given in italics. Where gh occurs in the pronunciation, it denotes the **ch** sound in the Scottish word "loch". Sometimes we've used the letter "r" in the pronunciation even though the word in question doesn't contain this letter; for example, we've given the pronunciation of "Egoli" as "air-gaw-lee". In these instances, the syllable containing the "r" is meant to represent a familiar word or sound from English; the "r" itself shouldn't be pronounced.

African In the context of South Africa, an indigenous South African

Aloe Family of spiky indigenous succulents, often with dramatic orange flowers

Apartheid (apart-hate) Term used from the 1940s for the National Party's official policy of "racial separation"

Assegai (assa-guy) Short stabbing spear introduced by Shaka to the Zulu armies

Baai (buy) Afrikaans word meaning "bay"; also a common suffix in place names, eg Stilbaai

Babalas hangover

Bakkie (bucky) Light truck or van

Bantu (bun-two) Unscientific apartheid term for indigenous black people; in linguistics, a group of indigenous Southern African languages

Bantustan Term used under apartheid for the territories for Africans

Berg mountain (range), as in Drakensberg

Bergie A vagrant living on the slopes of Table Mountain in Cape Town

Black Imprecise term that sometimes refers collectively to Africans, Indians and coloureds, but more usually is used to mean Africans

Boer (boor) Literally "farmer", but also refers to early Dutch colonists at the Cape and Afrikaners

Boland (boor-lunt) Southern part of the Western Cape

Boma An enclosure or palisade

Boy Offensive term used to refer to an adult African man who is a servant

Bundu (approximately boon-doo, but with the vowels shortened) Wilderness or back country

Burg town or village, as in Johannesburg

Burgher Literally a citizen, but more specifically members of the Dutch community at the Cape in the seventeenth and eighteenth centuries

Bush Loosely, any woodland or savannah with an element of wilderness

Bushman Southern Africa's earliest, but now almost extinct, inhabitants who lived by hunting and gathering

Bushveld Country composed largely of thorny bush

Cape Dutch nineteenth-century, whitewashed, gabled style of architecture

Ciskei (sis-kye) Eastern Cape region west of the Kei River, declared a "self governing territory" for Xhosa-speakers in 1972, and now reincorporated into South Africa

Cocopan Small tip-truck on rails used to transport gold ore

Coloured Mulattos or people of mixed race

Commandos Burgher military units during the Frontier and Boer wars

Dagga (dugh-a) Marijuana

Dagha (dah-ga) Mud used in indigenous construction

Dassie (dussy) Hyrax

Disa (die-za) One of twenty species of beautiful indigenous orchids, most famous of which is the red disa or "Pride of Table Mountain"

Dominee (dour-min-ee) Reverend (abbreviated to DS)

Donga Dry, eroded ditch

Dorp Country town or village (from Afrikaans)

Drift Fording point in a river (from Afrikaans)

Drostdy (dross-tea) Historically, the building of the *landdrost* or magistrate

Egoli (air-gaw-lee) Zulu name for Johannesburg (literally "city of gold")

Endemic Species whose range is restricted to a particular country, region or habitat

Exotic In a biological context, a species that doesn't naturally occur in any given area

Fanakalo or fanagalo (fun-a-galaw) Pidgin mixture of English, Zulu and Afrikaans used to facilitate communication between white foremen and African workers

Fundi Expert

Fynbos (fayn-boss) Term for vast range of fine-leafed species that predominate in the southern part of the Western Cape (see page 314)

Girl Offensive term used to refer to an African woman who is a servant

Gogga (gho-gha) Creepy-crawly or insect

Griqua Person of mixed white, Bushman and Hottentot descent

Group Areas Act Now-defunct law passed in 1950 that provided for the establishment of separate areas for each "racial group"

Highveld High-lying areas of Gauteng and Mpumalanga

Homeland *See* Bantustan

Hottentot Now unfashionable term for indigenous Khoisan herders encountered by the first settlers at the Cape

Impi Zulu regiment

Indaba Zulu term meaning a group discussion and now used in South African English for any meeting or conference

Indigenous A species that naturally occurs in an area

Inkatha (in-ka ta) Fiercely nationalist Zulu political party, formed in 1928 as a cultural organization

Jislaaik! (yis-like) Exclamation equivalent to "Geez!" or "Crikey!"

Joeys Affectionate abbreviation for Johannesburg

Jol Party, celebration

Jozi Affectionate abbreviation for Johannesburg

Kaffir Highly objectionable term of abuse for Africans

Karoo Arid plateau that occupies a large proportion of the South African interior

Khoikhoi (ghoy-ghoy) Self-styled name of South Africa's original herding inhabitants

Kloof (klo-ef; rhymes with "boor") Ravine or gorge

Knobkerrie (the first "k" is silent) Wooden club

Kokerboom (both the first and last syllable rhyme with "boor") Quiver tree – a type of aloe found in the Northern Cape

Kopje Dutch spelling of *koppie*

Koppie Hillock

Kraal Enclosure of huts for farm animals or collection of traditional huts occupied by an extended family

Kramat (crum-mutt) Shrine of a Muslim holy man

Krans (crunce) Sheer cliff face

Laager (lager) A circular encampment of ox wagons, used as fortification by *voortrekkers*

Lapa Courtyard of group of Ndebele houses; also used to describe an enclosed area at safari camps, where braais are held

Lebowa (lab-o-a) Now-defunct homeland for North Sotho-speakers

Lekker Nice

Lobola (la-ball-a) Bride price, paid by an African man to his future wife's parents

Location Old-fashioned term for segregated African area on the outskirts of a town or farm

Lowveld Low-lying subtropical region of Mpumalanga and Limpopo provinces

Malay Misnomer for Cape Muslims of Asian descent

Matjieshuis (mikeys-hace) Reed hut

Mbaqanga (m-ba-kung-a) A genre of music that originated in Soweto in the 1960s

Mbira (m-beer-a) African thumb piano, often made with a gourd

MK Umkhonto we Sizwe (Spear of the Nation) The armed wing of the ANC, now incorporated into the national army

Mlungu (m-loon-goo) African term for a white person, equivalent to *honkie*

Moffie (mawf-ee) Gay person

Muti traditional medicine

Near-endemic Species that is almost endemic to a particular country, region or habitat

Nek Saddle between two mountains

Nguni (n-goo-nee) Group of southeastern Bantu-speaking people comprising Zulu, Xhosa and Swazi

Nkosi Sikelel 'i Afrika "God Bless Africa", anthem of the ANC and now of South Africa

Nyanga (nyun-ga) Traditional healer

Outspan A place set aside for animals to rest; can also mean to unharness oxen from a wagon

Pass Document that Africans used to have to carry at all times, which essentially rendered them aliens in their own country

Pastorie (puss-tour-ee) Parsonage

Platteland (plutta-lunt) Country districts

Poort Narrow pass through mountains along river course

Pronk (prawnk) Characteristic jump of springbok or impala

Protea National flower of South Africa

Qwaqwa Now-defunct homeland for South Sotho-speakers

Raadsaal (the "d" is pronounced "t") Council or parliament building

Restcamp Accommodation in national parks

Robot Traffic light

Rondavel (ron-daa-vil, with the stress on the middle syllable) Circular building based on traditional African huts

SABC South African Broadcasting Authority

Sangoma (sun-gom-a) Traditional spirit medium and healer

Shebeen (sha-bean) Unlicensed tavern

Shell Ultra City Clean, bright stops along major national roads, with a filling station, restaurant, shop and sometimes a hotel

Sjambok (sham-bok) Rawhide whip

Southeaster Prevailing wind in the Western Cape

Spaza shops (spa-za) Small stall or kiosk

Stoep Veranda

Strandloper Name given by the Dutch to the indigenous people of the Cape; literally beachcomber

Tackie Sneakers or plimsolls

Township Areas set aside under apartheid for Africans

Transkei (trans-kye) Now-defunct homeland for Xhosa-speakers

Trekboer (trek-boor) Nomadic Afrikaner farmers, usually in the eighteenth and nineteenth centuries

Umuthi (oo-moo-tee) Traditional herbal medicine

Velskoen (fel-scoon) Rough suede shoes

Vlei (flay) Swamp

VOC Verenigde Oostindische Compagnie, the Dutch East India Company

Voortrekker (the first syllable rhymes with "boor") Dutch burghers who migrated inland in their ox wagons in the nineteenth century to escape British colonialism

ZAR Zuid Afrikaansche Republiek; an independent Boer republic that included present-day Gauteng, Mpumalanga and Limpopo provinces and which was Britain's main opponent in the Anglo-Boer War

Food and drink

Amarula Liqueur made from the berries of the marula tree

Begrafnisrys (ba-ghruff-niss-race) Literally "funeral rice"; traditional Cape Muslim dish of yellow rice cooked with raisins

Biltong Sun-dried salted strip of meat, chewed as a snack

Blatjang (blutt-young) Cape Muslim chutney that has become a standard condiment on South African dinner tables

Bobotie (ba-boor-tea) Traditional Cape curried mince topped with a savoury custard and often cooked with apricots and almonds

Boerekos (boor-a-coss) Farm food, usually consisting of loads of meat and vegetables cooked using butter and sugar

Boerewors (boor-a-vorce) Spicy lengths of sausage that are *de rigueur* at braais

Bokkoms Dried fish, much like salt fish

Braai or braaivleis (bry-flace) Barbecue

Bredie Cape vegetable and meat stew

Bunny chow Originally a curried takeaway served in a scooped-out half loaf of bread, but now often wrapped in a roti

Cane or cane spirit A potent vodka-like spirit distilled from sugar cane and generally mixed with a soft drink such as Coke

Cap Classique Sparkling wine fermented in the bottle in exactly the same way as Champagne; also called Méthode Cap Classic

Cape gooseberry Fruit of the physalis; a sweet yellow berry

Cape salmon or geelbek (ghear-l-beck) Delicious firm-fleshed sea fish (unrelated to northern-hemisphere salmon)

Cape Velvet A sweet liqueur-and-cream dessert beverage that resembles Irish Cream liqueur

Denningvleis (den-ning-flace) Spicy traditional Cape lamb stew

Frikkadel Fried onion and meatballs

Hanepoort (harner-poort) Delicious sweet dessert grape

Kabeljou (cobble-yo) Common South African marine fish, also called kob

Kerrievis (kerry-fiss) *See* Pickled fish

Kingklip Highly prized deepwater fish caught along the Atlantic and Indian Ocean coasts

Koeksister (cook-sister) Deep-fried plaited doughnut, dripping with syrup

Maas or amasi or amaas Traditional African beverage consisting of naturally soured milk, available as a packaged dairy product in supermarkets

Maaskaas Cottage cheese made from *maas*

Mageu or mahewu or maheu (ma-gh-weh) Traditional African beer made from maize meal and water, now packaged and commercially available

Malva Very rich and very sweet traditional baked Cape dessert

Mampoer (mum-poor) Moonshine; home-distilled spirit made from soft fruit, commonly peaches

Melktert (melk-tairt) Traditional Cape custard pie

Mielie Maize

Mielie pap (mealy pup) Maize porridge, varying from a thin mixture to a stiff one that can resemble polenta

Mopani worm (ma-parny) Black spotted caterpillar that is a delicacy among Africans in some parts of the country

Mqomboti (m-qom-booty) Traditional African beer made from fermented sorghum

Musselcracker Large-headed fish with powerful jaws and firm, white flesh

Naartjie (nar-chee) Tangerine or mandarin

Pap (pup) Porridge

Peri-peri Delicious hottish spice of Portuguese origin commonly used with grilled chicken

Perlemoen (pear-la-moon) Abalone

Pickled fish Traditional Cape dish of fish preserved with onions, vinegar and curry; available tinned in supermarkets

Pinotage A uniquely South African cultivar hybridized from Pinot Noir and Hermitage grapes and from which a wine of the same name is made

Potjiekos or potjie (poy-key-kos) Food cooked slowly over embers in a three-legged cast-iron pot

Putu (poo-too) Traditional African *mielie pap* (see above) prepared until it forms dry crumbs

Roti A chapati; called rooti in the Western Cape

Rusks Tasty biscuits made from sweetened bread that has been slow-cooked

Salmon trout Freshwater fish that is often smoked to create a cheaper and pretty good imitation of smoked salmon

Salomie Cape version of a *roti*; unleavened bread

Sambals (sam-bills) Accompaniments, such as chopped bananas, green peppers, desiccated coconut and chutney served with Cape curries

Samp Traditional African dish of broken maize kernels, frequently cooked with beans

Skokiaan (skok-ee-yan) Potent home-brew

Smoorsnoek (smore-snook) Smoked *snoek*

Snoek (snook) Large fish that features in many traditional Cape recipes

Sosatie (so-sah-ti) Spicy skewered mince

Spanspek (spon-speck) A sweet melon

Steenbras (ste-en-bruss) A delicious white-fleshed fish

Van der Hum South African *naartjie*-flavoured liqueur

Vetkoek (fet-cook) Deep-fried doughnut-like cake

Waterblommetjiebredie (vata-blom-a-key-bree-dee) Cape meat stew made with waterlily rhizomes

Witblits (vit-blitz) Moonshine

Yellowtail Delicious darkish-fleshed marine fish

Animal checklist

THE BIG FIVE

☐ African Elephant *Loxodonta africana*
☐ Black Rhino *Diceros bicornis*/White Rhino *Ceratotherium simum*
☐ Buffalo *Syncerus caffer*
☐ Leopard *Panthera pardus*
☐ Lion *Panthera leo*

THE LITTLE FIVE

☐ Elephant shrew *Elephantulus spp*
☐ Red-billed buffalo-weaver *Bubalornis niger*
☐ Rhinoceros beetle (subfamily Dynastinae)
☐ Leopard tortoise *Geochelone pardalis*
☐ Ant-lion (family Myrmeleontidae)

PRIMATES

☐ Chacma baboon *Papio ursinus*
☐ Samango (or Blue) Monkey *Cercopithecus mitis*
☐ Southern Lesser Galago *Galago moholi*
☐ Thick-tailed Galago *Otolemur crassicaudatus*
☐ Vervet monkey *Cercopithecus aethiops*

LARGER CARNIVORES

☐ Aardwolf *Proteles cristatus*
☐ African Wild Dog *Lycaon pictus*
☐ Brown hyena *Hyaena brunnea*
☐ Cheetah *Acinonyx jubatus*
☐ Spotted Hyena *Crocuta crocuta*

MEDIUM-SIZED CARNIVORES

☐ Bat-eared Fox *Otocyon megalotis*
☐ Black-backed jackal *Canis mesomelas*
☐ Cape fox *Vulpes chama*
☐ Caracal *Caracal caracal*
☐ Serval *Felis serval*
☐ Side-striped jackal *Canis adustus*

MONGOOSES

- [ ] Banded mongoose *Mungos mungo*
- [ ] Cape grey mongoose *Galerella pulverulenta*
- [ ] Dwarf mongoose *Helogale parvula*
- [ ] Egyptian mongoose *Herpestes ichneumon*
- [ ] Slender mongoose *Galerella sanguinea*
- [ ] Suricate (meerkat) *Suricata suricatta*
- [ ] Water Mongoose *Atilax paludinosus*
- [ ] White-tailed mongoose *Ichneumia albicauda*
- [ ] Yellow Mongoose *Cynictis pencillata*

OTHER SMALL CARNIVORES

- [ ] African wild cat *Felis lybica*
- [ ] Black-footed cat *Felis nigripes*
- [ ] Cape clawless Otter *Aonyx capensis*
- [ ] Civet *Civettictis civetta*
- [ ] Genet *Genetta spp*
- [ ] Honey Badger *Mellivora capensis*
- [ ] Spotted-necked Otter *Lutra maculicollis*
- [ ] Striped polecat *Ictonyx striatus*

LARGE ANTELOPE

- [ ] Black Wildebeest *Connochaetes gnou*
- [ ] Blue Wildebeest *Connochaetes taurinus*
- [ ] Common Eland *Taurotragus oryx*
- [ ] Gemsbok *Oryx gazella*
- [ ] Greater kudu *Tragelaphus strepsiceros*
- [ ] Red Hartebeest *Alcelaphus buselaphus caama*
- [ ] Roan antelope *Hippotragus equinus*
- [ ] Sable antelope *Hippotragus niger*
- [ ] Tsessebe *Damaliscus lunatus*
- [ ] Waterbuck *Kobus ellipsiprymnus*

MEDIUM-SIZED ANTELOPE

- [ ] Blesbok *Damaliscus dorcas phillipsi*
- [ ] Bontebok *Damaliscus dorcas dorcas*
- [ ] Bushbuck *Tragelaphus sylvaticus*
- [ ] Impala *Aepyceros melampus*
- [ ] Mountain reedbuck *Redunca fulvorufula*
- [ ] Nyala *Tragelaphus angasii*
- [ ] Southern reedbuck *Redunca arundinum*
- [ ] Springbok *Antidorcas marsupialis*

SMALL ANTELOPE

- [ ] Blue Duiker *Philantomba monticola*
- [ ] Cape grysbok *Raphicerus melanotis*
- [ ] Common Duiker *Sylvicapra grimmia*
- [ ] Klipspringer *Oreotragus oreotragus*
- [ ] Oribi *Ourebia ourebi*
- [ ] Red duiker *Cephalophus natalensis*
- [ ] Sharpe's grysbok *Raphicerus sharpei*
- [ ] Steenbok *Raphicerus campestris*
- [ ] Suni *Neotragus moschatus*

OTHER LARGE HERBIVORES

- [ ] African Elephant *Loxodonta africana*
- [ ] Black Rhino *Diceros bicornis*
- [ ] Buffalo *Syncerus caffer*
- [ ] Burchell's Zebra *Equus quagga burchellii*
- [ ] Giraffe *Giraffa camelopardalis*
- [ ] Hippopotamus *Hippopotamus amphibius*
- [ ] Mountain Zebra *Equus zebra*
- [ ] White Rhino *Ceratotherium simum*

SMALLER HERBIVORES AND INSECTIVORES

- [ ] Aardvark *Orycteropus afer*
- [ ] Bushpig *Potomochoerus larvatus*
- [ ] Cape ground squirrel *Xerus inauris*
- [ ] Elephant shrew *Elephantulus spp*
- [ ] Pangolin *Manis temminckii*
- [ ] Porcupine *Hystrix africaeaustralis*
- [ ] Rock Hyrax *Procavia capensis*
- [ ] Springhare *Pedetes capensis*
- [ ] Warthog *Phacochoerus aethiopicus*

10 REPTILES AND AMPHIBIANS

- [ ] African bullfrog *Pyxicephalus adspersus*
- [ ] African clawed frog (platanna) *Xenopus spp*
- [ ] Flap-necked chameleon *Chamaeleo dilepis*
- [ ] Guttural toad *Sclerophrys gutturalis*
- [ ] Leatherback turtle *Dermchelys coriacea*
- [ ] Marsh terrapin *Pelomedusa subrufa*
- [ ] Monitor lizard *Varanus spp*
- [ ] Nile crocodile *Crocodylus niloticus*
- [ ] Southern rock python *Python natalensis*
- [ ] Tropical house gecko *Hemidactylus mabouia*

20 MARINE AND AQUATIC BIRDS

- [ ] African black oystercatcher *Haematopus moquini*
- [ ] African jacana *Actophilornis africanus*
- [ ] African penguin *Spheniscus demersus*
- [ ] African purple gallinule *Porphyrio madagascariensis*
- [ ] African spoonbill *Platalea alba*
- [ ] Blue crane *Grus paradisea*
- [ ] Cape gannet *Morus capensis*
- [ ] Goliath heron *Ardea goliath*
- [ ] Great white egret *Casmerodius albus*
- [ ] Great white pelican *Pelecanus onocrotalus*
- [ ] Greater flamingo *Phoenicopterus ruber*
- [ ] Grey heron *Ardea cinereal*
- [ ] Hadeda ibis *Bostrychia hagedash*
- [ ] Hamerkop *Scopus umbretta*
- [ ] Lesser flamingo *Phoeniconaias minor*
- [ ] Malachite kingfisher *Alcedo cristata*
- [ ] Pied kingfisher *Ceryle rudis*
- [ ] Pink-backed pelican *Pelecanus rufescans*
- [ ] Saddle-billed stork *Ephippiorhynchus senegalensis*
- [ ] Yellow-billed stork *Mycteria ibis*

20 FOREST AND BUSH NON-PASSERINE BIRDS

- [ ] African fish eagle *Haliaeetus vocifer*
- [ ] African hoopoe *Upupa africana*
- [ ] Bateleur *Terathopius ecaudatus*
- [ ] Burchell's coucal *Centropus burchellii*
- [ ] Common ostrich *Struthio camelus*
- [ ] Crested barbet *Trachyphonus vaillantii*
- [ ] Grey go-away bird *Corythaixoides concolor*
- [ ] Helmeted guinea-fowl *Numida meleagris*
- [ ] Jackal buzzard *Buteo rufofuscus*
- [ ] Knysna turaco *Tauraco corythaix*
- [ ] Kori bustard *Ardeotis kori*
- [ ] Lappet-faced vulture *Torgus tracheliotus*
- [ ] Lilac-breasted roller *Coracius caudata*
- [ ] Marabou stork *Leptoptilos crumeniferus*
- [ ] Narina trogon *Apaloderma narina*
- [ ] Secretary bird *Sagittarius serpentarius*
- [ ] Southern ground hornbill *Bucorvus leadbeateri*
- [ ] Southern yellow-billed hornbill *Tockus leucomelas*
- [ ] Spotted eagle-owl *Bubo lacteus*
- [ ] White-fronted bee-eater *Merops bullockoides*

20 PASSERINE BIRDS

- [ ] African paradise flycatcher *Terpsiphone viridis*
- [ ] Black-headed oriole *Oriolus larvatus*
- [ ] Blue waxbill *Uraeginthus angolensis*
- [ ] Bokmakierie *Telophorus zeylonus*
- [ ] Cape longclaw *Macronyx capensis*
- [ ] Cape robin-chat *Cossypha caffra*
- [ ] Cape starling *Lamprotornis nitens*
- [ ] Cape sugarbird *Promerops cafer*
- [ ] Cape wagtail *Motacilla capensis*
- [ ] Common fiscal *Lanius collaris*
- [ ] Dark-capped bulbul *Pycnonotus tricolor*
- [ ] Fork-tailed drongo *Discrurus adsimilis*
- [ ] Long-tailed widowbird *Euplectes progne*
- [ ] Malachite sunbird *Nectarinia famosa*
- [ ] Masked weaver *Ploceus spp*
- [ ] Pin-tailed whydah *Vidua macroura*
- [ ] Red-billed oxpecker *Buphagus erythrorhynchus*
- [ ] Southern boubou *Lanarius ferrugineus*
- [ ] Southern red bishop *Euplectes orix*
- [ ] White-necked raven *Corvus albicollis*

Small print and index

A ROUGH GUIDE TO ROUGH GUIDES

Published in 1982, the first Rough Guide – to Greece – was a student scheme that became a publishing phenomenon. Mark Ellingham, a recent graduate in English from Bristol University, had been travelling in Greece the previous summer and couldn't find the right guidebook. With a small group of friends he wrote his own guide, combining a contemporary, journalistic style with a thoroughly practical approach to travellers' needs.

The immediate success of the book spawned a series that rapidly covered dozens of destinations. And, in addition to impecunious backpackers, Rough Guides soon acquired a much broader readership that relished the guides' wit and inquisitiveness as much as their enthusiastic, critical approach and value-for-money ethos. These days, Rough Guides include recommendations from budget to luxury and cover more than 120 destinations around the globe, from Amsterdam to Zanzibar, all regularly updated by our team of roaming writers.

Browse all our latest guides, read inspirational features and book your trip at **roughguides.com**.

Rough Guide credits

Editor: Helen Fanthorpe
Cartography: Katie Bennett
Managing editor: Rachel Lawrence
Picture editor: Aude Vauconsant

Cover photo research: Aude Vauconsant
Senior DTP coordinator: Dan May
Head of DTP and Pre-Press: Rebeka Davies

Publishing information

First Edition 2020

Distribution

UK, Ireland and Europe
Apa Publications (UK) Ltd; sales@roughguides.com
United States and Canada
Ingram Publisher Services; ips@ingramcontent.com
Australia and New Zealand
Woodslane; info@woodslane.com.au
Southeast Asia
Apa Publications (SN) Pte; sales@roughguides.com
Worldwide
Apa Publications (UK) Ltd; sales@roughguides.com
Special Sales, Content Licensing and CoPublishing
Rough Guides can be purchased in bulk quantities
at discounted prices. We can create special editions,
personalised jackets and corporate imprints tailored to
your needs. sales@roughguides.com.

roughguides.com
Printed in China

Help us update

We've gone to a lot of effort to ensure that this edition
of **The Rough Guide to Game Parks of South Africa**
is accurate and up-to-date. However, things change –
places get "discovered", opening hours are notoriously
fickle, restaurants and rooms raise prices or lower
standards. If you feel we've got it wrong or left something
out, we'd like to know, and if you can remember the
address, the price, the hours, the phone number, so
much the better.
    Please send your comments with the subject line
"Rough Guide Game Parks of South Africa Update" to
mail@uk.roughguides.com. We'll credit all contributions
and send a copy of the next edition (or any other Rough
Guide if you prefer) for the very best emails.

Acknowledgements

Philip Briggs: Researching this book provided Ariadne and I with a wonderful opportunity to spend time in many
reserves and parks we hadn't previously explored, as well as revisiting a long list of old favourites. We are grateful to all
those who helped make it possible. In no particular order, that includes Julie Brand, Yolanda Mdlatu, Robyn Dougans,
Rene Schonborn, Ronel le Roux, Lisa Ker, Louise Bussell, Helga Vermaak, Kary Pearson, Charlene Watson, Debbie Miller,
Bronwen d'Oliveira, Claire Roadley, Monique van Rensburg, Tracy Wittstock, Karen Odendaal, Wendy Gilder, Marietjie
Rippon, Bea Mtetwa, Karel Landman, Theresa Ker-Fox, Valeri Mouton, Sebeh Ndlovu. Rebecca Dladla, Cecillie Nel,
Portia Maduna, Colin at Saint Lucia Wetlands Guesthouse, Phillip at Santa Lucia Guesthouse, Theresa Gibbon, Michael
Holthuysen, Janie van der Spuy, Johan van Schalkwyk, Lucy Frankin, Riaan & Lizelle de Klerk, Natanja Berg, Marina Toerien,
Kelsey Pienaar, Tasneem Delate, Alison Morphet, Jessica Davies, Wynand du Toit and the innumerable guides, lodge staff
and others who contributed to making the experience such a pleasure.
Chris Leggatt: Special thanks must go to Liz Bazin for introducing me to the bushveld of Madikwe and its surrounds.

ABOUT THE AUTHORS

Philip Briggs is the author of more than a dozen guidebooks to various African destinations,
from Ghana and Ethiopia to Madagascar and Mozambique. He grew up in South Africa, and
currently lives in the village of Wilderness with his wife, the wildlife and travel photographer
Ariadne Van Zandbergen.

Major contributors

Chris Leggatt, who wrote the sections on Madikwe and Pilanesberg, has spent his life in
the outdoors. His thirty-year career as an adventure tour guide, coupled with his passion for
photography, has taken him to many wonderful locations throughout the world.

Photo credits
(Key: T-top; C-centre; B-bottom; L-left; R-right)

Index

L

M

Map symbols

The symbols below are used on maps throughout the book

International boundary	Information centre	Hide	Hot spring
Provincial boundary	Gate	Golf course	Waterfall
Chapter boundary	Fuel/gas station	Museum	Lighthouse
National route	Border crossing post	Picnic site	Vineyard
Road	Park authority office	Viewpoint	Park
Unpaved road	Mountain refuge/lodge	Windmill	Beach
Footpath	Sand dunes	Shipwreck	Swamp
Airport	Elephant sanctuary	Mountain range	Accommodation
Airfield/airstrip	Nature reserve	Mountain peak	Eating
Parking	Garden	Cave	Shopping
Place of interest	Battle site		